REASON AND IMAGINATION

REASON AND IMAGINATION

THE SELECTED CORRESPONDENCE OF LEARNED HAND: 1897–1961

Edited by

CONSTANCE JORDAN

OXFORD
UNIVERSITY PRESS

OXFORD
UNIVERSITY PRESS

Oxford University Press is a department of the University of Oxford. It furthers the University's objective of excellence in research, scholarship, and education by publishing worldwide.

Oxford New York
Auckland Cape Town Dar es Salaam Hong Kong Karachi Kuala Lumpur Madrid
Melbourne Mexico City Nairobi New Delhi Shanghai Taipei Toronto

With offices in
Argentina Austria Brazil Chile Czech Republic France Greece Guatemala Hungary
Italy Japan Poland Portugal Singapore South Korea Switzerland Thailand
Turkey Ukraine Vietnam

Published in the United States of America by
Oxford University Press
198 Madison Avenue, New York, NY 10016

Library of Congress Cataloging-in-Publication Data

Hand, Learned, 1872–1961.
[Correspondence. Selections]
Reason and imagination : the selected correspondence of Learned Hand 1897–1961/ edited by Constance Jordan.
p. cm.
Includes bibliographical references and index.
ISBN 978-0-19-989910-4 ((hardback) : alk. paper)
1. Hand, Learned, 1872–1961—Correspondence. 2. Judges—United States—Correspondence.
I. Jordan, Constance. II. Title.
KF368.H265A4 2012
347.73'2634092—dc23

2012013714

9 8 7 6 5 4 3 2 1

Printed in the United States of America on acid-free paper

Note to Readers
This publication is designed to provide accurate and authoritative information in regard to the subject matter covered. It is based upon sources believed to be accurate and reliable and is intended to be current as of the time it was written. It is sold with the understanding that the publisher is not engaged in rendering legal, accounting, or other professional services. If legal advice or other expert assistance is required, the services of a competent professional person should be sought. Also, to confirm that the information has not been affected or changed by recent developments, traditional legal research techniques should be used, including checking primary sources where appropriate.

(Based on the Declaration of Principles jointly adopted by a Committee of the American Bar Association and a Committee of Publishers and Associations.)

For Patty Doar

CONTENTS

EDITORIAL PRACTICE

The letters in this edition of Judge Learned Hand's correspondence are in holdings in various libraries, principally Special Collections at the Harvard Law Library (the Learned Hand Papers, the Oliver Wendell Holmes, Jr. Papers, the Zechariah Chafee, Jr. Papers, the Charles Wyzanski Papers), the Sterling Library at Yale (the Walter Lippmann Papers, the Henry Stimson Papers), and the Library of Congress (the Theodore Roosevelt Papers). Harvard's holdings, the most extensive, comprise sixty-five thousand items dating from 1892 to 1961, with a few family biographical items dating back to 1846. Hand's correspondence comes to approximately fifty thousand items and falls into three categories: letters to and from acquaintances on business and social matters, letters to close friends, and finally, letters to family members. They include single letters Hand wrote to an individual correspondent, and two or more letters on a particular subject exchanged between Hand and a second correspondent over a brief period of time; the latter I have linked together so that they form a sequence. With a given year, a sequence is represented by a number indicating the year in which the letters were exchanged, followed by its chronological place within that year as determined by the date of Hand's letter. Thus, his letter to Frankfurter, dated February 26, 1911, the second of the sequences in that year, is referenced as: 1911-2 To Frankfurter, February 26. Letters quoted from the Hand Papers are cited simply by Box and Folder numbers; those from the Chafee Papers and the Wyzanski Papers are cited as such with Box and Folder numbers; those from the Holmes Papers are cited as they are represented on microfilm. Letters quoted from the Lippmann Papers and the Stimson Papers are cited as from Sterling, with Box and Folder numbers; and letters from the Roosevelt Papers are cited as from LC, with Reel numbers. All other letters are cited as from particular libraries with full annotation.

Footnotes to each letter within a sequence clarify particular topics, including relevant books and articles; identify persons, events, and institutions mentioned in the letters; and provide cross-references to relevant letters within the correspondence. Footnotes on legal cases mentioned in the letters provide citations to judicial opinions, statutes, and law review articles; where appropriate, I have quoted passages from opinions and articles. I have translated words and sentences in French, Italian, German, and Latin as needed, and have left frequently referenced legal Latin phrases untranslated.

The letters themselves are in various formats. Letters in manuscript are represented in photocopies or microfilms of the original document and show a date of composition, usually reproduce the signature of the sender, and often but not always indicate provenance: because Hand wrote letters on official stationary at home, provenance is not in any case always certain. Letters in typescript (frequently in carbon copy) are represented in photocopies or microfilm of the original document that may or may not feature a letterhead indicating provenance. Letters that indicate no provenance I have left as they are.

Hand wrote longhand drafts for his secretary to type, signing the original typescript and leaving the unsigned carbon copy for his files (tp (typescript without signature)). This practice is exemplified in his 1920 letter to Zechariah Chafee, Jr. with its explanatory note from his secretary, Ms. Bergman, who in this case substitutes her signature for his. In some instances, he signs the carbon copy (tp (typescript) with signature). These letters sometimes contain notes or emendations to the text in Hand's handwriting. For letters from him that are unsigned, I have supplied a signature in brackets, guessing how he would have signed them based on his familiarity with the correspondent, e.g., [L.H.] for letters such as to Justice Frankfurter, and [Learned Hand] for correspondence such as to President Roosevelt. Many of the correspondents with whom Hand was friendly addressed him as "B"; with very few exceptions, he signed all his letters to them "L.H."

Letters are also represented in typed transcriptions of their originals in manuscript, some copying the signature of the sender (tr/ms with signature (transcription of a manuscript with signature)), others without the signature of the sender (tr/ms (transcription of a manuscript without signature)). Other letters are represented in typed transcriptions of their originals in typescript, some copying the signature of the sender (tr/tp with signature (transcription of a typescript with signature)), others without the signature of the sender (tr/ms (transcription of a manuscript without signature)). As with letters in photocopies of carbon copies that are missing specific documentation, I have guessed how Hand would have signed these transcriptions The character—manuscript, typescript, transcription—and location of every letter in a particular archive is indicated at its conclusion.

I have reproduced most letters in their entirety; however, I have cut portions of letters (indicated by bracketed ellipses) that comment on topics irrelevant to their principal subjects. I have silently corrected errors in spelling, punctuation, and typing. I have also omitted the address of the correspondent to whom Hand writes that occasionally appears at the conclusion of the letter. For guidance through this correspondence, I have followed the account of Hand's life in Gerald Gunther's biography, editing in full some of the letters he quotes in part and including many others he omits entirely.

I have included several appendices: biographies of individual persons mentioned in the correspondence or associated with events it describes; cases discussed in particular letters with the names and dates of the party to whom the letter is addressed; and a general bibliography.

PREFACE

Constance Jordan has done a great service to many disciplines through this collection of the often fascinating and brilliant letters of Judge Learned Hand. Even his casual letters are an important part of jurisprudence, constitutional theory, and the legal history of almost the whole of the twentieth century. She has recreated the remarkable and sadly lost culture of those learned, busy men and women who wrote each other essays of mixed philosophy and gossip in moments stolen from pressing careers.

But the main delight of the letters is in what they tell us about Hand himself. He is now almost unreflectively called the greatest of all American judges, the sculptor of the best of our legal doctrine, a master stylist whose judicial opinions are often poetry. We knew all that from the books that fill a lawyer's shelves. Jordan's collection tells us more. It show us a relentlessly introspective, constantly self-doubting man of quite amazing erudition who quotes Hamlet with the easy familiarity of self-identification. He is angry with judges and philosophers who suppose themselves in touch with "absolutes"—universal moral truths. But his letters betray him as only a reluctant and part-time skeptic who wanted all his life to find his own ethical absolute—the truth, that is, about the right way to live.

He thought he had found this in a deep and near paradoxical idea: that living well means, as he put it, converting means to ends by taking what might be thought of as instrumental traits—like wisdom, courage, and industry—as freestanding virtues valued for their own sake quite independently of whatever else they might help to produce. That means judging a life by the way it is lived, as we judge a musical or athletic performance—not by what it has produced by way of an independent lasting achievement. It may seem odd that someone so dramatically successful in achievement should subordinate success to craft. But it may have been a comfort to a man approaching old age, conscious of the transient character of any kind of worldly success and with no conventional religious faith, to think that living with integrity is success enough to stand up to mortality. It may also be pertinent that Hand, as he repeatedly admits in these letters, was bitterly disappointed in not having had the one achievement he most wanted: his own seat on the Supreme Court. He said, toward the end, that that disappointment finally evaporated; perhaps his deeply thought-out ethical theory helped.

Legal scholars will undoubtedly find great interest in an altogether different matter: the fascinating correspondence between Hand and his close friend of many years, Supreme Court Justice Felix Frankfurter, about the Supreme Court and race. Hand and Frankfurter had both come passionately to disapprove of judges who used the Constitution to overrule democratic legislative decisions that contradicted their own moral convictions. Frankfurter nevertheless joined the Court's 1954 unanimous decision striking down laws that required schools to be segregated by race. Hand wrote him, charitably, that he would probably have done the same in Frankfurter's place. The nation would have suffered from a divided opinion on this issue.

But Frankfurter wanted Hand's advice on another, even more delicate, matter: Frankfurter expected that in view of the segregation decision, another case would soon come before the Court testing whether the miscegenation laws of many states, which forbade interracial marriage, should also be overruled. Frankfurter thought not: that would be too great an assault on the conventional morality of large parts of the country. He wanted Hand to tell him that there would be no contradiction in his voting against racial segregation in schools, but not in marriage. Hand wrote a carefully worded reply. If one assumes that the school case was correctly decided, he said, then the marriage case would have to be decided the same way. Frankfurter, unhappy, tried to wriggle out of Hand's logic; reading his attempts in this collection is both amusing and sad. (In 1967, after Frankfurter's retirement, the Court unanimously struck down Virginia's statute making intermarriage a crime.)

In 1958, in his Holmes Lectures at his beloved Harvard Law School, Hand publicly stated his own opinion about race and the Constitution. He conceded that the 1954 segregation decision violated his lifelong convictions about judicial restraint and therefore acknowledged, glumly, that in his opinion the celebrated decision was wrong. Jordan reports in her introduction that this opinion was not popular. He knew it would not be. His integrity in nevertheless publishing it showed how well he lived, by his own measure of what that means.

Ronald Dworkin

ACKNOWLEDGMENTS

I have received most generous help over the years that I have worked on *Reason and Imagination*. I wish especially to thank the members of the staff of Special Collections at the Harvard Law Library: Leslie Schoenfeld, David Warrington, Margaret Peachy, Mary Person, and Edwin Moloy, Curator of Modern Manuscripts, who, from 2005 to 2010 answered my questions about letters in the Hand Papers, advised me on copyright matters, and gave me access to the collections I needed to see in order to complete this edition of Hand's correspondence. I am also grateful to Judith Schiff, William Massa, and Susan Gibbons for their assistance in locating letters in Manuscripts and Archives in Sterling Library at Yale and responding to my concerns about copyright; to Jennifer Brathovde and Patrick Kerwin at the Library of Congress for responding to my requests for information; and to Mary Robertson, Curator of Historical Manuscripts, and Sara Hodson, Curator of Modern Manuscripts at the Huntington Library, for their support and encouragement.

I wish also to thank Lisa Lucas, who did much of the basic research on the cases mentioned in the correspondence, and the many friends and family members who provided me with contacts throughout my work on this project and all kinds of Hand memorabilia, including letters, notes, and photographs: Patty Doar, Phyllis Seidel, Frances Morris, Susan Speers, Peter O'Malley, David and Lori Damrosch, and Jonathan Churchill with whom I spent many hours parsing Hand's prose and whose enthusiasm continues to inspire me. I deeply regret that he did not live to see this book in print. I am grateful to Judith Churchill for her support and introductions to persons Hand knew, including Ronald Dworkin, who kindly agreed to write the Preface to this volume, and to Barbara Gunther, who provided me with an initial contact at Oxford University Press. I wish also to thank my colleagues at Claremont Graduate University, Lori Anne Ferrell and Janet Brodie, who encouraged me to pursue this project at its earliest stages.

I have greatly benefited from the energetic efforts of my agents Ike Williams and Katherine Flynn of Kneerim and Williams, the interest of Jessica Picone in Learned Hand's correspondence, and the generous assistance of Michelle Lipinski, Gwen Colvin, Jennifer Gong, Ninell Silberberg, and Cassie Tuttle as this edition has gone through the publication process.

I wish further to thank the following persons and libraries for giving me permission to publish various letters I have included in this edition of Hand's correspondence: Susan Speers for letters from Augustus Hand; Mrs. Louisa Spenser for a letter from Grenville Clark; Alice Henkin for the wartime letters of Louis Henkin; Harvard Law Library for selected letters from the collections of Learned Hand, Oliver Wendell Holmes, Jr., Zechariah Chafee, Jr., Charles Wyzanski, and Bernard Berenson; Sterling Library at Yale University for selected letters from the collections of Henry Stimson and Walter Lippmann; the Seeley G. Mudd Manuscript Library at Princeton University for a letter from George F. Kennan; and the Harry Ransom Humanities Research Center at the

University of Texas at Austin for letters from Alfred A. Knopf. I also gratefully acknowledge copies of letters in the Library of Congress from Theodore Roosevelt, Harlan Fiske Stone, Felix Frankfurter, Harry S. Truman, and Warren Austin included in this edition of Hand's correspondence.

I have relied throughout this project on the support of friends and family, especially my sons Wilson, Andrew, and Geoffrey Kidde and my husband Edward Golub, who for five years has listened to me read aloud half a century of Hand's mail. My cousin Patty Doar has a special place in the history of this work, and it is to her that I dedicate it with affection and gratitude.

INTRODUCTION

If any judge is to strike the imagination of his time, I think you should and increasingly do

—Oliver Wendell Holmes to Learned Hand, March 10, 1931

A man well into middle age, notably successful in his life's work, Hand wondered if he should "try really to write." His question to his friend Philip Littell reflects a certain inquietude, a longing for closure, however particular: "the thought is not really buried until put into words." Once in words, a thought is no longer in the mind, to excite, frustrate, and perhaps even disturb. Hand's question is also understandable: his productions—opinions, articles, reviews—are firmly grounded in law and politics. Would another kind of writing be possible—history, philosophy? Years later, Bernard Berenson wrote Hand to remind him of what he might do: "I would urge you to write."[1]

In another sense, however, whether Hand should "try really to write" is a question answered by the sheer volume of his personal correspondence evident even at an early stage in his life—pages upon pages of letters to friends, notes to acquaintances, orders to businesses and public administrators, responses to queries and compliments from persons he knew and some he did not know. They testify that he did write; more important, as the correspondence published here shows, he was a master of English prose. It is not misguided to characterize his letters as literary. Many are brief essays on current events, often seen through the prism of their historical determinants, and on cultural affairs, often by comparison with those in England or in Europe more generally. They are addressed to the concerns and character of his correspondent, but rarely so limited in their scope or depth of reflection as not to entertain topics of general interest. Collectively, they punctuate those periods in which Hand chose to sequester himself from the business of work and the pleasures of society, and to gather his thoughts in order better to give an account of how he wished to be understood. For the most part, his letters depict him doing what he loved to do—talking (though on paper) to others. These conversations usually begin with a letter to Hand; its writer introduces a topic to which Hand will respond, often with digressions, objections, amplifications drawn from his own vision of life, distinct from yet also part of his view from the bench.

I have organized Hand's correspondence so that it falls into six parts: a Prologue containing letters that date from his graduation from Harvard Law School through his employment with Zabriskie, Burrill & Murray in New York City; four Parts, each comprising letters written successively during ten- to fifteen-year periods through the publication of *The Bill of Rights* in 1958; and finally, an Epilogue containing letters written in the last three years of his life. Accounts of events reflecting Hand's career on the bench are

1. 1933-2 To Littell, February 12; 1952-1 To Hand from Berenson, January 23.

given perspective by observations on politics and ethics, often made to persons outside the legal field. Henry Stimson's letter congratulating Hand on his appointment to the United States District Court for the Southern District of New York introduces letters describing Hand's activities on behalf of Progressivism, his position on the freedom of speech associated with his decision in *Masses* and amplified in correspondence with Oliver Wendell Holmes, Jr., and his engagement with issues arising in the aftermath of World War I and the League of Nations; those letters make up Part I of the correspondence. Letters on the role of judges and the courts in declaring legislation unconstitutional, the politics and legislation of prohibition, the effects of the economic depression in the United States, and Hand's elevation to the United States Court of Appeals for the Second Circuit are topics addressed in Part II. The legislation of the New Deal, including the treatment of immigrants and the status of aliens, the rise of fascism and the outbreak World War II, the postwar period together with prospects for world government, and the rise of Communism in Eastern Europe are discussed in Part III. Hand's retirement from the Court of Appeals, Senator Joseph McCarthy's work for the House Committee on Un-American Activities, the Supreme Court's decisions on segregation, and Hand's Holmes lectures at the Harvard Law School and their publication are among the events reviewed Part IV. The Epilogue includes letters from the two persons whom Hand had signally regarded with respect and affection, Felix Frankfurter and Walter Lippmann, and also letters to and from Alfred A. Knopf concerning the publication of *The Spirit of Liberty*. Certain topics recur throughout the correspondence: freedom of speech, the interpretation of statutes especially in light of the procedure outlined in Edmund Plowden's report on *Eyston v. Studd* (1574), judicial review, natural law, and the philosophical notion of *mediocritas* or the moral mean.

Hand's correspondents hailed from many quarters. The largest group consisted of men of his own calling, the law; the rest had a place in some field of public life: journalism, government, and education. To each, and especially to those of long standing like Felix Frankfurter, Walter Lippmann, and Bernard Berenson, Hand cultivated a particular literary style, one clearly designed to engage his correspondent on subjects of mutual interest.

To Frankfurter, with whom letters on issues in the law were predominant, Hand was at once a dedicated exponent of the legal philosophy of James Bradley Thayer and an almost raucously witty critic of judicial activism, whether of the *Lochner* era or as exemplified by members of the Warren Court. Hand expected Frankfurter to address his complaints, and Frankfurter would do so, often responding with his own criticisms. Considered as a whole, their correspondence covers a period of just under fifty years and represents an acutely focused commentary on issues in American law, especially the interpretation of the First, Fifth, and Fourteenth Amendments.

Letters to and from Lippmann are of a different character. As a young successful journalist, Lippmann fascinated the judge, who, from the moment of their first acquaintance in 1914, admired the younger man's energy and self-confidence and cherished their friendship in part because it gave him a chance to experience a public character that he himself was neither permitted to reveal professionally nor, more important, able to summon personally. Their correspondence is wide-ranging and speculative, Lippmann suggesting daring measures and Hand supplying prudent counsel. It also radiates a deeply felt affection, one for the other—at least until Lippmann's second marriage to Helen Byrne Armstrong in 1938. Hand's letters reveal that his subsequent distance from Lippmann followed his reluctance to meet Helen Byrne Armstrong's first husband and his own friend Hamilton Fish Armstrong. This break was eventually mended, but not entirely healed; their last letters, especially Lippmann's to Hand, show some of the old spirit, albeit in a muted way.

Of all Hand's correspondents, Berenson was perhaps least likely to have become intimate. A distinguished connoisseur of Italian Renaissance painting and long an expatriate living in Florence, Berenson exemplified virtues that Hand thought he himself lacked, particularly a temperament keen to enjoy the world's beauty and the knowledge to appreciate its representation in works of art. Suffering, by his own admission, from a rigid conception of art as a kind of engine of ethical uplift, a scripture mandating the moral life, Hand credits Berenson with allowing him actually to like looking at pictures. As they saw each other only on summer trips, and not at all during World War II, their correspondence is sporadic if also on occasion detailed and heartfelt. Hand's first letter to Berenson after the close of hostilities in Italy conveys his "utmost admiration" for Berenson's stoic conduct during his years of hiding from the Nazis in and around Florence.[2]

Three more correspondents figured prominently in Hand's life: Oliver Wendell Holmes, Jr., Theodore Roosevelt, and Herbert Croly, the founder and one of the editors of *The New Republic*. The Hand–Holmes correspondence shows the judge as touchingly reverential to the Justice, the Justice as condescendingly approving of the judge, and in all serves as a powerful illustration of how the audacious Civil War veteran had captured the attention and admiration of his colleagues by a jurisprudence mandating judicial restraint and promoting an Austinian vision of the law as expressing the power of the sovereign over the subject. This correspondence is continued almost in a deputized way in letters to and from Zechariah Chafee, Jr. of Harvard, who in his seminal work on the First Amendment, *Freedom of Speech* (1921), had applauded Hand's views in apparent distinction to those of Holmes, but finally followed the Justice rather than the judge. Hand's understanding of judicial review and the interpretation of statute, as conveyed in his letters to Frankfurter and Charles Wyzanski, extends well beyond what he took from Holmes, embracing, as it does, an appreciation of the imagination's role in the interpretation of the words of the law to the terms of the case to be decided.

Addressing issues relating to the Progressive movement, Hand's letters to Roosevelt reveal how deftly he tried to make Roosevelt embrace the social, economic, and political advantages that the nation could secure if only its citizens could be made to realize them in practice. Roosevelt's responses generally reflect his own political commitments and a self-confidence that Hand worried would be fatal to the cause. Hand communicated much of his dismay to Croly, whose book, *The Promise of American Life* (1910), had launched the Progressive program as a feature of American political thought. The sense of Hand's mostly anonymous contributions to *The New Republic* during this period is also registered in the Hand–Croly correspondence and provides rationales for judicial restraint, especially with respect to legislative reform of industry and the labor market.

2. 1945-3 To Berenson, February 18.

The genre of the letter is ancient—one could instance Cicero's *Letters to Atticus*—and also modern. Letters from heads of state, the clergy, and persons in all walks of life inform the history of the west and continue to provide cogent evidence of political attitudes to the present day. The constitutive features of the genre remain the same, however: it serves to substitute a literary presence for an actual absence, and it contends with meanings communicated over time and through space, however brief and limited. Even letters received within days of being sent (as were most of Hand's to Frankfurter) need to be understood and interpreted in light of changes that have occurred in the interim;[3] they require historical contextualization. When Hand writes to Frankfurter that "while I look back on my nineteenth century kit of feelings and beliefs, it is not with any complacent satisfaction at the changed times I have lived into,"[4] he recognizes the burden of acknowledging the effects of these changes. Read right through, however, Hand's correspondence has a novelistic dimension. As letters follow in sequence, they can be seen to have created character. Accounts of business become elements of plot, to be tested in light of public and official discourse, and expressions of passion, aroused, thwarted or satisfied, gain the interest and power of words spoken in dramatic dialogue. The reader lives in the present they have fashioned after an imaginative reconstruction of the dynamics that produced the correspondence in the first place.[5]

The conditions in which Hand exchanged letters with his friends and acquaintances are exceptional by comparison to those in which we write today. They wrote and received letters of various lengths, some essays on a particular topic, some no more than casual notes. They expected to keep the letters they received and sent for later reference, and even to circulate the letters of others to their friends and acquaintances. Intimacies are thus made public, like those in a telephone conversation that is wiretapped and overheard by a third party unknown to the speakers. Some of Hand's correspondence openly defies conventions of privacy: a letter he sends or receives comments on and is sent together with a second letter from a third party whose consent has apparently not been sought. That party's communication is therefore effectively intercepted, read by someone to whom he had no intention of writing.[6] Its intention may be merely to inform; it may also convey criticism. Thus Hand comments to Lippmann on British politics by reference to two letters sent to Berenson's friend Nicky Mariano and now passed on to him: "I am enclosing a letter which Nicky got from an Englishman called Robert Trevelyan that B.B. thought you might like to see. Also a letter to the *Guardian* by Clifford Allen who according to B.B. must be the real author of the Trevelyan letter. You will see that both are a

---

3. As Janet Gurkin Altman notes, a letter manifests a "temporal polyvalence": an act it describes is performed, then written down; it is dispatched, received, read and perhaps reread. EPISTOLARITY: APPROACHES TO A FORM 118 (1982).

4. 1950-2 To Frankfurter, January 20.

5. Robert M. Menuel and Christine L. Compson indicate such invention when they claim that from his correspondence with Holmes, "Frankfurter constructed another Holmes whose decisions invariably supported Frankfurter's reformist predilections." ROBERT M. MENUEL & CHRISTINE L. COMPSON, HOLMES AND FRANKFURTER: THEIR CORRESPONDENCE, 1912–1934, xxv (1996).

6. The practice is evidently ancient; *see* THOMAS E. JENKINS, INTERCEPTED LETTERS: EPISTOLARITY AND NARRATIVE IN GREEK AND ROMAN LITERATURE (2006).

defense of [Ramsay] MacDonald."[7] And including in his letter to Hand a letter from Frankfurter—in which Frankfurter states that he is "flabbergasted" at Lippmann's May 31 editorial in *The New York World* criticizing Holmes's dissent in the case of Rozika Schwimmer, who was denied citizenship because she was an "uncompromising pacifist"—Lippmann invites Hand to disapprove of Frankfurter's presumption: "Don't you think it's a bit trying?"[8] Agreeing in the matter of style but disagreeing in the matter of substance, Hand replies: "I think it is more than a bit trying, I think it is intolerable. Nobody has a right to address another, even an old friend, in that tone. It is quite likely that he [i.e., Frankfurter in supporting Holmes] is right. I am going to read the opinions with considerable care when they arrive, and I should rather guess that I shall come out that way."[9] Such letters can also reveal reasons for an event well after its occasion. Having assumed that Frankfurter's repudiation of Lippmann was linked to Lippmann's divorce, Hand learns its darker cause long after the fact: Lippmann's sympathy for Fascist attitudes toward Jews, announced in his columns in the World in the 1930s. In his letter to Hand, Frankfurter encloses the letter he wrote to Lippmann seven years earlier: "[W]hen, in your column for May 19, 1933, you described Hitler as 'the authentic voice of a genuinely civilized people' [...] something inside of me snapped,"[10] and also Lippmann's response: "the manner in which you have torn phrases from their context and ignored the historical circumstances in which the article was written, is inexcusable [...] [I]nstead of trying to clear up the misunderstanding at the time, you have waited nearly four years to raise the question. It is now too late to raise it."[11] For the most part, however, Hand's letters to and from his friends and acquaintances are both frank and tempered; though Hand is occasionally vitriolic in his criticism of opinion he considers shallow or ignorant, he is ready to listen to it. His modesty is striking; he is hardly ever entirely certain of himself. In time, this modesty comes to include a tolerance for other, though not all, ways of being, and to support a celebration of the enjoyment life offers.

Throughout his correspondence, the figure of Learned Hand the man, a person of many moods and diverse interests, remains in view; it is not easy to pin down or characterize in simple terms. In an early letter to his cousin Augustus Hand, he characterizes himself, rather aptly I think, in the words of the Roman poet and emperor Hadrian as *anima vagula, blandula, qui errat in locis* (a sweet wandering spirit who moves from place to place), and invokes a character that is capricious, moody, and resists a fixed identity.[12] The figure is facetious and self-deprecatory, but it conveys an image of the writer nonetheless, and perhaps especially of the writer at work, stating, revising, restating, and never entirely confident that the resulting work would not need to be done again. Privileging the experience of doubt and delay over certainty and action, Hand's letters promote the

---

7. 1931-3 To Lippmann, September 16.

8. 1929-3 To Hand from Lippmann and note 97, June 6.

9. 1929-3 To Lippmann, June 7.

10. 1943-3 To Hand from Frankfurter, April 27; *see* therein To Lippmann from Frankfurter, November 28, 1936. (In this Introduction, ellipses in quoted correspondence and articles by Hand are mine.)

11. 1943-3 To Hand from Frankfurter, April 27; *see* therein To Frankfurter from Lippmann, December 17, 1936.

12. 1924-1 To Augustus Hand, July 27.

practice of tolerance and the classical virtue of *mediocritas*. Surprisingly, perhaps, they also celebrate the anti-utilitarian concept of means as ends: what is valuable is the practice of a virtue, not the goal it realizes. The point goes to Hand's own way of understanding history as the creation and destruction and recreation of successively realized ends, which, owing to their transience really do not qualify as ends. What remains, in history, are the examples of actions and attitudes that have comprised what is memorable in human experience. Hence his frequent reversion to the concept of the ad hoc, what is appropriate in a particular situation but cannot or should not be raised to an absolute or a universal.

Hand's world is thus both built and mobile, deliberately constructed and casually realized, the effect of individual labor that is done and redone over time. It depends on striving to reconcile oppositions that may appear to be irreconcilable; it reflects a sense that what we see as real is actually the outcome of constructions we give our raw experience. He approaches this world with some diffidence. Trying to understand Robert Millikan's physics, Hand writes to Simon Flexner: "Does it not suggest that we may ultimately come to the idea that what we understand by external reality is after all no more than the extremely elaborate patterns which we can impose upon the phenomenal world?"[13] "Is there nothing in our craving for something 'objective'?" Hand asks Wyzanski.[14] Evidently not. "Really this is my credo, so far as I can say to myself that I have any—in our search for 'external' laws of nature we are doing no more than trying to devise successively and progressively intricate conceptual patterns to enable us enough to foretell the course of the flux and deal with it to our purposes. Those patterns, formulas, schemes, call them what you will, are the measure and test of any 'externality' and probably exhaust whatever meaning that may have."[15] Thus he appreciates Berenson's claim that "Landscape," like other renderings of reality, whether objective or subjective, is essentially a "fabricated idea"—fabricated but utterly compelling in its capacity to deliver the experience of great beauty. Hand's account of visits to Berenson's Tuscan villa illustrates his "pleasure" in reading in the raw data of topography a wealth of emotion—desire as well as disappointment: in that countryside particularly "there is written the long history of man with all its tragedy of endless labor and its persistent belief that, in the words of William James, life on any terms, however straitened and painful, is to be accepted as better than non-existence. That and the matchless splendor of the mountains and the whole vast collections of centuries gathered up and open to all to see will never have their equal." And then too, it is a reminder of time's passage: "I regret more than I can say that although every opportunity was open to me, I waited till I was 50 before ever I broke in upon it. True, that first descent from Silva Plana (I wonder if I have remembered the right name) to Como was even then an unforgettable and is a never forgotten experience of what the World did have and what I never availed myself of."[16] Rendered repeatedly in different and sometimes satirical terms, Hand's notion of a constructed reality composed of self-imposed patterns that give meaning to phenomena becomes the basis of a self-knowledge always

13. 1926-3 To Flexner, December 15.
14. 1945-8 To Wyzanski, December 16.
15. 1945-8 To Wyzanski, January 22, 1946.
16. 1955-3 To Hand from Berenson, August 8; 1952-7 To Berenson, August 5.

conditioned by humor. Returning from a European trip, Hand writes to Philip Littell that on setting out, he dreaded the "prospect of bustle and hotels and porters and the everlasting drip, drip of fees which one can never gauge properly"; he expected to be "jostled and harried and cheated, or [to] think I have been"; he knew that he would have "a haunting sense that I am missing much and am an ass to think about whether I am missing anything." Once back home, however, a compensatory, indeed a beneficent, plenitude will fill this void: "I shall come back and say that I have had a good time and *it will be true*."[17] True, that is, as a helpful fiction is true to its generous purpose; true, too, as any fiction that has disclosed its nature as fiction can be true to the reality that has given it voice and substance.

It is my hope that this edition of Hand's correspondence will give further depth and color to the judge's portrait already so brilliantly rendered in Gerald Gunther's biography *Learned Hand: The Man and the Judge* (1994, 2011). Drawing on a host of documents that include correspondence, Gunther's narrative history describes the causes and effects of the events that shaped Hand's career. To treat Hand's correspondence as a self-circumscribed collection of writing as I have done here is to undertake a different though complementary task, less invested in describing the causes and effects of events than in listening to assessments of such events, immediate, privileged, and personal as they inevitably were. And because this correspondence possesses a theatrical and arguably disputative quality, it resists conclusiveness; the questions the letters pose may be answered but often leave more to be asked. To bring to a narrative history evidence supplied by a correspondence is therefore to complicate it, leaving it open to the possibility of counterfactuals and in that way to make it a less perfect history.

Read as a single body of writing, Hand's letters, punctuated as they are by those of his correspondents, convey a thematic ambiguity, shifting as they do between positions critical and rational on the one hand and others conciliatory and imaginative on the other. His first letter to his cousin Augustus Hand illustrates his reliance on reason as a means to prove a point. He approves abstractly two positions: the "individualism" endorsed by contemporary Democrats and expressed as the politics of "laissez-faire," and the imperialism rendered as a global politics of "subject dependencies" and exemplified by colonies under the control of the United Kingdom. Yet his approval of "individualism" is qualified when considered in light of American experience: here reasonable inquiry reveals that "in a vast multitude of cases the State must and should regulate the conduct of individuals for their own welfare and modify the contractual relations which they assume towards one another." Similarly, he rules out for the United States the possibility of acquiring "subject dependencies" such as the Philippines in light of the vast abuses and inequities already visited on the peoples over which this country had de facto control: "When one considers the plight of the poor Indian, who had at least a better chance of making his woes come home to us than the Filipino will have, and when one considers the Negro, I can't see how he can have any very sanguine confidence in the beneficent effect of that glorious American liberty of which we talk so much."[18] Argument of this kind appears

17. 1929-7 To Littell, July 19.
18. 1898 To Augustus Hand, November 6.

throughout the correspondence; Hand objects, disagrees, demurs, and leaves it to his correspondent to appreciate his point of view.

By contrast, Hand's understanding of the imagination and the work it does is complex. Its most persistent and important reference is to the written word, principally in legal text but also as evidenced in literature generally. It is sketched initially in Hand's version of the English common lawyer Edmund Plowden's instructions on the interpretation of statute: "it is a good way when you peruse a statute, to suppose that the law-maker is present, and that you have asked him the question you want to know touching the equity; then you must give yourself such an answer *as you imagine he would have done, if he had been present.*"[19] Contending with Plowden throughout the last half of his correspondence allows Hand to claim an essential role for the imagination in determining how words can find meaning in real situations, how the circumstances surrounding both the enactment of a law and its subsequent applications—necessarily tempered in historical terms, both those that shaped the character of its maker and that of its interpreter—determine the particular significance of the law that the judge is to apply. In "How Far is a Judge Free in Rendering a Decision," an address delivered on the Columbia Broadcasting System in 1933, Hand admits that the "intent" of those who make law is hard to discover: "Strictly speaking, it is impossible to know what they would have said about it [. . .] All they have done is to write down certain words which they mean to apply *generally* to situations of that kind. To apply these *literally* may either pervert what was plainly their general meaning, or leave undisposed of what there is every reason to suppose they meant to provide for. Thus it is not enough for the judge just to use a dictionary":[20] "he must have the historical capacity to reconstruct the whole setting which evoked the law; the contentions which it resolved; the objects which it sought; the events which led up to it. But all this is only the beginning, for he must possess *the far more exceptional power of divination which can peer into the purpose beyond its expression, and bring to fruition that which lay only in flower.*"[21] Such imaginative projection need not—indeed must not—result in making law as a legislature does: while it may seem as if "a judge who is not 'literal' is 'legislating,' if he knows his business that is what he never does."[22] Imaginative projection is not a matter of "intruding one's own solution" on the case, however much this may be a temptation.[23] However difficult this may be in practice, "interpretation" must not become "enactment."[24]

Here, without becoming more explicit, Hand confronts the full force and dramatic effects of the "imagination" at work in interpretive reconstruction. The judicial work that takes place after a literal parsing of the words of the law, statute, or precedent, and before a decision as to how to apply these words to a situation more or less different than the one envisaged by the legislator or judge, is interpretive. The relevant question to ask of such

19. EDMUND PLOWDEN, COMMENTARIES OR REPORTS 467 (1779) (cited in 1951-1 To Frankfurter, January 15 (emphasis added).

20. 1933-1 To Frankfurter, January 23, note 10 (emphasis added).

21. *Thomas Walter Swan*, *in* THE SPIRIT OF LIBERTY: PAPERS AND ADDRESSES OF LEARNED HAND 217 (Irving Dilliard ed., 1960) (emphasis added) [hereinafter THE SPIRIT OF LIBERTY].

22. 1948-3 To Wyzanski, May 22.

23. 1952-5 To Wyzanski, April 13.

24. 1955-5 To Frankfurter, October 1.

interpretation is: How far is it also the work of the creative imagination pure and simple? The judge is "free" to reconstruct the "occasion" in which the legislator's or former judge's words were uttered in order to find their present application, but given Hand's strong warning against judicial "enactment," not too free.[25]

Engaging both reason and imagination, Hand's letters complement his understanding of how the law works with a philosophical position: a working skepticism predicated on an understanding of human experience as essentially earthbound and without knowledge of any kind of "Absolute," whether understood spiritually as a function of a transcendent will or morally as irreproachable dicta governing human relations. Here, Hand's earliest and most vigorous mentor is Holmes, whose outlook on life fascinates him and yet also proves to be bafflingly inadequate. For Hand, what is taken for truth is no more than opinion, and "opinions are at best provisional hypotheses, incompletely tested."[26] By contrast, Holmes offers an essentially personal and arguably dogmatic notion of truth as his own private collection of "Can't Helps"—beliefs that appear to be needed in order to more forward: "when I say a thing is true, I mean that I can't help believing it—and nothing more. But as I observe that the Cosmos is not always limited by my Can't Helps, I don't bother about absolute truths or even inquire whether there is such a thing, but define the Truth as the system of my limitations." Although philosophically this truth functions as no more than a self-mirroring register, it is for Holmes the presumption upon which social exchange can proceed: "I may add that as other men are subject to a certain number, not all, of my Can't Helps, intercourse is possible."[27] Proving too dire an assessment of human nature for his studied temperament, Hand in time transforms his own concept of truth into a creative principle without which a democratic society cannot thrive or properly function.

At its most extreme, Hand's "Absolute" is a self-canceling paradox. Complaining to Frankfurter of renewed activity by members of the political right, Hand expresses his frustration: "Old men, I know, must not 'crab' about the changes that will come even in their own absolutes, though these be confined to A SINGLE ABSOLUTE, i.e., THERE ARE NONE. We live, but do we learn?"[28] This rather moody extravagance renders the very idea of a divine creator problematic, and Hand seconds Berenson's rewriting of Genesis: "among *les mots les plus justes* that I have encountered for a very long time is your 'In the beginning was the Guess.'"[29] Yet Hand represents humanity as privileged; while it needs to reject "Absolutes"—the predicates of philosophy or the doctrines of religion—it profits from experience. In "Democracy: Its Presumptions and Realities," a speech delivered before the Federal Bar Association on March 8th, 1932, Hand reports a vision of history that is characterized by human "trial and error."[30] Man is a "wayward creature" for whom "the Absolute is mute: no tables come from Sinai to guide him; the brazen sky gives no

---

25. 1933-1 To Frankfurter, January 23, note 10.

26. 1918-2 To Holmes, June 22.

27. 1918-2 To Hand from Holmes, June 24.

28. 1955-7 To Frankfurter, November 25. Here, Hand refers to a philosophical principle. By contrast, in correspondence with Frankfurter on *Brown* in 1957, Hand regards the Equal Protection Clause as constituting an "absolute" with respect to civil rights for African-Americans.

29. 1956-1 To Berenson, January 29.

30. *Democracy: Its Presumptions and Realities, in* The Spirit of Liberty 101.

answer to his prayers." There are no fixed or changeless laws, not even those enjoining "self-abnegation," for "life is self-assertion" and will not endure silence or idleness. "Beware then of the heathen gods; have no confidence in principles that come to us in the trappings of the eternal. Meet them with gentle irony, friendly skepticism and an open soul." But this "soul" is also to reject despair. "Nor be cast down," Hand insists, "for it is always dawn. Day breaks forever, and above the eastern horizon the sun is now about to peep. Full light of day? No, perhaps not ever." But "if one watches sharply enough the paths that were so blind will become hourly plainer." In such mediated darkness "we shall learn to walk straighter. Yes, it is always dawn."[31]

I think Hand's appreciation of these figures reflects his boyhood education. To live "always" at dawn is itself a condition of the belief in the nature of history and historical time that is demanded of Calvinist Puritans, the branch of Christianity in which Hand was raised. His embrace of the virtues of temperance and moderation reflects his sense that history will provide its truths and the conditions in which settled and coherent societies thrive, but only retrospectively, at the end of time. As John Calvin glossed Romans 13.12—"*The night is past the day approcheth neere*"—the "day" to which Paul refers heralds an enlightenment not yet present but rather, as promised in scripture, always to come. "Hee comparath the knowledge of the life to come, which shineth unto us by the gospel, unto the morning. Day, here, as in many other places is not put for the light of faith [...] but for that brightnesse of the celestiall life, whose beginnings are now seene, in the gospell. The summe is, as by the spring of the day we gather, that the full light of the sunne is at hand."[32] For Hand, the experience of history indicates a "day" that, while not fully apparent within the compass of history, will nevertheless show within that compass the "paths" to take.

True, in his adult life, Hand was no advocate of Puritan morality. To Holmes he confesses: "I could never muster much enthusiasm for those worthies though I carry their blood."[33] Yet Hand, by his own admission a "timid, puzzled, old bourgeois,"[34] could not escape its influence or reject its curious discipline, engaging both hope and despair. As the tenor and substance of Hand's correspondence attests, a puritanical practice informed many of the actions of his life. Summing up Hand's character late in his life, Frankfurter alludes to "the constant and too often uncomfortable debate [...] between the Puritan and the Pagan" that troubled Hand's soul and reminded him just weeks before he died—confined to a wheelchair, blind in one eye, and worried because he had "taken part in only 25 or 26 cases" that year—that he was endowed with "Puritan conscience."[35] The light of the dawn and the uncertain certainties it gives was for him a constant.

---

31. Democracy: Its Presumptions and Realities, in THE SPIRIT OF LIBERTY 101–02.

32. A COMMENTARIE VPON THE EPISTLE OF SAINT PAUL TO THE ROMANES 176 verso, 177, written in Latine by M. Iohn Caluin, and newely translated into Englishe by Christopher Rosdell (1583).

33. 1913-1 To Holmes, April 21.

34. 1945-2 To Clark, February 8. Gunther sees Hand's self-confessed reticence as primarily owing to timidity; however, it also respects the Calvinist insistence that one lead a rigorously examined life.

35. 1952-8 To Hand from Frankfurter, November 13; and 1961-2 To Hand from Frankfurter, June 15.

Hand's recourse to the imagination as a source for the interpretation of the letter of the law has a moral as well as an intellectual reference. It reverts to his rejection of "absolutes" and his corresponding celebration of "debate," a "privilege" that "presupposes that there are no orthodoxies so absolute that they may not be wrong [...] it trusts that error will be best answered by not being repressed." Because no "mediating organon can be found to measure our values beyond our individual preferences, our chance lies in imagination, i.e., an ability to put ourselves in each other's place, and a gradual slackening of our own insistences."[36] It requires a sympathetic identification with the situation of others.[37] As Hand tells Frankfurter, "the prime quality for your Court is a power to put oneself in the position of others with whose interests and antecedents he disagrees,"[38] and it depends on "the spirit of moderation [. . .] the temper [. . .] which can understand and will respect the other side, which feels a unity between all citizens [. . .] which has faith in the sacredness of the individual."[39]More critically, it is linked to a willingness to recognize "the uncertainty of human hypothesis," and "how changeable and passing are our surest convictions."[40] In espousing such discipline, the Court needs to accept that it has no "duty to keep this society in the path of righteousness and high endeavor."[41]

Once released from its verbal bottle, this genie—at once the spirit of rational discrimination *and* imaginative invention—informs not only Hand's ideas about interpretation but also those conveying his sense of the role of the law in preserving human society. Insisting on the judge's detachment, Hand regards him as both artistic and visionary: he must use "as much imagination as is possible" in the way that a poet or sculptor might when he pursues his "vague purposes" among "an indefinite number of what you might call frames of preference."[42] Those who practice law fashion the future: "[they] are cast for the part of putting into words the vague yearnings which float half grasped in men's minds[. . .]; they will command in the end, no matter how much for the moment they must bend, for they alone are the interpreters of the spiritual essences which inspire the brains of men."[43] Eventually they contribute to the creation of a common will.

In an early and controversial exchange with Benjamin Cardozo, who complains that Hand gives him no credit for "interpreting the common will" in his decisions, Hand responds by explaining how such interpretation is possible. Reading an old text in order that it may be relevant to a new situation, a judge becomes a visionary: "No, I did not mean that you or other sages did not interpret a common will. I think you do. 'Interpret' is a baffling word. I am by no means sure that I know just what it means, but I should say that what you succeeded in doing was expressing ideas to which people would assent

36. 1952-5 To Wyzanski, April 13; 1954-3 To Wyzanski, February 2.

37. Defining justice, Hand invokes Ulpian: "Justice consists in the constant and perpetual willingness to render to everyone his rightful due. The rules of the law are these: to live honestly, not to harm anyone, and to give each his own." *Digest* 1.1.10 in 1957-5 To Frankfurter, April 24, note 187.

38. 1957-5 To Frankfurter, April 24.

39. *The Contribution of an Independent Judiciary, in* The Spirit of Liberty 164.

40. *Sources of Tolerance, in* The Spirit of Liberty 76.

41. 1957-5 To Frankfurter, April 24.

42. Quoted in Gerald Gunther, Learned Hand: the Man and the Judge 673 (1994) (citing Anthony Lewis, N.Y. Times, Apr. 11, 1959, at 1).

43. 1934-2 To Harry E. Stone, November 5.

when they became aware of them. If you are disposed to be a mystic you may say that the idea was there already; I should prefer to say that it was not, but that you made your beliefs theirs."[44] By making his beliefs an anticipatory reflection of the people's, the judge has a "representative character as a complementary organ of the social will"; his is a "free power by interpretation to manifest the half-framed purposes of his time."[45]

Because of the effects of the interpretative process, the body of law in a representative democracy evolves. Its ends may be unknown, its beginnings obscure, its growth spontaneous and unpremeditated, yet it has an organic integrity: "the whole of it has been fabricated in this way like a coral reef of the symmetry of whose eventual structure the artificers have no intimation as they labor."[46] For all its multi-directedness, this "structure" is coherent in itself and throughout its disposition. Nor does Hand doubt that for all the diversity in its development, the law is perdurable in principle. To Frankfurter, who jokes that the law he works on will be "deader than a dodo" in no time, Hand responds: "I don't agree that the stuff which we are dispensing will be deader than a dodo. It may seem so, but unless the whole works blow up, it will have had its part. I remember that Holmes once said to you that you would go on increasing the measure of rationality in an irrational world. I decline to believe that the lower depths of the coral reefs do not support the levels which rise above the sea."[47] Dispensing as always with any reliance on "Absolutes," Hand assumes that "'History' is our mainstay in legislation," and although it may be that "the past is so manifold and so inaccessible that we must always be uncertain what were the actual interests adjusted in the past," solutions that have "enjoyed a long acceptance" have "an authority which we are disposed to accept until they too greatly outrage some dominant group of present power."[48]

However instrumental in understanding how law should function, Hand's skepticism was less governed by the intellectual constraints exemplified by Holmes's "Can't Helps" than by the Justice's conception of humanity as merely biological: he regards mankind in his world as no more than a "fluid ganglion in a fluid universe, significant only as a part of I know not what."[49] The concept of humanity as a mobile mass of protoplasm supported Hand's belief that to seek stability is to invite disappointment; more important, it allows for a politics of moderation and tolerance. As he told the members of the Elizabethan Club at Yale on May 10th, 1941, the liberty of the individual to test and try the terms by which he lives is "an authentic demand of the spirit—*animula vagula blandula . . . quae nunc abibis in loca.*"[50] Seeking a basis for promoting "free discussion," Hand develops further the functions of reason and imagination by insisting that the "imagination" be purged and the "judgment" be ripened by an "awareness of the slow hesitant wayward course of human life, its failures, its successes [and] its indomitable will to endure."[51] Linked to the *anima vagula* and engaged in multiple responses to experience,

44. 1929-4 To Cardozo, June 26.
45. *The Speech of Justice, in* The Spirit of Liberty 14.
46. *Is There a Common Will, in* The Spirit of Liberty 53.
47. 1932-2 To Hand from Frankfurter, March 11; 1932-2 March 12 To Frankfurter.
48. 1958-3 To Wyzanski, December 9.
49. 1920-2 To Hand from Holmes, March 9.
50. *Liberty*, in The Spirit of Liberty 153.
51. *A Plea for an Open Mind and Free Discussion, in* The Spirit of Liberty 283.

the imagination as a heuristic faculty of mind fashions the moral virtues of "Tolerance" and "Moderation."

Hand's experience of a personal *anima vagula,* inhabiting, perhaps, a Holmesian cosmos of ganglia, was informed by a second and related figure: man as the product of an evolutionary process that featured at its inception a simian ancestor. Inviting Holmes to reflect on man as "ce méchant singe, *homo sapiens,*" a creature shaped by "various prejudices and accepted conventions,"[52] Hand must have known that his conflated image of a simian creature both naughty and wise would please his reader.[53] In fact, Holmes had endorsed Darwin's theories from his sophomore year at Harvard. But like his vision of his own wandering spirit, Hand's sense of man as simian is transformed, even redeemed, by its reconceptualization in positive terms. As he tells Berenson, "we are not now throwing coconuts at each other from the tops of the trees, not because by the opposition of our fifth finger [our first finger] has turned into a thumb, but because by some strange biological quirk [. . .] we got a habit of not responding immediately to all flashes from the environment. Those blockings or frustrations—which incidentally play such havoc with us individually now—that are the fruit of our delayed reactions have developed into inconceivably numerous possibilities of response." With a strange good fortune, these "possibilities of response" go to fashion "what we call 'mind,'" their effects compounded because all "thinking" does "violence" to our residual and "primitive" makeup.[54] In short, "by insistent scrutiny and by readiness to re-examine presently accredited conclusions [. . .] we have risen [. . .] from our brutish ancestors."[55] By "'monkeying around,'" always meddling with everything, we produce a human culture.[56]

"Monkeying" thus becomes the means by which society guarantees its future: "any organization of society which depresses free and spontaneous meddling is on the decline, however showy its immediate spoils." To "pry about at random" is to investigate the premises upon which a society can stave off stagnation. Without such inquiry, we shall come "to rely upon accredited bodies of authoritative dogma, and as soon as we come to rely upon accredited bodies of authoritative dogma, not only are the days of our Liberty over, but we have lost the password that has hitherto opened to us the gates of success as well."[57] Hand's man as monkey is naturally a liberal, that is, an opportunist, a tinkerer, as he defines him in a letter to Charles Amidon: "To me the liberal is the man who disbelieves in the power of the human mind to see far in advance and who is therefore rather limited to being an opportunist, that is, to taking advantage of this and that as it comes up, without far-reaching programs."[58] Thus the move to a human competence in the business of the world is engineered by our very simian attributes. The liberty man enjoys is less a matter of thought than curiosity, less a matter of planning than impulse.

---

52. 1920-2 To Holmes, March 7.

53. 1950-2 To Frankfurter, January 20. Quoting Holmes, Hand notes that Holmes attributes to "man a significance [not] different in kind from that which belongs to a baboon or a grain of sand."

54. 1950-1 To Berenson, January 8.

55. *A Fanfare for Prometheus, in* THE SPIRIT OF LIBERTY 294.

56. *At Fourscore, in* THE SPIRIT OF LIBERTY 258.

57. *Liberty, in* THE SPIRIT OF LIBERTY 152–53.

58. 1928-2 To Amidon, February 24.

In keeping with his celebration of monkeying around, Hand regards human resources as self-reflexive, engaged less in securing ends than in exploiting, testing, and entertaining the means to those ends. This is true to the extent that it yields yet another paradox, cribbed in part from Aristotle's treatment of 'prudence': [it determines] "actions concerning what is good or bad for man: for the end of production is some other thing [i.e., a product], but in the case of action there is no other end (for a good action is itself the end)."[59] In Hand's practice, ends recede into a future experienced as a series of progressive displacements; the means used to attain ends become ends in themselves. The process of securing means is itself beneficent. "Human wants" function as a safeguard against "depression," both personal and industrial. Contemplating the numbers of deities in the classical pantheon in a letter to Lippmann, Hand notes: "I rejoice in all these capacities of the human soul. I see in the proliferation of human wants the surest safeguard against suicide—and for that matter industrial depression. We started off little endowed, and if we had not achieved the faculty of making ends out of means, where in Hell should we be today?"[60] Hand's evident satisfaction in transforming the means to an end to an end in itself takes aim at a rare foible of Holmes's: "I want the enterprise of finding out to seem final and conclusive" as it will be if means can be ends. Holmes, by contrast, "seemed to me to be guilty of the contradiction by saying the limits of human knowledge are inherent, we can never reach the ultimate. Who was the lad who first showed up that faked humility?"[61] Professing appreciation of means as ends, Hand addressed The American Jewish Committee on January 29th, 1955, in uncompromising terms: "[Man's] reward is not so much in the work as in its making; not so much in the prize as in the race. We may win when we lose, if we have done what we can; for by so doing we have made real at least some part of that finished product in whose fabrication we are most concerned: ourselves."[62] The dictum becomes "gospel," the only one he knows how to preach: "that of sport for its own sake and within that [. . .] all that we undertake."[63]

Hand's letters reveal that his engagement with the law and its role in public life was at the expense of a more compelling interest in philosophy. Early in his career, Hand wrote to his uncle Richard Hand that he longed to be a philosopher but felt it imperative that he turn to law. Professionally, this was the life he had in view.[64] His regrets remain, however attenuated: "the soul which aspired to comprehend the universe is content to try bootleggers. After all, why not?"[65] Nevertheless, in letters to his friends Edward Burling and Philip Littell, he sketches the terms of a *modus vivendi*—a philosophy of sorts—that declares the individual to be the practitioner of particular virtues rather than the achiever of a defined goal.

To [Edward] Burling, he contests the usefulness of a utilitarian philosophy to secure the "Good Life": "The Utilitarians missed much [. . .] The reason I suggest is this. It

59. Aristotle, *Nicomachean Ethics*, VI, 5(1140b).

60. 1931-2 To Lippmann, May 31.

61. 1954-2 To Curtis, January 14.

62. *A Fanfare for Prometheus, in* The Spirit of Liberty 297.

63. 1937-4 To Wyzanski, December 28, 1937.

64. To Richard Hand, January 4, 1893; Box 110, Folder 6, Special Collections, Harvard Law Library.

65. 1923-1 To Cardozo, March 3.

makes no difference how biologically it came to be true, nevertheless it is true, that mankind has for aeons come so to confuse the means with the end that the means have become ends in themselves." Nor is it a mistake, Hand continued, outlining the process by which the exercise of a personal means creates a good—indeed, an unqualified "good in itself": "man is a curious animal who builds out of his own insides, so to speak: courage, which in origin was mediate and of itself neutral, becomes in time a newly fabricated good—*Güte an sich*, so to speak. Thus a man who possesses it has a sense of value in himself, quite independent of the safety he secures, of the recognition that he may get from his fellows. It is as direct and un-analyzable a good as the enjoyment of the senses themselves." The achievement is consistent with the forfeiture of ends and the embrace of a practice of whatever virtue that in time becomes exemplary. Hand concludes his assessment of means as ends by celebrating the satisfaction they give—not pleasure but a "higher satisfaction."[66] As he told the graduates of the Yale Law School on June 17th, 1931: "the Good Life begins only when one's satisfactions are not derivative but immediate; that what one gives one's time to should be an end in itself, not a means."[67]

Hand's letters to Littell speak to a different and more tranquil world than any Utilitarians could envisage. A meta-correspondence of sorts, they reflect on their own workings. They explore the resources given the imagination, that faculty of projection and sympathy, by indifference (in effect, close to a Stoic *ataraxia*), the habit of modesty, and an embrace of failure when that is clearly realistic. On board the steamer *Volendam* headed for Europe in the summer of 1929, Hand writes Littell that he was struck the day before with a thought that he had "something really new, a light upon conduct" but that it is now "quite gone" (a loss consistent with the status of fluid ganglion). The event prompts this reflection: "Out here in the sea nature impresses on me that at bottom the principle of indifference is fundamental. If one man chase his tail, that is for him the Absolute: God as Tail-chaser. If on the other hand, he is of hound blood, and contemplation is his food, that is Absolute: God as Hound-Dog. Whether there is at bottom some Higher Synthesis I cannot tell."[68] The "light on conduct" that Hand had hoped to convey, whatever it was, has been transformed, almost, it would seem, by the prismatic effects of the moment of its apprehension, into a series of colorful suppositions to which the appropriate response is—no particular response apart from that which enables a record to be made of the loss, of the failure to remember what had, at the moment, seemed of considerable value.

This insight leads to its correlates: acceptance and repose. In subsequent letters to Littell, the effort Hand makes to understand is chiefly retrospective, bound up with a sense of the desires that have been forfeited over time. Writing from Washington, DC, he confesses: "[D]elighting in the beauties of the mornings and evenings [. . .] I can see it is a good life as I could not have seen not many years ago. How our values shape themselves with our possibilities." He frames his vision by alluding to a past disappointment, one perhaps that might even recur in the future, that lies in wait, as it were, a potential

66. 1944-2 To Burling, February 6.

67. *To Yale Law Graduates, in* The Spirit of Liberty 85.

68. 1929-7 To Littell, July 19.

distraction from the effort at indifference and the contentment with a "world in which there can be no divine goddesses [. . .] I used to wish awfully that I could be on the Supreme Court; I used to wish this whenever I came here. I do not do this now. It amuses me to think of this; still more to wonder how much I might change back, if it by a miracle could become again possible."[69] The vision and its contentment gesture toward the state of classical *mediocritas*, a way of being that is especially privileged in Hand's last letter to Littell in the Harvard archive. There he warns of the dangers of aspiring to "perfection" in life—Is it hubris?—because it certainly courts failure. "I sometimes think you believe you have failed," he tells Littell. "Well, you have; everybody does, one way or another." But paradox immediately inverts this judgment and creates its opposite: "But really you have won." Why? "[B]ecause you have plied your craft as you saw it should be plied, even when you knew that you could not reach the quality you wished." By this existential calculus, failure, though it cannot be counted as success, realizes its own perfection. Those who recognize such failure in others "delight" in the "high-heartedness of the effort." They do not commemorate the end but the virtue summoned in trying to achieve it, the perfection inherent in trying and failing, in trying despite successive failures. "I choose that, and it is from you that I have had a repeated sense that I ought to keep loyal to it."[70]

Hand returns to the view of human failure and triumph in two addresses later in his career. In his speech to members of the Harvard Club on the occasion of his 80th birthday in 1952, he proposes as an ideal life's work not "redeeming the world" but something more personal, more modest: "It is enough that we set out to mold the motley stuff of life into some form of our own choosing; when we do, the performance is itself the wage [. . .] let us not fear failure: 'Tis not in mortals to command success but we'll do more, Sempronius—we'll deserve it'.[71] And deserve it we can; not necessarily in our harvest, but in the resolution with which we till the soil."[72] Throughout his life, Hand was committed, almost programmatically, to facing endeavors whose outcomes he sensed were doubtful, even precarious. But he stopped well short of a skepticism so radical that it disdained any permanent or stable point of repose; rather, he saw that to search for the deepest meanings in life created its own singular and irreproachable form of tranquility.

Beyond wondering whether he should "try really to write" and facing Berenson's insistence that he should, Hand's correspondence gives no indication that he ever took the possibility seriously; indeed, the reverse was the case. Whether from self-doubt or a reluctance to create a public persona, he regarded the prospect of publishing his essays and speeches with diffidence if not dismay. Asked in 1942 by the editor Edward C. Aswell if Harper & Brothers might publish his "occasional addresses," Hand replied that this would destroy his "peace of mind": "I never read one without an acute feeling of nausea."[73] Ten years later, Hand remained reluctant to credit his literary productions. On April 3rd, 1952, having agreed that Irving Dilliard should publish THE SPIRIT OF LIBERTY, Hand conveys his "great sense of gratitude" for his editor's "efforts to gather up and perpetuate these words

69. 1933-2 To Littell, February 12.

70. 1936-2 To Littell, July 10.

71. JOSEPH ADDISON, CATO, act 1, scene 2.

72. *On Fourscore, in* THE SPIRIT OF LIBERTY 262.

73. To Edward C. Aswell, April 25, 1942, in 1952-4 To Dilliard, April 3 and note 81.

of mine which have been scattered at random through so many publications," and he hopes the publisher, Alfred A. Knopf, will not suffer too great a loss on this account.

Given that The Spirit of Liberty is Hand's only extra-legal work to be published, its history is remarkable: by August, the book had sold 7,500 copies; by September, it had sold 9,000 copies; by October 19th, 1954, it had sold 20,000 more copies and been translated into Turkish and Greek. On January 2nd, 1957, Jean Paul de Dadelson of the International Press Institute wrote to Hand about the forthcoming French translation and the foreword intended for French readers.[74] A second edition was published in 1953, and a third, much augmented edition, was published in 1960.

The end of this story is no less impressive. Perhaps because his lectures on The Bill of Rights had received a generally negative response,[75]Hand continued to regard The Spirit of Liberty with diffidence. On January 20th, 1960, evidently unwilling to leave him without remuneration, Knopf sent Hand a check for $1,000; this check Hand promptly returned. As he stated to Knopf, The Spirit of Liberty was simply a collection of his "desultory talks"; the book could have been a "flop, and useful only as a 'deduction'"; that it had received "a certain degree of welcome" was to be credited not to what it contributed to its many readers but to Knopf's "backing."[76] Knopf, to his credit, appears to have taken Hand's gratitude as rhetorical. Undaunted and refusing to give up, Knopf sent Hand a case of wine on March 22nd. Whether because it would have been graceless to return a case of wine to its giver or because the prospect of enjoying a good Bordeaux pleased him, Hand accepted Knopf's gift, which he acknowledged on March 25th.[77]

At the end of his life, Hand clearly could not bring himself to recognize that his published essays and speeches were in fact "really written" in the manner and kind he had entertained in 1933 in his letter to Littell, when "really to write" was no more than a distant prospect at best: "I can see vistas of unknown relations that I have never even started down, but I know at least that they are there." Nothing in his words or tone suggests that he will start down any of the vistas he says he sees. Here, however, the reader may wish to pick up the narrative and recognize in Hand's letters to and from his many correspondents evidence of the "relations" to which he had gestured earlier—now known in and through the act of writing.

---

74. *See* 1960-1 To Knopf and note 3, January 20, 1960.

75. *See* To McGeorge Bundy, June 28, 1958, Hand papers, Special Collections, Harvard Law Library, Box 85, Folder 11. For Bundy's review, see 67 Yale L.J. 944 (1958).

76. 1960-1 To Knopf, January 27.

77. Correspondence on the publication and sales of The Spirit of Liberty with Alfred A. Knopf is filed in the Hand Papers, Special Collections, Harvard Law Library, Box 91, Folders 21–24, and with Irving Dilliard in Box 87, Folders 12–16.

REASON AND IMAGINATION

PROLOGUE

A better if less consistent social philosophy

—Learned Hand to Augustus Hand, November 6, 1898

A BETTER SOCIAL PHILOSOPHY: 1897–1908

The first four letters in this collection can be read as points of departure for journeys both intellectual and literary that Hand will take over the next half-century. To Thayer, Hand represents the disciplined student of the law, insisting that the language of the law must be both bound by the rules of logic and avoid recourse to metaphor and other figures of speech. He associates the logician with law that is applied, the poet with law that is made. Hand praises Norton for showing him the way to an essentially moralistic experience of art; in the company of Berenson forty years later, he discards this morality for an uncritical enjoyment of works of art. To his cousin Augustus Hand, he reflects upon their common family history. Rejecting the individualism of his father and uncles, all Democrats, Hand argues for the importance of a "social philosophy" that includes a role for the "State," and while he does not rule out the prospect of acquiring "subject dependencies," he doubts the ability of the American government to act in good faith. Finally, to his wife Frances, he proposes to neglect neither joy nor duty and rather to regard them both as essential to a life well lived.

1897

To James Bradley Thayer

April 12, 1897 Hale, Bulkeley & Tennant, Albany, N.Y.

My dear Mr. Thayer:[1]

The copy which you so kindly sent me of "The Presumption of Innocence in Criminal Cases" came to hand today, and I have just finished reading it.[2] Being already well convinced of the truth of your position, I cannot say that it was enlightening to me, but I don't see how it could fail to be convincing to those who have not had the advantage of hearing the substance of it before. I did not know but that you would insist more strongly upon the distinction between presumption proper and the rule determining how much proof is necessary to establish the case, but I understand you at the end to allow that however clearly the two must be discriminated in theory, there is no great harm in speaking of the presumption as requiring so much proof in one case, so much in another, to meet it. This seems to me fair. I remember that in the School we used to have it very flatly in our note-books that all presumptions were alike in that they ceased absolutely to have any bearing upon the case as soon as any relevant evidence was introduced, whatever. For purposes of teaching this is no doubt useful, but it would greatly confuse an ordinary lawyer in practice, I believe, who unites the real presumption with the rule which requires a certain quantum of evidence in each case to establish the opposite conclusion to that of the presumption. Nor does it involve at all the singular confusion in Mr. Justice White's[3] opinion of supposing that a presumption actually is a matter in any sense probative to the lay judgment, and to be classed among the ordinary facts from which inference is to [be] made.

Incidentally, I wish some one with the requisite patience and dialectic skill would write an essay upon the evils arising to the law from the use of figurative language. More pompous nonsense and pretentious question-begging goes stalking about our books in the form of poor metaphor than would confuse the clearest-headed. I wish

---

1. James Bradley Thayer (1831–1902): Professor, Harvard Law School, 1873–1902. Responding to Professor Samuel Williston's request that alumni report on "what Harvard Law School has meant to the profession," LH describes Thayer's instruction as he remembers it in 1949: "His course in constitutional law we held to be the fitting crown of the whole three years, although one did not get, or at least I did not, many working propositions out of it. But that was not the heart of it; what one did learn, step by step, was that most of constitutional law had been constructed out of circular propositions which justified the predetermined attitudes of the judges, who, being more often than not, primarily men of action, were unaware of the verbal traps that lay about them and into which they often unwittingly fell. I never felt sure how much of what we took away he meant us to get; for, so far as he ever committed himself, he was always tentative and moderate, as though dealing in an unpredictable medium on which no one could count. But the result was to imbue us with a skepticism about the wisdom of setting up courts as the final arbiters of social conflicts, which many of us, at any rate, always retained." HARV. L. SCH. BULL. Nov. 1949, at 8.

2. *The Presumption of Innocence in Criminal Cases*, 6 YALE L.J. 185 (1897).

3. Edward Douglass White (1845–1921): Associate Justice of the United States Supreme Court, 1895–1910; Chief Justice of the United States, 1910–1921.

that no decision could be authoritatively quoted unless it were in one of the formal syllogistic forms, the judge being required to state, by page and line reference to some standard work on logic, which form he was using. We might discover when he was making law, when applying it, and he might also know which he was doing. Besides, opinions might become shorter.

Thank you very much for the pamphlet: it is very refreshing to get a breath of the clear, systematic treatment of the School; it is only now that I can get no more of it that I realize fully how wholesome it was.

Very sincerely yours, L. Hand

P.S. It may perhaps interest you to know that owing to the death of Mr. Matthew Hale, I shall leave my present office soon and go into that of Mr. Marcus T. Hun of reportorial fame.[4] I think myself very fortunate in the change now that Mr. Hale is gone, because I believe I shall have as good an opportunity as I could have any where in this city.

ms with signature 10.16

1898-1

To Charles Eliot Norton[5]

July 1, 1898 — 25 North Pearl street, Albany, N.Y.

My dear Professor Norton:

I cannot let pass the occasion of your retiring from active teaching in Harvard College without expressing to you my individual gratitude to you for your instruction when I was there. I certainly cannot recall many facts in my experience which so entirely changed my point of view, and opened my eyes to a side of the world which had been quite shut off to them. As I concern myself with practical affairs more completely, I feel more and more the value of what you have given, though the vessel seems to become less suitable for the little it contains. You will therefore be glad to let me add my voice to those of the many in Harvard and out of it, whose ideals have been raised and whose appreciations have been developed by your teaching. I can only wish you many years of active happiness to yourself and of usefulness to your country and the world of letters.[6]

Learned Hand

ms with signature 7.19

---

4. Marcus T. Hun, the attorney in Albany for whom LH worked from 1899 to 1902.

5. Charles Eliot Norton (1827–1908): editor of the North American Review, 1864–1868; Professor of the History of Art, Harvard University, 1875–1898.

6. For LH's later view of Norton's instruction as stringently moralistic, see 1949-2 To Berenson, May 24.

To Learned Hand from Charles Eliot Norton

July 6, 1898 Ashfield, Massachusetts

Dear Mr. Hand:

Your letter has given me great pleasure and I thank you for it. It is a rare good fortune and privilege for a teacher to have to deal with ideas from the very nature of his subject fitted to quicken and inspire the hearts of his pupils, and thus to become associated in their minds with high interests and ideals. I trust that even in the most busy and dusty days some of these ideas may stay with you and prove serviceable. I hope that I may see you at some time again in Cambridge, and with all good wishes, I remain

Sincerely Yours, C.E. Norton

ms with signature 17.19

1898-2

To Augustus Hand[7]

November 6, 1898 Albany, N. Y.

Dear Gus:

[. . .]At present I want to talk to you about the political situation. I had a talk with Uncle Cliff[8] which was very exhilarating and delightful. Incidentally I may say that he and your father, and I suppose in this my father would have agreed with them, are to me very refreshing in that their ideas seem so neatly and clearly defined and so confidently accepted upon all political questions. Their doctrinaire individualism—to use a rather obnoxious phrase—has always seemed to me so sturdy and manly a political philosophy as we can hold, and when I contrast it with the amorphous mixture of socialism and laissez faire which is perhaps the most generally accepted belief of the present generation, I confess that aesthetically at any rate their beliefs have the advantage.

But you and I cannot be quite so naively confident in the policy of letting everyone alone, and must sacrifice robustness and lucidity of idea to what I in the end believe to be a wider scope, and a better if a less consistent social philosophy. I go with you in a belief that a general presumption of laissez faire is the proper basis of government, but I believe that you in turn will join me in believing that it is in no sense an inevitable principle applicable to all cases, and that in a vast multitude of cases the State must and should regulate the conduct of

7. Augustus Noble Hand (1869–1954): son of Richard Lockhart Hand, brother of LH's father Samuel, and LH's first cousin. Judge, United States District Court for the Southern District, 1914–1928; Judge, United States Second Circuit Court of Appeals, 1928–1953. He remained a close friend and ally of LH throughout his life. *See* 1924-1 To Augustus Hand, July 27; 1950-5 To Augustus Hand, August 8; 1950-7 To Augustus Hand, September 23.

8. Clifford Hand, the eldest son of Augustus C. Hand, the brother of LH's father, Samuel, and LH's uncle.

individuals for their own welfare and modify the contractual relations which they assume towards one another. In particular, I at least believe that in the matter of regulating the safety and healthfulness of factories and the maximum hours of work for women and children this obtains. As to the children you may urge that it is not a violation of the strictest laissez faire—they not being *sui juris*—but at least you must admit that it is a substitution of the governmental for the parental supervision and that that is a step in the same direction.

As to imperialism I agree with him[9] wholly in his feelings though I confess they seem to me to be rather frantically apprehensive[...]; that the possession of colonies *necessarily* implies the disruption of the Republic I cannot believe. There will doubtless be serious questions as to the status of the inhabitants and there will be—by far the most serious matter—a vast amount of corruption and disintegration of political conscience—if any exists—from governing them, but that there is no place under our form of government for a dependency which is not self-governing I do not believe. The territories before admission are given the right of self-government simply by the grace of the Federal government, which is in law as to them absolutely untrammeled as I take it. The Constitution affects the relations of the States only, until we come to the post-bellum amendments, and with their exception the Federal government is as unbound as is the Czar. So at least I believe, basing my belief upon what I conclude myself, and what Thayer told us in treating of territorial government.

So I am not so fearful of the supposed subversionary effect upon the government.

Then too, what of the moral effect? That the mere fact of ruling subject dependencies is not fatal to the democratic instinct, the British Empire seems to me to be a final proof, perhaps the purest democracy in England in the whole world, and an entire despotism in those parts of India in which the rajahs have been deposed.

So that really I think we must fall back upon the peculiar conditions of our country and I regret to say the inability we have shown properly to make a democratic government efficient. When one considers the plight of the poor Indian, who had at least a better chance of making his woes come home to us than the Filipino will have, and when one considers the Negro, I can't see how he can have any very sanguine confidence in the beneficent effect of that glorious American liberty of which we talk so much when applied to an uncivilized and inferior people. Moreover until we have learned to make our cities safer, e.g., from the contamination of their water supply, and free from the contamination of [their] moral ideals we are in no sense fitted to go abroad. Here we have in what most clearly and vitally affects every citizen, the independence of his judges, a very doubtful struggle for the very basis of society, and that final insult to civilization, Richard Croker,[10] adored by thousands of our citizens and almost worshipped. Charity begins at home. I think if we had anything but a pharisaical jellyfish[11] in the White House these things might be better felt[...]

Your loving cousin, Learned Hand

ms with signature 109.2

9. I.e., Clifford Hand

10. Richard Croker (1841–1922): head of Tammany Hall, 1886–1902.

11. William McKinley (1843–1901): President of the United States, 1897–1901.

1904

To: Frances Hand

July 5, 1904

Best of Women:

[...]I have been thinking about our talk on the way up[12] and the matter shapes itself in my mind somewhat like this, though I realize that words are a very poor means of transmitting all the facts because they are mere abstractions from a very intricate complex of feeling. It is with you as it has been with many other people to whom I have tried to justify my own ideas, that they have deemed very forbidding (the ideas) and have seemed so greatly a denial of the spontaneity and the freshness and the general realization of living. This is, I think, because they have become so in my case and of course in preaching the main influence is the preacher's personality. My preaching has seemed somewhat inhuman because I have not been able to show a successful example of the theories I advocate, because I have not done any real service yet, and because I have not coupled with my work the spontaneous and fresh living for living's sake that ought to go and does go along with it.

Now I think this would not be important at all so far as it concerns the rest of the world, but it is most important as concerning you who are always going to live with me, thank God. Because it seems to have an effect upon you, which is very reasonable and perhaps inevitable, of throwing you into the opinion that the doctrine I preach—that our lives should be attached to some service—is inseparably connected with a mutilation of the richer and more keenly sensitive portion of existence. All I want to insist upon is that this is not true, as I believe[...] A man may serve who fills his soul with all that is fullest and most wholly quivering with sensation, if only he keeps a certain ultimate purpose of service before him, not in the sense of such deliberate arranging of his life as to be a killjoy to himself, but in the sense that back of his daily life and through it lies a general sense of his responsibility outside of his purely personal aims and those of them he loves. I have not the least doubt that to anyone, who is conditioned as you and I are, the gratification of this sense of responsibility is a *sine qua non* of a happy life; that is, that it is what Kant called it a categorical imperative which cannot successfully be permanently disobeyed[...]

Of course I have no right even to preach to you in the art of living which you have already learned many times better that I shall every practice it—I say this with perfect sincerity—but I can see what I think is a danger which arises from me and as I believe from my mistakes, and that danger is that you should lose sight of what I believe you do feel when you are at the deepest with yourself and which I admit I hope that you feel; that any single person should not count for more than any other and that our efforts must be

12. LH writes this letter from Albany, where he is visiting his widowed mother, Lydia Learned Hand. He married Frances Fincke in December 1902; they moved to New York in December 1903, when LH joined the firm of Zabriskie, Burrill & Murray.

directed towards that conduct which realizes the greatest realization all round. This is awkwardly put, but to give an instance: I mean that if A and B were alone in the world for one day it would be wrong for A to use $100 for Ortolano and champagne if B were in need of Force, Flaked Rice or Bread. I need hardly add that this simile is not to be expanded into Communism.

Well, dear Chic, this is a long-winded harangue which hasn't really succeeded in setting me right at all with what I meant to say. Perhaps it may do more than it seems. Always keep in mind that I know the two precious things that have come to my life, even when I seem not rightly to value them; the great love of two women, a mother and a wife, which has opened me places which I cannot enter and which I only can see are higher and deeper and sacreder than anything else I shall ever have or that anything I can ever have or ever do. This, dearest Chic, I can and do always remember and it will never leave me[...]

Your loving Pucky B.

ms with signature, family collection

PART I

The old world was breaking up and the new world is trying to be born

—Learned Hand to Douglas MacKinnon, August 11, 1920

THE UNITED STATES AND EUROPE: 1909–1920

Hand's correspondence during these years illustrates his investment in the politics of the nation and after the outbreak of hostilities in Europe, his engagement with the policies of the European powers. His letters to Theodore Roosevelt on the Progressive movement convey his hopes and finally his despair that its programs of reform can be realized. At first an inspiration, Herbert Croly and his magazine, *The New Republic*, lose both force and credibility; to Hand, Roosevelt becomes ineffectual as a national leader. In 1911, Hand opens his life-long correspondence with Frankfurter by outlining the dangers of judicial review, a position he modifies over time but never abandons. For Hand, the legislature will always remain "the efficient organ of democracy." His first letter to Holmes suggests that the Justice has a purity of soul that is both engaging and intimidating; Holmes allows Hand to confront his own Puritan inheritance and to find it less than life affirming. Hand's response to the government's challenge to Max Eastman, the publisher of *The Masses*, begins his efforts to interpret First Amendment law. The advent of war, the negotiation of peace, the "preposterous" indemnities levied against Germany, Roosevelt's aggressive assertion of the victors' power, Wilson's support for Russia's independent government that he at the same time wants to outlaw, the possibilities to be realized by a League of Nations that the United States will not, in any case, agree to join—these are the subjects that concern Hand during the second decade of the century. The threat of Russian communism, transformed as American "socialism," creates variations on the common theme of a "Red scare" that Hand regards as frightening only insofar as it may destroy the liberties of nation from within. Mindful that the enemy may be a better man and support a better cause does not mean he should have any quarter: Holmes and Hand agree that "man's destiny is to fight." But Chafee's support of Hand's *Masses* opinion in his 1920 book, *Free Speech in Wartime*, prompts Hand also to find that even in wartime his own rule is good: "nothing short of counsel to violate law should be itself illegal."

1909-1

To Learned Hand from Henry L. Stimson[1]

April 7, 1909 Winthrop & Stimson, New York

My dear Mr. Hand:

I have been out of town for a few days and have so been delayed in sending you my hearty congratulations on your appointment as District Judge.[2] For the last three years I have been in a position where I could realize much more clearly than ever before the tremendous opportunities and responsibilities of such a position. Particularly is this so in a community like New York City, where on the one hand our greatest industrial problems are being constantly presented for solution before the Federal Tribunals, and where on the other hand there is at the same time such an absence of national spirit[...] In such a community the Federal Judge must face his great responsibilities with comparatively little help from his surrounding atmosphere; he must keep his mind and heart open to the progress which is taking place in other parts of the nation, and must by constant study keep abreast of a wide field of constitutional advance. It is a very sincere pleasure to me that the President has chosen to fill this most important position a man whose scholarly attainments, whose ideals, and whose industry are such as I know yours to be. Believe me with sincere regards,

Faithfully yours, Henry L. Stimson

tp with ms signature 39.18; Sterling, Stimson Papers, Reel 17. This letter and LH's response to Stimson are reproduced in facsimile in *The Remarkable Hands: An Affectionate Portrait* 143–46 (Marcia Nelson ed., 1983).

To Henry L. Stimson

April 8, 1909 2 Wall Street, New York

Dear Mr. Stimson:

I have received your most kind note of congratulation, and it has been very grateful to me to get such a word from someone who knows the solemn nature of the undertaking which I have sought and must now assume. All that you say about the position I believe I realize, insofar as anyone can realize it from the outside. In addition, I realize that I am yet quite unproven and must cope with matters which exceed in importance many times those with which I have ever had to deal. To keep courteous and patient, to try to think

---

1. Henry L. Stimson, 1867–1950: District Attorney for the Southern District of New York, 1906–1909; Secretary of War, 1911–1913; Governor General of the Philippines, 1927; Secretary of State, 1929–1933; Secretary of War, 1940–1945. *See* 1945-9 To Stimson, December 25.

2. After the Senate confirmed LH's appointment as United States District Judge for the Southern District of New York, he took the oath of office on April 30, 1909.

clearly and to work out my counsel with independence and industry: these are now what I can contribute to the President's experiment. I wish I might feel more entirely indifferent to the personal element in it, but naturally I can't quite eliminate that.

I know just how you feel and how you have felt, and your letter has really meant more to me than nearly any other I have had. It seems to me that I may be able to expect from you an understanding and a sympathy which I may need in the future, and I particularly want these and your good opinion, because of the esteem which I have for your character, your talents, and your ideals. It is from you and your kind that can come the only regard which will be the chief payment for the work I am to undertake. If I can deserve it, I know I shall win it.

Faithfully yours, Learned Hand

tp with ms signature 39.18

1909-2

To Herbert Croly[3]

November 5, 1909

Dear Herbert:

Your book came today, but of course I have not yet had time even to look into it.[4] I feel every confidence that I shall enjoy it very much. It is a great pleasure to find a person, and you, I think, are nearly the only one whom I have found who has in fact led successfully the kind of life that I once mapped out for myself and abandoned, perhaps through weakness of will, though I have never been certain that it was not wise for me personally to abandon it. I feel that you think out my thoughts for me, or at least help to, and in this book I hope to find them thoroughly worked out.

I am much caught up and whirled about in the "Wheel of Things" as the Hindoos called it, and it seems to me as though my life grew more and more superficial all the time, though not on that account unpleasant. I do not feel as though I ever really took time to master what I meant to, and that if I did, I should get hopelessly in arrears in the work which I must in some way dispatch. While this is a pleasant life to me, it is really, in a sense, a kind of intoxicant. I look forward to your book as a sort of bromo-seltzer, to help clear the head.

Faithfully yours, [Learned Hand]

tp 102.17

---

3. Herbert Croly (1869–1930): editor of *The New Republic*, 1914–1930. LH met Herbert Croly during the summer of 1908 in Cornish, New Hampshire.

4. Croly had sent LH an advance copy of The Promise of American Life (1910).

To Herbert Croly

December 3, 1909

Dear Herbert:

Come to dinner Tuesday, Friday, or Saturday; the other nights seem to be taken. If you can, come all three nights. I have not yet got far enough in the book to be able to discuss it intelligently, and indeed I can tell you quite frankly that up to the present time, I am lost in a maze of admiration at your excellent work. I do not believe that if I had to talk to you now about it, I could give you any ideas which would be of the least value to you. Not that I hope that I shall ever be able to discuss it on an equality with you, but I do hope that after I have finished it and digested it a little, I may be more intelligent than I could be at present. I mean you to believe quite literally what I say when I tell you that I consider it a most remarkable work of reasoning, and certainly it is the result of the best reflection which any man of my acquaintance and anywhere near my age has given forth, with perhaps the exception of Santayana.[5] I find that in my talk and in my thoughts about political matters since I have read it, I am constantly borrowing whole cloth what you say, which makes me feel a little sheepish, but which is inevitable I suppose. Of particular excellence I found your discussion of the history of political ideas up to the time of the Civil War. I am not quite so well satisfied with the chapters upon the specialists in business and in politics. I should have been a little better pleased if you had shown in more detail just what the political function in democracy of the boss really was. I agree with you that it is a necessary function, and I also think that it is a function rendered necessary through the shortcomings of the voter, so that it was quite excusable for the "Fathers" to leave it out of the political structure; in other words, the boss system is necessary because men are not public spirited and require a more or less refined kind of bribery to be held together in party affiliations. In reading your book, I feel as though you might have in mind some more legitimate function for the boss than that which it seems to me he fulfills, however necessary it may be. Perhaps I have not understood you.

Let me know which of the days you will come. We dine at seven-thirty. Fanny is in excellent shape and would like to see you very much. She is counting upon the Cornish trip but as you will remember, it is contingent upon our being able to dispose of the young one by that time, so that she will not need the constant attendance of her mother, for if she cannot be separated, her mother would have to stay with her as you can well see.

Faithfully yours, [Learned Hand]

tp 102.17

---

5. George Santayana (1863–1952): philosopher, poet, and literary critic. His work to the date of LH's letter includes The Sense of Beauty: being the outlines of aesthetic theory (1896) and The Life of Reason: or, The phases of human progress (1906). In later correspondence, LH mentions The Last Puritan: a memoir in the form of a novel (1935) and The realm of the spirit. Book fourth of Realms of being (1940). On LH's visit with Santayana, see 1937-2 To Berenson, September 17, 22.

To Learned Hand from Herbert Croly

Dear B.:

You may expect me Tuesday evening at seven o'clock[...]

Your reference to the book overwhelmed me. Is it really as good as that? Others have been generous in their appreciation of it, but none so generous as you. Naturally I hope that it is really good not merely because I have my own share of vanity, but because it needs to win friends. It is essentially a reconnoitering expedition into territory hitherto not very well occupied in this country, and I cannot expect to hold my ground unless I obtain support. I have absolutely no means myself of appraising the value of the book as a contribution to the principles which do or should underlie the American democracy. The idea, when it came to me, served to have some power. I worked it up, expressed it as candidly as I could, without tripping over any apparently dangerous obstacles. I have always hoped that it would win some converts, because then I should feel encouraged to seek other applications, and to fortify the position already assumed. But, of course, what I need above all is criticism, particularly from people who agree with me in certain fundamental suppositions. Whatever may be the value of the book, I am trying to keep a candid attitude towards its doctrines, and I don't believe that the force of a really weighty criticism would escape me, provided, as I say, my fundamental assumptions are not all wrong [...]

Chapters 6 and 7 need more re-writing than any others in the book. I shall look forward to Tuesday evening.

Faithfully yours, Herbert Croly

ms with signature 102.17

1910

To Theodore Roosevelt[6]

April 8, 1910

Dear Colonel Roosevelt:

I am recalling to you an acquaintance, long since past, to send you the book of my friend, Herbert Croly, *The Promise of American Life*, which goes under a separate cover. I hope that you will find in it as comprehensive and progressive a statement of American political ideas and ideals as I have found. I think that Croly has succeeded in stating more adequately than anyone else, certainly of those writers whom I know, the bases and prospective growth of the set of political ideas which can be fairly

6. Theodore Roosevelt (1858–1919): Assistant Secretary of the Navy, 1897–1898; commanded the 1st United States Volunteer Cavalry Regiment in the Spanish American War, 1898; Governor of New York, 1899–1900; Vice President of the United States, 1901; President of the United States, 1901–1908; presidential nominee of the Progressive Party, 1912. LH met Roosevelt in 1898. There is no record of his contact with Roosevelt during the latter's presidency, September 14, 1901 to March 4, 1909. *See* GERALD GUNTHER, LEARNED HAND: THE MAN AND THE JUDGE 64, 198–99 (1994).

described as Neo-Hamiltonian, and whose promise is due more to you, as I believe, than to anyone else. I do not suppose that you will agree with it all, but I should be much disappointed if you failed to be interested in much the greater part of it, if you could find a chance to read it.

With the highest regards, and always with most agreeable memories of the time when I used occasionally to see you in Albany, believe me,

Very sincerely yours, [Learned Hand]

tp 37.21

To Learned Hand from Theodore Roosevelt

April 22, 1910 The American Embassy, Paris

Dear Judge Hand:

I thank you for your letter, and look forward with pleasure to reading the book.[7]

Faithfully yours, Theodore Roosevelt

tp with ms signature 37.21

1911-1

To Herbert Croly

February 6, 1911 District Court of the United States

My dear Herbert:

[...]My dear friend, you are becoming an authority. I have no doubt that in a few years, myths will be established about you. Perhaps you will take on the form of the Sun-God. That is the common retroactive metamorphosis of heroes. What with the Colonel giving you such a splendid send-off, and a second edition coming out, you are quite the rage. Stimson is reported to have read the book over three times. I doubt not he could recite parts of it by heart, like the Colonel, except that I don't believe he can recite anything by heart. Sometimes I wonder whether he has a heart. The local insurgents are a forlorn hope, and just at present I think are in some danger of canonizing you. I find that by actual mention of my intimacy with you, I acquire a distinct political significance, the

7. Roosevelt wrote Croly a complimentary letter, which Croly then copied in a letter he sent to LH, dated August 1, 1910: "My dear Mr. Croly: do not know when I have read a book which I felt profited me as much as your book on American life[...] I shall use your ideas freely in speeches I intend to make. I know you won't object to my doing so, because my dear sir, I can see that your purpose is to do your share in any way for the betterment of the national life; that what you care for is to see this betterment secured. Can't you come in to see me at the *Outlook* office? I want very much to have a chance to talk to you"[...] (ms with signature 37.21).

only one that I have ever reached or expect to. Therefore, persevere, Seer of Dingleton,[8] and you will get even great honor than you already have[...]

Every month reassures me of the Colonel's position. No one, I think, in this country has anything like the real breadth of vision that he has, no one the foresight; granting his violence and his lying, his personal untrustworthiness, he is today the best patriot we have. It seems to me incredible that in the situation which the next ten years will bring us, he should not again come to the front. I believe he will, provided he lives and does not go crazy. It is a pity that the precious liquor is all in one chalice, but that is a condition which we have not made, and we must take it as it is. It is a pity, too, that we stand likely at any time to another campaign like that of last October,[9] utterly offensive to all men, destructive to itself and almost mad in its perversity. That, again, however, we can't help[...]

If you want a good book, get Gilbert Murray's *The Rise of the Greek Epic*, a course of lectures given at Harvard a year or two ago.[10] The best thing about Homer that you ever saw or dreamt of. Perhaps you don't care a damn about Homer. I am reading nothing and thinking nothing but how to construe statutes and work out laborious facts. I hope it keeps my wits sharp; it certainly keeps them narrow, and I suppose that sharpness is nothing but the ultimate expression of narrowness. Please never desert me, and leave me to be nothing but a word exchanger. It grows on me, and sometimes oppresses me, the extent to which the whole of our life is wrapped up in these words. Just think of it; all that I and all my tribe ever do, ever have done, ever will do, or ever can do, is to consider the meaning of words. The same is largely true of all of us. I don't wonder that I used to think the logos was a sacred thing, but I get sort of sick of it once in a while.

Please give my love to all the good party. I wish I might be by some Arabian carpet instantly transported into your midst. Being out of the counties of New York and Westchester, I could pour a Bacchic libation and take you all to my heart, not that you are not there anyway, but I can make it more manifest, were I there. Just at present we are having a lowering, blowing, caddish effort at a snow-storm. It's an ill-bred snowstorm, without the good manners to declare itself, content to be ill-natured, disagreeable, and offensive. I am glad you are away from such things.

Faithfully yours, [L.H.]

tp 102.18

---

8. Dingleton Hill near Cornish, New Hampshire, Croly's place of residence.
9. John A. Dix defeated Henry L. Stimson in the election for Governor of New York.
10. Gilbert Murray, The Rise of the Greek Epic (1911).

1911-2

To Learned Hand from Felix Frankfurter[11]

February, 1911 United States Attorney's Office, New York

My dear Judge Hand:

This will interest you if you haven't yet seen it: what [James M.] Beck[12] and the firm think serves as a good chemical test of a negative character. Truly, it all depends whose ox is gored.

Sincerely yours, Felix Frankfurter

ms with signature 104A.1

To Felix Frankfurter

February 26, 1911

My dear Frankfurter:

Beck assumes with some historical justification that the Fourteenth Amendment protects us against "Socialism." Of course, once you admit that a regularly passed act of the legislature may under some circumstances not be "due process of law," you have already got into a category which is vague and is indeed itself "legislative." If your judges are to say when such an act is "due" and when it is "not due," the only considerations they can appeal to, so far as I can see, are whether they approve of the purpose and result of the measure under consideration.[13] Beck, of course, doesn't mean that there are not a good many purposes for which property may be taken in turn, which have as their only sanction that the result is on the whole better for others, even counting the loss to the mentioned.

Now nobody has ever said that the Court might merely substitute its own will for the legislature's. So there you are; they have power to review, not to exercise their judgment independently. My own belief is that practically they ought not to exercise it at all. Of course, there is a reserved possibility, the class distinction between blue-eyed and black-eyed men, as Thayer was fond of saying, but that practically never arises. The fact is that legislatures don't pass laws that have no backing in some public sentiment. In a rare case,

---

11. Felix Frankfurter (1882–1965): Professor, Harvard Law School; 1914–1939; Associate Justice of the United States Supreme Court; 1939–1962. LH and Frankfurter correspond regularly for the next fifty years.

12. James M. Beck (1861–1936): Assistant U.S. Attorney General, 1900–1903; Solicitor General, 1921–1925; and Representative from Pennsylvania, 1927–1934. I have not identified the article that Frankfurter forwarded to LH.

13. LH comments on due process throughout his correspondence; see especially 1912-2 To Roosevelt, February 27; 1913-6 To Veeder, December 11; 1957-7 To Frankfurter, September 13. *See also* LEARNED HAND, THE BILL OF RIGHTS: THE OLIVER WENDELL HOLMES LECTURES, 1958, at 35–55 (1958).

the sentiment might be obviously merely an oppression; I cannot think of an instance, but I have no doubt there are such. To that extent there is room, a very ill-defined room, for "undue process of law."

So far as I know we could have "Socialism" tomorrow, if we wanted it. Doubtless, we could not send the Marshall to seize a factory and operate it by the State, but that is because those methods of proceeding are not customary to our laws. We can accomplish the same thing indirectly by so regulating it that it becomes valueless.

The fact is that all these stand-patters have no courage in their convictions. They regard private property as the cornerstone of existence, but have no confidence that they can justify it before the people at large. Their trust being therefore put in the awkwardness of constitutional amendments, they want to put the whole weight of government on nine elderly gentlemen at Washington. If they had any real confidence that their institution was beneficial, they would let it stand on its own feet, and live in such shape as it could. You and I don't quite love it as unreservedly as they—I may add for myself that I am speaking abstractly—and we are willing to let it be mauled about a bit. For myself, I have no delusions of the *vox populi vox dei* character, but I do believe that anybody is in firm equilibrium when his center of gravity is low, and if we can't make the "people" realize that the institution is worth keeping, it is in the end better to let it go by the board. It is a healthier political phenomenon for [Robert Martin] La Follette and his university,[14] from which he gets his ideas, to be prodding around here and there, trying to find out what it is all about, than for our Constitutional jawrey to talk a lot of platitudes about "Socialism," whatever that may mean, all designed to show that the beatitudes were delivered in Manchester[15] and not on the Mount. However, it is bringing coals to Newcastle to say all this to you[...]

Sincerely yours, Learned Hand

ms with signature 104A.1

To Learned Hand from Felix Frankfurter

March 2, 1911 Association of the Bar of the City of N.Y.

My dear Judge Hand:

Much the only good thing, from my viewpoint, Beck has done since he came here was to have occasioned your letter. It's refreshing, at least for an iconoclast like me, to read a consideration of the Constitution that doesn't consist of merely phrases uttered with dogmatic finality. Of course, I realize you were unrobed when you wrote; but even so, you made me feel that it's getting to be more and more respectable not to regard the Constitution as the last word on government, however much respect and historical affection an instrument of such long service may be entitled to.

---

14. Robert Martin La Follette (1855–1925): Governor of Wisconsin, 1901–1906; Senator from Wisconsin, 1906–1925. He advocated agrarian and urban reform, and promoted the cooperation of the state government with the University of Wisconsin in matters of social policy.

15. "Jawrey," i.e., talk. The nineteenth-century "Manchester school" consisted of English economists who advocated laissez-faire policies.

Much of the adulation of the Constitution, as you say, springs from the cowardly hypocrisy of the "them-that's-got" school. But there is still a goodly number of thinking people who balk at any Constitutional higher criticism with all the unreason of religious bigots. Blame for this, I think, rests largely with the universities. Teachers who have the acumen and honesty, the freedom from undue acceptance of tradition, like Thayer, are rare. What is to be expected from the men who year after year are indoctrinated by the teaching of a Simeon Baldwin or [William D.] Guthrie at Columbia? And the ablest portion of the Bar represents property, and therefore from that source—and that too, most of the time, with entire honesty though blurred vision—the protective property theory of the Constitution is insistently fostered.

I think for the next ten years there'll be little cause for complaint. The recent batch of Supreme Court decisions seems to me to indicate a real desire to pull in the reins. A very wide conception of the police power and a restrictive meaning of "liberty" and "due process" will allow practically every piece of legislation at all defensible (and what is very important, properly argued) to pass muster. Such an opinion, for instance, as [Charles Evans] Hughes[16] wrote last week in *C Bo v. McGuire*[17] on the liberty of contract shows very clearly that the Court is realizing acutely that "Mr. Herbert Spencer's *Social Statics*[18] was not incorporated in the Constitution" (or words to that effect). A story I heard the other day bears this out, and at the same time beautifully illustrates the real thought back of the Beck kind of talk. Shortly after his accession to the Chief Justiceship, [Edward Douglass] White said to a friend that he was thinking a great deal about his responsibility and that of the Court. He was somewhat oppressed with the realization, he went on to say, that "nine of us down here have power to thwart the will of ninety millions." When these remarks were repeated to a prominent financier, he curtly replied "what in hell does White think they're there for." Of course, coming from a Custodian of "the bulwarks," your last letter makes you impeachable, dealing though you were with abstractions and uttering merely intellectual aspirations. I shall jealously conceal your views with the hope that some day we may get you inside the house, past the unsuspecting Trojans. I am greatly appreciative of your letter and your kind thoughts of me back of it.

Sincerely yours, Felix Frankfurter

ms with signature 104A.1

---

16. Charles Evans Hughes (1862–1948): Governor of New York, 1907–1910; Associate Justice of the United States Supreme Court, 1910–1916; Secretary of State, 1921–1925; Judge, the Permanent Court of International Justice, 1928–1930; Chief Justice of the United States, 1930–1941.

17. I.e., Chicago, Burlington & Quincy R.R. Co. v. McGuire, 219 U.S. 549 (1911). In this Iowa state case appealed to the Supreme Court, the railroad had compensated an injured worker for his injuries through a corporate worker relief fund, and asserted that by accepting such compensation the employee was not entitled to any further relief, contrary to Iowa state law that specifically deemed unenforceable any contract between a railway and its employees that would restrict the railroad's liability in cases of employee injuries due to the railroad's negligence or willful wrongs. In an opinion authored by Justice Hughes, the Court rebuffed the railroad's arguments that it should be able to contract freely with its employees and that the Iowa law was an unconstitutional violation of the Fourteenth Amendment's Equal Protection Clause.

18. Herbert Spencer (1820–1903): English biologist, philosopher; his Social Statics (1851), addressed topics in social theory and human evolution. Frankfurter paraphrases a portion of Oliver Wendell Holmes, Jr.'s dissent in *Lochner v. New York*, 198 U.S. 45 (1905).

1911-3

To Theodore Roosevelt

May 8, 1911 District Court of the United States

My dear Colonel Roosevelt:

I met Mr. Sullivan at the station at Syosset on Saturday night on my way to Oyster Bay and learned from him that you were preparing an article for *The Outlook* on the *Employers Liability* decision.[19] He said you might be glad of a call from anyone who was interested in the subject, and as this has been for a long time a matter of concern to me I walked over yesterday morning to Sagamore Hill, but unfortunately found that you were at church. I am sending along a paper I wrote three years ago on the *Bakers'* case before I felt as tied up as I am now, which says some of the things I had in mind and which perhaps says all I would say myself, though it is now happily rather superseded by the later decision of the Supreme Court.[20] I entirely share your views on the whole subject, which is of the utmost consequences if the system of constitutional control by courts is to survive at all. It is strange that those very persons who generally most deplore the Referendum should as a class be eager for that control which renders the Referendum an absolute necessity.[21]

However, the matter goes much deeper than that. Mr. Thayer of the Harvard Law School, the father of the present Dean, used again and again to point out how the stiffness of the courts in their views of proper legislative experiments would tend to destroy the independence and character of the legislators themselves.[22] Have not events proved him too absolutely right? Of course, one may not press one course too strongly in accounting for the result, yet it is surely within moderate bounds to assign a part of the present bankruptcy of

---

19. This a reference to *Ives v. South Buffalo Ry. Co.*, 201 N.Y. 271 (1911), in which the New York Court of Appeals had ruled unconstitutional New York's workmen's compensation law, finding it violated employers' rights to due process. The 1910 state law made employers in extra-hazardous occupations—including tunnel construction, bridge building, on railroads, and work involving scaffolds, electrical wires, or explosives—liable for all job-related employee injuries, regardless of the employer's negligence. Prior to enactment of the law, employers were liable only when their negligence was demonstrated.

20. LH wrote on the *Bakers'* case or *Lochner v. New York* in *Due Process of Law and the Eight-Hour Day*, 21 HARV. L.REV. 495 (1907–08). The "later decision" is the Supreme Court's unanimous decision in *Noble State Bank v. Haskell*, 219 U.S. 104 (1911), also referred to as the *Oklahoma Bank* cases. The Court upheld the State of Oklahoma's right to establish a depositors' guaranty fund by requiring that banks chartered in the state deposit 1 percent of their average daily deposits in the fund to ensure repayment in the event of a bank's failure. Writing for a unanimous court, Holmes stressed that "an ulterior public advantage may justify a comparatively insignificant taking of private property for what in its immediate purpose is a private use." *Noble State Bank* at 110, 111. *See* GERALD GUNTHER, LEARNED HAND: THE MAN AND THE JUDGE 210–12 (1994).

21. As he would soon state in print, Roosevelt advocated the removal of judges who were "fundamentally out of sympathy with the righteous popular movement" by popular recall or referendum. *See* his *Workmen's Compensation*, 98 THE OUTLOOK 49 (1911).

22. Thayer emphasizes the limits of judicial power under the Constitution: "Under no system can the power of courts go far to save a people from ruin; our chief protection lies elsewhere." *The Origin and Scope of the American Doctrine of Constitutional Law*, 7 HARV. L. REV. 129, 156 (1893).

the legislative branches of the States to the irresponsible attitude they take towards grave and novel experiments, an irresponsibility due to their ability to throw the odium of conservatism upon the courts. I must say that little as I can believe in the principle of a recall of judges, I can well understand that the people should determine at all hazards to make the courts more responsible to popular feeling, so long as they assume to permit or to forbid meliorating measures through the general clauses of their constitutions and in accordance with their own political or economic views.

If the present temper of the Supreme Court endures, no one has just ground of complaint, but we have had here a sad reminder that it is not to be assumed that this temper is universal. I am quite certain that if it does not become more so, either the courts must give up their constitutional prerogative, a by no means unthinkable alternative, or they must change, or we shall have our constitutions codes of general administrative and substantive legislation, which seems a cumbersome form of making law and loses the enormous advantages of deliberation and amendment before enactment.

I trust you will excuse by the interest of the subject my intrusion on your time. What you say has so much weight that you must consent even now to interruptions from which a strictly private citizen is exempt. I am with much regard,

Very sincerely yours, Learned Hand

ms with signature, Theodore Roosevelt Papers, Manuscript Division, LC, Reel 106

1911-4

In a series of articles on trusts published in The Outlook, Theodore Roosevelt argued for prosecutions under the Sherman Antitrust Act of 1890. Based on the constitutional power of Congress to regulate interstate commerce, the Act made illegal "every contract, combination in the form of trust or otherwise, or conspiracy, in restraint of trade or commerce among the several States, or with foreign nations" and provided several enforcement mechanisms.

To Theodore Roosevelt

November 15, 1911[23] District Court of the United States

Dear Colonel Roosevelt:

I have seen the article in this week's *Outlook* entitled "The Trusts, the People and the Square Deal," and it seems to me that the implication that the Circuit Court is responsible for the failure to break up the community of ownership featured in the new tobacco companies needs a little supplementing.[24]

---

23. Two letters from LH to Roosevelt are dated November 15, 1911. Apparently, the first prompted a second, which states that the first, as emended by LH, is enclosed with a further comment and asks that they be published anonymously.

24. On the Tobacco Trust, Roosevelt argues as follows: "It is a vitally necessary thing to have the persons in control of big trusts of the character of the Standard Oil Trust and Tobacco Trust taught

The decree of the Circuit Court in the *Standard Oil* case distributed the stock of the constituent companies *pro rata* so that they were owned in the same proportion as the original stock and that decree the Supreme Court affirmed.[25] It is true that the Government did not appeal in that case, but the Supreme Court evidently did not consider itself limited thereby, because in discussing the relief to be granted, the Court said it was necessary to examine that afforded by the lower court "in order to fix how far it is necessary to take from or *add to* that relief to the end that the prohibitions of the statute may have complete and operative force." And thereupon the Supreme Court approved the decree which necessarily resulted in a community of ownership. So in the *Northern Securities* case[26] a *pro rata* distribution was approved by the Supreme Court, although the subject was not discussed at any length. And upon the Tobacco hearing, the Attorney General stated in open court that in view of these decisions he felt that he could make no objection to the plan upon the grant of community of ownership, but desired the matter held open for five years.[27]

The *Standard Oil* decisions of the Supreme Court, together with the position of the Attorney General, concluded the Circuit Court in the *Tobacco* case, except upon the proposal of the Attorney General for a provision holding open the reorganization for five years. Upon that point the Court was not bound by the authority of the Supreme Court, but its decision cannot be said to have in any sense approved of the feature of community

---

that they are under the law[...] [T]he results sought to be achieved are achieved only in extremely insufficient and fragmentary measure by breaking up all big corporations, whether they have behaved well or ill, into a number of little corporations which it is perfectly certain will be largely, and perhaps altogether, under the same control. Such action is harsh and mischievous if the corporation is guilty of nothing except its size; and where, as in the case of the Standard Oil and especially the Tobacco trusts, the corporation has been guilty of immoral and anti-social practices, there is need for far more drastic and thoroughgoing action than any that has been taken under the recent decree of the Supreme Court. In the case of the Tobacco Trust, for instance, the settlement in the Circuit Court, in which the representatives of the Government seem inclined to concur, practically leaves all of the companies still substantially under the control of the twenty-nine original defendants. Such a result is lamentable from the standpoint of justice. The decision of the Circuit Court, if allowed to stand, means that the Tobacco Trust has merely been obliged to change its clothes, that none of the real offenders have received any real punishment, while, as *The New York Times*, a pro-trust paper, says, the tobacco concerns, in their new clothes, are in positions of 'ease and luxury,' and 'immune from prosecution under the law.'" *The Trusts, the People and the Square Deal*, 99 The Outlook 12 (1911).

25. *See Standard Oil Co. of New Jersey v. United States*, 221 U.S. 1 (1911), in which the Court upheld the ruling that Standard Oil, a trust that effectively controlled the United States' oil industry, had violated the Sherman Act. In doing so, the Court modified the Act's prohibition on contracts and combinations in restraint of trade by finding that only contracts and combinations that were an "unreasonable or undue" restraint were unlawful, a distinction not found in the language of the Act. *See* 221 U.S. 87–88.

26. *See Northern Securities Co. v. United States*, 193 U.S. 197 (1904), in which the Court affirmed the circuit court's decree and dissolution of the holding company for the Great Northern and Northern Pacific Railway companies, noting specifically that the Sherman Act targeted all restraints of trade, both reasonable and unreasonable.

27. *United States v. American Tobacco Company* began in the circuit court. *See* 164 F. 700 (S.D.N.Y. 1908) and 164 F. 1024 (S.D.N.Y. (1908), where the defendant companies were found to have violated the Sherman Antitrust Act. On appeal, the Supreme Court approved dissolution of the Tobacco Trust. 221 U.S. 106 (1911).

of ownership, except in so far as the individual opinions of the several judges may be thought so to indicate.

Faithfully yours, [Learned Hand]

tp 37.21

To Theodore Roosevelt

November 15, 1911 District Court of the United States

Dear Colonel Roosevelt:

I enclose the letter.[28] I think it might be better to indicate your correspondent as a vaguely wise and competent person than as a lawyer. I can't deny I am a judge, but I have no doubt that a host of compurgators could be found to serve as oath-helpers to anyone who took issue that I was no lawyer. I believe that this letter states the facts accurately, though I am aware that the distinction, though absolute enough in fact, is a little too fine for the "Great Heart." Besides, perhaps the Great H. is righter than otherwise in bundling all in one sack and then giving the classic order of the Queen in Alice. Nevertheless, personal justice *is* a fine idea, even if it be a luxury which can only grow after bulk justice gets done.

Faithfully yours, Learned Hand

ms with signature, Theodore Roosevelt Papers, Manuscript Division, LC, Reel 117; also 37.21

1911-5

To Theodore Roosevelt

November 20, 1911 District Court of the United States

Dear Colonel Roosevelt:

I have read the galley proofs of "Conservation of Womanhood and Childhood" with very much interest and think that it is an extremely good article, as good as I remember

---

28. In a brief article entitled *The Tobacco Trust and the Court*, Roosevelt published LH's first letter, which he attributes to "a citizen of New York who by training, ability, and position, is peculiarly competent to express his opinion on the matter," with his own comment. He then adds the comment LH enclosed with his second letter, which he attributes to "a distinguished United States Judge": "The courts ought as far as possible to be relieved from the task of regulating the Trusts. It is not their business. They suffer in the process. It is of first important that the courts shall be universally respected. So long as their work is confined to doing justice between man and man it is not difficult for them to retain the general respect of the community and to deserve it. Whenever they are called on to do other things they are likely to lose it, and to some extent deserve to lose it. The fail when they are called on to pass upon questions of governmental policy precisely as they have always failed when they have been given many offices to fill. They fail because they are merely ordinary men, and they are put at work for which their judicial training probably makes them, if anything, a little less fit than the ordinary man." 99 The Outlook 13 (1911).

from your pen.[29] There are many things that it suggests, but of course the most important part for me is about the judges, and to that I wish I could object more than I can. I have said very often almost the same thing, and there is really none of it that I can disagree with. However, perhaps not very consistently, I cannot quite swallow the necessity of having public pressure put on a judge for any purpose, for it so utterly perverts the assumption which is fundamental in his function.[30] He should properly have no duty but to interpret words which have been used by the sovereign itself, and in doing that, I think it is fatal in the end to his integrity to try to find the sovereign's meaning except in its formal declarations. Of course, I am leaving out the duty of interpreting the customary law, where probably a certain legislative function is inevitable.

Really, we have got ourselves into the mess we are now in here in America by failing to remember how strictly our duties should be interpretive—Justice Holmes has said "literary," with his usual insight. In construing the vague clauses of the Bill of Rights, we have done the most damage, and something must be done to change it, but I really think that I had rather take them out of the Constitutions altogether than make the judges respond to any popular pressure, as distinct from the general political and economic beliefs with which the judge has grown up. The popular will, when clearly ascertained, cannot wisely be withstood in a democracy, but there are a good many occasions when, before it has been authoritatively expressed, a judge is tempted to interpret what he finds about him in popular form. Except in so far as that helps him to an honest interpretation of what has reached authoritative expression, I have not the least doubt that he should, and indeed he must, wholly disregard them. If he does not, he is just as much a usurper of authority if they be popular and even the matrix of future laws, as though he followed his personal, but unpopular, predilections.

Now to be perfectly frank with you, I think that the end of your paper would almost inevitably result in making people suppose that by some sort of popular pressure ad hoc, judges should be influenced in their decisions. A just man—and we could each name many—who thoroughly believed in the political theories of, say, Justice [Rufus] Peckham,[31] would quite rightly feel that come what might, he must be true to his convictions of what the authoritative expression of the community now was. I should say that he was doing all that he could do without compounding with his conscience, and I should urge him to

29. Roosevelt sent LH the proofs of his address entitled "The Conservation of Womanhood and Childhood" and delivered on October 20, 1911, in Carnegie Hall, in which he criticizes courts that have struck down legislation protecting workers, especially women and children.

30. By 1912, Roosevelt supported such measures as judicial recall (the people's power to remove judges) and the recall of judicial decisions (the people's power to overturn judicial decisions.) Roosevelt states that while "the judge should be independent," it is "[the people's] right and duty to see that the man is responsible to us, to the people[...] I do not believe that it is wise or safe to pretend that we have self-government and yet by indirect methods to permit outsiders to rob us of self-government[...] [The people] can not surrender the right of ultimate control to a judge any more than to a legislator or an executive." THE CONSERVATION OF WOMANHOOD AND CHILDHOOD 81–83 (1912). As published in THE OUTLOOK, the address omitted the passages on the courts that he had included in his speech; see 99 THE OUTLOOK 17 (1911).

31. Rufus Peckham wrote the opinion in *Lochner v. New York* (1905).

face the popular will at the very moment when I personally believed that his theory of the disposition of political powers was pernicious.

In short, there are only two ways of meeting the difficulty: one, by changing the formal expression of the fundamental law, as you suggest, and the other by securing such men as understand it in a different sense. The first is a so much better way of meeting the evil than the second, which lends itself to exploitation by men of facile convictions, that we ought to prefer it.

Indeed so inherent are the defects of the system which has grown up under the general clauses of the Bill of Rights, that I am feeling with increasing force that the evils which would result from their abolition might be less than those under which we now labor. The subject is so grave that anyone ought to hesitate a long time before committing himself to it, certainly a man with as little political experience as I. If Justice Holmes's opinion—I hope you will not get to hate that man's in my mouth—in the *Oklahoma Bank* cases[32] could become well riveted into all the law, that would solve the difficulty, but candidly, it leaves so little of the Bill of Rights that it remains *brutum fulmen* for the most part. In short, to appeal to the people not to endorse such opinions as the *Employers' Liability* cases[33] is to ask a remedy which is either impracticable, or, as I think, very dangerous; and it seems to me the end of the article will certainly be construed in that sense.

This is an unconscionably long letter, but if you belonged to a tribe, so now accursed, you would, I think feel as I do, rather sensitive.

Faithfully yours, Learned Hand

tp with ms signature and notes, Theodore Roosevelt Papers, Manuscript Division, LC, Reel 117; also 37.21

To Learned Hand from Theodore Roosevelt

November 22, 1911 *The Outlook,* New York

Dear Judge:

Evidently I must try to make my expression more clear. I absolutely agree with you as to bringing pressure to bear on the judges, but in Constitutional cases the alternative must be to secure the right of appeal from the judges. Take the New York cases to which I refer. My idea would be to have the Constitutional Convention provide that the people shall have the right to vote as to whether or not the judges' interpretation of the law in such a case is correct, and that their vote shall be decisive. Evidently I have to get you to come out again and talk this matter over with me. I am sincerely obliged to you for your note.

Faithfully yours, Theodore Roosevelt

tp with ms signature and notes 37.21

---

32. I.e., Noble State Bank v. Haskell. *See* 1911-3 To Roosevelt, May 8, and note 20.

33. I.e., Employers' Liability Cases, 207 U.S. 463 (1908). The decision of the Supreme Court in the first of these cases invalidated a statute that made all interstate carriers liable for injuries to employees caused by supervisor's negligence of defective equipment because it applied to intrastate as well as interstate activities.

1911-6

To Theodore Roosevelt

December 15, 1911 United States District Court

Dear Colonel Roosevelt:

I enclose the last opinion re Police Power,[34] not particularly good but important as one more stone on the cairn which marks the real decease of that once menacing ghost. Note it "is but another name for the power of government." If you should read the opinions which now regularly follow one another without dissent, you would feel that that Court anyway is safe for a long time from any danger of narrow usurpation. Of course, to one meditating on permanent dictatorship this may seem only an indication of flabby imbecility, but pray recall that boards of usurpers have always proved ineffective, and, besides, how much they might have interfered with your ruthless, vaulting ambition! At least it is good to find pliant tools, where one might have found stiff-necked competitors. Let this moderate your scorn for such abdication in favor of a "pure Democracy."[35]

Faithfully yours, Learned Hand

ms with signature, Theodore Roosevelt Papers, Manuscript Division, LC, Reel 120; also 37.21

To Learned Hand from Theodore Roosevelt

December 19, 1911 *The Outlook*, New York

My dear Judge:

I am really obliged to you for sending me that case. It seemed to me that the lines you underscored put the whole matter in a nutshell. It comes in the nick of time for me to

---

34. Mutual Loan Co. v. Martell, 222 U.S. 225 (1911). Justice Joseph McKenna's opinion upholding a Massachusetts employee protection law noted: "in a sense, the police power is but another name for the power of government; and a contention that a particular exercise of it offends the due process clause of the Constitution is apt to be very intangible to a precise consideration and answer[...] It is certainly the province of the state, by its legislature, to adopt such a policy as to it seems best. There are constitutional limitations, of course, but these allow a very comprehensive range of judgment[...] Legislation cannot be judged by theoretical standards. It must be tested by the concrete conditions which induced it, and this test was applied by the supreme judicial court of Massachusetts in passing on the validity of the statute under review." 222 U.S. at 233.

35. LH acknowledges Roosevelt's actual political power in a letter to Herbert Croly, dated January 24, 1912: "It looks to me as though the Colonel certainly is the Man of Destiny now. It is quite strange that the President [Taft] seems incapable of developing any strength. I really think he has not had a square deal. The good things that he has done have been interred long before his bones, and the evil seems to bedevil and cling onto him more than he deserves. I am sorry." *Cf.* "The evil that men do lives after them,/ The good is oft interred with their bones." JULIUS CAESAR, III, ii. (tp with ms notes 102.19.)

insert it in an article I have been writing about the New York State Court. My dear judge, I chuckled heartily over your allusion to the probable thoughts of the world-be dictator! Seriously, these decisions please me immensely, not merely because of the cases themselves, but because they represent the kind of attitude which if regularly taken means that any effort to assault the Federal judiciary will be abandoned; and therefore we shall preserve what is of inestimable value, the power of the Court *on great occasions* to steady our governmental structure by declaring what the Legislature or Executive can do and what it or he cannot.

Sincerely yours, Theodore Roosevelt

tp with ms signature 37.21

1912-1

To Norman Hapgood[36]

February 2, 1912 District Court of the United States

My dear Norman:

I felt a kind of spring of joy at the heart when I read this morning your paragraph in the February third *Collier's*, entitled "Minimum Wage." It seems to me in a very short way to strike at the very root of the matter. All I object to is the phrase, "low paid workers shall receive more than they earn." Distinctions between what they earn and what they get I always think a little unfruitful. However, that is a mere speck; the thing that pleases me is that I find myself so in accord with you and just the way you reach your results. A minimum scale in the first place gives us hope of meeting its cost by increased efficiency. Insofar as it does not, it enables us to know exactly who those are who are so inefficient that they cannot maintain themselves and bring up efficient children. These we now support in all sorts of indirect ways without knowing it. A minimum scale would force upon us the existence of these people, and by the burden of the taxes would make us face the necessity of preventing their perpetuation in my judgment. So I feel that it is in no sense vague humanitarianism, but quite as cold blooded as the wage fund theory[37] ever was. I want the minimum scale as a means of ascertaining who of the race is fit to survive, without mingling fit and unfit in a vague class half fed and half educated. Of course the minimum scale means the whole business: regulation of the wage, the working day, out-of-work pay, and accident insurance. I am not yet sure it means old age insurance; that just at present I am inclined to think is bad. Given an adequate wage scale, the mere fact of personal thrift is a great moralizer. However, I will be converted on that if you want.

36. Norman Hapgood, 1868–1937: editor of Collier's Weekly, 1903–1912; Harper's Weekly, 1913–1916; Hearst's International Magazine, 1923–1925.

37. The "wage fund theory," or more properly the wages fund theory, held that an employer uses a fund of money, or fixed amount of capital, to pay workers; so, if employees demand higher wages, unemployment of some workers will be necessary.

Between you and me it is hardly necessary to presuppose that child labor disappears absolutely.

My dear Norman, I do not know why I should spout these platitudes to you, who know much more about it than I, except that I love you and like to find that we agree.[38]

Faithfully yours, [L.H.]

tp 23.5

1912-2

To Theodore Roosevelt

February 27, 1912 University Club

Dear Colonel Roosevelt:

I have breakfasted and dined today with [George] Rublee,[39] and I am so pleased with his idea that I want to write you of how perfectly I think it answers the situation. I cannot help saying that the appeal to the people from judicial decisions has very seriously troubled me, not because it is "revolutionary," but because it seems to me to meet the evil in the wrong way. I can't see why Rublee's idea does not in much more thoroughgoing fashion than my suggestion go to the very heart of the difficulty.

All the veto power of the courts which can trouble what you want to do, and the rest of us who feel as you do, is bound up in the phrase "due process of law" which we all have in the Bill of Rights. It is by definition of that phrase that practically the whole damage has occurred. Having now an authoritative and unanimous declaration of the Supreme Court after the most amazingly latitudinarian canon,[40] what can be better than to suggest that it be written into the Bill of Rights as a definition. You would not want to take Holmes verbatim; there are other and shorter forms which have been constantly recurring. You may remember my sending you one opinion which was only a specimen. Besides, you need not commit yourself to any given phrase; it is enough that the interpretation should be finally fixed in the B. of R. itself, substantially embodying the best present doctrine of the Supreme Court. I confess if it came to actual reduction in the case of a given state, I

---

38. LH published two articles on the minimum wage in The New Republic: *The Hope of the Minimum Wage*, November, 20, 1915, at 66, and *The Legal Right to Starve*, May, 2, 1923, at 254 (published anonymously).

39. George Rublee (1858–1957): New York attorney, Federal Trade Commission, 1915–1916; Special Counsel to the Treasure Department, 1917; American Delegate to the Allied Maritime Transport Council, London, 1918–1919.

40. I.e., in the vein of Holmes's opinion in *Noble State Bank v. Haskell*: "We must be cautious about pressing the broad words of the Fourteenth Amendment to a drily logical extreme. Many laws which it would be vain to ask the court to overthrow could be shown, easily enough, to transgress a scholastic interpretation of one or another of the great guaranties in the Bill of Rights. They more or less limit the liberty of the individual, or they diminish property to a certain extent. We have few scientifically certain criteria of legislation, and as it often is difficult to mark the line where what is called the police power of the states is limited by the Constitution of the United States, judges should be slow to read into the latter a *nolumus mutare* as against the lawmaking power." 219 U.S. 104, 110 (1911).

should want it powerfully clear, but that's another matter. The genius of the idea is that it absolutely quiets the hardest-shelled Bourbon.[41] They always have banked on the Sup. Ct., and haven't yet waked up to the fact that that august body has been sadly treacherous of late, consistently, deliberately treacherous.

New York is, of course, a bad place to judge from, and we are apt to get a gloomy outlook, but still, with all allowance, I think that the present form of the recall of judicial decisions is much misunderstood and distrusted. I don't believe that would be your real purpose at all, if it could be once made clear, and I hope you will gradually be able to make Rublee's scheme emerge, and take the place of the other, that is, if you agree. I hope you liked Rublee. I have mentioned him to you but you never met him before, to know him. He has more sagacity and clearness of mind than almost any man I know. He could and would help a good deal in such matters[...]

The following suggestions occur to me as tentative definitions of "due process of law" or, what is the same thing, the "Police Power." None of them is taken verbatim from the reports, but they can be found in substance I think throughout them.

1. "an act of the legislature shall be deemed due process of law if it prescribe what can in any reasonable view be thought to serve the welfare or convenience of the people."
2. "an act of the legislature shall be deemed due process of law if it prescribe what it consonant with morality, or public policy, as understood by a majority of the people."
3. "an act of the legislature shall be deemed due process of law unless it certainly appear to have no possible relation to any public policy."
4. "an act of the legislature shall be deemed due process of law whenever it does not clearly prescribe what is beyond the scope of any reasonable view of the welfare or convenience of the people."

I rather prefer no. 4 or no. 2.
L. Hand

ms with signature, Theodore Roosevelt Papers, Manuscript Division, LC, Reel 131

1912-3

To Felix Frankfurter

April 4, 1912 District Court of the United States

My dear Frankfurter:

I was sorry not to get to the Law Review dinner, for I should have liked to hear what you said. Rublee said that it was much better than anybody else's discourse, and I dare say

41. I.e., arch-conservative.

that I shall agree with him when I have a chance to read it, which I have not had yet.[42] I wish I might know [Roscoe] Pound.[43] He impresses everybody who meets him, and all I hear agrees entirely with my general views.

I should not want to announce this publicly, but I am quite willing to tell you that I am really deeply disappointed in the Colonel and his candidacy. It seems to me as though he were falling into the same fatal attitude of mind which got him in 1910. Whether he changed then or whether that was the first time when his back was against the wall, I do not know, but nearly everything he is saying now fills me with regret and indeed with dismay. I wish he could be chloroformed for eight months and then elected. There is no doubt about it that as a campaigner he makes the judicious grieve. Even Rublee feels pretty unhappy about the fraud cry,[44] and Rublee is getting somewhat the feeling that he is in a crusade. That is a feeling which I cannot share. Nearly everyone wants to be known vaguely as a Progressive, and almost all really want to be Progressive. We are being bedeviled beyond any measure by sympathies and sentiments, and so far the result is only to tinker over the old machine. Meanwhile, many of the working people are kicking out the whole kit of institutions which have been achieved with so much trouble. I am sick of clamor, of mutual suspicion, and of abuse: what we need is *Licht, mehr Licht*! like Goethe. I am weary to death of the Rule of the People and a millennium created by constant elections and never-ending suspicion of authority. That does remind me of my dear old friend and bogey, the Paris Commune in 1793.[45] There is no better nidus for hypocrites to thrive. When will the day come that some courageous men will stand sponsors for a real program of "social justice" in the words of our leader? Can you see a single man who would really dare to commit himself to any plan like [that of] the Fabians?[46] Why have we nowhere any Fabians? Why aren't all of us Fabians? Just think how much of modern England they have directly made. Yet today the heart of Progressivism in the Mississippi would turn and rend anyone—if a heart can rend—who dared to take up anything of the sort, e.g., the Reciprocity Bill,[47] surely a very mild step. I say I am sick of the whole lot, either they are full of sound and fury and signify nothing; or they twist around a whirligig with prayers written on it, like the Grand Llama of Tibet, and think that they can exorcise all the devils within the four seas[...]

Faithfully yours, [Learned Hand]

tp 104A.1

---

42. In a letter dated April 2, Frankfurter enclosed remarks he had delivered at a Law Review dinner, noting "how much of the profession is still in the grip of conventional thinking." (ms with signature 104A.1)

43. Roscoe Pound (1870–1964): Professor of Law, Harvard University, 1910–1916; Dean, Harvard Law School, 1916–1936.

44. Roosevelt had repeatedly claimed that corruption and fraud—in favor of his opponent, President Taft—rendered many primary elections illegal.

45. I.e., the insurrectionary government in Paris that took control of the French government in 1792–1794 following the Revolution of 1789.

46. LH refers to the members of the Fabian Society, founded in the United Kingdom in 1884 to promote socialism, which included the writers George Bernard Shaw, Beatrice Potter Webb, and Sidney Webb.

47. The Reciprocity Bill represented President Taft's free-trade agreement with Canada in late 1910. It was submitted to Congress as a revenue bill in early 1911 and signed into law in July 22, 1912. LH goes on to describe this "lot" as telling idiotic tales, "full of sound and fury,/ Signifying nothing." MACBETH, V, v.

To Felix Frankfurter

April 11, 1912 District Court of the United States

My dear Frankfurter:

[...]I read your words at the Review Dinner and afterwards gave them to Rublee who wanted to look them over again. You were very moderate, perhaps too moderate. I think that the worst evil in the situation is not in the least what the Colonel supposes—that the popular will is being thwarted. The real evil arises from the injury to the most capable engine of government, the legislature. That is the idea which I should like to impress, and the idea which I'm afraid would have the least acceptance. Today in America we have little interest in the consolidation of power. I think I might be willing to press the case more strongly than you, yet I sympathize with you and assent to your moderation under the circumstances. It seems to me that you put it admirably. Had I been there I should, as too often I do, have been apt to raise needless opposition by too strong a statement.

Rublee gave me a long lecture the other day on my lack of faith after I had talked to him somewhat in the vein that I wrote to you. I felt genuinely humiliated when he was through, and I was a little more contrite than I have since felt. His complaint to me was that I was standing outside and merely barking, which put me in a fatuous position, but [that] I really was in sympathy with the movement as a whole and I ought to give that sympathy more expression. Well, I suppose he is right. I suppose I am in sympathy with the movement though I am pretty doubtful just what the movement is. It looks to me rather a recrudescence of bourgeois Jacksonianism than the kind of thing that I really want, but it is beyond human nature, or at least beyond my human nature, to become very kindly when nearly all the declarations of the leaders fill me with sadness and even with contempt. It is really shocking to have the Colonel keep repeating that [William Howard] Taft[48] believes in government by only a class of the community. There is just enough verbal truth in his statement, if you read over Taft's words, to allow it a faint casualistical [sic] color but that is all. If he really thinks that he is fairly expressing Taft's meaning, which he may think, it is a lamentable instance of his incapacity for understanding the opposition. The Illinois victory,[49] although it was surprising in size, has not given me the elation which it would [have] some weeks ago; indeed, it has not encouraged me much at all. I shall honestly try to get into a more happy frame of mind. I realize the truth of all that Rublee said, but so far have not been able to get my suggestion centers accurately at work.

Faithfully yours, Learned Hand

tp with ms signature 104A.1

---

48. William Howard Taft (1857–1930): President of the United States, 1909–1913; Chief Justice of the United States, 1921–1930.

49. The Republican Party conducted its primaries in the spring of 1912. Robert La Follette won two of the first four primaries (North Dakota and Wisconsin), and President Taft won the other two (New York and Nevada). Roosevelt won in Illinois on April 9 and subsequently also in Pennsylvania, Nebraska, Oregon, Maryland, California, Ohio, New Jersey, and South Dakota.

1912-4

To Herbert Croly

June 14, 1912

Dear Herbert:

I am enclosing under separate cover Volume 24 of the *Harvard Law Review* which contains the two articles written by Corwin on due process of law before the Fourteenth Amendment.[50] I have just read them over again myself, my first perusal being hasty. It is a very interesting paper. You will see that the real meat in the coconut historically was the old social compact theory[51] and the inherent limitation of legislative power, coupled with the somewhat similar theory that the grant of legislative power was itself of a limited character. I was right, therefore, in thinking that the present theory of due process of law, which supposes and treats it as a limitation upon acknowledged legislative power, authorizes the courts to examine the substance of the statute and in fact to determine upon its policy within any conceivable range of wise legislation as they understand it. There is undoubtedly a fundamental theoretical difficulty in the construction of the phrase, provided it is to apply to the legislature at all, and tradition is now too strongly rooted in American law to avoid that result. There is, however, an alternative which might not become fixed in the hands of strong judges, and that is that the phrase refers only to procedural requirements. I should myself be sorry to see the doctrine take root in that way. My own belief is that it had better suffer a general subsidence such as it now is suffering at the hands of the Supreme Court. This permits the dead to be burying their dead, and does not cause theoretical difficulties such as would result from any other system.

You will see that old Chancellor Kent was one of the worst sinners we have ever had.[52] I don't quite know why a person of so strong federalist proclivities should have so early distrusted concentrative power, but from what Corwin says he seems to have browsed about enough in International Law writers to get ideas of *ius gentium*[53] which confuse. I understand the same thing can be found in Blackstone though I don't know about Blackstone[54][...]

[L.H.]

tp with ms notes 102.19

---

50. *See* Edward S. Corwin's two-part article, *The Doctrine of Due Process of Law Before the Civil War*, 24 HARV. L. REV. 366 (1911) and 24 HARV. L. REV. 460 (1911).

51. Proposed initially by Thomas Hobbes (1588–1679) and endorsed subsequently by John Locke (1632–1704) and Jean Jacques Rousseau (1712–1778), social compact (or contract) theory held that civil government grew from society's need for mutual protection by a sovereign power to which all persons consented.

52. James Kent (1763–1847): Chancellor of New York State, 1814–1823. His *Commentaries on American Law* revived the body of legal principles and rules developed initially by the sixteenth-century English Court of Chancery under the concept of equity. Equitable jurisdiction was designed to correct the injustices caused by the formalism of the common law and relied on notions of what is naturally perceived as right rather than on precedent and the precise words of statute.

53. I.e., the law of nations, the common law shared by all peoples.

54. Sir William Blackstone notes that the *ius gentium* develops after men have formed "separate states, commonwealths and nations" and depends "upon the rules of natural law or upon mutual compacts, treatises, leagues and agreements between these several communities." WILLIAM BLACKSTONE, 1 COMMENTARIES ON THE LAWS OF ENGLAND 67–68 (William Carey Jones ed., 1916).

To Learned Hand from Herbert Croly

June 17, 1912 Cornish, New Hampshire

My dear B.:

Thank you very much for sending me the *Harvard Reviews* containing Corwin's articles[...] The interest of Federalists like Chancellor Kent in the establishment of a judicial despotism is easily explained. They wanted a strong government, but only or chiefly for the sake of protecting property and promoting its accumulation, and of course there was a reason: the distribution of sovereign legislative power among a couple of dozen little states with strong local interests and without any sufficient balance of classes in accumulated practical experience was bound to result in a lot of law-making unnecessarily and [illegible] destructive of property. Our pretence of divided sovereignty is at the root of trouble [more] than is usually supposed[...]

Faithfully yours, Herbert Croly

ms with signature 102.19

1912-5

To Theodore Roosevelt

August 11, 1912 Pointe à Pic, P.Q., Canada

Dear Colonel Roosevelt:

When I said to you last spring and year before that what I regretted in our present day politics was [the absence of] a party which should courageously face the social and economic problems of the time, I had no idea that within five months you would be leading such a party. It is the most inspiring time in my own political experience, and has the largest promise for good. You have succeeded in switching the radical movement from the mere distribution of political power to the actual issues for which political power exists at all. It was so easy to bear over the old straw, so congenial to American political traditions dominated by lawyers, and so convenient a way to dodge the real difficulties, that I was afraid no party could ever be brought to face the necessity. You have done it and you will immensely raise the tone of American politics for a generation, whether we win or lose. All true radicals should now come to us, even though we make many mistakes, for they have no other proper home. I am sorry that my hands are tied so that I cannot get more actively into this fight, but perhaps it is as well, for I am by no means sure that I could do very effectively that kind of work, and I should have to surrender the only work at which I seem to have been effective. However, I should be especially interested in bringing out my idea about the proposed industrial changes, even if it did not immediately answer so well in a campaign.

I believe the great value of the "Normal Rules of Industry" lies in the fact that they would consciously force upon the community the recognition of those as dependents who cannot produce what the Normal Rules require. In short, it would tell us who were fit to be the fathers and mothers of the next generation. By the way, if you haven't read the

Webbs' book, *Industrial Democracy*[55] (as you probably have long since), it would come in most pat just now. It may be out of print, at least I think I heard so. I should be delighted to let you have my copy which Croly has now, but which I should commandeer at once.

Rublee told me you said I should flop to [Woodrow] Wilson.[56] You see, good sir, you were a poor prophet; I am glad you so often disclaim the art. Nearly all of us are with you heart and soul. The greater part of the conscience and brains—under forty—of the country that I see are fine Bull Moose. Even at Mt. Kisco, where there are a good many of the Banderlog,[57] there is a fine small herd. "Der Anblick giebtden Engeln Stärke."[58]

Faithfully yours, LEARNED HAND

tp with tp signature and notes 37.21

To Learned Hand from Theodore Roosevelt

August 16, 1912 *The Outlook*, New York

Dear Judge:

I prize your letter. What is more, I shall use some of your expressions in my speech tomorrow. I am mighty glad I was a bad prophet about you and Wilson.

Faithfully yours, Theodore Roosevelt

tp with ms signature 37.21

1912-6

To Oliver Wendell Holmes, Jr.[59]

December 12, 1912 United States District Court

My dear Mr. Justice:

[Francis G.] Caffey[60] writes me that there is a chance of getting you to speak to us at the Law School Association dinner in February. I hope very much you may be persuaded.

55. SIDNEY & BEATRICE WEBB, INDUSTRIAL DEMOCRACY (1897).

56. I.e., Woodrow Wilson (1856–1924): Governor of New Jersey, 1910–1912; President of the United States, 1913–1921. For LH's criticism of his presidency, see 1957-3 To Frankfurter, February 3.

57. A tribe of monkeys; see RUDYARD KIPLING, THE JUNGLE BOOK.

58. From Goethe's *Faust*, literally: "Ihr Anblick gibt den Engeln Stärk"; "its countenance gives the Angels strength."

59. Oliver Wendell Holmes, Jr. (1841–1935): Associate Justice of the United States Supreme Court, 1902–1932. By the date of this letter, Holmes had published THE COMMON LAW (1881) and SPEECHES (1891).

60. Francis G. Caffey (1868–1951): Judge, United States District Court for the Southern District of New York, 1929–1951.

I do not believe you realize what a shining example and an encouragement you have been to us now for many years, from the beginning when you stood more alone than now.[61] We should like to show you that we can distinguish wisdom from solemnity, learning from volume, and political sagacity from a sluggish imagination and limited sympathies. If you will come, we will do our best to prove it to you.

Sincerely yours, Learned Hand

ms with signature, Holmes Papers, HLL, Reel 33, frame 77

To Learned Hand from Oliver Wendell Holmes, Jr.

January 2, 1913 Supreme Court of the United States

My dear Judge:

You and Mr. Choate more than anything else determined me to break through my habits and come to the Harvard Law School Association dinner in February. If I have given any encouragement to younger men they have paid it back, and give me too an intellectual companionship harder to find in their elders. I wrote a week or more ago accepting my invitation and when the time comes I hope that we may meet and talk.

Sincerely yours, O.W. Holmes

tp with ms signature, Holmes Papers, HLL, Reel 33, frame 135

1913-1

To Oliver Wendell Holmes, Jr.

April 21, 1913 Judge Learned Hand's Chambers

Dear Mr. Justice:

I got the volume of your addresses[62] some time since and read them with much pleasure. Two things stand out, the early and never to be forgotten experience of the war, and the impress of the Puritan spirit. I suppose men run to about the same raw stuff now as you all did then, but it is the world that counts and we never had a world like that. As to the Puritans I feel a little less sympathetic. To be sure I know chiefly the Connecticut brand, more Hell and less vision than yours had in Massachusetts, but I never could muster much enthusiasm for those worthies, though I carry their blood. For A. or B. it cannot be all cakes and ale, to be sure, but, as you say yourself, in the end the value of life

---

61. LH knew Holmes casually while he was a student at Harvard Law School. *See The reminiscences of Judge Learned Hand 1958*, Columbia Oral History Collection, part 1, Pickler Memorial Library, Truman State University. Hand's correspondence with Holmes begins with this letter in 1912 and continues until Holmes's death in 1935.

62. I.e., Oliver Wendell Holmes, Jr., Speeches (1913).

is the living of it, even if it does not stop here on earth, and the galvanometer of living is joy. Collectively we may trust our desires, or at least when we are told that we mayn't, we should ask the best kind of proof. I am sure we shall all individually get enough discipline and heroism, if we try to see that we take no more than is our share.

I am sorry to see that the winged words have come less often than they used. Remember there are those of us who will always look to you to tell us of the light on a wider horizon than our own. *Quorum pars sum.*

Faithfully yours, Learned Hand

ms with signature, Holmes Papers, HLL, Reel 33, frames 78–79

1913-2

To Winfred T. Denison[63]

June 10, 1913

My dear Denison:

First, a man is rash who is a prophet; second, a man is unpopular who has been a successful prophet; third, a man lies when he says he prophesied true. I am going to assume the role of all three, and that too without having read the decision of the court in the *Minnesota* cases.[64] Sooner than I had any expectation the court has taken what I called in my talks with you the Kent aspect[65] of Interstate Commerce, i.e., that the States may regulate it in so far as necessary for their domestic polity, subject to the supreme power of Congress. This is the only possible administrative outlet for the absurd distinction between "direct" and "indirect" which has been bothering us for three generations. I believe that the exclusive domain of interstate commerce which the states may not touch at all will gradually dwindle and the limited power of Congress will gradually extend so that in the end Congress will become the vehicle of regulation of so much of the commerce of the country as Congress itself may believe to require national control. For you must remember along with this doctrine will grow the other doctrine that the judgment of Congress itself,

---

63. Winfred T. Denison (1873–1919): Assistant United States Attorney, Southern District, New York, 1906–1909; Assistant United States Attorney General, 1910–1914.

64. In the *Minnesota Rate Case*, 230 U.S. 352 (1913), several railway company stockholders who objected to acts by the State of Minnesota to establish maximum charges for intrastate freight and passengers brought suit, claiming that the state's actions were an unconstitutional interference with interstate commerce. Writing for the Court, Justice Charles Evans Hughes noted that "[t]he power of Congress to regulate commerce among the several states is supreme and plenary," and that "under the established principles governing state action, the state of Minnesota did not transcend the limits of its authority in prescribing the rates here involved, assuming them to be reasonable intrastate rates. It exercised an authority appropriate to its territorial jurisdiction, and not opposed to any action thus far taken by Congress" 230 U.S. at 398, 431–32.

65. LH suggests that the position of the Court in the *Minnesota Rate Case* reflects the position of Chancellor Kent on equitable jurisdiction. *See* 1912-4 To Croly, June 14, note 52.

as to whether interstate commerce requires the regulations it proposes, will become almost conclusive, just as the judgment of the legislature is becoming conclusive as to what is a legitimate public policy. I believe this decision will prove a great step toward the consolidation of the national power, and the consolidation of it in the legislature where it belongs. From the various outlines of it that I have got thus far, I feel it was perhaps a better way out than to say as a matter of law that an intrastate rate might *sua sponte* become an interstate rate. On the whole, the "outlook gives the Angels strength."

Faithfully yours, [Learned Hand]

tp with ms notes 42.3

1913-3

To Felix Frankfurter

July 3, 1913 District Court of the United States

Dear Felix:

I am pleased about [Lindley] Garrison's interest[66] and have myself some hopes, for they are having some trouble in selecting from Connecticut apparently. I will have a word with Marshall here, who could perhaps do somewhat, would he.[67]

As your own affairs: I have been revolving it as I can and my impression—I can hardly call it a definite conclusion—is no.[68] That you will end there is eminently likely and desirable, but not now. You have had a wonderful experience in affairs, great affairs, but you cannot afford yet to let it slip. Nothing, in my judgment, will stand you in better stead for your purposes than just what you are getting. There is a very genuine reality in the suspicion of the practical man for the academician, though not so much basis as for the academician's scorn for the practical man. If you were really in the grind of routine, I should think otherwise—poor Stimson for example! My heart really bleeds for him—but you are not; you are learning what all our pleasant vaporings actually come to and it is really of inestimable service, not to be replaced, not to be equaled. Especially serviceable to the State as well as to you will this be, and in the next few years which are to be full of a good deal of half-baked stuff gathered from turgid brains alone. You will get power and certainty where you are for four years more.

Besides, the fight is now just on and you can actively help, particularly in conservation. Your place for a while is just where you are, where you will be cooking up facts at the very center of the web and learning how the mixed conflict of personal feelings and interests

66. Lindley Garrison (1864–1932): Vice Chancellor of New Jersey, 1904–1913; Secretary of War, 1913–1916. LH alludes to the vacancy on the United States Court of Appeals for the Second Circuit created by the resignation of Walter C. Noyes.

67. LH may be referring to Louis Marshall, attorney in New York City and president of the American Jewish Committee.

68. LH responds to the Harvard Law School's offer of a faculty position to Frankfurter.

with ideas actually works out. It will give you something to work on, and there is surely time enough ahead, if you have your life, to arrange them afterwards.

Pound is a temptation but he will keep. The precise chair I don't think of paramount consequence; you will be doing about the same thing whatever you are called, for the usual professional work won't take up all your energies. Perhaps I lie a little in that last sentence, but the difference is not enough to pay the loss. After this offer, you can certainly soon get a place there if later you want it, and anyway you wouldn't have to wait many years. Once there you will go ahead.

There is one feature, however, which I must suggest quite seriously and which you very obstinately ignore. It is that your present single state may not endure; just now I believe you when you say that you are absorbed in ideas, but it may not be always so. You ought to think of that, and try as you can to realize that other interests may come in. How will you meet those? A safe berth does make a difference *quoad hoc,* when the alternative is grubbing at the law. That is what gives me pause; on the rest I am pretty sure, as you see. What does Holmsey say? I suppose you have written him before now. It is wonderful to see you so exempt from the calls of pleasure and ease. If the will is trained against that, the rest is so simple, as I know to my cost.

Here now come the legions and phalanxes of the bankruptcy bar and my day of peace is over. Adios. God bless you.

Yrs., L.H.

ms with signature 104A.2

To Learned Hand from Felix Frankfurter

July 8, 1913 — 1727 19th street, Washington, D.C.

Dear Judge:

[...]You're a blessed friend to give me what you did on the Harvard business. I suppose one ought to take one's joys as one's buffets, or mostly outside on one's credit or blame and therefore not too hard. But the love has been generous in my friends. Gratitude is a poor irrelevant thing, but it symbolizes what I want to convey to you. Your reaction hit me hard—for you want for me the things I want in my sanest moments[...] My doubts come in as to my ability to have decent scope for four years more under this administration. With a man like [Louis Dembitz] Brandeis,[69] most decidedly. Otherwise, I'm very dubious. I'm afraid the period of saturation may be setting in for me here. They do want Democrats for one thing[...]

My own thinking on the Harvard thing—for my own clarification—I soliloquized and here it is. I really wanted to see what I looked like—that's why you may find me standing in front of the mirror[...] Stimson opposes because he thinks I ought to be in "the center of things" in New York (would practicing law as I would have to for a livelihood be the

69. Louis Dembitz Brandeis (1856–1941): Associate Justice of the United States Supreme Court, 1916–1939.

center of things for whatever I might contribute?) and Croly is afraid I'd become a "pillar" of society. Me—a pillar!

I'm particularly grateful for the friendship that prompts your reminder that things may change for me. I think I get its force[...] You're a great gift to me.

Faithfully, F.F.

ms with signature 104A.2

To Felix Frankfurter

July 18, 1913 District Court of the United States

Dear Felix:

Your judgment of your own place at Washington of course puts a new light upon the matter. If you are to be frozen out into a mere legal subordinate, most of the force of my argument disappears. That you alone can judge. I urge you however not too readily to assume that you have not and will not have the confidence of Garrison in the sense that you want it. I still feel that unless you are certainly to be relegated to the duties of a mere formal functionary, you should hang on. The kind of experience you will get cannot be found anywhere else. If there were danger of your getting bureaucratized, I should say so quickly, but that is not so, and I feel as if Harvard was always open to you. On the whole, I have not changed in spite of your letter, though I must say you have made me a bit groggy in the certainty that I felt before.

I wonder whether you are right about Wilson. It is easy to mistake mere indecision or better, a general vagueness of ideas, for far-sighted apprehension. His spoken words have indeed been disappointing. Terse thought I have not usually found in them or a keen edge of definite conclusion, but his acts have nearly all suited me to a T. In them, he has shown himself to be quick and sure, even when his sureness consists in inaction, e.g., re Mexico. So I have come to believe that he holds back from us his mind, and asks us to read it in his deeds[...]

Be good. L.H.

ms with signature 104A.2

To Learned Hand from Felix Frankfurter

July 22, 1913 War Department, Bureau of Insular Affairs, Washington

Dear Judge:

[...]Thanks very much for making me be sturdy in my thinking about myself. I wonder if fates won't be good to me for a talk with you sometime during the summer. Are you by any chance to be at Cornish the last of August or at the American Bar Association meeting thereafter?

Hasn't the new Central American policy unexpected virility? I am not prepared to have an opinion as to details, but in its essential concept, it is a refreshing departure from the Rule of Rhetoric. My best to you.

Faithfully yours, Felix Frankfurter

tp with ms signature 104A.2

To Felix Frankfurter

August 13, 1913 Windsor, Vermont

My dear Felix:

I leave here tomorrow for the West and shall be gone at least three weeks and perhaps longer[...]

Mexico looks to me worse and worse.[70] We ought, of course, to give the man on the inside all the benefits of doubt, and it may be that recognition would not save the day, but I must say it looks to me the proper play. Certainly we may say this: strengthen the hands of any particular blackguard and bandit that you think most likely, or at all likely, to stop the fire and to shoot successfully the other blackguards and bandits who aspire to power; forget the means they have used, murder or other, to get into the saddle—under penalty of involving your own country in a conflict which will certainly seriously compromise her future for a generation—forget the general moralities between man and man—and remember that your duties are to avoid entangling your country in what seems to be otherwise an inevitable war of the most dreadfully pernicious character, [involving] the subjection of people who, with all their infirmities, will be at once united by a strong national spirit which you must entirely destroy. Of course, if Huerta has not any chance, all this comes to nothing, but I should help anyone who had a chance just as far as I could without exciting against him jealousy as a Gringo favorite. I suspect that things are not going along on these lines[71][...]

Thine, L.H.

ms with signature 104A.2

1913-4

To Herbert Croly

October 14, 1913

Dear Herbert:

I got your letter of yesterday. There really isn't any news to give you. I have only spoken to two of the judges here about my nomination and they took it better than I

70. In February 1913, the liberal leader Francisco Madero was assassinated; the reactionary General Victoriano Huerta took control of the government.

71. "I squint a lot towards his general view of things Mexican." (ms note in Frankfurter's hand)

supposed.[72] I should not be surprised, however, if I had incurred a good deal of odium from a number of the older members of the bar, who must look upon the Progressive Party in general as anathema and think any judge who will lend himself to it is already condemned.

I was a little surprised to learn that Brandeis had told both George [Rublee] and Norman [Hapgood] that he thought I ought not to have done it. His theory was that a judge ought never to run for any elective office. It seems to me that this is perfectly absurd if it is to be extended to State judges, for logically it necessarily involves not running to succeed yourself for the same office. The theory that your impartiality is affected has undoubtedly something in it, in fact, is a good argument against electing judges anyway, but it seems to me preposterous when you have the institution, to lay down any such rule as that. I believe he confined it to Federal judges, but it seems to me just as absurd to apply it to Federal as to State judges, and certainly the strictest tradition up to the present time has not discountenanced it in the least. From what I read of Brandeis's articles which are coming out, I think he is going to stick his standard of disinterestedness so high that few of us can possibly hold office or even important position. Things will have to be run by people who are willing to sacrifice a good deal more than anybody that I know—unless it be Brandeis himself.

I had a pleasant lunch and hour afterwards with Felix the other day. Found him inspiring and in good form. I think he will probably go to Harvard. He does not seem to care much and I should doubt whether the job was appealing to him quite in the way in which it ought. Going into a thing like that, I should like to see him full of invention. I must say I do not see how he could be, for it seems to me all very hazy, but with such an active intellect as he has got I had perhaps expected more than I should.

I have neither done, seen, heard nor thought anything of interest or otherwise since I left you. Work, I am glad to say, is very light, so I have hardly had enough to keep me busy. I was rather discouraged when I went to Meray[73] to learn that my vacation seemed not to have given me the rest which I hoped. He found that I had a pretty low blood pressure, which indicated that I was still rather run down, and he has cut down all my tobacco and practically all my alcohol. He insists that I shall sleep out of doors and take regular calisthenics in the mornings. I fear I have been living a little on my capital for the last four years, since I have been judge, and that I do not respond quite as quickly to rest as I should. I feel now as though I did not much care, to tell you the truth, and I suppose that is one indication of the very difficulty, for if I were in good shape I should care more what happened. I hope in the course of time things will straighten out and I shall take a little more interest in life [...]

[L.H.]

tp 102.21

---

72. In a letter dated October 13, Herbert Croly asked LH about his decision to run for Chief Judge of the New York Court of Appeals on the Progressive Party ticket. (tr/tp with ms signature 102.21) *See* 1913-5 To Roe, November 7.

73. Meray was LH's personal physician. In a letter to the editor of The Journal of Outdoor Life dated October 27, 1913, LH asks "where in this town, if at all, I can buy beds so shaped that the head of the sleeper may be run out of the window, together with the fixtures, if any, which go with such beds." (tp 26.17) LH purchased a bed of this kind and slept in it during good weather for several years.

1913-5

To Learned Hand from Gilbert E. Roe[74]

November 6, 1913 55 Liberty street, New York

Dear Judge:

Pardon me for saying "I told you so."[75] I felt sure that your vote and that of Judge Seabury would be far in excess of the figure your suggested. I think the defeat of Judge Werner and the size of the vote which you and Judge Seabury received are the most significant facts of this election. Your vote is practically a vote of protest, as everyone understood you would not be elected, and also there was very little in the nature of party-solidarity to aid you. Had a campaign been made, your vote could have been doubled. Your vote represented a calm and deliberate judgment; there was no hysteria about it. It shows that there is a sentiment in this state demanding a change in the character of judges, which must be reckoned with. Just at present our politicians feel that they can ignore it. A little later they will be only too anxious to cater to it. Then we may have to fight as hard to preserve what is right in our law and procedure, as we now fight to get rid of what is wrong.

Yours sincerely, Gilbert E. Roe

tp with ms signature 37.13

To Gilbert E. Roe

November 7, 1913

Dear Mr. Roe:

I thank you for your letter. The result was in every way satisfactory, but votes are the hardest thing in the world to interpret. Now I should myself interpret the vote for Judge Seabury and me as made up of the minimum strength of the Progressive Party plus those disgruntled democrats who could not quite bear to vote the Republican ticket. The extent to which the *Ives* case[76] figured seems to me to be measured by the difference between Judge Seabury and me, which is only a few thousand votes. Of course, there was no

---

74. Gilbert Ernstein Roe (1865–1929): attorney, Roe & McCombs, New York, 1905–1910; counsel to Senator Robert La Follette, 1918.

75. LH ran as the Progressive candidate for the office of Chief Judge of the New York Court of Appeals in the election of 1913. The Democratic candidate, Judge Willard Bartlett, won the election over both LH and the Republican candidate, Judge William E. Werner. Judge Samuel Seabury, Progressive candidate for Associate Judge, was also defeated. See GERALD GUNTHER, JUDGE LEARNED HAND: THE MAN AND THE JUDGE 197–201 (1994).

76. Ives v. South Buffalo Ry. Co., 94 N.E. 431 (N.Y. 1911). *See* 1911-3 To Roosevelt, May 8, note 19.

ground in reason for any distinction between Judge Werner and Judge Hiscock, as both shared in that opinion,[77] but I don't believe that people cut quite so fine as that.

In some ways I am sorry about all this trouble over judges. As a judge myself I am very conscious of the fact that it is hard to be indifferent to the popular feeling, as it exists now, in those cases in which one ought to be indifferent to it. All of us must recognize, of course, that a judge is not the authoritative source of public opinion and that his first duty is honestly to try to get at the legislative meaning when it is written. There is no doubt in my judgment [that] a great deal of public feeling in this country at the present time strikes directly at that limitation of function. I believe that that feeling has arisen in large part through the very ill advised and lawless attitude of judges in the past in their constitutional decisions: men, for example, like [Rufus] Peckham[78] and [John Marshall] Harlan,[79] who fundamentally did not understand law, at least as I understand it, though they took quite opposite views. I am glad to see that you look with some concern yourself at just the problem. I agree with you that the time may come when we will have to fight hard to preserve what is right in our law. It will be harder for people like you and me because we will be charged with having caused exactly the excitement which at that time we shall be trying to stem.

Faithfully yours, [Learned Hand]

tp 37.13

1913-6

To Learned Hand from Van Vechten Veeder[80]

December 10, 1913 United States Court, Eastern District of New York

My dear Hand:

Since the receipt of your note I have been expecting from day to day to get over to your building to consult a book or two in the Law Institute Library, and in that event I had in mind dropping in to see you. In view of the delay perhaps I should assure you in this way,

77. William E. Werner (1855–1916): Justice, New York Supreme Court, 1895–1904. Frank H. Hiscock (1856–1946): Judge, New York State Court of Appeals, 1910–1916; Chief Judge, 1916–1926. Both Werner and Hiscock sat on the New York State Court of Appeals that had ruled in *Ives*.

78. Justice Rufus Peckham; *see* 1911-5 To Roosevelt, November 20, note 31.

79. John Marshall Harlan (1833–1911): Associate Justice of the United States Supreme Court, 1877–1911. In contrast to Justice Peckham, whose *Lochner* opinion for the Court was much criticized, Justice Harlan dissented in *Lochner* and was the lone dissenter in *Plessy v. Ferguson* (which established the "separate but equal" doctrine).

80. Van Vechten Veeder (1867–1942): Judge, United States District Court for the Eastern District of New York.

if assurance be necessary, that I had not the remotest thought of anything personal in your comments on the *Ives* case.[81]

With respect to that case I simply say that upon reading the opinion of [Joseph P.] Cotton's committee,[82] they did not assert that the constitutional question was free from doubt. And I understand that only one of the two western states have since enacted compulsory laws, while more than a score of states have avoided the constitutional issue by various expedients[...] I see no reason for treating the judgment in the *Ives* case with contempt. I have made no special study of the matter—I have been busy with my own problems. But if you will refer me to the same thing on the on the other side of the issue, I shall be glad to read it.

Faithfully yours, Van Vechten Veeder

ms with signature 44.6

To Van Vechten Veeder

December 11, 1913

Dear Veeder:

I have your letter of yesterday. I am glad you did not think that I was rude. You are quite right that Cotton had some doubts about the constitutionality of this law. He and I talked it over a little at the time, but if you could hear him talk now about the decision, you would have no doubt as to what his personal views were. His doubt was as to whether the courts had been educated up to that point, not as to whether there was any genuine doubt about the propriety of the law within the Constitution. There is no doubt, as I wrote you before, that when men like you feel as you do, that I have got twisted in my sense of indignation and otherwise at such decisions. I must have got into a biased and partisan frame of mind, and the question must at least be open to a good deal more doubt than I should have supposed.

I cannot refer you to anything to read which seems to me to clear up the matter, unless it be, for example, the *Oklahoma Bank* cases, which [Oliver Wendell] Holmes, Jr. wrote. These represent perhaps the most advanced doctrine, from my point of view. I should say that in general, the decisions of the Supreme Court in the last ten years had made impossible any such reasoning as Judge [William E.] Werner's, nor can I see the least distinction between a law which compels a man to guard his machinery and a law which compels him to pay for accidents which may occur in his factory. In either case, by running his factory he engages in an enterprise which, in the long run, will certainly insure injury to certain people. He should be compelled to spend a certain amount of money to minimize that risk, as we all agree, even though his workmen know all about it and accept it at the penalty of having no work at all. I cannot see why the state should not say as a condition

81. Ives v. South Buffalo Ry., 94 N.E. 431 (N.Y. 1911). *See* 1911-3 To Theodore Roosevelt, May 8, note 19.

82. Joseph P. Cotton (1875–1931): attorney, New York City; member of the New York State Commission on Workmen's Compensation, 1910; Undersecretary of State, 1929–1931.

of permitting him to engage in the industry, that he also should be required to pay them in case they are injured, a certain amount of injury being the inevitable result of the conduct of human being as they appear to be constituted.

Further, I especially deplore that kind of interpretation of such vague clauses as "due process of law" as takes away from the legislature the power to do those things which are recognized as within the legislative power in every civilized country of the world. It seems to me that that result alone is sufficient to show that the court must have been wrong in its construction of the clause in question. If there were any necessity for twisting or violating the plain language of the Constitution, more could be said, but the phrase "due process of law" is notoriously vague and uncertain. The idea that it embalms individualistic doctrines of a hundred years ago I believe myself to be heretical historically and very serious practically.

I daresay this seems rather vague; perhaps it is. My own judgment has always been that all decisions and all talk about the Bill of Rights were extremely vague. I could never make much of any doctrine about it, and in the secrecy of my own soul had always thought that men who had discussed it had never clearly attempted to come to an understanding with themselves. Frank Goodnow has the best ideas of constitutional law that I know. If you will read his little book on *Social Aspects of Constitutional Questions*,[83] or something else like that, you will get a much better defense of my ideas than I can possibly give; indeed, I have borrowed substantially what I believe from him. I agree that a great deal of it is very much in advance of what we can hope for during your life or mine, but I believe that most of it in the end will come true, and that we ought to work as much as we can for it, if our system of government is to endure.

Faithfully yours, [Learned Hand]

tp with ms notes 44.6

1913-7

To Learned Hand from Herbert Croly

December 13, 1913 — The Dupont

Dear B.:

[...]Everybody here seems to be filled with a holy terror of the President. There is no symptom of any effective opposition. The Democrats, knowing that they are a minority and comforted by the awful example of the Republicans, are resolved to keep together at any cost, and only under Wilson's leadership can they succeed. It looks as if he would get triumphantly through the present session, and that we will be rewarded with a practically undiminished majority in the next House of Representatives. He will deserve it. Whether we like him or not, he is giving to the country a most impressive precedent in resolute

---

83. Frank Goodnow, Social Reform and the Constitution (1911).

and effective executive leadership, which will be very beneficial to any equally strong successor. Up to date, his influence has been all to the good, but he is talking incautiously. He is laying down principles about constitutional government in Latin America and about his inability to urge any reforms, not contained in the platform which may haunt his path in the future. Mexico is his weakness; but he may slip out of the dilemma by recognizing the first constitutional soul who can establish any pretence of government in that distracted country[...]

Faithfully yours, H.C.

ms with signature 102.21

To Herbert Croly

December 19, 1913

Dear Herbert:

[...]We had a nice evening with Felix Saturday, and I am delighted to see how much Frances takes to him. To tell you the truth, I was in considerable hesitation as to whether she would like him or not, and I always find that however much my reason may tell me that she is wrong in her personal judgments, in the end I am very greatly influenced by them. I doubt whether I can very thoroughly like a person whom she does not. In any case, it greatly safeguarded my friendship with Felix to have her like him[...]

I do not wholly agree with what you say about Wilson. I grant that he is an extraordinary, impressive figure, and it may be that he is carrying the country with him, which I suspect is true.

I do not think that his influence has been all to the good, as you suggest. It is perhaps a little difficult to see in the present condition of Congress how so strong a man could fail to have the dominance which he exerts. But surely it cannot be a healthful political experience for a nation. Whether it is well so glaringly to show the deficiencies of Congress as he is doing is perhaps arguable. But he is an example of personal government and reliance upon the executive alone, which is much the worst of my time. I hear from all sources that Congress is absolutely supine before him. If he were a more sensitively responsible man, this, in a single instance, might not be so serious, although as an example it would always remain so. But he is not that: he is genuinely representative of the great mass of the people in his deep democratic feeling. But he is not in any sense responsive, and a president that exercises the power that he has should be not only representative, but [also] responsive. Besides, I am pretty well satisfied that at bottom he is not genuinely rational. I think his attitude toward people is governed by deep-seated prejudices, and although those prejudices are common to a great mass of the people of the country, they are nonetheless undesirable. This is one reason why Norman [Hapgood] so often judges men, and so seldom judges things. I think Washington is now a place where you get no hearing unless you come from the proper crowd, and in that respect I must look back with gratitude to our vivacious Colonel, who was much more widely sympathetic than the present incumbent is or ever can be. I believe that this is the secret of my own invincible dislike of him. I cannot get up any enthusiasm for him personally, although I will acknowledge nearly all the good things he has done. I was a little surprised to find that Felix had just the same feeling as I. We each of us were constantly cudgeling ourselves to get rid of mean and malicious dislike of him. I do not think it unreasonable, I think it is founded on what I say, and has a genuine basis. I am a little surprised that you should suppose that he could slip out of the Mexican situation by recognizing Villa or Carranza.[84] In the first place, they have already soiled themselves in such a way that he will not do it, and in the second place, it would do no good if he did, for their tenure will be much more doubtful than Huerta's. They are northerners, and I think it is generally accepted that no northerner can possibly rule Mexico. They are the merest brigands, who will be unable to set up any kind of government. When Huerta goes down—as seems most probable—there will be no way out for him; he will simply have to maintain his policy, as Phil [Littell][85] says, of ultimatums backed up by infinite patience until even his obstinate insistence upon peace may be broken down[...]

As ever, yours, [L.H.]

tp 102.22

1914-1

To Morris R. Cohen[86]

May 7, 1914 District Court of the United States

My dear Cohen:

I enjoyed the paper about "Law and Discretion" immensely.[87] It put plainly some things that I have had in the back of my head for a long time, but never quite got out. The logic of discretionary powers is most interesting. You probably know, when the chancellors started, everything was discretionary, but they developed their rules until they got, in Lord Eldon's time,[88] to a place where they needed equity upon equity. What we got, of

---

84. Pancho Villa (1877–1928) was a revolutionary leader in Mexico who fought against General Huerta and after his overthrow against President Carranza. For Huerta, see 1913-3 To Frankfurter, August 13.

85. Philip Littell (1868–1943): editorial staff, New York Globe, 1910–1913; editor, New Republic, 1914–1923. LH's letters to Littell are the most intimate in his correspondence and continue to Littell's death in 1943. *See Philip Littell, in* The Spirit of Liberty 180–82 (1960). Subsequent citations from The Spirit of Liberty are from this edition.

86. Morris R. Cohen (1880–1947): Professor of Philosophy at City College of New York, 1912–1938.

87. On the relation between law and discretion, Cohen observes: "The legalist's dilemma, either a rigid rule without discretion on the part of the judge, or else arbitrary caprice, does not [...] exhaust all possibilities. If it were true, there would be no middle course between absolutism and anarchy[...] Discretion in general, represents more or less instinctive evaluation or appreciation of the divers elements that enter into a complex; and such instinctive evaluation must precede conscious rule-making." 11(8) *Rule versus Discretion*, J. Phil., Psychol., & Sci. Methods 208–15, 212 (1914).

88. John Scott, Lord Eldon (1751–1838): Lord High Chancellor of Great Britain.

course, was a general revamping of the whole business, more in accordance with vague ideas of justice and speed. Discretion is a faith which, like other faiths, at once begins to develop its own church, which turns out in the end, like all churches, to be its shroud. It is the place where law ceases to appeal to formal authority and takes root from general ideas of morality. As you say, in those ideas themselves the same dialectic breaks out. A judge's discretion is the point in his system where he takes his nourishment directly from his mother—ethics.

Faithfully yours, [Learned Hand]

tp 102.14

1914-2

To Amos R. E. Pinchot[89]

May 29, 1914

Dear Amos:

I have received and read your letter to Dickson,[90] which I think a very capable production. However, I do not agree by any means that the Sherman Act is of value or that the Progressive Party should take its position against monopoly. That depends upon questions of fact which I'm in no position to judge. I have always suspected that there are monopolies possible which depend for their maintenance wholly upon economic efficiency, and which it would be an economic blunder to destroy. Whether the great trusts of this country are such or not is quite beyond my information or ability at the present time. I have never believed in trust-busting, and I think that the winter's work of George Rublee is going to show considerable effect in that respect. The trust-busting definition is at present pretty groggy, and the main movement is for a trade commission. Such a commission would inevitably tend to the licensing of monopoly, either in whole or part, as the case may be. I think that Brandeis has been substantially brought around on that subject.

However, this has not much to do with the subject of your letter, though it has more than I think you allow. If [George Walbridge] Perkins[91] is using the Progressive Party for the purpose of booming his own interests and the interests of the two corporations with

89. Amos Pinchot (1872–1944): supported Roosevelt's Bull Moose campaign in 1912; founding member of the National Committee to Uphold Constitutional Government, 1937.

90. This letter is not in the Hand Papers. LH may be referring to Joseph M. Dixon, chairman and campaign manager of the Progressive National Committee. The "letter" he indicates may have been a draft of the copy Pinchot would send to Dixon but that he also forwarded to Theodore Roosevelt; *see Colonel Roosevelt Is Loyal to Perkins; Resents Amos Pinchot's Attack and Considers Him Radical to Point of Foolishness*, N.Y. TIMES, June 12, 1914. For a full account of the Pinchot-Dixon controversy, see Harold M. Ickes, *Who Killed the Progressive Party*, 46 AM. HIST. REV. 306–37(1941).

91. George Walbridge Perkins (1862–1920): partner, J.P. Morgan & Co.; Executive Secretary of the Progressive Party, 1912. *See* GERALD GUNTHER, LEARNED HAND: THE MAN AND THE JUDGE 230–31 (1994).

which he is associated, he ought either to stop or get out. I think in this letter you have shown that he has been using his position to boom himself. I think there is palliation for this in the consistent attacks which have been made upon him, and which have made him, in fact, a matter of interest to the party. He is not to be altogether blamed for identifying these attacks with the party welfare. Upon the whole, I do not feel that your drive at him has much changed the situation as I understood it before. The question in my mind has always been whether he was an absolutely essential factor in the existence of the party. Taking one thing with another, I should be prepared to say that he ought to get out as chairman of the Executive Committee and as quite so prominent a figure as he is. I would not throw him off the Executive Committee. I do not think that in any organization which has got so little start as we have yet it is possible to begin throwing bricks at everybody you don't like. Perhaps this is about what you mean yourself.

Faithfully yours, [L.H.]

tp 35.1

To Learned Hand from Amos R. E. Pinchot

Saturday

Dear B.:

If you can mention any industrial monopolies which should be protected, I wish you would drop me a line. It seems to me industrial monopolies are fundamentally and logically wrong and wasteful. Railroads, telegraphs etc. come in another class. They are natural and not artificial monopolies. I know of no industrial monopolies which are natural and which have been formed to gain efficiency or which have gained it. What they want and get is the price-fixing power. The enclosed letter from George came a few minutes ago. Please return it after reading.

Yours, A.P.

ms with signature 35.1

To Amos R. E. Pinchot

June 1, 1914

My dear Amos:

Your requirement of me is quite beyond any promise which I made. I particularly said that I did not know anything about it and that I did not understand the facts, but that I suspected that monopolies were possible, depending upon economic efficiency. I think it perfectly possible, at least theoretically, that monopolies based on mere economic efficiency, once in control of the market, would succeed in keeping all others out. They would probably get this by what you call "price-fixing power." I am entirely ignorant about the industrial conditions in this country, and decline the assumption of your letter that I ever suggested that any of the existing trusts were of that sort.

I return George's letter, which seems to me to concern itself more with the effect that Mr. Perkins is having upon the opinion of the party than with the facts. George's whole effort this winter has been for a commission which shall have large powers to license contracts affecting competition.[92] The question all depends upon how large a market you are considering, and how complete control you have in mind. A combination of two merchants in a small village will effect a monopoly. On the other hand, there is no monopoly so absolute that at a certain point substitutes will not come in to control its price. What I particularly object to in the whole matter is the effort to deal with it in generalization. That is the reason why I am for a trade commission,[93] but as you will readily see, I know nothing about the subject, and what I think is of less conceivable value to anyone than any other single thing that I can imagine. This is the reason, probably, why I express myself in strong general terms.

Faithfully yours, [L.H]

tp 35.1

1914-3

To Learned Hand from Walter Lippmann[94]

June 8, 1914 Sebasco, Maine

Dear Judge:

I meant to get your blessing before I left, but I'll get it before I go to Europe. Francis and I plan a trip to Coney Island the night before I sail, July first. Won't you be our guide?

---

92. George Rublee worked to create the Federal Trade Commission early in 1914. In a letter dated June 9, LH asked Rublee: "what kind of monopolies in restraint of trade the Supreme Court has prohibited under the Sherman Act in its latest decision? I have before me a demurrer to a complaint under the Sherman Act which is troubling me a great deal. I have read over again some of the decisions and I must confess that I am in the most hopeless and absolute confusion[...] I can find absolutely no general rule which applies[...] The whole treatment of the act seems to me very discreditable to the administration of justice." (tp 107.4)

93. After the Commission had been created, LH wrote an editorial, anonymously, in THE NEW REPUBLIC. He described the Commission as focusing "not on possibilities, but on performance, not on monopoly, but upon unfair trade methods[...] In this Trade Commission Act is contained the possibility of a radical reversal of many American notions about trusts, legislative power, and legal procedure. It may amount to historical, political, and constitutional reform. It seems to contradict every principle of the party which enacted it. It seems to strike at the root of ancient American prejudice. But the opposition has been negligible, so negligible that it stirs a little wonder as to whether Congress and the press realize that the quiet phrasing and ingenuity of this bill were another Trojan House." *An Unseen Reversal*, THE NEW REPUBLIC, Jan., 9, 1915, at 7–8.

94. Walter Lippmann (1889–1974): journalist, author. LH probably first met Lippmann at the offices of The New Republic early in 1914, as Herbert Croly was getting the magazine underway; its first issue appeared on November 7, 1914. LH and Lippmann remained friends, though not without periods of conflict, until LH's death in 1961.

These are bleak days for you Progressives, I'm afraid. Why not join the Socialist Party? It never changes, has no ambitions, can't win, is not puzzled, and hasn't even one leader. That's what I call political stability[...]

Yours, Walter Lippmann

ms with signature 106.15

To Walter Lippmann

June 10, 1914

My dear Walter:

I have your letter of the 8th. So it is there that you have disappeared[...] I do not like your political sneers and I do not think they are sincere. My Progressive flag is nailed to the mast and I propose to play the Star Spangled Banner while the ship sinks. My position in the band is to beat the bass drum softly. I don't know what position you have in the Socialist Party; I suspect it is in the last line of water carriers, with a distinct tendency to desert at that.

When you get back shall I see you at all before you sail, except on the eventful evening? I don't wonder you busybodies have only a limited spare time for a *judex*, most of whose living hours are consumed in reading testimony. I now see why people in former times went to such extravagances in telling judges what great men they were. If they had not baited the hook in some such way, the poor suckers would never have bitten. Don't forget me.

Yours, [L.H.]

tp 106.15

To Learned Hand from Walter Lippmann

June 12, 1914 Sebasco, Maine

Dear Judex:

June 30th does then, and we promise to adapt the occasion to whatever you feel fit to do. I see that I am never in New York to give the judiciary exercise. There will be at least three days to do it before I sail, and I'll telephone when I get to town. I haven't seen a newspaper for a week, but somebody told me that [William Jennings] Bryan has gone off on a Chautauqua[95] and that Wilson has laid it down as a principle of mediation that when

95. William Jennings Bryan (1860–1925): Democratic nominee for President in 1896, 1900, and 1908; Secretary of State, 1913–1915. A supporter of biblical creationism, he appeared for the prosecution in the trial of John Scopes, who taught Darwin's theory of evolution in Tennessee. *See* 1925-2, To Lippmann, June 7, note 63. Lippmann may be referring to a summer seminar program offered by the Chautauqua Institution, founded in 1874 in New York State and dedicated to the furthering of American education.

Huerta steps out his first act shall be a visit to the White House to express his regrets for being what he is.

I spend my days reading proof, which is worse than testimony, writing out what I think about socialism, and reading a history of the French Revolution. I also chop wood twice a day and kill mosquitoes. John Hobson's new book—*Work and Wealth*[96]—has just come, and from what I saw in manuscript last summer I guess you ought to read it. Graham Wallas's book will be out June 17th.[97]

I hate to think of your upholding the existing order in the heat while I'm up here undermining it with the sea breezes blowing.

Yours, Walter

ms with signature 106.15

To Walter Lippmann

June 15, 1914

Dear Walter:

[...]You don't have to see the newspapers at all, except that you will be surprised to hear that the administration is very optimistic about Mexican mediation. At strange and wholly unexpected thing also has arisen. Huerta is supposed to be quite willing to retire, but for some reason which has not yet appeared he objects to having a Carranzista[98] in his place. On the other hand, Carranza has refused as yet to enter into the conferences and it is thought at Washington that he may be unwilling to have any cientifico [sic] provisional president. This unexpected dilemma has greatly upset the plans of the administration. Secretary Bryan, however, is reported as saying that he has the best possible hopes of a satisfactory outcome, and that so far there is no reason to suppose mediation will not turn out well. Some of us of more atrabilious temper wonder whether his certainty is so wholly justified as he thinks.

[...]My dear boy, don't trouble about my upholding the existing order in the heat while you undermine it in the cool. In the first place, that is as it should be, and in the second place, it is not so. I suspect I am doing a good deal dirtier work than you and that, too, with a very half heart. Why shouldn't I be uncomfortable for both reasons?

Don't forget me when you come through. You have so many of these stimulants that I am rather sorry you may get slack of sedatives.

As ever yours, [L.H.]

tp 106.15

---

96. J.A. Hobson, Work and Wealth: A Human Valuation (1914).

97. Graham Wallas (1858–1932): Professor of Political Science, University of London. Lippmann may be referring to The Great Society; A Psychological Analysis (1914).

98. I.e., a supporter of Carranza; for Huerta and Mexico. *See* 1913-3 To Frankfurter, August 13.

1914-4

To Felix Frankfurter

July 31, 1914

Dear Felix:

[...]Today my "psychology" is genuinely overshadowed by the terrible prospects of the general war. It obsesses my mind to think that where ten days ago there were millions of men engaged in peaceful and profitable pursuits, now apparently they are all to begin killing each other as rapidly as possible, so as I can see only because some Austrian nobles have decided that it ought to go on. The particularly hopeless part of it to me is that were I, for instance, in control of any of the other countries of Europe, I should feel myself perfectly helpless to take any other course than they do. Once the row of bricks begins [to fall], each brick is powerless to stand up. I cannot see how Russia can allow Serbia to be beaten, or Germany can allow Austria to be beaten, or France or England to allow Russia to fight it alone. It seems vicious circles, but I suppose perhaps it is all inevitable, men being men and land being limited. I have not a vast deal of confidence that the fundamental causes of war are going to be removed by Hague tribunals[99] or much of anything else. I doubt whether there is any other way finally of testing out which people is entitled to hold a country except those who are the strongest. That may seem a very brutal test, but I seem rather despondent; that I should live, perhaps to see it, I regret[...]

I wish you would tell me the result of your talk with Ted when you come here. I agree with you that his strategy has been of the very highest order. I compare it with Napoleon's campaign of 1814, in which he showed his greatest genius, although it was unsuccessful. Having created a successful diversion in the enemy's camp and discomfited the most formidable rival, he seems to be about on the point of annexing the other detachment. I cannot conceal, however, the fact that it seems to me the end of anything in the nature of a Progressive Party. Nevertheless, it was a good fight and I am not in the least sorry for it. I would like to find a new home. If you know any congenial political boarding house where we could live for a while I wish you would advise me of the number; I am quite sure that we could furnish it with some desirable company. I cannot myself quite take the Socialist Party seriously; I got over my religious *Drang* about twenty years ago. Ecclesiastical organizations, crusades, and revival meetings have since that time ceased to appeal to me.

Faithfully yours, [L.H.]

tp 104A.3

99. I.e., the sessions of the Permanent Court of Arbitration, established in 1899 and staffed by a permanent group of jurists to whom contending nations could appeal for settlement of disputes.

1914-5

To Felix Frankfurter

October 9, 1914 Albany, New York

Dear Felix:

You will now have had a week or two of work and will have begotten an enormous enthusiasm for it.[100] Don't be offended, *mon brave*, I know you quite well and I don't hesitate to prophecy. You will increasingly like it, and you will be successful in this as in what else you have undertaken. I rejoice in your energy, I associate myself in your pleasure, I fear nothing except that you may let the variety of your interests divert you from what will perhaps become the monotony of subsequent years.

I am faintly drawn to the study of the Philosophy of Law, and [have] begun by reading [Fritz] Berolzheimer's *World's Legal Philosophies*.[101] It is very hard for me to get up any interest in this aspect of law, which seems to me to be rather the belated expression of our moral ideas and to take its source wholly from them. That there are administrative limitations in the enforcement of these ideas, and political necessities, I agree; these seem to me to constitute all there is of *Rechts Philosophie*, but still I shall plug along a while, confident that when men like Pound think otherwise, my small rush-light has not illumined the vasty [sic] recesses. The conventional English skepticism has so long got hold on me that it will take some training to shake it off. I trust in the course of years that you will have plumbed depths I have never reached, and you will, I know, guide me to the bottom. Meanwhile, at your leisure ask Pound to give me a little course of easy steps, *gradus ad Parnassum*, for the tender beginner. If I can get anything out of it, I purpose to do it; the interest may come with exercise. At least it will be better than our American substitute, the fatuous floundering of the Supreme Court which goes by the name of Constitutional Law. Am I perverted that I alone of those who touch it have acquired such a contempt for that subject? I can scarcely think of a matter to which the human mind has been applied with less credit to itself than that. If it were from only a political attempt to disguise the necessity of a continued course of utilitarian adaptation of language to new needs, I could respect it, but the creatures who utter the stuff take it with the utmost seriousness. They suppose they are compelled by a rigid dialectic, that they are engaged in a deductive analysis (those of them who would know what the words meant) and their work is pitiable from that aspect; most of it would disgrace any capable boy of 20 who had been trained by you and your colleagues in HLS. I should honestly have much more respect for a trained pupil of St. Thomas [Aquinas] than for most of those worthy mastiffs. Looked at largely, regarding them as the wholly unconscious instruments of ideas they do not recognize, I can respect their work. As a political body, they indeed have a genuine dignity and value, but I am thinking of them not in the Balaam's Ass capacity but as conscious of what they are about.

---

100. Frankfurter began teaching at the Harvard Law School in September 1914. *See* 1913-3 To Frankfurter, July 3.

101. Fritz Berolzheimer, The World's Legal Philosophies (1912).

My dear Felix, as I write these words I am fearful that it may only serve to show my ignorance and my frivolity—I honestly am—but still that is what I think, nothing less moderate than that, and why should I not be frank with you? I cannot take seriously that solemn farce; it is the rarest thing in the world to find any honest avowal of the real reasons which dictate their decisions.[102] The reason [Edward Douglass] White is thought so good is because he is a Jesuit, a casuist, and a sophist[...] Even Holmesy, shrewd analyst that he is, has to conceal in part the main-springs. Out upon the accumulated mass of rubbish![...]

Having given birth to this monster of my soul, I am relieved. Poor old H. C. [Herbert Croly] is deeply cast down by your coerced defection. To be deprived of him "who more than any one else understands his point of view, and shares his convictions," was hard indeed. The rape of his little Benjamin by the hard-hearted [Ezra Ripley] Thayer[103] was a bitter blow. I was incontinently, brutally, unsympathetically joyous[...] Thereby I showed that I was, besides a tyrant, 1. a truant to the faith in ideas as the final directors of life; 2. a jealous mole who wanted other men to be kept out of the light just because I have got a life sentence myself; 3. an obscurantist, a believer in factory life without "Normal Rules of Industry," a dullard, a grind, a dry-as-dust, a soul-quencher, a German pedant, a blear-eyed, soulless, plodding son of Caliban without faith, vision, trust in life, or the generous aspirations and confident attacks of Sacred Youth[...] O Flippant, Diffuse, Treacherous, Disloyal Pen that has carried me away to the utmost limits of inconsequent insincerity, and that now I resolutely, resolutely, responding to my solemn, conscientious, stuffy old self, cast away into Cimmerian blackness till that pleasing whore, *Stultitia*, throw well again about me the embraces of her delusive arms.

Thy damned, but constant friend, Old Dog Tray[104]

P. S. What in Hell are you, F.F. esq., Prof. F., or Mr. F.F.? Beware to answer; I am a devil for correct address. By the way, now I am no longer "Judge Hand," but "Judge L.H.," God be praised.

L.H.

ms with signature 104A.3

1916-1

To Felix Frankfurter

January 10, 1916 — Judge Learned Hand's Chambers

My dear Felix:

[...]Here is an interesting point I succeeded in ducking the other day. The Chinese Exclusion Act says that a person of Chinese descent found in the country must prove he

102. Early the following year, LH identifies the "interests" of the Justices as determined by "the prejudices of that economic class to which all the justices belong" in *The Normal Inequalities of Fortune*, The New Republic, February, 6, 1915, at 5–7.

103. Ezra Ripley Thayer (1860–1915): Dean, Harvard Law School, 1910–1915.

104. LH refers to a poem by Stephen Foster (1826–1864) celebrating his faithful dog Tray: "Grief cannot drive him away."

is not an alien or if not, that he has the right to remain.[105] Is the connection between alienage and descent sufficient to justify an inference of fact which will allow the burden to be thrown on the individual? Suppose it had been Jewish descent. Suppose it had been English[...] I hate to use such an odious word between us, but (I whisper) would it be constitutional to compel a person of English descent to prove he was not an alien? May we make legitimate distinctions based only on race?

L.H.

ms with signature 104A.5

1916-2

To Learned Hand from Felix Frankfurter

April 20, 1916 Law School of Harvard University

Dear B.:

I'm here in Pound's Jurisprudence seminar and I know I'll never be a "jurist." All this stuff about rights and duties, the accumulated logomachy of centuries, wearies the flesh. And then Pound is too damn scholarly for me—he cares about what every Privatdocent has written. I'm not handicapped by learning and the result is I get much more out of my men in the Administrative Law by reading their work instead of pouring things into them.

It looks rather bad for Brandeis—worse than ever, for the Administration has allowed the thing to drift while the gang has been busy and flooded the country with that lying brief of [Austen G.] Fox.[106] Gee—but how deep prejudice and inertia and selfishness go, and how poor reason is used as a perverted instrument in their behalf[...] But now for jurisprudence—

F.F.

ms with signature 104A.6

---

105. The Chinese Exclusion Act, passed in 1882, provided harsh penalties for Chinese and persons of Chinese descent who were found to be in the United States unlawfully. In a series of cases, the Supreme Court upheld the Act's provisions, noting repeatedly that the right "to exclude or to expel aliens, absolutely or upon certain conditions, in war or in peace, is an inherent and inalienable right of every sovereign and independent nation." *See* Wong Wing v. United States, 163 U.S. 228, 231 (1896) (citing Fong Yue Ting v. United States, 149 U.S. 698 (1893)). Until *Wong Wing*, such punishments were meted out without a finding of guilt in a court of law; in *Wong Wing*, the Court held that punishments such as hard labor or the confiscation of property could be imposed only after a judicial trial determined the guilt of the accused, relying in part on *Yick Wo v. Hopkins*, 118 U.S. 369 (1886), in which the Court held that the protections of the Fourteenth Amendment which refers to "persons" are not confined to citizens.

106. Woodrow Wilson nominated Louis Dembitz Brandeis to the Supreme Court in 1916; Brandeis was confirmed on June 1. Frankfurter refers to charges against Brandeis made earlier by the New York attorney Austen G. Fox. *See* N.Y. Times, Mar. 29, 1916.

To Felix Frankfurter

April 29, 1916 Judge Learned Hand's Chambers

Dear Felix:

There are they who build the misty mansions for the soul, most of which are born to perish with them. They build like ancient cities, stratum on stratum, but we always hope that all is not lost each time. For me I never doubt that in the end a worthy habitation will be made, and men like Pound, numerous perhaps as coral worms, or nearly, will have built it.[107] There are they, also, who pass the torch along from generation to generation and these give light in a murky world by which the others can work. If you cannot lay the bricks, certainly your torch is bright. I am not prepared to say you will lay no bricks. (N.B. I seem to have got a little away from the mist, but only a pedant fears a mixed metaphor).

I am glad people are talking about rights and duties. When I came on we were all still joined by Charles (was it Charlie?) Austin and we dared not talk so, all save Langy,[108] who, like the old king in the lush verses my children repeat, "had nigh lost his wits," and lived way off beyond the moon with Plato in the absolute Truth Factory where he was a foreman. Everyone else was historical then, and the secrets of Jurisprudence, a word used with much circumspection and never without conscious if not express apology, all lay in Register of Original Writs. "Jurisprudence, my son, he's in the same contingent forms by which a slowly consolidating king's power happened to exercise its will first. Procedure is all there is of it. Once get the ways they used to do things and there is nothing more. Above all do not confused the vagaries of the supposed sociologist with the possible acquisition of a legal scholar." *Also sprach Zarathustra.* It would have been dew to parched lips for me to have been born twenty years later, or thirty. Do not despise, do not recoil before Pound and his splendid pageant of sonorous abstractions. You are not too old to join the gorgeous priestly procession of rationalism of which I see the banner tips already over the hills. When the archbishops of the sensuous sell out like [Henri] Poincaré, shall the mere mountebanks like [Henri] Bergson long delay? Take heart and jump on the bandwagon.

I cannot bear to think that Brandeis can lose. I was not so unqualified as thou and the *N[ew] R[epublic]*, but I never realized how much I felt till this morning I felt my heart stand still at the fear that in the end he might really lose. The triumph of the bunch will be unendurable. I can support being thought a pariah, a turncoat, a scurvy time-server, he

---

107. LH returns to the figure of the law as a coral reef in an address delivered May 11, 1925, at the American Law Institute in Washington, D.C.: "the whole of [the law] has been fabricated in this way like a coral reef, of the symmetry of whose eventual structure the artificers have no intimation as they labor." LH argues that what passes for the "common will" is no more than a "stock instance of a combination of custom and its successive adaptations. The judges receive it and profess to treat it as authoritative, while they gently mold it the better to fit changed ideas." He denies that statutes qualify as an expression of the "common will": "some carry something like the assent of a majority. But most legislation is not of that kind; it represents the insistence of a compact and formidable minority." *Is There a Common Will?, in* THE SPIRIT OF LIBERTY 47–56. On the "common will," see 1929-4 To Hand from Cardozo, June 25; on the figure of the coral reef, see 1932-2 To Frankfurter, March 12.

108. Christopher Columbus Langdell (1826–1909): Dean, Harvard Law School. Langdell instituted the case method of instruction, which exemplified a rigorous logic.

who sells out his own traditions, his own case, his own family, but I always fancy it against the background of unjust truth, the furious abjurations of gilded impotence. The real test is when we get it in the neck into the bargain.

Thine, L.H.

ms with signature 104A. 6

To Learned Hand from Felix Frankfurter

May 15, 1916 Law School of Harvard University

Dear B.:

[...]Your juristic letter gave delight a) to a potential Justice (Brandeis), b) to a jurist (Pound), c) to a philosopher (Cohen), and d) to a humanist (F.F.). If I rebel against learning once a month, will I fetch your cheeringly searching pen in return?

Thanks, Felix

[P.S.] Neither the philosopher nor I got your learned reference to Poincaré's sensuous sell-out to rationalism.

ms with signature 104A.6

1916-3

To Theodore Roosevelt

June 13, 1916 Judge Learned Hand's Chambers

My dear Colonel Roosevelt:

I have always felt that you were peculiarly the man for the present time; I was for you before, I am for you now without any question. Yet I hope you will not be persuaded out of your position regarding our nomination.[109] Hughes has it in his hands to make it possible for us to support him. If he will show a genuine sympathy for our general point of view and energy in the policies which are vaguely centered about our movement, we shall betray nothing in going with him. His past gives much cause for hope that he will, and your decision to give him the chance seems to me wise and patriotic.

If you run, you will do nothing to redeem the Progressive Party as such. It cannot endure as a third party and there will be three while the amorphous Democracy remains intact, if it can be called intact. Meanwhile, we must worry along with our former brothers so long as we stand equally, and do not have to assume the position of erring prodigals returned. If that be their conception of unity, we have no choice but to jump the

109. The Republicans nominated Charles Evans Hughes for President in June 1916.

reservation. Yet even then, if I go, I shall join the Amalekites;[110] I can see no room there for a third party.

I have no right to volunteer advice, but so many others are doing it, and you have been always so open to listen to all that I know you will not mind it. If Hughes has wisdom and makes it possible, I should like to see you actively with him. If he will trim and teeter, let him be anathema.

Faithfully yours, Learned Hand

ms with signature, Theodore Roosevelt Papers, Manuscript Division, LC, Reel 211; see also draft in pencil, 37.21

To Learned Hand from Theodore Roosevelt

June 16, 1916 New York City

My dear Judge:

That's a mighty nice letter of yours! I agree exactly with what you say. My own belief is that we shall have to support Hughes as against Wilson; but the vigor of our support must depend upon Hughes himself. With warm regards to Mrs. Hand,

Faithfully yours, Theodore Roosevelt

tp with ms signature 37.21

1916-4

LH's letter to Max Eastman represents his initial critique of restrictions on free speech instituted by the Espionage Act of 1917, just passed on June 15. The Act prohibited persons from conveying information or false reports with the intention of interfering with the operation or success of the armed forces of the United States or to promote the success of its enemies.

To Max Eastman[111]

June 27, 1916 Judge Learned Hand's Chambers

My dear Mr. Eastman:

I have your letter of the 26th asking me to say that I think *The Masses* ought not to be excluded by Ward & Gow from the newsstands.[112] I answer unhesitatingly that I think it

---

110. The Amalekites were the other party; in Genesis, they are the enemies of Israel. *See* 17 *Exodus* 8–10.

111. Max Eastman (1883–1969): publisher of THE MASSES, a paper supporting radical reform, from 1913 to 1917.

112. Responding to the news that Senator Thompson's Legislative Committee was considering whether Ward & Gow—a distributor of periodicals to newsstands in New York City—should exclude

ought not. I do not often see your paper, and as you probably can guess, I do not feel sympathy with your approach to the question of social and economic reorganization, or the means by which you seek to bring it about. That I prefer another way, does not blind me to the wisdom of giving you the chance to persuade men of yours. I have never seen anything in *The Masses* which did not have a sincere and genuine relation to these absolutely legitimate purposes. You will forgive my saying that parts of it have at times been extremely repellant to me, though never what you did yourself, but that in my judgment has nothing to do with this matter. Yours is a way, whether it is a good way or a bad way, of getting men to think and feel about those things on which it is most important that they should think and feel. I can conceive no possible defense for excluding you except either that such matters must not be discussed, or that they must be discussed only in a way which accords with the common standards of taste. One alternative is tyrannous absolutism, the other, tyrannous priggism.[113]

Sincerely yours, [Learned Hand]

tp 20.1

1917-1

To Learned Hand from Walter Lippmann

May 2, 1917 | 46 East 80th street, New York City

Dear B.,

I've hoped you'd guess and yet wasn't able to explain why I've been so elusive this winter. I'm to be married early in June to the girl with whom I've been in love since freshman year

---

THE MASSES from the subway and elevated newsstands, Eastman asked that LH send him a letter or telegram stating that it should not. (tp with ms signature 20.1)

113. The case against THE MASSES was brought by Postmaster General Albert S. Burleson, who charged the newspaper with criminal behavior under the Espionage Act. In a decision handed down in July, LH decided for THE MASSES and enjoined the postmaster from banning the newspaper from the newsstands supplying public transport. Masses Publ'g Co. v. Patten, 244 F. 535 (S.D.N.Y. 1917). The United States Court of Appeals for the Second Circuit overturned LH's decision in November. 246 F. 24 (2d Cir. 1917). In a second trial, *United States v. Eastman*, 252 F. 232 (S.D.N.Y. 1918), LH ruled that the September 1918 issue of THE MASSES violated the Espionage Act, specifically for its publication of a cartoon, "Having Their Fling," and a poem, *Young Lads First*. However, he also ruled "that the defendants were entitled to have the government enumerate the particulars of phrases in the charges, such as 'private solicitations' and 'public speeches.'" 252 F. at 232. *See* John Sayer, *Art and Politics, Dissent and Repression: The Masses Magazine versus the Government, 1917–1918*, 32 AM. J. LEGAL HIST. 42, 66–67 n.116 (1988). For LH's correspondence on the case, see 1917-3 To Lippmann, October 3; 1917-4 To Burlingame, October 6; 1919-3 To Learned Hand from Oliver Wendell Holmes, Jr., April 1. For an analysis of LH's view of this case, his differences with Oliver Wendell Holmes's interpretation of the First Amendment, and the eventual adoption of LH's position in 1969 in *Brandenburg v. Ohio*, 395 U.S. 444, see Gerald Gunther, *Learned Hand and the Origins of Modern First Amendment Doctrine: Some Fragments of History*, 27 STAN. L. REV. 719 (1975). For a history of *Masses* in relation to the question of free speech, see GEOFFREY STONE, PERILOUS TIMES: FREE SPEECH IN WARTIME (2004).

at Harvard. Her name is Faye Albertson[...] It's not news to me—It's always been one of the things that were sure and splendid. I'm very happy indeed.

Tell Mrs. Hand, but no one else till after the 18th of May—Just now I'm only telling the few people for whom I care most.

Yours ever, Walter

ms with signature 106.16

To Walter Lippmann

May 3, 1917

My dear Walter:

I didn't guess and it is a surprise, and yet, and yet. Tho' I am no reader of women's minds like F.H. or Louis Dow,[114] some things get even to me. Last winter—on 5th Ave. East side about 33rd st.—I did pass you in a big ulster and the woman was nestled up under your arms in a way! I said *Tiens, Tiens*, see Walter, he is like the rest of us after all. But you really aren't, you are a good deal like yourself and rather more than usually so to find your balance in your freshman year, even if it was only yesterday. I thought, notwithstanding the under-the-wing effect that evening, that all your evenings were being spent with E.M. House or Newton Baker[115] or other guys like that; I suspected you not, being a judge and a guileless fellow. It all seemed to me further corroboration of what a force of an important thing you were. And I was right, you were important and you are important, only I didn't know just where it was. I don't know yet, but I'm going to learn as soon as you will let me.

I always feel envious of people who are just in love—you aren't just, but never mind. I took mine neurotically, as I have taken most else, and it seemed to me fiercely serious. I couldn't have said like you, "sure and splendid"; they are good words, and I believe them quite literally. They are particularly good words for you, because, my hearty, they hit you off pretty well yourself. There, it is shameful to swipe to a man openly and I'll say no more, except that I wish I could say more and not be a little ashamed when I saw you next.

Thine, L.H.

P.S. The fearful secret shall be hid till May 15th, 1917, at midnight.

ms with signature, Lippmann Papers, Sterling, Box 12, Folder 499

---

114. Louis Dow, Professor of French, Dartmouth College.

115. Colonel Edward M. House (1858–1938): an advisor to President Wilson. Newton Baker (1871–1937): attorney, Baker & Hostetler, Cleveland; Secretary of War, 1916–1921; member, the Permanent Court of Arbitration at The Hague, 1928–1937.

1917-2

Following Germany's unrestricted pursuit of submarine warfare in January 1917, President Wilson announced a break in official relations on February 3, 1917. Congress declared war on April 6, 1917.

To Charles C. Burlingham[116]

June 26, 1917

Dear Charles:

[...]Harvard commencement was very moving. The regiment of the boys passed us, fine-looking fellows, and all of us old ones looking on much moved and ready at a word to dribble into tears, like the silly old sentimentalists that we were. You would have been as bad as the worst. If you had seen them and thought what the next twelve months might have for them, and been there yourself, safe and out of it, it would have been hard to keep a cool composure. Everyone felt the significance of the whole occasion. The college is hardly more than a camp, and those who are going to do nothing go around talking about what the others will do. [Herbert Clark] Hoover[117] was the star of the occasion and read (hopeless method) a speech of wisdom which touched the heart of the matter. The point was that there was plenty of willingness, but the condition of the willingness was that all should bear the burdens equally; if inequalities in war-burdens became glaring, the whole structure would fall. That is the secret, and I am not wholly confident that we shall succeed. His job is a particularly difficult and uncertain one. I do not know any case where price control—and that is in substance what he proposes—has been successful; certainly not in such a large community as our own. We shall see. It must be tried. If it only succeeds in part something will be gained. Woodrow [Wilson] at least has kept them well in hand, and it looks now as though the thing would go through. Hoover told me that if it did not, he would not undertake it for the present, feeling fully confident that inside of six months conditions would so have changed that he could get the powers on which he thinks any success depends. From the present outlook he will succeed and then we shall see, we shall see[...]

I suppose you saw that Felix Frankfurter had gone with [Henry] Morgenthau[118] to Egypt and further if possible, though no one can tell. The purpose is to try to find out the condition of Americans in Palestine, and also the condition of the Jews, American or not Americans, with an idea to alleviate their condition, which I suppose is very trying, and

---

116. Charles Culp Burlingham (1858–1959): attorney, Burlingham, Veeder, Masten & Feary, New York.

117. Herbert Clark Hoover (1874–1964): Secretary of Commerce under Presidents Warren Harding and Calvin Coolidge; President of the United States, 1929–1933. Hoover headed the operations of the American Relief Administration in Europe, 1917–1919.

118. Henry Morgenthau, Sr. (1856–1946): Ambassador to the Ottoman Empire, 1913–1916.

apparently to extricate such Americans as may be stuck there, if the Turks will consent. I do not envy him his companion and don't quite see why they selected him[...]

As ever, thine, [L.H.]

tp with ms notes 100.26

1917-3

To Walter Lippmann

October 3, 1917 Judge Learned Hand's Chambers

Dear Walter:

I sent a special delivery letter to Felix Monday night, supposing he was still in Washington. Please destroy it. It contained a letter to George Rublee, but I tried to get another to him last night when I learned that F. had left. These letters were about that everlasting judgeship. [Martin] Manton, the junior district judge, is announcing that they have promised the place to him, and it is quite possible.[119] I thought that if the wind lay in that quarter, F. and G. might be able to do something yet. Indeed, I had hoped that even Brandeis might be willing to raise a hand to prevent that, though I knew he would not do anything positive. I am getting convinced that I must be out of it; perhaps *Masses* was enough. I loathe this damnable job-hunting inexpressibly, but I want the job, so *que voulez-vous*? It is that way or none.

[...]Herbert [Croly] has told me about the proposed committee, and I want to go over it with you as fully as possible.[120] Much of it tempts me fearfully; only think of the time after it is over, and of the *vacuus viator*—i.e., L.H.—who must face the coming years with nothing, so far as I can see, for which he is in the least fitted lying at his hand. No more of this now, I will tell you just the possibilities. Of course, you will understand that H.C. did not say that I could be the third; he merely mentioned the chance.

Faithfully, L.H.

ms with signature, Lippmann Papers, Sterling, Box 12, Folder 499

---

119. Martin T. Manton (1880–1946): Judge, District Court for the Southern District of New York, 1916–1918; Judge, United States Second Circuit Court of Appeals, 1918–1939; convicted of bribery, 1939. LH was hoping for an appointment to the Second Circuit Court of Appeals. *See* 1918-1 To Frankfurter, January 9. For LH's eventual appointment to that court, see 1924-1 To Augustus Hand, July 27.

120. LH refers to a committee directed by Sidney Mezes, the brother-in-law of Colonel E.M. House, dedicated to negotiating with neutrals so that they would become allies of the coalition opposing Germany. The committee, known as "the Inquiry," worked in New York City. Despite LH's reference to Croly's interest in the committee's work, there is no evidence that Croly promoted LH's participation in it. *See* Ronald Steel, Walter Lippmann and the American Century 128–30 (1980).

1917-4

To Charles C. Burlingham

October 6, 1917

Dear Charlie:

[...]Teddy [Theodore Roosevelt] spoke last night and was awful. Did you see his terms of peace in this morning's paper? Nothing but fire and fury. Poland with a Baltic port, which of course means Dantzig, the papers this morning said, [together] with the whole Baltic coast, whatever that precious nonsense may mean; Transylvania to Romania, a Bohemian kingdom; Austria generally in fragments; England to keep all colonies; Alsace-Lorraine to France; "Italian-Austria" to Italy. Would that mean Trieste and the Isonzo? He would be capable of that. And a whacking indemnity for Berlin. Last, but not least, a precious pearl, Shleswig-Holstein back to Denmark. In other words, in order to make the world "safe for democracy," we are to undertake to right every wrong that has been done for the last four hundred years and create more grievances than before. My only surprise is that he omitted giving back Silesia to Austria. There never was a more shocking rape than that. Finally, he is going to erect an independent Finland and apparently an independent Lithuania. Yet it was he who got all the applause. I can't feel very encouraged when I see nothing better than the thinking of the stone-age, smashing everybody and smashing without any idea of what you really want, and when you are asked, a string of nonsense like that. And then more fury to everyone who disagrees. Apparently he and his kind may talk terms of peace, but no one else.

I was foolishly pleased at [Frank Douglas] MacKinnon's agreeing with my opinion, which I suppose was in the *Masses* case.[121] I think all this building, plus Veeder, is against me, although [Henry G.] Ward[122] does not commit himself. Gus thinks of it as nothing more than another instance of my natural perversity. The perversity is there all right, and God knows how much my subconscious self, which is no doubt a cross-grained critter, may have been fooling with my cerebral centers, but I never was better satisfied with any piece of work I did in my life. I do not mean that I was pleased with it as a judicial performance, but with the result. There is a bit of it that is arguable, no doubt; in the main outline I have been very happy to do what I believe was some service to temperateness and sanity.

As ever yours, [L.H.]

tp 100.26

---

121. Frank Douglas MacKinnon (1871–1946): Lord Justice of Appeal, 1907–1946.

122. Henry G. Ward (1851–1933): Judge, United States Court of Appeals for the Second Circuit, 1907–1924.

1917-5

To Learned Hand from Charles Merrill Hough[123]

December 22, 1917 United States Circuit Court of Appeals

Dear B.:

I return opinion in the *American Druggists' Syndicate*[124] with concurrence. I can't help saying that it is amazingly interesting to me, as illustrating your turn of mind, conscience, and affiliated ganglia. All that you say seems to me perfectly true, yet since I cannot perceive that you are establishing or expanding any fundamental principle of law, or doing anything that will be referred to or depended upon in future cases, I am (as many times heretofore) left behind, wondering why in the world you work so hard to arrive at an end which so far as this plaintiff or defendant is concerned might be so much easier reached.

The foregoing is not mere impertinent criticism, nor is it only persiflage; I seriously think you wear yourself unduly by unnecessary exertion, and I put this in writing rather than in talk because I have wanted to say it often, and can put it more shortly on paper than any other way[...]

Sincerely yours, C.M.H.

tp with ms signature 24.9

To Charles Merrill Hough

December 24, 1917

Dear Boss:

[...]I feel it as much as you do. It is something that is simply tied up with me generally. I see all these difficulties, I suppose I see too many; when I do see them, it seems to me that an adequate statement of the case requires their consideration and their answer. I can't *do* the work any differently. I have got to go into those things. Whether I ought to put into an opinion all of that kind of work that I do is a different matter, perhaps I ought not, perhaps it only makes it confused, but it is necessary for me to feel that I am doing honest work, to go through that kind of thing. That is the only test that I can bring for myself. I should like to talk the matter over with you, for I feel just what you do[...]

Faithfully yours, [Learned Hand]

tp 24.9

---

123. Charles Merrill Hough (1858–1927): United States District Court for the Southern District, 1906–1916; United States Court of Appeals for the Second Circuit, 1916–1927.

124. American Druggists' Syndicate v. Continental Specialty Co. of Baltimore, 249 F. 290 (2d Cir. 1918). In this contract dispute, LH's detailed analysis of the correspondence between the parties apparently exceeded the effort Judge Hough thought necessary to reach the decision that the judgment of the district court should be reversed and a new trial ordered.

1918-1

To Learned Hand from Felix Frankfurter

November 6, 1917 Copper Queen Hotel, Bisbee, Arizona

Dear B.:

So they reversed you in the *Masses* case. Well—I'd much rather take my chances, now and hereafter, with you than the reversers. I knew nothing of the case until I got back in August, and I haven't read either your opinion or the C.C.A.'s, but it's the one single act of yours that makes me most proud you're a judge.

We're getting all het up, losing not only our perspective, but also our sense of humor in this war for democracy. The manifestations of shoddy patriotism this trip reveals are wide and deep.[125] You would be surprised, even you, by the tyrannies that are exercised in the holy name of "loyalty." They behave as though the mere utterances of "the flag," "patriotism," "loyalty" are acts of devotion, and themselves the surest proof of what constitutes patriotism. The thing is so shallow and so pathetic as well as brutal. These old bags, who have fought labor and unions as poison for a decade, now wrap themselves in the flag, and are confirmed in their old bias and what the *N[ew] R[epublic]* calls "obscurantism" by a passionate patriotism. Gee—but it's awful; and then they wonder at the fecundity of the I.W.W.s,[126] the wobblies as they are picturesquely called. They breed the I.W.W.s—they and the neglect by the old-fashioned trade unions of the needs of the immigrant, non-English speaking seasonal workers of the West.

[...]I have seen or heard nothing of the judgeship. I wrote [William] Hitz[127]—your letter came after I left—but not a line from no one. I can't believe that Manton will be appointed. I'll hate to see you not get it. But—that you are you is the important thing even though (or because) this is a worldly world. By the way—are you aware that you captivated a whole battalion of women in Lyme? And Frances will agree that your covey was a particularly fine one[...]

Yours, F.F.

ms with signature 104A.7

---

125. Frankfurter, on leave from Harvard Law School and serving in the War Department as special assistant to the Secretary of War Newton D. Baker, refers to a trip he took to investigate the deportation of Mexican workers in Bisbee, Arizona, after they had struck against Phelps Dodge, the copper mining company.

126. International Workers of the World, a labor organization.

127. William Hitz (1872–1935): Judge, United States District Court for the District of Columbia, 1916–1931; Judge, United States Court of Appeals for the District of Columbia Circuit, 1931–1935.

To Felix Frankfurter

January 9, 1918 Judge Learned Hand's Chambers

Dear Felix:

Please forgive my failure for so long to write you. I had a rather anxious time in November and December as you have by now learned all about.[128] I got your Bisbee report and think that it was right. No doubt T.R. is mad, but we may not follow him at the present time.[129] I keep hearing about you from [Julian W.] Mack,[130] who told you what he said about [Thomas W.] Gregory[131] and my elimination. It is better not to touch it, for though I understand I have been out of it for long, G[regory] seems to have some unreasonable shimmer against you dating not from the B. report, but way back in the summer. Hitz will be able perhaps to give you the reason. The poor love, G., has this affair here all snarled up, and is dreadfully bored with it. He ought to have decided it six months ago; it would have given him less trouble. At least I hope he will select a better man than Manton.

I am ever so much obliged for your friendly interest and care about me in it. I don't believe that anybody could have pushed me over the line. I am an outsider, an *utlegatus*, a man out of frankpledge, and who can expect such a one to stand for preferment. I ought rather to be thankful that G.W.W.[132] ever thought of pulling me out of my obscurity to land me even here. The world doesn't like non-joiners, and I sometimes I wonder whether the world is not half right.

Most of the oxen that won't pull in harness well are at bottom egoists, and that's the reason they don't pull.

Most of W.W.'s last[133] I liked exceedingly. Of course, a good deal of it is vague, but it must be. This is a nearer approach to definition than we have had before, and all in the right way. I am not too much in love with the smaller nations, but I should grow more so if they do not insist upon being too damned national. It is easy to get up objections to all the suggestions, but they point where we must try to go, and there is no use in seeing all

---

128. LH refers to a bout with pneumonia.

129. Frankfurter wrote a memorandum to Newton D. Baker, arguing that the administration should open a discussion with the "constructive and responsible radicals" in the labor department. Frankfurter later joined the President's Mediation Commission. *See* Report on Bisbee Deportations (GPO 1918). *See* Michael E. Parrish, Felix Frankfurter: The Reform Years 90–95 (1982); H.N. Hirsch, The Enigma of Felix Frankfurter 55–56 (1981).

130. Julian W. Mack (1866–1943): Judge, United States Court of Appeals for the Seventh Circuit, 1911–1929; Judge, United States Court of Appeals for the Sixth Circuit, 1930–1940.

131. Thomas W. Gregory (1861–1933): Special Assistant to the United States Attorney General, 1913; Attorney General of the United States, 1914–1919.

132. George W. Wickersham (1858–1936): Attorney General of the United States, 1909–1913; President, American Law Institute, 1923–1936; President of the Council on Foreign Relations, 1933–1936. Wickersham nominated LH for the District Court in 1909. *See* To Learned Hand from Henry L. Stimson, April 7, 1909.

133. LH is referring to President Woodrow Wilson's "Fourteen Points," his plans for the postwar world, which he presented to Congress on January 8, 1918. His last and fourteenth point provided for the institution of a League of Nations: "A general association of nations must be formed under specific covenants for the purpose of affording mutual guarantees of political independence and territorial integrity to great and small states alike."

the specks you can on the sun. The Russian clause was especially good and wonderfully timely.[134] The freedom of the seas is open to some doubt in my mind. I am for it while the international police hold out, but I should, if I were an Englishman, want a little assurance of my own against its disruption at the first strain, which I should look for. Have you really got a picture of an international force coercing a nation determined to be recalcitrant? I can see a coalition doing so, but to imagine the contingents of those nations which are affected joining in or of their allies, presses my sense of "realism," as W[alter] L[ippmann] used to like to say, pretty far. How would the men in them fare if they ever wanted to go back home? It seems to me our best reliance is upon smoothing out the worst places where roughness exists. You know I have always been a Tory and a backslider upon this subject. Still we must try to put into practice the beginnings of such a thing; there lies the hope. Trust to the International Police and keep your powder dry. I suppose that is a horrible thing to believe. I wonder how far you really differ[...] Write me when you can, and best of all, come to N.Y.

As ever, L.H.

ms with signature 104A.7

1918-2

To Oliver Wendell Holmes, Jr.

June 22, 1918 Windsor, Vermont

Dear Mr. Justice:

I gave up rather more easily than I now feel disposed about Tolerance on Wednesday. Here I take my stand.[135] Opinions are at best provisional hypotheses, incompletely tested. The more they are tested, after the tests are well scrutinized, the more assurance we may assume, but they are never absolutes. So we must be tolerant of opposite opinions or varying opinions by the very fact of our incredulity of our own. (This may be left for deductive demonstration in accord with the inexorable rules of formal logic by E[dward] D[ouglass] W[hite], C.J.U.S.Supr.Co.).

You say that I strike at the sacred right to kill the other fellow when he disagrees. The horrible possibility silenced me when you said it. Now I say, "Not at all, kill him for the love of Christ and in the name of God, but always realize that he may be the saint and you

---

134. LH refers specifically to the sixth of Wilson's Fourteen Points, which called for "the evacuation of all Russian territory and such a settlement of all questions affecting Russia as will secure the best and freest cooperation of the other nations of the world in obtaining for her an unhampered and unembarrassed opportunity for the independent determination of her own political development and national policy and assure her of a sincere welcome into the society of free nations under institutions of her own choosing"[...] *See* http://avalon.law.yale.edu/20th_century/wilson14.asp.

135. On the occasion of the encounter, see Frederick R. Kellogg, *Learned Hand and the Great Train Ride*, American Scholar 471–86 (Autumn 1987).

the devil. Go your way with a strong right arm and a swift shining sword, in full consciousness that what you kill for, and what you may die for, some smart chap like [Harold] Laski[136] may write a book, and prove is all nonsense." I agree that in practical application there may arise some difficulty, but I am a philosopher, and if man is so poor a creature as not to endure the truth, it is no concern of mine. I didn't ask him; let the Galled Jade wince,[137] speaking reverently of course.

I sat under the Bo Tree, and these truths were revealed unto me. Tolerance is the twin of incredulity, but there is no inconsistency in cutting off the heads of as many as you please; that is a natural right. Only, and here we may differ, I do say that you may not cut off heads (except for limited periods and then only when you want to very much indeed), because the victims insist upon saying things which look against Provisional Hypothesis Number Twenty-Six, the verification of which to date may be found in its proper place in the card catalogue. Generally, I insist, you must allow the possibility that if the heads are spared, other cards may be added under that sub-title which will have, perhaps, an important modification.

All this seems to me so perfectly self-evident, self-explanatory, and rigidly applicable to the most complicated situations that I hesitate to linger upon it, lest I should seem tolerant of any difference of opinion concerning it. I greatly enjoyed my good fortune in meeting you on the train.

Faithfully yours, Learned Hand

ms with signature, Holmes Papers, HLL, Reel 33, frames 85–88

To Learned Hand from Oliver Wendell Holmes, Jr.

June 24, 1918 Beverly Farms, Massachusetts

Dear Hand:

Rarely does a letter hit me so exactly where I live as yours, and unless you are spoiling for a fight I agree with it throughout.[138] My only qualification, if any, would be that free

136. Harold Joseph Laski (1893–1950): economist; Professor of Political Science, London School of Economics, 1926–1950.

137. *Cf.* "We that have free souls, it touches us not; let the galled jade wince, our withers are unwrung." HAMLET, III, ii.

138. Holmes had conveyed his interest in Hand's letter to Harold Laski in a letter dated June 25: "I had a good talk with Judge Hand coming on [to Beverly Farms] which led to a characteristic and mighty good letter carrying on the talk." Laski responded in a letter dated July 5: he wanted "to make some comment on B. Hand's letter to you," which Holmes had evidently forwarded to him, and went on to object to Hand's idea of tolerance because it failed to deal with the utterly powerful man, who, believing he has the truth, is "out to slay all who think differently. If he and B. Hand were the last two men in the world, how could Hand secure the survival of toleration except by killing him?" Holmes replied in a letter dated July 7: "I don't see where your quarrel with Hand is [...] My thesis would be (1) if you are cocksure, and (2) if you want it very much, and (3) if you have no doubt of your power—you will do what you believe efficient to bring about what you want—by legislation or otherwise. In most matters of belief, we are not cocksure—we don't care very much—and we are not certain of our power. But in the opposite case, we should deal with an act of speech as we deal with any other act

speech stands no differently than freedom from vaccination. The occasions would be rare when you cared enough to stop it, but if for any reason you did care enough, you wouldn't care a damn for the suggestion that you were acting on a provisional hypothesis, and might be wrong. That is the condition of every act. You tempt me to repeat an apologue that I got off to my wife in front of the statue of [William Lloyd] Garrison[139] on Commonwealth Avenue, Boston, many years ago. I said, if I were an official person I should say nothing shall induce me to do honor to a man who broke the fundamental condition of social life by bidding the very structure of society perish rather than he not have his way, expressed in terms of morals, to be sure, but still his way. If I were a son of Garrison, I should reply: Fool, not to see that every great reform has seemed to threaten the structure of society, but that society has not perished because man is a social animal, and with every turn falls into a new pattern like the kaleidoscope. If I were a philosopher, I should say: Fools both, not to see that you are the two blades (conservative and radical) of the shears that cut out the future. But if I were the ironical man in the back of the philosopher's head, I should conclude: Greatest fool of all, thou, not to see that man's destiny is to fight. Therefore take thy place on the one side or the other, if with the added grace of knowing that the enemy is as good a man as thou so much the better, but kill him if thou canst. All of which seems in accord with you.

If I may repeat another chestnut of ancient date, printed in later years: when I say a thing is true, I mean that I can't help believing it—and nothing more. But as I observe that the Cosmos is not always limited by my Can't Helps, I don't bother about absolute truths or even inquire whether there is such a thing, but define the Truth as the system of my limitations. I may add that as other men are subject to a certain number, not all, of my Can't Helps, intercourse is possible. When I was young, I used to define the Truth as the majority vote of that nation that can lick all others. So we may define the present war as an inquiry concerning truth. Of course you won't suspect me of thinking with levity on that subject because of my levitical speech. I enjoyed our meeting as much as you possibly could have, and should have tried to prolong it to Boston, but that I feared my wife would worry.

Sincerely yours, O.W. Holmes

tp with ms signature, Holmes Papers, HLL, Reel 33, frame 138

---

that we don't like." There is no record that either Holmes or Laski pursued the subject further, perhaps because neither Laski nor Holmes had read Hand's letter carefully. What it said had not to do with *what* to do about what is considered intolerable but rather with *why* to be tolerant: "what you kill for and what you may die for some smart chap like Laski may write a book and prove is all nonsense." Thus unknown to "B. Hand" was his entry, by the proxy effected by Holmes, into a relationship with "Laski," who, in Hand's epistolary projection of possible events, could—by writing a book showing that based on new evidence, an opinion upon which Hand had acted was wrong—*validate* the very position of tolerance for which Hand argued. This entire episode is reported in THE HOLMES-LASKI LETTERS: THE CORRESPONDENCE OF MR. JUSTICE HOLMES AND HAROLD J. LASKI 1916–1935, at 159–61 (Mark De Wolfe Howe ed., 1953).

139. William Lloyd Garrison (1805–1879): editor of THE LIBERATOR; a founding member of the American Anti-Slavery Society.

1919-1

To David Hunter Miller[140]

January 13, 1919

Dear Mr. Miller:

I have just received your letter of December twenty-first and am glad that you think the report will be of any service, though it was hastily drawn and not at all complete.[141] It is possible that during this present Conference the subject of patents may be brought up, although I should think it extremely doubtful whether it was even mentioned at all. Our idea was that the best service we could render to the Commission would be to prepare a ready-made section, somewhat along the lines of the Russian and Romanian treaties which were the only precedents we had, except some work done by some Hungarian lawyers, of which we got hold. [Archibald] Cox[142] did practically all the work of drafting the sections and it seemed to me well done.

I want you to feel very easy about the change in plan. I had got to have great misgivings about going over, for I felt sure that I should have absolutely nothing to do when I got there. To be frank with you, I did not fancy the idea of spending five or six idle months around the Hotel Crillion while the work of this court needed help.[143] It is a pleasure to me to know that you wanted me to go over and we should have had a very interesting time, but in the back of my head I should have always had this sense that I ought not to be there.

I think there is a decided change in this country toward the President's peace. His welcome on the other side has made a great difference. You can tell it by the fact that his opponents in the Senate are singing in a much lower key than they were a month ago.

---

140. David Hunter Miller (1875–1961): Special Assistant to Paris Peace Conference, 1917–1919; drafted the covenant to the League of Nations, 1928; Judge, Permanent Court of International Justice, 1930; adviser to the State Department, 1931–1938.

141. In a letter dated August 1, 1918, Miller had asked LH to collect and evaluate international law on patents and trademarks. Hand agreed: on September 11, 1918, he responded to Miller's request by asking for information on the scope of the work; on October 7, 1918, he stated that he hoped to begin work by the end of the week. On October 22, 1918, having been asked to consider attending the Peace Conference, he wrote to say he was "accepting the position of delegate for patents and trade-marks to the Peace Conference if the State Department should select me. It therefore gives me very great pleasure to tell you that I shall be glad to undertake that work if the Department thinks fit. Will you please advise me as soon as it is definitely settled whether they wish me or not?" In a letter dated December 21, 1918, Miller thanked LH for his report on patents and trademarks and informed him that he would not be needed at the Peace conference. (tps with signatures 31.8) For a summary of LH's interest in the Peace Conference, see GERALD GUNTHER, LEARNED HAND: THE MAN AND THE JUDGE 262–63 (1994).

142. Archibald Cox, Sr., patent attorney in New York.

143. In a letter dated December 21, 1918, George Rublee describes the activities of the Peace Conference as a "mess": "the Hotel de Crillion, where the American Commission to negotiate peace is lodged, is a rabbit warren and the rabbits are running in all directions. [...]The men who have come over don't seem to care much about learning anything that they did not know in the U.S." (tp 107.4) LH later expresses regret on losing the opportunity to participate in the Peace Conference. *See* 1920-6 To MacKinnon, August 11.

Moreover, I believe, although without much positive evidence, that the sentiment in this country is slowly but certainly turning toward a genuine League of Nations; perhaps my wish is father to the thought. His trip over was one of the wisest things he ever did, and even those who opposed it at first have now in many cases been brought around. It was a bold thing, but he knew the conditions over there so much better than anyone else that his judgment has been justified by the facts.

Faithfully yours, [Learned Hand]

tp 31.8

1919-2

To Learned Hand from Oliver Wendell Holmes, Jr.

February 25, 1919 — Supreme Court of the United States

Dear Judge Hand:

Instead of the letter I intended to write to you some new work makes it necessary that I should confine myself to a word. I read your *Masses* decision.[144] I haven't the details in my mind and will assume for present purposes that I should come to a different result, but I did want to tell you after reading it that I thought that few judges indeed could have put their view with such force or in such admirable form.

Sincerely yours, O.W. Holmes

ms with signature, Holmes Papers, HLL, Reel 33, frame 139

To Oliver Wendell Holmes, Jr.

April 1, 1919 — Judge Learned Hand's Chambers

Dear Mr. Justice:

I have read *Debs v. U.S.* and the other case (i.e., *Frohwerk v. United States*)[145] and this is positively my last appearance in the role of liberator. I haven't a doubt that Debs was guilty under any rule conceivably applicable. As to the rule actually laid down, my dying

---

144. Presumably, Holmes refers to LH's first decision in *Masses*; *see* 1916-4 To Eastman, June 27, note 113.

145. LH takes up issues he addressed in *Masses*. Relying on its holding in *Schenck* (see below, note 146), the Court in *Debs v. United States*, 249 U.S. 211 (1919), found that an antiwar speech with the "probable effect" to prevent military recruiting was a violation of the Espionage Act of 1917, which made it a crime for a person to convey information with intent to interfere with the operation or success of the armed forces of the United States or to promote the success of its enemies. Again relying on *Schenck*, the Court in *Frohwerk v. United States*, 249 U.S. 204 (1919), underscored its finding that "a person may be convicted of a conspiracy to obstruct recruiting by words of persuasion" (*id.* at 206), and noted that the finding of a conspiracy to obstruct recruiting—not the success of such a plan—was sufficient under the Espionage Act. *Id.* at 209.

words are these, now already fast receding in the seas of forgotten errors—and a crazy Saragossa that would be, wouldn't it? All the mad freaks of past contrivance.

The thing against which the statute aims is positive impediments to raising an army.[146] Speech may create such by its influence on others' conduct. In nature the causal sequence is perfect, but responsibility does not go *pari passu.* I do not understand that the rule of responsibility for speech has ever been that the result is known as likely to follow. It is not—I agree it might have been—a question of responsibility dependent upon reasonable forecast, with an excuse when the words had another possible effect. The responsibility only began when the words were directly an incitement. If I am wrong about that, it is mere matter of history. I confess I have no present access to the history. Assuming that I am not wrong, then it was a question of intending the responsibility, and that was fairly a matter of better and worse. All I say is that since the cases actually occur when men are excited, and since juries are especially clannish groups—are they *societates perfectae?*—it is very questionable whether the test of motive is not a dangerous test. Juries won't much regard the difference between the probable result of the words and the purposes of the utterer. In any case, unless one is rather not in conformity, it will serve to intimidate—throw a scare into—many a man who might moderate the storms of popular feeling. I know it did in 1918. The rule coupled with [Albert S.] Burleson's legal irresponsibility certainly terrorized some of the press whose voices were much needed.

There, that is all! Absolutely and irrevocably all *in saecula saeculorum*! I bid a long farewell to my little toy ship which set out quite bravely in the shortest voyage ever made[...]

Sincerely yours, L. Hand

ms with signature, Holmes Papers, HLL, Reel 33, frames 91-96

To Learned Hand from Oliver Wendell Holmes, Jr.

April 3, 1919 Supreme Court of the United States

Dear Judge Hand:

Since your letter came I have been so busy propagating new sophistries etc. that I haven't had time to defend the old ones, and now I'm afraid that I don't quite get your point. As to intent under the Espionage Act: I believe I have said nothing except to note that under the instructions the jury must be taken to have found that Debs' speech was intended to obstruct and tended to obstruct—and except further that evidence was held admissible as bearing on intent. Even if absence of intent might not be a defense, I suppose that the presence of it might be material. Leaving that on one side, you say "the responsibility only began when the words were directly an incitement." I am afraid I do not know exactly what history you

---

146. LH invokes the Court's decision in *Schenck v. United States,* 249 U.S. 47 (1919). Schenck was prosecuted under the Espionage Act for printing and circulating flyers questioning military conscription. Although the flyers did not direct men who had been drafted to avoid military service, they did advocate a repeal of the Conscription Act. Noting that "the character of every act depends upon the circumstances in which it is done" (249 U.S. at 52), Holmes stated the "clear and present danger" standard to which he refers in his letter of April 3. Acknowledging that a time of war creates a special context and that speech that is protected in times of peace may not be so in times of war, the Court upheld Schenck's conviction.

have in mind—I don't see how you differ from the test as stated by me [in] *Schenck v. United States* (March 3, 1919): "The question in every case is whether the words used are used in such circumstances and are of such a nature as to create a clear and present danger that they will bring about the substantive evils that Congress has a right to prevent. It is a question of proximity and degree." I haven't time even now to recur to your decision but I take it that you agree that words may constitute an obstruction within the statute, even without proof that the obstruction was successful to the point of preventing recruiting. That I at least think plain. So I don't know what the matter is, or how we differ so far as your letter goes. With which I send you my blessing and don't hold you bound by your adieu to this stage.

Yours Sincerely, O.W. Holmes

ms with signature, Holmes Papers, HLL, Reel 33, frame 97

1919-3

To Ernst Freund[147]

May 7, 1919 — District Court of the United States

Dear Professor Freund:

Your article in last week's *New Republic* was a great comfort to me.[148] I had supposed that in holding such views about the Espionage Act I was in a minority of one in the profession, and that is rather too slim a party to carry a banner. You express my own opinion much better than I could myself and in your distinguished company I shall take heart of grace to believe I am right, even with the whole Supreme Court the other way. If you are interested in sports of judicial opinion you can find the judicial variant with which I tried to stop the way in *Masses Publishing Co. v. Patten*, 244 Fed. R. 535.

I own I was chagrined that Justice Holmes did not line up on our side; indeed, I have so far been unable to make him see that he and we have any real differences and that puzzles me a little.[149]

Sincerely yours, [Learned Hand]

tp 21.1

---

147. Ernst Freund (1864–1932): Professor of Political Science, University of Chicago, 1894–1902; Professor, University of Chicago Law School, 1903–1932.

148. See *The Debs Case and Freedom of Speech*, The New Republic, May 3, 1919, at 13–15.

149. LH later quotes Paul A. Freund, who criticizes Holmes's "clear and present danger" test as "over-simplified": "The truth is that the clear-and-present danger test is an over-simplified judgment unless it takes account also of a number of other factors: the relative seriousness of the danger in comparison with the value of the occasion for speech or political activity; the availability of more moderate controls than those which the state has imposed; and perhaps the specific intent with which the speech or activity is launched. No matter how rapidly we utter the phrase 'clear and present danger,' or how closely we hyphenate the words, they are not a substitute for the weighing of values. They tend to convey a delusion of certainty when what is most certain is the complexity of the strings in the web of freedom that the judge must disentangle." Paul A. Freund, On Understanding the Supreme Court (1949), *quoted in* Learned Hand, The Bill of Rights: The Oliver Wendell Holmes Lectures, 1958, at 60–61 (1963).

1919-4

To Raymond B. Stevens[150]

May 27, 1919

Dear Ray:

[...]What do I think of the Treaty?[151] I think it's a rotten treaty, but I'm for ratification of it, for I don't see any other alternative. That is where I separate from my friends on *The New Republic*. France and Germany are going to ratify, and if we don't it won't be because it's a rotten treaty but because it contains a League of Nations, and it seems to me that in this Hobson's choice we ought all to be for ratification.

Faithfully yours, L.H.

tp with tp signature 40.16

1919-5

To Learned Hand from Felix Frankfurter

November 4, 1919 — Law School of Harvard University

Dear B.:

You disappointed me very much on the two occasions that I came to New York after my arrival by being away on your various judicial vacations. No one I wanted more to talk with about the Treaty than you—and the more so when oblique rumors reached me about your views. I canvassed my own notions with Louis Dow at Hanover the other day, and we found ourselves of near enough common mind for men who want to think freely, and so I refuse to believe that you and I would be varying much in our appraisal of the different factors of the situation if we had a dialogue on it. I don't know when that can be, for I'm very much on the job here—write "a bigger and better" Law School than ever (larger in numbers and an extraordinary fine quality of men—two years older than usual and a deepened experience of life) though all sorts of Cassandras have croaked ill prophesies for the school.

But I have a personal appeal to make—and in this you simply mustn't disappoint me. Marion Denman and I want you to marry us with the minimum number of words that your

150. Raymond B. Stevens (1874–1942): special counsel of the Federal Trade Commission, 1915–1917; United States representative to the Allied Maritime Transport Council, 1917–1918; vice chairman of the United States Shipping Board, 1917–1920; member and then chairman of the Federal Tariff Commission, 1935–1942.

151. In letter dated May 26, Stevens asked LH what he thought of the Treaty of Versailles. (tp with signature 40.16) After negotiations at the Paris Peace Conference, the Treaty of Versailles concluded the hostilities of World War I. It was registered by the Secretariat of the League of Nations on October 21, 1919.

sense of the significant ones and the law allows. Since you are to be the agent or the symbol of Fate for us, we want to be Lovers with you—you're our second choice, for Holmes has no jurisdiction. If you haven't got it—get it, somehow, ad hoc or pro hac vice or through some legal fiction. Oh, yes, we want this jurisdiction of yours exercised on December 20th; probably that's a Saturday and it may be not till the following Monday the 22th (you see what a pair of casuals you'll be floating). Say "yes." We can then decide all the other two or three details—gosh, how I hate 'em! E.g., whether in your chambers or maybe Frances will lend us your study. And tell Frances she owes me a photo of the Holmes bas-relief. So you want to know the lady's address! Thus: 92 School Street, Springfield, Mass.

Thine, Felix

ms with signature 104A.8

To Felix Frankfurter

November 8, 1919 Judge Learned Hand's Chambers

Dear Felix:

No, it is not possible. I have looked at the statutes, and they only give power to a "justice or judge of a court of record." I think there is nothing on it, but it seems to me pretty clear that the words must refer to a state official[...] I am truly sorry for this is an office which I should take the greatest pleasure in doing you. I should, however, want very much to have the "bonds" hold. Not that I distrust you because of your previous divagations, but it is as well to have you nailed fast. The lady, I am sure, will entirely subscribe to my hateful implications. Having got this butterfly chloroformed for the nonce, we don't propose to have him wake up till he is well skewered in a vital spot.

Come by all means and have the wedding ceremony, if you will consent, in this somber judicial sanctuary. I would say most gladly the house, except that F.A.H. has been so poorly all this autumn that I don't want her to take on any more festivities than she can possibly help. We can have a very nice party down here at chambers, if you will. It would be a fitting setting for one who has so exclusively limited his activities to the perusal of the Supreme Court Reports, etc.[...]

No, we should not differ greatly about the Treaty, though I am very positively decided that we in America should ratify "as is" and as soon as possible. I have been getting well annoyed with the *N[ew] R[epublic]*, not so much because it differs, but because it shows its differences with some ill temper and with a kind of persistent irritation that seems to me to sit ill on a Journal of Opinion. In truth, I believe I am nothing like far enough from the Center to be in sympathy with its present temper. Perhaps I have been [illegible] them, or maybe I leaned more on the Left than I had, or maybe I have been moving to the Right, though if so it has been unconsciously. In any case they have lost a good deal of weight with me, and I think it quite likely I have been counted among the goats with them. Herbert [Croly] was so quite intolerable in June that I have found it hard to be as forgiving as proper magnanimity required. I have given up much talk with him on public questions, which in his case means a decided limitation of intercourse. Some of W[alter] L[ippmann]'s work has been excellent, but he is a Wilson chaser all the time—there is no closed season—and it has affected me unpleasantly. So you see, I am a good deal out of the whole running. I can flock with no Tories and my old crowd I am on the outs with—just a little. Fortunately, my fate as a political thinker does not seem to me of great consequence, and just at present anyway, I am greatly pressed with the ordinary routine[...]

I shall do myself the honor of advising the young woman of the terrible chances she incurs. It is never too late to recoil before her ominous decision. Trust me, I may save her yet.

L.H.

ms with signature 104A.8

To Learned Hand from Felix Frankfurter

November 29, 1919 — Law School of Harvard University

Dear B.:

After Holmes and you failed us we lost most of our interest in "the ceremony" and felt most like marrying ourselves. However—there is something to be said for your legal scruples. So [Benjamin Nathan] Cardozo[152] will speak for the Law. I have written him asking his approval that it be done in your chambers, so that, as I wrote Marion, you may be her witness that I was "signed, sealed and delivered." I'll let you know the exact hour on Saturday a.m. December 20th. I expect somewhere between 12 and 2. Tell me on your honor as a human being, whether you think a "marriage ceremony," any kind of one, is that last word in anesthetic operations. But, don't worry. I'll be there—and I don't want any [one] else there except you, if that will satisfy the law. You see when it comes to my private life I'm not much of Aristotle's social animal—though it relieves me to be told by Morris Cohen [that] Aristotle is wrongly quoted!

You did something to Marion—for your letters cheered her up mightily as these curious autobiographical revelations, called notes of congratulations, come in. And it made her less contented than ever that you're a Federal Judge of "inferior jurisdiction."

I badly want a long talk with you on our Treaty and the world. I wonder what you say to these remarks of mine made to [Thomas Nelson] Perkins[153] over two months ago. At any rate please send them back. And I should like you to know what a grand time I'm having because of all those circumstances which lie back of my correspondence with Perkins that I've asked Julian Mack to show you. I ask those political psychologists G[raham] Wallas and W. Lippmann why men who are not enslaved by worldly necessity are timid if not cowardly, and I get no helpful answer from them. Of course, Perkins is doing his best—but why doesn't he know the luxury of freedom.

Devotedly, Felix

ms with signature 104A.8

---

152. Benjamin Nathan Cardozo (1879–1938): attorney; Judge, New York Court of Appeals, 1914–1932; Associate Justice of the United States Supreme Court, 1932–1938. Cardozo figures prominently in correspondence between LH and Frankfurter during the 1950s, chiefly as a critic of the Fourteenth Amendment. *See Mr. Justice Cardozo, in* The Spirit of Liberty 129–33.

153. Thomas Nelson Perkins (1870–1937): partner, Ropes, Gray, Boyden & Perkins, Boston, 1899–1937; counsel to the War Industries Board, World War I; American Representative on the Reparations Committee.

To Felix Frankfurter

December 3, 1919 Judge Learned Hand's Chambers

Dear Felix:

First, as to details: Saturday December 20, 1919, bet. 12 & 2, exact time to be later fixed. Present: High Contracting Parties: M.D. & F.F.; Magistrate, Judge Cardozo (have already been "in touch" with him, O.K.); L.H. witness for M.D.:—(name unknown) witness for F.F.—an absolute *legal* necessity, per Cardozo J. (F.F. will see to this on peril of bitching the enterprise). F.F. will remember that he must get a license from City Clerk I think—penalty as before, bitching enterprise. N.B. Will M.D. & F.F. join L.H. immediately thereafter in a little luncheon at Lawyers Club—Private room. Present: the five persons involved? As to your queries: No, there are many anesthetic moments after matrimony. You can't expect to be alive all the time—even you.

Second, I have read [your] remarks to Perkins: they are persuasive but don't bring me round. It is too long a matter to set down here, but in short I say this. If U.S. had the choice of refusing to go in because the Treaty was too bad, then I could see a chance of doing a good stroke. The Senate didn't care about that; the question was not of enforcing a liberal attitude but an ultraconservative one. All we have accomplished, qua U.S., is to establish the precedent that we are opposed to any international order. Especially—the Treaty was sure to go through anyhow. This is in it; there was a chance of its holding long enough to be modified by "collective bargaining." Without us, the prospect is perilous. I know that the answer is it had better go, the sooner the better and by an upheaval. I think it very doubtful that the upheaval will result for a more liberal attitude, and what it may bring no one can tell. At present we need cement, not explosives.

As to reservations to the League: it seems to me that it is quite fantastic to suppose our commitments imperil us except as any possible commitments to a world organization permit us somewhat. We are in the world anyway. Article Ten[154] I should not mind seeing modified though I share George [Rublee]'s beliefs about its meaning. We have talked a good deal about it. No one would have objected to some interpretations, except that the importance of the League—very feeble at best—depended so much on the willingness we showed on going in. They have done a great deal to kill it as it is, whatever happens. I have no objection to any plan which gives the Senate a voice in the choice of delegates, or which gives anyone else. I prefer not to have them mere executive appointees. The others powers didn't care how we chose them and had nothing to do with the acceptance of the Treaty that I can see.

As a result of it all, we have lost our chance to modify and ameliorate the conditions imposed on Germany, which are, as you and I both agree, most menacing. I really can see in the attitude of *The New Republic* nothing but the intransigent position of those who will have no bread if they must put up with half a loaf. Their continued hostility to Wilson, full

154. Article 10 of the Covenant of the League of Nations: " The Members of the League undertake to respect and preserve as against external aggression the territorial integrity and existing political independence of all Members of the League. In case of any such aggression or in case of any threat or danger of such aggression the Council shall advise upon the means by which this obligation shall be fulfilled." *See* http://avalon.law.yale.edu/20th_century/leagcov.asp#art10.

of personal feeling, has bred in me feelings I don't like to have towards my intimate friends. I seldom have been surer that I was right about a public matter than about the ratification. At first, I was very wobbly, but time has taken it from me.

Lastly as to you and [Thomas] Nelson [Perkins].[155] I am not wholly clear on that. That you must do it, feeling as you do is clear enough. Whether I should feel bound to do so, I am not so sure. It is a question whether present agitation will serve any purpose or not. In the light of the prevailing strange beliefs and passions, I have a great deal of doubt of the value of any attempt to get people to think at all about Russia. After all, there is small service in nailing your colors to the mast in a cyclone. Of course, I know how easy it is to give a fair seeming of prudence to cowardice; no one can tell how far his own conduct may be unconsciously so dictated. I can only say my instinct—whatever its source—rather tends against agitation here and now looking to a change towards Russia, little as I personally share the common feelings. I suppose I was born to be in the Center, a little to the left, but in Le Marais.[156] Not a very stimulating position to occupy and without the joys of Freedom, as you say. Anatole says this in *M. Bergerat* somewhere: "Je comprends, c'est mon faiblesse; il y a beaucoup de face de ne pas comprendre."[157] There is a time when we should not weigh too nicely the pros & cons. Perhaps you have hit it right and that the time is full for a gesture of independence even when there are no traceable results to be got; I honestly don't know, I guess no. It must be a little disappointing not to have one's friends more courageous.

Thine, L.H.

ms with signature 104A.8

1919-6

To Oliver Wendell Holmes, Jr.

November 25, 1919 — Judge Learned Hand's Chambers

Dear Mr. Justice:

I was greatly pleased with your dissent in the *Abrams* case, especially with the close, which, if I may say so, was in your very highest vein.[158] I am quite confident that whether

---

155. Frankfurter objected to Perkins's response to the possibility of "Bolsheviks" at the Harvard Law School. For the controversy, see GERALD GUNTHER, LEARNED HAND: THE MAN AND THE JUDGE 360–61 (1994).

156. I.e., a marsh.

157. Anatole France's novel, M. BERGERAT: "I understand, that's my problem; there is a lot of face-saving in not understanding."

158. Abrams v. United States, 250 U.S. 616 (1919). Jacob Abrams and his co-defendants were convicted of violating the Sedition Act of 1918 for inciting resistance to the war and for advocating curtailing of production of materiel. In an opinion by Justice John H. Clarke, the Supreme Court affirmed the convictions, indicating a shift from the standard set forth in *Schenck* and in *Debs*. In the now-famous dissent written by Justice Holmes and joined by Justice Brandeis, Holmes argued that the requisite intent had not been proven (the defendants claimed their intent was to prevent interference with the Russian revolution, not to hinder the United States' war efforts against Germany), and

it is avowed or not, in the end your views must prevail after people get over the existing hysteria. It will not be the first time that you have formed the law by a minority opinion. I also agree with enthusiasm with your analysis of motive and intent about which there has been much too meager discussion in the books. It was with a strong emotion that I read your words, stronger because I had found so little professional support for my own beliefs, which would always have been expressed so, had I had the power to express them.[159] I cannot help feeling like thanking you, even though I recall the annoyance it gives me when anyone undertakes to thank me for what I may say in an opinion. I always want to answer, "You fool, I didn't do it, it just came that way, quite simply and inevitably. If you thank me, you only show that you haven't the remotest idea of what I am doing." So I shall refrain—expressly anyway.

Meanwhile the merry sport of Red-bating goes on, and the pack gives tongue more and more shrilly. I really can't get up much sympathy for the victims, but I own to a sense of dismay at the increase in all the symptoms of apparent panic. How far people are getting afraid to speak, who have anything really worthwhile to say, I don't know, but I am sure that the public generally is becoming rapidly demoralized in all its sense of proportion and toleration. For men who are not cock-sure about everything and especially for those who are not damned cock-sure about anything, the skies have a rather sinister appearance.

Faithfully yours, Learned Hand

ms with signature, Holmes Papers, HLL, Reel 33, frames 98-99

To Learned Hand from Oliver Wendell Holmes, Jr.

November 26, 1919 — Supreme Court of the United States

My dear Judge:

Your letter gives me the greatest pleasure and I am very much obliged to you for writing to me. Sympathy and agreement always are pleasant but they are much more than

---

that without the "present danger of immediate evil or an intent to bring it about[...] Congress certainly cannot forbid all effort to change the mind of the country" (250 U.S. at 628). Holmes concluded his dissent by noting that the First Amendment did not leave "the common law as to seditious libel in force" and that "only the emergency that makes it immediately dangerous to leave the correction of evil counsels to time warrants making any exception to the sweeping command, 'Congress shall make no law...abridging the freedom of speech.' [...]I regret that I cannot put into more impressive words my belief that in their conviction upon this indictment the defendants were deprived of their rights under the Constitution of the United States" (*id.* at 630–31). For an account of *Abrams* and Holmes's dissent, see *The Collected Works of Justice Holmes*, ed. Sheldon M. Novick (Chicago and London: University of Chicago Press, 1995): I, 70–73.

159. For LH's reservations on Holmes's test of "clear and present danger," see 1919-7 To Chafee, December 3; and 1921-1 To Chafee, January 2. Chafee saw LH's decision in *Masses v. Patten* as pointing out the "same situation" as that in *Abrams*: "it is not a question of judicial refusal to enforce legislation, but of giving it a construction which will not limit discussion beyond the express terms of the Act." *A Contemporary State Trial: The United States v. Abrams*, 33 Harv. L. Rev. 747, 770 (1920).

that when they come from one that I have learned to think of as I do of you. Accept my thanks.

Ever sincerely yours, O.W. Holmes

tp with signature, Holmes Papers, HLL, Reel 33, frame 142

1919-7

To Learned Hand from Zechariah Chafee, Jr.[160]

December 2, 1919 Law School of Harvard University

Dear Sir:

The Harvard Liberal Club of Boston is anxious to make some public recognition of the stand taken by the two Harvard men on the United States Supreme Court on the question of freedom of speech, and a dinner is to be given in their honor on January 12th at the Boston City Club. We should like very much to have you come as the guest of the Liberal Club and be one of the speakers[...]

I suppose the *Abrams* decision was the same kind of shock to you that it was to me. At all events, Holmes's dissent is bound to win against the unreasoning majority opinion as the years go on, and I console myself occasionally with Browning's "baffled to fight better." If the Circuit Court of Appeals had only sustained you, one of the worst pages in our history might not have been written. I am glad to think of Holmes, Brandeis, and yourself, all Harvard Law School men.

Sincerely, Zechariah Chafee, Jr.

ms with signature 15.26

To Zechariah Chafee, Jr.

December 3, 1919

My dear Mr. Chafee:

I have your letter of December 2nd. It does not seem likely that I shall be able to get away to Boston at the time you mention, January 12th, but I should like to do so and I will advise you some time early next month as to what the chances are. I do not think, however, that I had better make a speech. If you are going to have Justices Holmes and Brandeis there, and if they are going to speak, I should hardly feel like adding my mite to their plenitude. I am not much surprised at the *Abrams* case, although the doctrine laid down seems to be what you so well call the "tendency" doctrine, which seems to me entirely destructive of any genuine freedom. I must say, however, that on the facts it

160. Zechariah Chafee, Jr. (1885–1957): Professor, Harvard Law School, 1916–1956.

seems to me very questionable whether the decision was not correct. At first, upon reading the opinion, I was quite sure the majority was wrong, but the distinction seems to me pretty tenuous between the purpose to encourage resistance to the United States and merely to prevent the United States from overthrowing the Bolshevik party. Nothing could be more needed than Justice Holmes's opinion. I am delighted that it appeared. Naturally it is some comfort to find myself not in a judicial minority of one. I think I will look over the case more carefully once again, just for curiosity.

I do not altogether like the way Justice Holmes put the limitation. I myself think it is a little more manageable and quite adequate a distinction to say that there is an absolute and objective test to language. I daresay that it is obstinacy, but I still prefer that which I attempted to state in my first *Masses* opinion rather than to say that the connection between the words used and the evil aimed at should be "immediate and direct."

May I say what great pleasure I had in your article in the June number of the *[Harvard Law] Review*,[161] and that I have heard it highly praised by most competent opinion? I must discount my own opinion, as you treated me so well, but Graham Wallas and Benjamin Cardozo, both high authorities, have each expressed themselves in high praise of it, and I have no doubt there are many others. I wish I had known half as much as you do about the subject when I wrote my opinion; I could have made it so much better. But you know the conditions under which we had to decide these questions. I sometimes think that I never have learned any law since I left the school, and I am condemned by my own limitations when I come to take up a great subject like this. I think I can also say, without exceeding proper deference, that it would have been a great advantage to us all if, when the final dissent was written, it could have been written with more historical perspective.

Faithfully yours, [Learned Hand]

tp 15.26

To Learned Hand from Zechariah Chafee, Jr.

January 6, 1920 Law School of Harvard University

Dear Judge Hand:

[. . .]I was very much interested in what you wrote me about Justice Holmes's test and your own, and have been wondering whether it is possible to embrace them both in defining the constitutional limits of speech. Suppose we divide utterance as you do in the *Masses* case into (1) political agitation, (2) incitement to resistance to law or violation of law. If the policy behind the First Amendment is the attainment of truth through discussion, can (2) be excluded from its scope since the inciter wants a smash and not discussion? On the other hand, can we say that (1) is protected, subject to Holmes's test of "clear and present danger"? Of course, the 1917 Espionage Act, properly construed, did not touch (1) at all. The broadest possible view (short of absolute license for speech) would be this: (1) can never be punished; (2) can be punished only if it satisfies the danger test. This

161. LH refers to Zechariah Chafee, *Freedom of Speech in War Time*, 32 HARV. L. REV. 932 (1919).

seems to me the right view as a matter of expediency, but I doubt whether Congress is so closely restricted (apart from Supreme Court decisions on the matter, which show amazing readiness to treat much of (1) as if it were (2) and then smite it even if there is no danger). Hoping that you can come. I am,

Sincerely, Zechariah Chafee, Jr.

ms with signature 15.26

To Zechariah Chafee, Jr.

January 8, 1920 Judge Learned Hand's Chambers

Dear Mr. Chafee:

I am sorry to say that I have got myself tied up on a calendar with cases set every day which will prevent my going to Boston. I ought to have remembered the dinner when I was doing this, but frankly I did not think of it. Thank you very much for asking me to stay with you. I should have liked to do it.

As to the general question to be discussed, I should hardly feel like making a speech. In the first place, I have some doubt about the propriety of a judge's taking sides on such matters anyway. In this especial question it so happens that I have expressed myself officially in opinions which have met with almost unanimous disapproval by other Federal judges,[162] and it seems to me pretty clearly inappropriate that I should take part in what certainly may have the appearance of a protest against those which prevailed. I think I at any rate am disqualified, whether or not the same is to be said of other judges.

My view of the matter is about like this. The State—you see, I still cling to the old nomenclature—must regard with disapproval all conduct which tends to produce any violation of its laws. It may, and in my judgment must, permit a great deal of such conduct—utterances—notwithstanding their tendency, that is, notwithstanding the probability that it may produce a violation of law. This toleration, however, depends upon the fact that the utterances in question may have some other result than to produce the evil against which the law is directed. Utterances which can have no other results than to do this may therefore be unconditionally forbidden. It seems to me, I own, that the test of immediacy and directness, while in application it may be about the same as the other, I

162. Hand is referring to *Masses Publishing Co. v. Patten*, which was overturned by the United States Court of Appeals for the Second Circuit. LH may also be referring to *United States v. Kennerley*, 209 F. 119 (S.D.N.Y. 1913), an obscenity case in which Hand allowed a prosecution to proceed despite his reservations about the continuing applicability of the "Hicklin Rule" that courts then followed when determining whether a particular work was obscene. The Hicklin Rule is so named because it was stated by Lord Cockburn in *Regina v. Hicklin*, [1868], L.R. 3 Q.B. 360, that the test was "[w]hether the tendency of the matter charged as obscenity is to deprave and corrupt those whose minds are open to such immoral influences and into whose hands a publication of this sort may fall." *Id.* at 371. In practice, this became the question of whether a father could read the work in his own home (where children or the "weak-minded" might be present). The effect of applying this test was that a work could be deemed obscene either because of isolated passages or because of the possibility that such a work might fall into the hands of a child. LH's opinion in *Kennerley* presaged the decades of difficulty judges would encounter trying to define obscenity.

shall suggest is not strictly speaking correct; I say this with a genuine diffidence. I prefer a test based upon the nature of the utterance itself. If, taken in its setting, the effect upon the hearers is only to counsel them to violate the law, it is unconditionally illegal. By "counsel" I mean to persuade them that their interest or duty lies in violating the law. It may be that that analysis is inadequate, but it is the only one I have been able to find.

As to other utterances, it appears to me that regardless of their tendency they should be permitted. The reason is that any State which professes to be controlled by public opinion, cannot take sides against any opinion except that which must express itself in the violation of law. On the contrary, it must regard all other expression of opinion as tolerable, if not good. As soon as it does not, it inevitably assumes that one opinion may control in spite of what might become an opposite opinion. It becomes a State based upon some opinion as against any opinion which may get itself accepted. But it has been indubitably the presupposition of democratic states, however little they have lived up to it.

If so, nothing short of counsel to violate law should be itself illegal. There could be no objection to the rule of the Supreme Court, tendency plus a purpose to produce the evil, even though the words did not come to the objective standard, if one were sure of the result in practical administration. The chance that the State would lose any valuable opinion by suppressing those whose purpose was to produce a violation of law, while they kept on the safe side of counseling it, seems to me much too thin for practical estimate. My own objection to the rule rests in the fact that it exposes all who discuss heated questions to an inquiry before a jury as to their purposes. That inquiry necessarily is of the widest scope and if their general attitude is singular and intransigent, my own belief is that a jury is an insufficient protection. I think it is precisely at those times when alone the freedom of speech becomes important as an institution, that the protection of a jury on such an issue is illusory. The event seems to me to have proved this.

Therefore, to be a real protection to the expression of egregious opinion in times of excitement, I own I cannot see any escape from construing the privilege as absolute, so long as the utterance, objectively regarded, can by any fair construction be held to fall short of counseling violence. That much actually sinister utterance will pass is undoubtedly true, but the whole institution presupposes a balance of evils. In taking sides, I suppose one will range oneself according to one's degree of natural skepticism about opinions in general. For myself I think our chief enemies are Credulity and his brother Intolerance.

Sincerely yours, Learned Hand

The foregoing was written by Judge Hand and typed after he left. B.A. Bergman[163]

tp with ms signatures, Chafee Papers, HLL, Box 4, Folder 20

---

163. Ms. Bergman was LH's secretary; his signature here is in her hand.

1920-1

LH reports to Graham Wallas, who had just returned to England after delivering the Dodge lectures on the duties of citizenship at Yale University, that five Socialists who had been elected to the New York Assembly were prevented from taking their seats; on April 1, the Assembly voted to expel them.

To Graham Wallas[164]

January 17, 1920

Dear Mr. Wallas:

[...]You are by now back again in your old habits. What you said on the last lecture made me sorrowful, for I realized your disappointment. However, as I look back now at it, I am not surprised, as you were. I remember on your trip in 1914, you seemed to see here a good deal more that was hopeful than I did. I was ready to believe that your insight might be fresher and deeper than mine, perhaps for the very reason that you knew less about the country. But it is apparent now that I was righter than you. We never have had the foundations in this country, in my time, for a genuine sprit of toleration. It is a country where you are expected to conform, and if you don't, you are looked on with suspicion. We all knew this, or at least knew it at times and in spots long before the war taught us. Of course, I do not mean that we were not surprised by much of the intensity of feeling, and I confess that the last movement, which is to exclude the Socialists from the State Assembly, came with all the surprise of a great shock.[165] But the conception that America was a place of warm-hearted acceptance and toleration was always a mistaken one, I think, and the change is not so great as it seems. You were too kindly, and ought to have expected less.

It is hard to know on what one's judgments are formed in such matters, and I cannot give you any reasoned bases for my belief, which nevertheless exists, that the tide of intolerance has turned a little. At least, I think we are in slack water. The effort to exclude the

164. Graham Wallas (1858–1932): Professor of Political Science, University of London.

165. The Lusk bills were the products of the Lusk Legislative Investigation Committee, chaired by state senator Clayton R. Lusk. They would have barred a Socialist ticket in elections by changing the criteria by which a political organization would be recognized as a party for election purposes. In addition, they would have required a "loyalty test" for public school teachers and licensing of all schools (a thinly veiled effort to close the Rand School of Socialism), created a secret police bureau responsible for investigation of so-called "criminal anarchy," barred Socialists from holding any public office, and modified the oath-taking procedure for a member-elect of the legislature, thus allowing for the qualifications of such elected but not yet sworn members to be questioned and thereby delaying their ability to take office. *See Gov. Smith Vetoes Six Bills Aimed at Socialist Party*, N.Y. Times, May 20, 1920. See also 1920-4 To Smith, May 21. The following day, Governor Smith signed three other Lusk bills that incorporated parts of the Lusk committee's "Americanization plan," providing for educational programs for immigrants and scholarships for teachers to be trained in the special education needs of immigrants. *See Signs Three Lusk Bills*, N.Y. Times, May 22, 1920.

Socialists, although it may go through by sheer political force, has aroused a great many people who up to that time were complaisant. Hughes's attitude has been of great service,[166] and there have been voices from all over the country from somewhat unexpected sources. The Young Republicans are on record against it, and it will cause trouble among them if the countrymen force it through, as they probably will, to save their speaker's face. Indeed, I rather hope that the Socialists will be excluded, especially if it is done without any color of justification. For people will then begin to see the actual inferences from the excited fears in which they have indulged, and the currents, which I seem to see slacken, now will begin to run the other way. Do not despair of us, by any means. We are not very temperate, any more than our weather is temperate, but we shall stop long short of the logical implications of what we have been doing.

Faithfully yours, [Learned Hand]

tp 44.16

1920-2

To Oliver Wendell Holmes, Jr.

March 7, 1920 — Judge Learned Hand's Chambers

My dear Mr. Justice:

To-morrow, if I have not forgot my dates, brings again the anniversary of that day, so fortunate to us all, when you first saw the light. May I join with your other friends in expressing the pleasure I have that it will find you still engaged in the service of the state, which now of all times most needs you? I own that the moment does not seem very propitious to the labors of one who has never been a lover of catch-words and easy solutions, and who finds no *vade mecum* that easily concludes matters which are intricate, and depend upon the various prejudices and accepted conventions of "ce méchant singe," *homo sapiens.*[167] Still for that reason, we need you the more. The voice of reason—or should I say, borrowing from high sources, its light—is not, or ought not to be strident. In the end, we must insist, whatever the tumult, it must make itself heard, even if it is not at once attended to. No one is placed by nature, acquisition, and happy chance, where he can utter it so well as you. We listen for you, and rejoice at your speech; we should be cast

166. Charles Evans Hughes had defended the right of Socialists to sit in the New York legislature.

167. I.e., that naughty monkey, man. The figure of homo sapiens rendered to emphasize his primate character appears elsewhere in LH's letters; *see* 1950-1 To Berenson, January 8. In an address to the Elizabethan Club at Yale in 1941, LH elegantly redeems its regressive tendencies: "we rose from the ape because like him we kept 'monkeying around.'" *Liberty, in* THE SPIRIT OF LIBERTY, 144–54, 152. In an address to the Harvard Club in 1952, he links the attribute with the larger question of self-understanding: "as we have trained ourselves [...] 'to monkey around' have we learned to understand ourselves." *At Fourscore, in* THE SPIRIT OF LIBERTY 253–62, 258.

down if you were not there to tell us, as we cannot say it ourselves, what we think and what we hope for. Our constant hope is that you may continue to give us the evidence of your wit, your insight, your learning, and, what those who have eyes to see, find beneath all your passion for the paths of truth.

Sincerely yours, Learned Hand

ms with signature, Holmes Papers HLL, Reel 33, frames 100–101

To Learned Hand from Oliver Wendell Holmes, Jr.

March 9, 1920 Supreme Court of the United States

My dear Hand:

Not for the first time your letter gives me a thrill of pride and joy. During weekdays such emotions are legitimate, and may be accepted as the baits by which we are lured to keep going. It might be ill with us if in the religious moment when we see clearly, we did not realize the illusion of self-satisfaction. On Sunday a dame asked me to describe a gentleman. I said that the center of his being was the sin against the Holy Ghost, that he finally thought of himself as a little God over against the universe, as a person for whom certain things must and certain must not be, instead of a fluid ganglion in a fluid universe, significant only as a part of the I know not what.[168] But while we are at work, we must be allowed to lapse into pride if we work the better for it. So you help me in a way for which I am deeply gratified, even while you open the door to the Pit. I wish I could impart to your, I suspect, melancholy nature a like encouragement, which all that I have read of yours, or heard, or seen of you, quite equally deserves.

Sincerely yours, O.W. Holmes

tp with signature, Holmes Papers HLL, Reel 33, frame 143

---

168. Holmes repeats a version of this trope in a letter to Felix Frankfurter, dated April 25, 1920: "Absolute beliefs are a rum thing. I always wonder at a man who takes himself seriously all the time. I was repeating to Hand yesterday my old chestnut that a gentleman couldn't be a philosopher or a philosopher a gentleman. For a gentleman postulates himself as an ultimate over against the universe. I said to Hand that I thought that the sin against the Holy Ghost[....] Thought afterwards that if one were out for trouble with a paradox, one might put it: The sin against the Holy Ghost is self-respect." Holmes and Frankfurter: Their Correspondence, 1912–1934, at 88 (Robert M. Mennel & Christine L. Compston eds., 1996).

1920-3

To Paul D. Cravath[169]

May 11, 1920 District Court of the United States

Dear Mr. Cravath:

I quite agree with all you said in December 1918, so far as I have any right to an opinion about it all. After stripping Germany of her "tangibles," we can make her pay only through her labor, which means her excess exports. That she could pay the amount of that excess measure by pre-war standards seems pretty doubtful. Her economic organization was so closely tied up with her political that I should think it would be impossible to suppose she could regain a similar capacity till an indefinitely deferred and speculative future. Besides her loss of population has been not inconsiderable and of resources important.

But does it really make much difference what her capacity is theoretically, if she cannot be made to use it? It is to me merely incredible that after a few years any German government should endure which tried to load taxes with annual indemnities equaling even the lowest that have been calculated. If a Socialist government, it would look at such burdens as relics of a detested order then past; if an imperialistic, it would attribute them to the injustice of Germany's enemies and their purpose to destroy her. I do not believe that anything but the fear of immediate retaliation will produce a penny after five years. Before that period, I should guess that the resultant of international strains and stresses would long since have relieved Germany of any such fear. Indemnities, and especially the Reparation committee, would become, I should think, little more than a possible futile source of suspicion and distrust.

Little as one may like the present posture of France, I think one should concede it the merit of a realistic view of the situation, i.e., that nothing will be got which is not got while the army of occupation remains. As to the Germans themselves, I doubt whether any nation has ever believed that it has been in the wrong, or that any indemnity is just. If so, while perhaps we have lost nothing by an attempt to impose upon them such big indemnities, nevertheless our only chance was in small ones which they might have some selfish motive to pay. Those would have to be pretty small, wouldn't they?[....]

Sincerely yours, [Learned Hand]

tp 17.9

To Learned Hand from Paul D. Cravath

May 19, 1920 52 William street

My dear Judge Hand:

I read with very much interest your letter of the 11th inst. on the subject of indemnities. You are entirely right in your view that the only reasonable chance of the Allies

169. Paul D. Cravath (1861–1940): attorney, Cravath, de-Gersdorff, Swaine & Wood, New York City; Director of the United States Council on Foreign Relations, 1921–1940.

collecting an indemnity from the Germans is to keep it within such modest limits so that the burden of paying it will be less appalling to the Germans than the consequences of default. When I saw [John Maynard] Keynes[170] almost daily during the period intervening between the signing of the Armistice and the beginning of the Peace conference, he was disposed, under the influences of just such reason as you use, to favor a relatively small indemnity, say seven or eight billion dollars, payable within five or six years, on the theory that during that period the payment could be enforced by an army of occupation. He gave up that idea because he saw that after Germany's transferable assets had been absorbed and her credit destroyed, she could pay a substantial indemnity only in moderate annual installments covering a long period of years, and at best could not begin payments out of annual savings for several years.

At the request of Mr. Gay, I have prepared some observations on indemnities that will doubtless appear in the "post" within a day or two.

Very sincerely yours, Paul D. Cravath

tp with ms signature 17.9

To Paul D. Cravath

October 26, 1920 District Court of the United States

Dear Mr. Cravath:

Thank you for "Impressions of Germany,"[171] which I got this morning and read at once. I am pleased to find that your inquiries and actual experience so well confirmed the impressions that we had been getting here through inadequate information. We are seeing now the impossibility on the part of Britain, which is the strongest part of the world, to control even so small and feeble a people as the Irish, who for nearly forty years have not suffered any economic oppression and whose grievances are political though real. I think we may hope that it will not be long before the world will recognize the impossibility of keeping the German people in economic tutelage for an indefinite time. The real danger I fear in this country is entire indifference. Had we gone into the fray at once, bad though much of it was, we should have been in a stronger position to side with Britain and combat the present attitude of France, which I think nearly all impartial men recognize to be the most dangerous factor in the situation. I greatly hope that when Mr. [Warren Gamaliel] Harding[172] is elected those who have any influence with him will procure that result, which will be better late that never[. . .] Apathy seems to me to be our great danger, in this as in nearly every other question of moment at the present time.

---

170. John Maynard Keynes (1883–1946: economist; Lecturer, University of Cambridge; Director of the Bank of England, 1940–1945. Cravath summarizes Keynes's position on indemnities; *see* John Maynard Keynes, The Economic Consequences of the Peace (1920).

171. This article appeared first in the London Times in July 1919 and was subsequently published as *Impressions of the Financial and Industrial Conditions in Germany*, 92 Annals Am. Acad. Pol. & Soc. Sci. 5–12 (1920).

172. Warren Gamaliel Harding (1855–1923): President of the United States, 1921–1923.

What we need more than anything else is to try to understand how the German people is feeling. It is not necessary for us on that account to agree with them, nor do I think that is a serious danger, but if we can once realize that they regard themselves as victims of misfortune and not as a nation of justly punished knaves, we can better understand the effect of coercion upon them. But after all, isn't that kind of imagination the rarest thing in individuals? And is it to be expected from a self-sufficient, aggressive people like our own, who have never known and do not believe that this is a world of misery and terrors? I remember three or four years ago Graham Wallas wrote me a letter in which he ended up by saying that what the world needs most is religion. I am not quite sure that I ever knew what he meant, but if he meant that religion is a consciousness that human reason is a feeble rush-light to be blown out, then America needs religion more that anyone else. Of all who live, it seems to me we are most in danger of that senseless self-confidence amid the perils of being a human creature at all which the Greeks knew long since was the source of most of the undoing of mankind. I very sincerely hope that in the kind of work you have been doing since the war, you will continue. I think you have a position where you can get an unusual hearing, and your influence might be important. Its results might even console you for having to vote for Harding.

Faithfully yours, [Learned Hand]

tp 17.9

To Learned Hand from Paul D. Cravath

October 27, 1920 — 52 William street

Dear Judge Hand:

Thank you very much for your interesting letter. For a time I tried to persuade myself that the United States should insist upon revision of the substantive provisions of the Treaty of Versailles before becoming a party to it. I am now inclined to the view that we could not secure such a revision of the Treaty, and should become parties to it in order to work from the inside for its gradual revision. The present French Government would not stand for a revision of the Treaty, and I doubt if the Germans would accept a revised Treaty unless it were fairly satisfactory to them. I think they will be slow in giving up their present position of being able to urge, at least with plausibility, that the Treaty is not morally binding upon them because they had no voice in framing its provisions and accepted it under duress.

Very sincerely yours, Paul D. Cravath

tp with ms signature 17.9

1920-4

To Alfred E. Smith[173]

May 21, 1920

Sir:

Nothing has given me greater satisfaction for many months than your veto of the Lusk bills.[174] It is refreshing to learn that a public officer has the courage in the face of determined and vindictive opposition to assert his faith in free institutions. Shocking as it is that it should be necessary to show such courage, it is none the less grateful that you have been found willing to do so. All citizens who believe in popular government will not soon forget this check upon the most sinister and disintegrating influence that can beset a democracy, the attempt to establish political orthodoxy.

May I express to you my warm regard and admiration not only for this, but for your consistent liberalism in the discharge of your high office?[175]

Respectfully, [Learned Hand]

tp 39.4

1920-5

To Learned Hand from Felix Frankfurter

May 20, 1920 Law School of Harvard University

Dear B.:

[...]I was for [Herbert] Hoover—but he certainly is showing no grip to deal with things. I believe in him; I believe facts would have an impact on his mind and even move his naive generalizations about "socialism" and "initiative"—but he isn't doing anything with equipment, and letting a lot of personal friends influence him and in them I have no confidence. Alas—I think he threw away a great chance to be the Damocles sword over both parties. I'm about ready to vote for [William Gibbs] McAdoo, if I'll get a chance. I only hope [Leonard] Wood is dead—for Marion threatens she won't live in America if he becomes President[176][...]

---

173. Alfred E. Smith (1873–1944): Governor of New York, 1919–1920, 1923–1928.

174. For the Lusk bills, see 1920-1 To Graham Wallas, January 17.

175. In a letter dated May 25, Governor Smith thanked LH for his letter. (tp with signature, 39.4)

176. William Gibbs McAdoo (1863–1941): Secretary of the Treasury and Chairman of the Federal Reserve Board, 1914–1917; Senator from California, 1933–1938. Leonard Wood (1860–1927): Army Chief of Staff, 1910–1914; Governor General of the Philippines, 1921–1927. James M. Cox, having

Am I never going to have another talk with you? I should like to, much—for there is much I should want to think over with you.

My wife wants me to greet you! F.F.

ms with signature 104A.9

To Felix Frankfurter

June 6, 1920 Harvard Club, New York City

Dear Felix:

[...]I am for Hoover on any ticket, Soviet included, but I shan't have any chance to express myself[...] [Calvin] Coolidge[177] I hear excellent accounts of; if he is nominated I should guess I might wait a while before deciding between him and McAdoo. Of that second gent I am not too sure; his character gives me misgiving—give, misgive. G[eorge] R[ublee] pounds me deliberately determinedly and ruthlessly in the face when I suggest this. Naturally when I have picked myself up, brushed off my clothes and give way, I have greater misgiving than ever. G.R. is like all men of action; he cannot distinguish between persuading people and breaking their faces. The second is the best way to get your will; the first is the best way to accomplish the comparatively unimportant purpose of enlightening the people. For this reason G.R. could never be a democrat any more than H[erbert] C[roly] could be; or perhaps anyone else who ever leads or wants to lead. I am nearly the only democrat in the world, except Phil Littell and Holmes. It is fortunate, probably, that there are so few democrats or there might be nothing to eat or to wear. Real democrats get food and clothes only because they are so few that they get ignored in the general handout. If they were many enough to be noticed, they would be put in the cellar and would there be tolerant to each other till they starved to death.

So you are going Zionizing.[178] Someday you must show me what it all means. I agree with your Mrs.: Anything but Wood.

L.H.

ms with signature 104A.9

---

defeated McAdoo, was the Democratic nominee for President in 1920. Warren Harding, having defeated Wood, was the Republican nominee.

177. Calvin Coolidge (1872–1933): Vice President of the United States, 1921–1923; President of the United States, 1923–1929.

178. Frankfurter, with Brandeis, went to London to reconcile conflicts within the Zionist movement. In a letter dated July 22 and sent from "Zionist Organization" in London, Frankfurter writes that his earlier letter, dated June 6, was returned to him and that he encloses it with his letter of July 22, which he concludes as follows: "Thus far I have been busy night and day on Zionist work, but before long Marion and I hope to go to the Continent, particularly Germany. I am keen to understand what lies beneath the surface. If ever you want a real joy, cross the ocean with Brandeis. I cannot help thinking that he is a truly great man." (tp with ms signature 104A.9)

To Learned Hand from Felix Frankfurter

June 28, 1920 Law School of Harvard University

Dear B.:

Is Hamlet the only democrat? There is at least one man of decision on mundane matters that I know who I think is also a real democrat—Brandeis. He cares about convincing and he cares about educating and in fact he cares more than anything else for the processes of education which will enable our modern democracy to understand what public matters are about and then act upon such understanding[...]

I will be very glad some day "to show you what Zionism means." I can tell you the heart of it now in a few sentences. For some strange reason millions of Jews prefer to live and have children follow them. They prefer to live rather than die to be harassed in a way that makes existence not living—but more than that they prefer to live in the land they deem their home that they have dreamed about and longed for for two thousand years—strangely enough, not unlike the feeling of a Frenchman for France. In returning to the land of their fathers they don't want to dispossess anybody, to turn back the historical clock, to do injustice to anyone, for this land is capable of sustaining millions but has lain wasted and devastated for centuries. They now want to bring it back, and all those who have studied the situation, like General [Jan Christiaan] Smuts, who made a special study of it for the British Cabinet before they made their famous Balfour Declaration,[179] are convinced that it can be restored to its ancient days of milk and honey, but only by the people in whom the emotional pride is strong enough to overcome all the difficulties that have resulted from centuries of Turkish misrule. Incidentally, they may work out a civilization that will be worthwhile. That is the whole story. These millions of Jews feel about Palestine as other peoples feel about their native country and some of us feel we ought to do all we can to render effective the reconstruction of that land for its people. Incidentally, having seen something of eastern and western Europe, I am convinced that there is no other solution to the so-called Jewish problem and the continuance of millions of people. Some day I do want to talk without about it—if you are interested[...]

My very best, [F.F.]

tp 104A.9

179. Arthur James Balfour issued the Balfour Declaration in 1917, declaring British support for a national Jewish homeland in Palestine.

1920-6

To Frank Douglas MacKinnon[180]

August 11, 1920

My dear Mr. MacKinnon:

I'm a godless soul not to have answered your letter for so long, but it is not because I have not thought of it often and wanted to hear from you again. Since your last, our two peoples do not seem to have benefited their mutual relation much, do they? I am told that at present America is not *persona grata*. I can well believe and excuse it. Whatever they may believe to be their motives, I am entirely satisfied that the Senate has acted throughout in a spirit of pure faction.[181] They were greatly outraged by Wilson's ignoring them, in which he made a quite inexcusable mistake, and being a jealous, bureaucratic body, they were determined to assert their power at any cost. It would all have been very easy if Wilson had been less of an egoist and more accustomed to accommodation and compromise, as everyone who aspires to statecraft must be in my opinion. And so the fat is all in the fire, and we are an unhappy example of the dangers of wealth and security. Even at the last minute, Wilson could have accomplished the essence of what he wanted had he been willing to show any reasonable spirit of compromise. But he has always been a dour (shall I be offensive if I say, Scotch?) Presbyterian, who would have his way and all his way.

Just how far the election is going to turn upon the League I am blessed if I can tell. The politicians obviously think it will figure largely, for they are making it the chief issue. But you know how often they are mistaken about public opinion, and I find it hard to suppose that the ordinary exceedingly prosperous American is going to care anything about what seems to him so remote, or those who are not prosperous are going to be concerned about anything but getting prosperous. We shall see.

Harding seems to me impossible. His nomination represents nothing but an appeal to apathy, little Americanism, and the tacit assumption that the old crowd of wire-pullers playing in with the "big interests" is on the whole most to be trusted. All of what Theodore Roosevelt stood for in public life has been wiped clear off the slate by the party which he led. That party today stands just where it stood in 1900, when Mark Hanna and the little crowd of magnates for whom he spoke were the easy bosses of the whole country. The inner ring which was in control at Chicago scarcely concealed this attitude. Their appeal is to the prejudices and timidity on which they for many years found it safe to rely. They have no program, no policy, no ideas.

Wilson has personally made himself so hated that his party stands in the gravest danger, although they have gone as far as they could to repudiate his leadership. Open repudiation was of course out of the question, but they threw aside all the candidates whom he favored, and have clearly shown that they will not stand on the letter of his imperious insistence. In

180. Frank Douglas MacKinnon (1871–1946): Lord Justice of Appeal, 1907–1946.

181. I.e., in rejecting the Treaty of Versailles ending hostilities in World War I. For LH's view of the prospects ending the war, see 1917-4 To Burlingham, October 6; on the terms of the Treaty, see 1919-4 To Stevens, May 27; on the importance of the League, see 1919-5 To Frankfurter, December 3; on the economic problems attending the Treaty, see 1920-3 To Cravath, May 11.

other words, it is quite clear that they are willing to come to that compromise upon the League which all the other powers would have so gladly made. Their nominee is not inspiring,[182] although he certainly will have my vote as against Harding. He has shown a good deal of judgment and tact in his dealing with the labor situation in Ohio, and is supposed to have liberal tendencies, though that is a phrase which in the United States, as you probably know, means something much more conservative than what it means to you. I wish I felt better confidence in his chances, but the Democrats start with a handicap which I cannot believe they will overcome. If not, we are in for four years of stout Bourbonism—years which promise to present to us the most formidable questions of internal policy which we have experienced since 1865, years which ought to be met by the best thinking and the most courageous statesmanship that we can muster. We promise to meet it by a refusal either to think or to take any position. I suppose we shall get through, for we are so grossly rich that apparently we can with safety neglect all the common precautions in our public affairs of intelligence and character. Don't think from what I have said that I was not and in a way am not still an admirer of Wilson. He has done great things, and I suspect when history comes to be written after you and I are dead, it will be felt that he did as much as his powers admitted in the winter of '18–'19.

I don't know how you feel about the Treaty. To me it was conceived in a spirit of oppression and without any view to possibilities. I was glad enough to take all the German cash and property which we could lay our hands on, everything, as we say here, which was not "nailed down" was legitimate loot, but as for the indemnities, they seem to me merely preposterous, yet I never have felt, in spite of the disgust of my liberal friends, that it was possible during the period when the Treaty was made to make either England or France agree to any other terms. The pity of it is that we have dissociated ourselves from that execution where, if we had acted in good faith, we could have done much to support the present attitude of Britain and overcome what seems to be the excessively dangerous posture of present-day France. Besides, we have already done what we could to commit sabotage on the League. Most of its benefit rests in the spirit in which it starts, and we have been so churlish and shown such an ugly spirit toward the whole enterprise that we have hurt it as much as we possibly could. In my judgment we should have been of estimable service to those elements of British opinion which, so as far as I can gather, are now making themselves felt with increasing power and which I firmly believe in the near future will control British policy. All this, if Wilson had been supported, might have helped. I am far from going along with much of his policy. Only today he comes out with what amounts to an outlawry of the Soviets, no matter how long they may be established, and how obviously they have constituted a government. It seems to me to serve no purpose that he adds that he will recognize any government which the Russian people establish. He is taking just the attitude that the Powers did toward the French Republic which plunged Europe into twenty years of destructive warfare.[183] If the Russians are content with the kind of militant oligarchy they have got now, or if not being content they have not the public spirit to overthrow it, we do our best by our present attitude to consolidate its power and to give it the enormous support of all national Russian sentiment. I agree

182. James M. Cox (1870–1957): Governor of Ohio, 1913–1915, 1917–1921.

183. LH indicates the period from the inception of the French revolution, 1789, to the peace concluded between France, under Napoleon, and Austria, 1809.

with what Bertrand Russell said when he came back, that while it is an intolerable government, we are all doing our best to maintain and consolidate it, and this last announcement of Wilson is only another prop[...]

My wife, who makes all our decisions, has announced that next year the family is to spend the summer in Europe, and naturally I assent. If so, I shall have a chance to see you, which is indeed a pleasant prospect[...] Nine years is too long and I never should have waited so long except that while the old world was breaking up and the new world trying to be born, it was no place for an idle stranger. Indeed, I came within a shot of getting over in the Peace Conference myself under a feeble pretext that I was to be an expert on patents. I was delighted at the time not to go, for there was lots of work to be done here, and I knew that it would not be pleasant to kick my heels for two or three months about the Hotel Crillion without a single excuse for my existence. Afterwards they told me, however, that the billet was only a pretext, and if I had gone over it was with a more roving commission. But the Great White Father and Robert Lansing[184] settled it, and I was very well content. I should have liked to look in on you and get from your mouth what the last eight years had brought to pass. Perhaps you will not think me so incorrigible a correspondent as to cut me off altogether from your pen.

My family has been away for ten weeks, and I am just closing up the year's work to get off for seven weeks. I had almost said that I deserved it, but you must remember that if we got our deserts, none of us should escape hanging[185] and so I hesitate. Incidentally, I may add that if hanging should become a popular outdoor sport in America, I can think of no class in the community who would sooner play the premiere role than the Federal judiciary, and as it would be most handy, I do not see why they should not begin with the inferior judges. So far the prospects of wearing a hemp collar, however, do not alarm me. Of all the people who are likely to run amok I should think ours was the least, perhaps after yourselves. Barring Ireland, you seem to be able to effect your changes with a minimum of excitement, and after all that, in my judgment, is all there is of the art of government[...]

Faithfully yours, [Learned Hand]

tp 29.11

1920-7

To Learned Hand from Zechariah Chafee, Jr.

October 25, 1920 — 81 Irving street, Cambridge, Massachusetts

My dear Judge Hand:

The time is, I am glad to say, rapidly approaching when my book on Freedom of Speech goes to press. Would you give me the great pleasure of dedicating it to you? It was

---

184. Robert Lansing (1864–1928): Secretary of State, 1915–1920. *See* 1919-1 To Miller, January 13.

185. *Cf.* "use every man after his desert, and who shall 'scape whipping." HAMLET, II, ii.

really your opinion in the *Masses* case that started me on my work. I feel more and more that it was a staggering task to solve the problem as you did at the very outset of the war, with so few precedents and in such pressure and excitement, and also that if you had only been followed, a living public opinion might have developed in this country on the ultimate purposes of the war, which since the armistice we have fatally lacked. I have spoken of your judgment at the length in the body of the book, but I should like to place my opinion of it at the very start.

Sincerely, Zech Chafee, Jr.

ms with signature 15.26

To Zechariah Chafee, Jr.

October 28, 1920

Dear Mr. Chafee:

Your letter has really thrown me in more embarrassment than I have felt for long, indeed, as an old lady would say, I am all upset. That you should select me to dedicate your book fills me with an unaccountable measure of pleasure. Especially do I feel this in view of the very slight accord which my opinions ever received from the profession at large. It was indeed scarcely necessary to ask my consent to what I should deem to be a great honor, but as you have done so, I give it with much content and indeed with a sense of great humility. You must know that we who have left the School always look back to it as the "fountain of Honor." It is from there that we hope to get approval, and it is by their standards that we wish our work to be judged. It follows that they are like to be the best judges of its quality.

I cannot conclude without expressing my thanks to you for your kindness and repeating my very genuine sense of the unfitness which I have for the signal honor you mean to give me.

Sincerely yours, Learned Hand

tp with ms signature 15.26

To Zechariah Chafee, Jr.

December 3, 1920 Judge Learned Hand's Chambers

Dear Mr. Chafee:

[...]I have not yet got to the book, but when it comes I shall make free to attach the letter to it and shall always keep it with the greatest pleasure.[186] You cannot indeed know how satisfactory it is to me to have you say what you do. The case cost me something, at

186. Zechariah Chafee dedicated *Freedom of Speech* to LH: "To Learned Hand, United States District Judge for the Southern District of New York, who during the turmoil of war courageously

least at the time, and, as you know, it seemed to meet with practically no professional approval whatever. I kept up my hopes till *Debs'* case[187] and when the whole court affirmed that without laying down anything like what I thought was the rule, I confess I began to wonder whether I had not got some kind of wrong squint on the subject.

Later things turned a little the other way, but your very generous and, I must believe, exaggerated recognition of my views has been by far the most whole-hearted support I have ever got. It may interest you to know that when I was suddenly faced with the decision, I looked back with the greatest regret at my wasted days. "Here" I thought, "if you only knew enough, there is a place to state correctly, based on scholarship, what is the right rule. You don't know your job; you don't know anything about the history of the subject, and you must fire off your own funny ideas about what ought or ought not to be." If then I could have tapped the resources of the Harvard Law School I should have been a happy man. However, there was nothing very peculiar in that; I felt it so often and when a book like [Samuel] Williston's[188] comes out I frankly accept it and seek to learn no more. I dare say yours in its field will take its own stand as a similar authority. I shall surely read it, and if anything occurs to me that seems worth saying, I shall take great pleasure in letter you have it. With renewed thanks and the hope of an early meeting I am

Sincerely yours, Learned Hand

ms with signature, Chafee Papers, HLL, Box 4, Folder 20

1920-8

To Oliver Wendell Holmes, Jr.

December 20, 1920 Judge Learned Hand's Chambers

Dear Mr. Justice:

I have just got *Collected Legal Papers*[189] and have therefore not yet had time to read it, an omission I shall soon correct. Some I know, one at least I have heard, all I shall enjoy

---

maintained the tradition of English-speaking freedom, and gave it new clearness and strength for the wiser years to come." FREEDOM OF SPEECH iii (1920).

187. Debs v. United States, 249 U.S. 211 (1919). Decided in March 1919, *Debs* applied the "clear and present danger" test that had been established in *Schenck v. United States. See* 1919-3 To Holmes, April 1.

188. Samuel Williston, (1861–1963): Professor, Harvard Law School, 1895–1938. LH may have been referring to Williston's works on contract, COMMERCIAL AND BANKING LAW (1918); *see also* THE LAW OF CONTRACTS (1921–1922).

189. OLIVER WENDELL HOLMES, JR., COLLECTED LEGAL PAPERS (1920). In his review, LH declares that the "soul of Rabelais roams the earth gathering spirits for the Abbey of Theleme, those who are gay, nimble, courteous, feat, witty, amorous, simple courtly, kind, pleasing, happy, genial, wise, humble, tolerant, joyous. Now the initiated tell us that among these there is none he has more certainly chosen than the captain of Antietam, young then and young now." Learned Hand, *Review, Oliver Wendell Holmes, Collected Legal Papers*, 36 POL. SCI. Q. 528–30, 528 (1921). Holmes was evidently gratified by the complement, writing to Frankfurter on November 6: "I was feeling a little down and

as I always do what comes from the same source. I have been promising myself a trip to Washington soon during the winter, but the daily grind has hitherto always put it off. Probably I must now wait till spring[...]

Meanwhile time goes along and so much of the year is spent in sitting stupidly listening to the slow ooze of evidence which painfully shapes itself or does not shape itself into an organic form. Patience surely is the final confession of our limitations, and yet I would have it inscribed upon the top of every bench where the judge may always read it. If I had the trenchant blade of a [George] Jessel[190] or the incision of a Holmes perhaps I could safely penetrate at once to the very medulla of my prey and perhaps all further resistance. As it is, I must hew and hack till I land in the same vital spot; too often that makes the trophy a sorry prize. But we must work, each as we can, and it ill becomes a junior member of the Society of Jobbists[191] to complain. My wife says I shall lose my union card because I don't take the prescribed days of rest, but then she doesn't know how much of the time I spend upon the bench in suspended animation.

At any rate I shall have a quickened vitality in reading the book. If I were only Julius Caesar, I would rule on evidence and read it at the same time while I concealed it beneath the bench. But I am not. Please remember me to Mrs. Holmes and believe me as ever,

Sincerely yours, Learned Hand

ms with signature, Holmes Papers, HLL, Reel 33, frames 102–103

---

it set me up." HOLMES AND FRANKFURTER: THEIR CORRESPONDENCE, 1912–1934, at 127–28 (Robert M. Mennel & Christine L. Compston eds., 1996).

190. Sir George Jessel (1824–1883): Master of the Rolls, Court of Chancery.

191. The Society of Jobbists was the "society" composed of hard-working judges to which Holmes and Hand declared they belonged. For a definition of "jobbist," see Charles P. Curtis's review of the Holmes–Laski letters, quoting Holmes: his "job is the contribution to the general welfare and when a man is on that, he will do it better the less he thinks either of himself or of his neighbors." *The Holmes–Laski Letters, 1916–1935*, 63 YALE L.J. 266 at 273 (Mark DeWolfe Howe ed., 1953).

PART II

If a state legislature wishes to make a jackass of itself, it should have the responsibility for doing so rather than the Supreme Court

—Learned Hand to Felix Frankfurter, June 6, 1923

IN FOR DEMOCRACY: 1921–1931

Challenged to interpret the significance of events at home, Hand and his correspondents debate the role of judges and the courts. Supreme Court Justice Frankfurter and Judge Hand agree on the danger of the Supreme Court as it exercises the power of judicial review; the Court must not become a third legislative chamber. Hand's argument is that even a law requiring the people to conform to practices that offend a minority is legitimate, telling Lippmann that the state of Tennessee can forbid the teaching of evolution, however misguidedly: "we are in for democracy." He agrees with Frankfurter on the power of the legislature: a constituency has an absolute and unconditional right to elect the officers it chooses, and the attempt to prevent the Socialist Representatives Smith and Vare from taking their seats in Congress was therefore lawless. Legislation may not be wise or prudent—as is, for example, the Volstead Act prohibiting the sale and consumption of alcohol—yet it must be enforced. And although unpopular among certain constituencies, legislation regulating the wages and hours, as in *Adkins*, does not violate employers' rights under due process and is therefore law. The role of the judge is at best problematic. Holmes argues that judges should remain out of the fray, not meddle in burning themes; Hand agrees, at least in part, telling Frankfurter that a judge needs to interpret "the more permanent relations of men." But where to discern them? Persons in the law cannot avoid the question of particular interests—who has won, who has lost: the *cui bono* question. Yet we seek a "superintending and directing norm" in order to discover "unity." Cardozo writes that he thinks he has found a "common will" when he decides a case; Hand does not quite deny this but makes the claim futuristic, even prophetic: a judge can express "ideas to which people would assent when they became aware of them." Writing to the scientist Simon Flexner, Hand touches on a related kind of expression, also indebted to the work of the imagination. We project a "reality" upon the data that scientific experiment provides. Similarly, he confesses to his friend Philip Littell that he writes his own history selectively, from memories that respond to his desires.

1921-1

To Zechariah Chafee, Jr.

January 2, 1921 New York

My dear Mr. Chafee:

My life here is so full of interruptions that I have only just finished reading *Freedom of Speech*,[1] and that too without that chance for a continuous perusal which it deserves instead of in disconnected snatches now and then. It has more than justified all the hopes I had for it, and it will stand for an indefinite time as the most complete and satisfactory exposition of one of the most baffling subjects in the law. Indeed, how baffling it is I never quite realized till I had been over your pages. I kept feeling—did I write you so before?—that in writing my own opinion, which you have so kindly noticed, it was well that I knew no more than I did. Like the Heathen, I was saved by my invincible ignorance, and now that you ask me to suggest to you any deficiencies in your work I can really do nothing; certainly I can bring nothing that I do not carry from its covers.

As you so often point out, the decision in any given case will depend upon the relative values which the tribunal places on the importance of illumination in general through discussion, and the immediate purpose which is in danger. I doubt whether men will ever succeed at once in feeling intensely the necessity of accomplishing this thing, here and now, and in retaining enough detachment to remember that a precedent is a precedent, and that the first taste of blood is often the greatest danger. There will be a few who can at least believe of themselves that they combine the two, but their fellows will always put them in the church of Laodicea,[2] and relatively that is really the place for them—in my judgment the most honorable place of all. In any event, the result is that we must be content to worry through with as little inconsistency as possible, making prayerful protestations where we must, and securing heartfelt accord when there is no need for protecting those who talk unpalatably—that is, when they have no chance of success.

I am not wholly in love with Holmesy's test and the reason is this. Once you admit that the matter is one of degree, while you may put it where it genuinely belongs, you so obviously make it a matter of administration, i.e., you give to Tomdickandharry, D.J., so much latitude, that the jig is at once up. Besides even their Ineffabilities, the Nine Elder Statesmen, have not shown themselves wholly immune from the "herd instinct," and what seems "immediate and direct" today may seem very remote next year, even though the circumstances surrounding the utterance be unchanged. I own I should prefer a qualitative formula, hard, conventional, difficult to evade. If it could become sacred by the incrustations of time and precedent, it might be made to serve just a little to withhold the torrents of passion to which I suspect democracies will be found more subject than, for example, the Whig autocracy of the 18th century. We know very little yet about enormous aggregations such as our present U.S. How can one catch this fly and preserve it in

1. See 1920-7 To Chafee, October 28.
2. I.e., identify them as perennial doubters.

amber? What ritualistic phrase shall fix the place where discussion ends, and words by ex cathedra be said to have no power to enlighten? You have, I dare say, done well to take what has fallen from Heaven and insist that it is manna rather than to set up any independent solution. "Immediate and direct" is all we have; for God's sake let us not look it in the mouth.

Next as to Uncle Henry Clayton.[3] Did I tell you I always felt a little responsible? We were glad enough to get anyone who could legally sit on a bench, and he was fish because he swam into the net. Then I turned the D. Atty. loose on him as usual, and lo! A *cause celebre* to the honor of no one. But wasn't it a little *over* irresponsible? I fear I am not free from blame. On the law of that case in the Supreme Court I have reflected a little since reading your article in the H.L.R. and now your chapter, and you have brought me around. At first I was even guilty of what seems to be the universally conceded solecism that the Russian Expedition was part of the war.[4] In that you assure me that only poor [John Henry] Wigmore[5] is with me, respectable enough company usually, but a bit *toque* here. Well, will this content you? I am charging the jury with Uncle Henry and without his racy gift of speech. I say: you must find that the defendants intended to impede the war, and to do so you must decide either that they had that purpose, which in your places I should find they had not, or that they knew that in stopping the production of munitions till the Russian Expedition was given up, the war against Germany would inevitably be impeded. If you think that they understood that they could not stop munitions here without that result, that knowledge is enough special intent under the statute. As to the Russian Expedition itself: I charge you that while you may not review the wisdom or necessity of including a diversion, if it was intended to be a diversion in Siberia, or of the release of Czecho-Slovaks who might be made to fight, the U.S. must show you that it was intended by those who directed it as a part of the war with Germany, and they have showed nothing whatever about it. They might show it perhaps by calling those who directed it and letting

---

3. Henry DeLamar Clayton, Jr. (1857–1929): Congressman from Alabama, 1897–1914, and sponsor of the Clayton Antitrust Act, 1914; Judge, United States District Court for the Middle and Northern Districts of Alabama, 1914–1929. Clayton served on the United States District Court for the Southern District of New York in *Abrams v. United States*. The "net" to which LH refers is apparently *Abrams v. United States*, in which Jacob Abrams and his co-defendants were convicted of violating the Espionage Act. *See* N.Y. TIMES, Sept. 13, 1918. Zechariah Chafee was critical of Judge Clayton's role in *Abrams*: "The whole proceeding, from start to finish, has been a disgrace to our law, and none the less a disgrace because our highest court felt powerless to wipe it out." Zechariah Chafee, *A Contemporary State Trial: The United States versus Jacob Abrams et al.*, 33 HARV. L. REV. 747, 774 (1920).

4. The Northern Russian Expedition, i.e., the American North Russia Expeditionary Force, was a contingent of about five thousand U.S. troops who landed in Arkhangelsk, Russia, and fought the Bolshevik forces in the surrounding region during the period of September 1918 through July 1919.

5. John Henry Wigmore (1866–1943): Dean of the Northwestern University Law School. Critical of Holmes's dissent in *Abrams*, Wigmore warned of the danger of Bolsheviks and those sympathetic to revolution in the United States and cautioned against "this misplaced reverence for freedom of speech [that] should lead us to minimize or ignore other fundamentals which in today's conditions are far more in need of reverence and protection. [...]It will not do to let freedom of speech obscure for us the demands of other elements of liberty and safety." J.H. Wigmore, Abrams v. U.S.: *Freedom of Speech and Freedom of Thuggery in War-Time and Peace-Time*," 14 ILL. L. REV. 539, 559 (1920).

them tell you how it was a part of the war. If they had, you would have had to take their word for it, however mistaken as strategy you thought it, unless someone satisfied you that they might not be telling the truth about their own purposes. As no one has told you anything about it, I must take that phase of it from you[...]

Then, Deportations.[6] My God, but I never knew they were like that. That comes of never reading the papers, I suppose. Croly says it was all in his sheet, but at that time I was too mad with their intransigence about the Treaty to do them justice in anything. Your doubts about the constitutionality of any deportation as distinct from exclusion law I think I don't share. On the whole I believe that while the justification for freedom of speech is public enlightenment, historically the "right"—though I join you in hating the word—is vested in the speaker, and our legislatures can engage *ad libitum* in obscurantism, provided they don't impinge on an individual who can cry out. Now it is inhuman enough, and it has filled me with loathing to have to recognize it, but it is the fact that if I come here and don't get out my "papers" I stay on sufferance. I don't think we judges could intervene if they deported all aliens who ate with their knives. After all, a court which doesn't recognize the post "as a common right" is not going to strain at gnats like deportations[...]

Finally, for this grows quite unconscionably long—and written too—the last chapter interested me immensely. About a year ago I had this out with [Charles Evans] Hughes. Suppose this case: [August] Claessens[7] is about to take the oath to support the Constitution, etc. On the way up Capital Hill in Albany while arm in arm with two bishops he says that he knows that he must take the oath, but that it is all nonsense, he does it only "to bore from within." As for him, the shortest way is the best, and a General Soviet with an Extraordinary Commission of the modern equivalents of Fouquier-Tinville, Couthon, Saint Just and Anacharsis Clootz[8] is what he means to get and that P.D.Q. Meanwhile, he will do his best to befuddle the poor dunderheads up there and reduce their effort to miserable and ridiculous confusion.

Is this a question justiciable before the Committee on Privileges or whatever it is, and before the House, when the two bishops somewhat treacherously peach on Claessens? "No," says Carolus the justiciar (*ci-devant*), "No, not if Claessens once takes the oath. The test is the oath." Well, much as I should like to avoid the possibility, which became an actuality of letting in all the mischievous little tattle on which the Five were excluded, I find a little trouble in going along. It is a possible view that the (only) sanction is the

6. LH refers to the government's deportation of aliens in 1919, termed the Palmer raids after A. Mitchell Palmer, the Attorney General.

7. Claessens was a Socialist member of the New York Assembly. LH refers to actions contemplated under the proposed Lusk bills. *See* 1920-1 To Wallas, January 17; and 1920-4 To Smith, May 21.

8. I.e., Antoine-Quentin Fouquier-Tinville (1746–1795), a French Revolutionary lawyer and public prosecutor of the Revolutionary Tribunal; Georges Couthon (1755–1794), an associate of Robespierre, on the Committee of Public Safety that ruled Revolutionary France, 1793–1794; Louis de Saint Just (1767–1794), elected to the National Convention in 1792 and became its president in 1793; Anacharsis Clootz (1755–1794), elected to the National Convention; an advocate of the liberation of Europe in name of Revolutionary ideals.

oath—our conscience. Maybe that's the effect of *Bradlaugh's* case[9]—I don't know, but I confess it seems to me rather "strong doctrine."

Of course, I don't mean that they should go any further than to inquire whether Claessens *meant* to support the Constitution as C[laessens] *understood* it, but mayn't they go so far? This great man said no, and God forbid that a D.J. should say no. But he is entitled to doubts. You see I am for your faction, which, at least for N.Y., would admit no extra-constitutional tests, Savage C. J.[10] to the contrary notwithstanding.

Well, you will be glad at least that I have nothing more to say. You have I think done a notably admirable thing—naturally I am prejudiced—and you have preserved so excellent a good-humor and so much moderation that the book should have influence even in these less excited times. The work must have been severe and the material hard to get in convenient and condensed form. How did you manage to find the time? That is where you active fellows with jobs who write books puzzle me.

But the thing which is nearest to me is what will be least important to your other readers, that you selected me for a very honor. I must confess I can't help feeling a little danger in it. It is well and admirable to yield to enthusiasm, but I can't help wondering whether a good many years from now when you are old and I am dead, you may not pick up the book and reading the first page, smile with some amusement and some regret. You really will have nothing personal to regret, even if you would not then think of repeating it, but still if I were there then, and perhaps I shall come back to plague you for your thoughts because ghosts have no respect for freedom of opinion, I should feel a little as though I have passed off on you some false coin. Whatever *you* may come to feel I don't know, but you have made me feel very happy and you have pleased three little girls too, who I am glad to say have never regarded their father hitherto as much more than an elderly man with a not wholly reliable amiability, though buttressed with a taste for buffoonery.

Sincerely yours, Learned Hand

ms with signature 15.26

To Learned Hand from Zechariah Chafee, Jr.

March 28, 1921 Law School of Harvard University

My dear Judge Hand:

Your delightful letter of January 2nd ought to have been acknowledged long ago. There is so much in it that I would like to discuss with you. For instance, with regard to the test case you put of the New York Socialist—I wonder whether the legislative oath

---

9. Charles Bradlaugh (1833–1891): freethinker, elected to Parliament in 1880, refused to take the religious Oath of Allegiance required of all members and consequently forfeited his seat. In 1883, he took his seat, however, and eventually secured passage of a new Oaths Act, which substituted the "right of affirmation" for the Oath of Allegiance.

10. In 1824, John Savage, Chief Justice of the Supreme Court of New York, ruled that the Bill of Rights does not control state action; states need not observe such rights. *See* Charles Fairman, *The Supreme Court*, 21 U. CHI. L. REV. 40, 46 (1953).

ought not to be viewed in just the same way as the oath of a witness. If his whole bearing shows that he does not mean to tell the truth and does not take the oath seriously, I suppose the Judge might refuse to let him testify, but how far would the Judge consider his statements outside the court room to see whether they indicated an intention to lie: it all comes back to the main difficulty. How far, for the sake of protecting ourselves from an obviously bad man, shall we lay down a general rule which will also include persons whose wickedness is less certain. Of course, when you can put a high board fence around the bad men as you can for murder and many other overt acts, we can handle them very well; but in the sedition cases, the attempt to draw a boundary seems to baffle us all. I agree with you that Holmes's distinction would prove unworkable in many cases. The Jury would go over it rough shod. Thomas Reed Powell[11] feels this even more strongly than I do. Your test is surely easier to apply although our old friend Marc Anthony's speech is continually thrown at me in discussion. After all, we ought to take the best test we can find even though it will sometimes break down, and then prevent its breaking down by using channels outside the law to produce greater tolerance in judges and jurors and the public at large, so that when the next emergency arises we shall be better prepared. I have had a very interesting letter from Graham Wallas and enclose a copy of a portion which may echo some of your thoughts[...][12]

Yours sincerely, Zech Chafee, Jr.

tp with ms signature 15.26

To Zechariah Chafee, Jr.

March 30, 1921

Dear Mr. Chafee:

[...]I do not believe I quite understand what Wallas meant in his letter. The difficulty I find with him always is one of definition. Both in reading and hearing him I get very stimulating insights here and there, but I have always found it hard to find the main structure and outline of his thinking. I suppose that is my fault. When I was at college I used to spend a good deal of time in studying metaphysics, and perhaps then I could have got the outline of his thought better. Whatever facility I then had I am afraid has gone,

---

11. Thomas Reed Powell, Professor, Harvard Law School.

12. Chafee encloses the following: "Extract of a letter from Mr. Graham Wallas to Mr. Z. Chafee": "I wish that someone in the Harvard Law School, under Dean Pound's inspiration and your own, would undertake in the light of the newer psychology that general analysis of law as a social fact which no one has attempted (as far as I know) since Bentham. Your 'social interest' is an admirable step forward from Bentham's 'greatest happiness' principle; but I want something more. I want someone to ask what law aims at, and what means (habit, calculation, suggestion, classification, etc., etc.) it uses to reach its ends. Such an inquiry might find from the outset that certain social expedients, not now classified as law, use kindred means for attaining kindred aims, and that certain expedients now classified as law are not really *in pari materia* [i.e., of the same kind]. Above all it would make invention again possible in the science of law, especially in that use of law as the main instrument of international relationship which dominates so much of American idealist thinking."

and in common with most so-called jurisprudence I fear I have come to share the stodgy point of view of the conventional English-speaking lawyer that law consists of certain concrete and rather disconnected rules of convenience, dictated by considerations supposed to be applicable at the time they were first put into force. I wonder how far there are general principles which can be found applicable through the whole body of law. In my day, this was rather the accepted attitude. I understand that it is regarded now as superficial heresy. Well and good. Possibly we should gain much by following the Continentals. As least I am glad that Pound keeps insisting upon the essential punity [sic] of all law. If it turns out there isn't any, at least the time is not wasted. To a judge of the first instance who spends most of this time in settling questions of fact, it all seems pretty remote, but we look to you in the school to reform us out of our traditionalism.

Faithfully yours, Learned Hand

ms with signature 15.26

1921-2

To Learned Hand from Clarence Day, Jr.[13]

March 30, 1921 258 Riverside Drive

Dear Buck:

A magazine editor has asked me to write an article on morality and legislation, their separate fields. I am trying to do so in the following way: never mind personal views or details (except illustrative details), but *state some fundamental principle* so simply that it will help people's thinking. The editor had in mind these new Sunday laws which have been proposed. The principle I am trying to drive home is this: legislation and law-codes are at bottom a defensive machinery to protect men against each other—against being killed, robbed or cheated by others. Their object is protection. They have as a function making men *orderly*. Codes of morals, like religions, have the function of making men *good*. If religions try to tame men into being orderly, their true soundness is gone. It is not for them to help strengthen dominant political systems by teaching submission, etc., to their congregations. They should inspire them with a fiery wish to be good. Positive, not repressive, etc. Laws, on the other hand, should not concern themselves with making men good—being out of their province, it strains laws and makes them decay. Does this seem to you sound? Are there important exceptions? Don't bother to answer if you're busy, as of course you probably are. Let me call you up, and hear any comment you may off-hand have. If you have none, or don't feel like thinking about it, it's all right. (Leaves me that much freer!)

Clarence Day, Jr.

ms with signature 102.28

---

13. Clarence Day (1874–1935): essayist and contributor to the NEW YORKER; author of LIFE WITH FATHER (1935) and LIFE WITH MOTHER (1937).

To Clarence Day, Jr.

March 31, 1921

Dear Clarence:

The question you raise in your letter of yesterday is one that has vexed people a good while. The attitude you take, I think, is at present somewhat antiquated. It finds its best statement in J.S. Mill's *Liberty*, but it was the dominant theory all through the first three-quarters of the last century, and its chief exponents were the school of Jeremy Bentham. Their belief was that the State should intervene only to prevent men from using violence or fraud against each other, and that being done, they would get on better by being allowed free scope to their own devices.

Although this theory got to have nearly complete acceptance among social thinkers about 1870, there was always an independent band who repudiated it, and during the last fifty years these men have succeeded so far as today to have nearly everything their own way—except in America, where political thought is always a generation behind the rest of the world. It was recognized, for example, that the State could not afford to take that attitude toward children and delinquents, and the admission had other consequences, for there was no time at which one could say that education was over, nor was there a time in which one could say that all adults had passed beyond the need of effective protection. Furthermore, adequate protection involved more than freedom from violence or the grosser kinds of fraud. Their economic position might be such as to make them individually, at least, helpless against certain kinds of exploitation; their acquired habits might be such that they could not resist certain forms of addiction; the opportunities for their enlightenment which the State could offer might be such that they could always be made better citizens, and better able to protect themselves by what one may as fitly as anything else call an improvement in their moral characters. Although you will therefore still find people who would accept the nice distinction which you suggest, I scarcely think you would find among them many informed thinkers. For myself, I do not believe that there is any principle which governs the limits of State intervention. Nor should I for a moment be willing to say that the State was never justified in attempting the improvement of the "morals" of its citizens. The issue is mostly of the means at the State's disposal.

Prohibitory laws of all sorts depend for their sanctions at least for the most part upon force, and that means the ordinary machinery of justice.[14] In the United States this is woefully clumsy and ineffective, due largely to the character of the bench, the jurors, and the bar, and to an inveterate love for legalism which Americans confuse with liberty, except in times of war, when they lose all sense of liberty. Prohibitory laws, therefore, in my judgment, are idle unless in communities where the feeling is overwhelming against the prohibited practice. Besides, they have other evil effects. They proceed for the most part from a desire by a large part of the community to impose their will upon the rest, in very large part for the pleasure of imposing it. In all of us there is a good deal of the Puritan; it is the pleasure of the spectators and not the pain of the bear that troubles us. Besides, there is a good deal less harm in much that is prohibited than people are apt to think. We have a national complex against enjoyment which you, as a psychoanalyst, will have to fathom for yourself.

---

14. For LH on prohibition and the Volstead Act, see 1923-6 To Frankfurter, October 11.

But prohibition by law is only one form of State activity. Education is another means by which the same purposes can be accomplished, but it is as open to your objection as forcible prohibition. I give the illustration only as showing that the question in each case, to my mind, is purely practical one; first, is the aim a good one; second, can it be accomplished, and if so, what is the best way? For myself, I recognize no a priori distinctions between what the State may and what it may not do. A consideration most apt to be forgot by people who share my view is that the mere ability to go to hell in one's own way is an inestimable boon to most men. The State should be chary in taking it away, even in part. Does this answer what you mean?

As ever, yours, [L.H.]

tp 102.28

To Clarence Day, Jr.

April 23, 1921

Dear Clarence:

I thought the article in *The London Nation*[15] splendid. You have said what everyone who has any practical knowledge of courts knows to be true. In the end it is possible that we shall have valid objective tests of credibility, but there are none yet, and they would be strongly resisted, I fancy, by the most conservative of the professions. Besides, I don't know that there are any which are of any value. The experts will have to get over their own mutual suspicious and recriminations before the bar or bench can take any action.

What I wrote to you about the other thing could not have been of any value to you, unless it was to open up the complexities. Remember, I am not necessarily in favor of repressive legislation of any sort. My only position is that we must not attempt to deal with it on a priori grounds. Walter Lippmann is writing a book on Social Psychology. That was the proper approach. For instance, how far is it true that any purely repressive measures are desirable unless they give correlative outlet? If we take away rum, must we substitute something else? All such thoughts go very deep. All I am protesting against are any inalienable and inherent rights of man to get drunk, or even to dress himself in cap and bells, which I suppose theoretically he may do in the street, but which practically he could not get away with for a block. The police would arrest him, and the magistrate would put him away for thirty days because he was guilty of disorderly conduct.

Do you know anything about disorderly conduct? That is one of the strangest crimes of the law. As far as I can learn, though I don't know much about it, the petty magistrates are essentially kadis, who can put you or me in jail for no more than thirty days whenever we do what they think will cause offense to our neighbors. I should think outrageously unconventional dress would fall within that category. If I wear a light pink tunic and knee breeches striped with lavender and black, red silk stockings with a skull and cross-bones on them, and shoes with musical buckles, and to cap it I wear a hat with a bird cage full

---

15. This article is entitled *The Value of Evidence*, and it appeared in the March 19th edition of the journal; as Day notes, it is not his work.

of canaries on top and carry a blue parasol, on which sits a stuffed rooster, I guess it is a crime. It would stir up too much feeling. There is no law about it, but in practice I should find that the law was against me, even though I could prove beyond doubt that I was a social philosopher and not at all crazy. People would say that I attracted too much attention and made riots likely. Well, is that an undue suppression of my impulses? Are you against it or for it? The example is conceivably bizarre, but you can work out more practical suggestions in your own inimitable way.

Thine, [L.H.]

tp 102.28

To Learned Hand from Clarence Day, Jr.

! Buck!

I didn't write that *London Nation* article. It's by a man who signs himself "S"—don't know who he is, but he does good stuff. About disorderly conduct—it appears to include any unusual conduct? Because unusual conduct excites the herd. Hence instead of permitting it, and getting used to it, and thus growing a little less narrow-minded, they protect themselves from ever becoming cosmopolitan and urbane in such matters by forbidding anyone from doing anything that would bother them. At Yale, in snowy weather, I used to wear a pair of high russet boots—old riding boots I think they were. This made lots of jabber. Some said I did it to be conspicuous, some said I was fresh, some just put me down as a damn fool or hopelessly queer. Nobody considered the merits—pro or con—of wearing such boots in deep snow.

I value your example of unconventional dress. You have the most vigorous and outrageous fancy. Buck! "musical buckles"—my god[...]

[Clarence Day, Jr.][16]

ms 102.28

1921-3

To Learned Hand from Zechariah Chafee, Jr.

June 1, 1921 Law School of Harvard University

My dear Judge Hand:

I am very sorry indeed that they dragged you into that rumpus over the *Abrams* case.[17] I cannot see how any reasonable man could conjure up an insinuation of foul play out of

---

16. Day actually signs his letter with a small self-portrait, sketched in pen and ink on the lower right-hand corner of the page.

17. Chafee was examined by the Board of Overseers of Harvard University—which included Julian Mack, A.N. Hand, and Cardozo—for his article on the *Abrams* case; *see* 33 Harv. L. Rev. 747

the paragraph in my book dealing with the assignment of the case.[18] Of course, I knew from you when I saw you in Washington that you had arranged the calendar, but I saw no reason for naming you in that connection. My criticism was of the general lack of any system of specialized judges for Espionage Act cases[...]

Sincerely, Z. Chafee, Jr.

tp with ms signature 15.26

To Zechariah Chafee, Jr.

June 3, 1921

Dear Mr. Chafee:

I have yours of June 1st. Do not concern yourself at all about my share in the "heresy trial." There was no part that was unpleasant to me. As a matter of fact, we have no opportunity for specialization of judges in any of our trials, and if we had, public confidences are so slight in judges that it would be unwise to exercise it ordinarily, at least in political trials, where the selection would never be deemed to be for the reasons given. As matters stand, the District Attorney has it a good deal in his own hands when he will bring on a case, and in that way he can effectively select his judges. This has its serious objections, but the defendant is protected under the statute if he is willing to challenge a judge, and the convenience of having the calendar made up by the United States when it is the plaintiff in all cases is very real. I have sometimes thought over the propriety of having a general calendar as they do in the State courts, but have hitherto always been against it, and so have all the other judges.

I find Mack, A.N. Hand, and Cardozo so secretive about their share in the "[heresy] trial" that I can get very little satisfaction from them. They apparently all swore some dreadful oath that they would tell nothing and so far they have been very loyal to each other. They are free to tell what took place openly and at the hearing but I get very vague ideas even of that[...] Hoping some time in the near future to see you, I am,

Faithfully yours, [Learned Hand]

tp 15.26

(1920). President Lowell defended Chafee. LH refers to this "rumpus" as a "heresy trial." *See* Gerald Gunther, Learned Hand: the Man and the Judge 360–62 (1994); *see also* Michael E. Parrish, Felix Frankfurter: The Reform Years 126–27 (1982). On *Abrams*, see 1919-6 To Holmes, November 25.

18. Judge Henry Clayton decided *Abrams* in October 1918 in the United States District Court for the Southern District of New York.

1921-4

To Learned Hand from Felix Frankfurter

July 26, 1921 Hadlyme, Connecticut

Dear B.:

[...]There is one aspect about Taft's appointment that makes me very curious: how will that lazy bones be able to do the grinding, unrelenting work which the office requires.[19] Gawd—what "mashed potato" opinions (that's what [Elihu] Root called the style of his speeches) we'll get[...]

I hope you're having a good summer. My greetings to Frances! F.F.

P.S. I suspect Brandeis is too reticent to have told you what he told me: "Learned Hand's opinions are the best Federal Court opinions that come before us for review."

ms with signature 104A.10

To Felix Frankfurter

July 27, 1921

Dear Felix:

[...]Your doubt about Taft has occurred to me. I am wondering whether such a fat man, sixty-four years old, will be able to keep up with the work of the Court. I do not suppose that the administrative side is so important, and he will do it poorly. But I am wondering whether he has ever done any hard work and can take it up now.

My solution is, however, that the average of these worthies is about sixty-six or seven, and with the exception of [Mahlon] Pitney[20] and Brandeis, I do not believe they are any of them capable of really hard work. It is not necessary for Holmes, because he has a power of divination, and I do not suppose he does work hard or has had to for a great many years. In some way or other, they manage to get through with the whaling lot of stuff that they do. I think you will find that on the whole Major Tufto will make a noise like a Chief Justice which most everybody will say is fine stuff. Besides, I think (although I gather you don't agree with me), that when he was Circuit Judge he was professionally tiptop. I think his stuff was as good as we used to get in the ordinary line of work[...]

As far as I can find, the heretics will have to be content with an acquittal by silence.[21] I think that nothing will come out, at least that was the last I heard, though your letter suggests that something may have been published that I don't know. I had the queerest

---

19. Taft became Chief Judge of the United States on July 11, 1921.

20. Mahlon Pitney (1858–1944): Associate Justice of the United States Supreme Court, 1912–1922.

21. The "heretics" were presumably the faculty at Harvard who supported Chafee before the Board of Overseers. *See* 1921-3 To Chafee, June 3.

talk with Jim Byrne[22] a while ago in which he seemed to get himself all worked up, about what, I could not exactly understand. He seemed to be on the side of Chafee, but greatly concerned over what he considered the inaccuracies. That attitude makes me a little tired. I had it out with Gus lately. The good thing about old Gus is, that however much to me he may rave and curse, you will always find him in the end on the right side, and there is no doubt that he has a great deal more influence with the other side than people like you and me, who are regarded as radical. Radical—God save the mark! Think of anybody thinking me a radical, a man who always finds the new experiments too hazardous to be tried just now. That charge always amuses me.

Are the hysteria disappearing? Only because there is nothing on. They would appear again just as soon as anybody tried to start anything. I have not yet got away. Hope to leave about the middle of August.

My love to the fair bride. [L.H.]

tp 104A.10

To Learned Hand from Felix Frankfurter

July 29, 1921 Hadlyme, Connecticut

Dear B.:

You certainly know where to strike the ladies! Says Marion, "it's real han'some of him to call me fair bride after all these years!!" Please also tell her why anyone should call me "radical"; she thinks it's almost as funny as to call you that.

Big Bill's performances on the Sixth Circuit may be called "merchantable wares," but surely you don't call his work "distinguished." I just will not join the procession that regards Taft's judicial output as great: good, straight, competent stuff yes; but not more[...] The truth is that I saw Taft too closely during the Presidency (from 1911 to 1913) to have a decent opinion either of his brain or the quality of his convictions[...]

My fondest—and Marion is "for you" even without the latest handsomeness. F.F.

P.S. There was a statement exonerating Chafee!

ms with signature 104A.10

To Felix Frankfurter

August 31, 1921 Windsor, Vermont

Dear Felix:

You are a little hard on the old boy. Forgive his exaltation of his prerogative, and remember what constitutionalism did for the country during its first century. Remember

22. James Byrne (1857–1942): New York City attorney and founding member, in 1922, of the American Law Institute.

too that without some tribunal which has power to mark off the limits between State and Nation we should scarcely get along even today. It makes a vast difference whether this be done by Nine Elder Statesmen removed from political turmoil or by the several centurions of Congress and the States legislatures. Much has depended upon the mere authority of that "Great Tribunal." What we are troubled about is those damned Bill of Rights. Let us concentrate our attention and give credit where credit is due. It is only when a chance is given to those worthies to perpetuate their own ideas of economics that trouble arises[...]

By the way, I have just come from a fortnight's visit to Murray Bay. I did not see him [Taft] except to say howdydo, but he looked OK. I can't understand why he should treasure aught against poor little me, but apparently he does[...] I am in Dutch, I fear, with his nibs.

My regards to your fair preceptress. L.H.

ms with signature 104A.10

To Learned Hand from Felix Frankfurter

September 7, 1921 Hadlyme, Connecticut

Dear B.:

I'm sending you one of the late C.J.'s vacuous pomposities I just indulged in irresponsible amusement. But if you seriously call the sinner to repentance, here goes three articles of my constitutional credo: 1. "Nullifying legislation" as unconstitutional is not judicial usurpation but as [Charles] Beard[23] has shown, the exercise of power that Federal Courts were meant to have. Even that arch-democrat exalted the practice of colonial and sovereign state's courts in upsetting legislation as ultra vires. 2. Undoubtedly the Constitution served as a maypole around which national feeling could and did dance for a hundred years or so—certainly through the Civil War. It served the same purpose that "the Crown" did in England. 3. Even now we could not get on, as Holmes pointed out in his N.Y. Harvard L. School speech in 1913, without some tribunal delimiting boundaries between Nation and States.[24] I'm for S.C. doing that and it does it pretty well—except when its economic biases come into play, and still more its fears of the future. I quite agree we want to concentrate not on the Bill of Rights but on Due Process Clauses, because by their very indefiniteness they leave too much play to policy without the conscious recognition that it is policy.

I do wonder whether Big Bill does harbor thoughts agin' you—though, of course, he is romantic about "courts" and he is vindictive. But even he may learn a few things after he reads a good many of your opinions[...] I'd give a lot—more than that—for a whole day in the country with you. There are heaps of things I much want to talk of with you.

Fondly yours, F.F.

---

23. Charles Beard, An Economic Interpretation of the Constitution of the United States (1913).

24. *See* Oliver Wendell Holmes, Jr., Speech at a dinner at the Harvard Law School Association of New York on February 15, 1913, *in* The Essential Holmes: Selections from the Letters, Speeches, and Judicial Opinions of Oliver Wendell Holmes, Jr. 145–48 (Richard A. Posner ed., 1992).

Marion says she ain't no "preceptress"—she didn't suspect that you were one!—but thanks you for your greetings and sends hers. Both greet Frances.

ms with signature 104A.10

1923-1

To Benjamin Cardozo

March 3, 1923

Honored Sir:

I am returning herewith *A Treatise on Probability*[25] which you gave me, God knows how long ago. I read fifty pages of it, and that was enough to satisfy me that with any attention and time which I had at my disposal, it was not for the likes of a district judge. There was a time in my noble and masculine youth when I think I might have pursued the subtleties of Friend [John Maynard] Keynes in the hope of creating that delectable sense of exalted confusion, which I was pleased to call the study of philosophy. But now that time has passed, with all its dizzy raptures, and the soul which aspired to comprehend the universe is content to try bootleggers. After all, why not? Pigeons should not imagine themselves eagles, and salvation lies in the knowledge of one's limitations. At least there is a gain in happiness and that, we are told, is the test of the good life.

I wish I could have taken you around on either of the two visits to Holmes. You were away each time. I told him you had been in town, and he was, I think, genuinely disappointed to miss you. He knows about you and like the rest wants to meet you. Time has not affected his mind or his gallantry, but it has reached his body and he perceptibly grows feebler. You really must see him some time before he leaves us; obviously we cannot take long chances on anyone who is eighty-two, and you are each so "set" in your ways that it was a misfortune to miss this opportunity.

As ever, [L.H.]

tp 101.7

To Learned Hand from Benjamin Cardozo

March 10, 1923 | 16 West 75th street

Dear L.H.:

Your attempt to prove that you are not a philosopher has been duly considered. I regret to be obliged to state that it is a vain pretense. A philosopher you are, have been, and ever

25. John Maynard Keynes, A Treatise on Probability (1921).

will be. If I doubted it before, your letter would supply the proof of your ignominy. These are hard words, but true ones. I shan't tell the bootleggers. The fear of you and of the law as embodied in you would go out of their hearts, and they would scorn you as a highbrow. Poor wretch! Vainly trying to prove yourself a harmless mediocrity, struggling to get within the shelter of some comfortable and conventional dwelling instead of ranging out of doors in the cold as a free spirit. I'm on to you. You're the most confirmed philosopher I know. You're all stained and impregnated with philosophy. And when you call yourself a pigeon, I don't agree with you.

I wish I could have seen Holmes. He has been my hero, and I owe more to him than to anyone else. I hope he will live forever.

I'm pining for a sight of you. I'll look you up the first chance I get when the court is in recess.

Ever yours, [B.N.C.]

tp 101.7

1923-2

To Learned Hand from Felix Frankfurter

January 30, 1923 Law School of Harvard University

Dear B.:

The S.C. has unexpectedly advanced the Minimum Wage cases[26] to February 26th, and I'm therefore working at break-neck speed on the brief. Hence my imprudence in trying to graft some help from you. 1. What is the practice of your C.C.A. as to a member of the Court who did not partake in the decision of a case participating in the disposition of a motion for rehearing such a case? 2. If there be a practice is it set forth in some rule or decision, or how may its existence be established?

I appreciate a search may reveal all these in our Library—but I simply haven't the time. But don't you waste any—I thought you would know—off-hand.

The boys here are still full of your Sunday talk—the recurring phrase I hear is "there was no bunk about him." You have no idea of the pomposity of the Eminences that usually strut before the lads. I was piggish enough to have wanted to see more of you—but that much I was very glad.

Always, F.F.

ms with signature 104A.10

26. *See* Adkins v. Children's Hosp., 261 U.S. 525 (1923). In *Adkins*, the Court, upholding the earlier decision of the District of Columbia Court of Appeals, found the Minimum Wage Act to be an unconstitutional interference with freedom of contract under the Due Process Clause of the Fifth Amendment. Felix Frankfurter represented the appellants before the Court. Chief Justice Taft dissented, as did Justices Holmes and Sanford. On the minimum wage, see 1912-1 To Norman Hapgood, February 2.

To Felix Frankfurter

April 11, 1923[27] Judge Learned Hand's Chambers

Dear Felix:

The real need about that decision is not to get angry over it, but to have some idea what one ought to do. The whole thing we thought gained in 1912[28] is now thrown overboard and we are just where we were. I confess I did not expect it again. Of course, those five men were elderly, the youngest 55 (isn't [Pierce] Butler[29] that?), and it is not likely that any successors would follow them. Yet the danger persists, and I can't see anything we get out of the Fifth and Fourteenth Amendments in the least commensurate with that danger. I am opposed to the 7 to 2 rule, if applied generally.[30] I shouldn't want to have a State statute stand in the path of Federal power or vice versa because 3 judges stuck out for it. It seems to me the place to hit is the Amendments themselves. What do you think?

L.H.

ms with signature 104A.10

To Learned Hand from Felix Frankfurter

April 11, 1923 Law School of Harvard University

Dear B.:

Thank you ever so much for your note. You're a peach, as always! Of course, we must not "get angry" over this decision; but I know I can say with the fullness of at least my conscious feelings that not a trace of anger or personal resentment has gone through me since Monday. I have been trying to do exactly what has been occupying your mind—to see the thing in its impersonal significance, to try to understand what it means, the implications of what is involved with a total disregard of all the silly "sinister" talk. And my own mind has about found lodgment where yours has; namely, that the possible gain isn't worth the cost of having five men, without any reasonable probability that they are qualified for the task, determine the course of social policy for the states and the nation. For, of course, it is silly to assume that the ordinary questions of law that you and other judges

27. Perhaps this letter should be dated April 10, 1923; see Frankfurter's reply, dated a day later.

28. LH may have in mind Supreme Court decisions supporting workers' rights in 1911 and 1912: Southern R. Co. v. United States, 222 U.S. 20 (1911) (upholding a federal statute on railroad safety devices); Second Employers' Liability Cases, 223 U.S. 1 (1912) (sustaining the constitutionality of the law fixing liability for employee injury without reference to contributory negligence).

29. Pierce Butler (1866–1939): Associate Justice of the United States Supreme Court, 1922–1939.

30. In 1923, Senator William Borah introduced legislation requiring a concurrence of seven of the nine Justices in order to find an act of Congress unconstitutional. The bill was defeated, but Borah continued to voice his opposition to close decisions of the Court, particularly 5–4 decisions, characterizing them as "one man" decisions that inappropriately invalidated with work of the legislature. For a contemporary view of judicial review, see Alan H. Monroe, *The Supreme Court and the Constitution*, 18 AM. POL. SCI. REV. 737 (1924).

are concerned with, the mental habits, the stream of precedents, etc., that have come down through centuries, have any reasonable relevance to the kind of issues involved in determining whether a minimum wage law is included within "the vague contours" of the Due Process Clause.

I am, therefore, practically clear in my own mind that "the place to hit is the amendments themselves" in the aspect under consideration. You will be interested to know that this is the first decision as to which there was unanimity of opinion on the part of the Law School Faculty. I never heard such outspoken talk around a table as that which was uttered by some of the most conservative members of the Faculty. Even before this decision, [Eugene] Wambaugh[31] spoke to me about the use made of the Fourteenth Amendment, and I took down his words at the time. You will be interested in them, not because of their novelty, but because of their source: "It isn't fair to leave the delicate and intricate questions arising under the Fourteenth Amendment—questions composed of fact, opinion and matters of degree—to what are, in the long run, nine elderly gentlemen whom we would never choose for the determination of such questions. It is all wrong to turn the Fourteenth Amendment into a general revision of legislation. Each generation is entitled to be left to itself to become angels or asses."

[...]Those who are most concerned with the industrial consequences are insistent that I come on to New York before very long for a kind of stocktaking. I suppose you will agree that it is up to me to throw into the pool whatever I have, if only to serve as a fool-killer. Of course, we must have the benefit of your brain. I don't know whether you want actually to sit in on a conference (of course it will be a private one), but in any event, I will let you know so that I, at least, can get hold of you.

Yours, F.F.

tp with ms signature and notes 104A.10

1923-3

To Learned Hand from Felix Frankfurter

June 5, 1923 Law School of Harvard University

Dear B.:

I wonder how you feel about the Foreign Language decision?[32] For myself, I should have voted with the minority. Of course, I regard such know-nothing legislation as uncivilized, but for the life of me I can't see how it meets the condemnation of want of "due

---

31. Eugene Wambaugh (1856–1949): Professor, Harvard Law School, 1892–1925.

32. This is a reference to *Meyer v. Nebraska*, 262 U.S. 390 (1923), in which the Supreme Court ruled that the state's law prohibiting the teaching of foreign languages in primary school was an unconstitutional violation of the Due Process Clause of the Fourteenth Amendment. Holmes and Sutherland dissented in *Meyer* and in two other cases decided concurrently, *Bartels v. Iowa* and *Pohl v. Ohio* (consolidated as 262 U.S. 404 (1923)), with Holmes noting that such a curriculum restriction

process" unless we frankly recognize that the Supreme Court of the United States is the revisory legislative body. If legislatures of our polyglot communities in their folly deem it desirable to exclude foreign languages from our schools and the Fourteenth Amendment forbids them, I must say they are circumscribed far beyond what "fundamental principles of liberty and justice," by the most liberal conception of "fundamental," limit. The reasons that J.B. Thayer dwelt upon thirty years ago still hold. That kind of confinement of the activity of our legislatures shrinks their responsibility, and the sense of responsibility of our voters much beyond what is healthy for ultimate securities. The more I think about this whole "due process" business, the less I think of lodging that power in those nine gents at Washington.

Quite irrelevantly, some day I should like to have a long talk with you about the League of Nations,[33] because you are one of the few supporters I know who won't make me feel that I am talking with a Catholic or a romanticist[...] As one who from babyhood was bought up to have some understanding of the complexities of the European mélange, I shudder at some of my friends who are ready to take on all European difficulties with the smug assurance that we are particularly equipped to handle them[...] Of course, we and Europe are interdependent. But it does not follow that every European affair is our affair, though it might, like Sarajevo, reach world proportions. But, after all, it wasn't Sarajevo that produced the war, but the whole scheme of forces that preceded it. I am utterly impatient of this talk about "the United States" without regard to the fact that a few well-meaning or naive Americans may, not as a matter of law but in fact (see Lord Loreburn's "How the War Came"),[34] commit this country into all kinds of foolishness and force. This doesn't mean going to a storm cellar. But it also doesn't mean that because the League of Nations, as is, is good for Europe, it is good for us. I submit as one mode of expressing my point of view Philip Kerr's[35] observation: "America is part of the world but not part of Europe." However, this is too long and complicated a story, but I should like a lot to have a long go at it with you. People like Judge Clarke[36] seem to me passionately naive when they talk about international affairs, and people who talk as George Wickersham does—who in the same speech on behalf of the League's Non-Partisan association urges our adherence to the League and also espouses France's behavior in the Ruhr, saying Germany must be brought to her knees—make one ask oneself, "Who is loony now, Wickersham or me?"

Faithfully yours, F.F.

tp with ms signature and notes 104A.10

---

was "a question upon which men reasonably might differ, and therefore I am unable to say that the Constitution of the United States prevents the experiment's being tried." 262 U.S. at 412.

33. For LH's views on the League of Nations and the Treaty of Versailles, see 1919-4 To Stevens, May 27; on the League specifically, see 1920-6 To MacKinnon, August 11.

34. Robert T. Reid, First Earl Loreburn, How the War Came (1919).

35. Philip Kerr (1882–1940): Secretary to Lloyd George, 1916–1921; later Lord Lothian, British Ambassador to the United States, 1939–1940.

36. Frankfurter may be referring to John H. Clarke (1857–1945): Associate Justice of the Supreme Court, 1916–1922, who resigned in 1922 to support the League of Nations. Clarke wrote the majority opinion in *Abrams v. United States.*

To Felix Frankfurter

June 6, 1923

Dear Felix:

I quite agree with you about the foreign language cases, although I have not yet seen the opinions. Holmes and [George] Sutherland[37] make curious bedfellows, notwithstanding. I can see no reason why, if a state legislature wishes to make a jackass of itself by that form of Americanization, it should not have the responsibility for doing so rather than the Supreme Court. But then, like you, I am ultra-latitudinarian in such matters[...]

About the League: as you say, we should have to have more than occasional letters. I am by no means one of those who expect it to work out the safety of mankind, but I do believe that given ten more years of life, it is the most single factor in what Herbert [Croly] would call the "appeasement" of the world. We must be content with very small beginnings. I never could see in just what factor of the League its opponents found the danger of our being unduly mixed up in European troubles. I understand that it is now admitted that there is nothing formally in the constitution of the covenant which could enline [sic] us, but that it is the general mussing up, the haggling, the bickering, the trading which we should get into that would inevitably make us parties to one side or another. I agree in the substance of this criticism. My difficulty would be that our interest being, as you well put it, interdependent with those of Europe, we should do more wisely to intervene at the outset, where, at least with our present power and prestige, we should have an important, if not a dominant influence. I think the proponents of the League ought frankly to admit that this is an abandonment of our traditional theory, and should be content to defend their position upon the theory that it is better so.

Of course, it is perfectly obvious that in any first-rate scrap in the future we shall not be regarded in fact as neutrals, any more than the Germans thought us neutral before 1917. Formally, we shall be as little out of it if we do not join the League as if we do. Pragmatically, we shall not be out of it in either case, but before the scrap comes we shall have some say along with what to me is a certain eventual responsibility. Moreover, I wish to look at it more widely than from our own interest. I think we owe it to the rest of the world to take some part in arranging an orderly world. It seems to me quite clear that there is nothing practical in sight besides the League which makes toward an international order. I do not regard it in any sense as tied up with the Treaty, nor do I understand why the opponents of the League so much insist that it is. While I should have been for the ratification of the Treaty, like you, I do not like it in many of its details, but I cannot help feeling that to keep away from the most promising institution that has yet been organized, we are putting ourselves in an intransigent attitude, and are demanding of men more than we are ever likely to get. I dislike the word "practical" because it so often covers intellectual laziness, but I must own that in this case I should be disposed to use it. We cannot afford, in my judgment, to ignore and keep ourselves out of the only promising effort toward the purpose which we all approve, because it appears in a world which, certainly in our time and for many generations hereafter, is not going to be fundamentally different.

37. George Sutherland (1862–1942): Associate Justice of the United States Supreme Court, 1922–1938.

This letter has already gone a good deal further than I meant. Are you likely to be in New York at all before August tenth, when I get my vacation? Where are you summering? Please give my love to the fair bride and believe me,

Affectionately yours, [L.H.]

tp 104A.11

1923-4

To Felix Frankfurter

August 11, 1923 — Cornish, New Hampshire

Dear Felix:

I was glad to get your letter enclosing [Charles Fremont] Amidon's.[38] He is a worthy man and I regret to hear that in his later years he has fallen upon ill health, that his days of work are past. His loss ought to be felt, though it scarcely will be. However, that is the nature of the job and cannot be otherwise. At 51, I begin to feel that the difference between the greatest and the least of us is so little that the oblivion which reaches the least a moment sooner is not an evil in its speed.

His letter does not greatly impress me with perspicacity. Of course, one must have lived only in the world of men to know the wolfish substratum on which the structure rests, but I am in great doubt whether a repeated return to the busy hives is desirable for one whose work ought preeminently to be an interpretation of the more permanent relations of men. There is as great a danger in contacts with immediate passions—or beliefs as they are usually the same [illegible]. If we were trying to guide mankind, even then I should fear too exclusive touch with A. or B. There was everything true in Wilson's approach; he would have had a better chance to see his world if he kept it a bit away from him than if he plunged into it here and there. Where he failed was in a disposition which made that too easy for him, and the defect of that quality ruined him, but the quality was not a bad one. When it comes to a judge, the case is stronger for retirement. Holmes is, it is true, too naïve in his judgments of men; that comes from a nature which has too few suspicions. I suspect that he met in his youth for the most part people who did not try to overreach him. But, however that may be, his work owes its permanent quality to his detachment. He has not mixed too much with people who insist upon the unconditional validity of their present nostrums, or if he has, the background of his acquaintance with letters and history has kept him from the chief danger to a judge or to any other man who is looking for truth: the automatic self-affirmation of ideas, their acceptance for their beauty of structure, because they fit into one's sub-conscious predispositions.

I should not want a judge to be a hermit, it is true, but periodic descents, or, if we choose, ascents into the world of supposedly throbbing, immediate, and impervious life

38. Charles Fremont Amidon, 1856–1937: United States District Judge for the District of North Dakota, 1896–1928. His letter to Frankfurter is not in the Hand Papers. See 1928-2 To Amidon, February 24.

seem to me growing a little absurd as a corrective for over-scholastic trends. Marshall might have been a great judge, I think, for he had the qualities, but he seems to me, in fact, scarcely to have been a judge at all. He was a great state-maker, which means something very different and much more momentous.

I was arrested and set to a little thinking by your leader in *The New Republic* about the Amherst row.[39] The practical difficulties of making any such public statement as you suggested are very great. In the first place, without [Alexander] Meiklejohn's consent the college would have probably exposed itself to an action, [in] which the actual values could have been weighed only very grossly, and where the rest might have obscured rather than illuminated the truth, as authoritative formal decisions are too apt to do. But I pass that, for what really interested me was what the duties are of a board of trustees to the public at large. I feel the force, more than do a good many of my friends, of the argument that there is a true public interest at stake, and that it is no answer to say that the college's affairs may [illegible]. Still, the considerations properly governing a decision like this are often not such as to be defensible intuitively. Meiklejohn appears to have had a very rare ability to arouse the interest of young men in ideas. Whether this was by an easy appeal to their natural vanity, assuring them of their equal competence with those who had gone before, or whether he was a great teacher who could awaken a passion for learning I don't know. That is a question which publicity is not apt to clarify; the facts do not admit of argumentative demonstration, they depend upon personal estimate, at least very largely.

Perhaps you would be content with the avowal of the mere conclusion as a ground, yet you will agree that it would never have been accepted. Whether in the ensuing dispute anything could have been gained seems to me very doubtful. The truth is that a college board of trustees is a curious anomaly which represents nobody and nothing, so far as I can see. Nor is there any effective way I can think of by which the public interest can be recognized. You would see that administration would become impossible if every chief had to defend contributions by his appointments or dismissals. Much of human affairs must go on outside of that kind of determination, and lawsuits, however large the jury, cannot be in the end a substitute for personal confidence in leaders. I recognize the dangers well enough of any power which is not callable to an accounting, but the accountings must, I should say, be rather in the results than in the means, and among means I should be disposed to class the dismissal of a president.

As for this case, I have no sufficient information for a judgment. On the whole, from the people I am inclined most to trust, I think I should have voted as the board did. Of the wisdom of any attempt to bring the facts to the "bar of public judgment" there appears to me the greatest possible doubt[...]

Please remember me to your fair lady and to Mr. Justice [Brandeis] and Lady B.

As ever, Learned Hand

ms with signature 104A.11

39. Alexander Meiklejohn (1872–1964), the President of Amherst College, was dismissed by the trustees of the college earlier in 1923. *See* Gerald Gunther, Learned Hand: the Man and the Judge 331–32 (1994).

To Learned Hand from Felix Frankfurter

August 24, 1923 Chatham, Mass.

Dear B.:

[...]Your letter is very exhilarating, as is almost always the case whenever I hear from you. But for once I must file a series of dissenting opinions on the three issues which you discuss. First, as to Amidon's letter. I think you dispose of him much too easily. Of course, judges can't lead "busy lives," cannot either contemporaneously or intermittently be part of the world of strife and business about them. But that doesn't dispose of Amidon's position, which is how are judges, and particularly the members of the Supreme Court, to know and understand the subject matter of the litigations that come before them. They need not and cannot work in factories; they must know facts. For practically all cases that come before the Supreme Court, as you very well know, turn on economic and business facts. Questions of taxation, of public utilities, of industrial relations, of banking, are the issues in controversy. Their wise disposition necessitates the kind of extensive knowledge of economic and business facts and experience that Brandeis brought to the bench, and which he continuously replenishes by a continuous study of economic data.

It's no use covering up the situation by saying judges deal with "an interpretation of the more permanent relations of men." In practice how does that work out? You have had more than one occasion to say that the only two men out of the nine about whose opinions you care are Holmes and Brandeis. Why? Because the others—men like Taft and Pitney and [James Clark] McReynolds[40]—base their interpretation "of the more permanent relations of men" upon the very limited experience in affairs which they had before coming on the bench, together with the fallible experience of the past intended for different economic and social conditions but generalized and handed down uncritically in the form of "natural law." All of this very limited and partial judgment as to the "more permanent relations of men" is unconsciously reinforced and vindicated by the social atmosphere of like-minded people in which they move. Hence you get the *Lochner*, the *Adair*, the *Coppage*, the *Minimum Wage cases*; hence you get the whole history of the perversion of the Due Process Clauses.[41] As a matter of fact, a court did have one question before it that genuinely raised an interpretation of the "more permanent relations of men" during

---

40. James Clark McReynolds (1862–1946): Associate Justice of the United States Supreme Court, 1914–1941.

41. All the cases noted by Frankfurter involved laws that regulated the relations between employer and employee and were deemed unconstitutional violations of the freedom of contract under the Due Process Clauses of the Fifth and Fourteenth Amendments. See *Lochner v. New York*, 198 U.S. 45 (1905), which found that the New York statute capping bakers' hours at no more than sixty per week or ten per day was unconstitutional; *Adair v. United States*, 208 U.S. 161 (1908), which upheld the so-called "yellow dog" contracts that forbade employees from joining a labor union; *Coppage v. Kansas*, 236 U.S. 1 (1915), finding a Kansas statute banning "yellow dog" contracts unconstitutional; and the Minimum Wage cases of *Adkins v. Children's Hospital* and *Adkins v. Lyons*, 261 U.S. 525 (1923), in which the Court found unconstitutional the minimum wage law Congress had established for women and children working in the District of Columbia. See LH on the issues in *Coppage* in *Normal Inequalities of Fortune*, THE NEW REPUBLIC, Feb. 6, 1915, at 5–7.

the last few years, namely various cases raising freedom of speech. And how did they behave? They behaved like the mob—they were victims of what Rosebery[42] called, when speaking of the similar performance in Pitt's regime, "the ignorant ferocity of panic."

In my judgment, Amidon raises a question which is fundamental in the future of our judiciary and had better be faced: How are our judges to have knowledge of the subject-matter of the issues that come before them? How are we to establish professional traditions by which the Supreme Court will decide the legal controversies in the light of the surrounding facts, instead of generalizing the extremely meager or partisan experience of the Justices into "fundamental principles." [...]How I ask you, are we to guard against or counteract the confirmation of judicial views which come from the social contact of the judges? They meet, as Lord Justice Scrutton candidly pointed out in a thing I quoted from him in the June Law Review,[43] their own kind constantly. It's like calling yourself up on the telephone. I don't believe that even so incorruptibly critical a mind as yours is immune from the unconscious influence of his social surroundings. Am I wrong in thinking that even a judge with your tastes and liberality meets very largely only "the right kind of people"? Therefore I submit Amidon raises about as far-reaching a problem as any that confronts our profession and the American judicial system.

Holmes furnishes no answer; neither does Woodrow Wilson. Holmes is a "sport." He is, I am sure, the only genius that the history of the Supreme Court has thrown up, and no guidance is to be had from the appearance of one genius in over a hundred years. Moreover, it is a terribly fortunate circumstance of his genius that his mind is as skeptical as it is. Otherwise, I verily believe his total divorce from the world of facts might have made him as harmful a judge as he now is a very great judge[...]

Secondly, I am rather on the war-path about Meiklejohn's dismissal. Hardly any American episode since the Armistice has stirred me up as much as this has. My starting point is the conviction that Meiklejohn's performance at Amherst was the most significant educational achievement in our times. What he did was to send forth every year a goodly measure of young men instilled with the responsibility of thinking and of self-direction in a period unusually materialistic and engulfing[...] I am shocked that you should suggest that such power exercised over young men year after year and in the mass can conceivably be exercised by "an easy appeal to their natural vanity." I am sure that suggestion never originated in your generous mind. Feeling this way about Meiklejohn's spiritual power and achievement, I am naturally eager to force the fighting on the trustees. All the more so because I think I know all they have to say for themselves. One of them is one of my oldest friends, Stanley King, and upon his insistence we had a four-hour "jaw" about the whole situation. I am glad to say he disagrees with those of your friends who think that Amherst College is the private business of the trustees. That was

42. I.e., Harry Primrose, 6th Earl of Rosebery.

43. *See* Felix Frankfurter, *20 Years of Mr. Justice Holmes's Constitutional Opinions*, 36 HARV. L. REV. 909 (1923). Frankfurter quotes Lord Justice Scrutton's observations that "[t]he habits you are trained in, the people with whom you mix, lead to your having a certain class of ideas of such a nature that, when you have to deal with other ideas, you do not give as sound and accurate a judgment as you would wish[...] It is very difficult sometimes to be sure that you have put yourself into a thoroughly impartial position between two disputants, one of your own class and one not of your class." *Id.* at 917 (citing Lord Justice Scrutton, *The Work of the Commercial Court*, 1 CAMBRIDGE L.J. 6, 8 (1921)).

precisely the issue that was sought be ventilated by the open letter to [Dwight] Morrow[44] in *The New Republic*, which, by the way, although I instigated I did not write. I also completely disagree with your notion that the issues that are involved in the termination of an educational enterprise such as Meiklejohn was conducting cannot be made the subject matter of public controversy. That's a doctrine fatal to any public responsibility by educational authority. It's the familiar doctrine of all autocratic regimes that they must be trusted and that the facts cannot be disclosed[...] That's why I am so anxious that this issue be kept alive, that the trustees be compelled to state their case, that the facts may finally be sifted in the course of public discussion and the evaluation of them be frankly faced. Let's find out whether we believe, in the first place, that the trustees of our colleges may run them as they do their private businesses, and secondly, let's find out whether we really think that excellence as a banker or as a lawyer or as a shoe manufacturer are sufficient guarantees—afford enough understanding and leave enough time—for the conduct of a college in producing the kind of next generation we want[...] Have a good time—and the best to Frances.

Yours, F.F.

tp with ms signature and notes 104A.11

1923-5

To Walter Lippmann

September 5, 1923 Windsor, Vermont

Dear Walter,

Your article in *The Atlantic*[45] has met with so much enthusiastic assent up here that I thought you would like to hear of it. G. Rublee said it was the best article he had ever read; you can't beat that for commendation. Louis Dow and Ray Stevens felt it was unanswerable and entirely disposed of the case. It seems to me that Phil [Littell] joined in, but I can't quite recall whether he has read it. Well, that is a small chorus if you like, *quorum pars sum*, but perhaps it will make up in quality for its size. No doubt you have heard from it elsewhere. It seems to me to leave nothing more to be said, and in your best style, which I think you know means much in my mind.

Herbert [Croly] is here for a few days. He said it entirely "disposed" of the idea as it had hitherto been presented, but he has detailed [John] Dewey to reply[46] and the reply, as I understand, is to put a new face upon the notion which will make it tenable. I had scarcely time to get just what was in his mind, but so far as I did, it was that there should be a new

44. Dwight Whitney Morrow (1873–1931): attorney and banker; chief civilian aide to General John J. Pershing during World War I; Ambassador to Mexico, 1927–1930; Senator from New Jersey, 1930–1931.

45. Walter Lippmann, The Outlawry of War, Atlantic Monthly, Aug. 1923, at 245.

46. See John Dewey, *What Outlawry of War Is Not*, The New Republic, Oct. 3, 1923, at 149–52.

conference which should put it up to France to admit Germany into a community of nations. Out of this was to come a kind of society, with a court devoid of any compulsive sanction which by its judgments was to be competent to declare the right and justice of any dispute, and any nation disregarding the award by force was then to be an outlaw. How far this court was to profess to be enforcing preexisting rules, and how far it was to be free to settle disputes by its own ideas of propriety, I am not clear. Surely that is important. We are, it is true, used enough to courts which legislate *in petto* as all courts must, but I fear that these adherents of a court alone fail to recognize that it is the degree which in such matters counts. Throw away the duty of courts, or if one is disposed to be [illegible] the pretence to be applying rules which have some preexisting sanction of public assent, and their whole nature changes. Their authority would at once disappear as soon as their decisions had no greater professed authority than the beliefs of the judges as to what was proper and just. There ought to be something said just now to bring out that distinction; it is vital and has been forgotten amid so much talk of the initiative of judges.

As for the League: this seems to be its day of trial.[47] I can see nothing for it but a rigid insistence upon the letter of the covenant. If it has no power to prevent this kind of brutality, it is of no service in its main purposes. Today's papers seem to indicate that the row may be straightened out diplomatically, which is tempting, but I cannot help feeling sorry if it is not made a clean League affair. It seems to me as frankly brutal as Austria's conduct in 1914 and without the excuse that had of a long preceding agitation. This is the frankest grabbing we have had and bears out what appears in the last number of *Foreign Affairs* by that absurd person [Francesco] Coppola. "Italy knows her destiny and her needs. She knows too how to make good her decrees if she is baulked."[48] Think of it: Italy with water on every side of her to try out conclusions now. Has she had assurances of French support so as to isolate Britain? Is it all a part of the Ruhr game? I wonder whether you know anything about it.

I have a letter from Felix highly wrought over the Meiklejohn episode.[49] "Nothing has worked on me so much since the armistice." Well, we are differently made. I am not clear what the duty of publicity is in such a case. I can't quite work out how the cross issues which make the final resultant would be well clarified by a public statement followed by the general yawp on both sides. If the public has no power to do anything, at least the necessity of publicity is less; perhaps it does not disappear. Yet I should like to see more plainly what good here and now would come of it. I can see plenty of harm. I assume you are still at Wading River; you said you would not be back till October. I trust the new *mag. op.* progresses.

---

47. A reference to the French invasion of the Ruhr area of Germany in January 1923, in response to German failure to pay reparations after World War I. The French occupation of the area lasted until August 1925. For the institution of the League of Nations, see 1918-1 To Frankfurter, January 9, note 133.

48. LH paraphrases the final comments of Francesco Coppola on the status of postwar Italy: "Once more Italy has become conscious of he national and international strength. She has realized that her victory was unjustly mutilated and that it is her right to retrieve it. She is again fully conscious of her vital need for expansion and she is deliberately determined to satisfy it." Francesco Coppola, *Italy in the Mediterranean*, 1 Foreign Affairs 105–14, 114 (1923).

49. For Meiklejohn, see 1923-4 To Frankfurter, August 11.

I have got to give an address on October 15th, and I am trying to do it up here, but I am shockingly inept at such things, and there is a blight in [my] vacation that my will has not been able yet to overcome. Most of it is done, but not satisfactorily; I can't get any fire into it, I mean inward fire, any real interest. I only hope that that won't make it only smoke. How on earth anyone ever writes a book passes me, and here are you that are writing one after another. "Desperately hard thinking," per G. Wallas. Do you do your daily dozen in that each day? I suppose so; you have a good determination.

H[erbert] C[roly] seemed to me rather low though he looks well. This has become for him rather a dreary place, not a single disciple I think. Several of us are ghosts of our old selves to him. I can't help it, I have tried but it won't go. I hope he doesn't feel it, but if he does what can I do?

Thine, L.H.

ms with signature, Lippmann Papers, Sterling, Box 12, Folder 499

To Learned Hand from Walter Lippmann

September 18, 1923 Wading River, New York

Dear B.:

Your letter and one from George [Rublee] have set me up mightily, especially since I have stage fright when ever I get near a semi-legal subject. But this summer I've been reading [illegible] on the common law, and some textbooks, and Pound, and I'm going to come to you for more. I really like the legal mind, what I've seen of it, and I feel hopelessly, foolishly ignorant about it[...]

What you say of H[erbert] C[roly] and yourself parallels my own experience. Take that latest theory of his in the *N[ew] R[epublic]* two weeks ago about getting out of Europe. Would anybody know from his contemptuous attitude toward a Wilsonian war psychology that in 1917 H.C. was one of the leading rationalizers and expounders of the war for democracy? I can't stomach that sort of thing. If H.C. has changed his mind, as he has, he should confess or shut up, but should not in 1923 treat people who agreed with him in 1917 as damned fools. That's just one step worse than self-righteousness.

And while I'm blowing off: there's Felix, who bombarded me all through July about Amherst, assuming from the outset that anyone who wasn't pro-Meiklejohn was morally defective. I had no right, he told me, to attempt a report of the affair. My business was to interpret and judge. You'd think from our correspondence that he was the hasty journalist and I the calm, learned, professor. But what in Sam Hill has got into Felix to make him so suspicious, so querulous, and so argumentative? Enough. I quit writing to Felix in order not to quarrel with him. After I'd quit, he wrote and told me I hated inconvenience, and that was why I'd quit.

We'll be back October 1st. May we see you soon? This brings our best to Frances Hand and yourself.

Love, W.L.

ms with signature, 106.17

1923-6

To Felix Frankfurter

October 11, 1923

Dear Felix:

I have received the leaflet from your remarks on the prohibition amendment in *The Annals.*[50] I entirely agree with your position. It is very hard to make up one's mind about the whole subject. Practical experience here in New York disposes one to be despondent and to question the advisability of the whole experiment. On the whole, I have now come from a mild adherence to it to a mild opposition; at least in a community like this, the price seems to me much too high for the gain, and yet it was only yesterday when [John Holley] Clark, an Assistant District Attorney, after a survey of the number of saloons in the York, told me that he thought about seventy-five percent had gone out of business. You cannot disregard practical results like that.

While I entirely agree with your suggestion of the way out, I really think that it was not the primary purpose of the amendment when it was passed, but that that provision contemplated national action over the whole Union centered at Washington. If it had not been so, there was no need of the amendment. Congress already had the power to control the traffic in liquors between the States and by import. The purpose, I think, was to have both Congress and the States pass laws to control it. So I cannot escape the conclusion that for Congress to limit itself to its more proper functions is really to abandon the purpose of the amendment. The reason why I favor your view is, however, that experience has shown it is a bad mess as it is, and we have at least a literal compliance with the law in the way that you suggest. We shall be relieved of what seems to me to be prime vice of the whole affair, and that is imposing upon communities what they regard as the fiat of an alien and hostile power. I do not believe that it is wise criminal legislation and this instance seems to me abundantly to prove its unwisdom.

Indeed, I should go so far as to say that it was almost an unconditional canon of legislation that no conduct should be made a crime in any community in which it did not already have an overwhelming moral condemnation. I should define "community" as being any large territorial body which was conscious of a common individuality. That last is a vague phrase, but it is not necessary, I believe, to expatiate on it. You and I would probably agree on its definition. While as you of course know I have little sympathy with the talk about personal rights, I have a very abiding sense that it is a mistake to force upon people rules, however wise, against which they rebel. And so I

50. *See* Felix Frankfurter, *A National Policy for Enforcement of Prohibition*, 109 ANNALS AM. ACAD. POL. & SOC. SCI. 193–95 (1923). The Volstead Act, which enabled enforcement of the Eighteenth Amendment, was passed in 1918 and prohibited the sale and consumption of alcohol. In his article, Frankfurter argues that the Act must be enforced: "the solution must be looked for in the proper distribution of duties between the states and the federal Government." For LH on prohibitory laws, see 1921-2 To Day, March 31; 1923-6 To Frankfurter, October 11.

am entirely with you, though I suppose you would agree that for a long time the effort will be quite impossible, for there are enough fanatics to terrify Congress out of any such sane proposal[...]

As ever, yours, [L.H.]

tp 104A.11

1924-1

To Augustus Hand

July 27, 1924 — 107 East 64th street

Dear Gus:

I am leaving in a few hours and don't know whether ranch life will be conducive to writing letters, so I take this chance. As I have heard nothing to the contrary I assume that you decided not to come back here[...] I fear that your mother's death may be a severe shock to you. Why not? She seemed to have as much as, if not more to live for than ever before, and yet, think as we will, we do consign the aged to death unconsciously. It helps us and maybe it helps them. I rather think it does. At any rate, often they get a placidity which seems like an acceptance of their end. I am sure I hope it for myself and for those I love. Nothing could be more desired than the manner of her going. All this will I hope give you a sense of acceptance, which may resign you without too much regret. Surely we die slowly; the gradual fading out of even the strongest—like dear old Eliot,[51] who has lost his wife, poor fellow—is a dying by inches, pleasantly if we are successful, but certainly. And the end is so logical, so necessary being what we are, with new lives coming on and the possibilities of new adaptations coming with them. The longer I live the more appropriate it all gets to seem. If only the animal inside me would see it as the mind does, it would have the sort of beauty that there is in any absolute. But there's the rub; it is logical for others, but not yet for my own *anima, vagula, blandula, qui errat in locis.*[52]

Your mother was very kind to me. I used to feel that the house was a second home. Indeed, there was a time when little turncoat that I was, I used to think it much superior to my own. I believe she always liked me, and your and my relations to each other were pleasant for her to think of. With her has now gone all the group, and time will soon be eating up their memories as it will eat up ours, and should too, else this would be a vastly overcrowded world to work in. Yet the past is our own secure possession—ours personally

---

51. Charles W. Eliot (1834–1926): President, Harvard College, 1869–1909.

52. LH slightly misquotes lines in Hadrian, *Carmina* 25, which run: "Animula vagula blandula/ hospes comesque corporis/quae nunc abibis in loca/pallidula rigida nudula/nec ut soles dabis iocos"; "Wandering sweet soul, guest and companion of the body, to what places will you now depart, pale, stiff, naked, and not joke as you are used [to do]." THE FRAGMENTARY LATIN POETS, (Edward Courtney ed., 2003). LH cites these lines again in To Wyzanski, December 16, 1945, and as provoking "an authentic demand of the spirit" in *Liberty, in* THE SPIRIT OF LIBERTY 153.

like nothing else. I have thought a good deal of it since Harry Hun[53] died last March, before time had worked any real ill on him. To me he has an immortality and will have. That he shouldn't have it for others is quite irrelevant.

It begins to look as though I should get the "step" into the C[ircuit] C[ourt] of A[ppeals].[54] [...]So far as I can see there has been no particular choice between you and me, and just for that reason my longer service will count me in. At least, that's how it looks from the kind of gossip that goes around. But it is all *in fieri*, and he's an ass who counts on anything of the sort till actual precipitation. It has been an unpleasant thing to me, this matter of you and me in a kind of competition. I have wanted to get this place more than I should have wished I did, considering that my having it meant you wouldn't get it, at least for the moment. I wish my heart could have jumped more generously to say "I really want him and not me to have it." I rather think you have felt that way personally. Still we must be what we are, and it hasn't taken this to show me that you are more selfless than I, you old rooster. That is quite another story and not to be told now or probably even to you at all, except as you know it already. Besides, I think there is a genuine ground to hope that we may be together in that court, if not then perhaps still as D.JJ., anyway without any perceptible separation. That's the main thing[...]

And so, my gallant, adieu for the moment, as old Gould[55] used to say, and use thine aged leg to hop and skip, awkwardly like Audrey but with a good will.[56]

L.H.

ms with signature 109.13

1924-2

To Learned Hand from Felix Frankfurter

December 3, 1924 Law School of Harvard University

Dear B.:

Ever since I was entitled to have an opinion about the business of courts and especially the Supreme Court, I have entertained an eager conviction that you are among the very few on the bench who ought to be one of the Nine. I welcome, therefore, your appointment to the C.C.A. as the step on the way to Washington. You are needed there—not for any "sociological" reasons, but merely from the point of view of technical professional equipment. In the

---

53. Henry Hun, a physician in Albany and a brother-in-law of LH; his father was Henry Hun, an attorney for whom LH had worked in Albany before coming to New York.

54. LH was nominated to the United States Court of Appeals for the Second Circuit by President Calvin Coolidge on December 2, 1924, to the seat vacated by Julius Marshuetz Mayer. His appointment was confirmed by the Senate on December 20, 1924. See GERALD GUNTHER, LEARNED HAND: THE MAN AND THE JUDGE 275–77 (1994).

55. Charles W. Gould, of Gould & Willkie, the second New York law firm at which LH worked.

56. *Cf.* Touchstone (a clown, on the eve of his marriage to Audrey, a goatherd): "Trip, Audrey; Trip, Audrey." AS YOU LIKE IT, V, i.

meantime you will give a new and rare distinction—in increasing measure—to the Federal Reporter. I hope for you also, what I assume you will find, happy personal associations. The President and [Harlan F.] Stone[57] are, for this much, entitled to all our gratitude.

Faithfully yours, F.F.

ms with signature 104A.11

To Felix Frankfurter

December 5, 1924 142 East 65th street

Dear Felix:

Your aspirations for me go too far. The chances are so remote for the other step as to be merely in the realms of mathematical possibilities. If you reflect you will agree. But this is a change I have much wanted and am very much pleased to get now I have it[...] The real trouble is the speed which will, I fear, make sloppy stuff very likely—I was just going to say, despairingly, inevitable.

I can always rely so heavily and securely on your good wishes and friendliness that it gives me a warm sense of pleasure to see your handwriting, though I read your letters sometimes with a sense that I ought to be blushing in my saffron rug. I have just spent an afternoon hearing Williston defend his "Restatement"[58] before the council of the [American] Law Institute. Good God, how you can any of you really think that we judges know anything or are good for anything seems incredible. But after all, you haven't committed yourself so far; you've only said that I'm fit to go to Washington. As against that marvelous, that superb creature I have been seeing today, even that seems a little paltry.

As ever, L.H.

ms with signature 104A.11

1925-1

To Louis D. Brandeis[59]

May 28, 1925

Dear Mr. Justice:

When the whole Supreme Court agrees that I am wrong, and when they are led by you, I am afraid that such convictions as I may have in any point of law are not rugged

---

57. Harlan F. Stone (1872–1946): Associate Justice of the United States Supreme Court, 1925–1941; Chief Justice of the United States, 1941–1946.

58. Samuel Williston was the "Reporter" on the subject of contracts for the American Law Institute. *See* SAMUEL WILLISTON, RESTATEMENT OF THE LAW OF CONTRACTS, AS ADOPTED AND PROMULGATED BY THE AMERICAN LAW INSTITUTE (1932).

59. Louis Dembitz Brandeis (1856–1941): Associate Justice of the United States Supreme Court, 1916–1939.

enough to stand up against it.[60] You may think this "tosh," as the English say, but it isn't. I dare say there might be a case to the contrary, but for the moment anyway I don't recall any. As to this case, I am disposed be acquiescent[...]

I have really no excuses to offer. Perhaps when one gets reversed as often as a district judge does in the course of fifteen years, one accepts too easily the mistakes one makes. But after all, that's the condition of any peace of mind. One spawns one's ideas out on the world. Only a few survive; the mortality is so high as in other of the lower biological forms. I have become hardened to the death of these children of my brain, and can look on without compunction when they become the prey of higher organisms. You will say that this betokens irresponsibility. Well, perhaps so; one goes along as one can. What you said was very true, that it is better to do a little well than much ill. Only the conditions here forbid it. Moreover, I doubt if I should have discovered this for myself, even with leisure. The limits that nature puts on one's imagination are not much transcended by reflection. A little possibly; let me take what comfort I can from what leisure might have added.

I am much concerned, far more than about "my fate as a thinker," with the apparently steady increase in our country of the pressure for uniformity. I fear we are losing our freedom. The latest instance is this obvious effort to choke any expression of opinion by Americans abroad which runs counter to the authorities. It has filled me with Homeric rage. What ever the limitations of the Victorians, at least they had more nearly examined the notion that men might freely speak their minds than any other moderns, any others at all perhaps but Athens in her glory and her fall. These ready means of communication, are they not to make us a great communal flute in which artful governors can play what tune they will?[61] I confess that it seems rather a dark outlook. The one thing I want to see survive is the skeptical temper. I don't find much. But consistently, I must be skeptical of the catastrophic results of attempts at its suppression. There's the hope. I hadn't any purpose to write you such a long letter. Forgive me.

Faithfully yours, Learned Hand

ms with signature 100.3

---

60. LH refers to *Benedict v. Ratner*, 268 U.S. 353 (1925), in which the Supreme Court reversed the Court of Appeals' decision *In re Hub Carpet Co.*, 282 F. 12 (2d Cir. 1922), regarding the validity of an assignment of the company's accounts receivable as security prior to a company's bankruptcy. The original decree, which found the assignment to be valid, was issued by LH's court, the United States District Court for the Southern District of New York.

61. *Cf.* "blest are those/Whose blood and judgment are so well commeddled/That they are not a pipe for Fortune's finger/To sound what stop she please." HAMLET, III, ii.

1925-2

To Walter Lippmann

June 7, 1925 224 State Street, Albany, New York

Dear Walter:

[...]I am indeed very sorry to hear that you have had so much to concern you.[62] I would not have you write, because I know at such times how intolerably irksome it is to have to do such things, but I want to let you know that I have not forgotten you or your troubles[...] Maybe you have come acquainted with the men in the hospital. I am hoping for some "aperçus" on modern therapy when we meet. It must be a stimulating group, if your mind has been free enough to come into contact with it. It's with them that the great chance lies. We shall in the end know a good deal about this complicated chemical combination which has so strangely appeared in a tiny satellite of a modest star. That is, we shall unless the besotted Tennesseans and their ilk do not engulf us.[63] There a fine passage somewhere in Gilbert Murray where he says that the Greek always lived with the consciousness that he was in a little island likely to be overwhelmed by the seas of barbarism at any time. Finally it was. I have always felt that we were secure. The last ten years ought to give any one some pause. Still I think it will be O.K., but it's a long fight, and the end always uncertain.

I was amused that the *Oregon School* case[64] came out of their Nibs without a scratch. Even old Holmesy couldn't stomach that. Yet it's a little hard to see why if the State may say to Calvin Johnson "We won't let you keep your children out of school till we give the wiff [sic] the once-over, and see whether she is up to our curricular standard," why, if the State may say that, it mayn't say "On the whole, we decide that the education we want must be in our schools." Well, it's all a matter of degree, and as the Klan was at work, I can't complain at the lack of logical integrity. Had I been there, I should have been recorded in a "Me too," I fancy. One might as well confess that the "Nine" are a superior legislative house and be done with it. But let them be on guard that they assume no more

62. Lippmann was in Baltimore where his wife, the former Faye Albertson, was undergoing surgery for the removal of her spleen. Ronald Steel, Walter Lippmann and the American Century 216 (1980).

63. LH refers to the trial of John Scopes, convicted for teaching Darwin's theory of evolution in defiance of Tennessee's Anti-Evolution Act, passed in March 1925, and fined $100 by the presiding judge. William Jennings Bryan argued for the prosecution, Clarence Darrow for the defense. The decision was later reversed by the Tennessee Supreme Court (see *Scopes v. State*, 154 Tenn. 105 (1927))—not because the statute violated the state or federal constitutions, but because state law mandated that fines greater than $50 be determined by the jury, not the judge.

64. This is a reference to *Pierce v. Society of Sisters*, 268 U.S. 510 (1925). Oregon's Compulsory Education Act of 1922 required parents or guardians to send children between the ages of 8 and 16 to public school in the district where the children resided. The Society of Sisters, an Oregon corporation affiliated with the Roman Catholic Church, having established and maintained its schools, consequently suffered the loss of property (i.e., income) when parents removed their children to enroll them in public schools in conformity with the statute. The Court unanimously found that the statute violated the Fourteenth Amendment and that it "unreasonably interfere[d] with the liberty of parents and guardians to direct the upbringing and education of children." *Pierce*, 268 U.S. at 534–35. For LH on *Meyer v. Nebraska*, see 1923-3 To Frankfurter, June 6.

than an overwhelming consensus of the vocal folks will admit. That's a fine doctrine for judicial independence. I didn't mean to be so prolix.

L.H.

ms with signature, Lippmann Papers, Sterling, Box 12, Folder 499

To Learned Hand from Walter Lippmann

Thursday[65] Evergreen, Charles Street Ave., Baltimore, Md.

Dear B.:

[...]I want your advice badly on the *Tennessee* case.[66] [Thomas Reed] Powell[67] and Morris Cohen take the view, if I understand them correctly, that the constitutionality of the law ought not to be attacked. Such foolishness should be within the province of the legislature. Now I know this is progressive dogma, as we all accepted it in the days when the courts were knocking out the laws we wanted. Powell and Cohen are consistent, but I wonder whether we don't have to develop some new doctrine to protect education from majorities. My own mind has been getting steadily antidemocratic: the size of the electorate, the impossibility of educating it sufficiently, the fierce ignorance of these millions of semiliterate priest-ridden and parson-ridden people have got me to the point where I want to confine the actions of majorities. Down here on the edge of the South, the danger is more evident than in New York, where Heaven knows the Hylan business[68] is enough to make anybody question the old democratic dogma. At any rate we have to fight this Tennessee business somehow. What do you think?

I have another favor to ask of you. My book *The Phantom Public* is to be published in the fall.[69] It is now being set in type, and I had planned to send you a proof. You will have sailed before you can read it. I want to dedicate the book to you, and I am embarrassed because I feel you ought to have a chance to say no, and I am afraid you won't say no whatever your feeling about it. I'm quite prepared to believe you will think it crude and even unsound, because I have taken a flyer into a rather strange field of theory. Please be frank enough to say just what you would like best.

Yours, W.L.

tp with signature 106.16

To Walter Lippmann

June 10, 1925

Dear Walter:

[...]No, I think you are wrong about [the] *Tennessee* [case]. I have found no competent person who differs from Cohen and Powell. What I said about the *Oregon School* case

65. Probably some time early in June.
66. I.e., Scopes v. State. *See* 1925-2 To Lippmann, June 7.
67. Thomas Reed Powell (1880-1955): Professor, Harvard Law School.
68. Lippmann refers to the activities of John Francis Hylan, Mayor of New York.
69. THE PHANTOM PUBLIC (1925).

indicates my attitude. Left to myself, I should have swallowed even that, *a fortiori* this. Somebody must determine the curriculum. Who shall it be? The judges? Well, if so, only when the preponderance is overwhelming. It's a case in the end of protecting their independence, and nobody knows how important that is who has not served in the job. If they are to act at all in such matters, as to which I have some doubt, it must be only in the extremist cases.

We are in for democracy, and while I am as shaken as you, I ask for any available substitute. These are the conditions: a principle of continuity—that rules out dictators; enough power to insure stability—that in modern times means the acquiescence of great masses of the people; some assurance that intelligence in this conduct of government will not cost too much in selfishness and exploitation—that on the whole seems to me to forbid an oligarchy, though as to that I am open to conviction. On the whole, the principle of counting heads apparently insures the first and second, at least the first. If I could get far enough away, I might be more doubtful about the third, but at close range, I am disposed to guess that even the modern technique of suggestion will not allow such absolute exploitation as uncontrolled forever. Ignorance may yet overwhelm us, but I am laying my odds against it. We are still too close to the Great Spasm. I have yet to see any satisfactory substitute.

It is a little curious that you should have any doubts about my pleasure—that is really not the word—at your wanting to dedicate to me any book you wrote. It has given me a satisfaction greater than anything else I have learned for a long time. I don't need to read the proofs; I know you, and what you have said, even if I don't go along with it *pari passu*, will so nearly accord with what I think, at least after I have read it, that there is no chance taken. Besides, I don't suppose that one assumes a foot-to-foot concurrence in such matters. Now that you have suggested it, I can only say that it would be a grave disappointment to me if I didn't get what seems to me one of the greatest honors I have had.

Amen, L.H.

ms with signature, Lippmann Papers, Sterling, Box 12, Folder 499.

1926-1

To Learned Hand from Felix Frankfurter

April 6, 1926 Law School of Harvard University

Dear B.:

I have now had a chance to read Holmes's opinions, both in your patent case[70] and in the *Chile Copper* [case].[71] I am, of course, not competent to have an opinion in the patent

---

70. *Alexander Milburn Co. v. Davis-Bournonville Co.*, 270 U.S. 390 (1926), involved the question of identifying the prior inventor in a patent infringement suit. Frankfurter's identification of "your patent case" refers to LH's opinion in the original matter, *Davis-Bournonville Co. v. Alexander Milburn Co.*, 297 F. 846 (S.D.N.Y. 1924), which was affirmed by the Court of Appeals, 1 F.2d 227 (2d Cir. 1924), and then reversed by the Supreme Court.

71. *Edwards v. Chile Copper Co.*, 270 U.S. 452 (1926), involved how "doing business" is defined for purposes of determining taxes owed. For the district court, LH found that a corporation organized to

matter, but certainly the power and acuteness of Holmes in an unfamiliar field are amazing. As to *Chile Copper*, I'm arrogant enough to find myself in easy agreement with Holmes. In fact, I was surprised that you should have held otherwise. In this opinion, too, I thought Holmes showed evidence of a really fresh mental start. Pound tells me that you read a very fine paper indeed at the Yale Law Journal dinner.

Always yours, F.F.

tp with ms signature 104B.13

To Felix Frankfurter

April 7, 1926

My dear Felix:

[...]When the Supreme Court reverses me and especially when Holmes writes the opinion, I should be disposed always to cry "Peccavi." Even in a patent case, in a talk I had with him, he greatly jarred a very settled opinion of mine on which I had spent a good deal of thought. Of course, I do not assume to pit my judgment ever against his, though frankly he did not satisfy me. I think you were a little hard on me in the *Chile Copper* case. I had to pick my way as best I could between decisions which were obscure and left me very little guidance. I had no power to treat the case as I might have if it was *tabula rasa*. I should have to pick up too much now of the authorities I went over and the case at large to know how I should have decided in that case, but I remember at the time feeling very confident that I was right as the matter then stood. The whole thing is extremely artificial, and each case comes up to the Supreme Court with a free opportunity to do what they like. As I view it, Holmes treats a case substantially anew, and he by no means is as trammeled by what his court has said before as I was. I can make very little of the distinctions which seem to govern the Nine Elder Statesmen in their treatment of tax cases. Frankly, they seem to me given to all sorts of meaningless casuistry. I expect to have them disregard what they have said before, but it hardly seems proper for me to assume that they will do so. The result, of course, is often disappointing, but again I say, don't be hard on me for not coming to the result which you think I ought to have reached on principle. Like most other reversals,

---

finance another corporation's activities (as was the Chile Copper Co., a holding company for the Chile Exploration Co.) was not "doing business" because the activity of the defendant was not profitable on its own account. Chile Copper Co. v. Edwards, 294 F. 581 (S.D.N.Y. 1923). Following Holmes's lead in a previous Supreme Court case, *United States v. Emery-Bird-Thayer Realty Co.*, 237 U.S. 28 (1915), LH noted that the court must look to what a business is actually doing, not what it can possibly do under its corporate charter. LH's decision was affirmed by the Court of Appeals (Edwards v. Chile Copper Co., 5 F.2d 1014 (2d Cir. 1925)), but was reversed by the Supreme Court, which distinguished the matter from *Emery-Bird-Thayer Realty* and held, in an opinion by Holmes, that when a single business cannot be conducted without two corporations taking part, each must pay a tax. In a letter to Holmes dated April 7, Frankfurter remarked on the *Chile Copper* case: "I do think Learned Hand this time clearly went off the track and you showed him the true path in an unforgettable manner." Holmes and Frankfurter, Their Correspondence, 1912–1934, at 200 (Robert M. Mennel & Christine L. Compston eds., 1996).

when they come down I have lost too much of what I knew or thought I knew at the time to be in a position either to acknowledge my fault or to remain obstinate. I have left only the vague impression I had at the time of whether the case seemed clear or not. In this case, as I have told you, I did feel very clear. I daresay you know the old cases, and if you think that they did not bear me out, I shall have no excuse. If you do not, I reserve the possibility that had you been in my place you might have thought as I.

Need I say that your judgment on this or any other case is of great consequence to me? I wish I had a little more robust confidence in my own judgment. It has been a little disconcerting, I confess, to get two cracks in the eye in succession from my beloved *maitre*, but as he himself so fond of saying, life is nothing but a bet on your own guesses, and one must be content if one's batting average does not put one too far down.

As ever yours, [L.H.]

tp 104B.13

To Learned Hand from Felix Frankfurter

April 8, 1926 Law School of Harvard University

Dear B.:

Someone ought to take me out to an empty lot and give me a good whipping for writing to you as carelessly as I did the other day. For I should never have aroused in you—all too little conscious of your powers and the truly distinguished quality of your judicial output—the sense of personal dissatisfaction simply because I felt decisively in agreement with Holmes rather than with you in the *Chile Copper* case. Of course, I should not have sounded as dogmatically as I did, for I know enough to know what a quicksand the Supreme Court decisions in taxation cases furnish for the lower courts. That ultimate authority, the *Harvard Law Review*, as you probably noted at the time, sided with you (38 *Harvard Law Review* 113). I do think, however, the case illustrates a talk that you and I had many, many years ago about your attitude towards the language of Supreme Court opinions where the decisions are not absolutely controlling. I remember urging bumptiously against your humility that you are too deferential to both the language and logical implications of past decisions in threading your own way through the mazes of Supreme Court language, in that you try to forecast what they would do were they to feel themselves bound by their past talk, rather than to try to enlighten them by your independent thinking, where the issue is not foreclosed. I suppose I feel that rather strongly, partly because I value your thinking so much more than I do that of all but two of the members of the Supreme Court, and partly because I know that for them the law, in these public issues, is sufficiently fluid to be influenced by the direction which your thinking can give it.

Of course, the case which preceded the *Chile Copper* case warranted the conclusion which you spelled therefrom. What I meant to say, however, and what I do feel, is that Holmes's result is so much more sense than their casuistic logic in the past called for. Also, I wonder if I misconceive the judicial function in wanting you to put up to them the impulses of your reason, rather than to be mastered by what you conceive to be deference to the implications of their past performances. Of course, I am opening up a wide issue and perhaps an abstract one, because in each particular instance the ingredients that make the final concoction will be differently proportioned. But pace Holmes, general principles do decide concrete cases, provided you feel strongly enough about the general principles, and I have a notion—I may be wholly wrong—that you are unduly influenced by a desire to forecast what the Nine will decide in the light of their prior pronouncements. You attribute to them, I think, a greater regard for general ideas than their decisions justify.

Always devotedly yours, F.F.

tp with ms signature 104B.13

To Felix Frankfurter

April 14, 1926

Dear Felix:

Don't trouble about my sadness. I was really playing the baby act, I think. Forget it. The really interesting question is the one which you suggest in your letter, as to how far a judge of a lower court should try to spell out his conduct from the declarations of the higher court, over which I have puzzled a good deal. In theory, one ought to treat the opinions as controlling, and I certainly should do so if the Supreme Court did not so often make it impossible for me to know what they meant, and also make it so clear that they were not bound by what they had said. We are having just such an instance at present in relation to the Sherman Act, on the whole the blindest and most discreditable line of decisions, it seems to me, that they have ever given.[72] Perhaps the bold and proper way is to spell out the principles as you think them applicable and disregard the form in which they have been cast by the upper court. I do not know that particular reserve or timidity prevents me from doing that more often than I do. I suppose it may be the old tradition of our law by which we stepped from hummock to hummock without laying any clear path through the morass. The English judges were certainly loyal to their earlier declarations, but the system has really broken down by its own proliferation, and it is impossible any longer to take quite seriously what is said. Indeed, since I have been on an appellate court and have realized how little the members who do not write can control in practice the utterances of the man who is charged with the opinion, the whole assumption becomes more and more distasteful to me that the declaration of the court is the authority. I can only tell you that I will try to be free in my treatment of such matters, and yet, when all is

72. On the Sherman Antitrust Act, 1890, see 1911-4 To Roosevelt, November 15. Its application and the question of whether there were "good" trusts and "bad" trusts were ongoing causes of concern. LH may have been referring to two recent cases invoking provisions of the Sherman Act, *United Mine Workers v. Coronado Coal Co.*, 259 U.S. 344 (1922), and *Coronado Coal Co. v. United Mine Workers*, 268 U.S. 295 (1925).

said, and to come back to this very question of the interstate commerce clause,[73] unless I take them at their last word, they seem to me to have left the whole thing in such a jumble as cannot be cleared up by any present attempt to simplify and reduce it to its essential outlines. So you see, this is rather inconclusive letter. But in general, I will try to be good.

As ever, yours, [L.H.]

tp 104B.13

1926-2

In 1919, the left wing newsletter the REVOLUTIONARY AGE *published* the LEFT WING MANIFESTO. *In 1922, Benjamin Gitlow, the newsletter's business manager, was convicted of violating the New York Criminal Anarchy Law of 1902, and in 1925 the Supreme Court upheld Gitlow's conviction, finding that a state may forbid speech if its "tendency and probable effect was to bring about the substantive evil which the legislative body might prevent." Holmes and Brandeis dissented, noting that the "clear and present danger" test of Schenck—not a "tendency" test derived from Schenck—should apply.*

To Learned Hand from Charles Merrill Hough

July 8, 1926 — 2 Clement Road, Hanover, New Hampshire

Dear B.:

Holmes does cheer my soul every now and then by holding that darling infant of most judges—the injured laborer—to some standard of duty[...] I sometimes think that is some remnant of the soldier in him. But I cannot reconcile that view or his conduct in negligence cases with his (to me) conscienceless and easygoing sufferance of "imperial jaw" from every kind of social vermin. His dissent in the *Gitlow* case[74]—standing alone—could lead one to think him either daft or an enemy of his race and country—yet he isn't[...]

Thine, C.M.H.

ms with signature 54.34

---

73. The Commerce Clause of the U.S. Constitution states: "The Congress shall have power [...] to regulate commerce [...] among the several states." U.S. CONST. art I, § 8, cl. 3.

74. In *Gitlow v. New York*, 268 U.S. 652 (1925), countering the majority opinion, Holmes famously noted: "Every idea is an incitement" *Id.* at 673. For *Schenck*, see 1919-2 To Holmes, April 1, note 146. For Holmes on *Gitlow*, see THE COLLECTED WORKS OF JUSTICE HOLMES 92–94 (Sheldon M. Novick ed., 1995).

To Charles Merrill Hough

July 9, 1926

Dear Boss:

[...]I cannot see what your trouble is with Holmes. It seems to me that except for something of the sort that he suggests, the whole doctrine of free speech goes by the board. I had rather lose any right but that of the right to talk. I think it is in the end the most important—as it is probably the most dangerous—of all rights. I should join in that dissent. While I cannot share his hopes that his views will ever become law, I am all for keeping the flag flying, whether you would describe it as "red," or as I should describe it as "stars and stripes." Whatever they may be, certainly his views are not "conscienceless," nor are they "easy going." They proceed in his case, as he says, from a very deep conviction, a conviction about the relations of men to one another, which, whether they be right or wrong, practical or impractical, go as deep as any can into the very meaning of morality. They are not "easy going," at least not for the people who profess them. They become important only at a time when most men are greatly excited and intolerant, when they are quite as likely to turn upon those who wish to be tolerant as upon those who actively oppose them, perhaps more so[...]

Thine, [L.H.]

tp 54.34

1926-3

To Simon Flexner[75]

December 15, 1926

Dear Simon:

I was interested in the clipping that you sent me of [Robert] Millikan,[76] which I think you will agree bears out what I tried very imperfectly to say the other night. Does it not suggest that we may ultimately come to the idea that what we understand by external reality is, after all, no more than the extremely elaborate patterns which we can impose upon the phenomenal world? At first blush, one feels a certain sense of unreality in so eliminating what we have been accustomed to think of as external, but a pattern is an intellectual concept, and we are accustomed enough to think of the rules, for example, of geometry or

75. Simon Flexner (1863–1946): Director of the laboratories of the Rockefeller Institute for Medical Research in New York, and later one of the charter members of the Rockefeller Foundation. *See Simon Flexner, in* THE SPIRIT OF LIBERTY 195–200.

76. Robert Millikan (1868–1953): Professor of Physics, University of Chicago; President of the California Institute of Technology, 1921–1945. The clipping to which LH refers is not identified.

of logic, as being more external and enduring, if possible, than any other form of existence. Why should it rob the external world of its externality if we say that it resides in patterns which we may eventually succeed in showing to be the form of occurrence of phenomena? Indeed, must it not rather lie in such existence than in any sensations themselves?

If, as we seem to find, there are no enduring sensuous data, but, as we attempt to account for the flux of the world, we are driven more and more into formula, why should we withstand the conclusion that these formulae, and these only, make up our concept of externality? At any rate, that has for some time been the general conclusion towards which I tend, and I think it is not without its competent supporters.[77]

It was delightful seeing you and Helen the other night. I hope we will see you soon again.

Faithfully yours, [L.H.]

tp 52.36

1927-1

In 1920, Nicola Sacco and Bartolomeo Vanzetti were tried for attempted robbery and attempted murder in connection with a robbery and double homicide in South Braintree, Massachusetts; they were tried and convicted of murder in 1921 and sentenced to death. Their association with known Italian and Italian-American anarchists was seized upon by the prosecution during their murder trial, and many—including Frankfurter—believed that errors during the trial, including the focus on the defendants' political beliefs, warranted a retrial. Despite public outcry, international protests, the discovery of new evidence (including a confession by another man), and compelling examples of error by the presiding judge, Webster Thayer, the Supreme Judicial Court of Massachusetts upheld the conviction and denied requests for review and a new trial. Several attempts to secure a stay of execution from members of the United States Supreme Court were also unsuccessful: Justice Holmes authored a formal denial on August 19, 1927, noting that another Justice might be approached to grant a stay, but he would not; Brandeis declined to act because of personal relations to some of the people who had been interested in the case (including that he had allowed Sacco's wife, Rosina, to use his home in Dedham, Massachusetts, during the trial); Justice Stone and Chief Justice Taft, both on summer vacations, also refused to intervene. Sacco and Vanzetti were executed on August 23, 1927. LH responds to Frankfurter's article on the case, just published in the Atlantic Monthly.

77. LH speculates in the same vein a year later: "Even this obdurate and recalcitrant world is perhaps in the end no more than a complicated series of formulae which we impose upon the flux. If so, we are throughout its builders." *The Preservation of Personality, in* The Spirit of Liberty 44.

To Felix Frankfurter

March 10, 1927

Dear Felix:

I got today "The Case of Sacco and Vanzetti."[78] I hope when the occasion offers that I shall be able to read this. I know how much time you have spent on it and how much interest it has aroused. I find myself unconsciously tending more strongly than I wish I did toward the position of my order. Maybe it is because I know how much goes through that does not go through well. From all I can hear of the people who have most examined it, they agree with you in substance, that is, that these men did not have a fair trial. No doubt that ought to send it some way or another. The first interest of course is that justice shall be fair.

I believe that when I come to read this I shall be able to overcome any prejudice with which I may instinctively approach it.

Faithfully yours, [L.H]

tp 104B.14

To Learned Hand from Felix Frankfurter

April 8, 1927 Law School of Harvard University

Dear B.:

[...]I wonder if you know [Samuel Eliot] Morison, the Harvard historian (who was recently designated to write Harvard's history for the tercentenary in 1936) and was the first holder of the Harmsworth Chair at Oxford? I enclose a letter which he has just written to the *Boston Herald*, not because I want to add burdens to the work which I know is now pressing upon you, but merely to let you know how the very best mind and spirit of New England feels about the Sacco-Vanzetti business when not in the grip of bogies and fears about the onrush [of] Bolshevism into State Street.

Yours always, F.F

tp with ms signature 104B.14

To Felix Frankfurter

April 9, 1927

Dear Felix:

[...]I read your clipping about Sacco-Vanzetti with interest. To get a judgment upon this whole matter involves more inquiry than I have had any opportunity to make.

---

78. Felix Frankfurter, *The Case of Sacco and Vanzetti*, 139 Atlantic Monthly, March 1927, at 409–32. For Frankfurter's full argument, see The Case of Sacco and Vanzetti: A Critical Analysis for Lawyers and Laymen (1927). For the original decision, see *Commonwealth v. Sacco & Vanzetti*, 151 N.E. 839 (Mass. 1926).

Whether there ought to be a more adequate review of the motion for a new trial seems to be the immediate question. Perhaps there should in capital cases, but I hardly think so in others. My general impression from observation is that the eternal succession of applications for re-arguments, new trials, pardons and the like in the end promotes injustice rather than justice, if we mean at all what we say about our criminal law. I am in doubt whether at the present time, the temper of most communities being what it is, it is desirable to execute men at all. That is a large question.

Faithfully yours, [L.H.]

tp 104B.14

1927-2

To Walter Lippmann

September 7, 1927 Windsor, Vermont

Dear Walter,

I have owed you a letter for a long time, owed, that is, not in the ordinary sense, but because our friendship should not have allowed my silence for so long. Your father's death did not leave on my mind the impression that such an event, affecting you, would ordinarily have done. We consign those who have for a long time been hopelessly sick to our forgetfulness, perhaps just because it is the way of least pain to ourselves. When finally that which we have expected arrives, we feel that is not after all so bad, since it has become for so long a part of our world. Anyway, this is the only way that I can account for what may have seemed to you unfriendly indifference. I had attributed to you that acceptance which had established itself in my own mind unconsciously. I forgot what might have been the meaning to you of that final termination of the companionship about which your early feelings and thoughts must have so largely centered. My own mother lived to be over eighty, but for the last few years her life had been mere misery. I had looked forward to her death with unfeigned relief. Yet when she died, I felt a break which did not seem possible, and which before I should have thought irrational. So it may have been with you, and I should have considered it. Forgive me.

When your book came, which I galloped through at once, I remembered my neglect.[79] I enjoyed the book much, though I don't get from your occasional writing anything like that I do from your books proper. Why should I? It would be a sad comment on them if I did. These pieces are very effective bits of political polemic. They go much farther than that. Dear old Norman [Hapgood] can do much ineffective polemic. You never touch a subject without putting it in a new light, as Phil [Littell] very justly observed the other day. Nobody can read these and not be stimulated to some thinking of his own. Can you ask any more? [. . .]Still, because I believe that there is nobody, at least nobody I know, who is

79. Walter Lippmann, Men of Destiny (1927).

better fitted to read the meaning of Democracy right, I don't want to have you give too much of your time to this kind of writing, even though you seem to be able to turn it off with speed. We have talked this over before; you know that I think the continuation of your present life useful, but I should be sorry if the other were in any way prejudiced.

I have had a sad time of it up here about Sacco and Vanzetti. There is no exception to the ranks of the revisionists; all are convinced that justice went sadly wrong. I have not seen Phil so much moved since I can remember; it was good to find something which made him blaze into violence, or near it, even when one became oneself the victim, innocently, so far as one could see. I saw Felix at the Hanover Conference, but with a forbearance for which I felt very grateful, he did not even touch on the subject. I did have to sit at the table he got started, and it was to me exquisitely painful. Need I say as much to you? That he knew the case in its least details was of course true, but while that made it impossible to dispute with him, his conclusions at least to me were without weight, because it was so apparent that no more light could then come into his mind and that passion had seized all. What I needed was someone who could give me conclusions that I could accept. Plainly he was in no condition to do that. So far as in the swirling murk I can see at all, the men did not get a fair trial. Further, I doubt whether there was evidence to convict them. The foreign press has been extremely irresponsible, in my judgment, and would not have been so if the occasion had not been so apt to vent their hatred of all things American. To compare this to the Dreyfus case[80] seems to me wholly unwarranted, so much so that I can find small patience with it.

I was especially interested in your treatment of the case after the Lowell report.[81] Everybody up here was with you on that except Felix to whom it was monstrous, because even hypothetically it assumed that the report could be treated as emanating from human beings at all. At first, I too grasped at it as a way out, but later I became skeptical. The possible objection is so obvious that it is not necessary to state it. These men had come to be persons of great power in the community. Deviation in their instance would have been because they had in one way or another been able to set in motion great forces of opinion. When is it best avowedly to yield to such influence? That seems to me, a priori, to be unanswerable. I really never made up my mind about it in this case, but I incline to take your view. That is something of a concession from a judge. You can hardly realize how we cling for our own protection to our rigid impartiality. Without that, we know that our position would become at once untenable. Really the same considerations apply almost as strongly to a governor. That there may be occasions where he may yield that would not be available to a court is what I hold out to myself as a possible distinction, but I am very doubtful if he is himself clear. I should be willing to go to the extreme if a court were

80. Captain Alfred Dreyfus, a French Jew, was wrongfully convicted of treason in 1894. He was pardoned in 1899 and finally cleared of guilt in 1906.

81. Governor Alvan T. Fuller of Massachusetts appointed a board to review the *Sacco-Vanzetti* case headed by A. Lawrence Lowell, president of Harvard University. The board confirmed the jury's verdict of guilty and refused to recommend a new trial. Lippmann's editorial argued that the governor should commute the sentence to life imprisonment, New York World, Aug. 8, 1927. In a subsequent editorial published on August 12, Lippmann argued that because the testimony before the board was not public, a new trial was called for. *See* Ronald Steel, Walter Lippmann and the American Century 229 (1980).

concerned, and I dare say that you would also. One thing the whole thing has served to emphasize: we can expect no quarter from Europe. I wish I could impress upon this people how they were detested by the majority of mankind, and how eagerly they would unite, if the cost was not too great, to crush us. Our complacency terrifies me, just as their hatred makes me unwilling to go to Europe—I mean loath to go. Especially I feel this as regards the English, who have their blissful faculty of making one feel the Scythian manners and Scythian mores with which one is branded. These are stigmata that stick out all over one and ought to, if one has an ounce of guts. But I don't delight in stigmata of any kind. I can get the sense of what it feels to one of the oppressed race, with all its dangers to one's mental symmetry. I confess to a considerable Anglophobia just now.

As ever, L.H.

tp with ms signature and notes, Lippmann Papers, Sterling, Box 12, Folder 499

To Learned Hand from Walter Lippmann

September 11, 1927 Wading River, New York

Dear B.:

I'd have written to you long ago, but I have been writing so much this summer that I have almost had a revulsion against using a pen. All through July and August I worked nights and mornings on my book, and in the afternoons wrote at the office or at least edited the page. I am approaching the end of the book, not in final form for publication by any means, but at least in a form where I think the argument and the sequences hold together. I shall finish, I think, before we come back to town the last week in September. I shall feel as if I had been freed; having an unwritten book on one's mind is a form of tyranny which never lets me alone. I really don't enjoy anything or really want to do anything until it's done. Sometimes I think it must be a kind of compulsion neurosis.

That is the only reason I haven't written, for I have thought of you a great deal and missed you more than I can say. There is no one else with whom I am so much at home. All through the Sacco-Vanzetti horror I had you in mind especially, for there was no one who wasn't passionately prejudiced. I have not been so troubled about anything since 1919, when against what I really believe was my own deepest and best feeling I let irritation against Wilson's stupidity push me into intransigent opposition to the Treaty. The *Sacco* case was peculiarly difficult because I had so confidently assumed that the Lowell report would in no event mean the death penalty. The briefness of the time allowed for reaching an opinion, the atmosphere of horror and the very real danger of red violence followed by white violence, made me feel as if we were being rushed into the gravest kind of decision without freedom of mind to consider it. You know that I was never convinced that they were innocent. At the end, my feeling was (a) that Sacco might be guilty and Vanzetti less probably, (b) that the evidence against both was insufficient, (c) that the trial was almost certainly conducted in a prejudiced atmosphere, (d) that the governor, though probably sincere within his lights, was infected with the psychology of the class conflict which the case had provoked, (e) that a commutation was the wiser course even though one could sympathize with the governor's difficulty in yielding after the threats had been made. The event has shown that stability of this society is beyond anything we had imagined, for it was subjected to a strain which I thought ominous. One of the real lessons of the affair, if our conservative classes had insight, is that they are so strongly entrenched they could abandon their panicky state of mind and rule the country with some flexibility and ease. They sit upon the rock of Gibraltar and behave as if they were upon a raft at sea.

It is this timid forcefulness in our rulers which is most alarming. It is mixed with complacency as you say, but this complacency has more fear in it than confidence, I think. We don't feel sure enough of ourselves to admit that we are ever wrong, and so our instinct is to insist upon whatever it is that we think we want by main force and awkwardness. We are too powerful for our wisdom, and often I think we use our power to save ourselves the humiliation of trying to be wiser.

You completely understood my feelings about my father's death. I couldn't wish him to live more of the contracted and miserable existence which remained to him. When I received word of his death, I was relieved. And then suddenly, it seemed I forgot what he had been for two years and remembered him clearly as he once was. He was a very kind man with a kind of sweet humility and an unfailing good humor. He had so far as I knew no ambitions and no anxieties of any kind for himself, even when he knew that he was hopelessly ill. We were never very intimate, but affectionately friendly; he always let me do whatever I wanted to do even when he did not understand it, because he trusted me very much. When something I did got the obvious sort of recognition, he felt justified and was happy about it in a way which I had to pretend often to share.

I am looking forward to seeing you in October. You know we are going to live in 63rd street between Lexington and Third. Faye sends her best with mine to Frances Hand and you.

As ever, Walter

tp with ms signature 106.16

To Walter Lippmann

September 20, 1927 Windsor, Vermont

Dear Walter,

Your letter said a good many things that I wish I could have put as you did before you did it. I am not sure that you are not exactly right about Sacco-Vanzetti, and I wish that I could have come to a more certain conclusion with myself. I was aware at the time that I was really floundering about a good deal, but it was in the end, so far as I could see, because of the impalpable elements of the situation. I confess that when anyone asks me when we should make an exception in the ordinary course of judicial process, I can't give the answer. Yet that is exactly where the test of true statecraft comes in. It is just that that a real political leader must know. Perhaps the most important element that should determine his decision is the extent to which the opinion which counts with him will be outraged. If so, then we were all wrong *pro tanto* who supposed that this country was worked up over the case enough to make it a serious blunder to let things go on. What was really important, and all that was really important, was the effect upon foreign opinion. Now to say that—assuming the authorities were convinced that the trial was fair and that the men were guilty—still they should have made an exception, not because their own people were to be outraged, but because the world outside would be, seems to me a very doubtful proposal.

On the whole, I am persuaded that the only tenable attack on the case must have been confined to the merits of the conviction, taking all the proceedings as a whole. Probably the men were not fairly convicted, and the case remains a miscarriage of justice. There are so many such that we unfortunately cannot feel it as exceptional as we should like. Most of them are the other way; they result in the acquittal of the guilty, a thing we have got so used to that we do not turn a hair. I think that something could be said to show that a nation which has habituated itself to look with composure upon that kind of miscarriage must be prepared for miscarriages which work the other way with far most shocking results. I doubt if you can be sure that your inefficiency will always work for mercy. The disposition to be content with the introduction of passion of any kind into judicial procedure will not stop when it operates to release offenders. It will have its say equally when a victim is required. Nobody can know anything about the business and doubt that Taft was right in his extreme statement when he was in private life.[82] The administration of our criminal law is a disgrace to any civilized country, and this case is only an instance of how it can work against the individual, contrary to its usual course.

I despair of any relief because I am so thoroughly convinced that it is primarily due to the quality of the judge that reforms of procedure interest me not very acutely. How we shall advance much by putting a plastic, intelligible procedure into the hands of the boobs who will administer it as things are I have never been able to understand. If solemnly disposed, I should say that the administration of justice was a function of the general political level of the community, and that it was a matter of minor importance how it was formally organized. True, you could not do much with a bench of Marshalls under the procedure in some of the States, but it does not follow from that that you can do anything better with the most enlightened system when you turn it over to the cattle who apparently are going to use it as things are.

This whole thing seems now to be drifting into the realm of forgotten things. Such is our general apathy that I don't believe that even if they were to assassinate [Webster] Thayer[83] or [A. Lawrence] Lowell, as is still quite within the possibilities, it would provoke a very extravagant reaction. People are so under the magic of this unbelievable though actual prosperity that nothing which does not disturb that will disturb them. Incidentally, Al Smith has about as much chance of being elected as I have, unless we can get up a stump within the year. The outrage of our existence in the minds of Europeans is natural, but they are unreasonable nevertheless. They would manifest exactly the same responses

82. After Taft left the White House and before becoming Chief Justice, he continued his crusade for judicial reform in speeches and law review articles as Kent Professor of Law at Yale, 1913–1921.

83. Webster Thayer (1857–1933): Judge of the Superior Court of Massachusetts, 1917–1933, who tried Sacco and Vanzetti. Judge Thayer's life was frequently threatened following the Sacco and Vanzetti trial.

to the same situation. People want to be rich and comfortable, and are quite contented so long as they are. All of us reformers and betterers in general had best accept that with as good grace as we can. It ought not to be such a surprise to moralists who are never tired of telling us that we reach holiness only though our tribulations. Good, let us start up the tribulation factory; only I prefer to have you begin it, and when you have got it well going, I will come in and lend a hand.

Jesus, how I type! L.H.

tp with ms signature and notes, Lippmann Papers, Sterling, Box 499, Folder 12

1927-3

To Felix Frankfurter

December 16, 1927

Dear Felix:

You would be right in having me on the supposed court that you suggest to Walter [Lippmann]. I am too old a dog now to write down to "lawlessness and hysteria" almost any view that intelligent people in fact do hold. On the other hand, I think Walter was in substance right in saying that the momentum back of the Smith-Vare exclusion[84] was lawless, and came from an aspect of progressive political opinion in this country which seems to me to be its most sinister side. The fact that only twenty-three or twenty-five senators could be brought to vote in favor of Smith and Vare satisfies me at any rate that they had been terrorized, and that by a public opinion which was far too impatient to pay any attention to the real issues at stake.

I am not historian enough to say what the constitutional clause meant in 1787[85] or what the practice in Britain was in the preceding centuries, nor do I know what the precedents have been under our constitution or the state constitution. My views are therefore naive, but for all that they are very positive and based on what people used to call "the philosophy" of the situation. It seems to me intolerable, even if precedents permitted, that any representative body should have the power to exclude its own members because it thinks them unfit. [William] Borah's doctrine is a wedge for Pride's Purge or the exclusion of Socialists from the New York Legislature in 1920. [86] I do not see how any minority

84. In November 1927, the Senate ruled that the elections of William S. Vare of Pennsylvania and Frank L. Smith of Illinois were fraudulent because of the campaign expenditures made in their behalf. Denying them seats, the Senate disqualified them from serving. *See Fail to Fix Course on Vare and Smith*, N.Y. TIMES, Dec. 3, 1927.

85. The Constitution gave the power to each house to "judge [the] Qualifications of its own members." GERALD GUNTHER, LEARNED HAND: THE MAN AND THE JUDGE 396 (1994).

86. William Borah (1865–1940): Senator from Idaho. Pride's Purge: in December 1648, troops under the command of Colonel Thomas Pride forcibly removed from the House of Commons all those who were not supporters of the New Model Army and the Independents. On LH's view of the exclusion of Socialists elected to the New York legislature, see 1920-1 To Wallas, January 17.

is safe if he is right. You speak of compromise positions. Perhaps there are some, and if I had followed the discussion better I might know what they were. As I think you know, I am never in love with absolutes—though in this case I confess to a strong disposition towards one—and there may be some that I should think safe. Still, I must own that I am very skeptical and doubt whether I should ever be content with any doctrine which recognized the right of either house to do more than pass upon whether their members had been honestly elected and had the constitutional qualifications. I could never see why liberals take the other side; it had always seemed to me that they are just the people most likely to suffer[...]

Faithfully yours, [Learned Hand]

tp 104B.15

To Learned Hand from Felix Frankfurter

December 20, 1927 — Law School of Harvard University

Dear B.:

I daresay I am too far removed from the current of political opinion for a practical judgment, but I must say I am surprised that you should find at present a "lawless" momentum back of the Smith-Vare exclusion from a public opinion that is "too impatient" of anything except to cut off the heads of Vare and Smith. If you had said that *tempore* Roosevelt I could understand it, but for myself I see nothing but subservience to money these days in every shift of society and in the public press[...]

So when it comes to the power of the Senate over its membership, there is an historical setting to the constitutional clause; there are precedents and practice under it which, as a judge I think you would agree, entitle Senators like Borah and [Thomas J.] Walsh[87] to be treated as both conscientious and respectful of decency and right, and not merely as the instruments of "lawlessness and hysteria." Of course, such a doctrine lends itself to abuse; of course, it lends itself to the exclusion of despised minorities. We are back at the old issue of the denial of power because of the potentiality of its abuse[...]

The "compromise" I have in mind is a denial of the suggestion that the alternatives are either the specifically enumerated qualifications of the constitution or absolutism. The Senate of the United States must pass on the "qualifications" of its members, and that means judgment according to standards relevant to service in the Senate. I am aware that this a loose standard, but I think far less loose than the standards you must apply whenever you have a case under the Due Process Clause.

Faithfully yours, F.F.

tp with ms signature 104B.14

---

87. Thomas J. Walsh (1859–1935): Senator from Montana, 1913–1933.

To Felix Frankfurter

January 12, 1928

Dear Felix:

[...]You don't convince me. One can have all sorts of legislative devices one likes, and among these is one in which a representative assembly has the power to purge itself of those of whose moral qualifications it disapproves. The Constitution does not necessarily foreclose your interpretation, I dare say; at least, the precedents appear to allow it. What light Madison's journal or other contemporaneous documents throw I don't know. To me, the absolute right of each constituency to select the man it wants seems of greater importance than cooptation, even though only negative, among the members. It is an easy cover for faction, and so far as we have got, I have no confidence in the impartiality with which it would be exercised in times of stress. The unconditional right of each constituency to express itself by the man of its choice is closely akin to its right of self-government; we should accept the possibilities of its abuse, at least as against such correctives as are open. Such anyway is my very firm opinion. In some things I would be an absolutist, though not for absolutist reasons[...] Adios. My love to Marion [...]

[L.H.]

tp 104B.15

1928-1

To Felix Frankfurter

January 28, 1928 — Charleston, South Carolina

Dear Felix:

[...]I have had a chance to read nearly all of *The business of the Supreme Court*[88] and it has interested me more than I should have supposed possible. What an amazing mine of information it is! How extraordinary that anyone can find the opportunity for such detailed and thorough work! I regard it ruefully and reverently, as I did that work that you put out on the constitutionality of trying petty cases without a jury—really a definitive settlement of that question, in my judgment.[89] These are the kinds of work that enable us

---

88. Felix Frankfurter with James M. Landis, The Business of the Supreme Court; A Study in the Federal Judicial System (1927).

89. During Prohibition, the cost of federal jury trials for petty crimes in violation of the Volstead Act raised significant concern in Congress. One cost savings proposal called for the abolition of jury trials in such cases, which would be tried in (to-be-established) federal police courts, yielding a savings for New York state cases alone of approximately $50 million. In 1926, at the request of U.S. Attorney Emory Bruckner, Felix Frankfurter authored a memorandum addressing the constitutionality of conducting such trials. *See* Felix Frankfurter & Thomas G. Corcoran, *Petty Federal Offenses and the Constitutional Guaranty of Trial by Jury*, 39 Harv. L. Rev. 917 (1926).

to know what we are talking about. Generally we don't. I keep wondering, however, at the curious result of so much scholarship upon a subject matter which the actors knew as little or nearly as little about as we do when they produced it. To me, that is the constant antimony [sic] of legal history. You have got to have the Platonic approach of [Joseph] Beale[90] to relieve you of the sense that somewhere you are dealing with nonsense. You must believe in a superintending and directing norm that makes for unity and progressively reveals the *Geist*, in order to avoid the question, *cui bono*. Personally, I think Beale is one illegitimate son of St. Thomas Aquinas, his seed being miraculously preserved and in some Sacred Way entering the body of Beale's putative *père*. In short I think that his views are The Bunk on all such stuff. But maybe such work as this does enable us to understand the way things happen, even when they happen without real direction. Anyway, it is a most interesting matter and has amused me. I do wish I had had the chance to review it when it came out. They asked me to, but then it was impossible[...] I wish those who complain of *Sacco & Vanzetti* could be forced to see how dispassionate you can be when you are engaged in real research, and are not trying to accomplish a specific purpose [...]

L.H.

ms with signature 104B.15

To Learned Hand from Felix Frankfurter

March 14, 1928 — Law School of Harvard University

Dear B.:

Holmesy once said that he wrote only for those "learned in the art." From Olympus to *The business of the Supreme Court* is a steep descent—but it's true of us lesser mortals that one writes for very few in any serious effort. I'm not wanting in the humility of men whose judgment on *The business* is really important to me, important as a stimulus to future effort and as help to direction. You are one of those half dozen, and I'm immensely encouraged that you should think so well of the book.

[...]Your reference to the Sacco-Vanzetti book leads me to say a word. Nothing is farther from my purpose at the moment than controversy in what I'm about to say. I know the criticisms that have been widely made. But personally, I think that exactly the same spirit of scholarship which produces *The business* was behind the S-V [book]. I aimed at accuracy, and thus far no one—neither Wigmore, nor [A. Lawrence] Lowell[91] nor any one—has pointed out any omissions or commissions. If ever you know of anyone who is prepared to be specific in his criticisms, I should be genuinely obliged to you to let me have such criticisms; I don't mean criticisms of my characterizations, but of the data on which an opinion is based. For one of these days I hope to write a bigger book on Sacco and Vanzetti—an attempt at a definitive history of the case. And I crave

90. Joseph Beale (1861–1943): Professor, Harvard Law School.

91. A. Lawrence Lowell (1856–1943): Professor, Harvard Law School, 1898–1909; President, Harvard University, 1909–1933.

to be fastidiously accurate—as accurate and as scientific as you are good enough to find me in *The business*[. . .]

Always yours, F.F.

ms with signature 104B.15

To Felix Frankfurter

April 7, 1928 Judge Learned Hand's Chambers

Dear Felix:

It was kind of you to write as you did in answer to my letter in re *The business of the Supreme Court*. It was an A.1 bit of work which anyone has the right to be proud of. My allusion to *Sacco & Vanzetti* was, as you of course understood, not intended to suggest that that was not equally good. On that I am not competent to pass—nor is anyone who does not know the record and a lot more. Whether it is wise ever to prepare another book is to my mind open to question. I should have to talk that out with you and gain information. If that was really a judicial lynching, a great and flagrant miscarriage of justice, perhaps a permanent memorial ought to be written. I am in some doubt whether anyone so closely connected with it as the persons now living who have adequate information can do it with authority. But of all that anon.

The Senate has jumped in where angels should fear to tread and the Judiciary Committee has reported out a bill abolishing all jurisdiction based on diversity and on a "constitutional right."[92] They undoubtedly are not sincere and are actuated either by hostility to all Federal courts, e.g., George Norris[93] and Walsh, or they intend it as no more than a *ballon d'essai*. It has stirred up the boys here prodigiously and with reason, for such legislation is unconsidered and extravagant. The subject is full of genuine difficulties, to say nothing of high political explosives. It is going to be a truly troublesome matter to separate the wheat from the chaff, I mean to secure the right to a tribunal free from local bias while eliminating from Federal courts work which constitutionally is not theirs. I am not at all sure that when the reckoning is all made, much change will be found practicable. To make the test actual, real evidence of local bias would probably be invaluable in

92. In addition to having original jurisdiction for civil actions arising under federal law, the U.S. Constitution, or treaties of the United States, federal courts also have original jurisdiction in civil actions involving state law where the sum in controversy exceeds a statutorily mandated threshold (as of this writing, $75,000 exclusive of interests and costs) and where the matter is between: (a) citizens of different states; (b) citizens of a state and citizens or subjects of a foreign state; (c) citizens of different states and in which foreign states or citizens or subjects are additional parties; or (d) a foreign state (plaintiff) and citizens of a state or different states. *See* 28 U.S.C. § 1332. Assuming these conditions are met, the decision by a party to use diversity jurisdiction to avail itself of federal instead of state court also involves many strategic questions of civil procedure. Diversity jurisdiction is provided for in the U.S. Constitution (U.S. Const. art. III, § 2) and is also addressed in the Judiciary Act of 1789; despite this foundation, as a source of federal judicial power, diversity jurisdiction has long been a source of controversy. For a more detailed discussion of both the fundamentals of diversity jurisdiction and the controversies surrounding it, see Jack H. Friedenthal, Mary Kay Kane & Arthur R. Miller, Civil Procedure §§ 2.5-2.10 (4th ed. 2005).

93. George W. Norris (1861–1944): Senator from Nebraska, 1913–1941.

practice. To make it the mere charge of bias would probably become in the end a formality. Such a test is invidious at best and likely to arouse feelings which are disruptive rather than peaceful in the community as a whole. On the other hand, the spectacle of "equity receiverships" is preposterous and almost a scandal. What appeared is a genuine study of the subject by someone who is "Federalist" enough to hold fast to the central idea that every State (pace Laski), owes to its citizens as a prime function of its existence, a trial secure from local bias, and that the ordinary run of litigation, where there is no true ground to fear such bias, shall not be centralized. To bear the scales even between those two is no mean job and not to be solved by men of the intellectual attainments of Norris and Walsh, however pure in heart they may be.

As to "constitutional rights": now that the Supreme Court must more and more reserve itself for the large questions, I feel a little more positive, though of course no one is entitled to an a priori judgment. Federal tribunals should in the end determine Federal rights, and in practice the Supreme Court can't deal with all or nearly all. I should have to be convinced on that score; I tend to the crystallization point, but I shall not reach it, or at least a slight chemical change will always put me back into solution. I do complain, however, of such rash and irresponsible proposals. In the end they defeat their purpose, for they naturally arouse animosities; they have.

But I am biased. I don't much believe theoretically in *bonum judicis est ampliare jurisdictio rerum*,[94] but I may be a victim of my feelings. At least I discover more and more as time goes on how much these really control. Let me hope that the change is in introspective perspicacity and not in approaching senility.

There is much to say, but the pen will not carry some of it and the hand writes so much it wearies of setting down the rest. Today is a day off. Monday the mills grind again. It's quite a treat to feel the air pressure subside. It's a pity we meet so seldom, but you are often in my thoughts.

As ever, L.H.

ms with signature 104B.15

1928-2

To Charles Fremont Amidon

February 24, 1928

My dear Judge Amidon:

I was glad to get your letter of February 19th.[95] [Morris] Cohen's lecture was an interesting one and he is an interesting fellow, as you know if you happen to know anything about him. He seemed to me to identify liberalism rather with the forms which it had

94. Literally, "the good of the judge is to amplify the justice of things"; LH misquotes the usual rendering of the maxim: *boni judicis est ampliare jurisdictionem*: "it is the part of the good judge to enlarge his remedial authority." *See* ALEXANDER MANSFIELD BURRILL, A LAW DICTIONARY (1987).

95. Amidon's letter is not in the Hand Papers.

taken in the last two hundred years. I should define it rather as a frame of mind than as the espousal of any definite program. To me the liberal is the man who disbelieves in the power of the human mind to see far in advance and who is therefore rather limited to being an opportunist, that is, to taking advantage of this and that as it comes up, without far-reaching programs. For this reason he has always found his chief enemies in those ardent spirits who believe that men in the past were able to foresee universal rule or that those of the present can do the same. On the one hand, the Bolsheviks and the Fascists hate liberalism as they hate nothing else and with justice, for they know that the spirit of skepticism is death to their program. Similarly, Admiral Charles Peshall Plunkett and Mr. Ralph Easley hate liberals more than anything else because they know how corrosive is the influence of skepticism on the slogans in which they believe.

To my mind, the liberal in the end is the skeptic; he who insists on avoiding generalization beyond what the evidence warrants. It is for this reason that I regard Holmes as my ideal of a skeptic, and while I agree that Brandeis is of the same character, he has not to me the full quality, because although he believes as much as any man in testing his conclusions on the facts, I think that unconsciously his ardor at times carries him beyond the evidence. But I suppose this is sacrilege[...] With best wishes for your health and happiness, believe me,

Sincerely yours, [Learned Hand]

tp 48.15

1929-1

To Felix Frankfurter

April 25, 1929 Judge Learned Hand's Chambers

Dear Felix:

I remember seeing a letter from Holmes to you a number of years ago in which he said that he was confident that the upshot of what you would do in life would be to invest affairs with more rationality by your efforts. I have often thought that since, and I believe that it was true. You must not take too seriously such chance sayings as that of the other day. I suppose I am not much unlike other men when I find that generally, when my friends seem to impinge upon me, it is because they are touching spots that I have comfortably glazed over, but where I am really in conflict. They awaken those conflicts, and the result is disturbing. It is the common resort of most of us not to get to the source of the trouble, but to deny its existence and blame the occasion which might make us more truly aware of ourselves.

Brandeis once said to me that the chief virtue in a democracy was militancy. I will not go quite to that degree, for militancy so often breeds militancy and contention obscures judgment; yet I cannot deny the value of that virtue. It is easy to conform; years make it doubly easy. You are an influence which helps to stir me from that vice to which I suppose I am getting more and more prone. You will have to accept at times the price from one who has always been somewhat irritable, and, though perhaps you might deny it, at bottom disposed to be dictatorial.

But the truth will always remain clear to me of what Holmes said. I would at times wish that you did not so often espouse causes, but may not this be because I do not find the energy or the will—perhaps the courage—to espouse any myself? Do not think that this can obscure to me what you do, and what you will continue to do. There must be those who act; it is not enough to affect an aloofness which may be the cover for incapacity to make up one's mind. Do not believe that I shall ever fail to see these things in you; whatever at a distance I may feel, never do I meet you alone when my heart does not warm to your friendship.

L.H.

ms with signature 104B.15

To Learned Hand from Felix Frankfurter

April 28, 1929 — Law School of Harvard University

Dear B.:

Your words yesterday warmed my heart. For good twenty years now, I have had a solid and steadily growing affection for you apart from mere admiration for your great talents. And it has pained me to realize that from time to time I have irritated you and betrayed what I deeply care about. Yesterday, you brought me much peace by analyzing the source of "irritation." I suppose there is a *gaudium certaminis* in my nature. But know that at all times it is truly innocent, and I believe wholly unrelated, certainly in your case, to any statement of affectionate friendship.

Always yours, F.F.

ms with signature 104B.15

1929-2

To Oliver Wendell Holmes, Jr.

May 5, 1929 — Judge Learned Hand's Chambers

Dear Mr. Justice:

You have been much in my mind in the past few days; I try to put myself in your place and cannot see my way. And yet I have known for long that you are braced against the shocks of fate, and I am sure that you have that within you to meet this.[96] Indeed, I can hope that even now you will keep some part of that zest for living which has seemed to me, as to us all, an everlasting fountain of youth.

For myself I dare risk the charge of mysticism so far as to believe that there is an aspect of things *sub specie aeternitatis* by which human life may share the immortality of truth or beauty, of any pattern conceived and fitted to impose itself upon the flux. After all

---

96. LH wrote to Oliver Wendell Holmes on the death of his wife Fanny D. Holmes, on April 30, 1929.

science is fast coming to a place where it will offer us its formulas in coined symbols as the only "real" part of an "external" world. I can conceive no other rational immortality; at times at least I fancy I can conceive this. I shrink from imputing any of it to you for it is not clear, and I know your imperious craving for clarity.

Nor would I have you suppose that it or anything else hides from me your sorrow or your loss. For these I know there is no answer; I can do no more than tell you again what I have written so often before, of my admiration and my affection, of what you will always mean to me so long as I live.

Faithfully yours, Learned Hand

ms with signature 43.30

1929-3

To Learned Hand from Walter Lippmann

June 6, 1929

Dear B.:

Felix wrote me some days ago complaining that we didn't get sufficiently heated up about the *Schwimmer* case.[97] Here is the correspondence which follows. Don't you think it's a bit trying?

Yours, [W.L.]

tp, Lippmann Papers, Sterling, Box 12, Folder 499, and 106.18

---

97. In *United States v. Schwimmer*, 279 U.S. 644, 654–55 (1929), the Supreme Court denied citizenship to Rozika Schwimmer, a native of Hungary, because she was considered an "uncompromising pacificist." Holmes, joined by Justices Brandeis and Edward T. Sanford, dissented on free speech grounds: "She is an optimist and states in strong and, I do not doubt, sincere words her belief that war will disappear, and that the impending destiny of mankind is to unite in peaceful leagues. I do not share that optimism, nor do I think that a philosophic view of the world would regard war as absurd. But most people who have known it regard it with horror, as a last resort, and even if not yet ready for cosmopolitan efforts, would welcome any practicable combinations that would increase the power on the side of peace. The notion that the applicant's optimistic anticipations would make her a worse citizen is sufficiently answered by her examination, which seems to me a better argument for her admission than any that I can offer. Some of her answers might excite popular prejudice, but if there is any principle of the Constitution that more imperatively calls for attachment than any other it is the principle of free thought—not free thought for those who agree with us, but freedom for the thought that we hate. I think that we should adhere to that principle with regard to admission into, as well as to life within, this country. And recurring to the opinion that bars this applicant's way, I would suggest that the Quakers have done their share to make the country what it is, that many citizens agree with the applicant's belief, and that I had not supposed hitherto that we regretted our inability to expel them because they believed more than some of us do in the teachings of the Sermon on the Mount." 279 U.S. at 654–55. In an editorial in the New York World dated May 31, 1929, Lippmann argues against the decision, but on narrower terms. He insists that Schwimmer was not being treated as a native pacificist would have been treated under similar circumstances. In his reply to Lippmann, Frankfurter declares he is "flabbergasted" at Lippmann's position. For this exchange and Frankfurter's reaction to it, see Ronald Steel, *Letter on Lippmann and the* Schwimmer *Case*, 28 N.Y. Rev. Books (Apr. 2, 1981).

To Walter Lippmann

June 7, 1929 United States Circuit Court of Appeals

Dear Walter:

I think it is more than "a bit trying"; I think it is intolerable. Nobody has a right to address another, even an old friend, in that tone. It is quite likely that he is right. I am going to read the opinions with considerable care when they arrive, and I should rather guess that I shall come out that way. But the matter is not so clear as to justify any such extremity of language, and even if it were, it is not civil, and it really is not bearable.

I wish to God he wouldn't feel that every case was a signal for a moral crusade, or if he does, I wish his controversial manner would be a little more consonant with one's own self respect. I had a correspondence with him a while ago and a talk where I tried to press my point of view, but in the end I am afraid I wilted and showed my respect too frankly for his very great capacities and his generous enthusiasm for the right side on which he gets nearly always.

Again, it is a great limitation that one can never dissent from Holmes, Brandeis and Cardozo without being guilty of sinning against the Holy Ghost. I think his estimate of the ability of these three men is entirely justified, but it is preposterous to suppose that even the best men can never be wrong. It is almost a clansman's spirit, and it is certainly out of place in matters that justify and require any serenity or the contemplative spirit.

Yours, L.H.

P.S. I re-enclose the correspondence.

tp with ms signature, Lippmann Papers, Sterling, Box 12, Folder 499

1929-4

To Learned Hand from Benjamin Cardozo

June 25, 1929 Bar Building, New York City

Dear L.H.:

My thanks for your address,[98] which I have read with avidity. It is brilliant, but depressing. I seem to flounder worse than ever. Why can't you say that when I am doing my will, I am interpreting the common will, a process ever so much more respectable? I have always professed to be doing this, and now you tell me it was a sham, and maybe it was, though somehow or other, there are times when I do feel that

---

98. *See Is There a Common Will?, in* The Spirit of Liberty 47–56. *See also* 1916-2 To Frankfurter, April 29.

I am expressing thoughts and convictions not found in the books, and yet not totally my own. What you write has a quality so fine and so distinctive that it stands out above the common mass of lectures and addresses in a fashion to delight your friends. I don't know anyone else on the bench who can do it except Holmes, and he is pretty silent now.

I did mean to see you before going to Allenhurst, whither I expect to flee tomorrow, commuting more or less irregularly thereafter. I have had home worries of the usual sort, my sister having had a bad spell which has delayed our going away, and I was a good deal affected, too, by the death of my cousin, Edgar Nathan, of whom I was very fond. I shall try to get in touch with you for luncheon some day next week.

Ever yours, B.N.C

tp with ms signature 101.8

To Benjamin Cardozo

June 26, 1929

Dear B.N.C.:

Thanks for your letter of June 25th. You always give me so much more credit than I deserve that I feel a sham. But I like it just the same, more than you can know.

No, I did not mean that you or other sages did not interpret a common will. I think you do. "Interpret" is a baffling word. I am by no means sure that I know just what it means, but I should say that what you succeeded in doing was expressing ideas to which people would assent when they became aware of them. If you are disposed to be a mystic, you may say that the idea was there already; I should prefer to say that it was not, but that you made your beliefs theirs. That people in general have any thought or will about most things I do not believe, and the law is only one instance.

I am distressed to hear that things have not gone so well with you, and I am really grieved to hear of the death of Edgar Nathan, which I did not know of before. I had an acquaintance with him over some years. I greatly admired his dignity, gentleness, and intelligence. Had I seen more of him, I should feel a deep loss; as it is, I am genuinely grieved. He was a rare person.

Do let me know if you are in town. I shall be here substantially all the time until the thirteenth, when we all sail for Germany.

Faithfully yours, [L.H.]

tp 101.8

1929-5

To Felix Frankfurter

June 27, 1929 — Judge Learned Hand's Chambers

Dear Felix:

[...]I did enjoy those days as much as you, and I too shall long remember them.[99] As to Brandeis, I enjoyed seeing him and listening to him for he is really a great man. But one cannot really converse with him, for he never seems to want anything one has to give, and also he oppresses me in spite of his own passion for freedom. He wants it and would give it *in abstractu* to numbers, but he does not succeed in giving the impression in personal contacts that you have an equal right to your views as he has to his. I have never seen a really dominant person of strong feelings who did. Well, perhaps that's too comprehensive, but at the moment I think of none. It's a penalty of living that if you would permeate others with your beliefs you must press upon them. If you would get to them merely your temperament, your general approach, you need not, but your influence will be more diffuse, less apparent. I doubt if it is possible to say that one way is "better" than the other. Each one will proceed as his nature demands. If I were to favor the less positive, believing that conversion is better than persuasion, it is probably no more than the reflection of a somewhat lymphatic and diffident nature. I am not prepared to concede that truth is more obscured to it, but then I have always shared the views of that much abused man Pontius Pilate: "What is Truth"?[100] I remember that my father over forty years ago was somewhat of a Pilatian.

L.H.

ms with signature 104B.16

1929-6

To Joseph C. Hutcheson, Jr.[101]

July 2, 1929

My dear Judge Hutcheson:

I got your letter of June 24th some time ago, but did not answer it because I was awaiting your article in *The Cornell Law Journal*, which came only last night, and which I read

---

99. On June 15, 1929, LH wrote to Felix Frankfurter confirming a weekend visit—June 22 and 23—in Chatham, Massachusetts, at the house of Justice Brandeis, at which Frankfurter and his wife were also to be present. (tp with ms signature 104B.16)

100. LH actually quotes the opening sentence of Francis Bacon, *Of Truth*: "What is Truth; said jesting Pilate; And would not stay for an Answer." FRANCIS BACON, THE ESSAYS 1625 (1937). *Cf.* 27 *Matthew* 24; 16 *Mark* 15; 23 *Luke* 22–25; 19 *John* 15–16.

101. Joseph C. Hutcheson, Jr. (1853–1973): Judge, United States District Court for the Southern District of Texas, 1918–1930; Judge, United States Court of Appeals for the Fifth Circuit, 1931–1973.

with interest.[102] It is certainly in keeping with modern ideas, and has much in it that is true and suggestive. It is undeniable that the common law has been built up by generations of judges who have proceeded on what you very well call their "hunch," although all along they have professed to do no more than apply pre-existing rules. They have done this by all sorts of fictions and insincerities, generally apparent enough, but they have done it nonetheless. Further, I should be the last to deny that any of our conclusions were based upon reasons of which we were not fully aware. This is especially true, as you well observe, in cases like patents, and also, I think, in torts, where I find especial difficulty because of the casuistry involved in determining an indefinite standard of conduct, such as that of the ordinary person. All this I cheerfully admit, but I must say that it seems to me to be a confession of our weakness, and I doubt the propriety of raising it into a principle of conduct.

I have had this out at times with Cardozo who, deeply as I admire and love him, still leaves me a little unconvinced.[103] Is it not the duty of a rational man to know the actual basis of his conclusions, and, by such introspection as he can muster, to proceed rationally? The movement which has certainly gained great headway in the law schools, and which is pervading the bench, is a part of the anti-intellectualism of the times.

I have always also thought that there were genuine political perils in attendance. You and I hold our office on good behavior, and would probably not be willing to hold it on any other terms. We certainly have no warrant to impose on the community our own views of what is right, except as to minor decisions. The larger questions—social, economic, and political—are settled by men who are more responsive to popular pressure, and who ought to be in any community in which there are adequate safety valves. It is all very well for a man like you, with enlightened social views, to exercise a wide discretion, but take, for example, labor disputes. The difficulties, it seems to me, are that judges drawn from one economic class feel free to make the law on their own "hunches," and those hunches have corresponded to unconscious prejudices of their class. After all, civilization depends very largely upon the ability of society to work on general principles, and John Adams meant something when he said that he wanted a government of laws.[104] It has been applied foolishly often enough, but there lay in it a genuine advance for personal government.

What I am afraid of is that too great insistence by able and penetrative minds like your own on this judicial function will lead us to forget that law is something more majestic and authoritative than can proceed out of the mouth of any single living man. Please do not take what I say in criticism. I envy you the felicitous way in which you write, and your large background of information. In practice, I share your views. It may be that I do this

102. In a letter dated June 24, 1929, Hutcheson asks LH to consider his article, *The Judgment Intuitive: The Function of the 'Hunch' in Judicial Decision*, 14 Cornell L.Q. 274 (1929). (tp with ms signature and notes 55.4)

103. For an exchange between Cardozo and LH on interpretation, see 1929-4 To Cardozo, June 26.

104. "A government of laws, and not of men" (cited in John Adams, *"Novanglus" Papers, No. 7*, Boston Gazette (1774–1775)).

so much as to be especially fearful myself of the result, but I do think there lies here a possible danger. Thank you for thinking of me.[105]

Sincerely yours, [Learned Hand]

tp 55.4

1929-7

To Philip Littell[106]

July 19, 1929 S.S. Volendam

Dear Phil:

Tonight we shall have been a week out and still five hundred miles from Bishop's Rock. It's a slow boat, but I have enjoyed the lazy life and have, to my delight, not been pestered with this everlasting shining hour motif, which generally so bedevils my existence. The running down period is to me always a trying one; this has been relatively easy. Perhaps the sea disposes one to look at life more as a succession of moments than a realization of imagined forms. Anyway I have been surprised to find that I lost the itch so easily (being a Dutch boat there is no possibility of a double meaning).

It has made me think of you to be here; it has set me again to wondering at the curious dispositions of mankind and how you can hold them with so much justness, valuing each without acrimony or by virtue of their relation to your own. That is surely an achievement, in my experience unique. As I think of my friends, there is no one who can detach his own ethos from the estimate he puts on another's. With some it works in the reverse, of course, but that's of no moment, for the thing is to get the judgment pure.

This is really not what I started to say, though I am not so sorry for that. I had a much more stately and adequate thought the other day, when I was walking the deck. I said to myself that here was something really new, a light upon conduct, an aspect of himself and myself which Phil will be obliged to admit has been genuinely untouched hitherto between us. It will knock him dead to get this; it's a thought. But either it has quite gone, or if it was no more than this, the order of composition had intoxicated me. At any rate, the glory of it has gone and leaves not even a dying effulgence to the composer. I wished in some way to explain how my obsessions are really wound up on human nature more intimately, and, as poor Herbert [Croly] would say, more fruitfully than any others. But I cannot. Out here

105. In a letter dated July 10, 1929, Hutcheson responds to LH's critique: his article does not claim that "judging should be purely personal and uncontrolled by learning. On the contrary, it insists most vigorously that 'knowledge must precede understanding; understanding must precede judging,'" and that "it is safe for judges not only to state, but sometimes to make the law." (tp with ms signature 55.4)

106. Philip Littell (1868–1843): editorial staff, NEW YORK GLOBE, 1910–1913; editor, THE NEW REPUBLIC, 1914–1923. LH's letters to Littell are the most intimate in his correspondence and continue to Littell's death in 1943. *See Philip Littell, in* THE SPIRIT OF LIBERTY 180–82.

on the sea, nature impresses on me that at bottom the principle of indifference is fundamental. If one man needs to chase his tail, that is for him the Absolute: God as Tail-chaser. If on the other hand, he is of hound blood and contemplation is his food, that is Absolute, God as Hound-Dawg. Whether there is at bottom some Higher Synthesis I cannot tell. I confess the possibility teases me and tease me it always will. May there not be God as Hound-Dawg, Chasing his Tail *an sich*? After all, even hounds chase their tails when they are puppies. We have an absurd sense that maturity excels infancy. Why? Each is part of the pattern, and the pattern exists equally in every part and in no part. It is ridiculous to exalt the end unless we are to deny the true relevancy of the beginning.

All this has been bred by another frantic effort to understand, by a rereading, Whitehead.[107] I had thought I was familiar with the jabber of metaphysics, but it must have been all a mistake. Not only did Santayana[108] floor me but this chap puts the quietus in me beyond hope. Only here and there a shot of sunlight strikes me from the murk and leads me on. On the whole it's not, however, a very kindly light and leaves me much encircled by gloom.

The ship's company? Well, it is unusually uninteresting even for a ship's company. Pragmatic, middle-aged ladies, with definite ideas as to the places where we had best eat in London, or the merits of Bar Harbor, etc. etc. They disturb me unduly; I would do them some evil, as, for example, compelling them to read St. Thomas Aquinas all through. Horrid young men with a swagger and an imbecile look of self-importance. Slack-limbed young women who seem to throw their feet in front of them, uncertain whether each step may not be enough. On the whole, I have rather preferred the old, who at least have had drummed into them the sense that this is a world where there must be compromises.

Yes, it's been a pleasant trip, and I a little dread its conclusion with the prospect of bustle and hotels and porters and the everlasting drip, drip of fees which one can never gauge properly, and of quarrels about cabs and bills and the wonder what is the best route and what to see and what not to see. Some day, when my soul is re-embodied, I shall be a perfectly determinate, masterful person, whose executive competency gets the absolute maximum of enjoyment out of every minute. I shall invent a perfect determination and keep a score every day to prove to everyone that I have had the highest possible aggregate of happiness with no minus quantities whatever. I shall always go to the best of all possible hotels at the least of all possible prices; I shall combine in sagacious integrations all

107. Alfred North Whitehead (1861–1947): English philosopher and mathematician; Professor of Philosophy at Harvard University, 1924–1937. By 1929, Whitehead had published a formidable number of books: with Bertrand Russell, PRINCIPIA MATHEMATICA (2d ed. 1925) (1910); THE ORGANIZATION OF THOUGHT (1916); AN ENQUIRY CONCERNING THE PRINCIPLES OF NATURAL KNOWLEDGE (1919); THE CONCEPT OF NATURE (1920); THE PRINCIPLE OF RELATIVITY WITH APPLICATION TO PHYSICAL SCIENCE (1922); SCIENCE AND THE MODERN WORLD (1926); SYMBOLISM: ITS MEANING AND EFFECT (1927); and *Process and Reality:* AN ESSAY IN COSMOLOGY (1929). For LH's admiration of Whitehead, see 1942-2 and 5 To Frankfurter, January 29 and November 23. For LH's contributions to Whitehead's maintenance, see 1949-1 To Frankfurter, January 1.

108. George Santayana (1863–1952): Professor of Philosophy at Harvard University, 1889–1912, when he retired to live in Europe. Santayana's important works include THE LIFE OF REASON, OR, THE PHASES OF HUMAN PROGRESS (1906); THE REALMS OF BEING, 4 vols. (1927, 1930, 1938, 1940), and DOMINATIONS AND POWERS; REFLECTIONS ON LIBERTY, SOCIETY, AND GOVERNMENT (1951). For an account of LH's visit to Santayana, see 1937-2 To Berenson, September 17 and 22.

the desirable views, picturesque shots, noble vistas, and informing sights in the shortest possible routes. I shall have seen everything, forget nothing, and discover with informed moderation and a background at least as remote as the late Paleolithic, perfectly valuing all intermediate influences with strongly penetrating forecasts for the next two centuries. But I shall not do any of these things now; I shall be jostled and harried and cheated, or think I have been. I shall have a haunting sense that I am missing much and am an ass to think about whether I am missing anything. But I shall come back and say that I have had a good time and *it will be true*.

L.H.

ms with signature 233.29

1930-1

To Learned Hand from Felix Frankfurter

February 4, 1930 — Law School of Harvard University

Dear B.:

[...]I have very mingled feelings about Hughes C.J.—and little enthusiasm.[109] He *was* a good Justice, and I don't believe he will continue the recent reactionary lead. But—he is 68 and comfortable with the world; he won't have zest in his work and he is suspicious of L.D.B[randeis] and really not penetrating. Yes, I know he is a powerful advocate, but much more is needed.

Poor Stone must be deeply disappointed, but I suspected that the influences against him would be too strong. And also, I'm afraid this rules out anybody else from New York, both you and B.N.C[ardozo]. Altogether, I should have been much happier with Stone.

Always, F.F.

ms with signature 104B.17

To Felix Frankfurter

February 6, 1930 — Judge Learned Hand's Chambers

Dear Felix:

In the long run Stone would have been better, but it would have raised Hell in the Court, and I believe, though it is mere inference, that some of the worthies may have made such representations. I had heard that the old C.J. had freely expressed himself on the subject and was very set. I can't blame the President for yielding, though I don't doubt it cost him

---

109. Chief Justice William Howard Taft retired from the bench on February 3, 1930; President Hoover immediately nominated Charles Evans Hughes to succeed him.

a very genuine personal pang. Yes, I am sorry for Stone, who must have had much disappointment. But a man has only himself to thank if he allows himself to count on such things. 'Tis a world where the unaccountable is the most certain, and nobody over the age of consent ought to go along without that always in mind. What you say about me is comprised in the same. If anyone had been making a "book," he would have had to put me among the entries at mere odds. Personally, I should have put myself down as what the sports call "a long shot," but it is true I should have been on the "book." To have that "long shot" finally wiped off is a slight matter; in a sense it is as well that now it is closed. Anybody who is a judge and says that he would not like it is a damned liar, but then so is anyone or nearly anyone who says he wouldn't like to be President or King of England, I guess, or nearly another "face card." So we are made, little as it is creditable to us that we are.

As to Hughes: well, I share a little your doubts, but they all turn upon how "liberal" he may prove. No, he is not very penetrating, but he has numerous powers of industry, and my guess is that you are wrong about his lack of zeal. He appears to me to be an extraordinary youthful man of 68. If I thought he would reinforce the "three,"[110] I should be content enough.

The more I read Brandeis the higher and higher goes my esteem. He has some failings that I think you don't quite estimate, but they disappear in his work which today is of the very highest service. He sees further and deeper than any one else. By the way, O.W.H.'s work really does begin to show his years; it is not quite adequate any longer. This I know is terrible heresy, but I take my chances.

I have a very genuine sorrow at poor Taft's plight. I have an affection for his nature, straight and loving and loyal, for his kindness and his power of fine indignation. But I will confess to you now that your prognosis eight years ago was better than mine. While his influence on the Court, its working and its personnel, was of the greatest use, he fortified it in its most dangerous tendencies. God know where it will land if Hughes should disappoint us. We must have faith in him where we can.

L.H.

ms with signature 104B.17

1930-2

To Charles Evans Hughes

February 14, 1930

My dear Mr. Hughes:

It was only about a year ago that I had occasion to say in public what I thought of you, and there is nothing more that I am adding now. This, the last of the many honors which

110. I.e., Louis Dembitz Brandeis, Holmes, and Harlan Fiske Stone. Hereafter the initials O.W.H. refer to Holmes.

have come to you, is the natural and fitting complement of your whole life; it insures to the court a leadership which will maintain its prestige and give it the confidence of the whole people. The President has done the only thing which it was possible for him to do; he has demonstrated his wisdom and I hope you will allow yourself some personal gratification to go along with what I know will be the sense of the grave responsibility of the position.

Please accept my warm best wishes and he assured of my belief that in this as in every other post you have held the country will be the great gainer.[111]

[Learned Hand]

ms draft 106.7

To Learned Hand from Charles Evans Hughes

February 16, 1930 One Hundred Broadway

Dear Judge Hand:

Your very kind letter warms my heart. My plans for a future of relative ease and comfort have suddenly been disrupted. But I am girding up my loins, or, in more modern phrase, tightening my belt. I cannot express my appreciation of your words, which mean more to me than you can imagine.

Faithfully yours, [Charles Evans Hughes]

ms 106.7

1931-1

To Oliver Wendell Holmes, Jr.

March 8, 1931 Judge Learned Hand's Chambers

Dear Mr. Justice:

This annual event, which I have been in the habit of recalling to you for a number of years, has apparently become a national occasion this time.[112] I rejoice that it is so, both because I am always glad when the public, with its unsure judgment, now and then has a sense of true values, and because I cannot but suppose that it will bring satisfaction to you, however indifferent you may ordinarily be to such attentions. A judge does not often strike the imagination of his time; his work is cellular; collectively he and his fellows make a structure, but the artificers remain unknown. He must not complain of that; he

111. Chief Justice William Howard Taft retired from the bench on February 3, 1930; President Hoover immediately nominated Charles Evans Hughes to succeed him.

112. Holmes was 90 years old on March 8, 1931.

has his corresponding exemptions, yet it is agreeable to all of us when one achieves a distinction which is written so large as yours.

People have such vague notions of what a judge does, so easily confuse one even of your number with a justice of the peace, that it is notable when they proclaim that here is one whom the king delighteth to honor. I wonder whether you entirely realize how exceptional it is. It seems to me much to their credit that they should have got a sense of the quality of one who has not only never sought publicity but also whose work has been of a kind to prevent it. When I say that I find it curious, I know that you will understand the admiration which my surprise implies.

It is quite idle for me to add any words of mine; what I have so often said gains nothing by repetition. You cannot understand, I believe, how often I think of you, how much you are the model of what I should like to be. However, it can do no harm to say it once again; every year is permissible. I had hoped to get down this winter, but so far I have not been able. They keep us well employed, at any rate much employed, but I shall be there in May at any rate. Meanwhile I beg leave to associate myself in these current festivities.

Sincerely yours, Learned Hand

ms with signature, Holmes Papers, HLL, Reel 33, frames 126–127

To Learned Hand from Oliver Wendell Holmes, Jr.

March 10, 1931

My dear Hand:

There is time only for a line of affectionate thanks. Those I send. But I add if any judge is to strike the imagination of his time, I think you should, and increasingly do.

Sincerely yours, O. W. Holmes.

tp with signature, Holmes Papers, HLL, Reel 33, frame 159

1931-2

To Walter Lippmann

May 31, 1931 Salisbury, Connecticut

Dear Walter:

You wrote me a good letter from somewhere that I did not wholly grasp, en route, as I gathered, from Greece to Italy. Your trip sounded good; Gilbert Murray at Delphi was a really exceptional advantage. O, my God, those English and their God-damned Greeks! I am entirely clear that they would have bored the Greeks *à mourir* with all their decencies, their sentimental overlays, their reserves, their myoses,[113] if that's the way to spell it. I am

113. I.e., meioses.

so sick of the Greeks and the canting solemnities that prove how we owe the Ford car to Anaximenes! I am sick of them anyway; I revel in old Holmes, who very perversely and absurdly agreed with a timid suggestion of mine that it was not worthwhile fussing about them at all, but that we had best fill our fleeting moments with the last things the presses threw off. Horrid sacrilege upon the spirit of history, so precious, so imperative to be revered when I was reared. And yet there is something to be said even for that.

But this does not mean that I don't envy you; on the contrary, it proves perhaps how much I do envy you. Greek religions, Delphi supra, *par exemple*—so far I can gather after a very determined effort to read Jane Harrison[114]—was a kaleidoscope, a jumble, a patch-work quilt, and I simply cannot get interested in it. Just what were the processes and the various infusions by which people, "Pelasgians"[115] or "Thracians," changed from eating raw bulls and getting drunk on "cereal beverages" and killing "priest-kings" and having homeopathic fornication to make the crops and flocks increase till finally their successors from the north reached the "Prime Mover Unmoved"; all this you *can* get interested in, of course. But then I *can* and, curious as it seems even to me, *do* get interested in whether one should be allowed to tax as disbursements the premiums in attachment funds in the District Court. There are people who find it thrilling to herd dogs with "points." I rejoice in all these capacities of the human soul. I see in the proliferation of human wants the surest safeguard against suicide—and for that matter industrial depression. We started off little endowed, and if we had not achieved the faculty of making ends out of means, where in Hell should we be today?

So I don't complain that there are a certain number of buddies who labor at the Orphic gold inscriptions and Greek vases and chance allusions to Plutarch and Pausanias and Strabo,[116] seeking what is concealed amid their misunderstanding. But I don't really care a damn whether Dionysos was a Thracian because he was Brunios[117]—the brew god who became the wine god—or whether Orpheus came from Crete en route from Egypt or Lydia or Thrace again. Or whether the Eleusinian mysteries were "pure" and the Sacred Marriage was symbolic or as "dirty" as the dirty old Fathers wanted to make them, much to the chaste Jane's indignation. But I do protest against the veils which the English insist in throwing over the Greeks, and I insist that you put it much too moderately about Gilbert in your letter. Out with it: down with deference. They are haunted with the recollection of Victoria, and they do not know the Greeks because they will not. I appeal to Gilbert's pained allusions—for they are no more—to the prevalence of (not prevalence, only occasional lapsing into) those practices too revolting to a sound feeling Englishman even to be named. Is that the "Greek Point of View"?[...]

Enough of this. You will be more interested in what I can tell you of here than of my frothy comments about what you have seen and I haven't. But you will get very little, because the American scene is uneventful just now; you will find very little that you must

---

114. Jane Ellen Harrison (1860–1928): Lecturer, Newnham College, Cambridge, 1898–1922; author of PROLEGOMENA TO THE STUDY OF GREEK RELIGION (1903); and THEMIS: A STUDY OF THE SOCIAL ORIGINS OF GREEK RELIGION (1912).

115. Pelasgians, literally, are "sea-people" and are supposed to be one of the earliest tribes in ancient Greece; they eventually were displaced by the Achaeans, an Indo-European people from the north.

116. Plutarch, biographer and moral philosopher (46–120 AD); Pausanias, author of a *Description of Hellas*, c. 150 AD; Strabo, a geographer (64 BC to 19 AD).

117. I.e., Bromius.

catch up with. We roll slowly along down into our industrial caverns, everybody utterly dejected, sans teeth, sans hope, sans everything.[118] Nobody has any guts left; all sit and groan like the companions of Odysseus in Polyphemus'[119] cave. Occasionally, some irresponsible creature inveighs against the "lack of leadership," the "spinelessness" of those in command, but nobody pays any attention, and his voice scarcely rises above the low wailing. I never knew a time when the morale was so entirely gone; they expect anything and everything. Next winter is a specter, full of horrid doles and horrider Progressives. La Follette has been calling for a special session, for what God knows, except I suppose to point the finger of wrath at the guilty northeast and call for more taxes. Just how and when the automatic physiology of our nervous systems will begin to get sick of it all I don't know. I suppose there must be an end to the power of suggestion even in the most hysterical, but I confess there are no signs of it yet. I have got more used to it and face the possibility of entire industrial prostration in an almost frivolous spirit, though I know it will hurt a good deal more that I can realize sitting here for a pleasant weekend out of the hot city[...]

If I could only gather myself together, I might find something to say, but the older I grow the more bankrupt my mind appears to become. Poignant novelties heave on the horizon; I put out to capture them; it is a painful chase for an elusive prey, and when I succeed it's nothing but a bit of mass-produced old wreckage that has been knocking about every harbor in the world for centuries. Of course, I might try something connected with law, but I don't know enough, and to learn would be a superhuman job. Opinions are, I fancy, my "expression"; one can in them shoot off an occasional Roman candle without committing oneself too seriously. Besides, the audience is very unsophisticated and illiterate, so that criticism is not severe.

My love to Faye. F. is in Cornish for two months anyway.

That was a nice job the Sup.Ct. did in *McIntosh's* case.[120] But old Hughes really bellowed good and loud; I knew we should catch him and I confess to some disappointment that [Owen Josephus] Roberts[121] failed us, and so turned the day against us.

L.H.

ms with signature, Lippmann Papers, Sterling, Box 12, Folder 499

---

118. *Cf.* Old age is a condition "Sans teeth, sans eyes, sans taste, sans every thing." As You Like It, II, ii.

119. I.e., the cyclops encountered by Odysseus and his men; *see The Odyssey*, Book 9.

120. United States v. Macintosh, 283 U.S. 605 (1931). Macintosh, a Canadian-born applicant for U.S. citizenship, would not promise to bear arms unconditionally in defense of the United States unless he believed the cause to be morally justified. The district court had denied citizenship to Macintosh; the court of appeals had reversed the decision. Writing for the majority, Justice Sutherland noted that "[n]aturalization is a privilege, to be given, qualified, or withheld as Congress may determine" (283 U.S. at 615) and found that Macintosh's qualified acceptance of citizenship under the U.S. Constitution and the Naturalization Act was insufficient, reversing the court of appeals and affirming the district court's decision. Justice Hughes dissented, joined by Justices Holmes, Brandeis, and Stone, on the grounds that it was not clear to him that Congress had enacted a requirement that a naturalized citizen promise to bear arms in defense of the country. While not doubting that Congress *could* enact such a requirement, Justice Hughes did not find that requirement in either the Constitution or in the Naturalization Act.

121. Owen Josephus Roberts (1875–1955): Associate Justice of the United States Supreme Court, 1930–1948. Roberts joined the majority in *United States v. Macintosh.*

1931-3

To Walter Lippmann

September 16, 1931 Poggio allo spino, Consuma

Dear Walter:

We have been here two days and are leaving tomorrow.[122] It has been a delightful change from too much sightseeing which left us a little exhausted. I think we owe our invitation to you, who let B.B. know that we were to be hereabouts. It was kind of you to think of us, and really even I Tatti cannot be more delightful than these mountains. We would willingly stay longer, but as we sail in ten days and want at least six in Rome it will be time to move.

I am enclosing a letter which Nicky got from an Englishman called Robert Trevelyan[123] that B.B. thought you might like to see. Also a letter to the *Guardian* by Clifford Allen[124] who according to B.B. must be the real author of the Trevelyan letter. You will see that both are a defense of MacDonald[125] and that one looks to the possibility that he may be able to get a majority as leader of a Centre made up of the Liberals and additions from the Labour right and the Conservative left. I know nothing of English politics, but I confess that this seems to me somewhat fantastic. You will also observe that while Allen regards Mac's move as necessary, he puts it down to the beastly capitalists who would not have been content to leave their money in England had it embarked on the proper course through taxation with reduction of the dole. The English must have scapegoats like the rest of us, but it does seem a little trying when they seek to put their embarrassments down to the score of others, ourselves the most guilty presumably[...]

I have seen enough pictures to last me for a considerable season; maybe the days of incessant and indiscriminate gallery trotting are over for me. At least I cannot now leap from canvas to canvas with the joy that I used to feel, or think I felt. B.B. does promise us a Roman campaign, which looks exhausting, but as I have never been in Rome, novelty may supply the place of youth. We shall see.

I have had no news whatever from home, except the very discouraging stock quotations. I gather that nothing has happened, and that the spirit of all men continues to sag and get more melancholic, because nothing has. What a strange condition for us all. No one daring to make a start, no one willing to make a generous gesture. Little petty creatures like Hiram Johnson[126] who can frighten timid souls like H[erbert] H[oover]. You

122. LH writes from Bernard Berenson's house in Consuma, a short distance from Florence. Walter Lippmann introduced LH to Berenson in New York City in 1920. See GERALD GUNTHER, LEARNED HAND: THE MAN AND THE JUDGE 371 (1994).

123. Robert C. Trevelyan, an English poet and translator and a friend of Bernard Berenson.

124. Clifford Allen, Baron Allen of Hurtwood, a leading figure on the political left in the 1920s.

125. Ramsay MacDonald (1866–1937): Prime Minister, 1924, 1929, 1931–1935.

126. Hiram Johnson (1866–1945): Governor of California, 1910–1916; Senator from California, 1917–1945.

must have begun in the *Tribune* by now; maybe you have inclined your thoughts. I await the results.

My love to Faye. L.H.

ms with signature, Lippmann Papers, Sterling, Box 12, Folder 499

1931-4

To Bernard Berenson[127]

September 26, 1931 Piroscafo "Roma"

Dear B.B.:

All turned out exceedingly well and we are off in an hour or so from Naples[...] As I look back upon my trip, our visit to you is a precious interlude. I shall not forget the surpassing beauties of the Apennines as we saw them and of the delights of their light and shade. More especially, our welcome and the chances we had to come to know you and yours were rare, far too rare, and delightful. I confess that as I now turn to leave Europe, it is as it always has been, with very mixed feelings. America does indeed look bare and thin; one must think of its future and believe that in time it will become more interested in things of the spirit, less strident, less sure in its parochialism, more conscious of a common fate with the rest of mankind. I fear that nothing teaches us these things but suffering, and I am not sure that we should profit as we might by suffering. After all, when one has had dumped in one's lap the riches of this world as they have never existed elsewhere, how is one to realize that it is an accident, not derivable from some essential virtue? Do we not all attribute our good fortune to our qualities? And indeed, when is one to stop in the apportionment; I spare you a discussion of free will. To have even a part, however small, in the effort to impose reason upon the affairs of our country is something; we ought to think of it as much. A judge has at least that; he works no doubt in the microscopic dimensions but he works directly; what he does counts in human sweat or [illegible]. He does not talk *in vacuo*. That is a consolation; no doubt it ought to be more of a stimulus than long custom any longer allows. But it is essential that at times such a one should draw breath in another atmosphere; essential indeed, even in the narrowest sense, that he may properly carry on in his own job. This you serve to give me in ways that perhaps you cannot know; for this let me give you my warm thanks.

Please remember me most kindly to your gracious lady who always makes me feel that she likes to see me—what can be a better welcome? and to her whom I cannot resist speaking of as Nicky, at least behind her back. If a somewhat shop-worn judge is entitled

127. Bernard Berenson (1865–1959): art critic and connoisseur of Italian art; advisor to collectors and dealers on the provenance of works of art, whose principal residence was in Settignano, outside Florence. The first letter in the Hand–Berenson correspondence in the Hand Papers is Berenson's to LH, dated December 15, 1922; it is published in BERNARD BERENSON, THE SELECTED LETTERS OF BERNARD BERENSON 93–95 (A.K. McComb ed., 1964).

to select Egerias,[128] may she be mine. Again, my dear B.B., much thanks for all that you did to make our trip pleasant. I hope that the faint suggestion of your possible visit to America is not to go away as chaff in the wind.

Sincerely yours, Learned Hand

tr/ms with signature 99.12

1931-5

To Felix Frankfurter

October 14, 1931 Judge Learned Hand's Chambers

Dear Felix:

For several days after the casebook on Federal Jurisdiction[129] arrived, I did not know of your gracious act of friendship on the first page, else I should not have been so negligent in telling you of my pleasure at being so recognized. It was a flattering thing, my boy, and I feel its import; altogether it has pleased me very much.

This gives me an occasion for what in any event I should have wanted to write to you about. Morrow's death has been a crushing blow to George [Rublee], whose associations with him for the last five years was increasingly intimate, so that they really thought and acted much as one. Besides, he has had other hard luck, and is quite sad and discouraged.

Stimson had asked Morrow to head the Peace Delegation and Morrow had, I think, accepted. It would be a good thing, good for George, good for the country, if S. would ask G. to have a place on it. Of course, I do not mean as Morrow's successor; G. has no such public position as would justify that. But I do mean a place of some responsibility upon it, where his gifts could show themselves, gifts particularly in place in just such negotiations as the past has more than once proved. I am in no position to suggest any such thing to S., who always greets me as though in some vague way I were a lightsome and trivial grasshopper, but you have undoubtedly much weight with him. Does it commend itself to you to suggest to S. that this would be a useful choice? Maybe you don't feel free to do it. If so, amen. G. was, as you know, on the Naval Conference.[130] How he did I do not know. I may surmise that it was very well. Naturally I have not spoken to G. I do not even know that he would accept, though I should be willing to bet that he would. But even if he didn't, it would be a ray of light in what is at present a rather dull world for him. I lay this at your feet without more.

My love to the Peerless Lady. L.H.

ms with signature 104B.21

---

128. Egeria, a Roman goddess of fountains, counselor to King Numa.

129. Felix Frankfurther, Cases and Other Authorities on Federal Jurisdiction and Procedure (1931).

130. Stimson was chairman of the American delegation to London Naval Conference, 1930–1931, and would therefore have known George Rublee.

To Learned Hand from Felix Frankfurter

October 15, 1931 Law School of Harvard University

Dear B.:

It is invariably a joy to get a letter from you when you let your pen go. And even when it evokes such terribly sad reflections as fill me about Morrow's death. All you say about George finds the warmest response in me. After Joe [Cotton]'s death, I opened with Stimson the question of using George, and subsequently had a personal talk with him about George. The other day, after Dwight's death, as you will see from the enclosed correspondence with Stimson, I again raised the question of utilizing George. But you give my vague, general feeling a very concrete direction, and I shall now write Stimson, specifically urging that George be included in the disarmament delegation.

Incidentally, I think you are quite wrong in your feeling about Stimson's feeling towards you. Not that I do not understand the response that he arouses in you; I know very well the arctic atmosphere he manages to generate. It is the great limitation of the man. If he had even a jot of the dramatic chemistry of a MacDonald, a Lloyd George, or a T.R., he would really be an extraordinarily effective public man. As it is, the more I know about other public men, the more I feel justified in my own estimate of Stimson. There is an integrity and disinterestedness about him that the world needs as much as anything, because such integrity and disinterestedness are the parents of guts and judgment. At no point is his intelligence and insight obstructed or defeated by the subtle pulls of the ego. But I had better stop. For if I go on, as you doubtless will infer, I may make sundry remarks about MacDonald and Hoover. MacDonald in particular requires talk and not writing. Do let us see you when you come.

Yours always, F.F.

Please return enclosures

tp with ms signature and notes104B.21

To Felix Frankfurter

October 16, 1931 Judge Learned Hand's Chambers

Dear Felix:

It is hard to anticipate your own activities. You have already done about all that can be done, but perhaps making it specific will help. I see that you are quite as anxious as I am myself. I might have known it, in any event.

You cannot have a higher regard for Stimson's character or integrity than I have. I mean what I say. He is the veriest Roman of them all. I do not know enough about him to judge the suppleness of his intellect, which, judging from my little experience [I thought] was too rigid. I have always wondered whether diplomatic affairs were his forte. But of his absolute disinterestedness and courage I have never had the least doubt. He is a Regulus,[131] who, for his country, would be rolled down the hill in a barrel full of spikes.

I was pleased at what you let drop about Morrow. I did not mention his death to you, because I was not sure just how you felt about him, and frankly, I should have been pained if you thought of him less than I. Like all of us, he had his shortcomings. As a friend, he was at times trying; but for resourcefulness and fertility, quick insight and intelligence, I do not think I have ever seen his equal. Added to this, he was at bottom an absolutely pure-hearted man, willing to give himself to the end, as indeed he did. That he was indifferent to position I will not say; no doubt he had his vanities like the rest of us. But there was a simplicity and disinterestedness about him which could not be exceeded. I think Arthur Salter[132] was right when he said in *The Times* that there was no life in the world at the moment so important to the cause of peace as his. When I reflect that in seven months two lives like his and Joe's have gone out, when the Jimmy Walkers[133] still flutter over the dung-heaps, it makes me wonder how anyone can think that this universe is shaped with any regard to human destinies.

You may say what you like, but the President in the last four months has given evidences of a disposition which justifies the hopes of those of us who have continued to believe in him. I am sending back the copy of your letter to Stimson and his answer. I do not see that I can get on until the end of November, when I shall certainly see you. My love to Marion.

As ever, yours, L.H.

tp with ms signature 104B.21

131. Having evoked Marc Antony's eulogy of Brutus ("This was the noblest Roman of them all"), Julius Caesar, V, v, LH cites the example of Marcus Atilius Regulus, Roman general during the first Punic war, c. 250 BC. For his celebration as a Stoic hero, see Seneca, *De Providentia*, 3.9–3.11.

132. Arthur Salter (1881–1975): British politician and economist.

133. James John Walker (1881–1946): Mayor of New York City in 1928. Investigated by Judge Samuel Seabury, Walker resigned in 1932 after evidence of corrupt practices.

PART III

Really, the most stupendous performance that ever has ever been done on the Planet

—Learned Hand to Bernard Berenson, February 18, 1945

WORLD WAR AND WORLD POWER: 1932–1946

News of Holmes's retirement and Franklin D. Roosevelt's election opens this correspondence. Paramount are concerns about the economy. Frankfurter worries about how the nation's wealth and resources are allocated, and Hand alludes to the advent of National Socialism in Germany and of Communism in the Soviet Union. Both debate the constitutionality of New Deal legislation, a target of Republican criticism. Neither considers the Republicans fit to take power, but both see the danger of a nation made captive by the power of Roosevelt's personality. A focus on the interpretation of statutes leads Hand to articulate—at first in paraphrase and eventually by quotation—the seminal dictum of the sixteenth-century English common lawyer Edmund Plowden: "it is a good way, when you peruse a statute, to suppose that the law-maker is present, and that you have asked him the question you want to know touching the equity; then you must give yourself such an answer as you imagine he would have done, if he had been present." In his subsequent essays and letters, Hand considers Plowden's instruction with increasing emphasis on the role of the judicial imagination in reconstructing the legislative event and determining its present relevance.

Letters to and from Bernard Berenson reveal Hand's fascination with the cultural landscapes of Italy; their correspondence ends abruptly in 1941, when Berenson states that he writes *in articulo belli*, and it resumes only in 1945, when the Germans leave Italy and Berenson can emerge from hiding. Hand's letter to him on this occasion expresses profound admiration for Berenson's courage and resourcefulness during the war. Letters to and from Louis Henkin, Hand's former clerk, then serving with American forces in Sicily and afterward in Italy, further reveal the vast distance that actually separates Hand from the war in Europe and, at the same time, his emotional involvement in every phase of that war as it is reported in the public media. With the Allied victories comes correspondence that considers the conduct of government: how should it deal with national conflicts at home and international relations abroad? How best to serve the public interest and protect the peace? Hand differs from Frankfurter in seeing any kind of justice in the Nuremberg trials; he also acknowledges with praise Stimson's exacting role as Secretary of War, even as Stimson reports that the atomic bomb was his idea and explains why he endorsed it. The correspondence of this period closes with letters to and from Judge Henry T. Lummus of the Supreme Judicial Court of Massachusetts: there Hand explores the reasons for and the effects of Chief Justice Marshall's ruling in

Marbury v. Madison, and notes that he thinks it has allowed courts—in their "judicial review" of legislation—to decide matters more properly political. Lummus argues "natural law" guarantees judicial review, a claim that Hand interrogates throughout the rest of his correspondence; he both questions the practice of judicial review and disputes the status of natural law.

1932-1

To Oliver Wendell Holmes, Jr.

January 14, 1932 Judge Learned Hand's Chambers

Dear Mr. Justice:

Ever since I became a judge nearly twenty-three years ago, it is you to whom I have looked for guidance. When I wrote, it was you I was addressing; you were the audience whose approval I most wanted. When you agreed, I was content, though the rest might differ. Now that you are to be no longer there, this must go.[1] I shall continue as before, but half the zest is out of it. I can by no possibility be the same; that Court has forever lost its luster for me.

I must say this first; our personal losses are apt to loom largest. But I do not forget you or the wrench that this final yielding has caused you; I too must yield since you have so decided, for you know. Do not think that we shall not still find you, as you always were, our inspiration; we shall be able to see you and to know that what the body may deny, the spirit will replace. This will be so to the end; we shall always have you, even when time has finally taken you away. While those of us who have enjoyed the gifts of your kindness, your grace, your wisdom, and your dignity are still upon the earth, you will be to us the *preux chevalier*, the example of what, however dimly, we could have wished that we might be. Surely if life has any prizes, you have had them. What can we, who are your friends, ask more?

Sincerely yours, Learned Hand

ms with signature, Holmes Papers, HLL, Reel 33, frames 128–129

To Learned Hand from Oliver Wendell Holmes, Jr.

January 15, 1932 Supreme Court of the United States

My dear Hand:

A letter like yours would be enough to make one feel that one had not lived in vain—but I suspect that that question is none of our business. At all events, you have made my life happier and I am grateful.

Affectionately yours, O.W. Holmes

tp with signature, Holmes Papers, HLL, Reel 33, frame 160

1. Holmes retired on January 12, 1932.

1932-2

To Learned Hand from Felix Frankfurter

March 11, 1932 Law School of Harvard University

Dear B.:

Talk about being "secretive"! What's making a speech even to the Patent Law Association compared to the glories of grandfatherhood? Why have you kept such a golden mystery? And a boy at that[2] [...] If the lad is going to be a lawyer how much less nonsense he will have to study than did his granddaddy. For surely a great deal of the stuff that you and dispensing and that I am teaching will be deader than the dodo twenty-five years from now[...]

Always yours, F.F.

tp with ms signature 104B.22

To Felix Frankfurter

March 12, 1932 Judge Learned Hand's Chambers

Dear Felix:

I quite forgot to speak of the grandson. He is a month old and so far behaves as a person of such tender years should[...] I don't believe he will be a lawyer, but if he should be, I don't agree that the stuff which we are dispensing will be deader than a dodo.[3] It may seem so, but unless the whole works blow up, it will have had its part. I remember that Holmes once said to you that you would go on increasing the measure of rationality in an irrational world. I decline to believe that the lower depths of the coral reefs do not support the levels which rise above the sea.

I will send you a copy of my remarks as soon as I get them struck off, which will be done some time next week. I do not understand that the stuff is going to be printed, unless it appears in the *United States Daily*[...]

Love to Marion, L.H

tp with ms signature 104B.22

---

2. Jonathan Hand Churchill was born on February 11, 1932.

3. Frankfurter clarified his remark about the "dodo" in a letter to LH dated March 14, 1932, stating that only "some of the stuff" written on law would be dead. (tp with ms notes, 104B.22) However, he returned to the "dodo" image in 1951, stating that Hand's "actual decisions will be all deader than the Dodo before long, as indeed at least many of them are already." *A Great Judge Retires: American Law Institute Honors Learned Hand*, 37 A.B.A. J. 502, 503 (1951).

To Felix Frankfurter

March 16, 1932 Judge Learned Hand's Chambers

Dear Felix:

[...]You misread my remarks about the dodo. I was not touched off by that, nor did I interpret it as an indication that you thought the next fifty years would be those of revolutionary change, or that you were hostile to the present situation. I thought it was in line with a little note of wistful regret that I had been feeling in what you have written lately, a sense that you thought that what you might be doing was useless. It was this that I wanted to correct. I read it along with the letter of regret about your inability to inspire the young. I thought you might be getting despondent. But I ought to have known better than that. I ought not to have read your vitality in terms of my own.

As to the younger law teachers: they seem to me to have gone clean batty, along with the rest of their generation, in all forms of human activity especially the aesthetics. You can wait, but I have not the time. You will see the thing swing back again in my judgment, unless all the world has determined to go to hell in a hand-basket, which possibly it has. If I were to lay my finger on the rotten spot, I would say it was the sense of nationality.

Those birds in Washington are going to publish my remarks in something called *The Federal Bar Association Journal.*[4] I do not believe the *Harvard Law Review* will want them, and I should wince a little at having them in that august journal because they were dashed off a little irresponsibly. I am not at all sure how I should feel about them in a month or two. If I feel as I do about other things I have written, I should be sorry that they were not stillborn. I am apt to feel that way about my intellectual children, though thank God my children in the flesh are with me.

Parenthetically, I was rather surprised and grieved to have old Holmsey tell me he was glad he never had had any children. I could not make out exactly why, but so far as I gathered, it was because he thought the adventure of life was too ugly a gamble. This from him! I am inclined to put it down in some measure to compensation, as the Freudians say, but in any event, that is what he says.

I read the long opinions in the case about the Workmen's Compensation,[5] and Brandeis certainly floored them for fair. It seems to me one of the most unnecessary and wanton distinctions that they have got off of late and betrays a weakness in the Chief

---

4. In an address to the Federal Bar Association on March 8, LH reflects upon the conduct of a democracy. *See Democracy: Its Presumptions and Realities, in* THE SPIRIT OF LIBERTY 90–102.

5. This is a reference to *Crowell v. Benson*, 285 U.S. 22 (1932), in which the Court considered a claim under the Longshoremen's and Harbor Workers' Compensation Act of 1927, legislation providing a safety net to ensure that employees' compensation claims could be brought even where state law did not provide for such a claim. Distinguishing between the adjudication of "private rights" (one individual's liability to another) and "public rights" (matters arising between the government and individuals in connection with the functions of the executive and legislative branches), Justice Hughes wrote the opinion for the majority, upholding the ability of an administrative agency, under certain conditions, to adjudicate claims concerning private rights that arose from a federal statutory scheme, subject to judicial review. Hughes's opinion also distinguished between "jurisdictional facts" that a court must decide and routine findings of fact that could be decided by an administrative tribunal. Justice Brandeis's dissent took issue with the majority's assertion of a trial court's ability to

which I had hoped against hope might be in abeyance. Being a Baptist, however, is like being a Mormon—once you are it, you never can shake it off.

Faithfully yours, L.H.

tp with ms signature and notes 104B.22

1932-3

To Learned Hand from Felix Frankfurter

November 9, 1932 Law School of Harvard University

Dear B.:

Last summer you asked for references to cases in which the Supreme Court admonished the lower courts against giving decisions without opinions. Herewith is a list.

As to the election, I will indulge myself in only one remark. If you will read the speech of Hoover at Sacramento on Election Day you may, I think, agree that the country showed great wisdom in retiring him from the conduct of affairs. The poor man has the wrong make-up for the government of a democratic society. I cannot imagine a less appropriate speech for a President to make on Election Day. And the reason that he made it is that he has that great handicap for a successful man—an identification of himself with righteousness and the resulting persecution complex.

I did not during the campaign nor do I now expect the millennium from Roosevelt.[6] But those "soft" human qualities in him, which grated on so many people, may turn out to be one of the most important factors for a tolerably successful administration. Are we not apt to forget that perhaps the most indispensable function of a democratic statesman is the capacity to mediate among the feelings and irrationalities of his people? My fondest.

Always yours, F.F.

tp with ms signature and notes 105A.1

To Felix Frankfurter

November 10, 1932 Judge Learned Hand's Chambers

Dear Felix:

Thanks for yours of yesterday with the citations, which I have looked up. I agree in general with Brandeis that it is most unsatisfactory to dispose of cases without opinion. It always troubles me, though there are lots of appeals where there is really nothing to say unless one is to discuss the facts. I am thinking particularly of collisions in the admiralty, which, though they sometimes raise the most interesting questions of tort law that we

---

reexamine "jurisdictional facts," expressing pragmatic concerns about how such de novo trials could hamper the effectiveness of the Act and of the agency required to administer it.

6. Franklin Delano Roosevelt (1882–1945): Governor of New York, 1929–1933; President of the United States, 1933–1945.

have, are generally mere questions of credibility. We can say very little except that the question was for the district court and we will not intervene, and this we have said again and again and again. Even then perhaps it would be better to repeat that[...]

We affirm without opinion in about a fifth of all the cases. As I have said, a large part of these are admiralty cases where there is nothing to say beyond what I have suggested; while even as to these I am not wholly comfortable, it does not seem to me that what we might say would add to the comfort of the defeated party, and they never get to the Supreme Court so far as I know. It would add very perceptibly to our labors, which are quite enough now. Manton wrote eighty-six opinions last year, and I eighty-four.

I have no complaint about the result of the election. I do not share the fears of a good many that the advent of the Democrats will be disastrous, and I doubt whether it will have any perceptible effect upon the economic recovery, which is probably already under way though very slowly. I voted for Hoover and all the Republicans, without enthusiasm and without having informed myself about the issue. I read none of the speeches of either side except one of Roosevelt's, which George [Rublee] insisted upon reading to me, and which did not impress me. I quite agree with you that Hoover's crabbed and somewhat churlish nature was a great defect, and that Roosevelt's sunny optimism will be a pleasant change. If I should venture a forecast, my fear would be that he may prove incapable of making unpleasant decisions, and that he will be prone to rely upon the strategy, which he has in his own life found so successful, of a pleasant word to all. But as I have said, with so little information about him my opinion is of little weight. I rate him among what [William] James[7] used to call the "tender minded" rather than the "tough minded," and I have, perhaps for reasons that lie deeper than I know, an extreme leaning toward the "tough minded." One of the difficulties of a democratic society is the tendency of those who come to power to be of the other school. Hoover, whatever his faults, seems to me to look rather that way.

[Charles] Wyzanski[8] left me on Election Day. He is the paragon of law clerks, but if he had stayed through the year, I fear I should have been a nervous wreck. He twisted my poor old noddle around in so many directions, and proved so much deeper than I, that I was most of the time in a whirl. I liked him enormously. His independence and self-respect, his unwillingness to take a position in gross, the realism of his feelings and of his nature, and his entire absence of vanity, appeal to me enormously. I like to feel that he is one of my friends.

My best love to Marion. L.H.

P.S. About Roosevelt I try to remember always this. A man who has conquered such a terrible calamity as he must have somewhere in him *virtus*; when I reflect what it would have done to me, I must stand in respect of him. But the human soul is a curious mélange,

7. William James (1842–1910): Professor of Psychology and Philosophy, Harvard University, 1873–1907.

8. Charles Wyzanski (1906–1986): clerked for Augustus N. Hand, 1930–1931 and for Learned Hand, 1932; solicitor, Department Labor, Washington, 1933–1935; staff of the Solicitor General of the United States, 1935–1937; partner, Ropes & Gray, Boston, 1938–1941; Judge, United States District Court for Massachusetts, 1941–1971; Judge, the International Administrative Court in Geneva, 1950–1955. See LH's extensive correspondence with Wyzanski, which dates from December 18, 1932 to December 9, 1958. See also Wyzanski's tribute to LH: *Judge Learned Hand's Contributions to Public Law*, 60 HARV. L. REV. 348 (1947), in which Wyzanski identifies LH as *il maestro de coloro che sanno*, "the Master of those who know," i.e., the Aristotle in Dante's Limbo, that part of the inferno holding those without sin but unbaptized. *See Inferno*, 4, 131.

and what may be heroism in one may be no more than an unconquerable optimism in another. It is a pity that it was impolitic to emphasize this—by far the greatest claim in my opinion that he has upon our confidence. L.H.

tp with ms signature and notes105A.1

1933-1

To Felix Frankfurter

January 23, 1933 Judge Learned Hand's Chambers

Dear Felix:

I found the matter which you transmit offensive,[9] but I shall try to conform, notwithstanding my absence of "experience on the air."[10]

---

9. In a letter dated December 30, 1932, William Shafroth, advisor to the American Bar Association, invited Frankfurter to deliver a radio address on the topic "How Far Is a Judge Free in Rendering a Decision" for a series sponsored by the American Bar Association. Shafroth asked Frankfurter to have LH join him on this occasion. In a letter dated January 3, 1933, Frankfurter confirmed to Shafroth that he and LH would meet in a studio in Boston on April 9, 1933, to discuss the designated topic. (tp with ms signature 105A.1)

10. LH presented his address on May 14, 1933, on the network of the Columbia Broadcasting System. It conveys LH's understanding of how a statute or a precedent is to be interpreted: "The judge must therefore find out the will of the government from words which are chosen from common speech and which had better not attempt to provide for every possible contingency[...] [W]hat he really does is to take the language before him, whether it be from a statute or from the decision of a former judge, and try to find out what the government, or his predecessor, would have done if the case before him had been before them[...] The men who used the language did not have any intent at all about the case that has come up; it had not occurred to their minds. Strictly speaking, it is impossible to know what they would have said about it, if it had. All they have done is to write down certain words which they mean to apply generally to situations of that kind. To apply these literally may either pervert what was plainly their general meaning, or leave undisposed of what there is every reason to suppose they meant to provide for. Thus it is not enough for the judge just to use a dictionary." *How Far is a Judge Free in Rendering a Decision, in* THE SPIRIT OF LIBERTY 103–10, 106. LH is paraphrasing Edmund Plowden's instructions on the interpretation of statutes; *see* Eyston v. Studd, (1574) 75 Eng. Rep. 688 (K.B.) 695–702. (Frankfurter later provides LH with the exact citation; *see* 1951-1 To Learned Hand from Felix Frankfurter, January 13.) LH represents aspects of Plowden's commentary in *Reiss v. National Quotation Bureau*, 276 F. 717, 719 (S.D.N.Y. 1921): "if our Constitution embalms inflexibly the habits of 1789 there may be something in the point. But it does not; [the Constitution's] grants of power to Congress comprise, not only what was then known, but what the ingenuity of men should devise thereafter." *Id.* at 719; *see also* Borella v. Borden Co., 145 F.2d 63, 64 (2d Cir. 1944), *aff'd*, 325 U.S. 679 (1945) ("We can best reach the meaning here, as always, by recourse to the underlying purpose, and, with that as a guide, by trying to project upon the specific occasion how we think persons, actuated by such a purpose, would have dealt with it if it had been presented to them at the time."). See also 1941-3 To Learned Hand from Felix Frankfurter, July 30, note 81, on *National Labor Relations Board v. Federbush.* LH notes a fundamental conundrum plaguing the act of interpretation, that is: "how far the occasion which provoked the 'enactment' [of a law] and the purpose which infused it—be it constitution, statute, precedent or regulation—shall prevail to set its limits or to enlarge its comprehension[...] [The judge] must

Yes, I sometimes wish that I had been born in the eighteenth century, but I wish more that I could have been born in the twenty-first century. There are so many things now in the womb of time that I want to see born. How foolish! I should have the same regrets in the twenty-first century, and I should have had the same in the eighteenth century. The only satisfactory existence that I know would be to return, and have ten years every century. It would take ten years to get acquainted with the new situation. Besides, one could be so detached and so philosophic—and how damned unpleasant one would be too! No, on further reflection I am content. I don't want to be God and that would be too near divinity. In the whole, I had rather be this scuffling, passionate, discontented, craving creature that I am than seek the indifference of eternity.

Faithfully yours, L.H.

tp with ms signature 105A.1

1933-2

To Philip Littell

February 12, 1933 Washington, D.C.

Dear Phil:

I am stopping a couple of days at Ned's[11][...] We have been at the cabin; Louise, George, and I with a host of others. There was four inches—I decline to say were four

---

have the historical capacity to reconstruct the whole setting which evoked the law; the contentions which it resolved; the objects which it sought; the events which led up to it. But all this is only the beginning, for he must possess the far more exceptional power of divination which can peer into the purpose beyond its expression, and bring to fruition that which lay only in flower." *Thomas Walter Swan, in* THE SPIRIT OF LIBERTY 209–19, 216, 217. *See also* LEARNED HAND, THE BILL OF RIGHTS: THE OLIVER WENDELL HOLMES LECTURES 19–23 (1958). None of LH's admonitions are unproblematic. As Hans-Georg Gadamer observes, understanding the "whole setting" of an event that has occurred in the past is practically impossible, for "if we are trying to understand a historical phenomenon from the historical distance that is characteristic of our hermeneutical situation, we are always already affected by history. It determines in advance both what seems to us worth inquiring about and what will appear as an object of investigation and we more or less forget half of what's there—in fact we miss the whole truth of the phenomenon—when we take its immediate appearance as the whole truth." HANS-GEORG GADAMER, TRUTH AND METHOD 300 (Joel Wensheimer & Donald G. Marshall trans., 1975). LH's attention to the historical conditions in which the text he interprets may fashion its immediate relevance is evident when he considers Frankfurter's understanding of the Fourteenth Amendment in relation to *Brown v. Board of Education*, and implies his awareness of his own "hermeneutical situation," even though he would not have subscribed to that terminology. See 1957-7 To Frankfurter, September 25. Plowden's formula has not always been prescriptive. As Justice Robert Jackson observes: "We take the Act as Congress gave it to us, without attempting to conform it to any notions of what Congress would have done if the circumstances of this case had been put before it." Western Union Telegraph Co. v. Lenroot, 323 U.S. 490, 501 (1945). *See also* Archibald Cox, *Learned Hand and the Interpretation of Statutes*, 60 HARV. L. REV. 370 (1947); John M. Walker, *Judicial Tendencies in Statutory Construction: Differing Views on the Role of the Judge*, 58 N.Y.U. ANN. SURV. AM. L. 203 (2001).

11. I.e., Edward Burling; the company included Louise Burling and George Rublee.

inches—of snow on the ground; the sun was bright; purples were in the boles of the hapless trees. F.A.H. meant to come on; we both meant to get here Thursday night, but she fell sick of a cold and had to stay at home. We had been for three days at a little place called Salisbury in northwestern Conn. where we read and walked in a pleasant wintry countryside, comfortably housed. I have had a week's vacation, which I should best have liked to spend near you, but somehow the thought of the Windsor Inn seemed too forbidding.

Until then, my life had been very monotonous but agreeable. Work has been about as usual, save for the fact that my young secretaries make my wits dance to a somewhat livelier tune than before I had them, and so the work seems a bit harder than it used to. But I get more out of it, and I trust I put more into it. It does seem when I read it over as if there had been an improvement in directness and less affectation or literary effort. Phil, at the end of my life I am just beginning to see what it might have been to try really to write. It has a charm that for all my early years I was blind to; it is something anyway to learn that the thought one thinks one has is not really buried until it is put into words. One might think this so obvious a thing to be apprehendable at the outset. With me it was not; maybe I should have recognized it years ago, but I did not feel it as I have of late. That I should ever have learned to practice writing as an art I doubt. I can see vistas of unknown relations that I have never even started down, but I know at least that they are there; I can understand better what you, for instance, have meant than I used. My kind of writing is limited, but there are even so all sorts of modes in it; it gives one scope enough, if one can use it right. So the thing keeps up its interest; thinking out the details is, I fancy, getting a little harder. I find a disposition to yield to more superficial solutions than in earlier years, but I can still check it. Only the lift of thinking appears to be a little harder.

I have heard very little about you, except the very good news that you have been quite free of asthma, absolutely quit of it. Where did I hear that? From Margaret, I think. That was indeed a surprise, an unexpected added benison for Cornish to give you. I think of you and Fanny very often, see you reading alone and to each other, looking out on Dingleton [Hill] and delighting in the beauties of the mornings and evenings. It is a good life. I can see that it is a good life as I could not have seen not many years ago. How our values shape themselves with our possibilities. Do you remember Anatole France: "Elle fait ce qu'elle peut avec ce qu'elle a."[12] But that was said in an objective and so a hostile, at least an unfriendly spirit; the cuss found a superiority, a snobbishness in standing outside. What he ought to have reflected was that every standard of values, no matter how physiologically inevitable, was just as good as any other, if it was really a standard of values, if changes had not only limited possibilities of realization, but the very wants themselves. Of course, I agree that to him who is conscious of a feasible choice between values, all those in his universe here and now must stand in a hierarchy. I am not concerned with that. Is there a real difference between poetry and push-pin when A. cannot endure push-pin and B. hates poetry? That's not the heart of all morals; nobody seems to me to have answered that. So I am content now with a world in which there are and can be no divine goddesses, and the flash of an ankle will no longer stir me to unquiet. It is very hard, though, to keep open the memories enough to understand how the young are feeling. That I want to keep, because they do remain in my values.

12. French author and novelist, Anatole France, 1844–1924 (pen-name, Jacques Anatole Thibault): "She does what she can with what she has." I have not identified the work.

All quite obscure, Phil, but at bottom there is something in it; I put my finger in a real inquiry. I read a dreadfully crabbed bird called Moore, this summer—*Principia Ethica*:[13] read it twice. I don't think I quite understood it, and it did seem to me as though he could have said his say without so dreadful a dialectic all the time. But what I got out of it was that the "goods" were necessarily merely themselves, unanalyzable things. Put it most strongly: would the universe be better if the other side of the moon were a swill heap or Paradise? I presuppose that it is and always will be inaccessible to any sentience. He says yes; he thinks so. I say no; it is of utter irrelevance in the universe of "goods" or morals. "Good" relates to feeling and feeling alone. So it seems to me, though I agree that good things are merely what feel good; you cannot build them out of anything simpler. I should insist that unless they involved feeling they were not good, nevertheless. I merely take my arbitrary stand there; I doubt if anyone can find any "good" without overtly infusing it with the feeling of an observer.

How in Hell did I get into this? Just because I was writing about your life up there and that it seemed to me so pleasant, and that I was aware of the fading out of what used to seem so important and was not any longer. Here I am in Washington. I used to wish awfully that I could be on the Supreme Court; I used to wish this whenever I came here. I do not do this now. It amuses me to think of this, still more to wonder how much I might change back if it by a miracle could become again possible. There, that's an instance. *Elle fait ce qu'elle peut avec ce qu'elle a.* I don't see anything funny about that at all. Louis [Dow] does; I think he is too ready to interpret human conduct under the Fable of the Fox and the Grapes. It is really much more subtle than that and much more comforting[...]

This is a letter too long for anyone who is not presumed to have leisure; perhaps I ought not to put you in that class. You are not like Grampy,[14] who incontinently throws them away unread. But it has at any rate been a pleasure to me to write it, which counts for something, whatever the effect on you. And the little Duchess, present her with my deep goodwill and as much of this as you think she can tolerate.

L.H.

ms with signature 233.30

1933-3

To Felix Frankfurter

July 23, 1933 Albany, New York

Dear Felix:

It is extremely unlikely that I shall get to Cornish before we sail, and so I fear that I shall not see you for nearly a year.[15] In spite of the infrequency of our meetings this is a

13. George Edward Moore, Principia Ethica (1903).

14. Dr. Walton Martin, a family friend and physician.

15. LH traveled to Europe that summer; Frankfurter was to be the Eastman Professor of Law at Oxford University during the academic year 1933–1934.

regret to me, greater than I dare say you would suppose. I think of you very often, and your opinions have an importance to me which you probably do not know. Besides, I find, as who does not, that even in the case of those with whom one is familiar by long friendship, a short personal interview now and again is most important to keep one in contact with the course of other men's beliefs. So I repeat, I am truly sorry that I shall not meet you for so long. At 61 one cannot but recognize that time is on its inexorable flight, and that in the end the bird is bound to light.

I believe that your experience will bring you a great deal. Personally, I should wince at exposure to an Oxford atmosphere; I should dread the manifest lacunae which those acute and sophisticated souls would quickly discover, and I should inevitably make the mistake of trying to veil them by adopting the modes and tricks of the dons themselves, in which, though gifted with some power of mimicry, I should succeed only half, which is to fail. Nothing is more apparent to me than that an Englishman, at least an educated Englishman, does not value the imitation of English Kultur which an Eastern American at times knows pretty well how to assume. He is right. That kind of thing is better in the original than in the colonial version, and he knows it. His British complacency may be flattered by the tribute, but his respect is gone and he is quickly and rightly bored by finding a tiresome copy of what he is apt to be tired of in the authentic version. I have always yielded to this because I have always had a colonial deference to Europeans and to Englishmen especially, as my father had before me and brought me up to have, though he did not know it in such disparaging terms.

But the Englishmen whom I have seen really get a sense of a vital life out of Americans who are more truly themselves. Curiously enough, the kind I am thinking of are apt to be of the older immigrant stock, most closely akin in blood to the English, though we can find plenty of exceptions to that in the West. But they like the shock of new impacts, even when they don't agree with them. I rather fancy that Oxford is in an especial mood to be receptive to such collisions, little as one would select her. Maybe not. Anyway, whether she is or not, you are bound to be yourself wherever you are, and what you will give them will be the real American fruit, more real than what they get at a dinner of the Pilgrims. I think that they will like it, though many of the fine old crustaceans will certainly snort and some will sneer. Sneering is as congenital with them as with Pooh Bah. But unless I am wrong, they will like you and find in you something which, though they will probably not accept it, they will not be bored by. That's my guess. You, on the other hand, being a dab at "contacts," will make a hell of a lot of these and will come back with a correspondence for the future even greater, if that be conceivable, than what exists at present. You will be enriched, and you will give a quid pro quo. What more can anyone ask?

To what kind of America you will come back, I must own that I am quizzical about. On the whole, with the fullest possible recognition of my own inabilities to pass upon the issues, I am disposed to believe that Fearless Franklin has done the only thing that he could. I have no idea his brains are much less muggy about the whole business than my own. I do not for an instant suppose that he could stand any competent cross-examination by a hostile economist on any of the issues. He's a prime *sauteur*, as quick a cat and as full of shifts as a mongoose; he's a peerless politician. His very Boyscoutismus has made it possible for him to go on with a blithe irresponsibility which was essential and which a more scrupulous nature could not have put on. If this kind of job was to be done, he was par excellence the man to do it.

Was it to be done? I rather guess it was. Maybe if we had had a nation of patient cows, it would have been better to let things alone and feed the down-and-outers till we picked up. I am skeptical about the devices employed. But we had *homines sapientes* not patient cows, and you couldn't sit still. Just how it will come out I don't know, but we were in for something of the Efficiency Engineering type, and by God we are getting it.

But make no mistake: win or lose, our revered Constitution of checks and balances has gone. The American people is getting used to the idea that when the wind blows, the Captain is the boss and that what he says goes. If there is opposition, he goes "on the air" and bullies recalcitrants into line, just as they bullied poor old Germans to subscribe to the Liberty Loans in 1917. That lesson stuck. I confess I wince; it has too much resemblance to Russia, Italy, Japan, and Germany for my relish. I see a very small place left for the kind of *procedendo* for which I alone am suited and to which my heart is wed. I was struck with a piece by Keynes in the *New Statesman* where, while acknowledging that there must be drastic upsets economically if a shred of capitalism was to stay, he added that if the cost was to be the suppression of all dissent and the general atmosphere of the Big Bully, he was back to 19th Century Liberalism. That proved too ghastly a treasure for the editor, who commented on it with grief.

Well, the feel of the thing is not pleasant to me. I have abused old slobs too often for the principle of *obsta principiis* not to feel a little guilty when I invoke it, but really there comes a limit. If you once get used to brow beating the whole crew and the passenger list whenever the wind rises to a half-gale, your Beaufort scale will be half-gale whenever you don't have your way. I shouldn't mind so much if the way out was by upsetting capitalism, but Russia is not an encouraging alternative. And so I stand as I generally do, like Santayana: "perplexed aside from so much sorrow." I seem to be between an irresistible force and an immovable body, like a fly about to receive the swatter. On the whole it ain't so peaceful a state of mind; I can't quite dope it out. If Croly were here, he would have the key wouldn't he? I seem to see everywhere the specter of Fascism and I hate that something fierce; it stops my breathing apparatus. If they won't let me talk, I might as well die. And you may see in a few weeks that to talk dirty about the "Administration Program" will be disloyal. The note gets shriller all the time and the cheerleaders are yelling and jumping and clapping their hands harder and harder. "Now fellows, nine long cheers for the Rubber Dollar, etc. etc." I rather like their ideas but their "techniques"—Christ, how I hate that word—do not please me[...]

L.H.

ms with signature 105A.2

1933-4

To Bernard Berenson

November 11, 1933 Judge Learned Hand's Chambers

Dear B.B.:

[...]Just at present we seem to be at the turn of the tide. Roosevelt, in spite of some serious blunders, carried us on and gave us a little dash of self-confidence. It was sadly needed and the hypodermic worked.[16] But it took the form of too much bullying, and as was perhaps anticipated, it has provoked a good deal of resentment. The big fellows for a while professed to be cooperative though in fact they were not, only so scared that they were afraid to peep. Besides, they had more fat to live on, and they were offered the bait of freedom to combine, to be free of their *bête noir*, the Antitrust Acts. That went far to disarm them. But the little chaps, the small industrialists, got it both ways. Being "marginal producers," they were unable to raise wages and give shorter hours while holding prices level. Again, they hadn't the power to combine; they took what the big fellows saw fit to give them. Besides, they have to live by sniping anyway. They are unhappy, and though I am in no position to know much, I suspect that the marked change of sentiment towards the whole show has emanated largely from them. The big predatory boys were never at ease, and if they can find support for their discontent, I think they will join in a revolt. Add to this that the farmers are in open rebellion, almost a violent rebellion, and the set-up does not look too good for Fearless Franklin. Of course, the farmers want rotten money; they always have since 1785 when Shays' rebellion[17] so frightened the Massachusetts *bas-bourgeois* that it gave us a Constitution with some teeth in it. Again and again, they have cried for paper money and they have always been beaten. I am not so sure this time; the fashion is catching and we have not learned the joys of paying $2500 for a subway ride. The Germans and Austrians know all about that and don't want it again[...]

Yes, I agree that all this Hitler, Mussolini, Soviet religion is materialistic and to me it ain't pleasant, dear boy. However, I can't disguise from myself that I have so profited by the old patterns as to be inevitably corrupted. If I didn't know where the next meal was coming from and was likely to be thrown onto the street next week, I rather fancy that I should be relatively cool towards dangers of materialism. I have never been able to make my own hierarchy of values, let alone ours, for the world at large. I should be prepared to hear argument that the joys of Athenian citizens in 450 B.C. were more than a balance for the slaves and *perioeci* (I'm not sure about that spelling) or when they fed. If there were a sure way of marshalling those who could enjoy from those who could not, I will not say

16. LH may be referring to the "Recovery Program" Roosevelt outlined in his Fireside Chat on July 24.

17. Shays' Rebellion was an armed uprising in western Massachusetts from 1786 to 1787 consisting mostly of farmers protesting debt and taxes; it resulted in a call to reevaluate the Articles of Confederation and gave strong impetus to the Constitutional Convention, which began in May 1787.

that my democracy should survive. Besides, here at any rate, our system gives full play to the predatory fish and they seem to me limited in power to enjoy anything but the chase and the kill. A real "good," I dare say, though I'm a bit too anemic to share its delights. So, first, I am mixed about fundamentals, and second, I am not convinced that our blessed capitalistic democracies are less materialistic than [the regimes of] Stalin, Hitler, Mussolini & Co. I don't care for any of the partners, largely because they would cramp me, a divine soul, nearly 62 years old, and especially wouldn't let me express my ideas about whatever is the Good, the True, and the Beautiful. But when I go up to Sinai and begin to converse with the Patriarchal Gent whom your forefathers wished on the Western World, all these hills and valleys get a bit flattened out, and I'm in some doubt; I'm always in doubt.

This is a frivolous letter. It ought not to have been, for I was distressed to hear of your sister's death.[18] I never met her, but I know Perry and it grieves me to know that you and he will have suffered this loss. I hope that my condolence will not seem insincere after so much froth.

Please give my love to Mary.

Sincerely yours, Learned Hand

tr/ms with signature 99.13

1934-1

To Samuel Dickstein[19]

May 10, 1934

Dear Mr. Dickstein:

In conformity with your request, I am writing the substance of what I said on Tuesday as to the amendment of §19 of the Immigration Act of 1917, proposed by House Bill 9363, introduced April 26, 1934.[20]

---

18. Berenson's sister Rachel was married to Ralph Barton Perry. Berenson's reply to LH's letter, dated December 13, 1933, is reprinted in BERNARD BERENSON, THE SELECTED LETTERS OF BERNARD BERENSON 122–23 (1964).

19. Samuel Dickstein (1885–1954): Representative from New York, 1925–1945; Chairman of the Committee on Immigration and Naturalization, 1931–1947. In 1934, with Representative John McCormack, Dickstein formed the Special Committee on Un-American Activities to investigate supposed American fascists; in 1938, he was instrumental in founding the Select Committee on Un-American Activities with Martin Dies, Jr. as chairman, to investigate fascist and communist groups in the United States, which later, as the House Committee on Un-American Activities, focused on communist organizations.

20. On February 5, 1917, Congress had passed (over President Wilson's veto) the Immigration Act of 1917 (also known as the Asiatic Barred Zone Act), which added to the number of persons who were considered undesirable and thus to be banned from entering the country. The Act also designated an "Asiatic Barred Zone," a region that included much of eastern Asia and the Pacific Islands, from which people could not immigrate. Previously, only the Chinese had been excluded from

What I am especially interested in is the protection against deportation of aliens admitted at ten years of age or less, and some conditional protection for those admitted between eleven and sixteen. It is true that 5(a) gives the Secretary power to dispense with deportation, provided the alien be a person of good moral character, have not been convicted of a crime involving moral turpitude, and have not engaged in "subversive political agitation"; but if one turns to 2, it appears that of the twelve subdivisions stating the grounds for deportation, only three—numbers 1, 7, and 12—can fall within 5(a). There might be cases under subdivision 4 in which good moral character could be proved, but not many. Subdivision 10 could never apply, because the Secretary would not dispense with deportation in cases where deportation depended on his decision to deport. The result is that in cases where the alien is a person of bad character, has been convicted of a morally shameful crime, or is politically "subversive"—a most elastic phrase at best—no length of residence will protect him. This seems to me to result in extreme severity, and to presuppose a social irresponsibility which is dishonorable to the American people.

Speaking broadly, alien children become deportable only for conduct occurring after they are sixteen years of age; that will not be absolutely true, but it must cover the enormous preponderance of cases. If they have been brought here below the age of eleven, and have been reared indiscriminately with the native born, they are ordinarily indistinguishable from them; at least, it would be quite unwarranted to ascribe their criminal or immoral propensities to their foreign birthplace. They are as much mistakes of our own conditions as those who have been born here of the same stocks and environment; having admitted them before they could choose, and while they were perfectly malleable to their surroundings, we are in honor bound to accept responsibility for them. We cannot ship the native born elsewhere, we must deal with them; I submit that we ought not to disown their alien fellows because of the immaterial accident of birth. Deportation in such cases is an excessively harsh punishment, which in most cases is practically certain to effect their destruction so far as that has not already come to pass. Their formative years have been passed here; this is their home, ours are the only associations they know, the only habits to which they are used; generally, ours is the only tongue they can speak. To set them down in a foreign country is to banish them quite as effectively as it would banish any of us; they have by hypothesis already proved themselves unfit; we finish their ruin by putting them where it would be extremely difficult for even the best to adjust themselves. I append a list of decisions in which the Second Circuit has commented upon the unfairness of the present law.[21]

---

admission to the country. See 1916-1 To Frankfurter, January 10, on the Chinese Exclusion Act. At the request of D.W. MacCormack, United States Commissioner of Immigration and Naturalization, LH appeared before the Senate Committee on Immigration and Naturalization to express his opinion of the proposed bills on immigration.

21. LH's list of decisions runs as follows: "Cases in the Second Circuit discussing this question—U.S. *ex rel.* Mittler v. Curran, 8 F.2d 355 (2d Cir. 1925); U.S. *ex rel.* Klonis v. Davis, 13 F.2d 630 (2d Cir. 1926); U.S. *ex rel.* Kowalenski v. Flynn, 17 F.2d 524 (W.D.N.Y. 1927); U.S. *ex rel.* Mignozzi v. Day, 51 F.2d 1019 (2d Cir. 1931)." LH's oft-cited passage in *Klonis* sums up his views: "[W]e think it not improper to say that deportation under the circumstances would be deplorable. Whether the relator came here in arms or at the age of ten, he is as much our product as though his mother had borne him on American soil. He knows no other language, no other people, no other habits, than ours; he will be as much a stranger in Poland as any one born of ancestors who immigrated in the seventeenth century. However heinous his crimes, deportation is to him exile, a dreadful punishment, abandoned

Therefore if I could have my way, I would prevent the deportation of anyone admitted at the age of ten or less. As I have said, this would, speaking generally, not cover anyone who had not been here for six formative years, that is, between ten and sixteen; on the average it would cover those who had been here from five to sixteen. I should also like to see this prohibition extended to those who entered between eleven and sixteen, provided they had been here for five years[...] This would leave open harsh possibilities, e.g., the deportation of a child of sixteen, but that is inevitable if you proceed by general rule; such cases the Secretary could control if his discretion is preserved in the bill. My argument for this is the same as above, though possibly it is not so strong; the higher the age, the less the injustice[...]

May I take this occasion to thank you for granting me a hearing on a matter which, as I have said, I have long had at heart?[22]

Respectfully yours, [Learned Hand]

tp 57.5

1934-2

To Harry E. Stone[23]

November 5, 1934

Dear Sir:

I have your letter of November 1st, asking me to give you my ideas as to the share which a lawyer may feel that he has in the support and development of a civilized state.[24] We are apt to assume that the practice of the law, as it must fall to the lot of the ordinary lawyer whose first interest should rightly be to secure an ample competence for his family and himself, has no greater public significance than selling bonds or weighing sugar. For this reason, it has become common to direct generous minded young men to what is thought to be a higher social service. The profession in its more humdrum routine is contemned. It would certainly be beyond the compass of anything I have to say or of anything I have competence to say, to estimate the importance of agitation and propaganda, directed by compassion for distress

---

by the common consent of all civilized peoples. Such, indeed, it would be to any one, but to one already proved to be incapable of honest living, a helpless waif in a strange land, it will be utter destruction. That our reasonable efforts to rid ourselves of unassimilable immigrants should in execution be attended by such a cruel and barbarous result would be a national reproach." U.S. *ex rel.* Klonis v. Davis, 13 F.2d at 630–31.

22. In a letter dated June 1, 1934, D.W. MacCormack wrote to LH: "We finally got through most of our proposals, including that giving discretion in the case of children brought into the country before sixteen years of age. The sentiment, however, was so strong against any leniency that would benefit criminals that I felt it would endanger our whole program should we attempt to amend the deportation bill as you suggested. I am, however, in accord with your view that persons who have come in here as children and are the product of our environment should be considered as our responsibility and not as that of the country in which they chanced to be born and will, when occasion serves, present that view to the Congress for its consideration." (tp with ms signature 57.5)

23. Harry E. Stone (1883–1959): Dean, West Virginia University, 1922–1959.

24. In a letter dated November 1, 1934, Dean Stone asks LH for his view on a career in "law and public service." (tp with ms signature 62.1)

and indignation and injustice. Nevertheless, my impression is that, for the moment anyway, we are rather overstocked with both, or at least with those who profess them. Be that as it may, nobody can sanely deny that a critical outlook is an essential to any political efforts not bound to failure. The practice of law has always sharpened that skepticism without which no government can ever be healthy and which we sadly need just now. A body of lawyers, even those whom necessity will confine to the details of personal practice, forms an element in a state which has proved its value in the past and will prove it in the future. It is a humble role but most roles are humble, and to those who would fly high, much more is open if their wings do not fail. For lawyers are cast for the part of putting into words the vague yearnings which float half grasped in men's minds, and until we learn to communicate in something other than words, their proper use will be one of the highest functions of any society.[25] Lawyers who emerge will be those who know what words to use; they will command in the end, no matter how much for the moment they must bend, for they alone are the interpreters of the spiritual essences which inspire the brains of men. Some such interposition has always been a condition of the spread of the great emotional surges of the human spirit; they must become institutionalized because only so can any constantly communicable content be transmitted. Men will resent and resist this necessity; but they will not be able to escape. That necessity is the lawyer's opportunity and his justification.

Truly yours, [Learned Hand]

tp 62.1

1934-3

To Learned Hand from Felix Frankfurter

December 3, 1934 Law School of Harvard University

Dear B.:

[. . .]Let me congratulate you on having at last found a statute that is unconstitutional, at least unconstitutional in its operation[. . .][26]

Always yours, F.F.

tp with ms signature 105A.2

---

25. In an article for the HARVARD LAW REVIEW published in 1916, LH describes how a judge shapes the future: "[T]he judge has, by custom, his own proper representative character as a complementary organ of the social will [, . . . a] free power by interpretation to manifest the half-framed purposes of his time." *The Speech of Justice, in* THE SPIRIT OF LIBERTY 13–19; 14.

26. Referring to *Seelig v. Baldwin*, 7 F. Supp. 776 (S.D.N.Y. 1934), for which LH wrote the opinion enjoining the enforcement of a section of the New York state Agriculture & Markets law and a corresponding order of the state's Milk Control Board that regulated the price of milk sold in New York but sourced from out of state. The plaintiff milk dealer asserted that the regulation was an unconstitutional interference with interstate commerce because New York required that imported milk be sold at the same (higher) price as domestic milk, a program viewed as an attempt to give New York dairy producers an advantage by undermining out-of-state producers' ability to produce their milk at a lower cost and thereby compete in the marketplace.

To Felix Frankfurter

December 5, 1934 Judge Learned Hand's Chambers

Dear Felix:

[...]No, I was rather unhappy about that unconstitutional statute. I had a kind of feeling that my record ought to be clean, and it comes always a little hard for me when it is not. In twenty-five years this is only the second time, but I regretted it here less than in most instances, for it does seem to me that this kind of legislation, if lawful without the concurrence of Congress, would quickly Balkanize these United States. The effort to build up in each state economic barriers for the protection of the local industries seems to be a direct way toward an interstate protection system, and I am satisfied that our economic advancement in the past has been largely due to the free trade area which was insured. No such effort ought to be permitted without the concurrence of Congress, so I found a case that I could act on *con amore.* I can hardly imagine feeling so about the Fifth or Fourteenth Amendment[...]

As ever, yours, L.H.

tp with ms signature 105A.2

1936-1

To Learned Hand from Charles Wyzanski

January 7, 1936 The Anchorage, Washington, D.C.

Dear Judge:

[...]The "A.A.A." decision surprised me.[27] And because I find my prophetic insight less than I had thought, I am disappointed. But I do not regard the decision as a calamity. I, for one, take rather calmly decisions such as the *Child Labor* case,[28] the *Schechter* case,[29]

---

27. Wyzanski is referring to *United States v. Butler,* 297 U.S. 1 (1936), also known as the *Hoosac Mills* case, which challenged the constitutionality of the provision in the Agricultural Adjustment Act of 1933 that made it possible for farmers who reduced crop acreage to receive benefits derived from taxes on businesses that processed the commodities involved. Butler, a processor, refused to pay the tax. By a vote of 6 to 3, the Supreme Court declared the tax unconstitutional; Associate Justice Roberts authored the opinion of the Court; a dissent was authored by Stone, who was joined by Brandeis and Cardozo.

28. Wyzanski is referring to *Hammer v. Dagenhart,* 247 U.S. 251 (1918), in which the Supreme Court found that the Keating-Owen Child Labor Act, which prohibited the interstate shipment of goods that had been produced with child labor, was an unconstitutional exercise of congressional power. The Court found that Congress's power to regulate "commerce" among the states did not encompass the power to regulate production of goods; that power, under the Court's analysis, was reserved to the states under the Tenth Amendment.

29. Wyzanski is referring to *A.L.A. Schechter Poultry Corp. v. United States,* 295 U.S. 495 (1935), in which the Supreme Court, finding that section 3 of the National Industrial Recovery Act was an unconstitutional delegation of power by Congress, struck down the Act. For an analysis of this decision see GERALD GUNTHER, LEARNED HAND: THE MAN AND THE JUDGE 446–50 (1994).

and this "Hoosac" case in which the Supreme Court has insisted on keeping our system federal rather than national. (It is quite a different problem from those presented under the Fifth and Fourteenth Amendments.) I cannot therefore share all of Stone's indignation in his latest dissent. To be sure Roberts wrote a poor, hastily compiled opinion, but I am certain that his vision of the potential descendants of the A.A.A. statute, if it were upheld, was real. Once the revenue from taxes can be used to "purchase" action by farmers, it can be used to purchase action by other groups. And it is no answer to say that we can count on the "patriotism and conscience" of the Executive and Congress. For the question is one of power not between the national government and the people, but between the authorities of the United States and the authorities of the several states. To talk about "patriotism and conscience" under these circumstances is to ignore the psychology of every (or nearly every) politician and bureaucrat. Each member of that tribe always aims at a redistribution of power that will make him, even if only for a moment, kingpin. I have seen in the last few months many who would hesitate to take from people in business or in private life the power to conduct their own affairs, but none or virtually none, who would hesitate to take such power from other governmental authorities. *Vide* the Supreme Court itself!

Faithfully, Charles E. Wyzanski, Jr.

ms with signature 108.15

To Charles Wyzanski

January 9, 1936 Judge Learned Hand's Chambers

My dear Charles:

[...]It seems to me that the Court was pretty clearly wrong in the "A.A.A." decision, though I am not quite certain. Everybody agrees that Congress has power to spend money ad lib. I think that ought to be construed as including the power in its historic amplitude. It has never been suggested that a legislature with power to appropriate could not make the appropriation conditional in any way it chose, including among such conditions the conduct of recipients. As I understand Roberts' opinion, this was the vice of the statute. Congress would have had power to distribute among the farmers largesse as it chose. It did not have power to make the distribution conditional upon the reduction of acreage, because this invaded the powers of the states. Of course, it does invade the powers of the states. Economic sanctions are perhaps the best of all, but they are involved in the power to tax and appropriate unless it is limited in a way that has never before been suggested. Moreover, it seems to me that the distinction is futile in the end. Congress may select its beneficiaries according to their past conduct and gratitude; the expectation of benefits to come will be as potent a sanction as though the condition were imposed in advance. For example, would it be unconstitutional to lay down such codes as Congress saw fit, merely as model patterns of conduct? I suppose it would not, at least there would be no way of challenging it, as it would then carry no sanction. I should doubt whether the Court would go so far as to deny the power to Congress to distribute its gratuities in accordance with those who had conformed to these regulations. Certainly, that would be a plain invasion of the right of the power to appropriate as ordinarily understood.

I do not disguise from myself the fact that the power to appropriate for "non-enumerated" purposes can be made to change the federate system. The cat got out of the bag when the Sixteenth Amendment[30] was passed. When the Constitution was framed, people were interested in the power to tax and cared nothing about the power to spend, which they granted to Congress without limit. When we began to tax generally and finally got unquestioned power to do so, the economic balance was destroyed. I am not so much interested in retaining the federal form as I used to be. It has become to me somewhat an intellectual exercise less than a political conviction—this because with modern communication of all sorts I think in the end local interests have essentially ceased to be local. I am acutely aware of the dangers of a centralized government of a hundred and fifty or two hundred million people, but I do not see how we can save for our purely fortuitous states anything that in the end will be worthwhile. This is as yet with me rather a feeling that a conviction, but I seem to find myself rather more pointed that way.

Faithfully yours, Learned Hand

tp with ms notes, Wyzanski Papers, HLL, Box 2, Folder 6

1936-2

To Philip Littell

July 10, 1936 Judge Learned Hand's Chambers

Dear Phil:

I shall see you tomorrow and can tell you what I have to say about "necessity," which is nothing. Something touches me off in the second paragraph of your letter to write what I should not be able to say. I am glad when my friends grow old; it is not on their account, for I cannot deny that they become sadder, though with a resignation that perhaps makes that sadness more endurable than the agonized strivings of younger years. But I am thinking of myself when I say that I like to have them grow old. Perhaps I shouldn't if I had stayed young; perhaps it is secretly because, having taken their measure, I fear no longer the possible explosion of which everyone is theoretically capable when young. Anyway there is a quietness, an absence of assertion, an acceptance of the world which I would not have missed for much, which makes them dear to me as they were never before.

30. Passed in 1913, the Sixteenth Amendment provides that "[t]he Congress shall have the power to lay and collect taxes on incomes, from whatever source derived, without apportionment among the several States and without regard to any census or enumeration." Prior to passage of the amendment, attempts by Congress to tax income uniformly met with a mixed response by the Supreme Court depending on its characterization of the tax in light of the Constitution's requirement that "direct taxes" could be imposed only by a rule of apportionment (see article I, sections 2 and 9). The passage of the Sixteenth Amendment established the nature of income taxes as "indirect taxes," thereby eliminating the conflict with the aforementioned sections of article I.

You have been one of those—I don't remember any others—who set before yourself a standard of perfection. Perhaps it is *υβϱισ*[31] (where in Hell is the dictionary); always, at least, it is daring to recklessness. I sometimes think you believe you have failed. Well, you have; everybody does, one way or another. But really you have won; you have won because you have plied your craft as you saw it should be plied, even when you knew that you could not reach the quality you wished.[32] The disappointments that that has for the aspirant I need not tell you, who have lived so consistently for it, but the result upon others who have seen it, perhaps I can persuade you of. When we sum up a friend, we like most to think of those things about him which fill us with a sort of glowing approval; it is like looking at something handsome or well-executed, just as we feel almost a sense of love at a fine bit of sport. In more important things, such as the purposes which have actuated those whom we love, we single out with delight the same handsome performances. Only there is this difference, that we are chiefly interested in the high-heartedness of the effort, because what we love in our friends are the things which they have, what they go out for. Well, though all these years you have been to me an inspiration which probably you never knew, an inspiration to a perfection, which I knew, just as you knew, was impossible, and which an unsympathetic outsider would say would merely tease its possessor, idly and disastrously. We choose our own values and that ends it; I choose that, and it is from you that I have had—more constantly I think than from anyone else—a repeated sense that I ought to keep loyal to it. Performance is another matter; I don't like to think about my performance, and I pray God I may not be judged by it.

L.H.

ms with signature 233.31

1936–3

To Dean Acheson[33]

July 23, 1936

Dear Dean:

I read your speech at Atlantic City on July fourth with a great deal of admiration.[34] There is a notable grasp and certainty about it and a clarity of expression which makes me

---

31. I.e., *hubris*, overweening pride, recklessness.

32. LH returns to these ideas in a speech he gave to the American Jewish Committee on January 29, 1955: "[Man's] reward is not so much in the work as in its making; not so much in the prize as in the race. We may win when we lose, if we have done what we can; for by so doing we have made real at least some part of that finished product in whose fabrication we are most concerned: ourselves." *A Fanfare for Prometheus, in* The Spirit of Liberty 291–98, 297.

33. Dean Gooderham Acheson (1893–1971): Undersecretary of the Treasury, 1933; Assistant Secretary of State, 1941–1945; Undersecretary of State, 1945–1947; Secretary of State, 1949–1953. For LH's reaction to critics of Acheson, see 1950-1 To Frankfurter, January 20.

34. Dean Acheson sent LH a copy of his speech on Justice Roger Brooke Taney and judicial self-restraint delivered on July 4, 1936, in Atlantic City before the Maryland Bar Association. There he

eager to have you go in for this thing more than, so far as I know, you have hitherto done. I am especially impressed with the ease and confidence with which you deal with [Roger Brooke] Taney's work[35]; incidentally, you have much increased my own knowledge of that distinguished person.

I suppose the part that interests you most, as it does me, is the general considerations with which you conclude. I hope I need not assure you of my sympathy with your general attitude toward the constitutional function of judges. I should be disposed to go even further; as to the Fifth and Fourteenth amendments, I have long been of opinion that they mar more than they make. Giving an opportunity for strong-willed men to impose their own notions as to the proper resolution of class conflicts, they contradict the very presupposition of a democratic state as I can understand it. I am increasingly troubled, however, about the other constitutional function, that is, the apportionment of power between the Union and the States. There are some passages in what you said about that that I might want to qualify. I agree that Taney was right and Marshall was wrong in attempting to mark out a sphere which no state may enter regardless of the interposition of Congress, but although that would have been a very important qualification if it had got itself established, it would not solve the real difficulty—the extent of the eventual paramountcy of the Union. This is not place to discuss that. I am not sure that my own ideas are enough to be intelligible anyway; but some time perhaps I may have a half hour of your leisure—perhaps you can enlighten me; perhaps I can enlighten you. At least I know that we should be able to talk as I find few people, can, without fixed position and with receptive minds.[36] Meanwhile, please be assured of my great regard and admiration.

Sincerely yours, [Learned Hand]

tp 99.1

---

argued that "the giant stature which Taney assumes in the history of the Supreme Court is due chiefly to his insistence that the judge, in applying constitutional limitations, must restrain himself and leave the maximum of freedom to those agencies of government whose actions he is called upon to weigh." However, "the Court refused to follow Taney. Instead, it developed the now accepted rule that when the subject of regulation requires a uniform rule the federal government alone may legislate; in other fields the States may legislate until Congress acts; and in still others both governments may act. But the question in which class any particular subject matter belongs has been reserved exclusively for the decision of the judges." *Roger Brooke Taney: Notes upon Judicial Self-Restraint*, Dean Acheson Papers, Truman Library, Political and Governmental File, Box 8; 1, 9–10.

35. Roger Brooke Taney (1777–1864): Chief Justice of the Supreme Court, 1836–1864. Taney's most notorious decision, in the *Dred Scott* case, has tended to overshadow all his other decisions.

36. In a letter dated July 38, 1936, Acheson thanked LH for his comments on his Atlantic City speech and hoped that he could discuss them further at some later date. (tp with ms signature 99.1)

1936-4

To Grenville Clark[37]

October 31, 1936

Dear Grenny:

What you said is so far and away the best that anyone has said that it seems a shame it should not have more publicity.[38] Your sense of responsibility in making up your mind is of a piece with all your life and makes your friends value you increasingly as time goes on. I have sometimes wondered whether I was wrong in wanting you in [James Bryant] Conant's[39] place, but when you do anything like this, I realize that I was not, though I am indeed content with him.

To be less personal, I agree in detail pretty completely with your ways of reaching the result, just as I agree in the result, though with some misgiving. You give more approval to Roosevelt personally than I should, but then you know him and I do not. He seems to me too suggestible and too emotional a nature to be capable of anything I should care to call convictions, and so far as I can gather, he is nearly devoid of critical faculty, both because his mind seems quite at sea in dealing with abstractions, and because he is impatient of the obstacles which that kind of thinking puts in his way. I credit him with some real sympathy with oppression, but it seems to me very largely that of the social worker with whom he shares a truly vindictive feeling towards the ruling classes. (I am disposed to put down much of his venom towards them to the fact that he was unsuccessful at the bar.) Indeed, my chief hesitation about him personally was for a reason which does not apparently move you much—his willingness to fan incendiary animosities; he has repeatedly shown himself reckless and irresponsible in ways I shall never forgive him.

But I am quite clear—no, not that, I have hesitatingly concluded—that at the moment the Republican Party is not fit to take power, especially since it will not get any real power to govern at all. I entirely agree with you about the political necessity of a program of "Reform," doubtful as I am about its practicability. Such a program will be more likely to succeed in the hands of its friends than in those of a party which has been grudgingly

37. Grenville Clark, New York attorney.

38. On October 30, Grenville Clark sent LH "Notes on the Election: Second and Final Chapter," in which Clark states in part: "As to fiscal policy, I am uneasy about it but I do not think that with an increased opposition, a Roosevelt administration will run the country into serious financial trouble and thus produce too great a reaction on that score. As to judicial appointments, I made it clear in my notes that I think Mr. Roosevelt has not observed proper standards. This makes me uneasy, but I do not really believe that he would 'pack the Supreme Court with radicals.' Incidental to this, I do not really think that there is a serious constitutional issue[...] Accordingly, my misgivings on the above mentioned points do not outweigh the broader consideration I have in mind. This is that the net result of another Roosevelt administration would probably be to head off or ameliorate class division and tend to prevent ill-advised radical movements on a great scale. In the long run, this is what I think is most important." Clark's "Notes" are in carbon copy and included in 50.22.

39. James Bryant Conant (1893–1978): President, Harvard University, 1933–1953; Ambassador to Germany, 1953–1957.

driven to accept so much of it as it must, public feeling being what it is. It is a good program in its objectives and it may succeed; if it doesn't we are likely to have worse things as you well say. Just there is another reason which you do not mention, but which moves me a good deal. The program may go wrong; I am not at all quiet about finances. If the rate of interest should for instance begin to rise, the whole works would begin to tremble perceptibly. If it does go wrong, I do not want a conservative party in power any more than I do if we get into labor disorders, as we may. Our blithe friend has started this show, and he is the man to finish it—win or lose. At the present time, only Leftist governments ought to be in the saddle when periods of great strain come, as [Léon] Blum[40] has shown.

Finally I agree with your conclusion that if our Allerhöchster Boy Scout were sure to go over as "big" as he has before, we ought to vote against him. One of my daughters is going to vote just for that reason. I am not very satisfied that you are right in thinking that he will not get his old majorities, but I am going to chance it, partly at any rate because—given any kind of gamble—I had rather be counted on the mildly pink side. By the way, how do you get so het up about judges? Of all R.'s faults that which I mind least is "debauching the federal judiciary."

As ever, [L.H.]

tp 50.22

1937-1

To Walter Lippmann

September 10, 1937 Consuma

Dear Walter:

It was been a great disappointment to miss you here; our opportunities for seeing each other are so few and so short when they come that this chance seemed to me especially happy. We cannot stay, however; we sail on the 21st and want at least five or six days in Rome.[41] We have been here six days—all pleasant but today—and I need not tell you how pleasant days can be in these mountains. B.B. and I have had a number of good talks, he telling me of the conditions here, I trying to outline what they were with us, but it would have been better had we both been at hand to check off each other's judgments, perhaps modifying them in the process. Besides, I am very anxious to know whether the last four months have affected your opinions and how. As you know, I have never looked at the court controversy with quite your eye; in method and as an instance of arbitrary power, I should agree with you, but the issue as such does not have the importance to me that it has to so many of

40. Léon Blum (1872–1950): Socialist; Prime Minister of France, 1936–1937.

41. *See* 1937-2 To Berenson, September 17.

my friends. [Hugo] Black's appointment[42] was as insolent a defiance of respectable opinion as could be—a declaration of sans-culottism[43] plainer than any hitherto—but Black, as new member, did not shock me. Until we can arrange our institutions more in accordance with our professions, I shall not be overwhelmed by such perversions; the perversions which are inherent lead to perversions in detail. I can agree that John Marshall may have been necessary to make a nation out of fifteen or twenty parishes which liked to think of themselves as monadic nations looking up to God, but we are paying a heavy price for him now in a political metaphysic which is neither tenable a priori, nor tolerable in practice.

But, Walter, all this cannot possibly interest you. You have worked out your ideas as only they can be worked out when one composes a book and I understand that your last comprises this problem among much else. Insofar as you are discharging your artillery against totalitarian absolutism tempered by plebiscite, I am with you; it is only when a bench of judges is used to fill in the voids that I protest.[44] Besides, if we had been together all this would have occupied only a little of our time. It was precious time which I lost. Most of my trip has been spent amid the ministrations of elderly ladies—I say "elderly" in spite of the fact that sixty still seems to me not too irrevocably on the descending slopes. You see how far time has debauched my standards.

It is a little disconcerting to think that in three weeks my parole is over and I shall be in New York, preparing to serve another ten-week term. Will it not be possible in some way for us to see each other? I hope so. I hope that the leaden hand of routine will not so numb me that I shall not let the weeks run on, as I have. And yet that is what I have so often said to myself before. And what good did it do?

L.H.

ms with signature, Lippmann Papers, Sterling, Box 76, Folder 978.

1937-2

To Bernard Berenson

September 17, 1937 American Academy in Rome

Dear B.B.:

[...]I am to see the philosopher—Santayana—in a couple of hours. I wrote rather expecting that he would keep his impenetrability. To my surprise (a little), he said "come" and I go.[45] He wants to hear about the changes in feeling in the U.S.A; if I were only

42. Hugo Lafayette Black (1886–1971): Senator from Alabama, 1927–1937; Associate Justice of the United States Supreme Court, 1937–1971.

43. LH refers to the radical politics of the working class or Third Estate during the French revolution; this class wore trousers, not breeches, and thus were "sans-culottes."

44. LH refers to Lippmann's *Inquiry into the Principles of the Good Society* (1937). For LH's assessment of this book, see 1938-2 To Berenson, August 3.

45. LH and Frances Hand visited Berenson earlier in September; by the 17th, they were in Rome. There is no letter from Santayana to LH dating from 1937 in the Hand Papers.

Walter L., I should feel more competent. As it is, I fear I shall not really serve him, but it will be an interesting experience for me. Of course it's rather ridiculous being here for so short a time, but then traveling as I travel is ridiculous anyway. Besides, maybe all I do is ridiculous, and all that the sons of man do, if one really gets to cross-examining. I went yesterday to Subiaco, and saw where a young Roman, about A.D. 425, went for three years, lived in a cave,* and came out as St. Benedict. I am not sure that that was not as ridiculous as being a U.S. Circuit judge, though I agree that it had a good deal of result. But results, Good God, if we judge by results[...]

My love to Nicky; and the best of good wishes to you. L.H.

*Don't think I *believe* in that cave episode. L.H.

tr/ms with signature 99.15

To Learned Hand from Bernard Berenson

September 19, 1937 Consuma

Dear B.:

Happy to hear from you but eager to learn how your visit to Santayana went off. Do find time while on board to send me word[...] Walter's book is a marvel of statements, of argument, of appeal ending with something like liturgical fervor.[46] He himself is more delightful than ever, so discursive and informing and wise; but he seems to hang over the brink of a serious breakdown. I can't persuade him to remain here till he gets better. A demon urges him on as it does all destined to neurasthenia. Let me pray he may escape it [...]

Love to you both. B.B.

tr/ms with signature 99.15

To Bernard Berenson

September 22, 1937 "Roma"

Dear B.B.:

Your letter from Consuma reached me last night when I boarded this boat; your urgent request for an account of my call on Santayana I hasten to answer, for we reach Gibraltar to-morrow and that's the last chance. First, as to his appearance. Though he is 73 years old, he might easily pass for twenty years less. [But for] some fat—he has grown rather fat but is in no sense gross, and a thinness of hair, that too has not gone very far—he might indeed have almost passed for the youngster I used to know. This was very remarkable, like that curious giggle he has preserved when he hits off a good quip. He welcomed me in a very friendly, easy way, and we sat in his sitting room. It seemed to me a rather dreary place to live in, but he likes it and thinks the square with the Bernini fountain quite lovely. That is a strange judgment, as it seems to me. It was rather on the score

46. Walter Lippmann, Inquiry into the Principles of the Good Society (1937).

of an old friendship that we began—as coevals so to say. However, I did not mean to let it lie so, for after all, one's earlier teachers always retain a certain authority I find, and besides, I regard him as one of the most distinguished minds I have ever met, though I must own that like other metaphysicians, he is not uniformly and inexorably pellucid in expression. From that opinion I shall certainly not find you a dissenter.

His life is like an anchorite's. He does not dress in the morning—anchorites I suppose ought never to dress or undress at all. He does all his writing—two and a half to three hours—in his dressing gown. (Incidentally I have heard that persons who passed the door, when ajar, have heard pleasant chuckles when he tests a telling phrase. That has always seemed to me an agreeable picture; perhaps you won't like it.) Then he dresses and breakfasts and reads the papers; he has become a great paper reader. He always walks for an hour or so; then he comes back and reads, before and after dinner. He said that he was always glad to see his friends, for whom I think he has real feeling, but as you know he never dines out or visits. On the whole this is the complete philosophic life; serene, self-sufficient, abstemious, independent of others, and as nearly as may be, of things, finding ideas, abstract ideas, nutriment enough. It is exceedingly spare; the senses are nearly altogether denied, but the result does not seem to be meager, and happiness, as mortals may have it, is as nearly attained as is possible to those who are not of the "overborne," if you remember William James's division. If my own nature had not been so contradictory and my desires so vagrant, this would have been what I chose; it is the "spiritual life" without the fervor which almost inevitably corrupts it.

But I have told you nothing of what we said; it will be a little hard to do so. We talked a good deal about *The Last Puritan*;[47] he told me of its beginnings long ago when he was in Cambridge. Oliver had no prototype properly speaking—he was drawn fairly at large; Mario, I take it, was the same. The notion of the opposition between the "Latin" and the "Puritan" had been long in his mind; the book grew out of that, finally almost of itself. No other novel was now thinkable, because, as he said with a very engaging gesture, he had absolutely nothing more to say, that was his comment. He was, quite naturally, much pleased with its success—unaffectedly and without false reserve—and he had found handy the money which it had brought in.

We talked of his poetry. I disputed that he was only "almost a poet," as he once described himself. His disclaimer was detached and balanced; he conceded that he had some of the qualities, but he lacked the imagination—that last I interpolate a bit. We talked of the other young poets he had known in Harvard; they were all dead, died early. I did not know much of them, except Moody who was in my class; I cannot rate him as an authentic poet.

We talked a little of philosophy; the fourth volume, *The Realm of* ——— (I don't remember what), is substantially in the press;[48] *The Realm of Spirit* he is writing. That will finish his system, which, a little to my surprise, he spoke of as such. He has also become much interested in politics, and either proposes to write or is actually engaged in writing a book about it.

---

47. George Santayana, The Last Puritan; A Memoir in the Form of a Novel (1935).
48. Probably The Realm of Truth.

No effort at history or a scholarly analysis of the past, just the outcome of his own reflection upon what he has read and lived through. It will not, I should suppose, take a definite democratic position—one could hardly expect that from him anyway. I shall, however, be immensely interested in his definition of liberty, on which we touched. He spoke with respect of Russell, whom he rated much higher than Whitehead. Said that he understood "Process and Reality"[49]—the nearest to a boast that he got—and that Russell was right in saying that Whitehead really had his origins in Bergson; that surprised me.

He was dispassionate and generous towards friends in America, some of whom he thought had changed towards him. I liked my visit so much that I overstayed my welcome—an hour and a half. When I left I said: "I may write you; you needn't answer." He replied: "I may answer or I may not; probably I shall." There was nothing rude in this, and its frankness pleased me extremely. And there I leave him, I suppose forever. I feel a little abashed at having taken you so literally when you asked for an account of my visit. My excuse can only be that, besides wanting to comply, it has helped me a little to order my recollections by writing them down. When I left, though it would be false to say that in the usual sense I had had a good time, I did have a feeling of catharsis as from the society of an elevated person, elevated without being a bit inhuman.

I am distressed at what you say about Walter and to be frank, I find it hard to believe that you are right. In my experience people do not break down from work but from continued emotional strains. Of course, nobody knows the strains of anybody else and Walter may have plenty. But it seems curious that that level, unimpassioned wisdom should not be equal to whatever demands may be made upon it. And yet I will confess that at times I too have seen symptoms of stress in him. It would be a great shock to me. I don't see very much of him any more, and the time has long gone by when I had anything to contribute to his capacious mind, if indeed I ever had. But I estimate his judgment so highly that it would be grievous to me to have his strengths impaired.

I am sorry to hear that your trip to Vienna is to see the doctors, but at our time of life they become a more or less inevitable obbligato to living at all. Once more thank you for our delightful visit, which remains a bright spot as the shores of Europe are getting ready to fade into the East.

My love to Nicky, L.H.

tr/ms with signature 99.16

To Learned Hand from Bernard Berenson

October 6, 1937 Hotel Bristol, Vienna

Dear B.:

Thanks for a most entertaining letter posted at Gib[raltar] that I found waiting for me two days ago. Most interesting your account of the visit to Santayana. I am truly happy to

49. LH refers to Bertrand Russell and Alfred North Whitehead. See Whitehead's Process and Reality: An Essay in Cosmology (1929).

learn that he looked so young and vigorous and serene. Personally I wish him a long life and happy activity. Only I am no longer interested in what he has to say. Leisure fails me for reading commonplace, no matter how, like the chestnuts they are, they pop and smell savory in popping. For that sort of thing my mind is as *complêt* as Paris buses that stuck out signs to that effect.

Five and twenty years ago I told him that like a god he was careless of mankind and his retort was "Yes, an Epicurean God." But that is just what I meant. I could make endless comments on his remarks, but abstain because you are a busy man[...]

By the time you read this you will applaud yourself for expressing the conviction that work never breaks down a man. Nor did it break down Walter, as you know by this time. The strain he was under must have been awful. Not alone what he told me impressed me, but more still what Jane Wilmerding recounted. I hope he can disentangle himself and return to see the stars.[50] He has been in hell for many years[...]

The world situation is awful. Comic to let a second-class power in the Mediterranean continue to trouble more and more and more, when a good strong kick would bring peace in this part of the world at least. Thank Frances from me for her letter.[51]

Ever affectionately, B.B.

tr/ms with signature 99.16

1937-3

To Felix Frankfurter

October 7, 1937 Judge Learned Hand's Chambers

Dear Felix:

[...]F. and I had a good summer; plenty of music and all sorts of pictures, statuary, and buildings. The Italians are in a most dangerous frame of mind; they really think that Britain will not intervene and that they may not only tweak her nose but take away all her toys. The poor fish really believe they can do their will with her; that was the worst single thing I came to believe on my trip. F.D.R. made a ten-strike in the Chicago speech, just the right note at the moment. Growl but do not say when or if you are going to bite; that's another matter. But just now it pays for us to be nasty to show that we are not too "snail

50. Lippmann was about to divorce his wife; he married Helen Byrne Armstrong in 1938. LH knew Helen Lippmann's first husband, Hamilton Fish Armstrong, editor of the journal FOREIGN RELATIONS, who served with LH on the Council for Foreign Relations. *See* 1940-1 To Berenson, August 27.

51. See Berenson's brief response to this letter, dated December 26, 1937, *in* BERNARD BERENSON, THE SELECTED LETTERS OF BERNARD BERENSON 145–46 (1964).

conscious." Again, I incline my head in gratitude to you for the dedication, repeated once more.[52] My love to Marion.

As ever, yours, L.H.

ms with signature 105A.5

To Learned Hand from Felix Frankfurter

October 10, 1937 — 192 Brattle street, Cambridge, Massachusetts

Dear B.:

[...]Yes, it was necessary to growl. This business of being in the world and being indifferent to all that binds or severs its essential parts—and thereby binds or severs one's own moral unity, if I may use "tall talk"—well, not for me. At last John Bull appears to be fit to call Musso's bluff, for such I believe it to have been all along.

I crave for talk with you. Would it were soon. And Marion joins me in love to you.

F.F.

ms with signature 105A.5

To Learned Hand from Felix Frankfurter

Oct. 18, 1937 — Law School of Harvard University

Dear B.:

Even though I take what is in the newspapers with a cellar of salt, I cannot help hoping in the light of the recent dispatches that Anglophiles like you and me—who care about England not only because of intellectual and emotional congeniality, but also because politically she is the most civilized society—will not be disappointed in our belief that there are limits to what Britain will stand. I am not unfamiliar with the easy dilemma that the Fascist powers only know force, and it's no use talking unless you are prepared to go to war with them. These "either-or" reductions of complexity are much too simple for my taste. There are all sorts of things that can be done short of going to war. And I cannot rid myself of the conviction that Mussolini is a good deal of a blustering bluff, who gets away with murder so long as he is allowed to get away with it. The frame within which I place what seems the recent pusillanimous if not ignominious British foreign policy is the talk I had in London in August 1936 with the most responsible Service minister in the Cabinet, in the course of which he said, "I told Eden I don't care how he does it, but he must give me eighteen months of peace." These sands of time are running low[...]

Ever yours, F.F.

tp with ms signature 105A.5

---

52. Frankfurter dedicated the second edition of CASES AND OTHER AUTHORITIES OF FEDERAL JURISDICTION AND PROCEDURE (1937) to LH. *See* 1931-5 To Frankfurter, October 14.

To Felix Frankfurter

October 19, 1937 Judge Learned Hand's Chambers

Dear Felix:

[...]I do not believe that the Italians' attitude today is all bluff; I think they really believe that the British people will not fight and that they think they can take away Egypt and afterwards India. This is what disturbs me most. On the other hand, I recognize that this frame of mind can be changed: first by the armament which Britain is preparing and then by a steady and increasing pressure. I agree with you that there is too much simplification of the problem by amateurs, but I did not understand that you doubt that all that Mussolini and Hitler will recognize is a determined attitude, back of which there is a real and immediate possibility of war. The trick will be for Britain, having armed, to make that so clear that they will recede, and yet not to force them to too quick retreats. That will be where the statecraft will come in.

As to Japan, it may be indeed that you are right that Simon's unwillingness to back up Harry in '31 was the beginning.[53] I have always doubted it. Nobody was then prepared really to threaten Japan. I could never feel that it helped matters not to recognize their spoliations. In the end this will be inevitable unless they can be compelled to disgorge. The problem in the east seems to me far more troublesome than that in Europe. To show you, however, that I am in sympathy with your general attitude, I should like to say that I thought the President's speech on this matter timely and extremely useful.

As ever, yours, L.H.

tp with ms signature 105A5

1937-4

To Charles Wyzanski

December 28, 1937 Judge Learned Hand's Chambers

Dear Charles:

Thank you for the pipe which was really as fine a piece of briar as I had seen in very long; I like the shape of it too. It pleases me very much indeed to know that you think of me; I do of you often, and always in the hope that you are prospering and happy. A.N.H[and] or somebody said that it was trying to you to be pitched from aloft into the daily trifles of a practice[...] I can well believe it; I have never forgotten the despair that seized upon me in my early years of the law. The sordid spirit of the profession as I found

53. On September 22, 1931, Secretary of State Henry Stimson condemned Japan's attack on Manchuria which had occurred on September 18, and further asserted that the United States would support the League of Nations in efforts to guarantee peace. John Simon, the 1st Viscount Simon, was British Foreign Secretary during 1931.

it in Albany, the narrow little formalisms and the lack of any capaciousness of outlook, seemed insupportable. It may be doubly hard for you because you have come from so much more important activities. And yet I wonder whether there is any way to avoid those early years. At times I even permit myself to believe that they have some positive value, though for the life of me I can't see it, when, properly circumstanced, one might be going from strength to strength. The best I can see is that this is a world so full of maladjustments, in which chance must determine so much, that it is the part of wisdom to accept it as soon as one can. After all, nothing can take from one the chief joy, which is in doing the thing handsomely for the sake of doing it, as though it were a feat which paid for itself.

I remember years ago reading with disgust a lecture by [John] Ruskin to a graduating class at Sandhurst. He told the boys that the only defense for war was that it was a glorious game; fighting nothing but for fight's sake. Well, that remains—when the final balance is struck—as atrocious as it ever was; but now I can get a kind of glimmering of what the old fool—for Ruskin was a prodigious old fool—meant. I suspect that one reason why we all admire the English so much is because they, even the lower classes of them, feel so gamesome about life (if I may pervert that word). The more I live the more I seem to see that it is in the God-given faculty of treating one's own activities as sufficient in themselves that our best chance lies. It's for the moment the only gospel I know how to preach; that of sport for its own sake and within that I would include all that we undertake. That would have made me a freer man than I ever was, but I suppose it takes one more independent of others' opinions than I ever could have been.

Why should I so embark just over your handsome pipe? 'Tis done, nevertheless, and you must bear it. Come to see me whenever occasion allows and the spirit moves.

Sincerely, L. Hand

ms with signature, Wyzanski Papers, HLL, Box 2, Folder 7

1938-1

To Learned Hand from Harlan Fiske Stone

July 10, 1938 Jasper Park, Alberta, Canada

Dear Judge Hand:

I am informed that you are to give the Holmes Lectures at Harvard next winter, probably in February or March. Because they are the *Holmes Lectures* and because *you* are to give them, I have consented to give the dedicatory lecture which I understand will be of moderate duration (20 minutes or so) immediately preceding your first lecture. As I wish to utter no jarring notes, I shall be most grateful if at your convenience you will drop me a line giving some idea of the plan and scope of your lectures and making any suggestions which may occur to you as to the length and content of my talk. Well in advance I shall be glad to send you a copy of what I propose to say so that we may be certain that we produce harmony if not a symphony[...][54] The news of Cardozo's death came last night.[55] The public loss is for me a personal one also. If you could only be appointed to his place I could hope for a few years more of happiness in judicial work.

With warm regards, Harlan F. Stone

ms with signature 107.13

To Harlan F. Stone

July 18, 1938

Dear Justice:

I got your letter from Jasper Park on the 16th, which I had been expecting because [James M.] Landis[56] said I would hear from you. I had understood from him that you were to give one complete lecture—the first—and I the succeeding three. I suppose that they are meant to last 50 minutes, like a recitation. Don't you think you could take up that much instead of twenty minutes? It seems to me that never in God's world shall I be able to spin out 150 minutes, and if I have an extra 30, I shall bust. Think about it.

You ask me about my subject. As yet it is hazy in my mind; I am hoping to conceive next month and to bear the child about October 1st, but who can tell—I often assail high Heaven with my bootless cries[57] to be relieved, and wonder why in Hell I ever agreed to do this, but it's too late now and I have got to turn out something. I am here still at work at the mines, shoveling smoke, and I shall be for at least two weeks more: then I'll pitch in. So far as I have got, my idea is somewhat dreamily this. What do we really mean by liberty? We see cropping up in Europe societies whose idea appears to be uniformity for all—like an ant-hive. That uniformity is at first imposed and alien, but the effort is so to condition youth that it will not feel the social impact upon it as alien but as natural and harmonious. Conceivably it can be made to feel so: an irreducible and unchangeable human nature may be an illusion; what we have treated as constants may prove malleable and may be molded to forms we do not dream of. Will the result be a "free society"? Will it be "liberty"? Are not the ants and the bees perfectly free? "Thy service is perfect freedom," said St. Augustine, but mind: it was the service of God, *service and* freedom. Is there more in law than the command of the overwhelmingly powerful group? Holmes

54. In a letter to Dean James M. Landis dated August 9th, LH backed out of writing the lectures as planned. (ms draft, 56.18) For Stone's role in organizing the lectures, see ALPHEUS THOMAS MASON, HARLAN FISKE STONE: PILLAR OF THE LAW 331–32 (1956).

55. Justice Cardozo died on July 9, 1938. Known as the "cloistered cleric of the law" for his unyielding devotion to his work, Cardozo was diagnosed with a heart ailment during his final year on the New York Court of Appeals, a condition that worsened during his tenure as a Justice on the Supreme Court. *See Cardozo is Dead: New Heart Attack Fatal to Justice*, N.Y. TIMES, July 10, 1938.

56. James M. Landis (1899–1960): Professor, Harvard Law School; member, Securities and Exchange Commission, 1934–1937; Dean, Harvard Law School, 1938–1946.

57. LH paraphrases the opening lines of Shakespeare's sonnet 29: "When in disgrace with fortune and men's eyes/I all alone beweep my outcast state,/And trouble deaf heaven with my bootless cries."

would have said no; so would Bentham and Locke and Hobbes. Are there no objective determinants to liberty beyond freedom from control *felt* to be alien? If we say that there are, are we in danger the of raising up again the doctrine of "natural rights"?[58] If we do, would it be nonsense? etc. etc. Well, something like that. Three nice dressy packages all done up in pink ribbons. I can ask these questions and can't answer one; I am not sure they have any sense. All I know is that they are "pressing for an answer," and there ain't no answer, but they deserve talk if anything really does. *Sed de hoc quaere*. I don't expect to do it adequately but a substitute might be just as rotten. Anyway, that's about what I have in mind, if the germs will only get together and begin to proliferate.

You're a kind friend to want me alongside at Washington. I'm a bit overripe, but even now, you bet I'd try it if I had the chance and one of the main things would be that I think we could work together rather pretty. But my chances are not so good as for another job that I am going to tell you about in the strictest confidence—you are not to tell a soul, not even your wife. You probably do not know that I am being very seriously considered for the next Grand Lhama of Tibet. Of course, it's still all tentative, but the chance seems a good deal better than for the other job, and I have plumped for it. If I should land it, be sure to let me know the next time you are in Lhasa.

Poor B.N.C[ardozo], I could not wish that it should have been prolonged. And yet it is always so—isn't it?—that when Atropos finally does use her shears, it seems an act of violence. How gentle, how wise, and really, when all is said, how unhappy a soul! I don't think it was alone the shadow over him in youth: he never could have had any *body*; I doubt it he ever had any fun, though he could be gay and at times a little naughty. We ought all to strike roots down deep into the rich, smelly, black muck; his were all in the sweet pure air, like an orchid. That won't do; we came from the mud and we mustn't ever get quite out of it.

As ever, yours, [Learned Hand]

tp 107.13

1938-2

To Bernard Berenson

August 3, 1938 Windsor, Vermont

Dear B.B.

Here I am—since day before yesterday—with another year's work behind me and a rest of two months ahead of me. A letter from Nicky to F. admonishes me that I have not written you for months and months, and that you have always said that you were glad to hear from me. I really have small comments to make; probably you are as well informed

58. LH returns to the question of natural rights and the jurisprudence of Stone in correspondence with Charles Edward Clark. *See* 1948-2 To Clark, April 8.

as I about things over here, better maybe for Walter [Lippmann] has been with you and he really does know. Did he say that Roosevelt was as strong as ever, perhaps not literally but for all practical purposes? At least that is what I believe. It's very largely due to the collapse of the Republicans—utter, complete, irretrievable collapse. They have not an idea or a man; they give forth dull, hollow groans, *vox et praeteria nihil.* Even so, one might expect some resurgence or emergence of principles, old or new, in his own party. Nothing, quite nothing! And so he has an easy walkover, and while I know the dangers of prophecy, I believe he will have a third term. Nobody doubts that he would beat the boots off anybody today if he got the nomination, and I think he'd get that. We have craved a Messiah and we have one. On the whole I can't see anybody I would wish to substitute unless I could get the people differently minded. At least he can govern and that's the first need[...]

However, let me descend—or is it ascend? to more gossipy matters. Your letter to me on the ship about Walter long since explained itself. He acted rather curiously to me. He did come to dine, *solus*, in November, or even perhaps October, and we talked merely about the sordid side of getting a divorce, which I knew fairly well anyway, but not a whisper about the real project. That we heard about shortly afterwards in rather highly colored pictures, and twice F. tried to get him to dine, again *solus*. He evaded both times, though the first time he accepted and then backed out. So we concluded that he didn't want to come and we were right. I began to hear various pretty circumstantial accounts that the way he went about it was bad, but I have never allowed myself to form a judgment, nor shall I until, if ever, and it won't ever be, I hear from him his own account. No, that's really nobler and more judicial than I am or shall be; I shall say that I shan't come to any conclusion and I shall try to leave it open, but neither I nor any other man or woman can quite do that. The circumstantial stories did leave their effect on me and I do feel a little differently about him. Perhaps—for who really knows what controls his feelings—it was the book[59] that shared in the result. I found it a disastrously insufficient performance. How the man who had written the first half of the *Preface to Morals*[60] could have written that passed my apprehension. It seemed to me greatly padded, full of false reasoning which was quite easy to [illegible] and written without any of his former verve and movement. Now, was that because I had made up my mind subconsciously against him? I think not; my recollection is that I read the book before the Armstrong motif had developed in the bassoons. So I am a little apprehensive of our first meeting, for I haven't seen him since that dinner. He may think I have joined the pack against him, which at least I haven't, whatever defection you may choose to read into the above. I know that in all such matters outside judgments are not worth a good Goddamn. But the book will stand pretty well between us[...]

In a moment when the offer teased my vanity, I engaged myself to give three lectures next winter at Harvard. Now is the day of reckoning. They must be done up here in the green woods and the baking heat or they won't be done at all. Eben! Eben! What shall it be? Do you know at what I shall start? Scorn me not, friend, but know the worst. I propose

59. Walter Lippmann, An Inquiry into the Principles of the Good Society (1937).
60. Walter Lippmann, A Preface to Morals (1929).

to attempt to say something about Liberty and Law. Oh, I know, I know, it seems incredible, and probably I shall bear only a dead child, but that's what I am trying to conceive. Totalitarianism, collectivism, etc., etc., and all spun out of my guts. God, what a prospect! Enough; I can't bear to think of it, and you shall never, never be allowed so much as to whiff it[...]

My love to Nicky, and to Mary if she is with you. I get varying accounts of her, some bad, some good. I choose to believe the good, but I gather she is away now. Tell her when you write that I think of her often.[61]

Sincerely yours, Learned Hand

ms with signature 99.16

1938-3

To Learned Hand from Felix Frankfurter

July 25, 1938 Heath, Massachusetts

Dear B.:

Thanks to Julian [Mack], your talk on Cardozo came our way.[62] Reams will be written about him. But nothing will be said that will strike the jugular of his special quality more truly or more beautifully than your "something." Marion and I were profoundly moved by it—on the second reading aloud even more than the first. A good summer to you all.

Ever yours, F.F.

ms with signature 105A.6

To Felix Frankfurter

August 4, 1938 Windsor, Vermont

Dear Felix:

Thank you for your kind words about what I said. If it had anything like the merit you give it, it was because it was quite from the heart. He was indeed as wise a man as I knew—I mean in the law. Perhaps otherwise too, if in the end wisdom and goodness are one. As you know, there was a lot about his work I didn't like. I am absolutely confident that a judge cannot in the end avoid the responsibility of selecting some principles by which he will be bound. Merely to decide each case as though it were alone in the world will finally commit him to absolutism. He cannot forever disguise the fact that he is

61. Berenson's response, dated September 2, 1938, is reprinted in BERNARD BERENSON, THE SELECTED LETTERS OF BERNARD BERENSON 148–49 (1964).

62. *See Mr. Justice Cardozo, in* THE SPIRIT OF LIBERTY 129–33.

applying rules made by others to which he owes allegiance. He must find these and apply them; he cannot find them in anything but formal declarations. Cardozo was never willing quite to acknowledge this for himself; he winced at pressing the quivering flesh of humanity into any iron molds. That was all to the good, but it needed the supplement of a sterner streak—more ruthless if you will. One reason why he became the idol that he justly was is that today we are in such a turmoil that we recognize none of the traditional molds as having any authority. It was exceptionally fortunate to have him where and when he appeared. But he was appropriate for a transitional period.

L.H.

P.S. What period is not transition? (Comment of the Devil.)

ms with signature 105A.6

1939-1

To Felix Frankfurter

January 6, 1939

Dear Felix:

Yesterday carried me back a good many years. I saw again the eager, ardent youth just out of the law school, who used to come up to my chambers, a very green and timorous judge myself, and overwhelm me with the fertility of his mind and the warmth of his personality. That youth and I have had a long friendship, and through my admiration and esteem it has constantly deepened and grown. We have at times had our differences, but they have always yielded to affection and what I like to believe is essentially the same outlook. Now you are about to start upon what is almost sure to be a very distinguished career, more so even than the one you leave behind you.[63] You are sure to be a very notable judge; you may be a great one. You are at the top of your extraordinary powers; you have been through an amazing preparation for this service; you have the mind and an almost inhuman energy which I sometimes have feared might not find complete outlet in such a job. You understand that our safety as a nation depends upon our ability to carry over our habits without rupture into constantly changing scenes. Especially you are sanguine of success in that venture and that confidence will help to make it possible.

Finally, you start with an approval by the bar and the country, which is frankly the only surprising thing about it all. With such equipment, how can we help feeling that you are stepping into a shining career and that you will continue to be happy and useful, as you have been happy and useful before. I have thought of Holmes and of his pleasure if he is looking down somewhere from Valhalla. I have thought of Cardozo, serenely joyous, though hardly in Valhalla. I can speak for Stone's happiness, for he has told me of his

63. On January 5, 1939, President Roosevelt nominated Frankfurter to the seat on the Supreme Court vacated by Benjamin Cardozo.

hopes, and Felix, you have done it all yourself. You have done it largely no doubt because you were especially gifted, but even more so because in you burns the sacred fire, because you have zest and delight in this strange spectacle, because you will always be young. My grim Connecticut forebears would have been able to close by saying "God bless you and guide you." I think I will adopt their formula; it doesn't quite fit me, but I think I mean what they did and after all, where [can] we, poor wights of this tortured time, hope to find any consecrated formula of our own?

L.H.

ms with signature 105A.6

To Learned Hand from Felix Frankfurter

February 16, 1939 Supreme Court of the United States

Dear B.:

[...]For Marion and me it all seems unreal. I can hardly believe that less than a month ago I was still having classes at Cambridge. But then, I haven't had time to reflect or indulge even in the little introspection of which my shallow extrovert nature is capable. But when you come down here in the spring, perhaps you will put me too on your visiting list. I know I can count on Gus.

I have had a letter from you, which in good time I shall acknowledge with my own fist. For the present, let me say that none that came our way in the blizzard of communications touched me more deeply. And now, I must quit, for I am in the throes of my first opinions.

Thine, F.F.

tp with ms signature 105A.6

1939-2

To Charles Wyzanski

August 4, 1939 *à bord le Champlain*

Dear Charlie:

A letter of yours to A.N.H.,[64] which he showed me, contained a comment on what I said at Harvard in June that prompts me to write you just a line, for it made me think

64. On July 28, 1939, Augustus Hand wrote to Charles Wyzanski from New York City: "[...]As for the speech of L.H.: I think you mistake his real ideas. What he wants is not to have scholars active propagandists and militant reformers. I quite agree with him that it deprives them of the capacity to think steadily, and I deny that the fellow who doesn't act that way is an oyster living in his shell." (ms with signature, Wyzanski Papers, HLL, Box 2, Folder 3)

that I had not said what I meant. I certainly have no desire that a scholar shall be only a bookworm; on the contrary, I feel as strongly as you can that he must keep in touch with affairs. You mentioned Aristotle and I agree that in the "social sciences" it was right to send out bright young gents to all the cities of the Mediterranean and have them make surveys, etc., etc. What I was tilting against was the combination of scholarship and active propaganda—the Laski sort of thing. I am so sure that once you have embarked upon a cause—I mean as the promoter of the cause—you cannot have a truly detached attitude that I would divorce the two completely. Detachment and impartiality are at a discount with young intellectuals; I know it. I saw a review by Max Lerner where it bore that inevitable stigma of contempt, the inverted commas. I recognize, of course, that the words must be relative, that there is no such thing as entire detachment. But if we do not keep the font as pure as we can, how can we possibly get the water we need? That water, just at present, is the water of tolerance which can only come when one keeps oneself out of the mêlée. I am sure of very little but of this I am sure, that except as scholars can avoid the disposition to lead causes, they cannot be scholars, and that we need them bitterly at the time of these discontents.

We reach Paris tomorrow and sail home on September 15th. We shall be in France and England only. I think it may have been a mistake to come at all because of the great unrest which keeps us always on the anxious seat.

As ever, L.H.

ms with signature, Wyzanski Papers, HLL, Box 2, Folder 7

1939-3

To Senator Warren Austin[65]

October 20, 1939

My dear Senator Austin:

It is my invariable rule not to write letters to members of Congress about current matters because I think it improper for a judge. I am going to break that rule now, not indeed to urge any action upon you, but because I do not feel able to be silent about your manly declaration yesterday in the Senate;[66] the only one, so far as I have seen, which broke the supine and ignoble chorus of those who seem to believe that any ignominy, any concession should be patiently endured from or to ruffians and barbarians rather than risk war. I am proud that there was at least one voice which was raised against so craven an attitude.

65. Warren Austin (1877–1962): Senator from Vermont, 1931–1946; United States Ambassador to the United Nations, 1946–1953.

66. On October 19, Austin declared in the Senate that the United States should emend the Neutrality Act of 1935, which was designed to keep the United States out of a possible European war by banning shipment of war materiel to belligerents.

May I send you my warmest congratulations; you have made me less ashamed to be an American?[67]

Sincerely yours, Learned Hand

tr/ms with signature 66.29

To Learned Hand from Warren Austin

October 21, 1939 United States Senate

My dear Judge Hand:

I have received many letters which encourage me to sustained effort, but no letter that I have received is so weighted as yours is by the respect and esteem which I feel for the writer. I am grateful to you and positively helped by the knowledge of your cooperation.

Sincerely yours, Warren Austin

ms with signature 66.29

1940-1

To Learned Hand from Bernard Berenson

Dec. 10, 1939 Settignano

My dear B.:

This is to wish you and yours Merry Xmas and a Happy New Year. I do this with good cheer and sincerely. Things may get worse than ever before in civilized history[68][. . .]

Affectionately, B.B.

tr/ms with signature 99.17

To Bernard Berenson

August 27, 1940 Windsor, Vermont

Dear B.B.:

It is many months since I wrote you and what months they have been! Do not suppose, however, that you have not been in my mind often or in my speech; rather put it down to sluggishness, and until about three weeks ago to the general toil and coil of life that I

67. The Neutrality Act was emended on November 4, 1939, to allow supplies to belligerents, although U.S. ships were not allowed into combat zones.

68. The rest of this letter, in part describing a meeting with Santayana, is reprinted Bernard Berenson, The Selected Letters of Bernard Berenson 170–72 (1964).

should have failed. Perhaps it was meeting John Walker[69] at Southampton about a fortnight ago which gave the final push to my inertia. I have not for a long time met anyone who at once and without reserve so much captured me. It was not alone the obviously sound and well-founded abilities which he brought to his job ("How can B. possibly have any valid opinion about that?" you will say), but the delightful detachment of his general approach, even in such matters as his Catholicism where he could couple it with a perfect assurance, adequate to himself. I shall assuredly find means that the acquaintance so begun shall not lapse, unless he wishes it otherwise, which I dare hope he will not.

As for general comment, the most important things are taboo; and perhaps it is better so, for we can hardly mend them by speech, written or oral. I think of you at Vallombrosa and now that I have started this, find that F.A.H. has, quite independently, begun to write Mary. (Telepathy perhaps, except that I remain skeptical in spite of what I have understood to be indubitable evidence. Not very judicial.) Often I think of that country and of those beauties which it seems not improbable I shall not see again. It is all very well to ask me to live in memories, but I am not of that sort; I am greedy for more and always was from my childhood. Here we have our share of beauties too, but they are not the equal of yours in the valley of the Arico; and, that aside, there was something after all in what "Goose Norton"[70] used to say about the inevitable reflection upon any landscape of the history which overlaid it. (By the way, you remember that allusion: an entry in [Thomas] Carlyle's diary—"Goose Norton, came and would not go.")

But such laments are idle; you will be more interested in what I have to say of us here, which I fancy will be permissible interchange. If I were to believe those whom I personally encounter, [Wendell] Willkie will be elected.[71] To be sure, they all recognize that it will be a close race, but they trust to the nearly universal feelings of the *bon bourgeois* everywhere they go. F.D.R. has become the symbol of destruction, and they—like all of us—believe what they want. Personally, while I too am sure that the race will be close, were I descended from the Planet Mars to try to pick the winner it would be the Present Incumbent. I can't get out of my mind the aphorism of Al Smith four years ago: "Did you ever hear of anybody's shooting Santa Claus?" Both candidates are treating the war gingerly; each is afraid of the large section of people who see in it nothing more than a quarrel between Europeans in which we have no interest. That sentiment in my judgment is on the decline, but no one who is running for office can afford to disregard it unless he is willing to lose something for his principles. I should guess that we shall, taken collectively, be the creatures of events across the Atlantic, and that it will depend upon how things look on November first whether we shall plump for "isolation" or "near-isolation." That is one of the prices of democracy; you cannot have very long-range policies. Surely that theorem does not need much demonstration today, whether or not one thinks that there are countervailing advantages.

---

69. John Walker II (1906–1995): Curator, National Gallery, 1939–1956; Director, National Gallery, 1956–1996.

70. LH refers to Charles Eliot Norton, Professor of Art History, Harvard College. *See* 1949-2 To Berenson, May 24.

71. Wendell Willkie, Republican candidate for President, was defeated by Roosevelt in 1940.

As for the local issues: they are a good deal overridden by the foreign. The unions see in conscription an attack upon their "standards of living" and are generally hostile to it. Moreover, the emphasis upon production and more production tends or will, I think, tend to make people forget about the importance of distribution. Willkie bore upon that very heavily; it was old stuff, and true as scripture, but as I suggested above, in the end what people care about is the size of the slices of pie they get, and they are apt to forget that all slices must in the end come out of a pie whose size will govern even the slices.

In my judgment, Walter's voice is the sanest, the sagest, and the most prophetic which is being heard in the land. I wonder whether it is having much effect; I wish I could believe it, but I doubt. Strangely enough—it will seem unbelievably strange to you—I have had no converse with him for nearly three years, except for meeting him quite casually at a dinner over a year ago. It is a curious hesitation on my part, due to the version I kept getting of his treatment of Armstrong.[72] And yet I have never heard his side and of course never can, and if I did, I could never hear Armstrong's authentically, so that I should end where I began. I know all this very clearly and say to myself that when next I am in Washington I shall break through my ridiculous shyness, which no doubt he interprets in a very different way, and shall go to see him, but somehow or other I have never seemed to find the time. But I shall, I shall, when I am in Washington next October; it is too preposterous to leave things as they are[...]

My dear B.B., this does not seem to me to be a very successful letter. Maybe I have grown stiff in the mental joints; maybe it is a certain constraint upon me that has dampened my mind and spirit. But pray take it rather as an evidence of friendship than of epistolary achievement. It is only in this way that we are now able to communicate; I must make the best of it. Again I tell you, you and Mary and Nicky are often in my thoughts. Who knows, perhaps in some happier days we shall see each other again, and though as I said, the past is only the past, after all it is much. Please, give my love to both the ladies. (By the way F.'s letter was directed to Vallombrosa.) And believe me, B.B.,

Affectionately yours, L.H.

tr/ms with signature 99.17

To Learned Hand from Bernard Berenson

October 3, 1940 Vallombrosa

My dear B.:

Your letter of August 27th reached me yesterday and was worth waiting for. I seldom enjoyed one as much. What you say about Johnnie Walker went to my heart. I could not love him more if he was my son. He is as responsive as stimulating, as affectionate as the

72. Lippmann and Faye Albertson were divorced in December 1937; Hamilton Fish Armstrong divorced his wife Helen Byrne Armstrong in December 1937; she married Walter Lippmann in March 1938. For an account of the Hand–Lippmann rupture, see GERALD GUNTHER, LEARNED HAND: THE MAN AND THE JUDGE 496–502 (1994).

best of women and yet has very much of the maturing man about him. Part of his charm is the promise that he never will get over-ripe[...]

From all sorts of sources quite unrelated to W[alter], I learned long before the separation that Faye was bored with W. and on the lookout for entertainment. I doubt whether but for prestige and money leaving W. meant much to her. Of course, I know nothing of what the cost was to Armstrong, and I should not wonder but that Helen made up her mind to grab W. no matter what cost to a husband. Walter is such an innocent, an abstract mind, not very intelligent about things human—too human. Do get in touch with him again. He is worth it[...] May this find you in fit condition for your job. Love to Frances as well as yourself.

Affectionately, B.B.

tr/ms with signature 99.17

1940-2

To Charles Wyzanski

November 2, 1940 Judge Learned Hand's Chambers

Dear Charlie:

Thank you for MacKinnon's letter, which is quite in keeping with what I should have expected. I sent it to Frances who in turn sent it back; you may want to keep the copy or send it about more. There is a sublime composure about the British for which I can find no sentiment but awe. George Rublee said a terrible thing last summer—at least it seemed terrible to me, I wonder whether it will to you. I had said that whether Britain stood or fell her fight was one of the imperishable monuments to human virtue. To which he answered: "not if she falls, then nothing will have been done." L.H.: "What about Thermopylae?" G.R.: "The Greeks finally won." Well, if I really thought that, I should want never to have been born. The truth is that when my lights burn low—as they do quite often, I regret to confess—that is the outlook which presses itself upon me with terrifying force. I ask myself whether the fights have any value unless they lead to victory. And yet if that is all, what peasant slaves are we, who must lose most of our fights anyway? The play's the thing.[73] If I have any credo, it is that, little as I have lived loyally to it with all my petty pulling to get badges.

But dear Charlie, one old man ought not to talk that way to another. Maybe I do it because when I think of the incomparable freshness and courage of your own life, I feel as though I could speak to you with mutual understanding.

---

73. LH reinterprets two lines from a single speech: "Oh, what a rogue and peasant slave am I," and "The play's the thing" (HAMLET, II, ii) so that they reflect the virtue of "play" or the means to an end rather than the character of the end itself, whether that is a victory or a defeat. *See* 1944-2 To Burling, February 6.

I am voting for F.D.R. and while it would be too much to say that I do so *con amore,* I am getting relatively more comfortable about it. If only I could wean myself of my dislike for the complacent, self-righteous, self-seeking crew of social-workers who surround him, always caterwauling about their love for humanity, I should feel happier; and the worst of it all—yes, the worst of it—is that he himself believes that a bright smile, a happy mood, urbanity, and optimism are really about all that is necessary. Don't you long these days for some atrabilious T. Carlyle who with his hot breath could blow into the Limbo of infantilism whence they came all such shams, such phantasms of an undeveloped mind? Well, why do I vote for him then? It's a long story, centering substantially all on Britain; it's an effort at least to commit myself to ordeals which my prophetic soul assures me that I could not endure. Never mind, courage is concerned only with the "show."

L.H.

ms with signature, Wyzanski Papers, HLL, Box 2, Folder 7

1940-3

To Charles Wyzanski

December 27, 1940 Judge Learned Hand's Chambers

Dear Charles:

That looks like an extraordinarily good book[74][...] Democracy, my dear Charles, is the humanist form of association as yet unreceived by the anthropoid which you and I grace by being examples of him. But it is a *lux cerex,* a marginal utility, presupposing much that can be wasted. That is the reason it is "on the spot" today, and even I might live to see it eclipsed, for it rests upon the absurd assumption that the average man, if "uncorrupted," is able to choose wisely. Only in a society so far above danger from mistakes and folly that it can be mistaken or foolish nine times out of ten, is it really practicable.

Why anyone who has a sound heart should soberly wish to force his neighbor to do or believe more than he can convince him is for his interest, I never could see. That is the sin against the Holy Ghost, though all of us commit it every day. Recognition of this lies back of democracy and sanctifies it in spite of all its absurdities. But as Ortega says in a very moving passage, is *homo sapiens* fit for it? Prometheus suffered to give us Liberty, but we have never quite understood what it was, or shown that we could use it if we had it. If anyone asks me whether I believe in democracy, I feel like answering as the *leisleman* answered when they asked him if he could play the violin: "I don't know, I never tried"[...]

L.H.

ms with signature, Wyzanski Papers, HLL, Box 2, Folder 7

---

74. LH probably refers to JOSE ORTEGA Y GASSET, THE REVOLT OF THE MASSES: AUTHORIZED TRANSLATION FROM THE SPANISH (1932).

1941-1

To Bernard Berenson

February 22, 1941 Judge Learned Hand's Chambers

Dear B.B.:

It is most curious to be writing you in the present circumstances, so unreal, so circumscribed. Still, I think of you and Mary and Nicky very often, and my memories return to the happy hours I have spent with you all. At least these cannot be taken from us; sometimes I wonder whether we are ever to have any more[...]

It is hard to fill a letter with anything but trivialities, except that my life has been made up so largely of them that I should have no dearth. The work of our court has fallen off to no more than two-thirds of what it was, which has given me a chance to break away for a fortnight in Nassau. F.A.H. went there last week with the Rublees and Louis [Dow]. There is not anything to do there but lie in the sands and bake in the sun, but I can put in some of that profitably. I chanced the other evening to make a try at Santayana's *Realm of Spirit*,[75] the last of the "Realms"[...] I feel baffled. The succession of metaphors, that never-ending succession, gives me the sense of being in a mist which like a kaleidoscope constantly forms into beautiful shapes that at once dissolve and are followed by others. Even Whitehead with his extravagantly abominable terminology is not so maddening; one feels as to him that enough patience would master his meaning, but with George that beauty of manner—and there are sure spots of great beauty—engulfs the whole, at least for me. I wonder whether the professionals think they understand him. He could, so far as I can see, stop anywhere or go on forever, as he almost did. Is this really the most intelligible form in which to state the ultimates, if there are any ultimates?[...]

I wonder whether you ever hear of Walter [Lippmann]. You will think it strange—indeed I fancy you will deprecate it—but with one very unsatisfactory exception I have not seen him since October 1937. This has not been deliberate though he may think so, but because when he is here, which is not very often, or if it is, I don't know it, he does not tell me. I fancy that both he and Helen conjure up more resistance in their old friends than exists.[76] I believe that I went all over this with you before; never mind, if it should reach you that I was unwilling to see him or avoided him, disabuse yourself of it. It is not so. Besides, I get to Washington only three or four times a year, and when I go I am held incommunicado by the most terrible orders of what go by the name of conferences. I have not been following what he writes lately, but that is chiefly due to my being a very bad newspaper reader and to my affecting *The New York Times*.

Well, my dear B.B., it cannot be very gratifying to you to have me greatly drool along in this aimless way; yet *faute de mieux*, I have done so because it gives me some satisfaction, as it were, merely to stretch out a hand towards you, and what a long stretch it seems

---

75. George Santayana, The Realm of Spirit: Book Fourth of Realms of Being (1940).

76. Lippmann married Helen Armstrong in 1938. *See* 1940-1 To Berenson, August 27 and To Learned Hand from Bernard Berenson, October 3.

now! I should like to hear how you and Mary do; of her I got extremely favorable news some time ago, much to our delight. After all, whatever may happen, the sun shines and in ten weeks the New England woods will begin to take on their tender olives and faint dapple of russets, and your beautiful Italy will open more of her glorious pageant[...][77]

[L.H.]

ms 99.17

To Learned Hand from Bernard Berenson

May 2, 1941 Settignano

Dear B.:

[...]I write *in articulo belli*[...] Mary is incapable of moving or making any effort, and I am physically not much better. No question of our undergoing all the hardships of the journey to Lisbon and without Nicky, who being a subject here would not be allowed to leave. So this may be the last exchange of letters between us for a long time, perhaps forever. Life has been great fun and my zest for it is unabated. It has been delightful to know you and the likes of you.

I regret nothing except my own sins—not so many—and am ready to go on indefinitely or to end smiling—belly permitting. Should war begin I shall try to keep in touch with Lawrence Berenson and instruct him to give you our news.

Affectionate greetings to you both. B.B.

ms with signature 99.17

1941-2

To Raymond B. Stevens

May 29, 1941

Dear Ray-Ray:

[...]Yes, I am in essential agreement with you about [Charles] Lindbergh,[78] although I am not quite so savage.[79] He is an instance of how a person of limited education, gifted in

77. This letter is illegible from here on.

78. Charles Lindbergh (1902–1974): American aviator, author, inventor and explorer. Lindbergh was a member of the American First Committee, the foremost pressure group against American entry into the Second World War.

79. In a letter dated May 27, Raymond B. Stevens states that he has "an intense and comprehensive dislike" for Charles Lindbergh; evidently his remark reflects his plan to attend a Conference on June 26, not further identified, at which Lindbergh will be represented. (tp with ms signature, 80.13)

special lines and of limitless self-confidence, can become an extremely sinister figure. He could not have flown the Atlantic alone if he had not had the second two of these qualities, which, coupled with much persecution by the press and suffering, have turned him inward and made an acrid and complacent nature into bitter and perverse opponent of current opinion[...] You are not quite right in saying that he is "cold-blooded as a snake"; he has much inner fire with his very considerable mental acuteness. He is doing so much damage at the moment that it is hard for me to appraise him justly which I want to do, because in spite of all I have a deep regard for his wife.

The whole picture changed on Tuesday night with the President's speech, which set me up as nothing has for some time.[80] Now if there could only be some armed collision which would bring us at last into a real state of war, I should feel that we were safer. It sounds ruthless to say this, but the times call for ruthless conduct and we shall not be safe until we are at grips with those competent bandits who seem to be carrying everything before them. If we go down, at least it will be better to have had our try; we shall certainly go down much more painfully and shamefully if we stand aside now.

Yours, [L.H.]

tp 80.13

1941-3

To Learned Hand from Felix Frankfurter

July 30, 1941 New Milford, Connecticut

Dear B.:

I no longer try to persuade you of the felicity and distinction of your writing, but it gives me added pleasure to tell you with what relish I read your observations on "free

80. On May 27, President Roosevelt declared: "The pressing problems that confront us are military and naval problems. We cannot afford to approach them from the point of view of wishful thinkers or sentimentalists. What we face is cold, hard fact. The first and fundamental fact is that what started as a European war has developed, as the Nazis always intended it should develop, into a world war for world domination[...] For our own defense we have accordingly undertaken certain (obviously) obvious necessary measures"[...] *"We Choose Human Freedom," A Radio Address Announcing the Proclamation of an Unlimited National Emergency. May 27, 1941, in* THE PUBLIC PAPERS AND ADDRESSES OF FRANKLIN D. ROOSEVELT, WITH A SPECIAL INTRODUCTION AND EXPLANATORY NOTES BY PRESIDENT ROOSEVELT vol. 10, 181 (compiled by Samuel I. Rosenman, 1938–1950). Proclamation No. 2487, declaring an "Unlimited National Emergency" followed the President's address and concluded: "Now, THEREFORE, I, Franklin D. Roosevelt, President of the United States of America, do proclaim that an unlimited national emergency confronts this country, which requires that its military, naval, air, and civilian defenses be put on the basis of readiness to repel any and all acts or threats of aggression directed toward any part of the Western Hemisphere[...]" *Id.* at 195.

speech" in your *Federbush* opinion.[81] What sparkling and refreshing drink to a soul parched from a certiorari regimen. It's damn good!!

I assume that you are as delighted as I am that Stone was made C.J.[82] And it may again be the fate of Russian to save Europe. What a commentary the year since France fell is on the pessimistic and defeatist temperaments. Guts still make the difference! Wm. James knew that profoundest secret of "psychology." My fondest,

Ever thine, F.F.

ms with signature 105A.8

To Felix Frankfurter

August 6, 1941 Windsor, Vermont

Dear Felix:

[. . .]Yes, one can't help hoping that this may be the slack water that marks the beginning of the ebb. But I steadfastly refuse to assume too much. The more I read about the infernal thoroughness of those monstrous creatures, the more they scare the Hell out of me. "What a piece of work is man!"[83] How does a whole nation get so infatuated with a "Narcissus complex" that they can enslave themselves to enslave all the rest of us? And we with our loose ill-jointed society, how will it be possible that we can be welded into a real people? I fear the necessary blows of Fate on the anvil of Time; we have such a woeful

---

81. Frankfurter refers to *National Labor Relations Board v. Federbush Co.*, 121 F.2d 954 (2d Cir. 1941), in which the NLRB sought enforcement of its order enjoining the Federbush Company, an employer, from engaging in unfair labor practices and refusing to participate in collective bargaining with its workers' union. Responding to Federbush's argument that the NLRB sought to curtail its free speech rights by limiting the expression of the company's views about unions and unionism to its own employees, LH respected the Board's position: "No doubt an employer is as free as anyone else in general to broadcast any arguments he chooses against trades-unions; but it does not follow that he may do so to all audiences. The privilege of 'free speech,' like other privileges, is not absolute; it has its seasons; a democratic society has an acute interest in its protection and cannot indeed live without it; but it is an interest measured by its purpose. That purpose is to enable others to make an informed judgment as to what concerns them, and ends so far as the utterances do not contribute to the result. Language may serve to enlighten a hearer, though it also betrays the speaker's feelings and desires; but the light it sheds will be in some degree clouded, if the hearer is in his power. Arguments by an employer directed to his employees have such an ambivalent character; they are legitimate enough as such, and pro tanto the privilege of 'free speech' protects them; but, so far as they also disclose his wishes, as they generally do, they have a force independent of persuasion. The Board is vested with power to measure these two factors against each other, a power whose exercise does not trench upon the First Amendment. Words are not pebbles in alien juxtaposition; they have only a communal existence; and not only does the meaning of each interpenetrate the other, but all in their aggregate take their purport from the setting in which they are used, of which the relation between the speaker and the hearer is perhaps the most important part. What to an outsider will be no more than the vigorous presentation of a conviction, to an employee may be the manifestation of a determination which it is not safe to thwart. The Board must decide how far the second aspect obliterates the first" 121 F.2d at 957.

82. Harlan Fiske Stone became Chief Justice on July 3, 1941.

83. *Cf.* "What a piece of work is a man [. . .] And yet to me what is this quintessence of dust?" HAMLET, II, ii.

lot to learn. But there, you're right; the croakers of a year ago look thin and unreal now. And how one despises them!

If I had had the whole U.S. to choose from I should have made Stone C.J. Not that he's the greatest judge in these broad borders, but when all is weighed against all, he was surely absolutely the most available, and still I could wish he had more verbal chastity. Must all C.JJ. be so much "powerful figures" that they have to rape at least one word a day?

L.H.

ms with signature 105A.8

1941-4

To Sir Wilfred Greene[84]

August 16, 1941 Windsor, Vermont

Dear Sir Wilfred:

It was extremely kind of you to write me after your return home; I was glad to know that you had got back safely and pleased that you should have remembered me[. . .][85] I was indeed sorry not to see you on your way back through New York, though it hardly seemed possible that I should have that good luck, so manifold were the calls upon you.

The present moment one can't help feeling is propitious. Personally I have little interest in "peace terms" as such while matters are in this condition. But it was really a master stroke to forestall Hitler's next offer, which will come I suppose as soon as he can claim to have beaten the Russians, whether he does or not, for however little one may value any "peace terms," *some* "peace terms" are good as a war measure.

Over here we still hang fire in that curious way which I fear it the habit of democracies, a sort of "yes-and-no" attitude which distresses those of us who feel how vital it is for us not to wait, almost as much as it must you to whom the peril is more immediate, though in my judgment scarcely less threatening in the end. Roosevelt is doing all he can, but the attitude of the Republicans is incredible. They are denying all their past, and their position cannot possibly be excused; it is blind bitter partisanship, actuated in fact, whatever they may say, by hatred of the "foul fiend"[86] who by hook and crook has secured another four.

---

84. Sir Wilfred Greene (1883–1952): Lord Justice of Appeal, 1935–1937; Master of the Rolls, 1937–1949.

85. In a letter dated July 17, Sir Wilfred Greene states that he should have liked to have had "some quiet talk" with LH, as they have "many interests in common," and he expresses his "great pleasure at having met one whose name is so well known in this country"; he hopes to welcome him in England when the war is over. (tp with ms signature 72.15)

86. I.e., President Roosevelt. To describe the Republicans' fear of Roosevelt, LH invokes Shakespeare's character Edgar, who, disguised as "poor Tom," a madman, claims he is being persecuted by a "foul fiend." KING LEAR, III, iv.

I trust that sometime in less awful times and with more leisure I may have the good fortune to renew our acquaintance, which began so agreeably for me. Thank you once more for your letter.

Sincerely yours, [Learned Hand]

ms 72.15

1942-1

To Learned Hand from Felix Frankfurter

[December 1941–January 1942][87] Supreme Court of the United States

Dear B.:

How have you been able to stand all the dreary drool these lawyers get off for these 35 years?! And will I become inured to the boredom as the years go on? Will I become "conditioned" to this empty beating of the air without edification to mind or soul? These rebellious thoughts are stirred in me by a particularly wearisome argument in a case that a "learned profession" should be able to dispose of in 30 minutes all told![...]

Yrs., F.F.

ms with signature 105A.9

To Felix Frankfurter

January 6, 1942 Judge Learned Hand's Chambers

Dear Felix:

[...]I know how you feel; I used to think that I couldn't bear it and I had much more reason to feel so because, though the arguments are probably no worse than you hear, the consequences of what you do are so immeasurably more important. If you had had fifteen years as a D.J., you would know what a sense of fatuity really is. The only escape is the sort I used to get when I was a little boy doing "Algebra Originals"; when one writes, one does share in a kind of craftsmanship. That does not pall; Holmes used to say, you remember, "You get a chance at generalizing a little."

Of course, this is not what I ever really wanted. I drifted into the law and have always had a yen for other girls. "Our mistress" is a slut in my opinion, a disorderly, untidy, incoherent slut. We have got to keep her, I know. I have never really respected myself, trying to walk a tightrope all my life. If I could have looked ahead—and had had enough mathematics—I should have preferred physics. But there, that's what most old men say: "If I had ever really had my opportunity," etc., etc. And I don't truly feel so either; many a time I lie

87. This letter, undated, is written on nine pages taken from a small memo pad.

in bed and think what an amazing run of luck I've had and how strange it is that they have not yet found me out. Then I chuckle a little, and then wince, for after all I am not quite through yet.

L.H.

ms with signature 105A.9

1942-2

To Learned Hand from Felix Frankfurter

January 20, 1942 Supreme Court of the United States

Dear B.:

I assume in my ignorance that there are good biological reasons for men's shyness toward one another. But I don't have to be shy toward you, and so I should like you to know something now that it "can be told." There was, as you know, before the designation of [Donald M.] Nelson,[88] a good deal of gossip that [William O.] Douglas[89] would be translated into a Beaverbrook. Well, there were a few of us (as Lowell, A.L. used to say "we weigh heads and don't count them") who were determined to get you on the Court had that contingency occurred. And the G.W.F. would have had a tough time answering the case to be made for you—indeed only the calendar would or would have been urged, and the answer in *your* case would have been convincing. This note has no purpose except to let you know that fellows like the C.J. and I feel as we do—that *you* should be here and not a fellow like me, and, in any event, we wish to Pete you were here with us.

Thine, FF

ms with signature 105A.9

To Felix Frankfurter

January 21, 1942 Judge Learned Hand's Chambers

Dear Felix:

Yours of yesterday gave me a strong nostalgic sense as of something reminiscent and long past. Time was—and it lasted long—when I confess my aspiration was to go to the

88. Donald M. Nelson (1888–1959): Director, War Production Board, 1942–1945.

89. William O. Douglas (1898–1980): Chairman Securities and Exchange Commission, 1937–1939; Associate Justice United States Supreme Court, 1939–1975.

Supreme Court. There may have been a chance in 1930, though Bill Mitchell[90] meant me to think there wasn't, as I gathered it; but after that I put it out of my mind—at least that was true after 1932. It is strange to think that it should survive in yours or Stone's. I don't know; I suppose the honor of it and the reawakening of youthful desires would draw me very strongly; but after all, I shall be seventy next Tuesday and I have doubts that I could adjust myself so late. Perhaps so, but I can truly say that the knowledge you brought me left my feelings a little equivocal. Frankly, so many of them seem to use so unfamiliar an "organon" in reaching their conclusions that I wonder whether a man trained like me could have happiness or even converse with them.

I think of you very often, admiring the predominance you are acquiring among the judicious, who rightly enough grieve at some of the others. But I often wonder whether it must not be tough going and rather lonely work. I can only say by way of perhaps solace, that the longer you stick, the better you look to those outside, and that in the end you will have friends that will astonish and perhaps a little appall you. Meanwhile, perhaps what T.R. used to call the "Lunatic Fringe" may think you a traitor. What a bunch they are! I would say more, but let it be reserved 'til we meet. By the way, as the distance gathers around him, Brandeis grows in stature.

I will add in conclusion that I am sure at least of this: whatever vestigial hankerings remain for high place and office, I can yield *con amore* that that the gent of whom you spoke was not translated to that vital post.

I vary in mood about the war, but then every once in a while I ask myself to think back a year or to the summer of 1940, and then my soul rises on wings of confidence.

Mes amours à la belle marquise. L.H.

ms with signature 105A.9

To Learned Hand from Felix Frankfurter

January 26, 1942 1511-30th street, Washington, D.C.

Dear B.:

War throws everything that's civilized out of focus and so also distorts the values of youth and age. So much of the actual fighting has to be done by the young that we even forget that [Ferdinand] Foch was no lad, and that [Georges] Clemenceau was the will of France, though not its wisdom, as [Winston] Churchill, himself no chicken, is the will incarnate of Gt. Britain.

No, there is nothing more foolish than this business of setting up a calculus of preferences for the different instruments in the orchestra of life. But one does not have to depreciate the ardor and energy and liveliness and exuberance of youth to reflect, as I cannot help reflecting, that the men who have given me most pleasure and stimulus have

90. William DeWitt Mitchell (1874–1955): Solicitor General, 1925; Attorney General of the United States, 1929–1933.

been in the 70s and the 80s—Holmes, of course, and Prexy [Charles W.] Eliot, and Brandeis[...] They all "had something"—zest for life infused with long and enriched experience. And so Marion and I will drink to you tomorrow and to your continued zest for life, drawing upon it as you contribute to it your gay and meditative spirit.

Affectionately yours, F.F.

ms with signature 105A.9

To Felix Frankfurter

January 29, 1942 Judge Learned Hand's Chambers

Dear Felix:

Your note—with later Whitehouse [Whitehead?] postscript[91]—pleased me more than any other I remember ever having received from you; it made me feel how you really cared about me. I should have known that anyway, but this confirmed it very authentically. Yes, we do treat our years artificially, but then we treat everything artificially. I don't particularly mind that; apparently that is all that thinking really means. When I hear Charlie Clark and Jerry Frank[92] talking about "realistic" thought, I feel like the Tommy upon the Road to Mandalay:[93] "hell; what do they understand."

So I am content to accept the categories piously enough, and when the animal self insists that these perpetual revolutions of the earth are totally irrelevant, I dispose myself to taking on the conventions appropriate to this stage. I agree that inwardly it is not very convincing; in chatting with myself, I say that I can do my Fach better than I ever could before—though not so much of it—and I agree with you. But I shall conform as a good judge should to the accredited customs until they get themselves shoved out of the way with authority.

The postscript about Whitehead did set me thinking. There really is a man; there is a man whom I should really like to be like. When I was young, I aspired to be such a man, and it is something of a hardship that now I can't even understand what he says. Of all I have met, he seems to me to burn with the purest flame and to give to me the most authentic odor of sanctity. Thanks again, good friend.

My deepest to *la belle Marquise*. L.H.

ms with signature 105A.9

91. This addendum is not in the Hand Papers. Presumably, LH refers to Alfred North Whitehead here, as he does below.

92. Jerome New Frank (1889–1957): attorney, Levinson, Becker, Schwartz & Frank, Chicago, 1919–1929; attorney, Chadbourne, Stanchford & Levy, New York City, 1930–1933; general counsel of Agricultural Adjustment Administration, 1933–1935; special counsel to the Reconstruction Finance Association, 1935–1937; commissioner of the Securities and Exchange Commission, 1937–1941; Judge, United States Second Circuit Court of Appeals, 1941–1957.

93. "On the road to Mandalay" is a line in the chorus of Rudyard Kipling's poem *Mandalay*. LH's "Tommy" is the poem's "British Soldier."

1942-3

To Otto R. Barnett[94]

July 13, 1942

My dear Mr. Barnett:

I received this morning your very interesting letter of July 8th about the opinion in *Schenk v. United Aircraft Corporation.*[95] If I were to make over the patent law, I should want to have far more information about its effect upon invention and discovery than I have—or for that matter than I think anybody else has. As you will remember, the interjection of any notion of "invention" was a late comer in the patent law, the Supreme Court having for a number of decades required nothing more than novelty and utility. My guess is that the kind of invention you discuss is exactly that which should be stimulated, i.e., "persistent and intelligent search," checked by elimination through "trial and error." It may be that this has done more to advance the arts than perhaps even the great discoveries of men of genius. Whether that be true or not, I feel quite sure that discoveries of men of genius do not much need the stimulus of monopoly and that the kind of activity which you mention does. And so if I were recasting the world nearer to the heart's desire, I should not decide the cases in the way that I have tried to, i.e., by demanding a touch of uncommon imagination or something of the kind. However, I understand that the Supreme Court, in spite of the ambiguity with which repeatedly and from the earliest time it has stated the standard of invention, has always required something of that sort.[96]

I believe indeed that we shall get nothing satisfactory until we have an exhaustive examination of the actual workings of the present patent system, the kind of examination

---

94. Otto R. Barnett (1868–1945): attorney, Barnett & Truman, Chicago, Illinois.

95. Schenk v. United Aircraft, 43 F. Supp. 679 (D. Conn. 1941), *modified on other grounds sub nom.* Picard v. United Aircraft Corp., 128 F.2d 632 (2d Cir. 1942). LH's opinion received special attention because it was thought to reflect the heightened standard that was being applied when the validity of patents was in question. As LH noted: "Unless we are to mistake for invention the slow but inevitable progress of an industry through trial and error, and confer a monopoly merely upon the exercise of persistent and intelligent search for improvement, there was no invention in this." *Schenk*, 128 F.2d at 636. By contrast, Barnett writes that the Constitution proposes as patentable merely "discoveries" that may indeed be arrived at through "trial and error" and do not require a "flash of genius" or even "exceptional talents." (tp with ms signature and notes 66.45)

96. The "flash of creative genius" requirement was related to the "non-obviousness" required for patentability. The phrase was used in *Cuno Engineering Corp. v. Automatic Devices Corp.*, 314 U.S. 84 (1941, amended 1942): "[T]he new device, however useful it may be, must reveal the flash of creative genius not merely the skill of the calling. If it fails, it has not established its right to a private grant on the public domain." 314 U.S. at 91. Considered a very high standard, it suggested that research alone, without sudden insight, would not be sufficient to sustain a patent. The "flash of genius" requirement was later rejected by the Patent Act of 1952, which stated that "[p]atentability shall not be negatived by the manner in which the invention was made." 35 U.S.C. § 103. For LH on Patent and Copyright law, see Stephen H. Philbin, *Judge Learned Hand and the Law of Patents and Copyrights*, 60 Harv. L. Rev. 394 (1947). *See also* Paul H. Blaustein, Learned Hand on Patent Law (1983).

that would probably take the full time of a committee for a year or more. I would give such a committee power to examine all industrial organizations and to find out just how the system works. We are going along on assumptions which may have been valid in 1625 in a society which was unimaginably simple compared with our own,[97] and which may have stimulated the arts at that time, but we know nothing about what it is doing now. Without such a study, I have very little interest in the particular formulas which the Supreme Court from time to time adopts, swinging as it does from one side to the other. I need hardly say that this is no time for such an undertaking; after the war is decided—if it does not go against us—perhaps Congress could be induced to undertake something of the sort. With renewed thanks for your letter, believe me,

Very sincerely yours, [Learned Hand]

tp 66.45

1942-4

To Louis Henkin[98]

August 7, 1942 Windsor, Vermont

Dear Henkin:

[...]I did get through on Tuesday evening and came up here on Wednesday. When I say that I "got through," that is not quite true, because I took away a tough long case in which we have the briefs—a "statuary court" case, as [Julius M.] Mayer[99] used to like to call them—and I mean to get that done up here. But the work of the C.C.A. for the eighteenth term and time is complete. It had run very light indeed until May, when a sudden spate of saved up cases gushed upon us, holding us all through July. Even so, the total number was smaller than ever before except once, and it promises to be still smaller for the ensuing term. The war has taken the incentive away from litigants for some reason not wholly clear to me. It will revive in great volume after peace comes, provided the right kind of peace does come.

---

97. LH refers to the Statute of Monopolies of 1623, passed by the House of Commons in order to restrict the granting of monopolies by the Crown. The Statute declared monopolies void under common law, though it made an exception for invention patents. It is considered to be the starting point in the development of modern patent law.

98. Louis Henkin (1917–2010): United States Department of State, 1948–1956; Professor, University of Pennsylvania Law School, 1958–1962; Professor and University Professor, Columbia Law School, 1962–2010. Henkin was LH's clerk from 1940 to June 1941, when he resigned to enter military service. A corporal in the United States Army and stationed in Italy, he corresponded with LH throughout the war. LH responds to Henkin's November 23 letter from Fort Blanding in Florida.

99. Julius M. Mayer (1865–1925): Judge, United States District Court for the Southern District of New York, 1912–1921; Judge, United States Court of Appeals for the Second Circuit, 1921–1924.

I still have the fatuous sense of futility at sitting about doing crossword puzzles, and now just twiddling my thumbs while these terrific issues are being decided. The longer they go, the more fantastically vital they appear to me. I have been reading a history of the last seventy years of France and was immensely interested in the difference in temper of the Germans—including [Otto von] Bismarck who fought the war of 1870—from the same people now. Bismarck, in spite of all, was a civilized statesman; he really looked forward to a Europe in which men should exist on decent terms of live and let live with each other. He would never have yielded to those infantile dreams of world dominion and a sacred *Herrenvolk*, destined to enslave the rest of mankind. Something has happened, something deeply retrogressive, something that has led that people and I fear other peoples backward through millennia of accumulated habits to a far more primitive thinking, the thinking of rudimentary creatures, not really thinking at all, but a kind of hypnotic obsession due to the suggestibility of those who feel inadequate and unrealized and who make up in frenzy for the intolerable effort to face reality. As I think of it, it seems to me the most terrible visitation that has come upon us since at least the 15th century, because it goes so deep into the very foundations of all life except the most savage.

Indeed, even if the Nazi should win, their empire would fall apart in their own hands, for it has no natural basis; it does not admit of any statement except in terms which are so untrue as to be preposterous, and were it not for the terror of it ridiculous. To me, the most horrible part of all is to have it forced upon one that millions of human beings can, if caught young enough, be so indoctrinated with such nonsense that they gladly suffer death, mutilation, and incredible hardship to realize their *papier maché* paradise[. . .] And yet why should it surprise one: the mixture of the marauder, the frank pirate with the crusader has been a common enough phenomenon for ages, and that marauding does enter into the present German ethos very largely; it is not by any means all religious frenzy.

Well, my dear boy, I don't know what should have inspired me to pour out upon you such a flood of platitude. I suppose it is the oppression that so much weighs upon us all. Maybe it does not when one has taken on the job in any capacity of training to meet this curse in the only way it can be met. I can imagine that immersing oneself even in writing down the figures of fire control in a little book can be a release, or at least can satisfy one's sense of dignity at having some share, however small, in the effort to redeem the world. For really that is what it is; I know that you think so; I wish I felt more confident that the feeling was more general among your fellows.

In spite of the rather discouraging Russian campaign and the U boat successes, I can't help feeling that things are not so bleak as the faint-hearted keep saying. After all, they have got to do the job within ten or twelve weeks or they will never be able to do it. That is a large order.

If you can trust me with another letter, you might try me once more.

Sincerely yours, Learned Hand

ms with signature 73.5

1942-5

To Felix Frankfurter

November 23, 1942

Dear Felix:

Enclosed find my check for two hundred dollars to your order, as a contribution to the fund you are raising for Whitehead, which I said last night I would send you.[100] I have a very special feeling about Whitehead. If he is in anything approaching want again, will you please be sure to let me know?[...]

As ever, yours, [L.H.]

tp 105A.9

To Learned Hand from Felix Frankfurter

April 17, 1943 — Supreme Court of the United States

Dear B.:

The other day Mrs. Whitehead got a bad gash on her head which has put her in bed, and it was necessary to have medical attention and the services of a nurse. But I am passing on to you the comment that Marion made to me, namely, "What a lucky thing it is that they had B.'s check to meet the expense of this mishap, and that they have this sum as a nest-egg for the threats of illness which now will constantly hang over the pair."

This note is not intended to hint in a delicate way that the occasion has come for your generous offer to make some more money available to the Whiteheads. It has no other purpose except to say that bread cast upon the waters sometimes returns manifold.

Ever yours, F.F.

tp with ms signature 105A.10

---

100. Alfred North Whitehead and his wife were in need of financial assistance at this time, and Frankfurter and their other friends periodically contributed to their maintenance. On November 25, 1942, Frankfurter thanked LH for his gift of the previous day: "Seldom in your life, I suspect, have you put $200 to a more satisfying use than having it go anonymously as an offering on the altar of philosophy. I was not in the slightest surprised but nonetheless greatly delighted by your spontaneous readiness to lift the load a little from the shoulders of that gallant pair. Ever yours, F.F." (tp with ms signature 105A.10)

To Felix Frankfurter

April 19, 1943 Judge Learned Hand's Chambers

Dear Felix:

I have yours of the 17th. If you think you can get the enclosed check to the Whiteheads with as little information of its source as you did before I wish you would do it. Maybe $100 will be enough—you do not tell me how long she will be apt to have a nurse and doctor—but if it isn't let me know again. I have a sense about those people which is nearly unique; I think on the whole, I had rather have lived his life than any other that I have ever come in actual contact with, and I do not know him very well either[...]

Ever yours, L.H.

tp with ms signature 105A.10

1943-1

To Felix Frankfurter

January 11, 1943 Judge Learned Hand's Chambers

Dear Felix:

Just a word to say that out of all this effort to get me into the Court has come what has been especially gratifying to me: a sense of your regard and affection, which I suppose I ought not to have needed this to demonstrate to me. I shall never forget the warmth and the persistence with which you pressed me for the place, long after it was in the least probable that I could be appointed.[101]

As for the event itself, I have always been unduly sensitive to ambition, and even now I should be insincere to deny that this would have been a great pleasure. But I am sure that it would not have lasted after the first elation and delight in mere place and honor. As I told you, I have got too old to pull up my roots now and I should have always felt it a kind of selfishness to F.A.H. Except for you and Roberts—and possibly in the end Jackson[102]—I doubt if I should have formed any real ties, etc. etc. I am not really the Fox and the Grapes about this; I acknowledge that for years I wanted to make this step, not from any public spirit at all, but merely for the distinction of it. But those times were a good while ago and this flare-up always seemed to me out of place. The

101. For an account of Frankfurter's efforts to persuade President Roosevelt to nominate LH, see Roosevelt and Frankfurter: Their Correspondence, 1928–1945, at 671–77 (Max Freedman ed., 1967).

102. Robert H. Jackson (1892–1954): United States Attorney General, 1940–1941; Associate Justice of the United States Supreme Court, 1941–1954; chief United States prosecutor at the Nuremberg Trials, 1945–1946. For LH's view of Jackson's part in the Nuremberg trials, see 1946-1 To Frankfurter, April 14.

fact that it gave me such evidence of friendship from you was the best thing about it, and that was a great deal.

Affectionately, L.H.

ms with signature 105A.10

To Learned Hand from Felix Frankfurter

January 26, 1943 Supreme Court of the United States

Dear B.:

You beat me to it. I have been carrying a letter to you in my head ever since Rutledge's name went in[103]—but it takes time for me to get a longhand letter written. And so you beat me to it. But I'm glad you did—so that you wrote indeed as well as thought spontaneously.

I wanted to tell you that your regret at your not coming here is probably considerably less than mine. For even you know enough to know—apart from the pangs that uprooting would have meant for Frances and you—that your life on the Court would have been far from being dominantly congenial. And if you knew all I know, you probably would feel F.D.R.'s debtor.

But for me the regret is very deep. You may or may not know that one of the real ambitions of my own public concerns for now 25 years has been the yearning to see you on this court; that's where you have belonged as have only less than a handful of men during that period. And to me, of course, it would have been the pure joy of comradeship with a man whose very great gifts I admire and whose intellectual integrity in all its refined aspects I wholly esteem. "Es hat nicht sollen sein—es werd! so schön gewesen."[104] All of which is but the turn of the Wheel of Fortune—as is the absurdity of my being here and you not.

I salute you affectionately on your birthday. F.F.

ms with signature 105A.10

1943-2

To Louis Henkin

February 21, 1943 Judge Learned Hand's Chambers

Dear Henkin:

As usual I have let your last letter remain long overdue, and I have no excuse either for the work is very light. I have thought of you often, supposing that you were in or near

103. Wiley Blount Rutledge (1894–1949): Associate Justice of the United States Supreme Court, 1943–1949. On Rutledge, see 1957-5 To Frankfurter, April 24.

104. I.e., It ought not to have been this way—it is so obvious.

Africa, though God knows where you may now be, and trying in a futile sort of way to put myself in your place. The recent fighting in Tunis, where we met the enemy and apparently were not a match for him, particularly excited my imagination. I wondered what it would be like to find that they had got around behind me, and that my own crowd were separated from the main body, etc., etc. My general conclusion was that all such imaginings are useless; it has been my experience that one cannot really get any sense of how one will feel in a crisis until the crisis comes, and that must be immensely more true in war than in any other crisis. I suppose too that when you write your pen will be sealed against telling me how it all feels, and that I must wait until I see you to get such a faint realization as words can give[...]

Felix [Frankfurter] raised Heaven and Earth to try to get F.D.R to put me in Byrnes's place,[105] but F.D.R. had too much sense to do it, and while I should have been ass enough to accept, I am really greatly his debtor that he didn't. It would not be a pleasant place now with all the discords going on and I a man of peace. Do you remember the story—either Lincoln's or Mark Twain's—about the comment of the man whom the crowd tarred and feathered and then rode a rail? "If it wasn't for the honor of the thing, I should not have liked the experience." Well, that is about the way I feel. I will not deny that I am fond enough of tinsel to have liked it, but after a little, to a man of 71, it would have been too much uprooting and too contentious an atmosphere.

A great deal of talk about the Bill of Rights—as though people going to have a decent government by proclaiming how good they mean to be instead of being individually skeptical and tolerant. Much exaltation of T. Jefferson, to me always an unpleasant figure though an indubitably great one. A skillful demagogue, a most versatile and richly endowed human being, but a dweller in abstractions and at bottom, I suspect, not really a friend of the common man at all, but merely a creature conjured up out of his own egoism to shadow forth what he liked to think himself to be. But that won't do, will it? The censor may stop such heresy and put me in the coop.

Good luck, L.H.

ms with signature 73.6

To Learned Hand from Louis Henkin

March 30, 1943

Dear Judge:

I've taken this local stationery into the cab of a GHC and with that pit of protection from sand and sun I'm ready to acknowledge appreciative receipt of your letter of the 21st of February[...]

You ask of reactions to danger, and I wish I could answer in detail. At best it's really a personal problem and in our case, to a large extent, you're expected to look after yourself,

105. James Francis Byrnes (1879–1972): Representative from South Carolina, 1911–1925; Senator from South Carolina, 1931–1941; Associate Justice of the United States Supreme Court, 1941–1942; Secretary of State, 1945–1947; Governor of South Carolina, 1951–1955.

and you won't be put in the kitchen for being an ass and neglecting to wear your helmet. So too is the reaction, to speak of the fellow I should know a bit about—well, I never was a hero, I guess, and I'd probably go out of my way to avoid trouble[...] I confess a dread (not chronic, just one of those fears you talk about) of a Nazi with a bayonet, or capture. And yet, with a sort of youthful conceit that cannot viscerally be convinced of my vulnerability to the mechanical monsters of these mere men I'd rather not have to meet, I can walk through a mine field when I have to with comparative unconcern, go about my business with bombs falling, even neglect my slit trench when a lot of hardier, braver warriors pale at the first rumble of a plane motor and dive head first at the first alarm of shell fire. So it's a matter of personal difference. But you can feel terribly naked caught without trench or helmet 'neath an attack of strafing planes. You hug the road bank and "sweat it out"—yet since the waiting is of only a few moments, generally, the sensations are neither fear nor prayer nor real concern—something more akin to trying to hold time and world absolutely still, playing dead sensitively, and speaking as though ostrich-like that affords some protection. And if the predicament repeats, especially if you've had some fairly lucky breaks, you tend—dangerously—to a visceral confidence which whatever else helps through future ordeals and makes you more efficient because less worried. Then there's the reaction to enemy, all tied up with ideas of pacificism and war. I remember on Christmas Eve thinking suddenly of the more Christian version "Peace on Earth, Good will to men," and noting that my favorite carol is in the language of the enemy. I wondered then as I've often wondered since how the non-Nazis were doing over on the other side. When I hear "those bastards" about some stukas doing their job, I've thought of the German equivalent by some scared or angry youngster in Hitler's uniform. And yet when action of any kind is in progress, it fades[...]

This has been long and all at this end. I do want to express—well, I almost said regret. But it isn't really. If you had made the Court, dear Judge Hand, I'd probably go sticking my chest out over it and be glad for the old Boss! But even as you so well put it, it's better so. Especially now, when the Court's importance is temporarily overshadowed, the uprooting would hardly be worthwhile. We puisne[106] judges and Law Review bull-sessioners passed about many a tale on how it happened that Learned Hand—the greatest of them all, I've been told on good authority—never donned the Royal Purple of the Temple Beetles. Yet there's always something legendary added to the earned fame of the great player who for absurd reasons was never to be admitted to the big league[...]

My best to Mrs. Hand and C.C.A.2. Lou Henkin

ms with signature 73.6

To Louis Henkin

August 14, 1943 Pointe au pic, Province of Quebec

Dear Henkin:

It is such an unconscionable time since I wrote you that I have quite forgotten when it was. I have often thought of you in the meantime, contrasting the uneventful course of

106. Literally, *puis né* or junior; at law, of inferior status.

my own life with what may well have been yours, indeed, what in all probability has been yours. As I cannot do more than idly imagine what that has been, an exercise that can scarcely be interesting to you, I will tell you the news from the U.S.A. which, as I understand, all soldiers are greedy for. So far as I myself am concerned, there is little, as I have already suggested.

The term was lighter in the number of cases to be decided than any I have had in the nineteen years I have been on the court, but either they are getting more difficult, or I am getting slower, or the presence of Judge Clark and Judge Frank makes the work go more precisely and so take more time. Anyway, for some reason or other, I find that I work if anything harder than I used. I got through on the 6th and came up to Canada at once for a fortnight, half of which has passed. When I say that I got through, that is not quite true, for we carried away—T.W.S.,[107] A.N.H.—a very large case, sitting as a district court of three circuit judges. The U.S. has brought an action under the Sherman Act against the Associated Press, charging that it is an unlawful conspiracy in restraint of trade. The case has already developed to great length, and there has been a motion—by the plaintiff—for summary judgment. All three of us, having heard the matter for a whole day, decided to let it stand over until September. It has aroused a good deal of interest as you may imagine, and anything that touches the Sherman Act is, as you know, troublesomely vague[108][...]

You have probably heard that the people at large are what is called "complaisant," which means over-confident. I think that there is a truth in this. Our side has been successful recently in a good many places, and it can't be denied that to us who stay at home the prospect is brighter. We are especially impressed with the way in which the war is going in Russia; it seems as though the Germans must be definitely weakening. True, they may be merely retreating to other positions more defensible, but one can't help wondering whether that is all. Well, that coupled with the German bombings and the collapse of Mussolini have conspired to give us something more than we deserve of confidence. And I rather fear that there is some disposition to think that the war is "in the bag." It is almost inevitable that as the final event appears more and more certain, those who are far away, as we are, from the actual burden of it should become a little too sure. Everything possible is being done to correct this and our production continues at fabulous figures, notwithstanding.

Meanwhile, you must not suppose that the trials and sufferings of those who like you are bearing the whole ghastly weight of it are not in our minds; we follow every move[...] Don't bother to write, but if you should it would be welcome.

---

107. Thomas Walter Swan (1877–1975): Dean of the Yale Law School, 1916–1926, Judge, United States Court of Appeals for the Second Circuit, 1926–1975.

108. See *United States v. Associated Press*, 52 F. Supp. 362 (S.D.N.Y. 1943), *aff'd*, 326 U.S. 1 (1945), in which the Associated Press was charged with violations of the Sherman Antitrust Act stemming from the member newspapers' agreement to share resources in order to report news stories more quickly and efficiently. The United States Court of Appeals for the Second Circuit held that the Associated Press's arrangement, particularly the criteria to which potential member newspapers were subject in order to be admitted to the association, constituted an unreasonable restraint of trade, a decision the Supreme Court affirmed. On the Sherman Act, see 1911-4 To Roosevelt, November 15.

Roberts, the clerk of C.C.A., died yesterday; he has been sick for a month or two. We shall miss him badly. Good luck!

Sincerely yours, Learned Hand

ms with signature 73.6

To Learned Hand from Louis Henkin

August 30, 1943

Dear Judge Hand:

This Sicily thing has been over for two weeks, but for us that hasn't brought any change of situation. Now is the time of wait and rumor, and we lie around waiting for things to happen—an idleness neither relaxing nor restful.

It's been a funny campaign in some ways. I guess there was nothing funny—either amusing or peculiar—in the destruction and the waste and the casualties. I don't know what the figures are and I remember reading that our losses were light for the particular job undertaken, but I don't believe that at all. I don't know how you price these things, but my own feeling is that having landed successfully and with great good fortune, they had hoped for an easier, quicker, less expensive end. Still, it's done and I'm getting out of my department. What I started to remark about were the peculiarities. You capture a town, and every other house in it has a male speaking broken English after five to fifty years in New York, Chicago, Pittsburg, or Milwaukee. No soldier could fathom in his wildest dream what wild horses dragged them back here, but if you asked, it would probably be the combination of family and language and tradition that makes for belonging. They all have a brother or an uncle somewhere in the States, and every child old enough to mouth the word, young enough to drag weary bones, promises himself (at least to our hearing) "America"[...] Perhaps I'm not well versed in the history of conquest. But did the conquered Barbarians speak to the Roman soldiers of "our armies?" "How far did we get today?" Did they ask earnestly when the conqueror was to bring shoes and clothes? Did they express the fear that the Romans may decide not to occupy them, to go home and leave the poor conquered nation alone? They seem to dream of an independent country, Protectorate America, and I think I've been disillusioning those I've met by telling them we wouldn't touch them with a 3000 mile pole. They've tried to create in our minds what may or may not exist in theirs, the dichotomy between Sicily and Italy, to shed responsibility for the sins of the mainland. Since the weather turned from fair, Mussolini hasn't had too many friends. Before that I suspect the Sicilians' "Duce!!" was as loud as any, and they were ready to share in the glory of empire, though there were grumblings all along because nothing had been done for this island, because industry had not been brought into the Garden of Italy. When it was over they couldn't see how we might insist on treating prisoners who were Sicilians just like their fellow soldiers from the mainland. They were horrified at the possibility that we might fail to release immediately all those we captured[...]

It's easy to impose penalties if you can get another to execute. I wonder how much capital punishment we'd have if the judge had to do the executing or at least witness it, or how much perjury there'd be if the witnesses were made to do so. I realize that our civilization is too complex to carry the notion too far, but I wonder if a measure of it wouldn't help the cause of Justice, as I think it would an un-vengeful peace. May I ask for an opinion from you, sir?[...]

I hope this arrives to find you ready to start another term of the decency and good sense that mark a sane spot in this crazy, unholy mess. My very good wishes to Mrs. Hand, and the members of the court and especially to you.

Respectfully, Lou Henkin

ms with signature 73.6

To Learned Hand from Louis Henkin

October 31, 1943

Dear Judge Hand:

Your letter of August 14th crossed mine from Sicily, so now you must have read and forgotten whatever overflowed onto paper of my reactions to that one. Since then, much water under many bridges, and a bit under me too[...] Let me vitiate much of what follows by confessing that I generalize from very few particular conversations with peasants and with the townspeople that came into the Tambourro Flower Shop during the few days I took them in charge. Papa, it seems, didn't have much respect for the Fascists, but the center of my attraction, very pretty, 19 year old Filomena, sophomore at the University, admits Benito was a hero and the rah-rah of Fascism much to her taste.

[...]I don't think it was easy for them to forget the Pro-Nazi indoctrination of years, the bomb with which I destroyed their home, the brother I killed, the national pride we humbled. Their chief regret about the big game is that they started up with the rich and the mighty, Britain and America. No "moral" repentance I'm sure and yet what I said last time still holds. They've acquiesced in crimes the way our people en masse could do: in lynching, in oppression they don't see and may not believe. They've suffered, and they suffer still, more every day[...]

I hope this forces neither patience nor eyesight, and that it finds you in the best of health. I will be happy if you will give my best wishes to Mrs. Hand, and to Judges Hand and Swan.

Sincerely, Lou Henkin

ms with signature 73.6

To Louis Henkin

December 27, 1943 New York, New York

Dear Louis:

I got your two letters—one I suppose from Sicily and the other from Italy though I had to guess at the place each time—and I thought them extremely interesting as I should have expected. They asked me questions that I cannot conceivably answer. Of course, the Italians look to us as the Great Fairy Godmother. Why not? We have always been represented as Midases all. Their cousins and brothers and sons go to us, and come back lying about the streams of gold that flow down every street because that is expected of them. Then they see our tourists scattering the precious metal about as though the supply were unlimited. At last we have come to free them from the Tedeschi, whom they have always hated, and from whom they had to put up with every indignity during their infantile excursion into the land of the Brobdingnags.[109] Having tried to swell up to the size of an ox and burst in the attempt, what is left of them looks plaintively to those fortunate denizens in the "Land of Perpetual Effortless Plenty." I repeat, why not? And we shall have a rather hard time dealing with them, as has already begun to appear. I am not sure that this is relevant to your inquiries at all, but I hope it may be.

As to what we are to do, if we ever end this horrid business, I am at sea as usual. I cannot believe that an out and out vindictive peace, a "Carthaginian Peace,"[110] will in the end make for an enduring peace. It was natural for the Russians to hang the savages who massacred their comrades, but I wonder whether at the last that will serve to make Germans more understanding and tend to cure them of their notion that force is all. And yet I suppose that there is not the slightest chance that we shall not impose that kind of peace when we win; no, I will change that, I will say only that the chance is against it. Everyone says that Germany should be "disarmed" and it is hard to deny that that should be done, at least for a season. But I do not believe that the nations now together will continue to keep her disarmed, and the temporary disarmament at the end of the last war only led to a greater frenzy of armament when the restraint was off. You know, at times I have wondered whether the wisest plan would not be merely to take away all their territorial gains and leave the Germans with nothing more to show for their suffering and their efforts than their wasted cities and their lost and maimed young men. It would be harder for them to nurse a grievance out of that than if Hitler and Goebbels and Himmler and Goering were all hanged. I dread the invasion of Germany by the Russians; I dread the vengeance of the Czechs and the Poles. Yet all this hatred is natural and easily understood; I should feel so myself no doubt if I had suffered as they have. And yet, as I have said, if we are looking at a more tolerable society, to a world where men are not continually to kill, these retributions are not a good path towards it.

You may not have much news from here; in any case, I can give you my personal impressions. Roosevelt has lost control of Congress completely; it is arguable that he could do so well with a Republican one as with what he has. The Southern Tories are in full revolt and will do all they can to block whatever he wants. Maybe it is some evidence of this that he has officially announced that he is going to abandon the term, "New Deal."

---

109. Italy invaded Ethiopia on October 3, 1935, and occupied it until 1941. Brobdingnag is the fantastic land in which everything appears hugely out of scale in Jonathan Swift's GULLIVERS TRAVELS.

110. A peace that devastates the losing side, often used to describe the destruction of Carthage by Rome after the second Punic war. John Maynard Keynes's book on the Treaty of Versailles, THE ECONOMIC CONSEQUENCES OF THE PEACE (1919), described as such the terms the Allies imposed on Germany.

Going along with this change has been a general breakdown of the common interest as against special interests. It has come up principally about inflation; everyone is reaching for higher pay; the unions, the farmers particularly, as they have the most power. Slowly, the bulwarks against inflation yield, and we are in for a very considerable dose of it, though the best advised seem to think it will not go into a tailspin. What curious nonsense it is that a society will take its young men for death and mutilation at low wages during their most productive time, and yet will not put the necessary pressure on the rest of us to do our very small part, at best, by comparison. Of course, the chief reason here is that we have been so untouched by the war that we don't truly realize it. As [Robert] Patterson[111] said to me less than a year ago, a few bombings would do wonders for us.

I am afraid that this has seemed rather a dreary letter. Let it not be so; we are all satisfied that the thing will come out right. We do not doubt the cost, which next year will raise higher than ever before, but the fear which held us three years ago has gone and even though other fears may have appeared, they do not measure with that. We know, moreover, that we owe our release to you lads who have had to bear all the brunt of it. It is indeed impossible for us in imagination to get the reality of the least part of what you are doing, but we try, and we bear towards you an inestimable debt, which we now recognize and like other debtors are likely soon to forget. But whatever happens, my dear Louis, you will have a treasure of your own that you will never forget, for you have proved yourself a man.

Sincerely yours, Learned Hand

ms with signature 73.7

1943-3

To Learned Hand from Felix Frankfurter

April 24, 1943 Supreme Court of the United States

Dear B.:

[...]The question you raise about the tribe to which [J.B.] Matthews[112] belongs makes me feel less awed about the Ferrero's principle of legitimacy[113] which Walter Lippmann

---

111. Robert Patterson (1891–1952): Judge, United States District Court for the Southern District of New York, 1930–1939; Judge, United States Second Circuit Court of Appeals, 1939–1940; Under Secretary of War, 1940–1945; Secretary of War, 1945–1947.

112. J. B. Matthews served on the Dies Committee, dedicated to exposing Communist sympathizers in the United States. In a letter to Frankfurter dated April 23, 1943, LH had noted that Matthews, "a peculiarly savage witch-hunter [...] an ex-Communist," was attempting to undermine the professional status of Robert A. Lovett, Assistant Secretary of War for Air. (ms with signature 105A.10)

113. In THE PRINCIPLES OF POWER: THE GREAT POLITICAL CRISES OF HISTORY (Theodore R. Jaeckel trans., 1942), Guglielmo Ferrero states that principles of legitimacy, especially characterized by their power to instill feelings of confidence in a people, allow a people to trust the power and authority of their government.

had recently pronounced one of the profoundest contributions ever made in the whole history of political thought.

Ever yours, F.F.

tp with ms signature 105A.10

To Felix Frankfurter

April 26, 1943 Judge Learned Hand's Chambers

Dear Felix:

[...]So you keep up with Walter? I dare say I should do well to do the same, but I don't. My position reminds me of that of an old hymn I used to hear in my infancy: "Lord, it is my chief complaint, that my faith is weak and faint."[114]

L.H.

tp with ms signature and notes 105A.10

To Learned Hand from Felix Frankfurter

April 27, 1943 Supreme Court of the United States

Dear B.:

Since you ask about my relations with Walter, let me answer with pedestrian accuracy.

I don't know what your experience has been with him though the years, but in my case whenever I wrote him in praise of his writings—which was very often—I would get back the most incandescent words of appreciation both for my devotion and for my wisdom! But when intermittently I was at all critical of anything he wrote, I was put in my place and made to feel that I really did not understand. For my taste, he [became] more and more worldly-wise, and there set in an imperceptible alteration in our relationship. A, to me, incredible article on Hitler's "peace" policy snapped the cord and I ceased writing to him. The rest of the story is told in the enclosed correspondence.[115]

---

114. LH quotes the first two lines of the last stanza of *Hark My Soul It Is the Lord*, a hymn by William Cowper (1568–1619). The stanza's final lines are: "Yet I love Thee and adore/O for grace to love Thee more!"

115. Frankfurter encloses his letter to Lippmann, dated November 28, 1936, in the matter of Hitler's peace policy in order to account for Lippmann's reported belief that Frankfurter had "dropped" him. A portion of that letter asserts: "[W]hen, in your column for May 19, 1933, you described Hitler as 'the authentic voice of a genuinely civilized people'—I'm not unaware of the context—and likened the Reich's cold pogroms and the expulsion of some of its greatest minds and finest spirits, merely because their grandmothers or their wives happened to be Jewesses, to the fact that 'Jews have their parvenus,' then something inside of me snapped." (tp with ms signature 105A.10) Frankfurter also encloses Lippmann's reply, dated December 17, 1936, which defends the position he took in his column: "I am satisfied that the manner in which you have torn phrases from

Since I came down here we have maintained civilized relations, but the fire has gone out. As a matter of fact we see one another rarely and whenever we do, talk on the whole is desultory because he gives me the feeling of a man who is always worrying lest I might compromise him by my mere presence[...]

Ever yours, F.F.

tp with ms signature 105A.10

1944-1

The Atlantic Charter, signed by Franklin D. Roosevelt and Winston Churchill, Prime Minister of the United Kingdom in 1941, referred to the establishment of a future "wider and permanent system of general security," which then became the pretext for planning an international organization to keep the peace at a conference of the allied powers in Moscow in October 1943.

To George Wharton Pepper[116]

January 28, 1944

Dear George:

I will read your article with pleasure.[117] I share your unwillingness to apply force, but I do not see any escape from it, human beings being as they are. For an indefinite time I know of no way by which we can keep the world from lapsing periodically into the shambles which it is now, except by an alliance of the powers strong enough to make their will felt. If you ask me whether I am not aware that this will result in abuse of that power, I say I am acutely aware of it. The truth is, I have no great regard for *homo sapiens*, either as

---

their context and ignored the historical circumstances in which the article was written is inexcusable. It betrays a lack of personal goodwill which is emphasized by the fact that instead of trying to clear up the misunderstanding at the time, you have waited nearly four years to raise the question. It is now too late to raise it." (tp with ms signature 105A.10) The Frankfurter/Lippmann relationship may have suffered earlier that year. See Lippmann's letter to the faculty of Harvard University stating that professors should not be advisors to political office holders and LH's response to Lippmann's letter in a letter to Lessing Rosenthal, dated June 5, 1936, suggesting that Lippmann is specifically criticizing Frankfurter. ROOSEVELT AND FRANKFURTER: THEIR CORRESPONDENCE—1928–1945, at 330–31 (Max Freemann ed., 1967).

116. George Wharton Pepper (1867–1961): Professor of Law, University of Pennsylvania, 1893–1910; Senator from Pennsylvania, 1922–1927; President, American Law Institute, 1936–1947. *See* GERALD GUNTHER, LEARNED HAND: THE MAN AND THE JUDGE 414–15 (1994).

117. In a letter dated January 27, Pepper sent LH his article entitled *America and the League of Nations*, 3 J. COMP. LEGIS. & INT'L L. 21 (1921), and a second article by William Hard on World Union, READER'S DIGEST, Dec. 1943, at 1–15, to confirm that he thinks unworkable any "permanent alliance" among nations. Rather, he argues for "an inclusive organization with no commitments for the use of force" that would "let subsequent changes in the direction of what we think of as greater efficiency come about as the result of recognized need." (tp with ms signature 78.12)

master or servant, but it does seem to me that we are more likely to enjoy a regime of perpetual butchery if we depend upon nothing but periodical conferences.[118] But, upon this, as upon so many other subjects, like King Arthur: "All my mind is clouded with a doubt."[119]

As ever yours, [L.H.]

tp 78.12

1944-2

To Edward Burling[120]

February 6, 1944

Dear Ned:

Your letter was an interesting revelation of how your mind works.[121] Yes, it is true, as you have often told me, that I have been blessed beyond all but a very few men and that I have not profited by it inwardly. I think, however, that although what you call "chemistry" has had as it always does have much to do with happiness, more still depends upon the habits which the individual forms in childhood. The Freudians used to carry this notion to the most preposterous extent, saying almost that we were all really born equal if not free, and that circumstances had a clean slate to write upon in the case of each one of us. Obviously, we differ natively in psyche as much as in body; indeed, how could it be otherwise, now that we know as much as we do about the correlation of brain and mind?

But behind what you said there lurks a very serious omission, as I view it. I agree with you that if the value of life is to be measured purely hedonistically, that is to say, if it is a kind of balance sheet of happy moments against the unhappy or the merely neutral, intelligence is a doubtful asset. An un-fearful disposition, one which does not borrow trouble and which is contented with little, is probably the best possible insurance for the "Good Life" so measured. On the other hand, it has been a commonplace of all the great moral teachers, regardless of religion, that that is not an adequate way to measure the "Good

---

118. In his response dated January 31, Pepper declares that their positions are irreconcilable: "You infer that human beings will perform an agreement to use force for righteous ends. I infer that they will readily promise to do so and will renege when the time comes. If you are right, conference is a waste of time. If I am right, promises of collective security are a waste of breath." (tp with ms signature 78.12)

119. "I am going a long way / With these thou seest—if indeed I go— / (For all my mind is clouded with a doubt) / To the island-valley of Avilion; /. . . / Where I will heal me of my grievous wound." Alfred Lord Tennyson, Idylls of the King, "The Passing of Arthur," lines 424–432.

120. Edward Burling (1871–1966): attorney, Covington & Burling, Washington, D.C.

121. In a letter dated February 1, 1944, Edward Burling wrote LH: "I rather think misery depends upon some chemical adjustment[. . .] It may be that it is lack of intelligence that leads to happiness and that your acute intelligence produces misery." (tp with ms signature 100.16)

Life." The Utilitarians[122] did try to measure it so, and they made great progress because they had hold of a real truth, but they missed much—really the best part—and for that reason their morals have never really been able to take hold on most high souls. The reason, I suggest, is this. It makes no difference how biologically it came to be true, nevertheless it is true, that mankind has for eons come so to confuse the means with the end that the means have become ends in themselves.[123] The Utilitarians have inadequately realized the consequences of this, and it is on that account that their Utopia has always seemed tame, tepid, and tedious.

Let me take an instance. It may well be—indeed I should say that it was certainly true—that courage is reckoned a virtue only because, taking an average of those occasions on which a man should show it, it will prove profitable as a means of avoiding evil or achieving safety, either for himself or for others, including the society to which he belongs. The Utilitarians therefore say that courage is a virtue and is "good," not of itself but because its display is mediate to some "happiness" which its absence would forfeit. So far that is quite true; they are right. But where they are apt to miss out, I think, is that man is a curious animal who builds out of his own insides, so to speak; courage which in origin was mediate and of itself neutral becomes in time a newly fabricated good—*Güte an sich*, so to speak. Thus a man who possesses it has a sense of value in himself, quite independent of the safety he secures, of the recognition that he may get from his fellows. It is as direct and un-analyzable a good as the enjoyment of the senses themselves. Man has in this way immensely enriched the very "modest kit," as [C.L.?] Stevenson somewhere calls it, with which he started. This is what I think the great moral teachers have always meant when they speak of the "Good Life" as depending upon what one can make of oneself, not because that may be a path to some Elysium where other desires will be gratified, but because what one does make of oneself is the highest *Güte an sich*[...]

Well, when I talk with you, you seem to me to fear reliance upon this, as though it were a trap for the unsophisticated, a kind of counterfeit prize put off on the simple by those who want only to control their conduct. The absence of any belief in the reality of *Güte* does indeed make one melancholy and dreary, particularly when, like us, one gets towards the end. The world is not well adjusted to the "Good Life" on any other terms; but if one can once really come to believe that the acquisition for oneself of even a very modest equipment of the kind I mention, the whole face of things changes. I think I can call to witness for this a vast number of witnesses.

Do not suppose from what I say that I reckon myself among those few who have even that modest equipment. I do not; it is for that reason that I think of myself for the most part a failure. But I think that behind my individual fate, the idea of a world in which this kind of reward is possible and is not too infrequently gained makes the outlook far less

---

122. The subject of John Stuart Mill's essay *Utilitarianism*, this social philosophy endorses an ethical doctrine that evaluates the moral worth of an action by its contribution to overall utility.

123. LH commends his teachers at Harvard for urging not the achievement of an end but rather "satisfaction in the search itself." *On Receiving an Honorary Degree, in* The Spirit of Liberty 134–39, 138. Similarly, he argues that "the performance is itself the wage[...] In the work, moreover, we shall find our reward, and reward enough—on the whole the best of rewards—let performance fall as far behind conception as it may." *At Fourscore, in* The Spirit of Liberty 253–62, 261–62. *See also* 1936-2 To Littell, July 10.

dreary than it would otherwise be, and that apparently it is to you. So far as I can say that I have anything that could by any stretch be called a religion, this is about the sum of it. It does not follow that, when all is said, it was better that life came to this planet. Perhaps not, that is an unanswerable question, I suspect, anyway. But it is a complete answer to the despondency which takes form in the "Let us eat, drink and be merry, for tomorrow we die." At least there is a prize there to be won if you have the guts to win it, and this, I submit, gives one an enormous lift over the groundlings, however little one may be justified in counting oneself among the winners.

Well, all this your innocent pages have called out. Had I got such a letter from you, my courage would have failed me; I doubt if I should have pushed through it. Perhaps you will not and even if you do not, I shall not have lost my time; because these are things one does not say or think unless one writes them and while they are over fifty years old with me, it has helped me to state them again *in extenso*. I can only use this as a warning to you that you must be careful to stand away from the flood, if in the future you in some thoughtless moment make a little hole in the dam.

B.

tr/tp with signature 100.16

1944-3

To Learned Hand from Louis Henkin

March 9, 1944

Dear Judge Hand:

I am rather annoyed with our postal boys because the record for longest duration of a letter in transit was bestowed on yours of December 27th. It came about a week ago, however, and you must know I was very pleased to get it.

[...]The front has frozen me near a tiny mountain village for some weeks now. But soon I expect to go up to the mountain again (I've changed from Surveying to Artillery Observation), and I do so with definite regret, for this tiny spot will read in capital letters on my own map of the world. I should know better by now than to make friendships that must be severed, yet everywhere I allow myself to become attached to people, everywhere parting becomes "all we need of hell." There's a young doctor here, an intelligent man, who's taken my hand and led me into the village bloodstream. There I found great sadness because this particular place had the enemy too much and too long with them, and now I might say the same for us. There's not a family that hasn't lost a member to a shell or to kidnapping by the enemy; their homes are destroyed, the economy does not exist. They stand in fear before the smallest and meanest of allied soldiers, must succumb to indignities brought on by poverty and fear of us. Ordinary suffering of unknown nature to anonymous human beings weighs on us like a dull inexplicable weight. But these people are known and alive to me, and I stand helplessly by while they struggle with starvation, with the last bungle, with an atrocity by some allied soldier, all items that point accusingly at my comparative ease and wealth and freedom from fear[...]

I've been overlong again, dear Judge. But it's my one way of showing I was pleased to get your letter. I trust the Court is carrying on, that its members are well, that Mrs. Hand and you are enjoying the best of health and the height of good spirit possible in this confused day.

Respectfully, Lou H.

ms with signature 73.7

To Louis Henkin

September 21, 1944 Windsor, Vermont

Dear Louis:

It must be months since I have written you, months without any excuse[...] Meanwhile, what will you have been doing? God, I sometimes try to imagine what it is really like; every once in a while we do get a vivid, lurid picture which gives us what we like to believe is some approach to it. But I know that it is false, and for that matter, is not every description, however faithful, false? I can only say for myself that I can never tell anything about how I shall feel on any occasion by foreshadowing it; I have got to wait until it comes. And I suppose that is particularly true of that especially charming form of activity in which you are now engaged—communal and mutual murder. I have fancied you slowly, and with the utmost pains and weariness, working your way up the western side of the peninsula, and at the moment being engaged in trying to drive out the Germans from their fastnesses in the Apennines northwest of Florence. That country I know, unlike the country south of Naples, and it passes my imagination how it is possible to dislodge from those mountains a determined enemy, well equipped. Apparently, progress is really being made in spite of the fact that the Germans are still determined, at least in that region, and well equipped. Even at the other end of the line, where the chances look better to a civilian boob, they have succeeded in holding us up.

But, Louis, nothing can be of much less interest to you than my comments about your position and doings, even though I were to extend what I said to those charming folks who did such an exquisitely barbarous bit of lynching the other day in Rome. (I only pray that we over here, who have so often done more shockingly savage murders of Negroes, will not get self-righteous about that.) No, what you will really want to hear is news from home, and particularly about the election. F.D.R. did not do a very good job at the Convention; he tried to ride too many horses at once, and he fell between them. But it was a dreadfully hard situation. He could not have put over [Henry] Wallace,[124] as I suspect he would have preferred, and he could not have done with Byrnes, who was my favorite. [William O.] Douglas the South would have refused as much as Wallace, so he was up against it. Nobody seems to think anything of [Harry S.] Truman,[125] and the Republicans are doing their damnedest to spread it about that F.D.R. won't last out[...]

124. Henry Wallace (1888–1965): Secretary of Agriculture, 1933–1940; Vice President of the United States, 1941–1945; Secretary of Commerce, 1945–1946.

125. Harry S. Truman (1884–1972): Vice President of the United States, 1944–1947; President of the United States, 1947–1952. *See* 1951-4 To Learned Hand from Harry S. Truman, May 23.

After a man has been in the job for nearly twelve years, and such years as those, he has plenty of enemies. We are in a revolution anyway, and as the prospect of a peace gets nearer and nearer, F.D.R.'s chances get worse and worse. Things have been going so extraordinarily well in Germany and Holland that by the end of next month it may be apparent that all organized opposition is really over. Everyone agrees that that would have a very bad effect on F.D.R.'s chances. How far he has kept his hold except in the unions is the question; these I think he will have; those who think we are right to go in to the war, I should think he would also have. But the Nyes, the La Follettes, the Lindberghs, the American Firsters generally, they will be creeping out of their holes and whetting their knives. The odds still appear to be in his favor, but as I said, I am not too happy.

You may be amused to learn that the appeal in the case of *United States v. The Aluminum Company*,[126] which Caffey J. took four years to try and decide, has finally devolved upon Swan and the two Hand Boys to determine. It happened that the nine in Washington could not find six of their number who were not disqualified. That bench is lousy with ex-Attorneys General who had had a hand in the case, and it takes six to make a quorum. So Congress passed an act to make the C.C.A. decide, and said that the three oldest in Commission must sit!!! It is set down for January 2nd and there are to be 1500 pages of briefs. The record, which I hope to not have to look at all, is some 47,000 pages. We hope that we may be able to deal with it if we give two months to it, but I dare say that the poor wretch who has to write an opinion may be obliged to slop over still longer.[127] The calendar looks to be about the same size that it was last year; we sat only 22 weeks as against 27 when you were with me. But for some reason we work more slowly, and these weeks appear to give us as much to do as we used to have.

If you have any time that is vacant and the spirit moves you, pray let me hear from you, though I know I don't deserve it.

Sincerely yours, Learned Hand

ms with signature 73.7

1945-1

To Learned Hand from Felix Frankfurter

January 5, 1945 — Supreme Court of the United States

Dear B.:

There are even deeper reasons for any esteem of you as the most distinguished living judge in the English-speaking world, but I am moved to say that it is beyond the powers

126. [In] *United States v. Aluminum Co. of America*, 148 F.2d 416 (2d Cir. 1945), the government sought to break Alcoa's de facto monopoly of the aluminum industry by bringing a host of charges under the Sherman Antitrust Act. After a multiyear trial that began in 1937, the district court, in an opinion by Judge Francis G. Caffey, dismissed the government's complaint. *See* United States v. Aluminum Co. of Am., 44 F. Supp. 97 (S.D.N.Y. 1941). The district court decision was quickly appealed, and was affirmed in part, reversed in part, and remanded.

127. LH was that "poor wretch"; *see* 1945-4 To Frankfurter, March 24.

of all but the merest few to write such an opinion as yours in the *Cohen, Wachtel, Raffe et al.* case [sic],[128] assuming that there are any who can do it. And I say this all the more because I have misgivings about some of the manifestations in that and other cases that you tough guys reveal in criminal appeals. If you and Gus attribute such misgivings, as you doubtless do, to softness in me, please throw into the scales of your judgment of me the fact that I spent five years of my life putting people in prison or keeping them there, and that since [then] not a negligible fraction of my years has been directed toward reflection on what constitutes a civilized *and* effective system of criminal justice. But: the point of this letter is admiration for your opinions.

Ever yours, F.F.

ms with signature 105A.11

To Felix Frankfurter

January 11, 1945 Judge Learned Hand's Chambers

Dear Felix:

I carried about your letter all day with a sense of warm satisfaction. How could it be otherwise? I will not and indeed could not reply to the beginning of it; it would be idle to disclaim, for it would be so apparently in order to do so and so inevitably actuated by some kind of motive which would discredit it, however frank it might seem. I can only say that it gratified me deeply. Incidentally, I read over part of that opinion, and I do think I can be sincere when I say that whatever may be my merits, it did surprise me that you could have rated that performance as you did.

In re the second part: There is, of course, a real danger that we may get stuck in observing the essentials. I don't know any path to follow, rather be wary of all paths. For myself, I have disposed to press whenever we can against the exclusory rules of evidence and in that efficiency we should not differ. Wigmore does put them in a rational bases; I had supposed that hearsay, at least, was vestigially sacramental and Eddie Morgan[129] bears me out. Naturally, I am not competent in a matter of history, but I feel quite sure that we should allow our disputes in court to be decided by the same evidence which we should use in other serious concerns. As I apprehend, you have at times felt that we were too ready to disregard instances of arbitrary and overbearing action by the trial judges. I cannot plead not guilty, nor will I plead guilty. It is quite likely that the recollections of twenty years ago pervade me too much. I remember that then I felt strongly that in nine

128. Frankfurter refers to *United States v. Cohen*, 145 F.2d 82 (2d Cir. 1944), an appeal of mail fraud convictions by five of the original twenty-seven defendants, three of whom were Joseph Cohen, Mandel Raffe, and Bertram M. Wachtel. In addressing the appellants' contentions that the trial was, essentially, too complicated and the evidence too voluminous for the jury properly to weigh, LH's opinion (repudiating these contentions) has been frequently cited as a defense of the jury system in criminal cases, the role of the judge in admitting evidence, and the jury's role in considering it.

129. Edward M. Morgan (1878–1966): Professor, Yale Law School, 1917–1925; Professor, Harvard University, 1925–1950; Professor, Vanderbilt University, 1950–1962.

cases out of ten, these [instances] were fabricated almost altogether or at least raised to a grotesque importance. I know you will say that it is not so much that the innocent are punished, as it is that the habit of arbitrary and high-handed treatment of the accused corrupts the whole process. That I can't deny, and I can only inconclusively cite the platitude: *in media via ibis.*[130]

Thine, L.H.

P.S. You don't mention the Marquise.

ms with signature 105A.11

1945-2

To Learned Hand from Charles Edward Clark[131]

February 6, 1945 — Second Circuit Court of Appeals

Dear Learned:

[...]Did I tell you that at the Montague dinner I had the great honor of sitting beside Mr. Justice Johnston, Appellate Division, Second Department, who, after finding that I was on the court with you, offered me his deep heartfelt commiserations when he said, "Oh, he's a Red."

As ever, C.E.C.

tp with ms signature 101.28

To Charles Edward Clark

February 8, 1945

Dear Charlie:

[...]You filled my cup to overflowing. That anyone should think of this timid, puzzled, old bourgeois as a "Red" is a consummation for which I have wished many years. Now, at last, here is a boob silly enough to realize my ambition. The fly in the ointment is that, I suppose, the learned jurist would include as a "Red" anyone who believed in workman's compensation.

As ever yours, [L.H.]

tp 101.28

---

130. I.e., you will take the middle way.

131. Charles Edward Clark (1889–1963): Professor, Yale Law School, 1919–1929; Dean, Yale Law School, 1929–1939; Judge, United States Court of Appeals for the Second Circuit, 1939–1963.

1945-3

To Bernard Berenson

February 18, 1945

Dear B.B.:

I have very often thought of a passage in your last letter—just how long ago I cannot now recall—in which you said it would be indeed the last word you would ever be able to address to me.[132] I had a kind of melancholy suspicion that this might indeed be true: two men of our age who were to be completely isolated for a matter of no one knew how many years, were not at all unlikely to find it permanent. But Fortune, that strange bitch, has curious whimsies, and here we are (you after your incredible experiences, and I, just the same with time passing so much as before), once more able to communicate. I have had copies of several of your letters, and one of Nicky's, from Lawrence Berenson.[133] Also, Byba[134] has helped to put us au courant with your present status quo. "Incredible" I very deliberately mean to call your history under the Nazi domination; the skill, the patience, the *aequanimitas* which were required to see yourself through excite my utmost admiration. I had known that you were more largely endowed than most of those I had known to look upon this world as one in which intelligence was the only key, but I must own that I had not realized that your disposition had in it such a Stoic streak that you could sit in daily expectation of final doom, and still carry on undisturbed those activities which had been your custom in times of calm and security.[135] My neurasthenic soul humbly lays

---

132. I.e., Berenson's letter dated May 2, 1941, written before the Nazi occupation of Italy. LH had not received Berenson's letter sent from Settignano, dated January 5, 1945.

133. Lawrence Berenson, cousin of Captain Robert Berenson and of Bernard Berenson. *See* 1941-1 To Learned Hand from Bernard Berenson, May 2.

134. Byba Giulizni (Mrs. Henry Coster).

135. LH had read the account of Captain Robert Berenson, aide-de-camp to General Clark, who describes how he found Bernard Berenson in Florence in a letter dated September 6, 1944, forwarded to LH by John Walker on September 29, 1944, and preserved in the Hand Papers: "I have just come back from Florence, where I have been several times before in the last month or so, looking for B.B. I finally found him safe and well, and absolutely beside himself with joy seeing me. I actually got to him 7 hours after the Germans left the area where he was hiding. I am happy to say that B.B. is wonderfully well, considering everything. He has been hiding in a friend's house for a full year, not able to move outside for one minute. Imagine what he has been through. He is really remarkable. Rather than worrying about himself, he locked himself up with his books studying and writing. He came out having written two books, and a bunch of short stories. Mary, who is just about alive, is living at I Tatti. She is very old and weak and doesn't make much sense, but is still just as sweet and lovely looking in her tired old age. B.B. had to get out of his house and hide, but there was nothing Mary could do or anybody could do to her, so she stayed at I Tatti with the servants. Nobody bothered her at all. The Germans came to the house several times to drill her on where B.B. was, but she evaded them every time. The most remarkable thing was the way he hid his books and collections. They are all safe, with few exceptions. You just cannot imagine how these people have been living. Literally, nothing to eat. I dined with B.B. and his friends, who are extremely rich with a divine house. But this was our dinner, the big meal of the day. Plate of miserable bean soup first. The main course

before you the tribute of an unstinted praise—and, may I add without detraction—of surprise?

I scarcely know where to begin or what to take up after so long a lapse. Perhaps the most likely to interest you will be my own estimate of us here at home; you can hardly find any judgment of mine at this remove very enlightening as to Europe, the progress of the war or the hopes of a peace, although it is hard to separate these from an account of us, as will appear.

Shall I begin at December 7th, 1941, when the Japanese struck us while we were so negligently asleep? Possibly you were in more or less easy touch with us until Italy and we became enemies. Of course, we made the most of that "treacherous" and "foul" blow below the belt, struck in a time of "profound peace." Nonsense, my dear B.B., as you and I know. It is one thing to say that decency, supposing that to be among conventions of any kind of war, should require a declaration; it is another to scream, when, after being fully advised that the other chap does not fight like Tybalt "by the book,"[136] he has caught us off guard. However, moral indignation, justified or not, is a strong weapon, and we were very heartily in earnest in our sense of righteous superiority, rather a specialty of ours and J. Bull's anyway, is it not? Besides, after all allowance made for propaganda, the Japanese seem to have an added shade of bestiality in their notions of war, even over the Nazis; so, whatever the case at the outset, we soon got to have a justification for that crusade to make this sort of thing impossible in the future, which has now become prevalent, and is comforting to our persistent demand that *homo sapiens* shall throw off his simian trappings and do it now. At first, the Japanese seemed destined to make a clean sweep, and the Pacific Coast was very frankly scared and damn well scared. Each side of the country wanted to fight its own enemy, and there was much complaint about our share in the Nazi war. Besides, in very influential groups, especially in the Mississippi Basin, the Nazi war had always been regarded as a British business, and the old hatred of Britain flared up as it always does in a crisis. Do not think it is burned out yet. You know, it is allied a good deal with dislike of us here in the East: "damned snobs," "English boot-lickers," etc., etc. On the other hand, the Japanese were enemies of the "common people"; they were monkeys, hardly human, capable of the same atrocities as their cousins, the American Indians, and of the same fortitude, which made them so formidable.

How it happened that we did not throw all our effort against them I do not know. I suppose that Hitler and Mussolini had to declare war on us along with Japan, but certainly they did us a good turn, for if they had not, it seems to me quite possible that we might have let Europe go hang. Even as it was, it must have been the General Staff, seeing matters more detachedly, which forced so much of our efforts eastward. Or maybe it was F.D.R. himself. That strange creature, who in all matters which demand the least grasp

---

potatoes boiled and sliced with some sort of unattractive cream sauce, and a dried up piece of cheese for desert. You just couldn't believe it to be possible[...] Gen. Clark and I are going up to I Tatti within the next few days, and bring a "formidable" dinner with us, and really give B.B. and his friends a real treat." (tr/tp 82.38) On October 6, 1944, LH thanked John Walker for Robert Berenson's account of his uncle: "It is almost too good to believe. What a wise and balanced nature to be able to carry on under such dreadful peril." (tr/tp 82.38)

136. Mercutio describes Tybalt as "a villain that fights by the book of arithmetic." ROMEO AND JULIET, III, i.

of abstract reasoning is the lowest scholar in the primary grade, has—or at least in this instance he had—an ability to get the true balance of values and—an instance almost unique in his career—a courage to risk everything upon the cast, which may have been the determining factor. I have voted for him the last three times, though I could be his merciless critic, if there were any need of one, which, God knows, there ain't. At any rate, something turned us the right way, and we began our fabulous preparations which have not ended yet.

My dear B.B., this country of ours baffles me; I fancy that you may have grasped it better, being so long away, and out of the swirling eddies of passion in which we live who are here. A more undisciplined, ill-accorded group it would be hard to find, I say to myself: a mélange of all races, all traditions, all environments, swept together with a history of comfort, ease, and wealth such as has never descended on this creature since he jumped down from the trees and began to use his thumbs. And what did we do? Really, the most stupendous performance that ever has been done on the Planet, I mean of its kind, of mass production. Make no mistake about that; we have done it; somewhere, somehow, suddenly, as though inspired by some apparition, we did unite, and this inexhaustible flood of ingenious contrivances began to appear in absolutely incredible profusion. I am told that in kind they are by no means the best; that the Germans—you see I will not assume that Germans and Nazis are interchangeable terms though that may make you bristle—have excelled us in many weapons, and that we are in large measure imitators. So be it, that is a matter for the experts, and as usual they do not agree. It may be that our men are fighting with inferior equipment; I am not saying the contrary. The point is that we have poured out such a quantity of at least good stuff, if not the best, that we have been able to smother them, and that has done the trick. And do not suppose—certainly, you would be the last to suppose—that this took only the mere commonplace quality of drudgery. Somebody with a genius for organizing had to be there to keep everybody from stumbling over everybody else, and to supply the "assembly belts" so that the things rolled out of the factories with the spark plugs already snapping. There must be in some way a future for a society which can do that.

I can't quite keep the chronology straight, so I don't remember when the casualty lists began really to come in. Of course, naval fights don't count for so much, and for some reason, which I don't know, we seem to have had little trouble with the Japanese on the water. (I asked one of my old law clerks, who has been for over a year in command of a "destroyer-escort" and who utterly despises our naval high command, why this was; and his answer was that the Japanese were even more incompetent than we, and that it was our good luck that the Nazis had no fleet.) Well, that's not quite relevant. At least after June 6, 1944, D Day, the lists have been coming in, especially in these last months, and we are a sober people and a sad one. I do not see any evidence that our will has been blunted, but at times I feel glad that this, the real part of our ordeal, did not come until success was to all intents certain. Had we had to bear these losses while the result was in the balance, and with a chance to stop with some kind of compromise, I am not so sure. It would indeed have made a difference if our cities could only have been bombed. [Robert] Patterson, the Under Secretary of War who used to be on my court, said to me two years ago that he would gladly give the big plants in New Jersey if the Nazis would only send over a fleet of bombers. I suppose, if they could have done it, they might have been idiots enough to try. But though the sacrifices are now being felt all around each one of us, I think there is no doubt we shall see it through now. Not a corporal's guard could be mustered for anything but fighting to the "kill."

After that, what? Ah, who can guess that? "There are a kind of men," and perhaps some women, who profess to believe that we shall have lost "all we are fighting for" unless there emerges from this foul cauldron a "better world," where "war shall be outlawed." On the whole, I think that is the most mischievous group we have, even more so than the isolationists, because they are so God-damned righteous and aspiring. What I most fear is that they may refuse to have any truck or barter with a peace which does not match with their aspirations, and that they may in this wise play into the hands of those irresponsibles—few at present, I am glad to say—who may revert again to that noble concept: "What have we to do with abroad?" As usual these perfectionists have their slogans: "Power Politics" is one. Whenever a practicable scheme, which might tide us over for a couple of decades, is proposed, it is written off as that, as though power would not in the end decide and politics were anything else but a sense that each one could not have his own way. But I am not too discouraged; there is, certainly just now, a most hopeful disposition, which I like to believe is pretty general, not to demand perfection and not to repeat the errors of the League. There are plenty of stumbling blocks, and the temper of the army when it gets back home is an entirely unknown quantity; but if we were to judge just at the moment, there is reason to believe that the Senate would not oppose a system in which Britain and Russia and ourselves should be recognized for what we are, and should have the last word on paper as we are bound to have in the end anyway. Just how much the French will be able to upset the cart I can't tell. There isn't much interest here in them. Walter, for some reason I don't quite know—Helen perhaps?—seems to be extremely Francophile, though I am not really able to speak accurately about him, as I seldom read his stuff. (Indeed, we have completely drifted apart. Nothing in particular, no crisis, maybe no more than that I am perhaps losing energy for thought at my 73 years while he remains vigorous. But I will say in extenuation that others also have perceived in him an oracular tone.) But to revert, unless the fear of Russia—and that is not to be underestimated—interferes too much, it may well turn out that we shall have a set-up after the fighting stops that will be some assurance for a while. I don't know how you feel; for myself, I am a little of Holmes's opinion that men will keep killing each other for many centuries. I only differ from him in cherishing a hope that there may be a day when they will find another way. All I want now is that they shan't think that that can be done tomorrow. We seem to me pretty clearly, all of us, headed for a period of collectivism—we, probably last of all. I am not very sanguine that that can go along with democracy and I prefer democracy because it offers a way to fire out your rulers when you get sick of them without resort to machine guns, hand grenades, and the like. That may not seem much, but when one contrasts it with the only alternatives, it is enough, at least for me. But if government is to infiltrate individual fate, as it must in a collectivistic state, can it be left to the resultant direction of "pressure groups"? Of course, I know that there would be no "special interests." *Mais, cela, mon ami, me fait un peu reveur.*[137] (I don't quite see the relevancy of the last five sentences.)

137. I.e., but this, my friend, makes me somewhat a dreamer.

B.B., this is a ferociously long letter; I am sending with it a sort of translation, a typed version, which can be verified by comparison, if it seems improbable that I should have written such nonsense. Somehow the vision of the divine Nicky under the light of a smoky lamp, trying to spell out all this illegible "tripe," seemed to me more than human patience should be called on to bear. Maybe, *mon brave*, we shall meet again; but at any rate, this is the hand of friendship and of memory stretched to meet yours across all these dark abysms.

Au revoir, L.H.

tp with ms signature and notes 99.18

1945-4

To Learned Hand from Felix Frankfurter

March 11, 1945 3018 Dumbarton Ave., Washington, D.C.

Dear B.:

What an impressive performance your Alcoa opinion is![138] You admonish me that its sequelae may become part of my business, so I shall say nothing as to the merits—except to say that if a juristic Providence cares about such matters, it must have been a wise Providence that disqualified four of the Nine so as to put the case into your pen. Really, a superlative job!

[...]The European war is lasting longer than I thought it would—but now truly the end cannot be far off. And isn't it time for a fleeting visit from you?

Thine, F.F.

My love to Frances—and Marion's to both of you.

ms with signature 105A.11

To Felix Frankfurter

March 24, 1945 Judge Learned Hand's Chambers

Dear F.F.:

What a warm-hearted chap you are, and how you always respond to the stimulus of friendship! It was a dirty job, at which I took an unconscionable time and of whose outcome I was by no means always sure. It's too soon to tell yet, but I allow myself to hope that possibly neither side will ask for a rehearing. Indeed, I am not sure that "Alcoa" may

138. United States v. Aluminum Co. of America. *See* 1944-3 To Henkin, September 21.

not see the handwriting on the wall and prefer to "play ball" without friend F. Biddle[139] or his successor. *Quien sabe?*

[. . .] I confess it seems to me that we are pretty plainly headed for some fairly comprehensive collectivist ordering of industry; people don't want it, but they want what I fear they can't get without it. Can you have a collectivist democracy? The Future has all sorts of creatures in its womb—maybe that. And yet there seem to me great obstacles; a society in which the individual's fate is completely in the hands of government can scarcely manifest itself as a succession of resultants of "pressure groups": it won't stand up. But there, they say, in that bright day there will cease to be special groups, and Christ will be all in all. *Mais cela me fait un peu reveur.*

My love to the Marquise. L.H.

ms with signature 105A.11

1945-5

To Thomas K. Finletter[140]

April 2, 1945

Dear Tom:

I have not acknowledged your book[141] because I wanted to read it first, which I have now done. I am in entire accord with most of it; it seems to me extremely timely and most admirable in analysis and statement. Our amazing government, bred in fear and changed without system over a century and a half, is today inept, unwieldy, and archaic; of its many blemishes you have hit upon perhaps its most dangerous feature, the likelihood of periodic anarchy not infrequently realized in fact. Nothing would more tend to cure this than what you propose: the power of the President to dissolve Congress and "go to the country." Indeed, I am not clear that I would give him the option to struggle along with a hostile Congress if he wanted to hang on; it might be better to make dissolution automatic in the event of any important defeat of his administration. The temptation to stick on in office is strong and you know how the British Opposition is always charging that the Government is holding on only for a favorable time to be re-elected. I admit the difficulty of defining what would be an "important" defeat, but I doubt if that is insuperable.

---

139. Francis Beverley Biddle (1886–1968): Chairman of the National Labor Relations Board, 1935; Judge, United States Court of Appeals for the Third Circuit, 1939; Solicitor General of the United States, 1940; Attorney General of the United States, 1941–1945.

140. Thomas K. Finletter (1893–1980): special assistant to Secretary of State Cordell Hull, 1941–1943; deputy director of the Office of Foreign Economic Coordinator (OFEC), 1943–1944; consultant at the United Nations Conference on International Organization at San Francisco, 1945; chairman of the Air Policy Commission, 1948; Secretary of the Air Force 1950–1953; Ambassador to NATO, 1961–1965.

141. Thomas K. Finletter, Can Representative Government Do the Job? (1945).

However, these are details; the important thing is to insure against deadlocks and your scheme would do that.

I am a good deal more doubtful about your "joint executive-legislative" responsibility vested in a "joint cabinet." An executive is best fitted to make and suggest policies and measures, and—sight unseen—I should prefer not to let the legislature mess in upon it. Their function is better exercised, I would guess, in criticism, amendment, acceptance or rejection. The acts of a legislature—at least Congress—are, as you imply, pretty sure to be resultants of conflicting group pressures. I don't mind that personally; it probably gives about as sound a measure of where the actual political power lies as we can get and is a great insurance of stability. But in the process of logrolling, the general welfare usually gets lost. The President, on the other hand, has proved on the whole a better vehicle of the general will, a vague dumb thing anyway to be interpreted by him; indeed, it is often what he makes it. When he has declared and espoused a program, he must "put it over"; and then for the first time, I think, he should have to deal with Congress. That will disclose how far he has devised something that will withstand the shock of dominant group interests. What I fear is that your scheme would tend to blur the outlines of this conflict which I should prefer to keep sharp. Moreover, if our dissolution scheme were in force, I doubt if the need of any "joint cabinet" would exist; I should not then fear that Congress could be extinguished.

Indeed, what I fear more is that the party system may break up, for it seems to me that that, more than any other one thing, has been the cause of the failure of representative government where it has failed. There are always sure to be lots of minor divergencies of policy; and unless you can fuse enough of them into two groups, each formidable alone, you fall into government by coalition, which is government by kaleidoscope. The people soon get sick of that and look for dictators. France's decay was due more to that than anything else. If the minor issues can be absorbed within a party and only those remain which offer a choice between two, there appears to be far more chance of responsible government than by any other device yet achieved. We are in some danger as to that; the Democratic Party has long been an unnatural union of southern Tories and all kinds of groups whose color it takes litmus paper to detect.

Besides, as you say, we have no really national politics anyway. By the way, aren't you wrong about Congressmen? I never looked it up, but I have certainly understood for many years that any citizen of a state could run for any district in the state. Indeed, I knew a chap once who did. But the local tradition is so strong that nobody ever does except to run as a minority candidate in a hopeless district.

Why, oh why, did you not smite the preposterous and iniquitous gerrymander, the United States Senate? No use, you say. Yes, I know; but why not heave a brick at it? Excuse these incoherent remarks; one would have to give up a week really to do justice to your book. You are a good friend to send it to me.[142]

Sincerely yours, [Learned Hand]

tp 71.4

142. On April 5, 1945, Finletter responded by stating that his preference is to have "the President elected by the two Houses of Congress," "a cabinet composed of members of the Legislature," and "the head of this cabinet, who would be the Premier and *not* the President," with the power to dissolve Congress. (tp with ms signature 71.4)

1945-6

To Bernard Berenson

June 4, 1945 New York, New York

Dear B.B.:

[...]The utter and final collapse of Germany has left me in a frame of mind quite unexpected. When I try to reinstate the terror, for that is what it was, which I felt in the summer of 1940 and for that matter in 1941, I remember that I thought if the Nazis were only once checked and beaten, I should never feel afraid again. Now they have been annihilated and I must own that my anxieties, while far less, are by no means ended. (I wrote this so far about three weeks ago in Washington. Since then I know that you did get my letter). More nonsense is written here about the Germans than you could believe; no, not than you could believe because we should be ready to believe that any nonsense can be and will be written. What I particularly mean is the kind of nonsense that affects surprise—the worst of it is that the surprise is real—that the Germans show no contrition. They are not "ashamed," they are not "repentant," they have no "remorse." Good God, how can we ever live in a world where people have so little imagination about other people? I wonder if we Americans ever ask ourselves whether the South was "ashamed," or "repentant," or "remorseful" after the Civil War. And if not, why not? Can anyone ever point to any people who, being beaten, think it was right that they should have been and humbly ask to be put on the right path? Of course, it would not make so much difference if they didn't set out permanently "educating" the Germans. To take out a number of the high Nazis, as many as daren't do the job themselves, and shoot them out of hand—that is well enough, provided it is done soon and without any pretense of trying them for "crimes." Personally, my guess is that even that will not help the situation, say twenty years hence, but people are quite naturally eager for blood, and I don't much mind their having it, if in God's name or the Devil's they will only not try to dress it up with noble words. But if anything can more directly tend to revive or keep alive the whole brood of Satan than to start "educating" Germans forcibly and from the outside, I should like to know it. However, you can generally trust a general or a congressman to choose the worst of all possible courses.

Maybe it doesn't make much difference anyway. Unless signs fail—not "all signs" but I should say prevailing signs—your cousin Joe Stalin is going to have his way over most of Europe. We shall probably follow suit in time, though not, I fancy, till you and I are safely tucked way for a good while. My guess is that Britain and Sweden may not, Britain less that Sweden. I can't see any effective counter-movement which is going to preserve capitalism, and the extraordinary manifestation of Russian power will impress folks and make them forget the price of it in tyranny. I am quite sure that we here don't want Collectivism, qua collectivism; if you took a poll you would not find a corporal's guard for it. But we certainly do want, and shall want more, a constant correction of the evils of this world, of the "injustices" everyman has suffered, and the conviction is general that something called the "Government" was "born to set it right." If any one answers that that path leads in the end to the management of everything by the "Government" and that the "Government" is made of men like capitalists, he is written down as selfish, callous, and impervious to rudimentary humanity.

The real question, it seems to me, is whether we can have a Democratic Collectivism. Nobody ought to weep tears over the grave of Capitalism as such, though on the whole it has done more that any other economic system to help us make this a pleasant place to live in. But perhaps Collectivism will do better; we mustn't be set against it. However, I do permit myself to get rather dogmatic on the subject of the Totalitarian State, and if the price of Collectivism is to be that, I'm agin' it, and unless you have changed a good deal, so are you. But that will be the issue, I suspect, in the next thirty to fifty years, and I have some children and grandchildren, whose future does interest me[...] Otherwise, considering the fact that there are plentiful years to look back over, we do very well. My love to Nicky.

Affectionately, L.H.

ms with signature 99.18

To Learned Hand from Bernard Berenson

July 15, 1945 Settignano

Dear B.:

Thanks for letters of Feb. 18th and June 4th, letters that I like to read, real outpourings. I agree so much with all you feel and say as well as think that if it is tripe as you fear, then I fully share in producing it. Therefore little is left for me to answer, but I can offer a few marginal comments. Before beginning, let me thank you both for your sympathy over Mary and accept my regrets for the loss of Frances's nephew[...]

No doubt for centuries to come, men will want to kill each other. I don't see how they will go about it. Even now the sporting, ex-chivalrous aspect of war has faded out of existence. With rocket bombs, gases, microbes, etc., etc., destruction of an enemy will be possible for a while, but in a few decades it will be a question of who touches the button first. Then physical wars will cease, either because no bipeds will remain to make them, or that these have had the sense to stop them.

Distressing must be the talk about the Germans. Let me confess that what I heard the last time I was home, soon after the last war, made me so unhappy that it was one of the reasons why I decided [not] to return. Except for some weeks after Dunkirk, I never had a question about the outcome of the war. Indeed, it was faith in our victory that kept me going. From the very start, however, I dreaded the swelled head and the pretension of the populace after a totalitarian war and its economic and consequent social upheavals. It is this, as you say, that takes the shine out of all possible V-days.

Many of these remarks and their like I scribbled down in a diary kept during these war years. I may publish it. I wish you and Frances were here at I Tatti in this summer's prime, so golden, so opulent, so possessed by the spirit of Mother Earth. In eight days we go up to Vallombrosa to Nicky's cottage romantically hidden in the forest. You and Frances must join us as soon as traveling is free. Meanwhile mine and Nicky's most cordial greetings and remembrances to friends.

Ever affectionately, B.B.

ms with signature 99.18

1945-7

To Henry T. Lummus[143]

October 22, 1945

Dear Judge Lummus:

I have read with interest your opinion in *Bowe v. The Secretary [of the Commonwealth]*,[144] and of course I agree that you had no alternative under accepted principles to deciding whether the proposed law was in accord with the Constitution. I have forgotten just what our talk was, but I fancy I was saying that [John] Marshall's reasoning was not as inexorable, in my judgment, as it has appeared to most American lawyers. It is indeed true that English-speaking judges have from the earliest times assumed the power of declaring whether the acts of administrative officers were warranted under the law, statutory or customary; we have never had either here or in England any "Droit administratif." Even so, as I recall, there are reserves, but for argument I will assume that there are none. It was this analogy that appeared to our early judges particularly persuasive, and, as you know, *Marbury v. Madison*,[145] was foreshadowed in one or two of the papers in the Federalist, written, I think, by Hamilton.

Over fifty years ago, Thayer used to point out that the analogy was not so controlling as it seemed, and that Jefferson's view as a new question appeared equally tenable; i.e., each branch of government is charged equally with the courts with conformity of its conduct to the Constitution, and to submit its conclusions to the court is to give the court a determining and absolute authority. Indeed, the courts themselves have not pushed

143. Henry T. Lummus (1876–1968): Associate Justice of the Supreme Judicial Court of Massachusetts, 1932–1955.

144. *Bowe v. Secretary of the Commonwealth*, 69 N.E.2d 115 (Mass. 1946), in which the Supreme Judicial Court of Massachusetts considered the constitutionality of two proposed state laws. In addressing the questions presented, Lummus's opinion also explored the basis of the judicial power to hold statutes unconstitutional.

145. Authored by Chief Justice John Marshall, *Marbury v. Madison*, 5 U.S. (1 Cranch) 137 (1803), is often cited as the most important decision in U.S. constitutional law. In it, the Court established the authority of the judiciary to review the constitutionality of legislative and executive acts and orders; this power is not one enumerated in the U.S. Constitution, but instead stems from *Marbury*. For LH quoting Marshall in *Marbury*, see LEARNED HAND, THE BILL OF RIGHTS: THE OLIVER WENDELL HOLMES LECTURES 8–11 (1958).

Marshall's theory to its extreme; they have always recognized vaguely defined zones where it did not apply; e.g., they will ordinarily not go behind the returns as to the recorded vote of a legislature, nor will they review the action of the executive on what they choose to call "political questions." Surely these are untenable exceptions, if the doctrine is to be deduced from inescapable principles.

Whether our system has on the whole benefited us is indeed a debatable question. I should be disposed to straddle. During the first seventy years of our history, I suspect that it was essential to hold us together; it was a much needed centripetal force. Since the Civil War, I am disposed to guess, for I can do no more, that it has been a prejudice to our political development. I feel quite sure that this has been true so far as concerns the first Ten Amendments, but perhaps the Court or some similar tribunal is an inevitable necessity in a federation to hold the balance between the units and the whole; at any rate, Holmes used to think so. But in our case, it is hard now to see why Congress is not for all substantial purposes omnipotent anyway, having, as it does, the power of the purse, and control, direct and indirect, of all that moves over state lines. Moreover, I have an especial complaint of the effect their position has had upon the judges themselves. Being forced to decide matters which are in every true sense political as opposed to jural, they have not acquitted themselves with great credit. Indeed, there was no reason to expect that they should. Generally, they have pretty faithfully represented the interests of the groups from which they came; the present discords at Washington, while more frequent than in the past, are not new, and are, I believe, inherent in a system which fundamentally misconceives the place of the judicature in a democratic society.

Well, you could hardly have suspected that your innocent gesture would bring down on you such an avalanche, and if it is pardonable at all, it can be so only as an attempt to explain what may have seemed merely a chance remark.[146] Forgive me that I should appear to take myself so seriously, I really don't; the longer I live, the less importance I attribute to these generalizations, indeed to any generalizations. I want to say in closing what a satisfaction it is to me to know that I am going to see you more frequently, now that you are on the Executive Committee.

Sincerely yours, [Learned Hand]

tp 75.29

146. In a letter dated October 25, Judge Lummus rejects LH's position on judicial review, declaring that he sees "no hole" in Marshall's reasoning: the Constitution is law and not merely the source of precepts of policy, and it mandates restrictions on the power of Congress, e.g., a presidential veto kills legislation not passed over the veto by a two-thirds vote of the Congress. Illustrating his point, Lummus observes that by contrast, the English Constitution is merely a "conventional [...] restraint upon an omnipotent Parliament." (tp with ms signature 75.29)

1945-8

To Charles Wyzanski

December 16, 1945 Judge Learned Hand's Chambers

Dear Charlie:

You always select rather tough books for my Christmas.[147] I'm pleased with the compliment implied, but I am not always confident that I deserve it. I shall do my best on this one; my excursions into the borderland between modern physics and cosmology or epistemology or whatever the Hell it is, do not however encourage me to hope that I shall bring back very consumable fruits. By the way, have you tried Aldous Huxley's last—*Perennial Philosophy*[148]—I should put it aside at once were it not the work of one of the keenest minds I have encountered. Yet, when all is said, I simply cannot get any hold on mysticism. I feel that I may have some substance, I stretch out my hand, and I think I have something in it; then I open it, and lo! there is nothing, not even Compton's[149] cosmic ray. We are told—Aldous is at pains to repeat it—that it is idle to try to reach this beatitude by dialectic: one must live it and live it long, ascetically. So be it. That's what Hitler taught and taught successfully, and see what happened.

Is there nothing in our craving for something "objective"? Is it all the meandering of this *anima, vagula, blandula qui errat in orbibus?*[150] ("Orbibus" isn't right.) No, my "bet," as Holmes would have said, is the other way. But in this welter of agony and nonsense all bets are off.

I wish I might see you more often; you steady me and God knows I need it, though I were not unique in that.

Thine, L.H.

ms with signature, Wyzanski Papers, HLL, Box 2, Folder 8

To Charles Wyzanski

January 22, 1946

Dear Charlie:

I finished Schrödinger's book with some travail and nearly complete confusion. The physicist and biologist were too much for me for the most part, though I have dipped here

---

147. Erwin Schrödinger (1887–1961): What is Life: The Physical Aspects of the Living Cell (1944).

148. Aldous Huxley (1894–1963): The Perennial Philosophy (1945).

149. Arthur Holly Compton (1892–1962): Professor, Department of Physics, Washington University, 1920–1923, 1953–1962; Head, Office of Scientific Research and Development, 1941–1945; Chancellor, Washington University, 1945–1953.

150. I.e., [a] "wandering and deluded spirit that drifts here and there"; *cf.* Hadrian, *Carmina* 25: "animula, blandula, vagula." See 1924-1 To Augustus Hand, July 27, where LH substitutes "in loca" for "in orbibus" in the same phrase.

and there into modern physics, realizing that the concepts which they are now using are not more outrageous than those with which I became familiar as a boy and seem so only because I did not become familiar with them then. In short—and really this is my credo, so far as I can say to myself that I have any—in our search for "external" laws of nature we are doing no more than trying to devise successively and progressively intricate conceptual patterns to enable us enough to foretell the course of the flux and deal with it to our purposes. Those patterns, formulas, schemes, call them what you will, are the measure and test of any "externality" and probably exhaust whatever meaning that may have. That horrid little cad, Jeans, was not so far wrong when he said that God was a mathematician.[151]

The details of Schrödinger were so far beyond me that I fear I missed the force of his proof that the gene must be a molecule, protected in some as yet unfathomable way from the accidents which disrupt other approachably similar conglomerates of atoms and permit it to persist beyond any reasonable expectation. Perhaps if I had really studied it—I read over several parts twice, however—I should have understood this better, but really I did not need to, because I was quite prepared to accept his conclusion without any ability to check the steps. To accept it, that is, until some equally erudite and to me incomprehensible scientist came out otherwise. The modern notion that at the very base of things there is no uniformity, that each unit acts in an utterly unaccountable way, and that the only reliable "laws of nature" are statistical I must accept reverently. But I have never been able quite to see why you can build a world—on which, as John Dewey says somewhere, you "can safely lean back upon"[152]—out of the fact that given enough units all equally likely to jump about in any direction and in all directions, you will get a uniform pressure such as you do out of an enclosed gas. (Jesus, what a sentence!) Be that as it may, I accept it because I know it leads into vast mathematical ramifications which are infinitely beyond me[...]

But, Charlie, it all does go to show that the leisure you have found in your not too exhausting job well justifies your decision to take it.[153] I have been thinking of late that you may have been wiser than I when you knew that you wanted to give up your chances to lead the magnates more nearly to a sense of reason, and preferred to take up the duties of a D.J. You appear to be using the opportunities it has offered so fruitfully that I am disposed to believe you were right, and I quite wrong. After all, if this show goes on at all, as in a blind kind of way my guess is that it will, what it is going to need more than anyone else is the people who are not specialists and experts, but who in some transcendental way can pick the goddamn brains of such creatures and fit them for "human nature's daily needs." When I look back on nearly forty years of an enormous amount of detailed cerebration, most of it about on the level of cross-word puzzles, I do not personally find much exhilaration in the expert, in what Felix, in his baser moments, has permitted himself to call "expertise." I rather guess you have chosen the better part.

---

151. Apparently LH refers to Sir James Hopwood Jeans, the author of the steady-state theory, i.e., that matter is continuously created throughout the universe; *see* JAMES JEANS, THE MYSTERIOUS UNIVERSE (1930).

152. *See also At Fourscore*, *in* THE SPIRIT OF LIBERTY 259.

153. Wyzanski was appointed to the United States District Court for the District of Massachusetts in December 1945.

Gus tells me that the family has again taken a step forward: this time, a girl. Well, I have had three and can truly congratulate you, more directly than before because with real experience. My good wishes to Gisella. This incoherent ramble started nowhere and ends nowhere. But then that ought to make it "vital," for what else is life?

Thine, L.H.

ms with signature, Wyzanski Papers, HLL, Box 2, Folder 8

1945-9

To Henry L. Stimson

December 25, 1945

Dear Harry:

Ever since you resigned, I have had it in mind to tell you what you have meant to me through all these years that we have been friends. On this day it comes to me especially, for although the outlook is far from being full of Christmas cheer, when I think of what it might have been I know what we owe to all those who have kept us free, and to you, Harry, a great measure of that gratitude is due, always keeping yourself in the background, never flagging, never losing courage, never diverted by vanity or pique or ambition, utterly without thought of yourself, and that too without any large reserve of strength; your wisdom and your constancy went far to extricate us from destruction.

The public will not be aware of all this, or acclaim you as it does a returning general; your reward will be in that peace with yourself which is, after all, the best of all rewards and the rarest. Still I, who have for so long admired you for the qualities I envied—I want to tell you that we, your friends, know you, and that for us you stand with the few, the very few to whom we give an unstinted admiration and who make up those that give us pride to be Americans.

Affectionately, [L.H.]

tp 80.15

To Learned Hand from Henry L. Stimson

January 1, 1946 Huntington, Long Island

Dear B.:

When Mabel read me your letter of Christmas last evening, it made the eyes of both of us fill with tears; it was so kind and sweet and undeserved! You are certainly a good friend—and the years have taught me at least that thing—namely that the one best blessing of growing old is the friendship of old friends. I really don't deserve any thanks for the past five years of work; I really had a grand time—a glorious run for my money. During the last six months of it, I had a tight squeak of it with my increasing "coronary," but I just got across the goal line in time. I had promised [President] Truman that I would stay with him until the end of the war and the atomic bombs, which were my particular babies and which both navy and army were skeptical of, did the trick, and scared the Emperor into surrendering, thereby saving at least another year of war and another million of American casualties, not to mention the British, Russian, and Japanese casualties, which would have totaled at least two million more. These figures are not bunk, but the actual calculations of the Genl. Staff. So it was a cheap price for me to pay: six weeks in bed, and a couple or more months of convalescence! Well, thank you very much, dear old friend. I am already walking gingerly around, and hoping to get into New York occasionally very soon and seeing you. With deep affection I am,

Your devoted friend, Henry L. Stimson

ms with signature 80.15

1946-1

To Felix Frankfurter

April 14, 1946 — Judge Learned Hand's Chambers

Dear Felix:

[...]I do want to talk to you; I can't help asking myself whether I ought to take on another term. Perhaps I shall feel a little more picked up, perhaps I shall be able to find more significance than now appears in anything I am doing. At any rate, I shall like to talk it out with you, but I charge you by any regard you have for me that you be utterly and ruthlessly Rhadamantine with me! There is nothing which one gets less of, especially, as you will find when you have broken so far into the eighth decade as I, than the willingness of one's friends to take one up into the rocks and snows and let one look out. We shall see, no doubt, a vacation will put something of a new face on things. I remember that even Holmes used to get discouraged.

That Nuremberg business would be a farce if it were not so ominous.[154] I wonder if the gossip is true that Jackson promised F.D.R to take it on. It is not unlikely; F.D.R. would unhappily have been at his worst on such a matter. You know—and this you will certainly disagree with—much as I acknowledge what we owe to him and enthusiastic as I was to have him kept in office, now, after a year as I look back, he is not [seen] to be a pleasant figure, not a really likeable person. I don't believe that I could possibly have loved him; I disbelieve in his generosity. There: that's a bad note to close on; but I am telling what I feel. Always a doubtful course even with intimates.

Mon amour à la belle Marquise. L.H.

ms with signature 105B.12

---

154. LH was opposed to the Nuremberg trials, judging them "efforts to cloak vengeance in the robes of law." Gerald Gunther, Learned Hand: the Man and the Judge 469 (1994).

To Learned Hand from Felix Frankfurter

April 22, 1946 Supreme Court of the United States

Dear B.:

[...]If not my rough talk to you earlier in the year about your qualifications about the Labor Board jobs, perhaps the following two episodes will lead you to believe that I will be ruthlessly truthful to you in facing the issue that all of us have to face eventually—has the time come? These are the two incidents:

On the occasion of Holmes's seventy-fifth birthday, Mrs. Holmes took me aside and said quite out of a clear sky, "I want you to promise me something." I told her I could not imagine any promise she asked of me that I would not fulfill. "Promise me that when you see the slightest drop in the quality of his opinions that you will let me know. That day he will get off the bench." I honestly did not think the occasion had come during her lifetime. If you doubt that, reread his dissent in the *Schwimmer* case,[155] which he wrote within a month after her death. (How well did you know Mrs. Holmes? When she died Marion said with characteristic discernment, "In her way she was as great a personality as the Justice." She really was somethin'. Incidentally, I was more proud of that request from her than of any so-called honor that ever came my way.)

The other day Eddie Morgan was down here (This was before the resignation of Landis.) He said he was wondering whether he should stop teaching. I told him that I did not see any immediate occasion for doing so. To which he replied, "The difficulty is that I do not think anybody on the Faculty would tell me when the time came." I then suggested one of the men and he said he did not think even he would. To which I countered, "Well, will you ask him not to tell you but to tell me and I will tell you?" Eddie thought that was a fair arrangement and said, "I know you will tell me the truth."

This is the first time in my life in which I have taken the witness stand on my own behalf as a reliable person, so that I am all ready to listen to what you have to say. Of course I do not see you in daily work. But as you know, I have a good deal of evidence on you, both as to quantity and quality of products was well as the ruthless judgment of the young. Please believe one thing—I have no desire to have you or anybody else hang on just for the sake of hanging on. But I would have to deny my judgment if I denied that you seem to me on paper at the top of your form. Come along and we will have talk!

Ever yours, F.F.

tp with ms signature and notes 105B.12

To Learned Hand from Felix Frankfurter

April 23, 1946 Supreme Court of the United States

Dear B.:

1. What a fortunate going for Stone![156] (There have been physiological signs for the last two years that went unheeded.) And if he had chosen his own valedictory he could

---

155. For *Schwimmer*, see 1929-3 To Learned Hand from Walter Lippmann, June 7, note 97.

156. Harlan Fiske Stone died on April 22, 1946. *See Chief Justice Stone's Concept of the Judicial Function, in* The Spirit of Liberty 201–08.

not have done better than the last dissent he announced in the *Girouard-naturalization* case.[157] It expressed his essential attitude toward [...] the Court's function over a wide field.

2. God knows what is in store for the country, for I suppose only God knows the considerations that will move Truman.
3. Which leads me to say that you must acquit F.D.R of any share in Jackson's Nuremberg mission. Not a word of truth in the theory or rumor. It was wholly Truman's idea—and very proud he was of it. Bob J. felt it his "duty"; unconsciously, it was a welcome escape from the very unpleasant atmosphere of the Court[...]

Ever yours, F.F.

ms with signature 105B.12

To Felix Frankfurter

May 9, 1946 Judge Learned Hand's Chambers

[...]I didn't think I had begun to die at the top like an oak, as Dean Swift said and *did.* What I really want to talk about is whether I am not an ass to keep on "farting on the bench" as A.N.H. puts it when it seems to amount to nothing. Give me an honest job and I should be tempted. Louis [Dow] used to tell about a witness called in a French court with the following: "Monsieur, quel est votre occupation?"; answer in bold, loud tones: "Ramasseur de crottes."[158] Well, something like that might be good, but I suppose my back wouldn't stand it now[...]

L.H.

ms with signature 105B.12

157. Frankfurter refers to *Girouard v. United States,* 328 U.S. 61 (1946). Girouard, a Seventh Day Adventist who had petitioned for U.S. citizenship, agreed to take an oath of allegiance and to serve in the U.S. military as a noncombatant, but as a religious matter would not agree to bear arms in defense of the United States. His petition was granted by the district court and then reversed by the United States Court of Appeals for the First Circuit. The Supreme Court reversed the First Circuit's decision, finding that neither the Constitution nor Congress impose the requirement that an individual be willing to serve in combat as a condition of their citizenship. Justice Stone dissented, largely on the basis that the Court's decision overturned precedents that had been repeatedly affirmed by congressional actions. Many viewed Stone's reliance on precedents from which he himself had dissented an example of judicial restraint and deference to the legislative branch. In his dissent he was joined by Justices Frankfurter and Reed.

158. "Sir, what is your occupation?" "Street-sweeper." [Literally, "one who sweeps up manure."]

1946-2

To Learned Hand from Felix Frankfurter

June 20, 1946

Dear B.:

These six sentences[159] made me realize how unwittingly shrewd was Henry Ford's view of history, or at the least how very difficult it is to ascertain the truth and tell it! It may shock you to hear it, but each one of these six sentences is untrue as written and some of them egregiously false. And I could "document" beyond disproof what I have just written. I wish I couldn't!

Yours, F.F.

He was an honest man, intellectually as well as morally. He was a humble man, without ostentation or pretense. He was a kind man, ever ready to lend a helping hand. He was a dependable man, true to his ideals and loyal to his friends. He was a just man, tolerant, impartial, and fair. He was a courageous man, never afraid to defend what he believed to be right and oppose what he believed to be wrong.

ms with signature 105B.12

To Felix Frankfurter

June 26, 1946 Judge Learned Hand's Chambers

F.F.:

You, of course, had a much better chance to see Stone at close range than I, and I am scarcely in a position to offer the "disproof" which you say you have documents to demolish. Some of what Y.B. Smith said I have some independent doubts of—e.g., I doubt that he had great courage—but his failing in that I am disposed to treat very leniently, being in no position to throw stones.

"Intellectually" very few of us are completely "honest"; I am not sure that I could even state a standard. "Humble" I think he scarcely was, though I feel on surer ground in saying that he was not "ostentatious." I am a little surprised that you think him not "kind," for although nobody is "ever ready to lend a helping hand"—a mere rhetorical flourish so

159. This letter is handwritten on p. 6 of a copy of the tribute to Harlan Fiske Stone by Young B. Smith, Dean of the Faculty of Law, Columbia University. On May 16, 1943, Frankfurter noted in his diary that LH "finds greater uncertainty and lack of clear discussion in the opinions of Stone in recent years, more particularly since he as become Chief, and he attributes it to the fact that so long as he was with Holmes and Brandeis, and later Cardozo, he had the guidance of those great men. I said nothing to B. about that. In the first place, I had not thought of the matter in that light, and as I listened to him I realized that the matter is much more complicated than he is aware of." FROM THE DIARIES OF FELIX FRANKFURTER 242 (Joseph P. Lash ed. and notes, 1975).

far as ever I saw—[he was] kindly at least. I always found him [so] and so far as I ever knew, he always was. "Dependable," no; who really is? "Just, tolerant, impartial, and fair?" Well, he was not very tolerant of differences, but as things go he would get more than a pass mark on that too, I should think.

On the whole, if you will allow me an opinion in the face of what I acknowledge to be your stronger position, I think that you are testing him by a standard that few of us would survive. He was ambitious and he liked his ambition when it was satisfied. Do you remember T.R.'s answer to N. Hapgood's inquiry about M. or N.: "Colonel, is he an honest man?" "After the manner of you and me, yes; after the manner of John Hampden,[160] no." Be gentle, Mr. Justice; be not too censorious. Remember that in the Kleeg (is that the way to spell it?) light of God's eyes none of us look very unspotted, or only a few. But I am an "appeaser" anyway and I get more so day by day.

Mon amour à la Marquise. L.H.

ms with signature 105B.12

1946-3

From May 1946 to November 1948, the International Military Tribunal for the Far East conducted trials of the leaders of the Empire of Japan for crimes against peace, war crimes, and crimes against humanity that they were alleged to have committed during World War II.

To Learned Hand from Joseph B. Keenan[161]

October 23, 1946 General Headquarters, Supreme Commander for the Allied Powers

My dear Judge Hand:

In reading a selection of remarks in *The Practical Cogitator* I found your remarks under the heading "The Spirit of Moderation."[162] You may remember them:

"What is the spirit of moderation? It is the temper which does not press a partisan advantage to its bitter end, which can understand and will respect the other side, which feels a unity between all citizens—real and not the factitious product of propaganda, which recognizes their common fate and their common aspirations—in a word, which has faith in the sacredness of the individual[. . .] They are the last flowers of civilization, delicate and easily overrun by the weeds of our sinful human nature; we may even now

160. John Hampden was a Puritan Member of Parliament who led resistance to Charles I; he was killed fighting in the English Civil War.

161. Joseph B. Keenan, Chief of Counsel, at General Headquarters, International Prosecution Section.

162. *See The Spirit of Moderation, in* The Practical Cogitator, or The Thinker's Anthology 414–15 (Charles P. Curtis, Jr. & Ferris Greenslet eds., 1945). For the quoted passage, see *The Contribution of an Independent Judiciary to Civilization, in* The Spirit of Liberty 155–65, 164–65.

be witnessing their uprooting and disappearance until in the progress of the ages their seeds can once more find some friendly soil. But I am satisfied that they must have the vigor within themselves to withstand the winds and weather of an indifferent and ruthless world[...] Men must take that temper and that faith with them into the field, into the market-place, into the factory, into the council-room, into their homes; they cannot be imposed; they must be lived."

These words have meant very much to me here. We are trying to carry them into the courtroom in our International Trial against the Japanese. We are trying to put them into practice in our relations with the Associate Prosecutors from ten other nations. It did occur to me that they constituted an excellent formula for meeting many of the vexatious problems that are occurring in our own country as we live one with another and as we live with other nations.

I thought you might be interested to know that your words have reached far off Tokyo, and that they may bear some fruit in proceedings that you probably never dreamed of when you wrote them. With kindest regards,

Sincerely, Joseph B. Keenan

tp with ms signature 74.23

To Joseph B. Keenan

November 1, 1946

Dear Mr. Keenan:

Your letter of October 23rd leaves me quite abashed and makes it hard for me to answer beyond saying that I feel deeply gratified that anything I should have said could have a part, however small, in what is being done to bring ourselves and the Japanese to a better understanding. It is hard for us over here to be sure that we are getting the facts, but there seems to be no doubt that our army in Japan has done a most amazing work in promoting an accommodation on which to build. Unless we are misled, you have gone further on the path to a rehabilitation of this fearful world which lies about us than has been done anywhere else. Thank you indeed for your generous and warm words.

Sincerely yours, [Learned Hand]

tp 74.23

PART IV

That mood of toleration and compromise without which no human society can exist

—Learned Hand to Irving Dilliard, December 19, 1955

THE BILL OF RIGHTS: 1947–1958

Topics in law and politics concern Hand and his correspondents in this period: libel, searches, the standard by which to assess "good moral character," the privilege against self-incrimination, the distinction between property rights and personal rights, and finally, Hand's decision in *Dennis,* convicting Eugene Dennis and others charged under the Smith Act with advocating "the duty, necessity, desirability, or propriety of overthrowing the Government of the United States or of any State by force or violence." Writing for the court, Hand followed a modified formulation of Holmes's clear and present danger test: "In each case [courts] must ask whether the gravity of the 'evil,' discounted by its improbability, justifies such invasion of free speech as necessary to avoid the danger." To Frankfurter, Hand considers the effect of his ruling, confessing that he would not have charged Dennis at all: "Personally, I should never have prosecuted those birds: 'the blood of martyrs is the seed of the church.'" His sense that the country is divided between those more liberal on the East coast and others principally conservative in the "Mississippi Basin" and the West, conveyed repeatedly in letters to Berenson in Italy, is exacerbated by his dismay at the activities of Joseph McCarthy directed against Communists and their sympathizers. He reflects on the merits of philosophical detachment, specifically from Marxist ideology, as well as on Holmes's insistence that *homo sapiens* is a creature of little significance considering the general scheme of creation. He champions the practice of skepticism and the habit of scrutiny not only to friends like Frankfurter, but also to acquaintances like the scientist Julian Huxley. From 1952, three topics are persistent points of focus: judicial review, natural law, and the Supreme Court's rulings in the cases involving segregation. To Wyzanski, Hand argues that judicial review risks substituting judicial preferences for the interpretation of statute and precedent—implicitly this raises his own emphasis on the role of the imagination in understanding old texts in light of new situations. To Lippmann, Hand rejects the idea that natural law has any place in jurisprudence; in response, Lippmann insists that a "public philosophy" consists of "assumptions which have to be accepted in order to live in the historical, and conceivably unique and passing political order." In correspondence with Frankfurter, Hand supports the Court's decision in *Brown* by invoking the Equal Protection Clause, understood as an "absolute," and he maintains that it invalidates not only segregation but also anti-miscegenation laws; Frankfurter denies that *Brown* was decided on such an "absolute." Hand therefore declares *Brown* unconstitutional. Nevertheless, he states that had he been on the Court, he would have supported its decision in *Brown*. Hand's *The Bill of Rights*—lectures delivered at the Harvard Law School in 1957—prompts criticism of his position on judicial review. To Frankfurter, he insists that courts should "content themselves with confining the legislatures to the work cut out for them by the specific limits found elsewhere than in the Bill of Rights." To Wyzanski, he turns to experience rather than philosophy for guidance and seeks as "our mainstay in legislation" the variable records of "History," the accumulated experience of the ages, rather than the fixed principles of "Natural Law" whose authority is assumed to be valid, everywhere and at all times. Concerned that its obligation to regulate "the life of the individual" will reduce the power of the law to envisage new ways of seeking justice, Hand admits to Lord Evershed that while "interpretation is not yet quite become a matter of the text 'in one hand and the dictionary in the other,' as Holmes once put it [...] the more detailed we get the less room there is for the imaginative projection of the author's purposes to occasions undreamt of when he wrote." As Hand has repeatedly observed to readers of his letters and articles, it is in such undreamt of applications that the law demonstrates its relevance to an evolving social order.

1947-1

To Learned Hand from Walter Lippmann

January 27, 1947[1]

I send you my affectionate greetings and every possible good wish and I hope now that the world is beating a path to your door that you will let yourself believe that now and then the world does know what's what. Helen joins me in congratulations to Frances and yourself.

As always, Walter Lippmann.

Western Union telegram, Lippmann Papers, Sterling, Box 76, Folder 978

To Walter Lippmann

January 28, 1947 — Judge Learned Hand's Chambers

Dear Walter:

It all seems absurd, even for lawyers, but if anything could make it real, it is to have you join. What judges say—if they are really any good—in a given instance is about as interesting as the specifications for building a bridge, but I have noticed that if they get old enough, just because they have not angered the run of folks as they went long, there is an accumulation about them which gets to look imposing and there you are. It's passing strange but it's welcome just the same. Only you have to go in for the distance runs; judges are no good at sprints though some think they are.

You do not know how much your wire has meant to me. Time and distance have indeed separated us, but I shall never forget our friendship and I shall always treasure this evidence that it persists.

Affectionately, L.H.

ms with signature, Lippmann Papers, Sterling, Box 76, Folder 978.

1947-2

To Norman Cousins[2]

February 8, 1947

Dear Mr. Cousins:

I have your letter of the third, with the article suggesting the passage of a law making "Group Libel" a wrong, about which you ask my opinion.[3]

---

1. This was LH's seventy-fifth birthday.

2. Norman Cousins (1915–1990): journalist, New York Evening Post, 1934–1940; journalist, Saturday Review, 1940–1942; editor-in-chief Saturday Review, 1942–1972.

3. Cousins's "article," an editorial, is addressed to "The Senators and Congressmen from New York, and to their representatives in the New York State Legislature." It reads in part: "What is

I am quite certain that creating such a law would be undesirable. As a civil wrong for which damages would be the remedy, it would be practically a dead letter; there would be few or no cases in which the plaintiff could prove that he had been actually damaged. A jury might indeed give what in other actions for defamation are called "punitive" damages, but these are not damages at all but penalties and are really a disguised way of punishing the wrongdoer to the profit of the person alleged to be the victim. The law is indeed so settled; but for myself, I should be glad to see punitive damages abolished everywhere and certainly they should not be extended. If anything of the kind you suggest is to be done, it ought to be by way of criminal libel and that too I should be against. It is quite true that the kind of defamation you have in mind has that tendency to promote disorder, which has been the conventional justification for all criminal libel; yet if one thinks through the working of such prosecutions in practice, I should suppose that their effect would be rather to exacerbate than to assuage the feelings which lie behind the defamation of groups. The verdict of a jury, even assuming that it was possible to have a really impartial trial, which it would not be, would not satisfy those who sided with the losers and would only serve further to arouse the fanaticism of those who sided with the winners, and the trials themselves would be occasions for violent propaganda on both sides that would fan the flames. The passions which lie at the root of such utterances do not have their basis in evidence and will not yield to it, and any issues capable of being presented in a court which do depend on evidence would have to go back far into history and be quite beyond the grasp of a jury of men and women unskilled in such inquiries. There is no remedy for the evil but the slow advance of the spirit of tolerance, and I believe that the suppression of intolerance always tends to make it more bitter. This is a result most unsatisfactory to ardent natures and it may be wrong; I can only tell you what I believe.[4]

Sincerely yours, [Learned Hand]

tp with ms notes 69.16

---

happening is not unlike what happened in Germany and many other nations after World War I, when freedom of speech was used against minority groups and eventually against freedom of speech itself, when civil liberties built up painfully over generations were exploited by the few in order to deny civil liberties to the many[...] There is an approach to the problem[...] We suggest group libel. By group libel we mean laws which would enable groups to protect themselves against untruthful and harmful actions. These laws would give members or representatives of a group the right to institute proper legal action against its defamers." Saturday Review, Feb. 1, 1947, at 20. Paragraphs two and three of LH's letter were published in the Saturday Review, Mar. 15, 1947, at 23.

4. Only a few years later, Justice Frankfurter would write the majority opinion in *Beauharnais v. Illinois*, 343 U.S. 250 (1952), in which the Court upheld the constitutionality of an Illinois statute that made it a crime to exhibit in public the "depravity, criminality, unchastity, or lack of virtue of a class of citizens of any race, color, creed or religion." Addressing concerns raised in LH's letter to Norman Cousins (and by the dissenting Justices in the 5–4 decision), Justice Frankfurter noted: "That the legislative remedy might not in practice mitigate the evil or might itself raise new problems would only manifest once more the paradox of reform. It is the price to be paid for the trial-and-error inherent in legislative efforts to deal with obstinate social issues." 343 U.S. 250 at 262.

1947-3

To Learned Hand from Felix Frankfurter

May 8, 1947 3018 Dumbarton Ave., Washington D.C.

Dear B.:

You wisely do not read, I know, U.S.S.C. decisions unless you have to. Well, you don't have to read these and if you do, you may not approve of what I have written. But I hope that you will not disavow my undebtedness to you[...]

Thine, F.F.

ms with signature 105B.13

To Felix Frankfurter

May 10, 1947 Judge Learned Hand's Chambers

F.F.:

Your brethren have done something which in the end they will have to repent,[5] although that would not be exceptional nor would it be in ordinary circumstances very serious. On the other hand, coming as it does in a period when it is of the highest importance that we do not imitate the methods of those whom we fear the most, and when there are indications that our fears are likely to make us do just that, the decision is really serious. Of course, you are right as a trivet and your opinion will be an enduring monument to your wisdom, your scholarship, and your statesmanship. I have, as you know, on some occasions not seen eye to eye with you on these matters, but in this instance I really do not understand how anyone can take the majority's view in whose bowels there is any fire of freedom. Worse: this is the kind of thing on which totalitarianism lives and without which I rather guess it cannot live, though that's not too sure. I get very down about the future, as I have told you; I am especially skeptical of the possibility that the large or complete measure of collectivism, which is surely ahead of us, can exist without totalitarianism as the end product. Such *démarches* as these do not tend to lighten my anxieties.

Of course, there always was a bad penumbra about the right of search ancillary to an arrest; I was never satisfied to allow, as an incident, any "search," *stricti juris*, except of the very person of the person arrested. That did not mean that things visible without opening

5. LH comments on *Harris v. United States*, 331 U.S. 145 (1947), in which the Court held that under certain circumstances, a search incidental to an arrest may extend beyond the person being arrested to the premises that are under his or her immediate control, regardless of whether the premises are residential or commercial, noting additionally "that abuses sometimes occur is no basis for giving sinister coloration to procedures which are basically reasonable." 331 U.S. at 155. Justice Frankfurter, along with Justices Murphy and Rutledge, dissented: "[T]o find authority for ransacking a home merely from authority for the arrest of a person is to give a novel and ominous rendering to a momentous chapter in the history of Anglo-American freedom." *Id.* at 164.

receptacles, etc., and within his immediate reach, so to say, could not be taken. One can put instances where it would be silly to deny the right to seize, for really that should be the only question open in such situations. A man, apprehending arrest, empties his pockets, and the stuff lies open before the officers. Or it is in his desk or it lies on a chair in the room, etc., etc. Like most else in law, we cannot deal with the inevitable variety of occasions by general propositions; we must not be pedants and we must not let the exceptions eat up the underlying purpose. I have never felt very comfortable about the borders of this incidental power, but I must confess that such an extension of it as this throws me clean out of the boat.

And to have those crusaders for the underdog—Black and Douglas—go wrong![...]

L.H.

ms with signature 105B.13

1947-4

To Learned Hand from Felix Frankfurter

October 21, 1947 3018 Dumbarton Ave., Washington, D.C.

Dear B.:

[...]You are too knowing of history—of the non-Toynbeean[6] course of man's long endeavor—to warrant despair. As a matter of fact, I have no doubt we have the cards in this Russo-American "game." I wish I were as sure we have the players. Not that I do not deeply, deeply respect Marshall.[7] But—

Our love to you both. F.F.

ms with signature 105A.13

To Felix Frankfurter

October 24, 1947 Judge Learned Hand's Chambers

No, I don't fear that we have not the cards, though like you I doubt our players. But my fears reach deeper. The last thirty-five years in retrospect make me tremble for the

6. The English historian Arnold Toynbee presented history as the rise and fall of civilizations rather than the history of nation-states or ethnic groups: a civilization thrives when challenges are met; correspondingly, it falters when challenges are evaded or ignored. His A STUDY OF HISTORY was published in ten volumes from 1934 to 1954.

7. George Catlett Marshall (1880–1959): Army Chief of Staff, 1939–1945; Secretary of State, 1947–1949; Secretary of Defense, 1950–1951. On June 5, 1947, Marshall spoke at Harvard University and outlined what would become known as the Marshall Plan. This plan offered the European nations, including West Germany, $20 billion in economic aid to assist in rebuilding and establishing manufacture and commerce.

possibility of any stable order which will retain a semblance of what you and I and most other decent folk would call civilization. As I walk along the streets or read the papers, I can't resist asking how this creature, necessarily and properly immersed in his own affairs, is ever to direct a common fate and whether he can hope for better than the alternation of anarchy and tyranny.

I don't think it is much of an answer to say that all old men have thought that way. Maybe they get wise with their years. I came across an aphorism of Joubert the other day, whoever the Hell he was: "Il n'y a rien de bon dans les affaires humaines que les sentiments des jeunes et les pensées des vieux."[8] That isn't quite right, but it will serve.

After all, although the past when we go back to it does assure us—as your quotations thrown at me some time since were alone enough to show—that we have always lived on a narrow shelf so far as we have gone, we ought to be chary about any notion of "Progress" as the ancients were. I shouldn't for a moment have agreed to that on July 1, 1914, but by God, what has succeeded has shaken me to the bottom of my never secure foundations.[9]

Go along, my dear, on your "horse-power"; you are among our present White Hopes—*spes blancissimus* (if it is masculine). I suppose seen from within, the *Sancti Novem quorum pars tres* look more fantastic than they do even to us who are working in the engine room and never get on the bridge. Nevertheless, what comes out seems to me not usually so damn discreditable as it does to Cousin Augustus. And by the by, last month I had an hour or more with Wiley [Rutledge] and I wish to retract a little my scorn. No, I can't yet say that his initial outfit was by any means "top drawer"; he's a dull fellow. But the transparent goodness of the cuss and so far as I could see the utter absence of vanity quite captivated me. In the end I suspect that that last quality is apt to bring more goods to port than anything else. You and I have seen more goodly ships stick on a reef because the skipper was arranging his necktie, so to say, than for any other fault. I like to put it that if the ego subtends too much of the angle of vision, it is as bad as though one had cataracts. And who of us escapes? Oh, God, make me really not think I am "momentous"! And yet he won't change me a bit.

I love thee. L.H.

ms with signature 105A.13

To Learned Hand from Felix Frankfurter

November 21, 1947 — Supreme Court of the United States

Dear B.:

[. . .]My thoughts have turned to your recent observations on man's "progress" and his hopes for the future with much more eagerness than they have to most of the matters to

8. I.e., there is nothing any good in human affairs except the feelings of the young and the thoughts of the old. LH refers to the work of Joseph Joubert, eighteenth-century French essayist.

9. On June 28, 1914, Archduke Franz Ferdinand of Austria was assassinated; this action precipitated World War I.

which I have had to give my time. What wouldn't I give for a talk with you on these themes on a walk uptown from your courthouse to 65th Street? Even my optimism has been subjected to critical scrutiny. I feel more rather than less the obligation of effort and the opportunity through effort of furthering the decencies of life, at least within limits. But that is so because the task seems to me less and not more promising than I thought it, say twenty-five years ago.

In this connection, you will be interested in a talk I had with Brandeis in the early days of the Nazi regime, when their cruel and barbaric driving force had become painfully and plainly manifest. I asked him whether he had ever realized how thin the veneer of so-called civilization was when a country, so far advanced as was Germany in all sorts of directions that we associate with intellectual and moral progress, could so quickly revert to barbarism. He replied with an intensity of sadness: "No, I never did and I know no one who did excepting only one person, and that's Holmes. We used to think that Holmes was naive about affairs and the world in general, but I now realize that he saw more deeply into the nature of man than any of us." Apart from all else, wasn't that a handsome acknowledgment for Brandeis to make? There I shall have to leave the matter until opportunity for talk is more propitious.

Ever yours, F.F.

P.S. After Walter L.'s pilpulostic "Cold War," how refreshing Ham Armstrong's wise and sturdy "The Calculated Risk."

tp with ms signature and notes 105A.13

1947-5

To Learned Hand from Felix Frankfurter

December 6, 1947 Supreme Court of the United States

Dear B.:

I await with an eagerness bordering on impatience the full text of your opinion in the *Repouille* case.[10]

---

10. *Repouille v. United States*, 165 F.2d 152 (2d Cir 1947), in which the United States Court of Appeals for the Second Circuit reversed an order granting naturalization to Louis Repouille, who had been convicted of second degree manslaughter within the five years prior to his petition for citizenship for killing his brain-damaged son with chloroform. LH noted in his opinion for the majority that although Repouille had otherwise "conducted himself as a person of 'good moral character'" during the five-year period and that the jury in the criminal trial had chosen to convict Repouille of a lesser crime even though the evidence would have supported a conviction for first degree murder, it was incumbent upon the court to find that Repouille did not meet the "good moral character" standard the court had established in *United States v. Francioso*, 164 F.2d 163 (2d Cir. 1947). In *Francioso*, the United States Court of Appeals for the Second Circuit had noted that in determining "good moral character," the court should follow "not those standards which we might ourselves approve but [ask] whether 'the moral feelings, now prevalent generally in this country' would 'be outraged' by the conduct in question: that is, whether it conformed to 'the generally accepted moral conventions current at the time.' In the absence of some

Apart from all the questions that arise in connection with mercy killing, my interest is aroused by the psychological-judicial problem that confronted you, namely to what extent may a judge assume that his own notions of right moral standards are those of the community? But if it is his job—as you and I believe it to be—to divine what may rightly be deemed the standards of the community, by what process is he to make that divination? How and whether should he look for disclosures of the community's mores? I struggled with that problem last year in the *Willie Francis* case[11]—the abortive execution of a murderer through mischance—for I personally deemed it shocking that a State should insist on a second go for its pound of flesh. But I felt confident that while to me it was a barbaric thing to do, that would not be the feeling of the community, whether the community be Louisiana or the United States at large, and that therefore, I had no right to find a violation of the Due Process Clause. Since in your wisdom you do not read opinions of the Supreme Court until they turn up in the course of business, you may care to take a look at it, 329 U.S. 459.

Ever yours, F.F.

tp with ms signature and notes 105B.13

To Felix Frankfurter

December 9, 1947 Judge Learned Hand's Chambers

F.F.:

[...]I am enclosing a copy of our opinion in the *Repouille* case. I suppose I should have realized that it would get a good deal of publicity and be thoroughly misunderstood. Perhaps this has been accentuated by Jerry's[12] to me *outré* dissent. I assume that he expected the district judge, *sua sponte*, to call the Cardinal Bishop Gilbert, an orthodox and a liberal rabbi, Reinhold Niebuhr, the head of the Ethical Culture Society, and Edmund

---

national inquisition, like a Gallup poll, that is indeed a difficult test to apply; often questions will arise to which the answer is not ascertainable [...] We can say no more than that, quite independently of what may be the current moral feeling as to legally administered euthanasia, we feel reasonably secure in holding that only a minority of virtuous persons would deem the practice morally justifiable while it remains in private hands, even when the provocation is as overwhelming as it was in this instance." *Repouille*, 165 F.2d at 153. It is notable that in reversing the order, the court did so without prejudice to Repouille's filing of a subsequent petition for citizenship when the five-year window of review would no longer include the manslaughter conviction. *Repouille*, 165 F.2d at 153–54.

11. The *Willie Francis* case to which Frankfurter and LH refer is *Louisiana ex rel. Francis v. Resweber*, 329 U.S. 459 (1947). Willie Francis was convicted of murder in Louisiana and sentenced to death by electrocution. At the time of his execution, a malfunction prevented the electrocution from succeeding, and he was returned to prison and his execution rescheduled. The Supreme Court found that neither the double jeopardy provision of the Fifth Amendment, nor the prohibition against cruel and unusual punishment of the Eighth Amendment, nor the Equal Protection Clause of the Fourteenth Amendment were violated by the state in issuing a new death warrant. Frankfurter's concurrence rebutted the assertions of the four dissenting Justices that Francis's due process rights had been violated. For Frankfurter's dissent, see 329 U.S. at 466–72.

12. Judge Jerome Frank dissented, objecting to the standard used by the majority and the precedential effect of the decision. *See Repouille*, 165 F.2d at 154–55.

Wilson, to be all cross-examined, ending in a "survey." I don't know how we are to deal with such cases except by the best guess we have[...]

I have read your opinion in the *Willie Francis* case and I think it most admirable, but you know what I feel about the whole business of judges as final arbiters on such matters. Our Constitution in this aspect has debauched our courts, diminished our collective responsibilities, and falsified the whole basis of civilized society. The nearer I come to my end, the more certain I am that a Bill of Rights administered by a bench is what William James called Santayana's philosophy: "The perfection of rottenness."

Thine for the Common Man, [L.H.]

tp with ms notes 105B.13

To Learned Hand from Felix Frankfurter

December 11, 1947 Supreme Court of the United States

Dear B.:

Your opinion in the *Repouille* case is a shining example of "form" as part of "substance." The way in which you state the elements of the problem makes persuasive—to me inevitable—the conclusion. It really is fantastic to assume that the kind of confused ethical judgments you would get from Jerry's imagined panel of experts would be a dependable basis for a judicial judgment on such an issue as you had before you or the comparable issues raised by such a case as that of *Willie Francis*[...] As for the Bill of Rights: I could not agree with you more. After he came down here, I had a long correspondence with [Benjamin] Cardozo, evoked by a remark of mine that I would settle instanter on a repeal of the Due Process Clause. There was a fascinating debate in the House of Commons on the Irish Home Rule, which died on the eve of the First World War, provoked by a proposal to include a due process clause. It brought all the heavy legal guns into action and they did a fine job in showing the mischievous uncertainties under due process on this side of the ocean. And when the Australian constitution was under discussion, the Australians likewise profited by our example and did not include mischievous features of our Bill of Rights. And yet you might be surprised, unless you knew, to learn the number of people, otherwise sensible, who are now promoting the Equal Rights Amendment categorically proscribing no discrimination because of sex. When one asks some of these proponents whether they would deny states the right to make provisions for the guardianship of children whereby mothers would be preferred to miscreant fathers, whether no requirements could be made for the support of wives by husbands, one is told that of course the Amendment would not hit that sort of thing because impliedly there would be these exceptions! One of the strangest things about our people is the way in which they blow hot and cold regarding the judiciary. Nothing is easier than to gain applause for attacks upon lawyers and judges, often with good reason, and nothing is more habitual than to leave the most delicate problems of statesmanship for determination by judges[...]

Ever yours, F.F.

tp with ms signature 105B.13

1948-1

To Felix Frankfurter

January 16, 1948 Judge Learned Hand's Chambers

F.F.:

May I highly commend your concurrence in *Haley v. Ohio*?[13] (Also the letter about Whitehead.) I am, as I have often told you, very lukewarm about self-incrimination.[14] I always think of what G[eorge] Rublee said fifty years ago; when he read it, it seemed so damn silly that he thought he must have read it wrong.

You don't agree and maybe you are right. After all, these things are mostly visceral. But on what happens to a man under arrest your guts and mine move—doubtful simile?—alike. I suppose it would go too far to make inadmissible everything said after arrest which was not in the presence of a judge, etc., etc., though I confess that temptation is strong in me to go so far. But this goddam questioning for hours under Klieg—is that the right way to spell it?—lights outrages me. Such things are only next door to torture: to me they would be.

Did you see that the Alsops[15] said that the high Democratic Politicoes have told W.O. D[ouglas] that he could be V.P. candidate? I read it with mixed feelings[...] My love to the Marquise.

Thine, L.H.

ms with signature 105B.14
P.S. I shall be *76* in eleven days!

To Learned Hand from Felix Frankfurter

January 21, 1948 Supreme Court of the United States

Dear B.:

Believe me if I tell you that though I am neither satanic nor angelic, a combination of temperament and experience have made me as indifferent to praise as to blame except from the very few whom I deeply respect. None more so than you do I respect, and when you commend "highly" an opinion of mine, I feel comforted and encouraged. I am particularly

---

13. Haley v. Ohio, 332 U.S. 596 (1948). In *Haley*, the Court set aside the conviction of a 15-year-old African American whose confession to murder—the key evidence in his trial—was made under duress.

14. The privilege against self-incrimination depends on a provision in the Fifth Amendment which states that "No person... shall be compelled in any criminal case to be a witness against himself" and is derived from an ancient maxim of the common law: No one may be required to appear against himself (*Nemo tenetur prodere seipsum*). *See* 1954-5 To Griswold, March 17; 1956-4 To Frankfurter, March 28.

15. The syndicated columnists Joseph and Steward Alsop, who in New York City wrote for the New York Herald Tribune.

pleased that the *Haley* opinion should have evoked your commendation. You will not be surprised to hear that in this environment it is not easy to be as explicit as possible in stating in an opinion what we do when dealing with these due process cases[...]

You attribute to me more regard for the privilege against self-incrimination than I entertain. I wonder if you saw my opinion last term in *Adamson v. California*, 332 U.S. 46?[16] I am not sure I would originally have held that even in federal prosecutions the privilege precludes comment on the failure to testify. On the other hand, I don't know how I would today go on that question in view of what was written here before I came[...]

Ever yours, F.F.

tp with ms signature 105B.14

1948-2

To Charles Edward Clark

April 8, 1948

Dear Charlie:

I have yours of yesterday[...] I do not understand that any of the questions need an answer.[17] I can say, however, that I have a number of times talked with [Harlan Fiske] Stone and I certainly gathered that he very definitely held the opinions I attributed to him.[18] Of course, I may be wrong. I know that before Cardozo died, he told me that he

---

16. In *Adamson v. California*, 332 U.S. 46 (1947), Admiral Dewey Adamson, charged with first degree murder, chose not to testify on his own behalf. The prosecutor argued that his refusal could be seen as an admission of guilt under a California statute that allowed the jury to infer guilt in such cases. On appeal, the Supreme Court upheld the ruling of the state court, stating that rights guaranteed under the Fifth Amendment protecting against self-incrimination did not extend to cases brought in state courts. Justice Black dissented, arguing that the Fourteenth Amendment should be interpreted to mean that the Bill of Rights applies to citizens of all the states.

17. In a letter dated April 2, Clark comments on the view of civil liberties expressed by Harlan Fiske Stone, which were, he claims, misunderstood by LH. As evidence for his position, Clark cites LH's address in *Chief Justice Stone's Conception of the Judicial Function*, 46 Colum. L. Rev. 696 (1946), in which he sees that LH attributes to Stone views that are those of Frankfurter but not of Stone. Clark, further instancing *Minersville School District v. Gobitis*, 310 U.S. 586 (1940), in which Stone dissented from the decision of the Court upholding the constitutionality of the flag salute and recitation of the Pledge of Allegiance in schools, observes that "Stone, J., really started the view that there is presumption of constitutionality in statutes restricting civil liberties." (tp with ms signature 101.33)

18. LH comments on Stone's regard for civil liberties: "He could not understand how the principle which he had all along supported could mean that when concerned with interests other than property, the courts should have a wider latitude for enforcing their own predilections than when they were concerned with property itself." *Chief Justice Stone's Concept of the Judicial Function*, *in* The Spirit of Liberty 201–08, 206. *Cf.* Stone's statement in *United States v. Carolene Products Company*, 304 U.S. 144, 152 n.4 (1938), in which he asserts that "the review of statutes directed at particular religious or

agreed with me that the jurisdiction of the Supreme Court on questions like the so-called "Bill of Rights" had proved disastrous.[19] I don't know that there is any way we can find out whether I was right about Stone. I guess I shall have to let the wise guys fight it out in the reviews.

As ever yours, [L.H.]

tp with ms notes 101.33

1948-3

To Charles Wyzanski

May 22, 1948 Judge Learned Hand's Chambers

Dear Charlie:

It is a perplexing question where to draw the line; I agree that there is really no line to be drawn. We are all subject to inevitable "passional" bias,[20] but we are more apt to yield when we have espoused a cause or even openly committed ourselves to it. A judge's job is to try to reconstruct the attitudes, the aims, and the conscious or unconscious limitations of other men. I agree that their words are only a part of his material, and it is just because they are, that in the extremely difficult task of imaginatively projecting what they would have done, faced with this instance, he should strip himself, so far as that is possible, of any disturbing feeling, of any feeling except that of historical reconstruction out of most impalpable sources.[21] All this is being denied by shallow people, like Rutledge for instance, who, seizing upon an unfortunate phrase of Holmes, proclaims that he means to "legislate." The Yale Law School has it as Article One of its credo. It is a most disastrous notion to gain currency for, although in application it may seem that a judge who is not literal is "legislating," if he knows his business that is what he never does. It is curious to see a fellow like Jerry[22] assume a sophistication which he hopes will secure him against the appearance of simplicity by putting law and fact in quotation marks, as though a judge were free to innovate as he wishes.

---

national or racial minorities ... may call for a correspondingly more searching judicial inquiry" (citations omitted); for an analysis, see JOHN HART ELY, DEMOCRACY AND DISTRUST: A THEORY OF JUDICIAL REVIEW 75–77 (1980). *See also* Jerome Frank, *Some Reflections on Judge Learned Hand*, 24 U. CHI. L. REV. 666 (1957).

19. In the Holmes lectures, LH would specifically question whether "a legislature is a priori less qualified to choose between 'personal' than between economic values ... [t]here have been strong protests, to me unanswerable, that there is no constitutional basis for asserting a larger measure of judicial supervision over the first than over the second." LEARNED HAND, THE BILL OF RIGHTS: THE OLIVER WENDELL HOLMES LECTURES, 1958, at 51. *See also* 1958-1 To Frankfurter, February 10.

20. For the concept, see WILLIAM JAMES, THE WILL TO BELIEVE, AND OTHER ESSAYS IN POPULAR PHILOSOPHY (1898).

21. LH invokes the instructions of Edmund Plowden. *See* 1933-1 To Frankfurter, January 23, note 10; 1951-1 To Learned Hand from Felix Frankfurter, January 13.

22. Judge Jerome Frank.

Well, my position is only this, that our very delicate task we cannot properly discharge without a maximum of abstention from what Holmes once wrote me, as I remember it, were the "hot spots." I think you don't agree, and when you don't, I am always uncertain. But then—not to flatter you—uncertainty is a word (or a flower?) which grows rank in my garden.

Thanks for your bon voyage, L.H.

ms with signature, Wyzanski Papers, HLL, Box 2, Folder 8

1949-1

To Felix Frankfurter

January 1, 1949 Judge Learned Hand's Chambers

Dear Felix:

Of course I am willing to contribute to the purse for Mrs. Whitehead;[23] in fact, I had had her in mind before you wrote. I am enclosing a check for $100, not $200, because I fancied that you wanted to keep the gifts even. As he slips into the past, Whitehead's figure does not get smaller in my mind. I wish I could say that he became increasingly lucid: at times I think that I am not as able to understand abstractions as I used to be, but maybe not. His method was the right one, I do not doubt; he tried to coin a terminology which would be free from colloquial and so disturbing suggestions, and to use it consistently. The bane of philosophy has been that it must speak in the words of creatures who have worked their way out from the grunts and cries that accompanied their responses to their environment, and these all carry emotional obbligatos that destroy them for thinking purposes. On the other hand, it is so frightfully difficult to keep in mind the new and desperately alien significances of his vocabulary that, personally, after a few pages, I resign.

But why should I abuse you with this kind of stuff; he remains for me the perfect philosopher which is the perfect saint in my own brand of hagiology. On the whole, I think I should rather have lived his life than that of any other person I have ever been acquainted with[...]

L.H.

ms with signature 105B.14

23. In a letter dated December 15, Frankfurter asked LH to contribute to a fund for Mrs. Whitehead. For LH's support of Whitehead, see 1942-5 To Frankfurter, November 23.

1949-2

To Bernard Berenson

May 24, 1949

Dear B.B.:

I am a slow reader and have little or no leisure what with this and that, all in detail trivial. So it has taken me a good while to read the *Aesthetics* and the *Sketch*,[24] and the jerky way I have done so prevented my really measuring the first. I am—I need not tell you this—quite unqualified to pass judgment upon it, and indeed I was reduced to demolition by the amazing store of learning on which you can call and especially as you do so largely only by allusion—the proper way. It leaves one who like me has never really learned to read anyway with a stunned sense of helplessness, and yet there emerges from it a consolatory thought, for when all is said, you give one the right to trust to his untutored feelings. That is a boon greater than perhaps you can realize. When I came to Harvard College almost sixty years ago, there never entered a greener fledgling, with a pathetic, pathological suggestibility, which incidentally he was never to shake off. Those Puritans ruthlessly seized hold of my flaccid self, and chiefly through C[harles] E[liot] Norton, made me think that the enjoyment of art was possible only by a discipline which made a Yogi seem like a voluptuary. "Art" was something to approach with awe and humility; it must never be a mere spontaneous outgoing and only the cognoscenti were entitled to say that they had any likes or what those would be if they did have any. I suppose it came from the confusing of Art with Morals, for Norton, as you know, took his inspiration from Ruskin. Well, B.B., the damage they did me has never been undone and can't be; I shall never break the evil domination of connoisseurship, but you have at least shown me that beyond the bars of my moralistic cell is a land of sunshine and spontaneous joy, "life enrichment" as you like to call it, which, if the repressions of my background have prevented me from sharing, has at least in passing moments been mine own. Thanks for it; thanks also for saying that you don't detect forgeries by looking at the length of the metatarsal joint of the left little finger.

As for the *Sketch*: I especially liked some noble passages at the end; I wish that I too had some consciousness of that IT. Alas, I have none; what stand out in unexpected relief are the diffidences and the disappointments because you failed to convey yourself to others. I knew, of course, that like everyone else who is any good, you thought of yourself as a failure—aren't we all?—but I didn't realize that you included personal relations. That still seems to me very strange[...] My love to the wholly adorable Nicky.

Thine, [L.H.]

tp 99.20

---

24. I.e., Bernard Berenson, Aesthetics and History in the Visual Arts (1948); Bernard Berenson, Sketch for a Self-Portrait (1949).

1950–1

To Learned Hand from Bernard Berenson

December 28, 1949 Settignano

Dear B.:

[...]My thinking—if cerebration can be graced with a high-falutin' word—is absorbed by the problem of the topsy-turvydom which now reigns supreme. That the Politboro should say with Milton's Satan "Evil be thou my good" does not surprise, nor that the dumb, driven cattle should moo and bleat after them, and go to slaughter muttering "Holy, Holy, Holy Lord God, Stalin is Thy Name," but that so-called intellectuals not under close constraint—friends of mine here in numbers and in France—should advocate the Soviet religion, and be inscribed propagandists thereof or hopeful fellow-travelers gets me. I can but settle down to the belief that this Russian disease takes hold of the best the way the Spanish influenza did in 1918-1919, and that it is of the same nature in another sphere. It is terrifying and alarming, as once Soviet apostles, there is no evil they will not commit to bring about their own goal.

Cheerful reflections as 1949 goes and 1950 approaches! Fifty years ago to a day we moved into this house.

Yours, B.B.

tr/ms with signature 99.20

To Bernard Berenson

January 8, 1950

Dear B.B.:

[...]I was especially interested in your surprise at those of your Italian friends, cultivated, lettered, and intelligent who are Communists. I have also found that difficult to comprehend, although the local hysteria in this country has now reached such a peak that there are few who would dare to acknowledge any Communist inclinations if they had them. We are in a convulsion, likely in the end, as are most such violent reactions, to do more towards fostering what we have come frantically to dread than if we could keep better hold on ourselves. We especially dread the spread of the gospel, recognizing, as in our bowels we do, that it is a living faith, however Saturnine and false. I have tried to understand it, and as is usual with all of us I fear have come to write it down as part of my preconceived and long held beliefs—or should I more modestly say assumptions?—about the constitution of this poor wretch, *homo sapiens*, specimens of which you and I are among, not by our own choice. Shall I engage, B.B., in telling you or trying to tell you what I mean? It was last week because I felt so abashed at the resounding string of clichés in which a similar effort resulted that I destroyed that embryo of my brain. You, through your most undeserved kindness in writing me, have all unwittingly become the father of this equally commonplace offspring which I have not stifled before birth. So here goes.

We are not now throwing coconuts at each other from the tops of the trees, not because by the opposition of our fifth finger [our first finger] has turned into a thumb, but because by some strange biological quirk, which for aught we know may have been dish of cosmic rays that hit our genes, we got a habit of not responding immediately to all flashes from the environment. Those blockings or frustrations—which incidentally play such havoc with us individually now—that are the fruit of our delayed reactions have developed into inconceivably numerous possibilities of response. That is the physical aspect of what we call "mind" in its other aspect. But all thinking is violence to our "basic" or more primitive makeup, and we never engage in it or at least only a very select and few of us can engage in it without an imperious demand, itself often grounded in equally primitive urges as those which it must overcome.

The relief of finding something which will take the place of the "intolerable labor of thought" with all its attendant sense of futility makes us the prey of the most obscene and monstrous faiths from which, if thinking were not itself such a perversion of our nature, thinking would protect us. I believe that your intellectual friends, just because of their habit of "intellectualizing," are the easiest victims of Marx. They have today only two escapes from their world of Trial and Error in which all that we have hitherto relied upon has come into just suspicion. For we have burrowed so deep and are so God-damned smart in our burrowings that nobody who is inflexibly reasonable can be confident of much if anything. The juster he is rationally, the more unbearable becomes the outlook. One escape is into the bosom of the Holy Mother and it is curious that over here there is a not inconsiderable number of the kind you mention that have chosen that; I dare say that in Italy, where She is more intimately known, they are fewer. Anyway, the other escape is into the hairy embraces of that strangest of all strange deities, the enraged egoist, Karl Marx. I don't particularly wonder that once the vision of a liberated World has seized upon one, one can treat all the frightful agonies of the steps mediate to realization as necessary. After all, the Jesuits were nearer the truth or rather were more candid than my Puritan ancestors when they recognized that there are no moral absolutes which must inevitably be obeyed, regardless of the occasion.

It all comes down, I believe, to whether we have the guts to face the universe with a consciousness that it is a perpetual question-mark, and that, to crib from Isaiah Berlin,[25] the great man is he who can make "the paradox of yesterday the platitude of today," except that he should have added "while he himself recognizes that his platitude of today may well prove the paradox of tomorrow." For this is a reversible formula. My despair, when I do despair, which is oftener than I wish, is grounded in the fact that it does seem as though the last achievement of mankind was a detachment, a skepticism, an aloofness from conviction, which has proved the best road and nearly the only road that has led us out of the trees as I said. Consistently, you may reply, I should say that it is debatable whether we had better not have stayed there in contentment, if it was in the least

25. Isaiah Berlin (1909–1997): Professor of Social and Political Theory, Oxford University. LH may be recalling Isaiah Berlin's dictum: "Genius means the power of rendering paradoxes as platitudes," delivered in his lecture "Berkeley's Theory of the External World" (1934). *See* Isaiah Berlin, unpublished lectures, Hilary Term, 1947, *available at* http://berlin.wolf.ox.ac.uk/lists/nachlass/matter.pdf.

that of our arboreal progenitors. As a consistent skeptic, I must admit that, of course; and also as a consistent skeptic, I must be skeptical as to the supreme value of skepticism and that too I shall try to be. Indeed, I find it a most satisfactory way of evading any intellectual commitments, leaving me free to play in any other boy's backyard if only I keep from him the fact that what he takes as real, I think is play—or *perhaps* is play.

Well, B.B., that is the dose you have innocently brought upon your devoted cranium by your blameless comment. I shan't do it again for a brief time; I shall leave you undisturbed by such limitless garrulity. I know that when I get a letter anything like as long as this, it is only by the most determined exertions, which my sense of loyalty to the villain who wrote it can command, that I manage to master it.

My love to the most adorable Nicky, who is often in my thoughts. In a few days I shall be 78—to you a juvenile age no doubt, but after all, although I know that it's not a question of years, mine begin to count. F.A.H. joins me in every good wish.

Affectionately, L.H.

ms with signature 99.20

1950-2

To Felix Frankfurter

January 15, 1950 — Judge Learned Hand's Chambers

F.F.:

You knew Keynes, and as I recall you liked him.[26] I never knew him and "instinctively," which only means that I assumed him to be "too damn superior," I did not like him. I have just finished a tiny book of 100 pages of two essays now posthumously published and I want to make an abject *volte face*.[27] So far as he was not amused, he would be a little irritated at what I shall now call him: a "very good man." What I had falsely imputed to him was a cold, arrogant scorn of all lesser endowed creatures and an over-weaning confidence in his own powers. Much of this judgment was true, the last was absolutely just, but as a whole it altogether omitted, as I now see, a capacity for warm acceptance and genuine liking of the vague, unanalyzed, and unformed springs of feeling and intuitive apprehensions which I had always assumed he held in withering contempt.

The second of the two essays: "My Early Beliefs," does go to support a good deal of the first conclusion, what I am saying is properly to be attributed to his maturity; yet I suppose what comes out in the end—at least what is primal and comes out at the end—must

26. On March 6, 1950, Frankfurter briefly responded on the subject of Keynes: "You warmed my heart by what you said of Keynes and it was generous of you to write me of your revised view of him. I cared deeply about him. He and I became fast friends at the Paris Peace Conference. I brought over his ms. of *The Economic Consequences* [*of the Peace*]. He could appear intellectually superior, but he was a truly generous and tender spirit. I speak from experience. Yes, I read that posthumous little book of his." (ms with signature 105B.15)

27. John Maynard Keynes, Two Memoires (1949).

have always been in the weave. Anyway, if you haven't read the book already let me send it to you; it has refreshed me as little I have read recently. Contrast it, for example, with anything which I, at least, have read of the equally redoubtable, intellectually, at any rate, Bertie Russell, and B. emerges a chilly, disembodied wraith whose "passional" life was absorbed in seducing young women and exhibitionary exploits, apparently in aid of freedom but more importantly in presenting Bertie as champion of freedom. Well, perhaps that's a little unfair, but there is something in it nevertheless. And now Keynes could write: of course, I knew that before, but I had quite forgot it.

Did you ever read *Principia Ethica*?[28] I did, twice as I remember, being stumped both times, at least in large measure. He seems to have been the inspiration of Bloomsbury and a strange inspiration. I can't imagine his gentle soul falling in with the ethos of those hard-finished young geniuses and it is strange that he could have become their god, then and in a sense even to the end, with Keynes[...]

L.H.

P.S. I think the Republicans are acting with such inconceivable savagery that Dean [Acheson] will come out, in spite of his unhappy Chinese inheritance.[29] But it is all very awful. L.H.

ms with signatures 105B.15

To Learned Hand from Felix Frankfurter

January, 1950 — 3018 Dumbarton Ave., Washington, D.C.

Dear B.:

[...]You did well to write Dean a cheering note. As an old Washington hand, he is hardened against the slings and arrows of ignorance and malice and reckless partisanship. But [he needs] the encouragement and sustained confidence of friends in a letter, and this is a cruel town.

Ever thine, F.F.

ms with signature 105B.15

To Felix Frankfurter

January 20, 1950 — Judge Learned Hand's Chambers

F.F.:

Thanks for Dean's speech; he brings a note of wisdom, competence, and humanity into public affairs which is substantially lacking elsewhere. The violence of the attacks upon him is distressing evidence of the savagery of modern life. While I look back on my

---

28. LH probably refers to George Edward Moore, Principia Ethica (1903).

29. Frankfurter forwarded to LH Acheson's speech to the National Press Club, Crisis in China—An Examination of United States Policy, delivered on January 12, 1950. *See* Dean Acheson, "The Theme of China Lost," Present at the Creation: My Years at the State Department 355–58 (1969).

nineteenth-century kit of feelings and beliefs, it is not with any complacent satisfaction at the changed times I have lived into. Quite the contrary; in all that makes for human progress, if there is such a possibility, those days appear to me better than the regnant faiths to-day. None of us of that time were unaware of the terrible failures of the system as it was—well, no, that's too strong, of course. Better: the wise and imaginative knew the lacks and the woeful callousness all around us. But the ethos of those days forbad so ready a resort to violence: violence of feeling, violence of expression, violence of suppression, violence in action of every kind.

Perhaps this feeling is merely a symptom of every old man's lessening vitality. All people of my age are subject to it. I remember how amused I was at old George Holt[30] when he wrote of the "incurable baseness of mankind." O.W.H. escaped it, but then he started at scratch by not attributing "to man a significance different in kind from that which belongs to a baboon or to a grain of sand."[31] That didn't require any marked retrogression as the years piled on. And yet after all discounts are made for my own "personal equation," I can't help thinking that "objectively" I have a good deal to justify my despondency. So that when I look at Dean and his work, my soul dares again to take wing at its own low altitude and to believe that there may be at least a fighting chance that man has a significance, different, and I dare hope, better, than a baboon, whatever "better" may mean. And for myself I am disposed to be unsuspectedly dogmatic about what "better" does mean[...]

Thine, L.H.

ms with signature 105B.15

1950-3

To Walter Lippmann

July 18, 1950 — Judge Learned Hand's Chambers

Dear Walter:

Your "piece," as old Ned Martin used to call his articles, in today's *Tribune* so completely accorded with my own views that I feel that I must tell you so.[32] I have thought through all

---

30. George Chandler Holt (1843–1931): Judge, United States District Court for the Southern District of New York, 1903–1914.

31. In a letter dated August 30, 1929, Holmes admitted to Sir Frederick Pollock: "I only mean that when one thinks coldly I see no reason for attributing to man a significance different in kind from that which belongs to a baboon or a grain of sand." The Holmes-Pollock Letters: The Correspondence of Mr. Justice Holmes and Sir Frederick Pollock, 1874–1932 vol. 2, 252 (Mark De Wolfe Howe ed., 1941).

32. On July 3, 1950, in his column *Today & Tomorrow*, Lippmann proposed a "cardinal rule": that the United States should not engage in "borderland struggles [...] not of our own choosing and where no decision can ever be had." (quoted in Ronald Steel, Walter Lippmann and the American Century 470–71 (1980)). The "feint" LH refers to is the looming conflict in Korea: North Korea invaded South Korea on June 25; the forces of the United Nations, including those of the United States, then undertook to counter that invasion.

this troubled time myself very ignorant and very incompetent, so that I do not permit myself to have what I should venture to call "opinions" on international matters. Perhaps I impute to people like you a greater background of information than you have, but little as that may be, it so overshadows anything on which I can base a judgment that I am much pleased when I find that by chance I am in accord with what better informed men believe.

From the very day this damn thing started I have feared that it was a feint, and a damn clever feint to draw us into the East so deep that we could not do our part in Europe. I concede that we had to act with our existing commitments, but why did we ever get committed, and mayn't we be able to get out with only the seat of our pants torn off—an ignoble result, but better than being stuck in the flypaper for good? Indeed, as *res nova*, I have never been able to see why we should not do better practically to let Asia go; we can't play Atlas and it will only take three or four months of Russian occupation of Europe to extinguish all that we draw on for our spiritual sustenance. The role of the Republicans appears to me really infamous; I cannot imagine voting for Taft, maybe not even if Henry Wallace ran against him. Though that I confess would be a hard one.

Well, all this is not important: the worries of an old gent of 78 can safely be disregarded; but I did feel as though I wanted to tell you what particular bats were flying about in my belfry and I thought that I might so far impose upon you in the name of our former, alas, intimacy which distance has ruptured. My love to Helen.

Affectionately, L.H.

ms with signature, Lippmann Papers, Sterling, Box 76, Folder 978.

To Learned Hand from Walter Lippmann

July 23, 1950 Bernard, Maine

Dear B.:

I have been very depressed by the whole business and it cheers me up a bit to know that you are in the same boat. The question whether we should have put an army into Korea is not one which calls for special expert professional inside super-duper top secret information. The simplest facts that everyone can know are the most important: How far is in? How many soldiers have we? How many have they? If we fight there, could we also fight in Europe? The truth is, however, that our unprofessional opinions are also those of the best professionals. This decision was made by MacArthur [and] Truman, not by [Omar] Bradley and [Forrest] Sherman or by the British top soldiers. Whether the Russians planned it this way or not, they have us in a military trap and can draw us deeper and deeper into Asia (via China). The only way out of the trap is with British-Indian diplomacy. But the Republicans won't let Acheson encourage this British-Indian to extricate us. Are you coming up to Mr. Desert this year? I hope so. I'd love to see you[...]

Always yours, W.L.

ms with signature 106.19

1950-4

To Felix Frankfurter

August 5, 1950 Judge Learned Hand's Chambers

F.F.:

Yours of July 30th received and contents noted[33][...]

Well, after much travail I did get through with the "Communist appeal"[34] and now the rest lies in the lap of the nine Gods, *quorum pars esti*. I will say nothing about it save this one surely blameless comment: that without the fantastically competent help of the Peerless Paragon, Hugh Calkins,[35] this Old Grab Bag of Antiques would have completely crumpled. True, our mutual Effusion was hideously drawn out; you will have to grant me a compassionate lenity when you read it. I will make no excuses; a master would not have been so garrulous, I know, I know; I can only say of myself what Thayer used to say in exegesis of a particularly obscure decision: "It is as it is; and what ever it is, this is it."

L.H.

ms with signature 105B.15

1950-5

To Learned Hand from Augustus Hand

August 3, 1950 Elizabethtown, New York

Dear B.:

I have just read your fine opinion in the Communist case.[36] Of course I did not know anything about some of the minor objections to the rulings. I never believed

---

33. This letter, missing from the Hand Papers, presumably reported the Frankfurters' pleasure in visiting England.

34. I.e., United States v. Dennis, 183 F.2d 201 (2d Cir. 1950). In 1948, Eugene Dennis, general secretary of the Communist Party USA, and eleven members of the party were charged with violating the Smith Act, passed in 1940, which made it a crime for anyone "to knowingly or willfully advocate, abet, advise, or teach the duty, necessity, desirability, or propriety of overthrowing the Government of the United States or of any State by force or violence." Judge Harold R. Medina of the Court of the Southern District of New York found Dennis and his confederates guilty. See 1950-5 To Learned Hand from Augustus Hand, August 3 and To Augustus Hand, August 8, 1950, for a discussion of the case; see also 1951-6 To Frankfurter, June 8.

35. Hugh Calkins, attorney, LH's clerk from 1949 to 1950.

36. United States v. Dennis, 183 F.2d 201 (2d Cir. 1950). The decision was later affirmed by the Supreme Court; *see* Dennis v. United States, 341 U.S. 494 (1951). For LH on *Dennis* in relation to the First Amendment, see LEARNED HAND, THE BILL OF RIGHTS: THE OLIVER WENDELL HOLMES LECTURES, 1958, at 59–61. See 1950-4 To Frankfurter, August 5 for LH's response to the case, and 1951-6 To

the constitutional objections to the act under which the indictment was found would stand and even the "Barnyard fowl" will sustain you, I am very sure. The thing that bothered me most was the objection to the panel. How far the Supreme Court might go as to that I didn't know in view of some of the nonsensical utterances of the late [Frank] Murphy.[37] His removal and that of the sinless but most awful Rutledge "from our midst" and the dangerous times are going to uphold the panel. Why [Harrie Brigham] Chase[38] wanted to write I can't see. I don't think he is vain and crazy to be seen of men. Perhaps some of the points need not have been fully dealt with, but I am inclined to believe it was safer to do what you did. Anyway the job was a big and hard one, and the opinion very satisfactory to me[. . .] My best to all of you.

Affy yrs, A.N.H.

ms with signature 109.17

To Augustus Hand

August 8, 1950 Windsor, Vermont

Dear Gus:

Your letter pleased me a great deal; the job was a hard one and according to my habit especially at the end of the term, I was in doubt all the time before it was filed whether I should be able to get it done or should not have a stroke, etc., etc. A shaming and constant mood nowadays.

Don't blame Chase; he was not content to give any further authority to the constant obbligato—"clear and present danger"—and he really had a good deal on his side. The Nine Saints had again and again said that *Gitlow v. New York* was O.K., although they kept repeating the sacred rubric as though there was no inconsistency, and the last emanation, May, 1950, written under the name Vinson, C.J.,[39] surely treated it as law.

It seemed to me, and Tom [Swan] agreed, that this had come to be a kind of shibboleth that it was inviting trouble to disregard or not to take as authoritative. But no one ought

---

Frankfurter, June 8 for LH's assessment of Frankfurter's ruling in the case before the Supreme Court.

37. Frank Murphy (1890–1949): Governor General of the Philippines, 1930–1933; United States High Commissioner of the Philippines, 1935–1936; Governor of Michigan, 1937–1939; United States Attorney General, 1939–1940; Associate Justice of the United States Supreme Court, 1940–1949.

38. Harrie Brigham Chase (1889–1969): Judge, United States Court of Appeals for the Second Circuit, 1929–1954. With Thomas Swan and LH, he heard *United States v. Dennis* and wrote a concurring opinion (183 F.2d at 234), agreeing that the convictions should be affirmed but disagreeing on LH's and Swan's interpretation of the scope of the Smith Act and its relationship to expression protected by the First Amendment. Chase argued that a narrower interpretation of the Smith Act was mandated by the Supreme Court's decisions in *Gitlow v. New York* and *Whitney v. California*; and because those decisions were still "good law," the court was bound to follow their lead.

39. Frederick Moore Vinson (1890–1953): Judge, United States Court of Appeals for the District of Columbia Circuit, 1938–1943; Director, Office of Economic Stabilization, 1943–1945; Secretary of the Treasury, 1945–1946; Chief Justice of the United States, 1946–1953.

to blame Harrie for "hewing straight to the line," especially as he felt very keenly about the whole case. For myself, I believe that the prosecution was a mistake, and I can't help wondering whether it was more than a move in the election, for remember that the indictment was filed on July 20, 1948. I do not believe that it will do any good to put these men in jail; I am a firm believer that "the blood of martyrs is the seed of the church,"[40] any church. If one means to go in for suppression, one can suppress, it is true, but only when the job is done much more thoroughly than in this way; e.g., the Albigenses in the 13th century, the Heretics in Spain in the 16th, the Communists themselves today with their policy of thorough [suppression] everywhere. But nobody would tolerate such a Root and Branch business here for long and everything less is, I suspect, worse than useless. But with all that we judges have nothing to do. Black, J. will dissent on the jury point; I rather think he will be the only one.

L.H.

ms with signature 109.17

1950-6

To Julian Huxley[41]

August 8, 1950 Windsor, Vermont

Dear Mr. Huxley:

I am sorry to have delayed so long replying to your prospectus, "Evolutionary Humanism," but I had to wait until my official duties gave me a chance.[42] Of course you are right in wishing to make accessible to people generally the results of the vast stores of specialized knowledge about nature, including ourselves, which has developed and must needs develop in separate, non-communicable compartments. Without any liaison between these, without any trustworthy interpretation of them by which the results can be made understandable to those who have no specialized background, these acquisitions must remain no more than means—one might say, "tools"—by which to effect our purposes. They do not and cannot enlighten us as to what our purposes should be. In other words, they do not enable us to adjust our lives in accordance with the true structure of our nature.

---

40. *See* Tertullian, third-century Roman theologian: "Plures efficimur quotiens metimur a vobis: semen est sanguis Christianorum" (we multiply whenever we are mown down by you: the blood of Christians is seed). *Apologeticus*, L.

41. Sir Julian Sorell Huxley (1887–1975): evolutionary biologist; Secretary, the Zoological Society of London, 1935–1942; Director-General United Nations Educational, Scientific, and Cultural Organization, 1946–1948.

42. In letter dated simply May 1950, Huxley asked LH's opinion of an enclosed "memorandum," perhaps the prospectus for Huxley's EVOLUTIONARY HUMANISM (1954). (tp with ms signature and notes, 73.33)

I understand that you wish the "Institute" which you propose to prepare this specialized knowledge so that it shall be available to the ordinarily intelligent person, and that from this you hope that we shall procure a better comprehension of ourselves and become able to direct our conduct more nearly in accord with the truth. With such a project I am most heartily in accord. President Conant of Harvard has some such notion, as I understand. He believes that the teaching of the history of science can be made to have exceptional value, not because of the information which it will impart, but because through it the student may learn the method by which alone any reliable conclusions can be reached, and particularly how tentative most if not all conclusions must always remain. That seems to me to be also the chief benefit from teaching history, for while it would be untrue to say that history teaches nothing except that there are no lessons of history, I can scarcely imagine a more useful contribution to social judgments than to realize that all or substantially all those remedies which more or less spontaneously suggest themselves for present evils have been often tried before without turning out to be the panaceas which their proponents expected. The mark of a civilized man is his awareness that truth is a matter of trial and error, and that he never arrives at final, impregnable verity.

The trouble is that this temper does violence to our deepest inherited habits, for conditional responses are a late acquisition, alien to our primal patterns of conduct. God forbid that I should talk biology to you of all persons, but one does not have to be a biologist to know that the mood of suspended judgment, of the Scotch verdict, "Not Proven," is of almost all things the most hateful to mankind. Indeed, the abhorrence to me is the single most difficult and baffling factor in our present world. The last forty years have shown that we are no less susceptible to epidemics of fabricated creeds than we were in the Middle Ages, and I find it hard to see how we can mend that susceptibility.

I am not sure how far, if at all, what I have tried to describe corresponds to what you have in mind in the "Institute," but so far as it does, I should warmly welcome it. On the other hand, as I have just suggested, I am at a loss as to ways and means. I take it that you have in mind more than scientific generalizations in different fields or, if any such are possible, similar historical generalizations. Rather, you wish to spread the habit of thinking as those have thought who have made such generalizations possible. Yet how to make that habit anything but a pallid competitor for the exhilaration of a breed into which one can plunge without more of the "intolerable labor of thought"—that is where I have always failed to find an answer.

In the hope of making clearer what I mean, let me say in conclusion that I deem it supremely important for people to believe that the methods of science and of history, as distinct from the actual information acquired, are the only methods of any genuine human progress. One of the promising approaches to success lies in making them see how those material triumphs on which modern men are apt to rely all directly followed upon the habit of suspended judgment. The purposes in whose realization or defeat all life consists can be grasped only by the kind of scrutiny which depends upon that habit. How that habit can be inculcated I do not know and perhaps as a strong believer in it, I ought not to presume to know. Nevertheless, inquiries designed to learn how it can be inculcated would have permanent value, even if they proved that it could not be inculcated.

I trust you will forgive me the inadequacy of this answer; at any rate it may prove that my delay has not been because of indifference.

Sincerely yours, L. Hand

tr/ms with signature 73.33

1950-7

To Augustus Hand

September 23, 1950 Windsor, Vermont

Dear Judge:

[...]I am more and more shocked at the behavior of the Republicans; they have lost all sense of moderation—even of decency—in their efforts to get hold of Congress and I think it quite likely that they will succeed.[43] Then what an amazing situation will our Constitution have got us into with its timidity at granting power to any official or to its legislature. Think of it: here we are at one of the most, perhaps the most critical positions in our history, and there is likelihood that for more than two years we shall have no responsible government, the executive checked by the legislature, and the legislature checked by the executive. It appears to me that a frenzied panic is spreading further and further about any sentiment which even squints at change. The women are worse than the men and that ain't saying much. Imagine tolerating to say nothing of covertly supporting such inconceivable obscenities as McCarthy[44] and Jenner;[45] L. Saltonstall[46] at last in part redeemed himself. And yet, when I look over the scene as a whole, strange as it seems to me, that ungenerous, cold, and self-seeking little creature Dewey[47] appears to be the best bet we have[...]

Love to Susie, L.H.

tr/ms with signature 109.17

43. In February 1950, the Senate authorized the Subcommittee on the Investigation of Loyalty of State Department Employees, chaired by Senator Millard Tydings, to investigate charges by Senator Joseph R. McCarthy that members of the Communist Party of the United States of America (CPUSA) were working in the State Department. Concluding its investigations in July 1950, the Committee determined that McCarthy's charges were groundless: there were no Communists in the State Department. The Senate's vote on whether to accept the report was split along party lines.

44. Joseph McCarthy (1908–1957): Senator from Wisconsin, 1947–1957; chairman, Senate Permanent Subcommittee on Investigations examining evidence of Communist influence in the United States.

45. William E. Jenner (1908–1985): Senator from Indiana, 1944–1945, 1947–1959.

46. Leverett Saltonstall (1892–1979): Governor of Massachusetts, 1939–1945; Senator from Massachusetts, 1945–1967.

47. Thomas E. Dewey (1902–1971): Governor of New York, 1943–1955; Republican candidate for President of the United States in 1944 and again in 1948. *See* 1956-5 To Frankfurter, September 2.

1950-8

To Learned Hand from Bernard Berenson

November 5, 1950 Rome

Dear B.:

For a month I have been doing my morning exercises and brushing my teeth with one eye enjoying the light playing on the dome of St. Peter's and with the other the rhythm of the Alban Hills gliding down in soft slopes to the sea.

Iris Origo[48] told me yesterday she saw you a few days ago and that you had talked wisely about [Alger] Hiss[49] and witch-hunting. From other sources I hear that you had made an interesting summing up of a communist trial. Doubtless it is in print. Send me a copy.

Rome is given up to pilgrims and the last few days have witnessed an orgy of magic that the world scarcely has seen before, certainly not on such a scale. The choreography of the Church will never be attained by laymen. And the fervor, the ecstasy of the crowds processioning [sic] in the gorgeously lit, noble, early Christian basilica: it was at once a display of what "religion" still means to people and of the wide-flung allegiance the Roman Pontiff can count on. It has been a tremendously impressive parade to "give the Soviets pause." They can find no substitute to what the Church offers to satisfy the anthropologic need for magic. Once again I have reveled in Rome, its churches, its galleries, its views, its street-corners[...]

Best greetings from Nicky and myself to both of you.

Yours, B.B.

tr/ms with signature 99.20

To Bernard Berenson

December 10, 1950

Dear B.B.:

I sent you the other day a printed copy of my opinion in the Communists Appeal.[50] I did so only because you asked it in such a way as to make me think you wanted it. Even so, I was doubtful, remembering the feelings which similar tenders had produced upon me when judges sent me their cerebrations. But you don't have to read it; it ain't interesting. Opinions fall within Charles Lamb's classification βιβλια αβιβλια,[51] along with actuarial tables and reports of the Interstate Commission.

---

48. Iris Origo (1902–1988): author of: LEOPARDI: A BIOGRAPHY (1935) and THE LAST ATTACHMENT: THE STORY OF BYRON AND TERESA GUICCIOLI (1949).

49. Alger Hiss (1904–1996): U.S. State Department official, accused of being a Soviet spy in 1948 by the House Committee on Un-American Activities, convicted of perjury in connection with this charge in 1950. *See* 1951-2 To Frankfurter, January 29, note 58.

50. United States v. Dennis, 183 F.2d 201 (2d Cir. 1950), *aff'd*, 341 U.S. 494 (1951).

51. I.e., in a book, [there are] books.

On the surface things go on as before, but everybody is really worried and nobody knows what to do. We are caught between the realities and the necessity of not too openly running counter to the infantile beliefs of so many of our fellows. Perhaps it was wrong to go into Korea, though I still think as I did at first, that we had no alternative. However, we have made an honest effort, we did what we engaged to do and it has proved too much for us. I cannot believe that it is wise to persevere throwing in all we have while it will count least and giving up any hope, at best thin enough, to protect Western Europe. Yet we seem to be bedeviled by clichés: "there must be no appeasement"; "we must not yield to aggression"; "to fail now is to abandon our principles"; "we must be true to what our honor demands," etc., etc. I fear we shall lose whatever friends we have, God knows we have not too many, and shall embark whatever strength we can muster in the very worst place to put it—Asia, leaving nothing for Europe which is infinitely more important to us. It is hard for me to comprehend why the articulate feelings have become so orientally directed but apparently it is so. I have hoped to get a rational defense for the conviction that at all costs we must prevent what has already happened, the spread of Communism over that continent, and so far I have heard nothing but the kind of generalities I have mentioned. If I were to guess the real basis, it is made up in part of our past fighting against Japan, in part of a strange sense that we are a kind of foster parent to China although we have always treated them as inferiors, and in part of the worship of General MacArthur. The last factor has been tied in with the Republicans' impotent fury at being excluded from power for 18 years, and at the egalitarian policies of the dominating influences in the Democratic Party. Moreover, somewhat subtly running through all this is the latent and smoldering dislike of the Eastern Seaboard by the Mississippi Basin and the Pacific Coast, and a belief, well enough founded as you will yourself remember, that the East truckled and toadied to Europe, particularly England, and was exasperatingly condescending to all the U.S. west of the Alleghenies. I think you will agree with me that people do not take sides so much because of their economic interests as because of some wounding of their self-esteem. I have understood that one of Le Rochefoucauld's maxims was: "Pourvu que l'amour-propre soit satisfait, le reste n'importe pas."[52] The longer I live, the more of human conduct appears to me understandable in those terms. I think that a very considerable part of our present orientation—excuse the pun, it was not intended—is owing to our feeling of superiority to the Chinese and inferiority to the Europeans[...]

In spite of all the anxiety our industry has been prosperous as never before. The fantastic rise of the share market is in large measure owing to inflation and the fear of that inflation which is absolutely sure to come, but it is surprising that there have never been larger dividends or more material prosperity. I can't help looking at it as a kind of *Danse Macabre,* a sort of winding-up of an era, the feverish vitality which may precede collapse, but whatever it is, here it is. I wish I could enjoy it more, but at least one thing appears to me certain, a "call" upon future dollars is the worse kind of investment.

My love to Nicky: I trust this will find you restored beyond what you were when you wrote last. L.H.

tr/ms with signature 99.20

52. "As long as self-esteem is satisfied, the rest is unimportant."

1950-9

In 1944, Judith Coplon, who worked for the Foreign Agents Registration section, was recruited as a spy by the NKGB, i.e., the People's Commissariat for State Security. In 1949, FBI agents detained Coplon as she met with Valentin Gubitchev, a KGB official employed by the United Nations, while carrying what she thought were secret U.S. government documents; in actuality, they were fakes, planted in her purse at the order of J. Edgar Hoover. Declared guilty of espionage by the United States District Court for the Southern District of New York, Coplon's conviction was reversed by the United States Court of Appeals for the Second Circuit.

To Mary McKeon

December 28, 1950

Dear Miss McKeon:

I have your letter about the *Coplon* case and I can understand why you are troubled about the result; and because you were not abusive, I am going to try to explain it to you.[53]

It is a rule—well settled by the decisions of the Supreme Court—that evidence which the Government secures by its own violation of law it may not use against the person whose rights have been invaded.[54] An extreme example of this would be in case a United States marshal were to break into the house of an accused person and seize his papers; the Government would not be allowed to use the papers against the person whose house had been entered. The same thing is true of documents found upon the person of one who is unlawfully arrested as was Judith Coplon. That was one ground for the reversal. The other was that during the trial it became necessary for the Government to depend

---

53. United States v. Coplon, 185 F.2d 629 (2d Cir. 1950), *cert. denied*, 342 U.S. 920 (1952). In an undated letter, Mary McKeon (an unidentified correspondent), evidently wishing to know why Judith Coplon deserved a retrial, asked LH to give her the reason: "Figure it out and try to do something about it. Would you write to me and tell me what's to be done about it?" (ms with signature 69.8) In stark contrast to McKeon's civil request, persons angry at LH's decision wrote him frankly abusive letters, some of which are preserved in the Hand Papers. They include excerpts such as the following: "How much did the Jews of New York pay you 3 [i.e., LH, Thomas Swan, Jerome Frank] old spies and traitors to free the low vile Coplon thing"; "You old S.O.B. You are as much a spy as she is; may you suffer the tortures of the damned and burn in hell; our sons are being killed for such as you"; "Did you think when you turned loose the Coplon bitch you would get a big hand from the people? The good old U.S.A. is still a Christian country and we pray God to send us another Hitler; he not the dirty louse you are; let the kikes reward you for distinguished service to the Jews; 80 percent of the spies and traitors exposed are Jews; they are a despised race and always will be; no credit to you to be honored by them, it only proves what a yellow cur you are to sell your oath to traitors; our sons will remember this when they return from Korea." (mss 69.8) After several attempts at retrial, the government dropped the case in 1967.

54. LH refers to the exclusionary rule in criminal procedure under which evidence that is obtained in violation of the guarantees and protections of the U.S. Constitution must be excluded from evidence in a criminal trial: "The right of the people to be secure in their persons, houses, papers, and effects, against unreasonable searches and seizures, shall not be violated, and no Warrants shall issue, but upon probable cause, supported by Oath or affirmation, and particularly describing the place to be searched, and the persons or things to be seized," U.S. Const. amend. IV.

upon evidence which it was unwilling to let her see. The Constitution provides that a person accused of crime is entitled to have all witnesses, who are called against him, brought into court at the trial.[55]

Thus in these two instances the rights of the accused were violated, which is entirely consistent with her guilt. Perhaps, if you reflect, you will agree that it is not desirable to convict people, even though guilty, if to do so it is necessary to violate those rules on which the liberty of all of us depends.

Truly yours, [Learned Hand]

tp 69.8

1951-1

To Learned Hand from Felix Frankfurter

January 13, 1951 Supreme Court of the United States

Dear B:

Is the Plowden reference you want (re "Equity of Statute") *Eyston v. Studd*, Plowden 467?[56][...] As to W.L.: it would be fun to have an evening on him. For he is an interesting psychologic study—raises issues and problems that transcend the individual.

But now—to work! F.F.

ms with signature 105B.16

---

55. "In all criminal prosecutions, the accused shall enjoy the right...to be confronted with the witnesses against him." U.S. CONST. amend. VI. In *Coplon*, the trial judge had stopped an investigation of the person informing against Judith Coplon, despite the possibility that this informant might be one who had wiretapped her telephone, thus preventing her from confronting him. Discussing the significance of withholding evidence in *Coplon*, LH states: "[I]n truth, it is extremely unlikely that [Ms. Coplon] suffered the slightest handicap from the judges refusal. But we cannot dispense with constitutional privileges because in a specific instance they may not in fact serve to protect any valid interest of their possessor[...] Few weapons in the arsenal of freedom are more useful than the power to compel a government to disclose the evidence on which it seeks to forfeit the liberty of its citizens. All governments, democracies as well as autocracies, believe that those they seek to punish are guilty; the impediment of constitutional barriers are galling to all governments when they prevent the consummation of that just purpose. But those barriers were devised and are precious because they prevent that purpose and its pursuit from passing unchallenged by the accused, and unpurged by the alembic of public scrutiny and public criticism. A society which has come to wince at such exposure of the methods by which it seeks to impose its will upon its members, has already lost the feel of freedom and is on the path towards absolutism." 185 F.2d at 638.

56. In a separate note to his letter, Frankfurter provides LH with the exact wording of the sixteenth-century English lawyer Sir Edmund Plowden's directions on interpreting statutes: "And in order to form a right judgment when the letter of a statute is restrained, and when enlarged, by equity, it is a good way when you peruse a statute, to suppose that the law-maker is present, and that you have asked him the question you want to know touching the equity; then you must give yourself such an answer as you imagine he would have done, if he had been present," COMMENTARIES OR REPORTS 467 (1779). The distinction between reading a statute in a sense that is either "restrained" or, conversely, "enlarged" is a feature of much commentary on sixteenth-century English common law. *See* A DISCOURSE UPON THE EXPOSICION & UNDERSTANDINGE OF STATUTES WITH SIR THOMAS EGERTON'S ADDITIONS, (Samuel E. Thorne ed., 1942). LH had paraphrased without attribution Plowden's directions in an address he delivered on the Columbia Broadcasting System on May 4, 1933; *see* 1933-1 To Frankfurter, January 23, note 10.

To Felix Frankfurter

January 15, 1951 Judge Learned Hand's Chambers

F.F.:

Yes, that's it; especially that part of the note which says, p. 467 [Plowden]: "it is a good way, when you peruse a statute, to suppose that the law-maker is present, and that you have asked him the question you want to know touching the equity; then you must give yourself such an answer as you imagine he would have done, if he had been present." That, I submit, is "all the law and the prophets"[...] The Sainted Bennie,[57] for all his jurisprudential writings, seems to me to have written no more than "Variations on this Theme."

Thine, L.H.

ms with signature 105B.16

1951-2

To Felix Frankfurter

January 29, 1951 Judge Learned Hand's Chambers

F.F.:

[...]The enclosed will amuse you; you are in high company.[58] The advanced guard of obscurantism is making sally upon sally. They are right; this is their great opportunity. Yet though they will win many battles, in the end they won't win the war. Strange is it not, how the two living faiths today repeat each other so completely in ways and means. I feel like praying every night: "Oh God, preserve my skepticism, make me skeptical, God, especially about your being the One who is managing this mess. And for that matter, God, please put an end to all 'true believers.' I don't confine that to your devotees; I want to include Karl Marx's just as much. God, I will concede a point: I want much more to include them. Can't you do them in first and then take a swat at your own?"[...]

---

57. I.e., Benjamin Cardozo.

58. LH encloses Archbishop J. Francis A. McIntyre's article—*Says Justice Holmes Befuddled America*, published in the N.Y. Times on January 29, 1951—in which McIntyre blames two United States Supreme Court Justices, Felix Frankfurter and the late Oliver Wendell Holmes, Jr., for having "confused" the American people with "'whimsical evaluations of justice and equity...based on a purely social concept.'" They have thus "morally fostered irreligion and atheism, and in doing so substituted confusion and uncertainty for principle and high purpose." McIntyre specifically alludes to Alger Hiss, a State Department official accused of being a Soviet spy in 1948 before the House Committee on Un-American Activities, as "'trained in the rules of Justice Holmes and Justice Frankfurter'" and asks for a return to "'the Ten Commandments, supported by natural law,'" which he defines as "that inborn instinct in man which determines right from wrong." In 1950, Hiss was convicted of perjury in connection with this charge.

Don't answer this—I forbid it—I was 79 on Saturday and the saddening effect has not worn off. Also I am on the water cart. "Life is a tale told by an idiot full of sound and fury," etc.

Thine, L.H.

ms with signature 105B.16

1951-3

To Learned Hand from Felix Frankfurter

April 2, 1951 3018 Dumbarton Ave., Washington, D.C.

Dear B:

My tongue is supposed to be ready but when my feelings are deeply engaged, I'm choked. And so you must have noticed that I said not a word when you told me of your early retirement. It is not only a long, long stretch in your life but also in mine that you are terminating. Intimacy of outlook and purpose in what has been so much of our lives—our profession—we formed early, at least I felt with you, and by healthy growth, affection and intimacy of friendship evolved. And now, for nearly twelve years you have been the only colleague, as it were, I've had here. Hughes, with all his austerities, gave me satisfaction while it lasted and Bob Jackson gives all I get now. But he is, with all his charm and spontaneities and honesty, not an intellectual meal. (Stone had professional equipment, but he really was, believe me, a petty man. And Roberts delightfully naive.) And so you have been my intellectual companion on the Court, very much so in my soliloquies, partly fed by the stream of your opinions. That now will cease—but not my affection for you, my resort to you as "a frame of reference," above all my wishes for your continued flourishing in new forms of the great vitality, the exuberant inquiry and skepticism that are still in you. Fructify them and triumph over all the mess of the world by wresting from its chaos your own private world of peace and pleasure.

Thine, Felix

ms with signature 105B.16

To Felix Frankfurter

April 8, 1951 Judge Learned Hand's Chambers

F.F.:

Of course, I knew how much we think and feel alike about fundamentals and what is the warmth of our regard for each other; both these have been growing for many years and have never before been what they are now. But it did surprise me to have you say that I filled any such place in your universe of discourse. Indeed, it was clear that there is not much now in the Court that could stimulate or refresh you, but you have so many contacts that I had never ventured to believe that among them I could very positively contribute. And this has been more of a solace to me than you may believe, for you will find, I think, when it becomes plain to you that the curtain is inevitably soon coming down, that the play in retrospect has been at best inadequate and at worst tawdry. That is not an inverted egoism; at least, it's an almost universal experience. To find that among the few whose judgment is competent there are those who see it differently is a comfort: "Maybe," one says, "my judgment is too weighted to be reliable."

Don't suppose that the spate of stuff that has been pouring out of me all these years has necessarily dried up. I intend to keep a footing in the job, sitting in the district court where I shall be my own master and say what lies in my [competence] without need of compromise. It seems a little mean to say so, for I like them both, but the prospect that I shall not have to accommodate myself to Charlie [Clark]'s morbid sensitivities or to Jerry [Frank]'s garrulity is a relief. That I have in me possible emanations into other fields I doubt: expression is difficult for me, little as you may think so, and to pin down in pretty cases any of the fluttering moths that fly about in my belfry, seems, at the moment anyway, more than I can muster. We shall see; it isn't important. My God, I have been so "shot in the arse with luck" as John Henry, Cardinal Newman would have put it, that it is hard to believe I can end "in the red."

Don't, I pray you, suppose that, whatever happens, this step is going to make any difference between you and me. Some of what you wrote sounds as though you thought so. That's an error; as Holmes used to say, what we have is κτημα εσ εσι.[59]

Thine, L.H.

ms with signature 105B.16

1951-4

To Learned Hand from Harry S. Truman

May 23, 1951 The White House, Washington, D.C.

Dear Judge Hand:

Your impending retirement fills me with regret, which I know is shared by the American people.[60] It is hard to accept the fact that after forty-two years of most distinguished service to our Nation, your activities are now to be narrowed. It is always difficult for me to express a sentiment of deep regret; what makes my present task so overwhelming is the compulsion I feel to attempt, on behalf of the American people, to give in words

59. I.e., a possession beyond all others.

60. In a letter dated May 15, LH wrote to President Truman declaring his intention to retire from "regular active service." *Introduction, in* THE SPIRIT OF LIBERTY xxv.

some inkling of the place you have held and will always hold in the life and spirit of our country.

Your profession has long since recognized the magnitude of your contribution to the law. There has never been any question about your preeminent place among American jurists—indeed among the nations of the world. In your writings, in your day-to-day work for almost half a century, you have added purpose and hope to man's quest for justice through the process of law. As judge and philosopher, you have expressed the spirit of America and the highest in civilization which man has achieved. America and the American people are the richer because of the vigor and fullness of your contribution to our way of life.[61]

We are compensated in part by the fact that you are casting off only a part of the burdens which you have borne for us these many years, and by our knowledge that you will continue actively to influence our life and society for years to come. May you enjoy many happy years of retirement, secure in the knowledge that no man, whatever his walk of life, has ever been more deserving of the admiration and the gratitude of his country, and indeed of the entire free world.

Very sincerely yours, Harry S. Truman

tp with ms signature 81.10

To Harry S. Truman

May 24, 1951

Dear Mr. President:

Your letter about my retirement quite overwhelms me. I dare not believe that it is justified by anything which I have done, yet I cannot but be greatly moved that you should think that it is. The best reward that anyone can expect from official work is the approval

---

61. Five days before Truman wrote his letter of regret, LH had addressed the American Law Institute in Washington, D.C. His speech was taken down by a stenographer and published in the WASHINGTON POST on May 27, 1951: "My friends, our future is precarious. I do not know if you remember the time 11 years ago in 1940 when we were here on the eve of those dreadful days when it seemed not unlikely that the whole of all that which made life precious might be overwhelmed. Today we stand in as much danger as we did then, and although it is not from us that the heaviest sacrifices are demanded, yet we have much to answer for. I like to hope—although I agree that we can have no certainty, still I like to hope—that we have a good chance, a splendid fighting chance and much assurance of victory, but on one condition, that we do not go to pieces internally. It is there I think that you and I may be able to help. Because, my friends, will not you agree that any society which begins to be doubtful of itself, in which one man looks at another and says: 'he may be a traitor,' in which that spirit has disappeared which says: 'I will not accept that, I will not believe that—I will demand proof. I will not say of my brother that he may be a traitor, but I will say, 'Produce what you have. I will judge it fairly, and if he is, he shall pay the penalty; but I will not take it on rumor. I will not take it on hearsay. I will remember that what has brought us up from savagery is a loyalty to truth, and truth cannot emerge unless it is subjected to the utmost scrutiny'—will you not agree that a society which has lost sight of that cannot survive?" *The One Condition, in* THE SPIRIT OF LIBERTY 223–24.

of those competent to judge who become acquainted with it; your words of warm approval are much more than I could conceivably have hoped to receive. I can only tell you of my deep gratitude, and assure you that your letter will be a possession for all time for me and for those who come after me.

Respectfully yours, LEARNED HAND

tr/tp with ms signature 81.10

1951-5

To Learned Hand from Walter Lippmann

May 17, [1951] 3525 Woodley road, Washington, D.C.

Dear B.:

I have known or some weeks that you were going to retire, and I have been turning over in my mind the fine letter that I would write you when it was announced. Now that I face the letter it all sounds fine enough, but not for a personal letter to anyone I have known so long and loved so much[...] I do hope, now that you will have more free time, that we'll see you both either in Washington or up in Maine. If you come to Mt. Desert Island or anywhere near it this summer, why don't you pay us a little visit?

As ever, Walter Lippmann

tp with ms signature 106.19

To Walter Lippmann

May 21, 1951 Judge Learned Hand's Chambers

Dear Walter:

When I got back I found your letter of the 17th, which of course I had not seen yesterday when we had that unsatisfactory opportunity for any real talk. What you write brings back to me in long retrospect our friendship from the time when I was what now seems to me still a young man and you were the gifted stripling for whom, as we then knew, there awaited a long career of great distinction. It has always seemed to me curious that you should feel for me the esteem that you express; I am never with you without feeling that you must come to think its foundation weak. That you have not done so and still can with such obvious truthfulness speak of anything I have done as you do, although it gives me a strange sense of unreality, nevertheless has the deepest satisfaction. I can only thank you as I have before and try to believe that you may be right.

Affectionately, L.H.

tp with ms signature, Lippmann Papers, Sterling, Box 76, Folder 978

1951-6

To Felix Frankfurter

June 8, 1951 Judge Learned Hand's Chambers

F.F.:

Now that the mists have in part—gad, not much—lifted, I am once more impressed with the inefficiency of our political scheme which puts judges at the top of the deeply contentious issues of our society. You were the only one who saw the thing in its true light.[62] Indeed, all the rest, even Jackson, seemed to me to beat the air. Douglas[63] scarcely made coherent sense to my thinking. Personally I should never have prosecuted those birds: "the blood of martyrs is the seed of the church." So far as all this will do anything, it will encourage the faithful and maybe help the Committee on Propaganda.

As *res integra*, I think that Holmes—*nomen clarissime et venerabilissime*—(spelling uncertain)—for once slipped his trolley on "clear and present"; at most a mere side spark anyway.[64] I should, however, not take your view that it was a balance of interest in each case which judges have no business to mess in with. I did follow just that in what I wrote, taking your lead because I thought the stream of talk was too strong to make head against otherwise. But I have never felt satisfied that there was not an adequate qualitative distinction, baffling as any rule must become in application. I tried to state it years ago in the *Masses* case but have had to abandon it.[65]

---

62. In *Dennis v. United States*, 341 U.S. 494 (1954), Frankfurter joined the majority in affirming the decision of the United States Court of Appeals for the Second Circuit, but wrote a concurring opinion in which he addressed in detail what he called the "ultimate issue" of the case: "In enacting a statute which makes it a crime for the defendants to conspire to do what they have been found to have conspired to do, did Congress exceed its constitutional power?" 341 U.S. at 518. Answering this question in the negative, Frankfurter noted that the validity of the Smith Act under the First Amendment depended on a balancing of interests made by Congress, and that because Congress's conclusion—embodied in the Smith Act—was not "outside the pale of fair judgment," it should be respected. *Id.* at 540; *see also id.* at 517–61 (Frankfurter, J., concurring).

63. Justice Douglas dissented, 341 U.S. 494 at 581. Justice Hugo Black also dissented. *Id.* at 579.

64. LH makes specific Holmes's concept of a "clear and present danger": "It is a way to describe a penumbra of occasions, even the outskirts of which are indefinable, but within which, as is so often the case, the courts much find their way as they can. In each case they must ask whether the gravity of the 'evil' discounted by its improbability, justifies such invasion of free speech as is necessary to avoid the danger." United States v. Dennis, 183 F.2d 201, 211–12 (1950).

65. *See* 1918-2 To Holmes, June 22; 1919-3 To Holmes, April 1; 1919-6 To Holmes, November 22. On the *Masses* standard, Gunther observes: "[I]n 1969 [. . .] in *Brandenburg v. Ohio*, the Court established a new standard of speech protection, a standard in which incitement to lawless action—Hand's *Masses* standard—became a central prerequisite for justifying convictions under the First Amendment." Gerald Gunther, Learned Hand: the Man and the Judge 603 (1994).

So far as the Constitution goes, I cannot see why it should protect any speech which contains "aid, abetting, counsel" etc. to *violate* any 1aw. If that is mingled with otherwise permissible speech, I would leave it to Congress to require the utterer to separate the wheat from the chaff. Holmes was wrong, I think, when he said that every argument is an "incitement"[66]; that was too loose a use of language, for incitement more properly means making yourself a party to the venture, an accessory. Maybe in the end the crux is purpose; I rather think it is and I am as aware as you can be how unreliable a litmus test that is. Still, we do use it all the time and the definition is in terms that go back to Bracton:[67] same ritual. I tried to put it up to you folks in *Falcone's* case, 311 U.S. 205,[68] but Stone wouldn't quite face the music. Curiously enough, Douglas, in *Nye v. U.S.* 336 U.S. 613,[69] embalmed an old effort of mine which I can't help thinking is the only exit here. But then one gets in love with one's own children especially as the shadows lengthen[...]

Thine, L.H.

ms with signature 105B.16

---

66. Holmes's provocative statement, "Every idea is an incitement," was part of his dissent in *Gitlow v. New York*, 268 U.S. 652, 673 (1925).

67. LH refers to Henry of Bracton (1210–1268): Justice of the assize, 1245–1266; Chancellor of Exeter Cathedral, 1264–1268. In discussing criminal charges and procedures, Bracton distinguishes between the principal actor, one who commits an illegal act *propter factum* (by reason of the deed itself) and an accessory, one who does so *propter forciam* (by reason of assistance). The accessory either gives the help, *auxilium*; or advice, *consilium*; or instruction, *praeceptum* that causes the victim's injury or death. De legibus et consuetudinibus Angliae. English and Latin. On the Laws and Customs of England vol. II, 360, 389 (Samuel E. Thorne trans., 1968–1977).

68. United States v. Falcone, 109 F.2d 579 (2d Cir.), *aff'd*, 311 U.S. 205 (1940). In *Falcone*, LH decided that "a seller did not become a conspirator by selling goods to a buyer who, as he knew, intended to use them to commit a crime." *Id.* at 421. "It is not enough that [the seller] does not forego a normally lawful activity, of the fruits of which he knows that others will make an unlawful use; he must in some sense promote their venture himself, make it his own, have a stake in its outcome. The distinction is especially important today when so many prosecutors seek to sweep within the drag-net of conspiracy all those who have been associated in any degree whatever with the main offenders. That there are opportunities of great oppression in such a doctrine is very plain, and it is only by circumscribing the scope of such all comprehensive indictments that they can be avoided. We may agree that morally the defendants at bar should have refused to sell to illicit distillers; but, both morally and legally, to do so was *toto caelo* different from joining with them in running the stills." *Id.* at 581.

69. In *Nye & Nissen v. United States*, 336 U.S. 613 (1949), affirming a Ninth Circuit Court of Appeals decision that upheld the conviction of owners of related corporations on charges of conspiring to defraud the U.S. government, Justice Douglas approved the definition of "aider and abbettor" that LH established in *United States v. Peoni*, 100 F.2d 401 (1938), quoting LH's observation that aiding and abetting another in a crime means that a defendant must "in some sort associate himself with the venture, that he participate in it as in something that he wishes to bring about, that he seeks by his action to make it succeed," 336 U.S. at 619.

1952-1

To Learned Hand from Bernard Berenson

January 23, 1952 Settignano

Dear B.:

Take my congratulations on having reached your 80th birthday and my good wishes for many more[...] How are you shaping your "leisure"? Not by waiting for odd jobs, no matter how important. You must take up with something continuous if only for an hour a day. Do not let a morning come when you stretch, ask yourself what you are going to do.

I would urge you to write. The very little of your prose that I have read assures me that you have a style which all must envy who try to write. There is a freshness and learning and force in it that almost has vanished. Why not use it to tell what you have experience and concluded? It would give you great satisfaction once you are cranked up, and make life zestful.

Then you should keep going two or three books at a time, and look forward to taking them up. These be the comments of your senior by seven years, who not only admires but loves you.

Ever affectionately, B.B.

ms with signature 99.21

To Bernard Berenson

February 17, 1952 Judge Learned Hand's Chambers

Dear B.B.:

I scarcely deserved that letter of yours, written so as to reach me on my birthday; I had owed you one for long and have no excuse for my neglect except a sort of lethargy which creeps upon me increasingly, I fear. I take your advice very seriously; I am well aware that it will be dangerous in the years that remain to have a vacant mind and an empty life. There has, so far, been no apparent danger of this; indeed, at times I seem to have more "business"—rather, more "busyness"—than before I retired. True, a good deal of it is trifling stuff, but then every active life is made up largely of trifling stuff. As to writing, which you suggest, I have indeed thought a good deal about it, though very inconclusively. I should like best to deliver a set of lectures at the Harvard Law School, designed to show how the American doctrine of constitutional law has worked in which the courts have the last word. It would be directed at the assumption that there is a "Natural Law" whose tenets can be apprehended and applied as jural commands.[70] You may be surprised that I think it important to beat that old dead lion again, but make no mistake, he is by no means dead. Not only is the Holy Mother arousing him to roar loud, support for him and such notions comes from strange quarters. When you and I were growing up all these theories we thought to be finally disposed of, but we were wrong. St. Thomas Aquinas and the Stoics are coming back, horse, foot, and dragoons.

The thing that holds me back is that to do even a half-way thorough job demands far more scholarship than I have, and an amount of labor which would require one to put aside all, or substantially all, my judicial work—something I am not yet ready to do. And yet it teases me to attack it, for some such conceptual background is inevitable, if courts are to continue applying such vague counsels of moderation as the "First Ten Amendments" as though they had a fixed ascertainable content. The function has debauched our courts and perverted the assumptions of our democratic society. I don't so much cleave to that, but I submit that a hidden paralogism at the basis of any system will develop in it disturbing anomalies, and prevent the working out of any constituent plan, good or bad. There is always evil in that.

I need hardly tell you that we in this country continue to move about in entire confusion. I cannot myself understand our preoccupation with Asia, which, I believe, would in the end prove a weakness to the Kremlin, if it ever fell into the Kremlin's maw. But, that aside, I keep repeating Churchill's dictum: "First things first": it is Europe which should be our concern. But the interest, at least the vocal interest, appears to be more in Asia. Certainly that is true of the people at large, though not, I think, of the Administration. At a guess I should say that [Robert A.] Taft[71] is more likely than not to get the Republican nomination, and that will mean Truman will be the Democratic candidate once more. Which would win I should not care to have more than a nickel on; but, if forced to bet, I should put my money on Truman. Taft is the darling of the Safe, the Sane, the Sound Bourgeoisie, and the triple-distilled venom from the Fair Deal and the New Deal does, it is true, loom large because of its intensity. But I question how far below the upper income "brackets," as we call them, it goes; and indeed when I say that Taft is their darling, I mean that they take him as the chalice for their precious liquor, not that anybody particularly loves him for himself. A good many of them like in the same way even that old cobra, Hoover, whose teeth are pretty well gone, but who can still spit poison and does.

If Taft were to get it, we should in the end pretty well back out of Europe, probably. It would not be a case of confessed scuttle, but you will find, I think, if that happened, that any push and drive of the present really promising program will disappear. Without energy of conviction and deep concern for the fate of Europe, we shall just peter out and leave it to roll on its own wheels to its own unbewept fate, congratulating ourselves that we have never been so corrupted by Communism. Well, that is my gloomy prospect;

---

70. For LH on "Natural Law," see The Bill of Rights: The Oliver Wendell Holmes Lectures, 1958, at 2–3, 33–34; *see also* 1953-2 To Kennan, April 21; 1955-1 To Lippmann, March 7; 1955-3 To Berenson, August 25; and 1958-3 To Wyzanski, December 9.

71. Robert A. Taft (1889–1953): Senator from Ohio, 1939–1953.

maybe it is too dark, and after all, Taft has not won even the nomination yet, to say nothing of the election. All goes well with us [...] It does not look very likely, however, that we shall get to Europe this summer.

Affectionately, L.H.

N.B. I got so infatuated with the exuberance of my own verbosity that I filled the last page without having left any space to send my adorations to the divine Nicky. Let them now, as they should, be the introduction to all that I have to say. I prostrate myself before her in abject devotion.

ms with signature 99.21

To Learned Hand from Bernard Berenson

April 25, 1952 Settignano

Dear B.:

Let me congratulate you on the blushing honor that is to be bestowed on you—better late than never. For once in a blue moon a D.C.L. will not lie.[72]

I wish it were bringing you back to Italy where you have not remotely outstayed your welcome. I feel as if we still could find more to say to each other than most others can draw forth.

In your fine letter of February 17th you spoke of your interest in *ius naturalis*. For my part I "Suspicion" [sic; i.e., suspect] the word "nature" and all its derivatives in matters sociological, etc. etc. It means only what we take for granted without need of discussion, as a matter of course, like the expectation that when you stand on the ground it won't give way under your feet, etc., etc., etc. Why the Jesuits are fighting so hard for it I cannot understand unless we accept their sly contention that "Nature's Law" was implanted in our heads *numine Dei*. By the way do Jesuits or Rousseau coincide in the cult of NATURE?

Truman is not such a bad boy. The average American sprung from nowhere, yet sitting fairly decently on the most fool-proof throne yet invented. Given human nature, the which is 95 percent cannibal, we can be proud of what we have been doing for 150 years, and not least in the last 6 or 7. I don't shoot at Truman. He has been doing his best. I want to see you again. Shall I? Life for us oldsters is so precarious and mine now seems ebbing fast away. In rain or shine, and with my best to Frances.

Affectionately, B.B.

ms with signature 99.21

---

72. Berenson may be referring to the honorary degree of Doctor of Civil Laws that Cambridge University was to award LH in June.

1952-2

To Elliot Richardson[73]

February 29, 1952 Judge Learned Hand's Chambers

Dear Elliot:

[...]Your article in the [*Harvard Law*] *Review*[74] I read a good while ago, and it seemed to me, granted the condition of the decisions as they are, as good as could be done. However, as I think I have told you, I dissent from the whole approach to the problem of Free Speech which the Supreme Court has adopted during the last thirty-five or forty years. Constitutionally speaking, it is a simpler problem than is involved in any of the other "Natural Rights," for there is here a difference in kind between what the Constitution should allow and what it should not. I would make the purpose of the utterer the test of his constitutional protection. Did he seek to bring about a violation of existing law? If he did, I can see no reason why the Constitution should protect him, however remote the chance may be of his success.

My reasons may sound didactic and too generalized, but here they are. Every society which promulgates a law means that it shall be obeyed until it is changed, and any society which lays down means by which its laws can be changed makes those means exclusive. If it did not do so, the alternate implicit means, being by hypothesis themselves not unlawful, must become part of the means in fact accredited. I hate logic in government—it reminds me too much of Edward Douglass White—but I must confess that what I have just said seems to me no better than a pleonasm. If so, how in God's name can an incitement to do what will be unlawful, if done, be itself lawful? How do words differ from any other way of bringing about an event? I don't mean, of course, that it is not often hard to distinguish purpose from bringing about a result to which we are indifferent, but we do that in all sorts of situations. Every occasion is an example in which we accept as an excuse for doing harm to another some personal interest of the actor, for it is always a condition that the actor must be pursuing his own interest. Of course, I do not mean that it would be wise to punish all utterances whose purpose is to provoke unlawful conduct. Much of it is much better to ignore; too repressive a policy though in itself lawful may often discourage legitimate and even profitable discourse. But that, I submit, is not a constitutional objection or at least it ought not to be; it is a question to be decided ad hoc in each case by balancing the opposing considerations and should be left to Congress, unless, indeed, we are of that school which believes that the courts should review the compositions of conflicting interests which the legislature may make and substitute their own.

So much for what may certainly be repressed: i.e., any utterance designed to evoke disobedience to law. There is another field about which I am not too sure. Perhaps the

73. Elliot Richardson (1920–1999): Undersecretary of State, 1969–1970; Secretary of Health, Education, and Welfare, 1970–1973; Secretary of Defense, 1973; Attorney General, 1973; Secretary of Commerce, 1976–1977.

74. *Freedom of Expression and the Function of the Courts*, 65 HARV. L. REV. 1 (1951).

Constitution does not in all cases protect a man, even though it is not his purpose to provoke disobedience, if the effect of his utterance too plainly will do so. Although you may wish only to persuade your audience to confine themselves to lawful means, it may be plain that they will be moved to resort to unlawful means. Personally, although I recognize that there may be border cases, I should prefer to make purpose the absolute test: no purpose, no wrong. In any event, as a practical matter it would be pretty safe to do so, because it is so seldom that serious danger exists when such a purpose is absent. When I say "serious danger" I mean the kind of danger that a free society ought not to feel itself competent to deal with without forcible repression.[75] My warm regards to your future partner.

Affectionately yours, L.H.

tp 94.24

1952-3

To Edward C. Carter[76]

March 10, 1952

Dear Mr. Carter:

Thank you for your letter of the 6th with its enclosure from *The Nation*.[77] My first impression was one of satisfaction that [Owen] Lattimore[78] stood up to those members of the committee who were not interested in getting at the truth but only in discrediting

---

75. On March 8th, Richardson responded: "As a practical matter, utterances intended to provoke unlawful conduct would be likely to escape prosecution if the probability of actual harm were negligible. It is probably true, moreover, that unintentionally harmful utterances are rare. But how much should these considerations influence judicial enforcement of the Constitution? Apart from all this, should the protection afforded by the First Amendment be allowed to turn upon the Speaker's state of mind? It is 'speech' that is protected." (tp with ms signature 94.24)

76. Edward C. Carter (1878–1954): Officer of the YMCA, 1902–1922; member of the Institute of Pacific Relations, 1926–1948; chairman of the Russian War Relief Fund, 1941–1945.

77. On March 6th, 1952, Carter sent LH a page from an article on Owen Lattimore by Freda Kirchwey, which reads in part: "Owen Lattimore spoke for all free-minded Americans when he launched his lusty counter-attack on the McCarran Internal Security subcommittee [...] He has challenged the courts to test the accuracy of the charges against him, and his own honesty. The McCarran committee, like the House Un-American Activities Committee, has welcomed the testimony of the most suspect witnesses—men and women processed by the Communist Party machine who have recanted and turned state's evidence. The reputations of high government officials and other citizens of standing have been laid waste by a word from such witnesses [...] Their power has been further fortified by the backing they have had from committee members and counsel, from Joseph R. McCarthy, and from outside pressure groups like the China Lobby. The result, as *The New York Times* said last Saturday, has been to build up a 'corrosive atmosphere of mistrust and suspicion throughout the country and particularly within the government of the United States.'" *See* Freda Kirchwey, *Lattimore Strikes Back*, THE NATION, Mar. 8, 1952, at 216–20.

78. Owen Lattimore (1900–1989): Lecturer in History, Johns Hopkins University.

witnesses, and who have made testimony before a committee of Congress a dreadful ordeal.[79] As I have come to think it over, it seems to me that it was a mistake for him to return in kind the sort of treatment that they gave; that only led to mutual recrimination in which the committee had every advantage. True, we cannot tell how soon, if at all, the public will begin to react against such abuse of power, but my guess is that the best chance will be for the witnesses to retain their composure and dignity, so far as they can under such provocation, and to answer the questions as though they were put in good faith.

I do not remember what I said to you the other night. Possibly it was the opposite of this, and it is of course quite possible that if so, I was more right then than now, but this is my second judgment. I don't see how anyone can be very certain of either opinion. Thank you for your kindness in writing me.

Sincerely yours, [Learned Hand]

tp 86.33

1952-4

To Irving Dilliard[80]

April 3, 1952

Dear Mr. Dilliard:

The *Spirit of Liberty*—i.e., ten copies—came yesterday, and I was delighted at its make-up and appearance; it seems to me that the publisher could not have done better.[81] I do hope that his loss will not be great.

Now that it is all over, I wish to repeat what I have tried, not very effectively I fear, to tell you more than once before: I mean, my great sense of gratitude to you for all your efforts to gather up and perpetuate these words of mine which have been scattered at random through so many publications. As I read them over last night, I got a sense that for whatever they may be worth, at least here they could be found by anyone who had enough interest in them to want to have a look at them. I was a good deal surprised to see

79. Senator Joseph McCarthy accused Lattimore in 1950 of being a Soviet agent. Lattimore was subsequently cleared of charges. In 1952, however, a federal grand jury indicted him for perjury because he had claimed to a Senate internal security subcommittee that he had not promoted Communism. All charges were dropped in 1955. *See* Owen Lattimore, Ordeal by Slander (1950).

80. Irving Dilliard (1904–2002): journalist and editor of the St. Louis-Post Dispatch, collected and edited LH's occasional essays and speeches for The Spirit of Liberty: Papers and Addresses of Learned Hand, published by Alfred A. Knopf initially in 1952 and later editions in 1953 and 1960. For the book's publication history, see 1960-1 To Knopf, January 27.

81. LH was evidently reluctant to have his nonlegal work published. On April 24, 1942, Edward C. Aswell, an editor at Harper & Brothers, asked permission to edit and publish LH's "occasional addresses." (tp with signature 72.23) On April 25, LH thanked Aswell for his interest but replied that to see his addresses in print would destroy his "peace of mind": "I never read one without an acute feeling of nausea." (tp 72.23)

how much I had repeated myself; yet I was reconciled, because I saw that that made for a certain continuity—more than I had expected.

All this is not important, but what is to me most important is that you should have thought it worthwhile to go to the trouble you have taken to try to put my notions in a permanent form. I don't understand it, but that does not make my satisfaction any the less.

Sincerely yours, Learned Hand

P.S. Some day, when we meet again, which I trust may not be long delayed, I will try to put the *Dennis* opinion—"clear and present danger"—so that, maybe, you will think we had no alternative. Many is the time that I have declared valid a law I should never have voted to pass.

L.H.

tr/tp with ms signature 87.14

1952-5

To Charles Wyzanski

April 13, 1952 Judge Learned Hand's Chambers

Dear Charlie:

[...]I have never said, so far as I know, that a judge must not seek about for standards which the words do not express.[82] Interpretation is a baffling process, and I shall not try in a letter to define what I think it to be. I have tried more than once and am not likely to make any better fist of it now that I am in the sere and yellow leaf.[83] The bottom of what I have meant to say about it is that it is not a license for the judge to enforce his own choice or solution of the conflict of interests before him. My own view is that he must project imaginatively from what sources he can find the probable solution by which the authority who uttered the words would have met the occasion which has arisen, and which has not been expressly provided for. I think I am as aware as you can be of all the hazards involved, but it does seem to me that that is *toto caelo* a different process from intruding one's own solution. My complaint against our constitutional function is that it compels us to attempt this duty without anything that can be called a jural principle at all, with nothing more than a counsel of moderation. I am thinking especially of the Fifth and Fourteenth Amendments, but if I had time, I should not despair of including the First. Some of the others, e.g., the Sixth, are not subject to this criticism.

As for the "clear and present danger" postulate: I dissent from it in principle and in origin. You know my reverence of O.W.H. It is much more abject that yours, for he fits

---

82. LH evidently responds to a typescript of Wyzanski's essay entitled *A Trial Judge's Freedom and Responsibility*, specifically on questions of interpretation, free speech, and Holmes's formula, "clear and present danger." Delivered as the Annual Cardozo Lecture at the Association of the Bar of New York in July 1952, it was published in 65 HARV. L. REV. 1281 (1952). *See also* CHARLES WYZANSKI, JR., WHEREAS: A JUDGE'S PREMISES: ESSAYS IN JUDGMENT, ETHICS AND THE LAW 9–24 (1964).

83. *Cf.* "My way of life/ Is fall'n into the sere, the yellow leaf [...] " MACBETH, V, iii.

into my set of morals and beliefs better than into yours. But this stone, which by some strange chance, or as I should say mischance, "the head of the corner," was thrown out *en passant* to explain the affirmance of a conviction which a little later he and Brandeis would not, I fancy, have affirmed. When O.W.H. later said that every argument was an "incitement" or was it "instigation"?—he permanently perverted the whole question, and left us to wallow in a morass that we are not likely to get out of just because of the immense prestige of his name and Brandeis's, and of the very natural and highly commendable indignation which our incredible antics have now aroused.[84] No one can feel any more indignation about them than I; I even ask myself whether they may not be the beginning of the end. All old men do that.

I hesitate to write what I am now going to, because it is indeed an act of arrogance to assume that one has an answer where so many have failed. I ask you to excuse the categorical way I put it and to interpolate all the "it seems to mes," "I am disposed to thinks," "so far as I am able to see," etc., etc., that would make it more seemly. They are there, all right, but they impede discourse, and when I write to one who in any event knows me and my temper, I believe that they are not necessary.

The privilege of debate, discussion, and unsanctioned expression presupposes that there are no orthodoxies so absolute that they may not be wrong. Or else if there are any such, the only justification for questioning them is that the ensuing debate may bring the utterer to the right belief. Whenever a society commits itself to this principle, it has no infallible orthodoxy, or it trusts that error will be best answered by not being repressed. However, there is one orthodoxy which is inevitable: that conduct which a society forbids it does not permit. If it provides means for changing its prohibition, it should be understood to forbid other means. While the prohibition stands, only the permitted means are lawful. Any kind of effort directed to procure change by the permitted means is therefore lawful, none other.

So far I am dealing in tautology. What of speech as a means? There's the rub. I draw the line between that kind of speech which from the earliest time, e.g., Bracton, has been taken to make one an "accessory."[85] (You can find it still in our Criminal Code.) In our court we have tried to define it several times, and strangely enough [William O.] Douglas adopted our definition in our opinion. It has been an effort to describe that attitude towards a project by which one adopts it as one's own purpose and seeks to bring it to pass. It makes no difference whether the "overt act" be verbal or material; words may be the very best of all means to bring the end to pass. There can rationally be no meaning in saying that a man is positively protected in a verbal attempt to bring about conduct which is itself forbidden. All preliminaries whose purpose is to effect the result are parts of its authorship, and the law is concerned only with authorship.

It follows that whenever a man attempts by words to bring about an unlawful act, at however remote a time and however feebly, he has no protection from the "privilege of free speech." It may be the height of folly to interfere—more often than not it is—it was unwise

84. The "clear and present danger" test was first presented in *Schenck v. United States,* in which the Supreme Court upheld Schenck's conviction under the Espionage Act. *See* 1919-2 To Holmes, April 1, note 146.

85. For Bracton, see 1951-6 To Frankfurter, June 8, note 67.

in my judgment in the *Dennis* case. But that is a question of more or less; the utterer has no "right" to speak, merely it may be prudent not to stop him; e.g., people won't understand that he did not have such a "right." It may also be a good reason, for that too-repressive repression, even of what could be repressed, will frighten people who in fact will keep within the bounds of "discussion"; i.e., who do not attempt to bring about forbidden conduct. That again is a matter of wise toleration or of conduct not to be seriously apprehended.

But, you will ask, suppose a man utters what he knows will in fact provoke forbidden conduct. He means to show how desirable it is to get rid of the prohibition; he ridicules it, he denounces it. Suppose he is advised that in his audience there are those who will surely take what he says as a cue for unlawful acts. What then? I would answer that unless he seeks to bring about that result he is free to go to the limit. That is the privilege of free speech and it is a dangerous privilege to grant. I will revert to the parallel familiar enough in torts. A. causes B. damage; suppose his own interest to be an excuse, though his act be deliberate, it will toll that privilege if his net is not for the purpose of protecting the interest. It is the purpose that counts; there never can be a legal purpose to bring about a forbidden act.

The only place that I can find for "clear and present danger" is the doubt whether in all possible settings one has the privilege of saying what one will so long as one's purpose is right. I confess that that goes a great way—maybe too far. If it is too far, then I concede that something like "clear, etc." is necessary. But practically those are not the cases that make the trouble. The decisions which raise the outcry are substantially always those in which the accused is doing his best to provoke a forbidden act: he has associated himself in the venture, whether near or far in the future. I cannot agree that anyone ever has a privilege to do that, yet nearly all the complaints are of convictions of such. As I have said; often—indeed, usually—I would pass by such things, but only because on the whole they seemed to me either trivial or the prosecution [of them] likely to be misunderstood.

I feel like Pascal: "I am sorry to have written so long a letter; I didn't have time for a short one."[86] Thine, L.H.

ms with signature, Wyzanski Papers, HLL, Box 2, Folder 9

To Learned Hand from Charles Wyzanski

April 20, 1952 39 Fayerweather street, Cambridge, Massachusetts

Dear Judge Hand:

I have wrestled with the part of your letter of April 13th that deals with "the clear and present danger" test in free speech controversies. And though I am not unmoved, I am un-persuaded.

Let me begin by striking at what I regard as the weak joint in your armor: the doctrine that there is no difference in the test for political as distinguished from other forms of speech,

86. "Je n'ai fait celle-ci plus longue que parce que je n'ai pas eu le loisir de la faire plus courte." Blaise Pascal, *Letter 16, in* LETTRES PROVINCIALES 1657 (H.F. Stewart ed., 1920).

purpose, and effect. I concede that as to the non-political arena, the state which outlaws conduct has the power (and the sanction of experience as well as the sanction of the common opinion of thoughtful men) to outlaw any speech delivered with the intent of furthering that conduct. If the state forbids murder, larceny, etc., it can punish a defendant who urges another to kill or steal, even though the proposed crime is to be committed a decade hence. To punish the speech may be foolish, for there is a chance of repentance or change of purpose and plan. And ordinarily as the common law of attempts has developed, the lawmakers have chosen to ignore solicitation to commit a crime at some remote date. (See O.W.H.'s Lowell lectures.) But this is up to the lawmaker and has no constitutional overtones.

In the political field, experience, history plus philosophy, has introduced considerations which are not present in ordinary controversies as to conduct and misconduct. Of course, a state has the right to forbid persons to use force or also—and this is important—passive resistance to alter the form of government, or even to prevent the execution of a particular law. Does it follow that the state is warranted in outlawing speech deliberately aimed to encourage such active or passive resistance? Before invoking the analogy of the ordinary criminal law as an answer, I submit certain distinctive considerations applicable only to political discussion. All political talk is more than criticism or historical analysis or prophecy. It is advocacy. The speaker intends, if only to a limited degree, to persuade. And if the law or institution at which the speech is directed is sufficiently fundamental and the speaker sufficiently sophisticated, he must recognize that the change he advocates will not be effectuated without active or passive resistance to the law as it now stands. He who advocates the abolition of slavery or of private property or of imperial control of a colony knows that at some stage something in addition to the force of reason must be applied to accomplish his end. He himself may not be prepared to take the intermediate steps, but it is his purpose to arouse his hearers, of whom he knows some are bolder spirits. If the test be the test of ordinary criminal law, he is guilty. But society, or at least our community, has not felt justified in so strict a view, because free speech in the political area has so many advantages. Complete suppression of incitement to resistance would deprive us of creative ideas, novel insights, and ordinary outlets for disgruntled men. We have laid it down that the advocacy of disobedience or violent change shall go unpunished unless the circumstances show that the speaker intends that his audience shall act, if not forthwith at least before the audience can be dissuaded. Or at least, this is how I read Brandeis's gloss in *Whitney* upon "the clear and present danger test."[87]

Of course, if the speaker or the audience have at their command weapons, the paraphernalia of resistance, or a foreign ally ready to spring into the melée, the authorities can reasonably conclude that there is no time for dissuasion and punishment is timely. Perhaps in *Dennis* the proof was available that the USSR was ready to take a violent course in our domestic affairs and that the danger was immediate. But the proof was not before the 1940 (?) Congress which enacted the Smith Act. And I had supposed it was not before any court that heard or reviewed the case. So I should have voted with Black and Douglas JJ[...]

Affectionately, Charlie

ms with signature 108.17

87. I.e., Whitney v. California, 274 U.S. 357 (1927).

1952-6

To Edmond N. Cahn[88]

May 12, 1952

Dear Professor Cahn:

I have read the reprint of your article, "Authority and Responsibility" and have been much interested.[89] I have no defense for my inconsistencies; as my future continues to foreshorten, I hope I become increasingly less concerned about my fate as a thinker. However, there is a real difference between us which can lead to much difference in result. No one could have deeper regard than I—I was about to say reverence—for John Chipman Gray,[90] but I wish to put myself as reverently as I can in opposition to the passage which you quote from *The Nature and Sources of Law*. One of the most constant factors—I was almost about to say the only constant factor—in "interpretation" is the imaginative projection of the concrete situation upon the generalized statement which comes before the judge as his imperative. Two possible approaches are quite different: (1) shall the judge use his private conclusion of what is "right"; or (2) shall he attempt to hypostatize what the authors of the words would have said had they been confronted with the occasion. In my judgment much of the failure of our American jurisprudence is owing to the adoption of the first approach, and I had forgotten that Gray ever espoused it. When such language as "good moral character" is adopted as the standard, perhaps the issue becomes practically impossible to apply, and I concede that it is less so if the judge is to look to his personal notions of right or propriety. But as I view it, that only means that such a standard is a bad one, though hardly more so than lots of others we have to wrestle with.

It would take a good deal more than the compass of one letter for me to attempt to justify this conclusion, which some of the best minds of my acquaintance repudiate. Perhaps some time when we have an opportunity to talk it over, I can make a more plausible defense for it than obviously at the present it has in your mind. Thank you for sending me the reprint.

Sincerely yours, [Learned Hand]

tp 85.25

---

88. Edmond N. Cahn (1906–1964): Professor, New York University Law School.

89. In a letter dated May 5, 1952, Cahn asked LH for an assessment of his article, *Authority and Responsibility*, in which he criticizes LH's decisions in *Iorio v. Day*, 34 F.2d 920 (2d Cir. 1929), and *Berlandi v. Reimer*, 113 F.2d 429 (2d Cir. 1940), asserting that they gave weight to "the common conscience" and so "seriously distorted the court's function, because instead of exercising such influence as he [i.e., LH] could to raise the morals of the marketplace to a level approaching his own, he expressed an attitude of resignation [. . .] [His] opinion [in *Berlandi*] lends aid and comfort to those who would palliate the practice of evil." *Authority and Responsibility*, 51 COLUM. L. REV. 838, 841 (1951). See Edmond Cahn's further criticism of LH on judicial review in THE MORAL DECISION: RIGHT AND WRONG IN THE LIGHT OF AMERICAN LAW (1955).

90. John Chipman Gray (1839–1915): Professor, Harvard Law School, 1869–1913.

1952-7

To Bernard Berenson

August 5, 1952 Cunard Line, R. H. S. "Mauretania"

Dear B.B.:

I am at long last on board this ship bound home; I ask myself why and especially why I did not leave the island of Great Britain. The answer is not easy; in fact I do not quite know it. On the whole, I am disposed to put it down to the fact that at 80 I do not feel quite up to being pushed about in crowded hotels, where if one does not book oneself in advance and follow the schedule rigidly, one may have to put up with a shambles for a berth. I have very repeatedly thought that we should go to France and then to Italy where I could have seen you; but frankly the effort and the eternal piecing together in a rigid pattern, inflexibly impractical, seemed to me rather more than I could face. So here I find myself confined to the unsatisfactory means of communication by writing and bound back home to arrive in mid-August. We have spent more time in London than anywhere else, enough so that for the first time I began to feel a little at home there. My better acquaintance with the people more deeply imbued me than ever with a recognition of those qualities which have always satisfied me that spiritually they stand at the top. On the other hand, I must own that even in the space of eight months since I was last here, they do not accept the new order to which they are subjected with that absence of querulousness which I so much admired in them and which I did not find at all among our countrymen when the "New Deal" began to strike them. They do "grouse" a good deal, I mean the exploited upper classes.

But that is only a detail and they have been terribly tried, so that in the whole picture it has not assumed a dominant importance; they remain tolerant, brave, considerate, and civilized; sometimes I ask myself whether any other people can claim as much. But still I do not love the land as I love Italy; beautiful as are the long reaches of meadow and cultivated fields, and romantic as are the Scotch moors with their endless succession of color, there is to me more in the pleasure I get as I look upon any landscape in Italy. There is written the long history of man with all its tragedy of endless labor and its persistent belief that, in the words of William James, life on any terms, however straitened and painful, is to be accepted as better than non-existence. That and the matchless splendor of the mountains and the whole vast collections of centuries gathered up and open to all to see will never have their equal. I regret more than I can say that although every opportunity was open to me, I waited till I was 50 before ever I broke in upon it. True, that first descent from Silva Plana (I wonder if I have remembered the right name) to Como was even then an unforgettable and is a never forgotten experience of what the World did have and what I never availed myself of[...]

You were more than kind to write me that you could understand why I did not go to Italy. I have felt a kind of guilt at not doing so, which I tried to explain, however unconvincingly, at the outset. I will not try again.

Affectionately, L.H.

ms with signature 99.21

1952-8

To Learned Hand from Felix Frankfurter

October 26, 1952 Supreme Court of the United States

Dear B.:

Whether the "mass media" have drowned out individual voices or we've had no voices to make themselves felt, the fact is that in recent years no influential voices have been heard on behalf of Reason. Happily you have acquired authority appropriate to your powers, and you could not have employed your well-earned authority to more needed ends than the use to which you put it in your Albany address.[91] And so I do not even begrudge the effort that you may thereby have withdrawn from work on the Holmes Lectures, all the prose which as you know, I much covet from you[...] Love to Frances. Please send me the full text of the Albany address.

Ever yours, F.F.

ms with signature 105C.17

To Felix Frankfurter

October 30, 1952 Judge Learned Hand's Chambers

F.F.:

I suppose I ought to have seen that the tail end of what I said at the "Convocation" would get the publicity it did. As matter of fact, it was not entirely relevant to the main theme, which was the need of some study of the "Humanities" as preparation for political duties in a democracy. It did seem relevant enough, however, to drag in as a kind "stinger" in the coda what I most fear in the present time: McCarthy and his Cartesian Crew. (Peace to the Shades of the Great Blaise [Pascal]). Sometimes I ask myself whether a deep demon does not really lead me to publicity "stunts" while my public upper cortical centers strike noble attitudes in apology. Which is the Real Self?

---

91. In an address delivered at the University of the State of New York on October 24, 1952, LH argues that the "humanities" are essential to political wisdom: "The imagination can be purged and the judgment ripened only by an awareness of the slow, hesitant, wayward course of human life, its failures, its successes, but its indomitable will to endure." Implicitly criticizing the politics of McCarthy—"Risk for risk, for myself I had rather take my chance that some traitors will escape detection than spread abroad a spirit of general suspicion and distrust, which accept rumor and gossip in place of undismayed and unintimidated inquiry"—LH concludes by quoting passages on wisdom from the *Apocrypha* 7:22–3, 8:8–9, 11–12. *See* A Plea for the Open Mind and Free Discussion, *in* THE SPIRIT OF LIBERTY, 274–85, 276. *See also Sources of Tolerance, in* THE SPIRIT OF LIBERTY, 66–83.

But that's enough of that. I do shy off the lectures and I suppose I am taking chances, for all my friends, so it seems, of anywhere near my time have either gone off the deep end or are getting thromboses or slow cerebral palsy or other unpleasant preliminaries to what the docs euphemistically call "terminal pneumonias." I dread meeting you, for, damn you, you will be arousing me to "my better self," a phantom whom I should like to be rid of for the time that remains. Meanwhile I do always look for what you say and morally go along with it, unless it be some comment about myself [...]

Thine, L.H.

ms with signature 105C.17

To Learned Hand from Felix Frankfurter

November 13, 1952 Supreme Court of the United States

Dear B.:

Of course, the newspapers would quote what they quoted and with good reason. For you uttered views with unusual felicity and weight regarding what might be called the overreaching issue of our day. I use that big adjective because our attitude towards the nature of man—that is really at the core of the business—not only is what is ultimately at stake in our conflict with the Russians but is also at stake in the way in which we manage that conflict. I think it is not too difficult to demonstrate that the practical, day-to-day actions that are taken or ought to be taken are referable to one's outlook on the central issue. I do not think it was dragged into your convocation address. It flowed inevitably from your main discussion and was its appropriate coda.

But don't palm off on me the Puritan aspect of your nature. Don't charge me with trying to arouse your "better self." I know something about the constant and too often uncomfortable debate that goes on inside you between the Puritan and the Pagan. I daresay I know it because, within my limited capacity, I have been watching that struggle going on for these many years in Marion. But you fellows must expect to pay for your rich natures. In any event, in your more reflective moments at least, remember that while you fellows pay for it, we are the beneficiaries of the personalities compounded of these contradictions and conflicts. I don't mean to deny that I want you to do the Holmes Lectures. Nor even to deny that I want you to do them not merely for the satisfaction which I know you will have once you have done them. I also want them because I am confident you can do not a little to dissipate a good deal of the nonsense that is now current as "liberalism." If I had the good fortune to have a chance of jawing with you we would talk of many things, but I have to intermit.

Ever yours, F.F.

tp with ms signature 105C.17

1953-1

To Felix Frankfurter

March 20, 1953 Judge Learned Hand's Chambers

Dear F.F.

[...]I wish I felt freer to talk to you about the Vincent episode but we all promised each other, and I think rightly, that we would say nothing about it outside.[92] It is, however, proper enough for me to say that when [John Foster] Dulles[93] called me on the telephone and said that he did not need us, I replied: "Is there any gift that you can think of that you would like that I can give you?" My dear friend, I do not think I ever have been so much "philogrobolized" by any mass of incoherent documents as those, on which I put in three or four weeks' work in January[...] The volumes of verbiage almost broke the back of one of the smartest boys I have had for a long time. But of all this more when we meet. My love to the Marquise.

Thine, L.H.

tp with ms signature 105C.18

To Learned Hand from Felix Frankfurter

March 25, 1953 Supreme Court of the United States

Dear B.:

[...]Please recite on "philogrobolized." All I can get out of the O.E.D. is the use of the word in a quotation from Rabelais. How did you come to annex it? Not that I have not long been aware of the range and richness of your vocabulary, but I am curious about this particular one[...] You can't come down here too soon for the pleasure of Marion and myself.

Ever yours, F.F.

tp with ms signature and notes 105C.18

To Felix Frankfurter

March 30, 1953 Judge Learned Hand's Chambers

Dear F.F.:

In re "philogrobolized": the judgment of Panurge[94] was by all odds more like the opinions of Chief Justice White in the *Standard Oil* and *American Tobacco* cases than any other

---

92. At the request of Secretary of State Dean Acheson, LH chaired an advisory review panel to determine whether the decision of the Civil Service Commission's Loyalty Review Board, which found that John Carter Vincent, a career diplomat, had demonstrated a doubtful loyalty to the government of the United States, was correct. Before LH's committee could reach a determination, Dulles cleared Vincent.

93. John Foster Dulles (1888–1959): Secretary of State, 1953–1959.

94. LH refers to Book Three, chapter 43, of The Histories of Gargantua and Pantagruel by the sixteenth-century author François Rabelais; there, Panurge, in the character of the learned fool,

opinion that I know or have even heard of.[95] I must refer you to it because any attempt at a summary would be criminal.

There had been a great lawsuit between the Lords Suckfist and Kissbreach; it had gone on, as I remember, for twenty years and all the jurists of France had delved into it and groped about in it. Finally, the exhibits and the testimony had grown so great in bulk that it required twenty mules to carry them. The jurists having debated and debated, and quarreled and quarreled, finally declared that they were at an end. They were completely "philogrobolized," and so they asked Panurge to give judgment. That he did expeditiously and with a torrent of judicial wisdom which has never been equaled. I do not mean that it never will be, for I apprehend that there is a suit, now pending in the Southern District of New York, i.e., *United States v. The Investment Bankers*,[96] that ought to, and as I fervently pray may, match in bulk and complexity and in wisdom the French precedent. When it is done, if it ever is, I shall expect of your Court a judgment comparable, yes, by God, equal to that of Panurge. I suggest that there will be no impropriety in your all getting out your Rabelais and pursuing that celebrated judgment and considering whether you ought not to take it as at least a model of whatever you collectively say. Indeed, it would be highly desirable to have each one write such an opinion. Opinions under the Sherman Act are by all odds the most important work of our courts; I rejoice to think that their size and numbers have crowded out lesser controversies which merely concern the ordinary troubles of mankind and do not give opportunity for far-reaching stratospheric flights into the Empyrean. In consideration of which, Mr. Justice, I have the honor to subscribe myself, as ever

Yr humble and obedt servt always at your command. Hand of Shoreham[97]

tp with ms notes and signature 105C.18

1953-2

To George F. Kennan[98]

May 21, 1953

Dear Mr. Kennan:

I have not the good fortune to know you personally, although I have read some of your writings, but your address to the Princeton alumni last February has added so much to the

---

defends the jurisprudence of Judge Bridlegoose, who decides cases by a roll of dice, on the grounds that the decisions of Bridlegoose are never overturned.

95. *See* Standard Oil Co. v. United States, 221 U.S. 1 (1911), and United States v. Am. Tobacco Co., 221 U.S. 106 (1911). Both cases were brought under the Sherman Antitrust Act and yielded extensive and complicated opinions from the Court.

96. This is a reference to *United States v. Morgan*, 118 F. Supp. 621 (S.D.N.Y. 1953). The court's opinion ran to 204 pages.

97. LH assumes the name he might have had in sixteenth-century England; his father's family homestead was in Shoreham, Vermont.

98. George Frost Kennan (1904–2005): United States Foreign Service, 1927–1952; ambassador to the Soviet Union, 1952–1953; Professor of Historical Studies, Institute for Advanced Study, 1953. For LH on Kennan as a "mature thinker," see 1954-8 To Frankfurter, July 12.

admiration that I had already felt for you that I must tell you of it. I have no acquaintance with current international affairs except such as comes from a superficial and cursory reading of the newspapers, but I have been many years a judge and that from time to time has compelled me to think about constitutional issues, which in some of their aspects are quite like international questions. What you deprecate—the belief that such conflicts can be dealt with by a resort to wide generalizations—I too have come to believe is the surest path to failure. I dread, perhaps most of all, the upright, devoted man of principle; and if you have been exposed, as perhaps you have, to the way in which the courts have generally dealt with those broad admonitions of moderation that are crystallized in the early Amendments, you may have found much to bear out your misgivings about our general habits of thinking.

A time of such serious demoralization and confusion as this inevitably predisposes men to seek refuge in inspired declarations, ample enough to give room to the immediately desired solution. It is a strange and disconcerting symptom that the younger lawyers, who are apt to have so large a part in the conduct of public affairs, are reviving "Natural Law"[99] which we of my own generation believed was a ghost forever laid in the nineteenth century. I was especially interested that the chief antidote you suggested was as large a dose as possible of the "humanities." I have often thought that if our judges had known more of history, poetry, the plastic arts, and literature generally, they would have avoided many of those effusions that have not only confused their decisions, but have confirmed the profession at large in the belief that at a pinch there is always some *vade mecum* to lead us out of our perplexities.[100]

It is more of a comfort than you can realize to me, whose work is necessarily substantially done, to know that such as you, in the full tide of your powers, are coming on to teach the only gospel that in the end can save us: that human affairs are always a tangle, not only of fact but of conflicting values insusceptible of treatment save by patience, tolerance, imagination, and above all by the wider horizons opened alone by an acquaintance with our still enmeshed savage inheritance.

I hope you will forgive so very long a letter; I can offer no excuse except that you have stirred in me a gratitude too warm to suppress.

Sincerely yours, [Learned Hand]

tp 91.14

---

99. For LH on "Natural Law," see 1952-1 To Berenson, February 17.

100. Hand emphasizes the importance of the humanities and social sciences to the law in his address to the Juristic Society of the University of Pennsylvania Law School in June 1930: "I venture to believe that it is as important to a judge called upon to pass on a question of constitutional law to have at least a bowing acquaintance with Acton and Maitland, with Thucydides, Gibbon and Carlyle, with Homer, Dante, Shakespeare and Milton, with Machiavelli, Montaigne and Rabelais, with Plato, Bacon, Hume and Kant, as with the books which have been specifically written on the subject... Judges must be aware of the changing social tensions in every society which make it an organism; which demand new schemata of adaptation; which will disrupt it, if rigidly confined." *Sources of Tolerance, in* The Spirit of Liberty 66–83, 81. Similarly, in his address to the University of the State of New York on October 24, 1952, LH observes: "[the humanities] are fitted to admonish us how tentative and provisional are our attainments, intellectual and moral; and how often the deepest convictions or one generation are the rejects of the next... The imagination can be purged and the judgment ripened only by an awareness of the slow, hesitant wayward course of human life, its failures, its successes, but its indomitable will to endure." *A Plea for an Open Mind and Free Discussion, in* The Spirit of Liberty 274–85, 83.

To Learned Hand from George F. Kennan

May 29, 1953 — 2714 Quebec Street, Washington, D.C.

Dear Judge Hand:

It is difficult for me to describe the feelings with which I received and read your kind letter of May 21. They were not just ones of gratification; chief among them was rather a strengthened sense of responsibility in the face of the tasks that fate seems to have placed upon me. I know that you have no reason to flatter people and are too wise to make serious misjudgment of the value of ideas. For this reason, I accept what you say not only as a mark of kindness and encouragement for which I am deeply grateful, but also as a timely warning that have taken on myself a great deal in venturing to speak to people as I have, that many of them are beginning to look to me with confidence and expectation in time of great confusion and bewilderment, and that this represents a heavy responsibility to which I shall never be fully adequate, and to which I may prove not adequate at all unless I hold myself to rigorous standards.

It was never my ambition or plan to become a teacher and philosopher. Of the things I have said to people that evoked public comment and approval, many seemed to me at the time to be only poor re-statements of propositions that were either self-evident or were part of the basic fund of moral precepts with which I supposed most Americans had been provided and in which I am sure many people are still far better versed than myself. What had surprised me is that assertions so elementary should prove so useful to people, and I can only assume from this that education in our time has been even poorer and the process of forgetfulness even greater than I had supposed. If so, this again simply emphasizes the responsibility of those of us on whom these precepts seem to have left a deeper imprint.

I enclose the text of some remarks I recently made at the University of Notre Dame, which you might wish to note. When I drafted these two speeches, the one at Princeton and the one at Notre Dame, I was not yet familiar with the address which you delivered before the Juristic Society of the University of Pennsylvania Law School in June 1930. I have now read that address, and am happy to feel that some of the things I mentioned had been noted much earlier, and expressed much better, by someone wiser than my self.

Very sincerely yours, George Kennan

tp with ms signature 91.14

1954-1

To Learned Hand from Bernard Berenson

December 31, 1953 — Settignano

Dear B.:

I cannot let the year end without telling you why I do not write oftener. I have discovered the reason at last. It is this: a day seldom passes that I do not carry on long talks with you. To write them down would take the rest of the day. So I give up. I do not write at all[...]

I make sounds and hope for the resurrection of a presidential authority and the fight against a "hick" of a Senator. At bottom it looks like a fight between a senate and executive for conduct of foreign affairs. I am surprised at the tolerance of McCarthy on the part of so many acquaintances at home. Every good wish to you both for 1954. May it bring us together.

Ever affectionately, B.B.

ms with signature 99.22

To Bernard Berenson

January 3, 1954

Dear B.B.:

[...]We are in a hopeless division over here, a division that I fear the Democrats will seize upon to their advantage. It is not that I love the Republicans more, but at this juncture I do dread that paralysis that has often struck us when we can have no government at all because Congress and the President are of opposite parties. The Republicans have themselves of late been displaying the most shameless partisanship, apparently hoping to play upon the success of the unspeakable McCarthy—a success that continues to amaze me as I learn the extent of it. As I analyze it, though I am not sure that I am right, it has a background that cannot be understood in Europe, and that perhaps even you, who have been away so long, may not have fully grasped. It does take the form of a genuine panic about Russia, and something vaguely disruptive and vastly infecting of which Russia is the immediate expression: Communism. Communism is not much examined, but the loyal feel that it is the outgrowth of a long tolerated mood of skepticism about the fundamental tenets of the Good Life. It shades into and is in the end indistinguishable from "Subversiveness," and that in its turn is Heresy, which must at all costs be suppressed. You and I are "Subversives"; so is everybody else who disagrees with those elemental tenets of the American Way of Life—whatever these may be. Behind all this facade is, I believe, the deep cleavage of feeling between that part of the people who live west of the Appalachian Range and the Atlantic Coast, especially this City of New York. It is, more over, a reaction against the twenty years during which "That Man" (F.D.R) surrendered us to alien waves of opinion and agitation in which we surrendered the traditions that had made us what we are—God help us.

Well, that may be wrong, but I can get a good many witnesses to confirm my view. And, indeed, it is not a feeling from which the East is free either, there is plenty of it in New England too. But I rather think that the strength of it is across the Range. Eisenhower[101]

101. Dwight David Eisenhower (1890–1969): Supreme Commander of Allied forces in Europe, 1943–1944; Chief of Staff, 1945–1948; President of Columbia University, 1948–1950; supreme commander of the Allied Powers in Europe, 1951–1952; President of the United States, 1953–1958.

you must judge with the utmost lenity; his position is nearly impossible. He cannot rule as a coalition-president—that won't wash—and he has really not even a slack wire on which to walk. He is not a clever man but he is something better than that—he is a just and a selfless man really bent on doing all he can for his people. Granted the impossible position he is in, I am rather disposed to think that he is about as well fitted for the job as we were likely to get. The call of all the wise ones has been for more "positive action"; "he does not know what he wants, or what to do," etc., etc. Good God, does not everyone in any public office—even a judge—know that kind of critic?[...] My love to the beloved Nicky.

Affectionately, L.H.

ms with signature 99.22

To Learned Hand from Bernard Berenson

January 9, 1954 Settignano

Dear B.:

[...]Your account or rather picture of the political situation at home sounds as if it was going to resemble what already has been the case in France for years, is now definitely taking place here, and even threatening England. Even there both leading parties are threatened with splitting up. It would look as if, except in W. Germany, parties could no longer hold together, or that faction rather than common interest is going to dominate. Or is it political impotence based on the fanaticism of nihilism?

What can you hope from a government which rouses the population to madness over a trivial matter like Trieste, or falls victim to mass fury that threatens its position in world politics as is the case with Italy and Trieste. And France, sunk to an absolute indifference and yet expecting us to prevent Germany from reasserting herself as the strongest power save Russia on the European Continent: good sense should lead them to recognize the inevitable and to try to make friends with Germany! So be good children and plan to join us in Venice.

Love to you both, B.B.

ms with signature 99.22

To Bernard Berenson

January 24, 1954

Dear B.B.:

[...]I always lapse into political vaporizing when I write you, hoping that you will be interested in any sidelights from home. I think I told you in my last that a conservative reaction is underway, based a good deal upon the latent but violent dislike of the Atlantic Seaboard by all the country west of the mountains. Indeed, there is more in it than that: all the welled-up anger and frustration of twenty years at F.D.R. and [his] successor are striving to assert themselves. They are finding a frenetic ultra-nationalism the most convenient tool at hand, and I fear the Republicans are prepared to use it without scruple or decency. McCarthy still stalks about unimpeded, and everyone is afraid of him. [... I] wish I could hope that he would in the end be disclosed as T. O.[102] was, though I don't want him whipped at a cart's tail.

Don't be hard on Eisenhower. At your distance from here, he may indeed look feeble and indecisive but to my mind that is an inadequate judgment. He is declaring himself with more and more vigor, and has staged a top-notch fight about the "Bricker Amendment."[103] Presumably you know about that, but on the chance that you do not I will try to give you the outlines. It is a proposed amendment to the Constitution aimed at circumscribing the Treaty Powers of the President. The Conferences of Yalta, Tehran, and Potsdam[104] are the horrendous examples, the "gory heads" shaken at us to right us into a kind of paralysis of power over international questions with the hope that the executive may not enslave us. It is 1787 all over again: a speech of Holman,[105] one of the chief proponents of the change, reads almost verbatim like Patrick Henry's speech against the Constitution in the Virginia Convention. The really deadly section is what has come to be known as the "which" clause. This would make impossible any treaty by which we gave as a consideration to another nation any provision favoring their nationals that involved any change in the municipal law of the states. Every state would have the power to cancel the treaty *pro tanto*, for it would be *brutum fulmen* in all states that did not affirmatively accept it. It would be extreme to say that this would make all treaties impossible, for it would not affect those in which our *quid pro quo* was something that lay within the scope of our federal as distinct from our state resources, but it would put an end forever to any mutual concessions of internal domestic privileges. And yet, such is the fantastic obsession of many of the good bourgeois—the "common man" doesn't know what it is all about—that the American Bar Association voted for the damn thing by a large majority!! *O tempora; O mores*!!!![106]

Well, that gives you some notion of how far we have got from any internationalism. And yet there are donkeys—and highly intellectual donkeys at that—who wish us to attempt an international state shaped in the image of our own Union. But, I know, I know, it's bad for an old bloke like me to pour out his grievances to another old bloke like you. Somehow, some time, we may pull out of it. I am not so dreary as I seem. After all, we do seem to keep up—so far—this fabulous industrialism of ours, and if we can keep it going, that may pull us out. Love to my adored Nicky.

Affectionately, L.H.

ms with signature 99.22

---

102. I.e., Titus Oates, English fabricator of the Popish Plot.

103. The Bricker Amendment, sponsored by Senator John W. Bricker of Ohio, was designed to restrict the scope of treaties with foreign governments; it failed to pass the Senate in 1954. The Committee for Defense of the Constitution by Preserving the Treaty Power was composed of attorneys, legal scholars, former cabinet members, and others in the business community who opposed Bricker's proposal. *See Leaders to Fight Bricker Proposal*, N.Y. TIMES, Dec. 28, 1953, at 3.

104. Tehran, December 1943; Yalta, February 1945; Potsdam, July and August 1945.

105. Frank E. Holman (1886–1961): President, The American Bar Association, 1948–1949.

106. "Oh the times, Oh the customs." Cicero, *Oratio in Catilinam Prima*; the first oration against Catiline.

To Learned Hand from Bernard Berenson

January 31, 1954 Settignano

My dear B.:

[...]I am alarmed by your encouraging view of Eisenhower. The fact is that I recall Grant, his popularity, and his failure. It led me early to study the soldier as statesman. I have discovered precious few. Even Caesar seems to have been a failure after all his conquests, not knowing what to make of a world at his feet [...]

You are prodigiously photogenic. I enclose a reproduction of a photo. Please do send me the photo itself. I want to put it with my *lares* and *penates* to my left. Despite snow and sleet and cold and wind, it is very beautiful here in a wintry way and I enjoy it with my eyes, my lungs, and my feet.

Love to you both, B.B.

ms with signature 99.23

To Bernard Berenson

March 21, 1954

Dear B.B.:

I sent you a photograph some time ago, which may, however, not have arrived before this, because it went by ordinary post. I think that it is the one you spoke of.[107]

Things here with us do not seem to mend. I can't say that they grow worse, but it would be wholly wrong to suppose that they grow better. We seem to be teetering with a depression, in the face of which the stock market chooses to grow higher and higher. The only explanation I can think of is [that] the people have come to believe that the only way out for us is the same chosen elsewhere: inflation. You simply cannot get people—the "people"—to consent to tax themselves. The Democrats are taking an unconscionable advantage of the Republicans and will probably succeed in spite of Eisenhower's admirable effort to avoid more indebtedness.

It is strange and sad to feel repelled whichever way one looks. If one looks to the Democrats one sees, or thinks one sees, a typical egalitarian party that will deny nothing to the ordinary voter, and will not hesitate to endanger the whole stability of the country by financial excess. If one looks to the Republicans, one sees as fantastic and outrageous an appeal to primitive passions as we have ever had there. Feeling that they have nothing else to gain, they are willing to back the unspeakable McCarthy, and the worst of it is that they may be right. Not only are they correct in thinking that they do have nothing else, but the amazing and appalling thing is that this is an issue that has the most extraordinary support. You would not believe the kind of people who approve of what he is doing.

I put it down to something quite different than, or at any rate quite additional to, Communism. The well-fixed Tory, the sound Bourbon, has been building up a concentrated

107. LH refers to Alfred Eisenstaedt's photograph of him, now on the cover of the first edition of Gerald Gunther, Learned Hand: the Man and the Judge.

fury for twenty years. All the frustration, all the impotence that he suffered during the Roosevelt era, has now found an outlet, and, after the manner of all Bourbons, he has forgot nothing and learned nothing. Here is an issue come from Heaven to help him keep his accidental advantage of Eisenhower's personal popularity. Appeal to the atavism that lurks in us all, abandon all our professions of a rational society, and win on the issue of our desperate peril from within: "Nous sommes trahis." That's the ace that will win the jackpot. McCarthy is a symptom rather than a cause.

Well, that's my guess, and you ought, I think, not to blame Eisenhower too much for what looks at your distance like flaccid lethargy. If you knew the strength of the feeling here you would, I believe, realize what a tiny margin he has, and perhaps you would feel like me that a return of the Democrats would be a doubtful cure. I fill my letter with all this dreary stuff because you have given me to believe that you want to hear this aspect of our world over here, even when it comes from one so ill placed as to appraise the situation.

The day approaches when we leave on the Andrea Dorea for Naples: April 17th [...]We mean to try to get rooms at your hotel, the Europa [in Venice], and I trust that, D.V., this may be the fruition of long hopes.[108] My love to Nicky.

Affectionately, L.H.

ms with signature 99.23

To Learned Hand from Bernard Berenson

March 23, 1954 Settignano

Dear B.:

I can't thank you enough for the photo of your good self. You are photogenic as few. I mean the photo seems to draw out on your face all that one loves best in you[...]

Ever the same, B.B.

ms with signature 99.23

1954-2

To Charles P. Curtis[109]

January 14, 1954

Dear Charlie:

Your letter and its enclosure were very welcome indeed; I read your review with much pleasure and profit. The profit was particularly that it confirmed me in my original

---

108. LH and FAH returned to the United States on June 5; they were unable to fulfill plans to meet Berenson in Venice.

109. Charles P. Curtis (1891–1959): Massachusetts attorney, editor of THE PRACTICAL COGITATOR, 1945; *see* 1946-3 To Learned Hand from Joseph B. Keenan, November 1, note 162.

unwillingness to read the "correspondence."[110] I already felt that all that I should get that I wanted I already had, and that a good deal that I did not want I might get. I was, however, glad to see that O.W.H. kept his fond disciple at a greater distance than I had feared, and was vaguely aware of the net that was being thrown for him. The unsuspecting and naive simplicity that was at the bottom of him apparently came out here again and again, and when one tries to sum him up, that remains the most endearing of his moral qualities.

As a philosopher, he never deeply impressed me; what did completely overwhelm me was his matchless craftsmanship. But penetrating as that is, to me he did not carry it over when he went out of our specialized job. Didn't you ever get a little weary of standing abashed before the size of the universe? If one starts philosophizing, must one not *in primis* distinguish between the universe of value and the universe of the actual? Mind you, I don't mean that the littleness and transience of our powers do not too often affect the realization of our values. They cabin, crib, confine them, and we must reckon with them. But I insist that values per se are absolute, peremptory, and final, and that one ought not to have the slightest respect, deference, acceptance, or rejection of masses of electrons and protons, however immeasurably large and at speeds of hundreds of light-years a year. It is I who am the uncontrolled dictator of the "good"; it is my good—this is the one *sacro egoismo*. True, I must recognize your "Good" just as I must my own future "Good," which is quite as alien to me at the moment as yours. Indeed it is accommodation of all "Goods" that is the rational meaning of all living.

Well, perhaps I was wrong in thinking he did not agree to all this, but the emphasis on "things" made me wonder. Take for instance your quote of 1895 about the soldier's faith.[111] Do you like it? I never have; perhaps it did strike close to what he liked to call "the jugular" but still it missed it. It was only because and if the soldier had made the sacrifice his personal, egoistic affirmation that I count it. I don't of course mean that as a means, a tool, to the realization of other folks' good it may not count, but he must make that realization his realization. Somewhat the same temper appeared in his self-abasement about the scope of human knowledge, how little of it we can have, etc. You remember about the mouse who used to say: "I am in the bosom of the universe." Again, I missed a less humble approach. I don't of course mean a false estimate of how short a distance we have got in fact; call it a millionth of a centimeter. But I want the enterprise of finding out to seem final and conclusive. Not seldom he seemed to me to be guilty of the contradiction: by saying "the limits of human knowledge are inherent, we can never reach the ultimate." Who was the lad who first showed up that faked humility?

---

110. LH refers to The Holmes-Laski Letters: The Correspondence of Mr. Justice Holmes and Harold J. Laski, 1916–1935, with a foreword by Felix Frankfurter (Mark De Wolfe Howe ed., 1953). For Curtis's review, see 63 Yale L.J. 266 (1953).

111. *See* Holmes's Memorial Day Address, Harvard University, 1895: "I do not know what is true. I do not know the meaning of the universe. But in the midst of doubt, in the collapse of creeds, there is one thing I do not doubt, that no man who lives in the same world with most of us can doubt, and that is that the faith is true and adorable which leads a soldier to throw away his life in obedience to a blindly accepted duty, in a cause which he little understands, in a plan of campaign of which he has little notion, under tactics of which he does not see the use." Charles P. Curtis, *The Holmes–Laski Letters*, 63 Yale L.J. 266, 274 (1953) (quoting Holmes, Speeches 59 (1934)).

As for Laski, he was a marvel; his facility was uncanny. At one time I knew him well, though I never liked him, trusted him, or had the least confidence in his conclusions. Maybe it was because the poor wight was so pathologically sensitive to the opinion of others that he could never detach himself from how he appeared. Whatever the reason, that seemed to me to corrupt all he ever did, all at least that I ever read, which was not much, it is only fair to say[...]

Thine, L.H.

tp with tp signature 86.21

1954-3

To Charles Wyzanski

February 2, 1954 Judge Learned Hand's Chambers

Dear Charlie:

I have read *The Hedgehog and the Fox*[112] and am in the midst of Sherrington.[113] I must own that the last "Book" of *War and Peace* always seemed to me plain ungarnished [sic] nonsense, and I don't think that I.B. has done anything to redeem it. However, he never touches anything without illuminating it and this is no exception, particularly to me who know nothing of Tolstoy except from his books. I did let myself get enmeshed in "Determinism v. Free Will," which does not baffle us today so much, owing, I think, to our freedom from the Augustinian necessity of squaring Personal Sin with a Divine Benignity. With that out of the way, the debate has for long seemed to me only a bit of logomachy.

More interesting is the confusion from which T. never emerged of trying to appraise human desires and values, so that there might be a preference between them that would have authority "objectively." This is to me enormously absorbing, especially at the present time when most of the current molds have been broken and people are faced with the irreconcilable raw and imperious demands of our animal nature. One thinks of the savage solution of O.W.H.! "When two men want the same thing strongly enough, the only thing to do is for one to kill the other and take it." Personally, I am doubtful that any mediating organon can be found to measure our values beyond our individual preferences, which are as absolute and "unobjective" as the values themselves. Our chance lies in imagination, i.e., an ability to put ourselves in each other's place, and a gradual slackening of our own insistences. That doesn't look promising at the moment; its place has been filled by conventions that have been able to survive until they gathered a hypostatical authority of their own, so far as its place has been filled at all. The gravity of our present crisis is the

112. I.e., Isaiah Berlin's study of Leo Tolstoy's War and Peace, The Hedgehog and the Fox; An Essay on Tolstoy's View of History (1953).

113. Probably Charles Scott Sherrington, Man on His Nature (1951).

extinction of nearly all these placebos, so that we are faced with our naked primeval natures[...]

I doubt that I shall ever try to write that "Lecture" or "Lectures" for the H.LS. The more the clouds revolve in my cranium, the less likely it seems that there will ever emerge anything worthwhile. I see from a little dipping here and there that there is a substantive body of legal opinion that shares my nihilistic attitude towards Constitutional Law after the model of the U.S.A., and I can hardly think it desirable to add to the spate. Besides, I rather think that it leads to the kind of stuff I have been writing to you now, and surely I have no place in the company of the competent in these fields. On the other hand, there is an itch that may lead me in the end to scratch, even though it leads to no more than taking off a little of my own skin. Somehow, sitting in the admiralty or equity "parts" of the D.C. for the S.D.N.Y. does not make *mon coeur délater avec joie.*[114]

Until we meet, L.H.

ms with signature, Wyzanski Papers, HLL, Box 2, Folder 9

1954-4

To Learned Hand from Felix Frankfurter

March 3, 1954 3018 Dumbarton Ave., Washington, D.C.

Dear B.:

[...]I don't know when anything so drained my almost romantic faith in Reason as did the Stevens-McCarthy affair,[115] the humiliating acquiescence of our rulers in the indecencies of a demagogic bully and their failure to safeguard those impalpable but decisive presuppositions of our national life.* Putting all moral considerations to one side, I am completely stymied in trying to understand what "they" think they are doing from their own viewpoint of the "prudent" and "practical." I give it up, except that stupidity, I believe, plays no inconsiderable part. "*Gegen die Dummheit Kampfen die Götter selbst vergebens.*"[116] If I tell you that the chief concern of "the White House staff" was "not to get the President involved," you have some measure of the *Dummheit*! And the hell of it is that I remain of the conviction that Ike is a *good* man—a right-feeling, decent creature to whom all the McCarthy business is loathsome or at least highly repellent. You remember T.R.'s crack about Taft: "Yes, Bill Taft means well, but he means well feee-bly."

---

114. I.e., my heart swell with joy.

115. In April 1954, McCarthy's exchange of charges with Secretary of the Army Robert T. Stevens led to the appointment of a special subcommittee. Chaired by Karl Mundt of South Dakota, the investigative proceedings became known as the Army-McCarthy Hearings. For LH's earlier responses to McCarthy, see 1952-3 To Carter, March 10, and 1954-1 To Berenson, January 3.

116. I.e., "With stupidity the gods themselves struggle in vain." FRIEDRICH VON SCHILLER, THE MAID OF ORLEANS, I, vi.

[...]You should have no disquietude about *Remington*.[117] The fact is that three of us voted to hear the case: the fourth didn't because of the extreme views, expressed by that essentially lawless Black, indicated the hopelessness of agreement even among those who were outraged by the Gov't's behavior. As you know I'm dead against voting dissent from denial of certs.[118] I crave for talk.

Ever yours, F.F.

*Though not at all mystical, somehow I felt as though *I* had done some grievous wrong when Stevens collapsed.

ms with signature 105B.20

To Felix Frankfurter

March 8, 1954 Judge Learned Hand's Chambers

F.F.:

It is hard, as you say, to keep one's balance in these times. Plainly "there's something rotten in the state of Denmark,"[119] so rotten that I find it difficult not to let my imagination rove down deep into the Inferno. The most discouraging part of all is how pervasively is

---

117. LH twice sat on panels for appeals by William Remington. A government economist, Remington had been accused of membership in the Communist Party and of passing information by Elizabeth Bentley, a former Soviet spy. In *United States v. Remington*, 191 F.2d 246 (2d Cir. 1951), *cert. denied*, 343 U.S. 907 (1952), the United States Court of Appeals for Second Circuit, in an opinion authored by Judge Thomas Swan, unanimously overturned Remington's conviction on perjury charges stemming from grand jury testimony during which he denied being a member of the Communist Party, finding several errors in the conduct of the original trial and in the instructions given to the jury. Prosecutors continued their pursuit of Remington, charging him with five new counts of perjury stemming from his first trial. In an opinion by Judge Augustus Hand, Remington's conviction on two of the counts was upheld by the United States Court of Appeals for the Second Circuit. LH authored a dissent. United States v. Remington, 208 F.2d 567 (2d Cir. 1953), *cert. denied*, 347 U.S. 913 (1954). Among Remington's prosecutors was Roy Cohn, who had gained notoriety as a member of Senator Joseph McCarthy's investigations on the House Un-American Activities Committee. In November 1954, Remington was murdered in prison by two fellow inmates. On LH's view of the case as revealing "his personal sensitivity to civil liberties issues," Gerald Gunther instances LH's "eloquent outrage at what he called 'oppression and deceit' in grand jury proceedings in his dissent from the affirmance of a perjury conviction of William Remington, a Commerce Department official accused by the ex-Communist witness Elizabeth Bentley [...] With his two respected colleagues, Gus Hand and Tom Swan, against him, with his personal as well as judicial sensibilities engaged, he labored through 14 drafts, ever responsive to criticism, ever questioning whether his outrage was justifiably that of a judge as well as a man." Some Reflections on the Learned Hand-Felix Frankfurter Correspondence, The William Winslow Crosskey Lecture in Legal History, The University of Chicago Law School (Nov. 18, 1976); ©Gerald Gunther, typescript, p. 26. For extensive commentary on the case, see GERALD GUNTHER, LEARNED HAND: THE MAN AND THE JUDGE 592–24 (1994).

118. I.e., on certiorari petitions, which seek discretionary review from an appellate court: Frankfurter rejects the practice of voting dissent when a court has denied such a petition.

119. *Cf.* "Something is rotten in the state of Denmark." HAMLET, I, iv.

running this mad hysteria. Hardly a day passes that I do not get some evidence of our quite unconscious drift away from all that we have professed and much that we have practiced from the beginning of our history. On the other hand, I am not prepared as yet to say that Eisenhower has left undone what he ought to have done. My one reason for voting for him was that he seemed the only chance of avoiding either an eclipse of the Republican Party or its surrender to the Tories. It is the only possible opposition and no positions can in the end survive without some successes. So far as I can see, a multi-party democracy won't do. Eisenhower's position has been from the start almost inevitably untenable; he has been called in to walk a slack wire and now it is a wire jostled from below. I know, I know: you need not add to the scorn that I receive from nearly everyone, *ma femme comprise*, who says that the need is now for "One act of daring and courage." Who am I to say that that is not the proper prescription? Jack McCloy wrote me a letter the other day as follows: "Shades of Harry Stimson! J.J.McC." And yet I am not satisfied that Eisenhower is following the wrong course. Timidity? Perhaps. Tell me where prudence ends.

Besides, we are really up against the autonomy that is inherent in our system of Separated Power. There cannot be any doubt, I submit, the Congress has "power," *in abstractu*, to inquire ad lib. into whatever it may pass laws about, and nobody can doubt, I should think, that an honest search—though in my judgment an altogether unnecessary one, or almost altogether—into the "infiltration of Communism" is within the ambit of possible legislation, little as I should welcome what is apt to come on. It's a question of the "abuse" of this power, evident enough in fact to all decent people I should think, but not, at least expressly, left to the President to pass on. "Strong" Presidents have done so quite often, and since the courts cannot or at least will not (so I assume, though God knows just why I do), I will agree *arguendo* that it is part of our constitutional theory that all presidents may at the pinch. *Eh bien*; "you pays your money, and you takes your choice." When does the time come to say: "You son of a bitch, every decent man knows that you are abusing your powers, and I am going to tell you to go to Hell with my compliments." Good: "the People will respond." Will they? They haven't yet, though it's quite true that the stimulus of a plangent gesture (Query: whether "gestures" can be "plangent") might do the trick. All I can say is that from the background of a timid nature, I am not sure that he has overstayed the right moment. "What a piece of work is man!"[120][...]

We leave on April 17th for Naples and all points north and east. I have written what I suppose is my last opinion in the C.A. That gives me a little "fall" feeling: "Othello's occupation"[121] and all that sort of thing. Don't forget to give my love to the Marquise.

L.H.

ms with signature 105B.20

120. Hamlet, II, ii. *See* 1941-3 To Frankfurter, August 6, note 83.
121. Believing Desdemona unfaithful, "Othello's occupation [is] gone." Othello, III, iii.

1954-5

To Erwin Griswold[122]

March 17, 1954

Dear Dean Griswold:

Thank you for yours of the 13th with its enclosures.[123] I agree that it ought not to go against a teacher or anyone else that he has invoked his privilege. A privilege means that the law does not entitle the questioner to an answer and it must surely be a rare occasion when it is morally indefensible to refuse to answer what may endanger the recusant. Maybe there are cases where one might say that it is a moral duty to risk the danger and disclose the truth. I should hate ever to impose that duty on another and congressional investigations, as now conducted, are not among those occasions.

The real doubt is whether the answer would expose him to danger, i.e., whether he is claiming his privilege in good faith. The trouble with that is the trouble we always have when the issue comes up in court; i.e., ordinarily it is impossible to decide the issue without violating the privilege, if it should turn out that the claim is being made in good faith. And so it seems to me that for practical purposes we ought never to charge it as a wrong against a recusant, except in those rare cases where we can be sure that he knows that he has no privilege.

I am not too much in love with the privilege as it exists. The real abuses are examinations not presided over by what I will call a "full-fledged" judge, i.e., not a commissioner, etc. We let these go on and much worse than these: examinations in camera by district attorneys, the police, and the F.B.I., without the presence of counsel. It is there, I submit, that the opportunity lies for oppression, and there, I suspect, we should again and again find real "third-degree" practices. I think that I should be willing to make incompetent all admissions or confessions, and indeed all questioning, except publicly before my "full-fledged" judge and with the protection of counsel. On the other hand, I have never felt that an examination of the accused in open court would result in abuse, certainly when we remember that it could be reviewed on appeal. At least I should think that the other side ought to be allowed to use a refusal to take the stand as evidence against the accused. That is what we put in Eddie Morgan's "Model Code"—Rule 233.[124] It has for long seemed to me that we strain at a gnat and swallow a camel.

---

122. Erwin Nathaniel Griswold (1904–1994): Solicitor General of the United States, 1967–1973; Dean, Harvard Law School, 1946–1967.

123. Griswold sent LH a copy of his speech on the Fifth Amendment; it is not in the Hand Papers. *See Educator* [i.e., Griswold] *Praises Fifth Amendment*, N.Y. Times, Mar. 17, 1954.: "'It may be a serious error of judgment for an academic person to claim the privilege of the Fifth Amendment, or to refuse to answer questions, but the conduct, regrettable as it is, does not show the existence of treason, espionage, sabotage or any other serious crime.'" For the privilege against self-incrimination, see 1948-1 To Frankfurter, January 16, note 14.

124. *See* Model Code of Evidence, as adopted and promulgated by the American Law Institute of Philadelphia, Pennsylvania, May 15, 1942.

As for these congressional "investigating committees" with their paraphernalia of Klieg lights, snapping cameras, and television—they are a sinister symptom of "*facilis est descensus Averni.*"[125]

Sincerely yours, [Learned Hand]

tp 88.40

To Learned Hand from Erwin Griswold

March 18, 1954 Law School of Harvard University

Dear Judge Hand:

Thank you very much for your letter of March 17th. I am inclined to think that I would take a rather more favorable view of the privilege against self-incrimination than is indicated in your letter. This is because, as I see it, the privilege is of very great importance in protecting the right of dissent. As far as burglary and arson and using the mails to defraud, I might well agree with you. In these areas, the privilege may well be a nuisance and an obstruction to justice. But in other areas, some of which have been of historical significance and some of what we are seeing example of currently, the privilege may well be an important protection of the individual against the organized power of the state. I do not see any very good way to distinguish with regard to the privilege between the two types of cases. In order to have it for the dissenters and the heretics, it seems to me that we may well have to have it for the burglars. I fully agree with you that our present situation leaves considerable room for abuse in the matter of examinations by the police and others without the participation of a proper magistrate. Thank you very much for your comments.

Cordially yours, Erwin H. Griswold, Dean

tp with ms signature 88.41

1954-6

To Felix Frankfurter

June 5, 1954 Hotel de France et Choiseul, Paris

F.F.:

I received two days ago your copy of the Chief Justice Earl Warren's opinions in the "Segregation cases" expedited by their exuberant expenditure of stamps.[126] They were

---

125. LH cites Virgil: "facilis descensus Averno / noctes atque dies patet atri ianua Ditis; / sed revocare gradum superasque evadere ad auras, / hoc opus, hic labor est"; the descent into Hell is easy; day and night the door of dark Hell stands open, but to recall your steps and to ascend to the open air, this is the task, this is work." AENEID VI, 125–129.

126. *Brown v. Board of Education*, 347 U.S. 483 (1954), was a consolidated opinion addressing segregation cases from Kansas, South Carolina, Virginia, and Delaware; *Bolling v. Sharpe*, 347 U.S. 497

welcome. I agree that Fred [Vinson] and Earl[Warren][127] are to the last degree not "fungibles," with all that you imply. Apparently we have achieved a leader with a capacious outlook and inability to reinstate, measurably, the outlook of the indifferent observer. (I don't know why I said "*re*-instate.") He has, I should judge, relatively a small capacity for verbal analysis, but at any rate he avoids the hideous facility—vide, E[dward] D[ouglass] White for example—of stating the conclusion in the premises. What he says will not satisfy the "eggheads," at least it should not if they are real eggheads as few are, but it will lead to no confusion although it leaves your August Body with as pretty a job as I can imagine. Talk of the unwillingness of the Court of Chancery to superintend the execution of a building contract! You have let yourselves in for an enterprise than which it is impossible to imagine a "than whicher."

Had I been one of you *Divi Novem*, as I need not tell you I have always longed to be, though, thank God, no longer, I should have found difficulty in escaping the result you all, *mirabile dictu*, reached. (Apparently in some measure through the personal influence of Earl.) It is difficult for me to avoid the conclusion that the Fourteenth Amendment meant to cover such interests as a separation by race in so primary an activity as education. I should, however, have struggled my utmost to get away from that result and maybe I should have found the ingenuity to see a way out. After all there stood the earlier decisions![128] I say this because of my abiding and ever increasing conviction that an enforced "pause" in revolutionary changes—an enforced "pause" that I am coming to believe may be a condition upon the very continuance of democratic societies—ought not to be lodged in a court that professes and must profess to be interpreting the "meaning" of a written instrument.

Corruption is inevitable in imposing that duty upon a body that must be really a third camera, and I think it is pervasive and disables it from its primary and essential duty of interpretation. The fantastic divagations of the Yale Law School—some of them are, indeed, a pathological example of this—but they are nevertheless examples and not divergences. You can see in the case of Black and Douglas in your own milieu how we may slip into the position of *deus ex machina*, and Rutledge and Murphy left us only by what, were I devotedly disposed, I could but deem a Direct Intervention. I hesitate to classify the other five or six *notabili* who make up the balance, save to except Jackson, who has almost

(1954), involved segregation in the District of Columbia. A unanimous decision, *Brown* held that the "separate but equal" doctrine as announced in *Plessy v. Ferguson*, 163 U.S. 537 (1896), was unconstitutional, violating the Equal Protection Clause of the Fourteenth Amendment. *Bolling* came to a similar conclusion that was based on application of the Fifth Amendment's Due Process Clause, noting that the concepts of equal protection and due process were not "mutually exclusive." 347 U.S. at 499–500. The cases were argued in December 1952 and again in December 1953. Throughout subsequent exchanges on segregation, LH and Frankfurter refer, sometimes with quotation marks, to the "Segregation cases" on the one hand and to the "Segregation decision" or "Segregation case" on the other, that is, presumably, to *Brown v. Board of Education*. For clarity and consistency, I have supplied all these references with quotation marks.

127. Earl Warren (1891–1974): Governor of California, 1943–1953; Chief Justice of the United States, 1953–1969.

128. As context for its decision in *Brown*, the Court noted several cases in which it had considered the "separate but equal" doctrine in the context of public education. *See Brown*, 347 U.S. at 490–92.

persuaded me to forgive his Sin Against the Holy Ghost: Nuremberg. (But you don't agree about that).

Great and radical changes in a people's settled habits ought not to depend on a possible temporary and small majority of what it is not unfair to call a totalitarian assembly, though it be selected by universal suffrage. Right and wrong, justice and injustice, are too much the creature of past accommodations, "appeasements," if you like, to be upset without better evidence of an enduring and deep present discontent. But a court—I protest it, Mr. Justice—is not the organ to impose the hand of delay. The British Parliament Act of 1911[129] was not such a bad step, if only the Peers had been appointed for life.

I think on the whole—how silly it is to say "I think"!—rather, I guess that your decision will be a setback in the reconciliation of the two races. When people try, as we did after the Civil War, to manage such conflicts by generalizations enforced by political sanctions, they almost always go wrong. You will find yourselves in an infinite coil of administrative difficulties, if I am not mistaken, and you will have to eat the real meaning of what you have said unless you are willing to face the forcible suppression of some of the deepest prejudices, biases, atavisms, call them what you will, of large communities that are not bluffing.

Well, you didn't let yourself in for all this, I fancy, and I need not tell you not to take it seriously. As I said, in your place I believe I should have joined. Although if the U.S. chooses to announce eternal propositions, who am I, who have hired out to do what they say, that I should tell them that although that might be the right way in 1787 or 1867,[130] it ain't so today?[131][...] What I shall do when I get back, which will be before you get this, God knows. No doubt he will instruct me. My deepest regard to the Marquise.

L.H.

ms with signature 105C.20

1954-7

To Charles Wyzanski

July 2, 1954 Windsor, Vermont

Dear Charlie:

[...]I have read with interest your speech,[132] though it does show me how far your generation has diverged from mine. As is so often the case, I cannot help thinking

---

129. On August 10, 1911, the British Parliament deprived the House of Lords of its absolute power of veto on legislation.

130. 1787: the final meeting of the Constitutional Convention; 1868: the passage of the Fourteenth Amendment.

131. *See also* Learned Hand, The Bill of Rights: The Oliver Wendell Holmes Lectures, 1958 54–55, and 1956-2 To Frankfurter, February 26, and 1957-7 To Frankfurter, September 13.

132. Process and Pattern: The Search for Standards in the Law, address at the fiftieth anniversary of the Graduate Schools of Indiana University (Apr. 30, 1954).

that the difference in the end is for the most part, perhaps altogether, verbal. You say that today no teacher of law would adopt Langdell's formula or for that matter, Holmes's. Well and good, but I wonder whether the present teachers are talking about the same thing. In our day we meant to confine ourselves to those rules or doctrines—call them what one likes—that carried the sanction of force after the issues had been decided as controversies in tribunals having the recognition of the government. These we called "law," and it is hardly fair to us to suppose that we were not aware that so defined, "law" was the precipitate of a solution that contained all the ingredients you so tellingly mention. The fact that this precipitate is to be enforced by such tribunals—you see I am avoiding the word "courts"—means that they must have some especial quality, and it is that quality or those qualities that are important to young men primarily interested in becoming members of a profession that is to protect individuals in invoking or resisting the incident of the sanctions avoided. It is a very troublesome thing to give these men an adequate grasp of the scope and multitude of the propositions that they must deal with, and the question is whether it pays to go further.

I do not indeed mean that they should not learn how cloudy are the outlines of the propositions they are taught or that they should not be forcefully admonished of the latitude accorded those who are to decide what are their limits on concrete occasions. But again, it is a mistake to suppose that we were not made acutely aware of this, though I must concede that Langdell did not show much evidence of it. Where I diverge from much of present day teaching—I do not know how much—is in believing it desirable to include more than the recognition that "law," as I would teach it, is subject to the kind of influences you so well describe. I would not try, except in the most superficial way, to make part of my curriculum what those influences were, their origins, and their tendencies. This I would abjure, not because I thought they were not relevant, but in the interest of a parsimony that is necessary, time and cost being what they are. I would therefore still center the cases and the discussions in the technical magazines, and also, as we certainly did, in the historical growth of the doctrines and the reasons for their acceptance. I would not stress how well they matched present day needs, because it seems to me that this carries one into the empyrean.

I particularly liked what you said about custom and precedent as an important, perhaps the most important guide when one embarks upon ascertaining the ideal norms to which we should direct our course, assuming, *arguendo*, that one should so embark at all. That carries me far a-field indeed, so far that I feel sure that you would not follow me. It is the pervasive incommensurability of values that makes so desirable the permanence of those compositions of the resulting conflicts that have got themselves well enough established to be generally acquiesced in.[133] Efforts to set up new compositions—I

---

133. LH regards "values" as "cautionary warnings against the intemperance of faction [...They] demand the appraisal and balancing of human values which there are no scales to weigh [...] values are incommensurable." *The Contribution of an Independent Judiciary to Civilization, in* The Spirit of Liberty 155–65, 160–61. *Cf.* "Most of the issues that mankind sets out to settle, it never does settle [...] they are incapable of solution properly speaking, being concerned with incommensurables." *A Plea for the Open Mind and Free Discussion, in* The Spirit of Liberty 274–85, 81.

should like to beard the lion in his present den by calling them "appeasements"—at once disclose the absence of objective standards for the appraisal of values, and are apt to result in long periods of disorder. I do not mean indeed that there is no place for radical changes; the mere march of technical discoveries makes that inevitable. But I do mean that the notion that there are absolutes that can be used for such appraisals is baseless, given our present knowledge of ourselves. Decades perhaps centuries hence we may have learned enough about the workings of our psyche to set up an objective ethic. I doubt it—but to my mind, it only befogs us to suppose that we have anything like it to rely on now.

There: that's the *confessio fidei* of a senile old thing who fears change even more than he used to and whose chief motive always has been to play it safe anyway. So be it, at least I want to be granted the awareness of my limitations, disconcerting as they may have become.

Aspen seems to me a most desirable place to "vacate" in. Ned Burling was there two years go and said that you captured it by storm. He was so lyric about your performances that at times he seemed a little incoherent. Go on, *mon brave*, to new triumphs. My kind regards to the partner of your joys and sorrows.

Affectionately, L.H.

ms with signature, Wyzanski Papers, HLL, Box 2, Folder 10

1954-8

To Learned Hand from Felix Frankfurter

June 24, 1954 Charlemont, Massachusetts

Dear B.:

You know my deep sympathy with your outlook on the Fourteenth Amendment. I once shocked Cardozo by saying that I would favor, on balance, the repeal of that Amendment and had wished that only the Thirteenth and Fifteenth had issued from the Civil War. But since we have it, we have it, and I literally go through torture from time to time. Frequently I wish that Holmes and Brandeis had not permitted the "liberty of contract" lads to push them into accepting an extension of Due Process beyond procedural (with all its fringe difficulties as to what is "procedural") limits. But I expect less trouble than you fear about the decretal sequels of our decision. There will be serious difficulties, of course, but they will be largely localized: Mississippi, Georgia, South Carolina and spots in Tennessee, Arkansas, etc. I am assuming, of course, that the USSC will continue to behave wisely. Shaping decrees is peculiarly a function of wisdom!

This year you must come here[...] Our love to you both. F.F.

ms with signature 105C.20

To Felix Frankfurter

July 12, 1954 Windsor, Vermont

F.F.:

[. . .]The truth is that we need a very thorough overhauling of our political ideas—"Philosophy"—and that we can't have without reassessing the significance of our aesthetic. We in the U.S. are still adolescents, as appears acutely in this whole business of letting China into the U.N. Kennan is one of the few mature thinkers in the U.S.A. that I have chanced upon, perhaps because my reading is too scanty. The necessity of defending what you don't believe, e.g., Dulles's present unwillingness even to "recognize" China, must be a maddening feature of political life. As for your Court: some body, somewhere in the system, was an absolute necessity qua its federal aspect and there was no other organ of government at hand. Hamilton's and Marshall's reasoning was patently untenable, but although perhaps they believed it, they had the belly-sense to know what must be done, and perhaps on the other hand that was what they in fact went on anyway when it comes to the "Liberties of the Subject" (copied from your address and out of the Indian Constitution). I was immensely delighted to learn that those birds had put them in for what alone they can be, what, if I may quote myself, are "Admonitions of Moderation," and what I should like now to change into "Hesitations to Break through the Customs." Have you read Brogan's *The Price of Revolution*?[134] Good Book.

But none of this was for you: it leads straight to and almost lands in the abdication of the Court's review under the First, Fifth and Fourteenth Amendments. Thayer was really not so far from that, though he never liked broad verbal commitments, and Holmes, if forced in private, would have agreed, don't you think? You knew him better that I. I used to talk all this over with Bennie while he was in Albany, and I could never get him to agree. However, it hangs in my fast-decaying cranium that before he died he once told me that in the end he had actually come to think that these "Cardinal Charters of our Liberties" were on balance "more of a hindrance than a help," and maybe he didn't.[135] As to myself I find more and more often apt what Henry V said at Agincourt: "Old men forget and all shall be forgot but he'll remember, with advantages, the feats he did that day." The keystone there is that dreadful "with advantages."[136]

[. . .]There are birds flitting about who say that Bob Jackson and Stanley [Forman Reed][137] were not really convinced in re "Segregation" but yielded in order to avoid a dissent. I respect that attitude. The longer the thing simmers in my guts, the less I like it. I am now asking myself contrary to what I first wrote you whether I could not have found an honest way to stick by the precedent. At a guess, I might, but on the other hand, if I

134. D.W. Brogan, The Price of Revolution (1951).

135. LH refers to Benjamin Cardozo. *See* 1948-2 To Clark, April 8.

136. *Cf.* King Henry v. speaking of the soldier who fights with him at Agincourt. Henry V, IV, iii.

137. Stanley Forman Reed (1884–1980): Solicitor General of the United States, 1935–1938; Associate Justice of the United States Supreme Court, 1938–1957.

had found the Brethren irretrievably against me, I think I should have kept my mouth shut[...]

L.H.

ms with signature 105C.20

To Learned Hand from Felix Frankfurter

July 21, 1954 Charlemont, Mass.

Dear B.:

[...]It is a long story how unanimity was achieved in the "Segregation cases" and not at all a dramatic one. It could not possibly have come to pass with Vinson, which does not remotely mean that [Earl] Warren drew votes out of his hat. At the heart of the business was the wise and skillful ways by which the cases, which came to the Court from the different States and the District at different times, were dealt with so as not to have them come on for final disposition until they could all be heard together and were finally ordered to be reargued with specific questions put to counsel at this Term of the Court. One of these days I will tell you the story, but I will tell you that if the "great libertarians" had had their way we would have been in the soup.

Ever yours, F.F.

tp with ms signature 105C.18

1955-1

To Walter Lippmann Judge Learned Hand's Chambers

March 7, 1955

Dear Walter:

I got a good while ago the copy of your book that you sent me and I read it almost at once.[138] I have delayed writing you about it, not because it did not interest me, but largely because my own mind was so uncertain about the matters that you discuss that I was in doubt whether I had anything to say worth hearing. It is useless to wait any longer, however, for at my age one's mind does not tend to clear up, and indeed I fear that the interval has not helped me much. At the start let me say that you show a most impressive background of reading and reflection, which gives what you say initial impetus and power. I was much impressed.

Part One. I share with you great concern especially in the catastrophic possibilities about us, at the prevalent barbarism of so much that goes on in our popular assemblies

138. Walter Lippmann, Essays in the Public Philosophy (1955).

especially at Washington. I also share your belief that we should have the chance of better government if the "Executive" were freer from the immediate domination of these assemblies. Yet I wonder whether there is any evidence that they have degenerated in recent times. That is a question of history and I have not the adequate background for a judgment, but so far as I know, the violence of faction and blind partisanship was as great in this country, at any rate, a hundred or a hundred and fifty years ago as it is now. The dilemma seems to me to be that he who pays the piper calls the tune and we should all, I fancy, agree that the power of the purse ought to be in the popular assembly, if we are to continue our democratic experiment at all. For that reason I do not see much chance, institutionally anyway, of freeing the "Executive" without the recurrence of that impasse that arises so often here and in France. So far, the best device is, I think, the kind of parliament that Britain put together early in the nineteenth century, which subjects each member of the "legislature" to the need of getting elected again when the "executive" loses its majority. That does not indeed hit the root of the evil, but that and the whole tree lie in the nature of us all.

Part Two. As I look back on the masters who trained my youthful thoughts, they did not or at least I did not understand them to believe that there were any ascertainable general principles of government that could be made to serve as guides for the solution of concrete problems; we used to think that we had put the quietus on "Natural Law."[139] In that we have indeed proved to be quite wrong, as the strong renascence of what seems to be an equivalent is proving. I find it, for example, in so good a book as McIlwain's *Political Theory of the Western World* (that may not be quite the title)[140] which you know. It is cropping up all around in legal philosophy, quite independently of any theological background; it is an outstanding movement of the time. You know the literature much better than I. If I have understood you, you share at least the basis of that belief; you do think that there are enduring and ascertainable concepts of "civility" without which no society can reach a tolerable Good Life. Frankly, I cannot agree. I do not mean, of course, that we do not have the Kantian basic principle: A counts for as much as B and no more; Prince and Pauper stand alike; we must love our neighbors as ourselves. (I particularly like your emphasis upon future generations in this connection). But in the end, I adhere to the notion, well though rather brutally stated by Holmes, that in politics and for that matter in ethics, we are always faced with the insoluble problem of striking a balance between incommensurables, and that for the solution there are no standards or tests save what will prove the most nearly acceptable compromise, what will most accord with existing conventions.

Maybe at long last some fixed standards or tests will emerge; theoretically, it is not impossible that we may come to find some, should our physiology go deep enough. Out of it could then perhaps come an adequate ethic and aesthetic on which politics could depend. But all that is centuries away. Strangely enough, all this comes out, or so I think, when one examines our own constitutional system with the Supreme Court on top as the

139. Charles P. Curtis identifies Lippmann's "public philosophy" as a kind of "natural law" in *A Natural Law for Today and the Supreme Court as its Prophet*, 39 B.U. L. Rev. 1, 39 (1959).

140. LH probably refers to Charles Howard McIlwain, Growth of Political Thought in the West from the Greeks to the Middle Ages (1932).

final negative authority. I promised [Erwin] Griswold of the Law School to write some lectures about it, and I have tried, but so far I have failed, for the deeper I go, the more enmeshed I get. Perhaps your way out is possible, but for the moment I cannot see my part in that direction.

I feel quite sure that *The Public Philosophy* will be very successful; thousands of people are apprehensive and confused, and will find reliance and strength in what you say. Indeed, I read yesterday in *The New York Times Book Review* that you have leapt at once into the "best sellers" list. You are likely to stay there for a long while. Certainly you have a contribution "more life enhancing," as B.B. likes to put it, than my own forbidding gospel.

I heard some time ago that you had got worn down and went to the Massachusetts General, but I was glad later to learn that you had gone west to get fit again. You are certainly too valuable a factor in our present time of disorders to take chances with yourself.

Affectionately, L.H.

tp with ms signature, Lippmann Papers, Sterling, Box 76, Folder 978.

To Learned Hand from Walter Lippmann

March 12, 1955 Ojai, California

Dear B.:

Your letter reached me here in California where I am recuperating rather successfully from getting myself much worn out, in good part at least, I think myself, from trying to swim so long against the currents of public opinion with which my job is concerned. No doubt other pastures always seem greener, but sometimes I wish I had a profession, like law or medicine or chemistry, which has a recognizable subject matter and methods [. . .] perhaps that is what sent me off looking for a public philosophy.

Your letter gave me great pleasure and also much relief. I knew you could not agree, but I was afraid you would disapprove of the attempt. There are a few things which I'd like to say. In regard to Part I: am I wrong in thinking that the wars of this century are the first great wars waged by governments elected by a general suffrage, and that there is a causal connection between this and the ruinous and inconclusive character of these wars? No doubt you are right that the power of the assemblies is not a new phenomenon in this country, e.g., the civil war and reconstruction. But their power in the conduct of great wars, except for revolutionary France, is modern.

Part II, where I found I had worked myself into country that was new to me, is not meant to say that there are general principles for all societies everywhere and always. The good society for an orthodox Hindu has basic assumptions which are radically different from those on which western constitutional democracy rests. What I call the public philosophy are the assumptions which have to be accepted in order to live in the historical, and conceivably unique and passing political order to which we belong. I hope and believe, though it is perhaps pretentious, that these necessary assumptions can be elucidated.

Always affectionately yours, Walter

tp with ms signature 106.19

1955-2

To Charles Wyzanski

May 13, 1955 Judge Learned Hand's Chambers

Dear Charlie:

First, let me say what I did not have the chance to say the other day: how admirably I thought you spoke of Gus at the memorial meeting.[141] Nothing is harder than to write that kind of speech; usually it goes off into empty eulogy that leaves no impression of the man, and serves only as a kind of vapid incantation by an accepted ritual. One got a sense from what you said of the person you were talking about—an uncommon achievement—and withal a sense of the affection and esteem that you had for him[...]

Thanks for the Indiana speech which I have read now for the second time with great interest;[142] you draw upon a background of information that I envy more than you will believe. As to your underlying thesis, however, I fear that we do not see eye to eye. I recognize how much of present-day thinking, especially by those who are of your generation, follows yours, and it tinctures my diffidence with even more skepticism than is native to me. This is no place to put down such justification as I should in any case be able to muster, but let me try to state (far more categorically than in fact I feel) the outlines of my reasons for an opposite belief. Do not impute to them the confidence that they may appear to have.

"Law" is that part of morals that is enforced by violent sanctions; what is not so enforced is not "law." That is, of course, merely a definition not an announcement from Sinai, but one is free to define one's terms. Anyway, it avoids the confusion of including in "law" precepts that carry other sanctions, e.g., social approval, the satisfaction of inner attunement to one's society, and other similar controls. Reason has only one place in morals and therefore in "law." It serves the same purpose in judgments between individuals that prudence does between future and present values of the same individual. Conflicts between the values of different individuals should be adjusted as though they were the arbiter's own values. No one has said this more succinctly than in the words: "love thy neighbor as thyself." So far, reason may be said to be a determinant, for it strips the choice of irrelevant circumstances. However, this is a canon without content, for

141. Augustus Hand died on October 28, 1954. Wyzanski spoke on May 4, 1955, at the New York County Lawyer's Association and the Association of the Bar of the City of New York. *See Augustus Noble Hand, in* Charles E. Wyzanski, Jr., Whereas: A Judge's Premises 65–78 (1965).

142. *See* 1954-7 To Wyzanski, July 2.

values are immediate unanalyzable data, aside from their causal relation to other values. There is no common measure between them except the preference of one to whom both exist as values, and the preference is itself as immediate and underived as the values, which are not divisible into fungible units, and so cannot be quantitatively compared.

We proceed on the assumption that we are all so much alike that what is the preference of A will be so of B, and while between individuals that is usually untrue, statistically it may be true. In any event, it must be assumed in any ethic. To our native or animal values must be added those postulates of mutual adjustment or compromise that have got themselves accepted in any given society, and endure until with changed tensions, new ones get themselves substituted. "Law" is a part of these postulates, and they should be relatively stable because they gather an adventitious value of their own, greater at times than the native values whose conflicts they compose. Indeed, their value may be supreme, so that a man gladly dies for it. To quote Holmes: "the highest virtue is to stake all upon a generality that you know may be shown false tomorrow." However, when we ask for any "principles" of law, there are none outside those that happen to have got themselves accepted. So far as that acceptance embodies "Reason" in the sense I have tried to describe it, it is the best available, given the cultural status of the society where they obtain; we should be slow to change them because such authentic commands are difficult to impress on a society, but to repeat, they have no other compulsive sanction.

The work of judges strongly disposes them to substitute their personal compositions of social conflicts for those current, for it is difficult imaginatively to project a "common will" in any situation. That makes our job hard enough; let us at all costs eschew any effort to make our own compromises prevail; let us avoid being torch-bearers to a better world. That is judicial chastity—an overrated virtue ordinarily, but vital in a judge. I think this was what Holmes meant when he said to me what you quoted, and by the way he put it even more offensively to the true "Liberal": "My lad, that is not my job. I am here to play the game according to the rules."[143]

Oh, oh, Charlie, you really didn't deserve all this. In the future it should warn you not to stimulate the garrulity of the aged; as their controls weaken, they clutter up paper "something horrible." Also sprach Zarathustra.

Thine, L.H.

tp with ms signature, Wyzanski Papers, HLL, Box 2 Folder 10

To Learned Hand from Charles Wyzanski

May 14, 1955 39 Fayerweather street, Cambridge, Massachusetts

Dear Judge Hand:

Your practice of the judicial office will always make your theory of it appealing and persuasive. What you say of the nature of law seems to me so plainly right in most if not all of its aspects in the Second Circuit that I don't enter even a *dubitante* on that

143. *See A Personal Confession, in* The Spirit of Liberty 302–11; LH quotes Holmes at 307.

jurisdiction. But what has always seemed to me troublesome is whether your definition and approach can do much to illumine the faith of the legislator or administrator when not sitting quasi-judicially. Are his acts not law? J.C. Gray's negative answer seems to me to rest on arbitrary distinctions which would not be accepted except at certain stages of the history of common law, and then not by philosophers, anthropologists, or even jurists outside the Anglo-American profession.

If the legislator or administrator is formulating and even to an extent applying law, has he no standard to guide his power?

I am deeply grateful for your words about my remarks at the exercises in honor of Judge A.N. Hand. My wish to acknowledge his greatness so far exceeds my power to portray it that I cannot say that I was myself at all satisfied with my talk. Yet every hour I have spent in reflecting on his qualities has given me a stronger and a better command of myself. Gisela and I send our best to you and Mrs. Hand.

As ever thine, Charlie

ms with signature 108.18

1955-3

To Learned Hand from Bernard Berenson

August 8, 1955 Vallombrosa

Dear B.:

I am sorry you had to give up coming abroad this summer. I kept hoping you after all might be induced to join us here or in Venice. I have not yet digested the disappointment of your not joining us more than a year ago. Shall we ever meet again I wonder?

"Natural rights"—is one of my recent rereads. I forget whether in *Aesthetics and History* or *Seeing and Knowing* I have tried to make mincemeat of Nature, the out-of-doors, as our landscape.[144] I have tried to say that it was a complicated, highly elaborated artifact.

I believe any notion of nature and natural is equally artificial. Thomists even more than Stoics [affirm]: The Lord implanted in us a perfect sense of right and wrong, just and unjust, [as] the law of "Nature." Let believers in such myths read about the uppermost reaches of the Amazon and learn what real nature is like in Man and his world, his surroundings, his landscape. Only look at the darkening little men with their God-implanted sense of justice, right and wrong. How indignant they are that brother or sister has had a bigger share of cake, how outraged if immediate "justice" is not done them, and how full of *saeva indignatio* if they receive no cake at all. The child instinctively wants not to be under-privileged[...] To be over-privileged makes him as happy as the

---

144. Bernard Berenson, Seeing and Knowing (1953). For Aesthetics and History, see 1949-2 To Berenson, May 24.

cat that has swallowed the canary. I am ninety and within me I still have the infant's sense of justice and accusing sense of right and wrong.

It is time we dropped theology and need to possess, and approached problems anthropologically and psychologically. On what these teach us we can try to build up an ethic based on the fundamentals of human nature. Let me hope you do not sweat and groan too much trying to decipher the above.

Affectionately, B.B.

ms with signature 99.24

To Bernard Berenson

August 25, 1955 Windsor, Vermont

Dear B.B.:

Your letter of the 8th was forwarded to me while F. and I were in Northeast Harbor, Mount Desert, where we were spending a fortnight and whence we returned two days ago. It is rather over-"social" a place, but the relief was great to F. to be where she did not have to order meals and help prepare them. Yesterday I also received the copy you sent me of the *Bibliografia*[145] with an inscription that moved me very deeply. It will be one of my prized possessions. You ask when we shall meet. I too often ask myself that question. I remember well, B.B., the day we left I Tatti—three years ago wasn't it? and F. and I went to your bedroom to say goodbye. You said: "When shall we three meet again?"[146] and I felt the grave possibility that you were expressing[...] Maybe in the early spring we may yet arrange it, especially if we can get the Kings[147] to go with us again.

I am interested in what you again say about "Natural Law" and Walter's book.[148] I saw him three times in Mount Desert but we never had a chance to talk out his ideas. His chief preoccupation is with the dangers of an omnipotent legislature whose reflection of the immediate desires of the majority may sweep aside the accumulated habits, conventions, if you like, of the society in question, whatever that may be. I quite agree as to those dangers, and the question should not be confused with "Natural Law," if by that one means any body or code of postulates detailed enough to serve as guides in governing that are to be regarded as permanent and immune from the changing conditions to which all human affairs are subject. Even so, I can't help thinking that the way Walter puts it is misleading; but the chief trouble I find is in whom we shall vest the power to halt or at least to postpone the will of the legislature. After all, he who pays the piper calls the tune, and nobody today would want to take the purse away from the electorate. If he did, he would have a brief political life.

---

145. Bibliografia di Bernard Berenson, published in Italian by Electa Editrice (Milan), 1955.

146. *Cf.* "When shall we three meet again? / In thunder lightening or in rain?" Macbeth, I, i.

147. I.e., Edith and Frederick King, friends of LH and Frances Hand, who accompanied them to Europe in the summer of 1954. This trip appears to have been the occasion of LH's last meeting with Berenson.

148. Walter Lippmann, Essays in the Public Philosophy; *see* 1955-1 To Lippmann, March 7.

I suggested to Walter that perhaps the British Parliament Act of 1911 might have been a passable compromise: i.e., a suspensive veto by an aristocracy. But what kind of aristocracy? Our "Founding Fathers" were acutely aware of what Walter so much dreads and thought they had provided against it. They did not succeed by what they meant to provide, but at times I wonder whether they may not have done so by a means that they did provide, though not for that purpose or for any other purpose whatever, but only because they could not otherwise have got the Constitution adopted. I mean a senate in which each state has an equal vote. True, there is no other such egregious anomaly on the face of the planet, egregious, I mean, to any theory of democracy, define it as one will. And yet the result is to divide the political power of Congress into sections that do not, speaking widely, have the same economic interests. The uneven representation of the agrarian areas gives them a disproportionate power and tends to prevent the urban areas from having their way. I wonder whether there may be something of service in this, undreamt of as it was by the Founding Fathers.

As Walter is going to visit you this fall, you will have a chance to sound him out better than I had. Do not underrate his book: true, it is no "solution," but there can be none. Its importance is that it has set people thinking. As for me, all I want to do is to try to show that whatever may be the need of some restraining, of a delaying organ in the political machine, it is undesirable to select the courts for the purpose. But enough of this: perhaps you have already found it too much. I inflict it upon you only because it teases me at the moment. But the way, I like greatly your notion that "Landscape" is a fabricated idea. I must have missed it when I read both *Aesthetics and History* and *Seeing and Knowing*. My warmest regards to dear, dear Nicky.

Affectionately, L.H.

ms with signature 99.24

1955-4

To Felix Frankfurter

September 15, 1955 Windsor, Vermont

F.F.:

[...]For my sins I went down—Tom came up and drove me—to Charlie's conference last week. It was exhausting and tiresome, nothing of any consequence. The C.J. was there, and Felix, I can't help it (*ich kann nicht anders*), he is not a distinguished party. Allowing for your love affair, I must in the end set it down as *une affaire du coeur*. I don't mean that things being as they are, he may not be a benison, a soothing ameliorator, an influence necessary, etc., etc. But if so, that only goes to prove what seems to be getting to be accepted more and more: i.e., your August Body is not a court at all, but that third camera with the power of veto without which Walter thinks democracy is doomed. Well and good: I am, God knows, an old man and perhaps that may be the best result that we should and can expect. Still, I can't help looking back longingly to the hard unflinching dialectic of O.W.H.

If it is necessary to have this new organ, mayn't we be a little more frank about the substitution? Is there really nothing more in "interpretation" than Fred Rodell[149] et al. allow? Is it all a dishonest attempt to cover one's assertion of one's own influences? Let us, I suggest, divide our courts into two: one to be a genuine brake on our legislature, the other to be a truly final jural tribunal with the same limitations as are imposed upon courts of instance[...]

My reverential obeisances to the Marquise. L.H.

ms with signature 105C.21

To Learned Hand from Felix Frankfurter

September 16, 1955 3018 Dumbarton Ave., Washington, D.C.

Get me straight, Boss!

Of course the C.J. "is not a distinguished party"[...] He *is* a "benison," not a "soothing ameliorator, an influence necessary etc." I have to be blunt to make myself clear. He is a benison because he is a straight-forward, honorable character, as Vinson was not nor was, I'm sorry to have to tell you so, Stone[...] Warren is all homespun—all wool and a yard wide, does his work, is candid about his limitations, and in every way, except intellectual leadership, behaves as the head of our Court should. But don't be silly in using O.W.H. as a yardstick[...]

Yrs. F.F.

P.S. I assume you know that Adenauer's Germany *has* your system of two courts—one, the *Verfasssungsgericht.*

ms with signature 105C.21

1955-5

To Felix Frankfurter

October 1, 1955 Windsor, Vermont

F.F.:

I suppose it did seem like an "outburst," and I regretted it almost as soon as I had let it out.[150] I thought it would give comfort to Charlie W[yzanski] and Walter L[ippmann] and the rest who seem to me to be edging about, if not more, to a belief that we must look

149. LH refers to Professor Fred Rodell of Yale Law School, a longtime critic of the legal profession in the United States. *See* FRED RODELL, WOE UNTO YOU, LAWYERS! (1939).

150. LH is probably alluding to remarks he made on a paper delivered by Frankfurter at a conference. I have not identified the paper or the conference.

to the judges for our political inspirations. They have, so far as I can find out, a very large following, among whom, I feel fairly sure, are many judges.

Your remarks until the very end filled me with comfort and admiration; it was a splendid job, the best I heard, though I was not there at all on Saturday. What caused the "outburst" was that it seemed to me, and for that matter still does when read "in tranquility," that unless we keep the meaning of "law" very strictly, and if you will, even pedantically, to what Holmes said—was it not he?—"the command of him whom the sheriff will obey,"[151] we get into inextricable difficulties. Of course, we may define one's terms as one chooses, provided one uses them consistently, but if one includes within law those factors, political or ethical, that lie behind, influence, and indeed determine the final content of the "commands" that one's society treats as authoritative and indisputable, *quoad* the application of force, it is difficult to distinguish interpretation from enactment. Nobody knows better than I how delusive is that will-o-the wisp, "Interpretation"; yet at least as I view it, in this distinction, slippery as it is, lies the whole of the measure of a judge's duty. I think you will agree with me as to this; surely no one of the "nine" has given better evidence of a determination to find the obscure path. I am constantly "selling you" to anyone who will listen as the real expositor and exponent of just this.

But is it not a part of it that we should not think of those formative influences that in the end make "law" as part of "law" till they emerge in what professes itself to be the imperative word, already lettered by those upon whom authority to do so has been expressly conferred?

When you discredited Austin, I must confess my heart missed a beat. Maybe I am the last living Austinian, which would indeed be strange, as I have him only at second hand. I once spoke of Holmes as being "Austinian," and brought down Sir Frederick Pollock[152] on my head, apparently with the assent of O.W.H. himself. I did not indeed mean to class H. with A. in his barren a priori deductive aspect; I was aiming at H.'s insistence as I had understood it, and still do, that we must seek the "meaning," horrid word, of what had been laid down for us and that we must stop there.

Your instances of the way English and Colonial courts "interpret" statutes, which for them are always concededly imperative, seem to me rather to bear me out than the contrary. They assume (I take it from you) that those customary courses that have had long acceptance are to be supposed to apply until there can be no dispute that they do not. Well, I call that my beloved "Interpretation." So far as it can be honestly availed of, I would use it in the Fifth and Fourteenth Amendments, but it still does seem to me that they may not be used as part of what *is* "law," but only as a way to know what law *is*. Is that mere verbal pedantry? Maybe, but I am unconverted and believe that it is a most

---

151. LH invokes John Austin, Professor of Jurisprudence at the University of London, who argues that that law was the expression of the sovereign's authority. "According to [Austin], the characteristic feature of law, properly so called, is a sanction or detriment threatened and imposed by the sovereign for disobedience to the sovereign's commands." OLIVER WENDELL HOLMES, JR., *Trespass and Negligence*, *in* THE COMMON LAW 81–82 (1881).

152. Sir Frederick Pollock (1845–1937): Professor of Jurisprudence, Oxford University, 1883–1903. Pollock published THE PRINCIPLES OF CONTRACT (1876), THE LAW OF TORTS (1887), and, with F.W. Maitland, THE HISTORY OF ENGLISH LAW BEFORE THE TIME OF EDWARD I (1899).

important bit of casuistry and our best escape from the Blacks, the Douglases, and not a few of the Yale Law Schoolers.

It is against this rock that all the little craft, in which I have impotently tried to launch something that might weather the seas as a Holmes Lecture, have dashed themselves. I am discouraged, especially after the Bicentenary. I don't mean to include your piece[...] But make no mistake. Though I should be dishonest to say that I did get what seemed to me a setback out of some of what you said, it did not diminish my regard or affection for you.

I go back to New York tomorrow. L.H.

ms with signature105C.21

To Learned Hand from Felix Frankfurter

October 10, 1955 Supreme Court of the United States

Dear B.:

I wish I had burdened you with reading my paper in ample time before its delivery. Not only would I have saved your heart from missing a beat, I would have saved myself the danger, however remote, of giving comfort to those whom I regard as my enemies not less than yours. If there is one conviction about which I am as passionate as you can possibly be, it is the rejection of the belief that "we must look to the judges for our political inspirations." When Charlie Wyzanski expressed such belief of the Court's function, I was rather appalled and not the less so, I suppose, by the fact that he told me so in a schoolmasterly manner (this, in disapproval of my *Dennis* opinion) as though he was charged with that message by God on Sinai.

Had I the remotest notion that I was straying outside the strict confines of what I believe to be the business of judges, I could easily have avoided phrasing myself as I did by confining the term "law" to the scope to which you confine it, and to which I have been confining it, I think, on my job. It may interest you and perhaps relieve you a little to learn that what I said gave considerable displeasure to Gus's "children of light,"[153] including among them, to my surprise, some of the younger men on the Harvard Law School faculty. It would not be fair of me now to rephrase my paper, but I have added a footnote not to placate you, but to put myself to myself in the clear.[154] It is an addition to my disavowal of "a brooding omnipresence," and will read as follows: "It might further avoid confusion to restrict the term 'law,' particularly in a judge's mouth, to the commands of society which it is the duty of courts to enforce, and not apply it to those decencies of conduct which should control other branches of government but are without judicial sanction.

153. Augustus Hand referred to persons who took "Natural Law" seriously as "Children of Light"; *see* 1 *Thessalonians* 5:5 and *Ephesians* 5:8.

154. Responding on this point in a letter to Frankfurter dated October 12, LH observes: "Your proposed footnote would, I should think, remove any possible doubts that might arise, and indeed I am not sure that it was necessary at all. I dare say I was hypersensitive anyway"[...] (tp 105C.21) In a letter dated October 13, 1955, Frankfurter replies: "I am relieved that my footnote does the job." (tp with ms signature 105C.21)

But perhaps law has so established itself as a portmanteau word that clarity does not require too pedantically restrictive a use of it, so long as no doubt is left as to the circumscribed scope of the judiciary's function." Whether or not this repairs any damage that you think I have done, I am truly grateful to you for spelling out what troubled you in what I said. In saying this, I can assure you that I am not trying to fudge or blur any difference between us, for I am not conscious of any.

In any event, all this only emphasizes the importance that you say your say. Whatever else you may be worrying about, for heaven's sake dismiss all thought that what you say might be what the onward-and-upward lads may call "old hat." For that is precisely what it should be. Wisdom doesn't call for novelty, it calls for wisdom. The fact that you will expound it will be of prime importance and of enduring influence. In the realm of thought, as in other realms, there are fashions. And the present blabber-mouthing and loose-mindedness will not rule forever. Those who are of our way of thinking are entitled to the powerful reinforcement which you will bring.

Ever yours, F.F.

tp with ms signature 105C.21

1955-6

To Harley M. Kilgore[155]

October 6, 1955

Dear Senator Kilgore:

I am enclosing herewith my answers to your interrogatories, and this letter is an attempt to state my general position.[156] The questions do not in my judgment hit the real difficulty which is, I believe, that the evils covered by the phrases "restraint of trade" and "monopoly" ought not to be left to the courts until after Congress has taken a more definite position as to what it wants. There are, as everyone knows, two interests involved: economic and political. I mean by "political" the indirect social effects of a change from an industry operated by a number of small independent units to an industry operated by a few great units, even though these compete. Courts are competent to decide the first question: i.e., whether the prices charged by a combination are greater or less than those that would be charged if it did not exist; in short, whether the combination is beneficial to the consumer. True, there are formidable difficulties even about that: e.g., the appraisal of existing plants. Nevertheless, these are not insurmountable, and they present only questions of fact, little competent as a jury often is to decide them from evidence which

155. Harley M. Kilgore (1893–1956): Senator from West Virginia, 1941–1956; Chair, Antitrust and Monopoly Subcommittee of the Senate Committee on the Judiciary, 1955–1956.

156. In a letter dated September 30, Kilgore asks LH for answers to the Subcommittee's questionnaire on "the extent to which the policy of maintaining competition should be enforced in the first instance by courts or by an administrative agency." (tp with ms signature 91.18)

may be extravagantly voluminous and baffling. I should much prefer that some preliminary sorting and arranging of the evidence with tentative findings should precede the trial of this issue in accordance with procedure that the Supreme Court approved in *Ex parte Peterson*, 253 U.S. 300.[157] The subject matter of such causes of action is usually altogether unfamiliar as well to the judge as to the jury, and any adequate understanding of it demands an inordinate time; moreover, the conditions that obtain in a jury room with its Babel of twelve voices are quite inconsistent with its rational treatment.

However, although the economic question is vital, it is not as important as the "political" one and as to that much more searching questions arise. What will be the impact upon the social habits of these affected by the proposed combination? Obviously, a completely nationalized industry makes the most far-reaching changes, which it needs no argument to prove that Congress alone should impose, even though only one industry be involved. I do not see why the same considerations that are relevant to that question are not relevant to steps in that direction. For one reason—I am quite sure that the nationalization of any industry becomes more and more likely as the competing units become larger and fewer. Moreover, even if the final step is never taken, it is certainly one thing to be independently engaged in business and another to be employed by others. Again, to be employed in a small business is different from being employed in a very large one. It is not necessary to elaborate these differences and I agree that conflicting interests are involved, but my point is that the relative appraisal of these and an eventual decision between them are of the very essence of what we ordinarily call "legislation." To substitute a court is not to ask it to interpret any "law," but to impose upon it a duty that should pre-suppose a responsiveness to current needs, desires, and habits strikes at the foundations of its most important attribute—detachment from social pressures.

The fact that the present statute rests upon the ancient phrases "restraint of trade" and "monopoly" has been enough to protect it from the objections that proved fatal to the National Industry Recovery Act in *United States v. Schechter*, 295 U.S. 495.[158] Apparently, the words were thought definite enough when confined to their common-law meanings, uncertain as those were, but they have not been so confined in the step-by-step interpretation of the Acts. As so transmuted, they would now, I fancy, be open to the charge of undue "delegation of power" to Congress were they expressly incorporated into text. Under our constitutional system I should suppose that it would not do to make the conclusions of an administrative tribunal the substitute for indefiniteness in a statute, even though it were impossible to deal satisfactorily with the situation in any other way. But I am not sure that it is not possible to find some general principles definite enough to pass muster as adequate declarations of purposes, and so to serve as guides to such a tribunal in their proliferation. That would, of course, demand Congress's taking

157. I.e., *Ex parte* Peterson, 253 U.S. 300 (1920). The Supreme Court confirmed the ability of a judge to hire an auditor for the purpose of simplifying issues related to business accounts and other matters pertinent to a case, under the court's supervision, in order to assist the jury in making its final determination. Such assistance amounts to opinion evidence and is not unconstitutional, because the parties' Seventh Amendment rights are not compromised.

158. I.e., A.L.A. Schechter Poultry Corp. v. United States, 295 U.S. 495 (1935). *See* 1936-1 To Wyzanski, January 9.

a position, however elastic might be its terms, upon the "political" factor I have mentioned, and I cannot help thinking that something like this is inescapable unless the law is to be left in its present amorphous situation.

It follows, if I am right, that things will not be very much bettered until Congress declares what form it wishes industry to take, and that no paraphernalia of amended procedure, pre-trial appeal, and this and that, will in the end be more than palliatives.

I trust I have not exhausted your patience; you could hardly have anticipated so exuberant an answer.

Respectfully yours, [Learned Hand]

tp 91.18

1955-7

To Learned Hand from Felix Frankfurter

November 13, 1955 3018 Dumbarton Ave., Washington, D.C.

Dear B.:

The Commies are not alone in knowing about 'infiltration' and its deft practice. These Johnnies have the advantage in enlisting gullibility because they operate *ad majorem gloriam Dei.*[159] One would suppose that they had sufficient platforms of their own without utilizing the House of non-sectarian Law... They know not what they do.

F.F.

ms with signature 105C.21

To Felix Frankfurter

November 25, 1955

F.F.:

Of course they are pushing their propaganda now. We are all so confused about this and that that poor baffled *homo sapiens* is reaching out for GOD in his most authoritative form. The Catholics have removed Delancy—as good a juvenile judge no one could get—because he did not enforce the law! All around there are evidences of a lapse into "eternal general principles of ethical finality."

159. The motto of the Society of Jesus.

There, there! Old men, I know, must not "crab" about the changes that will come even in their own absolutes, though these be confined to A SINGLE ABSOLUTE, i.e., THERE ARE NONE.[160] We live, but do we learn?

I have not yet read Dean's book;[161] but I fancy I shall disagree a good deal. How can I agree with one who admires Woodrow Wilson?

L.H.

ms with signature 105C.21

1955-8

To Irving Dilliard

December 19, 1955

Dear Irving:

I have read with much interest your article in *Harper's* about the Supreme Court,[162] and have observed in it as in all your writing an invincible fairness, entire adequacy of information, and the most admirable clarity. Given your premises, I could not more entirely agree, but there is a very fundamental difference in our outlook that seems to me worth stating, though I dare say you know it anyway. Am I not right in thinking that throughout your article you are assuming that the Supreme Court, and indeed courts in general, are the protectors of those "Civil Rights" without which I agree that any society will collapse into anarchy after a more or less extended period of tyranny? That assumption is, I think, on the increase; I sometimes wonder whether it may not today have captured a majority of the younger students of law and government in this country. It presupposes that we may not trust legislatures to preserve our liberties, and that we must look to the courts. Now it may be that somewhere in our system there ought to be an organ whose function it is to act as a brake, a clog, a flywheel upon the hyper-responsibility to popular pressures of Congress and the state legislatures. Lippmann in his last book[163] shows a conservative's concern over the absence of anything of the kind, and the Founding Fathers were full of such apprehensions. Certainly one would have to be far surer than I am of the good sense and justice of the People to deny that something of the kind may not be desirable, although at the moment I should be disposed to guess the other way.

160. LH is addressing the idea of "Absolutes" in a philosophical sense. In letters to Frankfurter on *Brown*, dated September 13, 1957 and later, LH insists that the Fourteenth Amendment functions as an "absolute" with respect to civil rights for African-Americans.

161. Dean Acheson, A Democrat Looks at His Party (1955).

162. Irving Dilliard, *Warren and the New Supreme Court*, Harper's, Dec. 1955, at 59–64.

163. Walter Lippmann, Essays in the Public Philosophy (1955). *See* 1955-1 To Lippmann, March 7.

Be that as it may, I am entirely satisfied that however imperatively we may need such a restraint, we must not use the courts for the purpose. In proportion as we do, we shall impair the discharge of their most vital function: i.e., to be detached interpreters of the will of others. That this is not the present attitude towards them appears in all sorts of ways. For example, Earl Warren may by the grace of God turn out to be in all respects a top judge, for legal learning is not always a prerequisite of that, but he was not appointed to be a judge at all, and his success will not be measured by whether he is a judge, but by how far he will succeed as a moderator in the social conflicts of this time. During the last eighty or ninety years the Supreme Court, under the pretence of interpreting the "Bill of Rights" (with repeated shifts in its underlying convictions), has been constituting itself as a third camera with a veto.

In addition to the fact that at long last this will prove inconsistent with its independence and will destroy its moral authority, it is a basically erroneous view of the nature of the issues involved. The supposed verities that are the putative "basic" tenets of human society had their origins in the generalization of past specific conflicts of which the terms were human values and therefore incommensurable. We dress up these accommodations so as to extend them beyond their occasions, because in that way we escape confessing that we must always make choices that have nothing behind them but our preferences. As universal principles they have no content; they can do no more than write large and with authority that mood without which no human society can exist—the mood of toleration and compromise, when persuasion has failed.

"There, there," you will say, "Old Boy, you are getting a little too positive and hypertension is bad for the elderly." Maybe also you will agree with my wife who said to me the other day: "After all, you are only a phony liberal."

[L.H.]

tp 87.16

1956-1

To Learned Hand from Bernard Berenson

January 21, 1956 Settignano

My dear B.:

Congratulations on your 83rd birthday and many happy returns. To me well on my way to 91, 83 seems young[...] I wish the year might bring you here again to let me enjoy your presence, than which I know nothing more stimulating, more entertaining, more completely enjoyable. When you do come, I want to discuss "Nature" and "Natural" with you. It is a fascinating subject, knowing the naiveté of philosophers particularly of the now so admired Middle Ages[...]

The international situation seems more confused, more nearly tangled than ever. The talking shop in N.Y. is the most elaborate foolometer [sic] the world has ever known. The Lord have mercy on us! With love to you both and fervent hopes of seeing you soon.

Ever, B.B.

ms with signature 99.24

To Bernard Berenson

January 29, 1956

Dear B.B.:

Many thanks for your letter on my 84th (not, alas, 83rd) birthday. It came and went as they all do, and with the most damnably accelerating frequency. What you say of my society fills me with the greatest pleasure, impossible as the appropriateness of those adjectives appears. All goes about as usual here except that I find, unhappily, a steady decline in my power to work. That is to be expected, I know; indeed, I should be more than satisfied that it is not more. But you will know what I mean, even you, the Indestructible. Yes, it was a bit of a blow to find the eye—right one—go bad. The doctors say that the other is not likely to follow suit, and it has improved perceptibly in three weeks and more, but I cannot read with it at all, and it has rather "put me down," so to say[...]

We could not get on any boat going to the Mediterranean in April, but we have now got a passage on a Queen on May 9th to Paris. It will seem silly to you, I know, but I feel as though this were a wild adventure for so mature an old gent. My love to Nicky.

Affectionately, L.H.

P.S. By the way, among *les mots les plus justes* that I have encountered for a very long time is your: "In the beginning was the Guess." 'Twould perhaps be too daring to finish it for publication, but between ourselves I do: "and the Guess was with God, and the Guess was God." You meant it, I know, but I like to write it out. If this half-transmuted Ape, this *homo sapiens*, could only believe that, most of his troubles would be over.

ms with signature 99.24

1956-2

To Felix Frankfurter

February 26, 1956 Judge Learned Hand's Chambers

F.F.:

[...]I have been reading—no, that is not quite true, rather hastily "going over"—the recent constitutional decisions of your court, especially those on the First Amendment, and the experience has been nothing short of sobering. I think you know already my estimate of you, but it can do no harm to tell you explicitly how much I have admired all that you have said. You are indeed to my thinking the one member who comes out not only unspotted, but always with the only attitude that in the end will save the court if it is to be saved at all (about which I must own at times I have my reserves, unless it can be staffed very differently from what it ever has been). How it can retain any authority in the public mind with such divergences and such plain uncertainty of its own beliefs and duty, it is hard to see. And yet again and again I find people, Charlie Wyzanski among them! who seem to suppose that, if it will only be true to its best ideals, we shall have a force to guide us out of our darkness: a torch? Good God, a series of pointers each in a different direction.

I read for the first time the "Segregation case,"[164] and with great unwillingness could not help answering my own question to myself that, regrettable as I think the result, I did not see how, had I been called on to vote, I could have failed to concur. And I wish to withdraw what I fear were slighting words that I wrote about Warren. Of course, when I broach that whole subject to you, I need not add, I hope, that I neither expect nor want you to say anything. I recognize that you will and must be still as a sphinx.

Thine, L.H.

ms with signature 105C.21

1956-3

To Julius Cohen[165]

March 14, 1956

My dear Sir:

I have your letter of the 11th.[166] The quotations which it contains about what I said on May 30th, 1955[167] at the meeting of the American Law Institute are at least in substance correct, although obviously I cannot vouch for their exact verbal accuracy. Your question is whether my views were determined in any sense by what I consider the "prevailing moral sense of the community."

---

164. LH refers to *Brown v. Board of Education.*

165. Julius Cohen (1911–2005): Professor of Law, University of Nebraska, 1946–1957; Rutgers University, 1957–1981.

166. In a letter dated March 11, Julius Cohen asked LH to comment further on his statements on sodomy delivered at a meeting of the American Law Institute, as reported in TIME magazine. (tp with ms signature 97.29) There, LH had urged that private homosexuality not be prohibited by law because "criminal law which is not enforced practically is much worse than if it was not on the books at all," and because sodomy "is a matter very largely of taste and is not a matter that people should be put in prison about." TIME, May 30, 1955, at 13.

167. In 1955, the American Law Institute met from May 18th to May 21st.

That of course calls for my guess as to what in fact is the "prevailing moral sense" on this subject. In answer I may say that I think it strongly reprehends such conduct, but that disgust is a larger element than moral condemnation. As to how far our decision was determined by our estimate of the "prevailing moral sense," I can only answer that that was indeed taken into consideration, but that we distinguished very definitely between mutual conduct repulsive to the current mores but not directed against another person and conduct that is an invasion of another's legally protected interest.

Sincerely yours, [Learned Hand]

tp 97.29

1956-4

To Felix Frankfurter

March 28, 1956 Judge Learned Hand's Chambers

F.F.:

I cheer your stand, as you must know I would, about the privilege against self-incrimination.[168] Black and Douglas are frankly not judges at all: "to such favor will my lady come."[169] I am getting a bit obsessed about this step by step invasion of other folks' duties by these conceited, willful, obstinate, self-satisfied men, wholly without humility, moderation, or background.

But do you really believe that the privilege itself is desirable? I don't. I agree that nothing is to be more deprecated than questioning of an accused out of court and after arrest; I would go the limit under your McNabb rule.[170] But in an open court, protected by a judge and an attorney of his own, I would allow the accused to be questioned. Possible abuses? Of course. Have we not had enough of government based upon possibilities? Besides, it is historically all wrong, isn't it? It all came from the Star Chamber and the Ecclesiastical Commission as I read my Wigmore.[171] It was the ex parte examination that was the abuse; I could more entirely do away with that. I would even forbid all such.

---

168. For LH on this privilege, see 1948-1 To Frankfurter, January 16, and 1954-5 To Griswold, March 17.

169. *Cf.* "Let her paint an inch thick, to such favor will my lady come." HAMLET, V, i.

170. *See* McNabb v. United States, 318 U.S. 332 (1943). The Supreme Court reversed the federal murder convictions of three members of the McNabb family, who were held without access to counsel and questioned over the course of several days before their arraignment. In an opinion authored by Justice Frankfurter, *McNabb* established the rule that confessions obtained after an unnecessary delay in arraigning a suspect after arrest would be excluded from evidence.

171. The Court of High Commission, an ecclesiastical court established by Henry VIII to enforce the 1534 Act of Supremacy, required subjects to swear an oath of loyalty to the monarch; those who refused were tried before the Star Chamber, a court where the ceiling depicted stars. On the privilege,

I thought that Griswold much overemphasized the value of the privilege in his book.[172] Protect it as it is, of course we must—a *lex scripta est.* I am only wondering how far you really feel its importance. That in writing you should show respect for it of course was right and it was very wise. Nothing seems to me sillier, however, than to assimilate it to "torture," as the monkeys do. Indeed, I agree with Eddie Morgan that all privileges, being suppressions of truth, when one professes to be deciding rights—yes, and criminal liabilities too—on what is the truth, are to be jealously suspected. The one that, if I had *tabula rasa*, I should look at with least suspicion is that of priest and penitent. There! That's noble of me, from the outer rank of heretics where I belong.

Thine, L.H.

ms with signature 105C.21

1956-5

To Felix Frankfurter

August 28, 1956 Windsor, Vermont

F.F.:

There is plenty I want to write you about, and I don't quite see why I don't take the time to do it. Here I am really doing nothing but fussing, fussing, fussing over some utterly inscrutable stuff intended eventually to be two lectures which refuse to get born. The truth is that as soon as one tries really to reach to the bottom, one finds oneself (or at any rate I do) saying either pointless platitudes, mere personastic [sic] tautologies, or going off the deep end[...]

As to your two printed addresses:[173] Imprimis, although I recognize that your opportunities to know F.D.R. were immensely greater than mine, and although I agree with the place in history that you assign him (I voted for him three times), I simply cannot accept your estimate of him *sub specie* mere "man." But more of that when we meet. Secondo, [James Barr] Ames[174] was a noble lovely bird, and no one could bring to his work a more consecrated spirit; but I always felt about him what William James felt when he left Chautauqua: "What, no murders, no robberies?" Erasmus spent ten days with Bishop Fisher[175] and thus entered in his diary: "I cannot say how often I regretted that I had

---

see John Henry Wigmore: *Nemo Tenetur Seipsum Prodere* (No One is Bound to Betray Himself), 5 HARV. L. REV. 71 (1891) and *The Privilege Against Self-Incrimination; Its History*, 15 HARV. L. REV. 610 (1902).

172. LH refers to ERWIN GRISWOLD, THE FIFTH AMENDMENT TODAY (1955).

173. For Frankfurter's address, *Franklin Delano Roosevelt*, delivered at Roosevelt's graveside in Hyde Park, New York, on Memorial Day, 1956, see ROOSEVELT AND FRANKFURTER: THEIR CORRESPONDENCE, 1928–1945, at 750–52 (Max Freedman ed., 1967).

174. James Barr Ames (1846–1910): Professor, Harvard Law School, 1872–1910. *See Dean James Barr Ames and the Harvard Law School, in* OF LAW AND LIFE AND OTHER THINGS THAT MATTER: PAPERS AND ADDRESSES OF FELIX FRANKFURTER, 1956–1963 (Philip Kurland ed., 1956).

175. Dutch humanist Desiderius Erasmus (1466–1536); John Fisher, Bishop of Rochester (1469–1535).

agreed to stay ten days; the continuous atmosphere of so much holiness was more than I could endure." I had the same feeling about Brandeis. No more now.

L.H.

ms with signature 105D.22

To Learned Hand from Felix Frankfurter

August 30, 1956 — 3018 Dumbarton Ave., Washington, D.C.

Dear B.:

Your letter, which I've just read, makes me wish imperiously that I could get at you at once. And so I'm dashing this off—I hope, guided by reason. What you need, what your lectures call out for is a caesarian, and if I felt free to leave Marion for three days, when it isn't essential to do so, I'd turn up at Cornish and knock at your door. I mean this, I really would. For I have little doubt that you are foolishly discontented with what you have written, that you are looking for the philosopher's stone, that you are trying to demonstrate the un-demonstrable. Ultimately, I mean in the final reaches of reason, are not all conclusions (I'm not talking of the bloodless concepts of mathematics, etc.) up against it in any way that may fairly be called question-begging? You've thrown William James at me (what a delicious creature he was); I saw something of him "poisonally," not as a lecturer, so I'll throw him back at you. In an admiring comment on one of [Josiah] Royce's books, he wrote: "But it makes youthful anew the paradox of philosophy, so trivial and so ponderous at once." That's true of all jurisprudential writing and it is inescapably true of what you so fairly and so foolishly belabor, our Constitutional Law. The torture through which you are and have been going in your lectures, and I in my less metaphysically scrupulous and less competent way in some of my opinion-writing, is the best proof, no, is proof enough for mere mortals, that it isn't merely "a cover for doing what we want." I say it again, and not remotely in a smarty mood, that your lectures cry out for a caesarian. Trust what you have so conscientiously put on paper even if you can't or don't trust yourself.

Thine, F.F.

ms with signature 105D.22

To Felix Frankfurter

September 2, 1956 — Windsor, Vermont

F.F.:

Your letter came to me with a two-fold interest: first, I was much gratified with the background of friendship and affection that it showed; and second, I was disturbed by the strength of the counsel that it contained. It was indeed most warming to have you speak so ardently to me about what I should do, even to the extent of suggesting that if you had been free, you would have come up here to insist that I should dispatch this my job, no matter what its shape. Only a close friend who was deeply interested would do that[...]

There! Enough, and too much! I have never told you how glad I was that Harvard at long last woke up to the scandal of not giving you the LL.D.[176] I will someday tell you how baffled I have been for years at the curious attitude "they" evinced. I could never place the composition of that "they."

My love to the Marquise. L.H.

P.S. September 3

Am I wrong in thinking that [Richard Milhous] Nixon[177] is the *ne plus ultra* of the Old Guard spirit that T.R[oosevelt] rose against and that for once filled my then relatively youthful spirit with political ardor? The General has the enormous advantage in a democracy of not being too far above John Q. Public mentally: he thinks and he feels like the "common man," and the "common man" feels more affection for him than he has for anyone who has been in the White House in my time. Besides, one of the few things about which I feel sure is that democracies can't go along if they run into "splinter parties." Four years out of 24 is not enough to keep a party alive; this is a prime reason for voting Republican. Besides, as Scotty Reston[178] so well said, there is not much difference between the two anyway unless one looks at their "principles," and God knows "principles" are what I most abhor, politically, morally, or any otherly.

But this Nixon sticks in my crop[...] What he said about Communists and philo-Communists was as bad as the speech that Dewey made at Hartford—"twenty years of treason stuff"[...] Have you any help to offer me?

L.H.

ms with signature 105D.22

1957-1

To Herman Finkelstein[179]

January 27, 1957 Judge Learned Hand's Chambers

Dear Herman:

It is indeed difficult to know how to answer your letter; I shall try to do so, and I make it really to all of my law clerks for whom, if I am not wrong, you were

176. Harvard University awarded Frankfurter an honorary Doctor of Laws degree on June 14, 1956.

177. Richard Milhous Nixon (1913–1994): Representative from California, 1946–1950; Senator from California, 1950–1952; Vice President of the United States, 1953–1961; President of the United States, 1969–1974.

178. James B. Reston (1909–1995): journalist, N.Y. Times, 1939–1940; correspondent for the United States Office of War Information, London, 1942–1945; diplomatic correspondent, N.Y. Times, 1953–1964; associate editor, N.Y. Times, 1964–1968; executive editor, N.Y. Times, 1968–1969; vice president, N.Y. Times, 1969–1974.

179. Herman Finkelstein (1903–1990): General Counsel of the American Society of Composers, Authors and Publishers, 1952. He was the first of LH's clerks on the United States Court of Appeals for the Second Circuit.

writing.[180] As I come near to what must in the nature of things not be very far from the finish—in the home-stretch, so to speak—I ask myself what I have to be grateful for; and that young men of such exceptional and elected probity and intelligence as you are, all of you, should be able to think about me in the way you write; that appears to me to be an award, a kind of accolade, that is as satisfying as any I have had or could get. For, after all, you saw me when I was on my job, when I was putting out whatever I had, and, while I should not have wanted to take your judgments as of the years you were with me, now, you say that in retrospect you have not changed. I do not see who could have a better chance to appraise me; and—strange as it does seem that the appraisal is what you say—I will accept it and try to think that I do so with humility, though you have done your best to make that impossible.

I wish I knew better than I do what the whole show is about; I wish, in short, that the years had brought wisdom, or at least a measure of illusion of wisdom. All I can see that we do best when we think of ourselves as aiming at some construction, some embodiment, some objective impress in and upon the world about us that bears a resemblance to what appears to us fair and just and understanding and imaginative of others. You have all shown me examples of that purpose; most of you have already shown me successful realizations of it. I owe you more than you will be able to realize unless you too in your turn may have the good fortune to encounter young stars like yourselves to help you over the high stiles and the boggy paths.

Thank you all, know that in the years that may remain I shall not fail to remember what you have done for me.

Affectionately, Learned Hand

ms with signature 88.5

1957-2

From Felix Frankfurter to Learned Hand

January 25, 1957 Supreme Court of the United States

Dear B.:

Respect I've always had for age; at least I do not remember the time when I didn't. And rather early I gave myself as a reason that one who has lived long must have endured much. But for one who reached the years you will reach on Sunday, I felt more than respect: it was awe bordering on reverence. I do so no longer. Beginning with my experience with Prexy Eliot, of whom I saw not a little in his full vigor in his nineties, I've had too many friendships with men in their nineties for awe to have survived[...] As for the late eighties—they are too numerous to mention.

180. On January 26, 1957, Herman Finkelstein wrote a birthday letter to LH which included remarks on LH's former clerks: "we keep tabs on each other, and never meet but that the central topic of conversation is one that must be the envy of any other group." (ms with signature 88.5)

And so I salute, as does Marion, with joy, not with awe. You have given me much during all these years—nearer fifty than forty—and mostly not as an oracle of the law (I do not minimize your contributions to the profession to which I have given my devotion), but as one of the most delightful manifestations of the gayeties and depths and mysteries of the human spirit. Long may you wane! So says, warmly, Marion and your venerable friend,

Felix Frankfurter

tp with ms signature 105D.22

To Felix Frankfurter

January 28, 1957

Dear Felix:

Your letter is added assurance, though I needed none, of the regard and affection you have for me. It is among my most prized possessions, and, as you say, has endured for many, many years which makes it more and more so. Old age hasn't much to recommend it, but there are ameliorations notwithstanding. What? Well, for one thing I think one gets a little more the sense of anonymity, by which I mean that no matter what you have missed and the inadequacies of your past, it really is not so important as it used to seem. It would in any event have been indistinguishable in a few years if you had always hit the bulls-eye. Then too the urgency of this and that, the emotional drives so much lessen.

I don't think that this is quite the same as humility; it is less personal than that; it is a kind of acceptance—half acceptance anyway—of *Dinge an sich.* Holmes once told me that he was glad he had had no children, and when I ventured to ask why this is what he answered: "This is not the kind of world that I should want to bring anyone else into." No, I don't quite mean that either, and I am quite sure I don't want to die any sooner than I shall[...]

My love to the Marquise, affectionately, L.H.

ms with signature 105D.22

1957-3

To Felix Frankfurter

February 3, 1957 — Judge Learned Hand's Chambers

F.F.:

Your article in *The London Times*[181] really calls for a better answer than I feel qualified to give, for it leads inescapably into how we are to estimate statecraft, and although in a

181. Frankfurter's article reads in part: "[W]hatever may be the fluctuations of historical verdict, Wilson will surely join the company (the Father of his Country apart) of his three greatest

sense that in one of its limited aspects has been my job, the more I fuss over it, the less I feel able to get hold of any reliable fundamentals. I read it over again, this time aloud last night to F.A.H., [Nelson] Dean Jay, and his wife, and we all were struck with the great skill and beauty of the style; it is the best piece I remember of yours. However, that's not the point; you ask me how far I agree, and I am afraid that I am especially ill-qualified to agree or disagree, because, as time has passed, Wilson has become increasingly for me the type of statesman which I most distrust, and individually a most repellant human being, on the whole the American president for whom I have achieved the greatest personal dislike. It was not always so; I used to regret the bitter and discreditably petty venom that T.R. poured out on him, and I voted for him in 1917 though with complete lackluster.

But let me try to answer what you asked. It is a hard thing to prophesy and maybe you are right in putting him beside Jefferson, Jackson, and Lincoln in the sense of where he will stand in our permanent set of waxworks. I should guess otherwise, but God knows, I set no store on my powers of divination. He had, and I should say that it was his deepest failing, the gift of inspiring others, particularly women, with a sense of the loftiness of his moral principles and his searching penetration into the Realm of Righteousness that so often gets a kind of passionate loyalty that will make its object for the time being an absolute and dominating leader. Wilson felt this about himself. I like to think that when in a crisis he went into the closet to pray, he wrestled with the angel like Jacob—was it Jacob?—and the fight was real and crucial to him in its event. But (here comes in my evil bias), it was a sham fight. When he came out, God had told him where lay the RIGHT, and it was exactly what Wilson's subconscious had all along really decided upon. Such men are often irresistible, and the deep vice of them is that in a world where at most we have to barge along with the best guesses we can make, we know how little really lies back of them, and we crave more than anything else someone who gives us assurance that "He knows about it all, He knows, He knows." Wilson had a genius for creating that response.

If you ask me whether in a democratic society we can get along at all without such leaders, I must answer that I don't know. But this I do feel sure of: they maybe a necessity, but it is terribly costly palliative for our cowardice in being unwilling to face the necessity of moving forward, although we can see "but one step ahead across a void of mystery and dread" (G. Santayana), and to trust our straight path till something to the left or right gives us only as conditional a warrant for turning. If you tell me that human beings will never accept that as enough, I certainly shall not deny that you may prove right, but I do say that the kind of men like Wilson are soothsayers, misleaders of the

---

predecessors—Jefferson, Jackson, and Lincoln [...] His stature in the history of his country derives from the fact that he permanently influenced the direction of its affairs both within itself and in its global relations [...] Wilson's place in world history is tied to the fate of the ideal for the promotion of which he gave his life—organized peace. If it be the destiny of mankind increasingly to adjust by rational methods the inevitable clash and confusion of interest among the different peoples of the world, however agonizing the travail and checkered the efforts, Woodrow Wilson's name will surely be recognized as one of the most eloquent and resolute promoters of such a consummation. If, on the other hand, an era more ghastly than the Dark Ages is to be the lot of man, Wilson's fame will be obscured by it and his name will survive only as a nourishing hope to those who will start anew the toilsome journey toward reason." Felix Frankfurter, *Woodrow Wilson, A Devoted Champion of Organized Peace*, The Times of London, Dec. 28, 1956, at 7–8.

children of men, and that our one chance is to be content with the provisional, the tentative, the approximate, the compromise, accepting these as the best we can expect. (By the way Isaiah Berlin's *The Inevitability of History*[182] may interest you.)

Wilson will probably be remembered, as you say, as among those who pushed along that organization of nations without which we are headed in the end for mutual suicide. He will not deserve it; indeed, it was his colossal self-righteousness that ruined what might have been a promising start. Nobody ever destroyed his own child by his own vanity more completely. There was not a syllable of any new idea in it; it had all been thought out, so far as that is necessary after one really is seized by the purpose, over 200 years before, maybe earlier. I am not versed enough in history to know. But he aroused the forces that enabled his enemies, ill disposed as they were, to defeat him. No, I cannot go along with you, though I recognize that in many fights he was on the right side. If he had had Lincoln's humility, his gifts were real enough to put him high. But he hadn't, and so, do you mind if I consign him to the Pit?[...]

And, as ever, my love to the Marquise. L.H.

ms with signature 105D.22

To Learned Hand from Felix Frankfurter

February 6, 1957 Supreme Court of the United States

Dear B.:

You remember the outburst of the Victorian Bishop who controlled his own expletives when a careless waitress poured the gravy over him instead of into the plate, by saying: "Will some layman utter the appropriate curse?" You uttered full-throatedly all the things about Wilson that I uttered and suppressed. Not only is it true that "in the give-and-take of the spoken word" you and I would find ourselves only in negligible difference of emphasis. More than that, I am rather proud but also a bit surprised that you did not discover beneath the surface of what I wrote that I greatly disliked the cuss. Why am I proud? I will tell you.

When Sir William Haley,[183] about a year ago, asked me to write a piece on W.W. on the anniversary of his birthday, I wrote to him to say that I was far from being an idolater of Wilson and indeed that I took a very critical view of him. He replied that that was precisely why he turned to me. Maybe it was vanity, but I hope not wholly, that I convinced myself that I should like to put my judicial capacity to the test for myself. Could I re-examine, after all these years, my own old reflections and feelings about W.W. in the light of the relevant literature, his own voluminous writings and the books of importance that have been written about him, constituting as they do a sizeable library? For the better part of a year, on and off, I read and reexamined and reflected. The result you have seen.

182. LH may be referring to HISTORICAL INEVITABILITY (1954).

183. Sir William John Haley (1901–1987): Director-General of the British Broadcasting Company, 1944–1952; editor of THE TIMES, 1952–1966.

He never was congenial to me as a person (and I saw something of him close to, during the year I was with Lindley Garrison). I entered upon the enterprise of doing the piece with considerable dislike of him, but in an endeavor to be as fair-minded as I could on the basis of the materials which seem to be relevant. I hope that you do not find in the light of the confession that I have made about my feelings toward him that what I wrote is hypocritical or at least manifests the unconscious hypocrisy of satisfying one's own sense of fairness by bending unduly backward. I wish we could have the give and take of talk because I am prepared to defend the judgments regarding "statecraft" which I have expressed (fully agreeing with you about the difficulties of making estimates in that realm), although I came out of a year's living with him, as it were, with even a greater dislike of him than that with which I began. I wholly agree with what you say about his "gift of inspiring others, particularly women, with a sense of the loftiness of his lofty principles," etc. It is that that really grates me about him: his rancid morality, his self-righteousness. I am rather surprised that you make no mention of discerning this feeling about him, however gently or deftly expressed, in what I wrote. But he is also to be judged in relation to measures and movements and influences to which he was tied, and his significance in their context has to be assessed.

Of course, your faith is mine: "that our one chance is to be content with the provisional, the tentative, the approximate, the compromise, accepting these as the best we can expect." Gosh, how deep this cuts[...]

Affectionately yours, F.F.

tp with ms signature 105D.22

1957-4

To The Harvard "Veritas" Committee

March 28, 1957

Dear Sirs:

I have received your letter with its enclosures regarding the appointment of Dr. Oppenheimer[184] to the William James Lectureship in Philosophy.[185] It concludes with the

184. J. Robert Oppenheimer (1904–1969): Director of the atomic energy research project at Los Alamos, New Mexico, 1942–1945; chairman of the general advisory committee of the U.S. Atomic Energy commission, 1946–1952; director of the Institute for Advance Study at Princeton, New Jersey, 1947–1967.

185. In early March, Arthur Brooks Harlow, a New York City attorney, writing to Harvard alumni on behalf of the Harvard "Veritas" Committee, objected to the appointment of Dr. J. Robert Oppenheimer to the William James Lectureship in Philosophy for 1957. Stating that the "Veritas" Committee was constituted "to serve the cause of Truth" and that the committee believes "that our University, along with other American educational institutions, has been the target of Communist and subversive infiltration," Harlow questioned the propriety of Oppenheimer's appointment: "This scientist, because of fundamental defects in his character, was denied security clearance by the U.S.

expression of a hope that those to whom it is addressed will indicate their "support and advice and counsel." Although no doubt it does not require an answer, certainly it excuses one from an alumnus, who could not more completely disagree with your effort, or think it more to the disadvantage of the University.

I have read a considerable part of the evidence in the hearing and of the "Statement" of the Atomic Energy Commission, but any adequate discussion of the case would go much too far a-field. I need say no more than that I am wholly satisfied that Dr. Oppenheimer is qualified morally, as he certainly is professionally, for the position for which he has been chosen. I should say no more, were it not for the statement of the purpose of your Committee. This says that it is "to serve the cause of Truth," yet there immediately follows the statement: "We believe that our University has been the target of Communists and subversive infiltration." I can only read this as meaning that "the cause of Truth" must be kept safe from becoming a target of "subversive infiltration," and I cannot imagine a postulate more at variance with all that I value about Harvard. We do not conduct a kindergarten; the premise derived from all our history is that we shall teach students to think for themselves, and that if we do, they will be able to detect "infiltrations," good or bad. We do not seek to teach truth, but how to think; that is the chief difference between ourselves and all totalitarians. Anything else would be a surrender of our most precious possession and make us unfit to exist. You may use this letter for any purpose you see fit.

Truly yours, [Learned Hand]

tp 90.38

1957-5

To Felix Frankfurter

April 24, 1957 Judge Learned Hand's Chambers

F.F.:

I thought the "Mirror of Justices" one of the best things you have done, especially well written.[186] It is a little hard to have an independent opinion as to your thesis, because, as you say, one has to be one of the *Sancti Novem* and to know what it feels like. Anything I say you must take as consciously reserving that element. I am disposed not to agree with you that a preferential position should not be granted to a person with prior judicial experience, although I am entirely in accord with what I assume to have been a large part

---

Atomic Energy Commission[...] It seems strange that a man of his highly questionable moral background should be selected for this distinct honor in the field of philosophy, a study so closely identified with ethics and wisdom[...] How did this extraordinary choice happen to be made? Some individuals, or groups, must have been responsible for forwarding this strange selection to the members of the Board. Members of the 'Veritas' Committee feel constrained to find out who and why." (tp with ms signature 90.38)

186. *See The Supreme Court in the Mirror of Justices*, 105 U. PA. L. REV. 781 (1957).

of your object: to answer the suggestion that the Constitution should impose any such condition upon appointment to your Court.

The right answer, of course, turns upon what one thinks are the duties of that Court; in that I believe we are nearly in accord, though apparently not as complete as I had supposed. I cherish what is, as it seems to me, less and less believed: that even in construing the Constitution, we should concern ourselves with "Interpretation," and that that presupposes an imaginative projection of the purpose of the authors of any document upon the concrete occasion that calls for decision. This is not an impossible or fantastic attempt as to most of the Constitution, but it is utterly impossible practically as to those parts of the Bill of Rights that are now so frequently invoked. These are only admonitions to the sense of fair play—that is, that the lawmaker shall not favor himself or his group merely because they are his. As to these, I can see no room for judicial intervention except on the theory that that was not in fact the temper of those who uttered the command. That is an inquiry impossible practically; the result is "noli me tangere."

If that be right, the prime quality for your Court is a power to put oneself in the position of others with whose interests and antecedents he disagrees. That is the *suum* that he must learn to "tribuere" to "cuique," and it is not "Interpretation."[187] A prior experience as judge is, I believe, of sensible importance in the discharge of such a function. Of course, the main factor is the emotional balance of the individual, but practice, habit, and an enforced sense of obligation conduce to produce such a frame of mind. Moreover, if it ever became recognized that in the great key questions the role of even your Court was never to intervene unless it were sure that the measure before it had not been enacted in what I may call "Good Faith," its duties would be diminished to those parts of the Constitution to which we may apply the intellectual process that I have called "Interpretation." A court so reduced would on the average profit, I should think, by being recruited by men who, if they knew their job, had practiced that kind of "Interpretation." Those whom I most dread, even when, like Wiley Rutledge, they are men of the most impeccable disinterestedness, are the men who conceive it to be the chief part of their duty to keep this society in the path of righteousness and high endeavor. Jerry, for whom I had a very deep affection, could never pass against himself such a self-denying ordinance.

Of course, if there is not such doctrine of rigorous self-limitation, then the men one needs are those with insight and vision, and they seldom are found doing the daily work of the lesser courts. On the whole, I cling to the craftsman, though I believe I am in a small minority[...]

Give my love to the Marquise. Tell her she is often in my thoughts. L.H.

---

187. LH quotes a cardinal maxim of the law: "*Iustitia est constans et perpetua voluntas ius suum cuique tribuendi. Iuris praecepta sunt haec: honeste vivere alterum non laedere, suum cuique tribuere*" (i.e., "Justice consists in the constant and perpetual willingness to render to everyone his rightful due. The rules of the law are these: to live honestly, not to harm anyone, and to give each his own"). Ulpian, *Digest* 1.1.10. Reflecting upon how difficult a task this is, LH considers once more the question of values: "How are you going to tell what his own is? Does anybody know? As they say in English, 'My submission, my Lord, is that you can't measure values.' Values are incommensurables. You can get a solution only by a compromise." *A Personal Confession*, *in* The Spirit of Liberty 302–31, 307.

P.S. I have only one "complaint" to make of your paper: you included that incredible creature, Edward Douglass White, among your emergent justices. Oh, Oh!

ms with signature 105D.22

To Learned Hand from Felix Frankfurter

April 30, 1957 — 3018 Dumbarton Ave., Washington, D. C.

Dear B.:

[...]I refuse to believe that you could insert this paper's edge between the differences of your view of the judicial function and mine. The years here, especially since Hughes's days, have only confirmed the general outlook I derived from Thayer's Essay in 7 Harv. L. Rev.,[188] deepened by immersion in Holmes's opinions and the thinking to which I was led by my intimacy with Holmes and Brandeis (the latter did occasionally depart from his own strong, wise belief in the very limited scope of our job), my talks with you, and above all, my years here, which have made [me] intolerant [of] such essentially uninformed arrogance regarding the role of the Court that Charlie Wyzanski entertains. I shocked the gentle Ben Cardozo, in some correspondence we had, in suggesting that I wished the Court had found the Due Process Clause of the Fourteenth Amendment, once they departed from its narrow procedural scope, too vague for judicial application. Gawd! When I think how decisions have come to pass here during my time and the virtues that are deemed to inhere in them, I can't help but recall Bob Jackson's robust language, when he had to be lassoed not to get off the Court: "If I'm to work in a whorehouse, I'd rather go back to private practice." But so long as so much of our business must concern itself with these "admonitions," as you rightly characterize them, what you say of the reasons for giving judicial experience "a preferential" value loses almost all its force. Moreover, I wasn't treating the subject speculatively. I set myself the task of making as objective an appraisal as I could of the 75 Justices of whom I could freely speak, and what I wrote is, I believe, a fair estimate of their qualities and performance here.

I expected you to hit me over the knuckles about White. I share your opinion of his writing. But he is bigger than what he wrote, or, rather, how he wrote. Read for instance, Taft's estimate of him, 257 U.S. XXIV.[189] He had an instinct for the jugular; compare his opinion with that blabbermouth Harlan's on the one hand, and Holmes's on the other, in *Western Union v. Kansas*.[190] And also, White was a force on the Court beyond what he wrote.

Ever yours, F.F.

ms with signature 105D.22

---

188. I.e., *The Origin and Scope of the American Doctrine of Constitutional Law* (1893).

189. *See* William Howard Taft, *Proceedings on the Death of Chief Justice White*, 257 U.S. xxiv (1921).

190. I.e., John Marshall Harlan (1833–1911): Associate Justice of the Supreme Court, 1877–1911. *See* Holmes's dissent in *Western Union Telegraph Co. v. Kansas*, 216 U.S. 1, 52 (1910).

1957-6

To Felix Frankfurter

August 15, 1957 Northeast Harbor, Maine

F.F.:

[...]I have read or at least "been over" the batch of June opinions and they are discouraging. I do not, however, in the least blame you for joining in the results more often than you would have done had you been alone. I am satisfied that the Court has slowly but certainly assumed a position from which public opinion looks for it to guide the fundamentals of the national life in the right paths. Perhaps it was inevitable that this should come about, once it became settled that it was to have the last word about the validity of a statute of Congress or a state. It is hard to expect that men will be able to restrain their impulse to impose their own solutions upon others. The longer I live, the more I tend to agree with Acton.[191]

However, they are really digging their own graves—rather, I will say cutting away the support of their authority—because it will in the end come to a question of controlling their personal predispositions in one way or the other. Indeed, that is already true in a sense, for the election of appointees depends largely on their political, or, as I should put it, upon what James used to call their "passional" beliefs. Nothing is more difficult, indeed nothing is much more nearly impossible than "Interpretation," by which I mean the imaginative projection of another's answer upon an occasion that he did not anticipate, but for which he provided a command, cast in general terms. How many men have you known who would not, though quite honestly and unconsciously, intrude upon that function the deep urges that pressed upon them personally? Yes, I can think of some, but it would be hard to find as many as my fingers and toes[...]

Well, dear boy, this has been a rambling screed. I feel discouraged and do not make a good correspondent. 85 is probably too old, Felix, though with your super abundant vitality I do not think you need fear it. Your eleven years juniority prevents you from as knowing quite what I mean! Sometime we must talk about Mark Howe's *Holmes*.[192]

My love to the Marquise; she is often in my thoughts, as are you. L.H.

ms with signature105D.23

---

191. LH reflects on Baron John Dalberg-Acton's maxim: "All power tends to corrupt, and absolute power corrupts absolutely."

192. Mark De Wolfe Howe, Justice Oliver Wendell Holmes, 2 vols. (1957).

1957-7

To Learned Hand from Felix Frankfurter

September 8, 1957 3018 Dumbarton Ave., Washington, D.C.

Dear B.:

It is a propitious even if not happy day for me to turn to you for helping wisdom. I hope you can spare time and energy, and that your inclination will move you to do so, to tell me with particularity what you would do in my place were the constitutionality of the conventional [anti]-miscegenation statute[193] before you. I ought to put only one qualification in your disposition of the problem: you are to accept loyally the Court's decision on school segregation. I shall be much obliged to you. Of course, I won't tell you that I foresaw a Governor [Orval] Faubus,[194] but I can honestly say that I expressed my strong conviction that we shall be in for a long process, and probably with some ugly episodes. That's why I so strongly urged the phrase "with all deliberate speed" from Holmes's opinion in *Va.* and *W. Va.*[195] Why the phrase wasn't quoted and the case cited—the indication of a long drawn-out litigation—is another story.

Thine, F.F.

ms with signature 105D.23

To Felix Frankfurter

September 13, 1957 Windsor, Vermont

F.F.:

I got yours of the 8th only on the evening of the 11th, or I should have answered earlier, though I am not clear that the question is already *sub judice*. First, I must say that I have never read any of the anti-miscegenation statutes, and what I have to say is based upon the following understanding. There are several states that have not only made invalid the marriage of Whites and Negroes, but have made such marriages a crime, I am assuming a felony, though it does not matter. The only federal question is whether such statutes are prohibited because they "deny equal protection" to Negroes, and, I should suppose, equally to Whites. I know indeed that in the "Segregation cases" the Due Process

193. Many states had enacted anti-miscegenation statutes upheld by courts as valid exercises of a state's police power, protected by the Tenth Amendment.

194. Governor Orval Faubus of Arkansas; he called out the Arkansas National Guard to prevent the integration of Central High School in Little Rock in 1957.

195. In *Virginia v. West Virginia*, Holmes wrote: "a State cannot be expected to move with the celerity of a private business man; it is enough if it proceeds, in the language of the English Chancery, with all deliberate speed." 222 U.S. 17, 19–20 (1911).

Clause was held to apply, else segregation would have been valid in the District,[196] so that for these purposes the Fifth Amendment must be taken as equally applicable. You tell me that I am to take the decision *au pied de la lettre*, so I shall assume that the Due Process Clause was necessarily involved in it. May I however, think more in terms of equal protection than of due process?

I shall have to say, incidentally, in order to make clear what I mean, that I rather think I should have gone along with the "Segregation decision," though I should have wished to know a great deal more than I do about the enactment of the Fourteenth Amendment. My concurrence would have depended upon how far the history of years following Appomattox[197] justified me in thinking that the Amendment was passed in a spirit of extreme, indeed extravagant, egalitarianism in favor of Negroes. So far as all their legal rights were concerned, they were to stand upon an absolute equality with Whites. As they are taxed and otherwise subject to all laws in whose making it was assumed that they should have the same voice as Whites, there should be no distinction in the opportunities open to them, so far as any state law was concerned. Negroes, indeed any other persons, have a recognizable interest in being exempt from race discrimination. That may be unreasonable, but it is an indubitable "value," and, as such, being not peculiar to Negroes, it may not be ignored. (Maybe the same would be true if Negroes only regarded it as a "value"; that is not in fact relevant.)

If what I have said is true, I cannot see how we can possibly say that it does not deny "equal protection" to Negroes to forbid their marriage with Whites. It may be that there are good reasons for such a denial; Negroes may be biologically inferior, though, so far as I know, anthropologists do not say so. They may be culturally so backward that it is desirable to suspend intermarriage until they catch up. Neither of these considerations is relevant, as they would be in my own judgment were the question one of due process. They are not relevant because we are to read the Fourteenth amendment, *quoad* Negroes, as an imperative command by the Nation, that, so far as concerns the laws of a state, their race must not be considered as a determining factor, regardless of the "values" at stake.

Marriage is an institution that depends upon the state law; the privilege of marrying is a "legally protected interest"; the state may attach to it any conditions that seem to it appropriate, and the Constitution has nothing to say about what these may be. However, there is this exception, based upon the Fourteenth Amendment, that a state shall not make race—Negro race—one of those conditions. If a state passed a law that in fact impinged generally on Negroes more than Whites, it would be valid, provided the test was not obviously false and a disguise. But as soon as it appeared in any way that a court could recognize that it was intended or applied as a racial test, the Nation having stepped in in 1868 and imperatively forbidden it, we must accept the result, good or bad.

That is what I cannot avoid concluding, and I must own that it is to me a most unwelcome result. It is an instance of imposing on our constantly varying society, like all

196. The District of Columbia is under federal law; see the Court's discussion in *Bolling v. Sharpe*, decided simultaneously with *Brown v. Board of Education. See* 1954-6 To Frankfurter, June 5, note 126.

197. Confederate General Robert E. Lee surrendered to Union General Ulysses S. Grant on April 9, 1865, in Appomattox, Virginia. Relevant Amendments were ratified in following years: the Thirteenth in 1865; the Fourteenth in 1868; and the Fifteenth in 1870.

societies, a generalization that covers all sorts of occasions, each having its own congeries of pros and cons. No doubt all law is inevitably somewhat subject to that defect; it is impossible to foresee and provide for all the mutations and variants of a purpose that at large we wish to realize. However, when you inscribe in your fundamental charter such a prohibition, and there is no honest way to say that it is not intended to be enforced just as it reads, what alternative have you? Personally I think that the whole kit of ideas embodied in the Bill of Rights ought not to have had the sanction of "law" behind them, for law means force—at least to you and me, though apparently not to Charlie Wyzanski. If I could see any honest way of escaping the conclusion that the taboo on race discrimination was an "absolute," I should seize upon it. I do not see any and the "Segregation case" has closed it, if there was one I do not see[...]

I go down some day during the week of the 30th. I should finish those thrice-accursed lectures and then go back with contentment, if not with zest, to what Cousin Augustus used so feelingly to describe as "farting along the bench." I saw Arthur Goodhart[198] last week, who said that we Americans acquitted ourselves without discredit in London, save for your Brother [Thomas Campbell] Clark, who spoke for an hour and a half! "Angels and Ministers of Grace defend us!"[199] My love to the Marquise.

Thine, L.H.

ms with signature 105D.23

To Learned Hand from Felix Frankfurter

September 17, 1957 3018 Dumbarton Ave., Washington, D.C.

Dear B.:

You were most generous of your time, thought, and energy to write me so fully on miscegenation, and I'm truly deeply grateful. No, it is not immediately here, but vividly in the offing. We twice shunted it away, and I pray we may be able to do it again without being too brazenly evasive. The outcome, whatever it turned out to be, bodes no good for anything that you and I cherish. That the nation's highest judicial tribunal should be concerned with such an issue casts for me about as unhappy a light as is afforded by the tasks the Fourteenth Amendment puts on the USSC—or the Court assumed when it did not hold that the questions thereby raised are no more fit for judicial determination than is the guaranty of a "republican form of government." Your reasoning and the conclusion to which it led you make me extremely uncomfortable, because I may have to yield to the force of what you say, and deep within me I do not want to. Being the kind of creature that my training for half a century has made me, and not like—say I, I hope not, Pharisaically—others, I may well reach your conclusion, however much I may shrink from it.

---

198. Arthur Lehman Goodhart, Professor of Jurisprudence, Oxford University, 1931–1951.

199. Thomas Campbell Clark (1899-1977): Associate Justice of the United States Supreme Court, 1949–1967. LH quotes Hamlet's words on seeing his father's ghost. HAMLET, I, iv.

The Fifteenth Amendment, the right to vote, is explicit, dogmatic, in ruling out color. (That's why I was for the restricted voting provision in the new Civil Rights Act,[200] and am very glad they lopped off the Reconstruction "civil-rights" incorporation.) The Fourteenth makes no reference to color, however much regard for the right of "the blacks" (as O.W.H. always spoke of them) may have been the generating source of the enactment. (I shall be sending you shortly the most dependable account of the enactment of the Fourteenth Amendment proposal, written by a former law clerk of mine, [Alexander] Bickel, who made it first-rate for my needs while he was with me and then manicured it for a Harv. L. Rev. paper.[201]) You are quite right in putting "due process" to one side. We had to draw on that in the Fifth to avoid the absurd conclusion that the States can't have segregation, but the D. of Col. may!

But since "color" is not as such in the Fourteenth, why do you rule out relevant considerations of "classification" regarding "equal protection"—except by the starting point (as one of those ultimate question-beggings in all sociological reasoning) that color is absolutely barred as a basis of "classification" allowed by "equal protection"? Is the answer that IT IS!! the iron intellectual prison within which the Fourteenth confines me? God knows, I know what intellectually offensive conclusions this business of "equal protection" sometimes produces. I enclose the latest sample![202] From all of which you will infer how hard I shall work, within the limits of judicial decency, to put off decision on miscegenation as long as I can, just as [Robert] Jackson and I worked astutely and persistently in putting off a head-on decision on segregation *an sich*, as against "separate or equal." But that's another story—how short sighted some of the lads were in their eagerness to precipitate the present situation ten years ago! I have been so wary to avoid touching your sensibilities regarding the Holmes Lectures that I hardly dare tell you of my satisfaction to be told by you that you are reaching port with them.

My fondest to both of you, F.F.

ms with signature 105D.23

To Felix Frankfurter

September 25, 1957 Windsor, Vermont

F.F.:

The plot thickens; I had not thought of the Fifteenth Amendment, and at first blush I was much impressed by your suggestion that it specified "race and previous condition of servitude."

---

200. The Civil Rights Act of 1957 established the Civil Rights Section of the Justice Department and empowered federal prosecutors to obtain court injunctions against interference with the right to vote, and a federal Civil Rights Commission with authority to investigate discriminatory conditions and recommend corrective measures.

201. Bickel states that the Court, recognizing that "the record of history, properly understood, left the way open to, in fact invited, a decision based on the moral and material state of the nation in 1954, not 1866." *The Original Understanding of the Segregation Decision*, 69 HARV. L. REV. 1, 65 (1955).

202. This "sample" is not in the Hand Papers.

Besides, if the Fourteenth is to apply only as an admonition to the States, why make it exceptional when "race" is concerned? If on all other occasions the State legislatures are free to balance the values as seem to them appropriate for their communities, why is "race" to be singled out for special treatment amid a congeries otherwise undifferentiated? When I looked at dates, however, it seemed to me that the Fifteenth did not help much. Congress passed it on February 27th, 1869, nearly three years after it had passed the Fourteenth, and nearly two years after it had been ratified. I should regard it as a very tenuous inference that the contrast indicated that the Fourteenth had not originally been intended primarily to protect Negroes. It is possible that the later Amendment was intended to strengthen the Fourteenth: "We did mean the Fourteenth to apply to Negroes, but only so far as it applies to all persons; now we say as to Negroes that their suffrage is to be protected, regardless of any other considerations." There is great force in this, though the question still remains how far a later Amendment is to be taken to construe an earlier.

But all this, though it has changed my attitude about the Integration case [sic] and perhaps my earlier assent to it, is beside your point, for you said that I was to accept that decision as correct when the [anti-]miscegenation statutes came up. If it is correct, I should suppose that it could stand only upon the view I tried to state before: i.e., the Fourteenth is to be construed, *quoad* Negroes, as though intended specifically to prohibit all discrimination based on race. You throw out by way of escape the Court's abdication when "Political Questions" are at stake: e.g., the "Referendum" decisions and Taney, C.J., about the Rhode Island constitution.[203] I do think that it would be proper and wise to resort to this doctrine when the question comes up, as it will, about enforcing integration by the use of arms. In short, you might say: "We have said what the Constitution requires of the States, but we will not attempt to pass on the means that the Nation may use to enforce our interpretation."

However, will that do when the [anti]-miscegenation laws arise? That depends, I suggest, on what sanctions are invoked to enforce them. I do not see how you can escape, for example, deciding as to the marital status of a White and a Negro so far as that comes up civilly. On the other hand, may it not be consistent when any criminal prosecution comes up to say that the enforcement of the Fourteenth Amendment by a State presents a "Political Question" outside the scope of the Court's authority? That whole doctrine is indeed quite amorphous logically, but it is a precious bit of casuistry, not to be disregarded in these days. Indeed, as I wrote you before, there is no way without resort to force to bring all these beggars to heel: let Congress cut off their federal appropriations.

How I should have voted in the "Segregation cases" I can't tell, for, as I said before, I should want to know more about the post-war history. It is rumored that Jackson and Reed both were personally of an opposite opinion on it, but more silent when they found too large a majority the other way. If so, I think that they were right. Thank God we have

203. In *Luther v. Borden*, 48 U.S. 1 (1849), the Court refused to endorse suffragist theories of popular sovereignty. Chief Justice Roger B. Taney declared such matters to be political questions committed by the Constitution to the political branches of government (Congress and the President) for resolution.

not another Dred Scott decision.[204] I am deeply concerned with the situation as is. I hope the Court will find a way to avoid passing on the validity of any means used by the President to stop the utterly disgusting conduct of the Southern ruffians. But again, as to miscegenation, I don't see how you lads can duck it, and when I think of the whole lot, minus you and John [Marshall Harlan],[205] I am not filled with joy. ([Charles Evans] Whittaker[206] is still an unknown.)

I leave here today week: F.A.H. a day later. I am not clear what I should do after I get through with the Lectures. I doubt that I shall be needed in the C.A., and the prospect of sitting in the D.C. is not too alluring. I certainly am not equipped by desire or experience to attempt any extended writing; besides, I am too old. Incidentally, I am increasingly inclined to ask myself whether constitutions that assume to distribute political power into separate compartments are practicable anyway. There must be some authority, I agree, to say when one "Department," as Hamilton called it, oversteps its boundaries, and that involves a definition of the indefinable, because all generalizations are really valueless, at least in government. We might still get along, were it not for our accursed legacy of the eighteenth century that believed in "Inherent Rights," but we can escape that only by abandoning them as jural commands with any external sanction.

Thine, L.H.

P.S. Since writing this I have received the copy of [Alexander] Bickel's *Harvard Law Review* article. A hasty glance over it shows me how much I ought to know and don't, in order to have any opinion of the "Segregation cases," but I don't see that it changes the question of miscegenation.

L.H.

ms with signature 105D.23

To Learned Hand from Felix Frankfurter

September 27, 1957 3018 Dumbarton Ave., Washington, D.C.

Dear B.:

If further discussion of miscegenation bores you, read no further, and I won't remotely hold it against you. If not, I respectfully submit:

Yes, I wanted you to start with the "Segregation decision." But that case did not rest on the absolute that the Fourteenth in effect said no state law differentiating between colored and non-colored is forbidden, even, if you please, in relation to what may be

---

204. In 1856, Chief Justice Roger B. Taney delivered the majority opinion in *Dred Scott v. Sandford*, 60 U.S. 393 (1857), which stated that any person descended from black Africans, whether slave or free, was not a citizen of the United States according to the U.S. Constitution. The Court, however, was split; six Justices concurred and two dissented. LH expresses relief that in *Brown v. Board of Education*, the Court's decision was unanimous.

205. John Marshall Harlan II (1899–1971): Associate Justice of the United States Supreme Court, 1955–1971.

206. Charles Evans Whittaker (1901–1973): Associate Justice of the United States Supreme Court, 1957–1962.

called "inherent rights." It did not suggest that educational facilities involve "inherent rights"; it did insist that separate state "educational facilities are inherently unequal," and the State cannot thus discriminate in the facilities it supplies. I'm confident that as comprehensive a proposition as yours in dealing with miscegenation—that distinctions between different biological strains, colored and "white," are now out—would not have commanded unanimity. I know I would not have agreed to it, nor, I'm sure, would several others, perhaps even a majority would have balked. And is "freedom" to marry an "inherent right"? Not a few Northern States have restrictions on marriage for which, I suspect, there is no biological foundation. What about restraints on marriages by cousins and uncles and nieces and the like? Only the other day was the prohibition against marrying a deceased wife's sister lifted in England, though under Jewish law such a marriage was, I believe, enjoined!

I do not appreciate why you read the Fourteenth in effect as prohibiting a state-commanded elimination of disregard of the color line a wiping out of any "rational" discrimination (including among "rational" grounds an understandably entertained deep feeling which does not counter a predominant national interest as public education was cogently made to prevail). The historic gloss of the Fourteenth would have to be compelling, and the C.J. was wholly justified in speaking of "the inconclusive nature of the Amendment's history." (347 U.S. at 489). Or am I all cock-eyed?[207]

Ever yours, F.F.

ms with signature 105D.23

To Felix Frankfurter

October 10, 1957 Judge Learned Hand's Chambers

F.F.:

[...]I have tried to think out your problem about miscegenation, but I find it opaque. One possible way is to say, as I said before, that the "Segregation case" meant that race must not be a determinant of any "legally protected interest" of a Negro. I find it difficult to escape that, after reading Bickel, which you sent me, not that that enlightened me except that it left the issue without historical interpretation.

Another way might be to pass the buck to Congress and the President; i.e., declare that the Fourteenth Amendment made what you say is the law, but adding that enforcement involved "political questions" that you birds will not touch. You have never straddled that way, but is it impossible? Or suppose you say that unlike segregation, miscegenation is

207. Frankfurter's query seems casuistical: he asserts that the Court can order the desegregation of schools but that this order does not mean that it is eliminating the color line per se. In 1967, the Supreme Court unanimously ruled in *Loving v. Virginia*, 388 U.S. 1 (1967), that anti-miscegenation laws are unconstitutional.

ipso facto a "political question," and you won't even pass on it at all. I think it is more "loaded" than segregation.

The fourth way would be to say that miscegenation involves a balance between conflicting values, and under the Equal Protection Clause you will not try to review the choice allowed to the States. I am for that to the extreme in due process or equal protection also, so extreme that I believe courts should abdicate all review except on occasions, substantially impossible, when they can say that the legislature did not make an honest effort to reach a compromise—the best practically available.

But, as I said before, I can't reconcile that with the "Segregation cases." So I am afraid that I am not helping at all, but merely repeating what I said originally; i.e., that in the setting of 1868 the Equal Protection Clause *was* an "absolute," much as I revolt from all of them. I suppose I *must* say something about all this in my goddam lectures.

Thine, L.H.

ms with signature 105D.23

To Learned Hand from Felix Frankfurter

October 12, 1957 3018 Dumbarton Ave., Washington, D.C.

Dear B.:

[...]As to miscegenation. I wish much we could have talk, and if it weren't for the fact that I don't want to be away from here unless more or less of necessity (not that there is any concern about Marion except that it's such a lonely pull for her for such stretches of hours), I'd go up to see you. In lieu of talk, let me put a few things:

1. It will interest you, I believe, to learn that Bob Jackson strongly played with the idea of leaving enforcement to Congress, i.e., Sec. 5 of the Fourteenth. He found that it just wouldn't write. He tried it, tried hard for a considerable time, drafted and redrafted, and finally gave up and agreed to court opinion. (Incidentally, I don't suppose I have to tell you what a lot of hogwash has been written and uttered on the C.J.'s share in the outcome—that he 'done' it either by cracking the whip or by his winsomeness or both.)

2. Frankly, I fail to understand why Bickel's excellent article should lead to the conclusion that race differentiation was made an absolute irrelevance by the Fourteenth. As I understood his finding—he made that study for me while I was worrying about the problem—it was that the boys on the Hill left the scope of the Fourteenth for the Court's "interpretation" (I can't even spell the word!)

3. Nor can I agree, or rather nor can I read the "Segregation decision" as an absolute. Is it an absolute on "equal protection" to have concluded that "in the field of public education the doctrine of 'separate but equal' has no place? Separate educational facilities are inherently unequal (347 U.S. top of p. 495)?"

4. Finally, please don't take amiss a reference to your "goddam lectures." Of course I have no view on whether you "must say something about all this." But for the love of Mike don't say anything that lawyers and the cynical, unscrupulous Bill [William O. Douglas] can quote as the clear view of "the greatest living judge" that the "Segregation decision" covers miscegenation!!

Ever yours, F.F.

ms with signature 105D.23

1958-1

To Felix Frankfurter

February 10, 1958 Judge Learned Hand's Chambers

F.F.:

The Lectures went off far better than I had expected. I did expect a substantial audience the first night, but a diminishing return each of the other two. It was not so; apparently the stuff went down their throats with less effort than I should have thought.

What I meant when I said that I thought you might not go as far as I was that as I in the end came out [and declared]: the courts have really no part to play in the First, Fifth and Fourteenth Amendments unless they can find that the legislature was not actuated by an uncontaminated desire to give each man his due (*suum cuique tribuendi*).[208] Values are incommensurables and the business of legislation is to strike such a balance that it will be as well accepted, by and large, as is possible, given the prevailing conventions.

Courts have no means of judging legislative motives and an inquiry into them would be utterly "political," if they had. Thus in practice they should keep away and content themselves with confining the legislatures to the work cut out for them by the specific limits found elsewhere than in the Bill of Rights, at least those critical amendments I have mentioned. I did think that you would not agree to such a sweeping treatment. Nearly everybody seems to wish to keep more. I relied very strongly, as strongly as I could within bounds of decent respect, with your fight against distinguishing economic from "personal rights" or "civil liberties." The "Jesus Choir" of your NINE will think my work the most errant heresy, if they ever read it.

Anyway, the damned things are done and my relief is very great[...]

The lectures will be on sale—Harvard University Press—on March first.[209] My love to the Marquise.

Thine, L.H.

ms with signature 105D.23

---

208. *See* 1957-5 To Frankfurter, May 24 and note 187.

209. I.e., LEARNED HAND, THE BILL OF RIGHTS (1958).

To Learned Hand from Felix Frankfurter

February 13, 1958 Supreme Court of the United States

Dear B.:

The accounts that have come from Cambridge of the impressive success of your lectures have greatly rejoiced Marion and me. To have freed yourself of the albatross that they must have been around your neck all these years must in any event have been a great relief. But to have delivered them as triumphantly as you patently did ought to give you deep satisfaction that should last beyond the day, even though it cannot transmute the intermittently recurring gloomy ingredients of your nature. Time does after all make its exactions, and for you to have achieved an intellectual success which you could not, I am confident, have bettered twenty years ago enhances the intrinsic measure of the accomplishment. From what I am told, I infer that your peroration will be something that a good many of the students who heard it will cherish and recall for the rest of their professional lives.

One reason why you ought to find a source of relief in not having been on this Court is that you would have had one helluva time whenever you would have been called upon to act in these Due Process cases. Thus I doubt very much whether in the end you would have held out against the decision in the "Segregation cases." On the basis of some of the attitudes that he manifested during the short single term that Jimmy Byrnes was on the Court, I am bold enough to believe that even Byrnes, had he stayed on the Court, would no more have dissented than [Stanley] Reed and Tom Clark dissented. The fact of the matter is that Bob Jackson tried his hand at a justification for leaving the matter to # 5 of Art. XIV, "The Congress shall have powers to enforce, etc." and he finally gave up. Indeed, I cannot square your present attitude toward the "Segregation cases" with views you expressed to me about the miscegenation statutes. I myself do not see, at least not yet, why as a matter of intellectual honesty in starting with the "Segregation cases" the invalidity of the miscegenation laws follows[...]

Ever yours, F.F.

tp with ms signature 105D.23

To Felix Frankfurter

February 22, 1958

Dear Felix:

Your letter of the 13th is more than usually moving, which is saying a good deal. It is true that the boys responded satisfactorily to my closing words which came "from the heart," as I remembered my old teachers; i.e., seven or eight men as "pure" as I have known human beings. Nonetheless, what I really cared most about was how far I had got the right answers. What I tried to say is what I have got—sometimes I think all I have got—out of now nearly 50 years on the job, and not many will agree with it.

First, as to the "Segregation cases." Of course you can't "square" my attitude with what I wrote you about the miscegenation statutes—a good while ago. Of course you can't; nobody could because it doesn't "square." In excuse I plead: (1.) You asked my opinion, based on the assumption that the "Segregation cases" were right, (2.) At the time, I wrote you I thought the result was inevitable. It was only when, very regretfully and under the proper pressure of that Law Clerk to Beat all Law-Clerks, Roland [i.e., Ronald] Dworkin and one or two others who said "You simply cannot duck that one," I took up the pros and cons as best I could, that I saw, or at any rate thought I saw, that you were right in saying that your court had not treated the Fourteenth Amendment as making race an "absolute" as I had supposed. The rest was then easy, but the result pretty plainly wrong, as I viewed the constitutional powers of courts.[210]

I was acutely aware of the position of men like yourself, and you are quite right in supposing that had I been one of the NINE, I might have kept my goddam mouth shut when I found six of them against me. "No more Dred Scots for us," I might have said. That must be a common predicament, and it comes, as you will agree I know, precisely from the notion that courts are to point the way to a better life. Of course, there is little chance of agreement about that. Political pole stars are so often clouded; at any rate, I have never see any. However, on the whole, viewed now from a distance of two, or is it nearly three? years, I should guess that it would have been better to mess it all up. It is that anyway; but I am your slave as to that: you know the alternatives and I don't. The truth is that your *confrères* are a bunch of ruthless demagogues. No, I don't mean all, of course, but enough to ball up the whole show. For years it was my greatest desire to be one of you and I am still uncertain whether my change of feeling may not have a Freudian "compensatory" factor in it, (you know, the "fox and the grapes" stuff), but I am sure that now at 86 I couldn't possibly make the grade, and I have always thought that it was too late 16 years ago, when you tried so hard to get me in, instead of [Wiley] Rutledge (wasn't it)[...]

"And yet, and yet," as Graham Wallas used to say, I am not as despondent as Bertie Russell, *par example*; I don't believe we are going to blow the Hell out of each other.[211] I am still with E.M. Forster: "Two Cheers for Democracy!" Show me something at once available and not worse.

I have been confined to the house since Monday with bronchitis. I am not a good patient: fussy, "nervous," and apprehensive. "Silly old ass"; yes, I guess so, but it is much satisfaction to think that you like me. As ever, I always think of the Marquise when I am writing to you: indeed, it is to her as well as you that I write. If you can find God, messing around in the protons, electrons, neutrons and positrons, tell Him that it wouldn't be such a bad idea to take time off to bless you both.

Thine, L.H.

ms with signature 105D.23

---

210. LH refers to Ronald Dworkin, Professor of Philosophy and Frank Henry Sommer Professor of Law, New York University. For LH's position on *Brown*, see RONALD DWORKIN, TAKING RIGHTS SERIOUSLY 137–47 (1977).

211. *See* GRAHAM WALLAS, THE WISDOM OF THE WEST: A HISTORICAL SURVEY OF WESTERN PHILOSOPHY IN ITS SOCIAL AND POLITICAL SETTING (1959); *see also* POWER: A NEW SOCIAL ANALYSIS (1962).

1958-2

To Raymond Evershed[212]

April 7, 1958

Dear Evershed:

I got your kind and much too flattering letter about my Holmes Lectures[213] and under separate cover a copy of your Maccabaean Lecture for which many thanks indeed.[214] I have forgotten why I imposed upon you the burden of my own lectures; it was, I think, at the suggestion of someone in Cambridge while I was there that perhaps you might care to read them. In any event, I rejoice, since it resulted in getting both your answer and your lecture.

As to the last, I am in entire accord with you about the course of the "Law," not only apparently with you but also certainly with us. We have slowly but steadily become accustomed, either by statute or even more by what we call "Administrative Tribunals," to regulate the details of the life of the individual, so much so that the duty of courts is being more and more circumscribed into what you well describe as a "grammarial" function, but I don't quite see how this can be avoided. We must deal with the conflicting interests of countless individuals and can do so only by some sort of generalizations. It is not so much that tolerable overall patterns cannot be found as that the necessary information to make them gets more and more beyond access by judges unassisted by specialists. The specific issues are often not troublesome except as they pre-suppose a general background of acquaintance with the subject matter as a whole, which judges cannot have, and so it turns out that their decisions are irreviewable.

Did you chance to read Lord Radcliffe's addendum to his Reith Lectures?[215] He feels the difficulty and finds the temper of your people slowly changing by the surrender of those ancient conventions that have hitherto been the strength of your society, certainly the most successful anywhere, at least for the last two centuries. True, interpretation is not yet quite become a matter of the text "in one hand and the dictionary in the other," as Holmes once put it; after all we don't write in a coined diction like the scientists and colloquied words always carry what James used to call their "fringe." Still, the more detailed

---

212. Lord Francis Raymond Evershed (1899–1966): Master of the Rolls, 1949–1962.

213. Evershed thanks LH for a sending him a copy of The Bill of Rights and notes that the English press has indicated that LH criticizes the Supreme Court for its decision in *Brown*. Observing that the "judicial function" of the Supreme Court is different from that of the High Court in the United Kingdom, Evershed explains: "On our side, I think much trouble arises from (1) our strict rule of *stare decisis*, even in the H.C., and (2) what you call the 'unconditional imperative' of Parliament, plus the tendency of Parliament draftsmen to go into minute detail. The result is that the main judicial function tends to be that of the grammarian. I don't know how the knot, even vicious circle, can be stopped." (ms with signature 87.40)

214. The lecture was published under the title, The Impact of Statute on the Law of England (1957).

215. Lord Cyril John Radcliffe (1899–1977), published the Reith Memorial Lectures of 1951 as The Problem of Power (1952).

we get the less room there is for the imaginative projection of the author's purposes to occasions undreamt of when he wrote.

On the other hand, we do have a good residuum of what one might call "open-ended" legislation, not "implemented," as we like to put it here, by commissions and the like, and these still permit and indeed require authentic choices and by courts. But the old days of the masters, like Mansfield,[216] are gone and the game is correspondingly less entertaining. Besides, one can't help asking oneself whether it may not all end in the suffocation of the individual and if so, whether our democratic societies can survive. Over here at any rate, government is largely the resultant of conflicts between special interests whose compromises are necessarily a matter of give and take, and are largely undetermined by the interests of society as a whole. Brandeis used to think that any community begins to decline as soon as it gets large enough to make the emergence of its directors no longer depend upon the personal acquaintance of the directed. That was certainly a chimerical ideal, especially now when such tiny groups would not have the slightest influence upon the vast masses in whom political power is and will be vested. I must own that when I look forward, I can only see "as in a glass, darkly"[...]

If Lady Evershed should remember me, please give her my best wishes. Thank you again for your letter and lecture; and in the hopes that we may before too long meet once more, believe me,

With high esteem, [Learned Hand]

tp 87.40

1958-3

To Charles Wyzanski

December 9, 1958

Dear Charlie:

Your Chicago lecture may not be "required reading," but it is an amazing production[217] when I realize that you put it out during intervals in the full work of a busy district court, to say nothing of all sorts of interruptions such as your trip to Rhodes and the other jobs you have assumed. It astounds me that you have such a background of "jurisprudential" reading and even more that it has remained mobilizable as it has. It does me little good any longer to read, for I forget as soon as I finish.

However, it is your thesis that I want to say a few words about, for unless I have misread you, maybe we are not in entire disagreement. Like you, I regard "History" as our mainstay in legislation and I object to calling it "Natural Law" only because one then

216. Eighteenth-century English jurist William Murray, the first Earl of Mansfield.

217. Wyzanski delivered *History and Law*, the third Ernst Freund Lecture at the University of Chicago Law School on December 1, 1958. *See* 26 U. CHI. L. REV. 237 (1959).

assumes that its authority is valid, *semper et ubique.* I use the word, when applied to law or morals, as a corrective of those current compromises or adjustments that get themselves accepted in the clash of immediate conflicts. I agree that the past is so manifold and so inaccessible that we must always be uncertain what were the actual interests adjusted in the past. Nevertheless, the important thing is that as solutions they have enjoyed a long acceptance, and this gives them an authority which we are disposed to accept until they too greatly outrage some dominant group of present power. Why persistence should give such authority is another matter. I suspect that an animal like *homo sapiens*, through long "Natural Selection" has been made "conformist," because only those who conformed survived. However, that aside, most people are aware of the "burthen of the mystery [. . .] of all this unintelligible world,"[218] and crave solutions that they know are beyond their own capacity. So they cleave to those that have the support or the apparent approval of those who have gone before.

I meant in the [Holmes] Lectures that if one did look behind such generalizations, they appear to have been inferences from data quite as inaccessible when they originated as the data on which we must act at present, and that rationally all we can say is that they have induced general compliance and not provoked successful resistances. If we were not so constituted that our individual satisfactions were much the same over wide areas, it would be impossible to give them even this authority. To me, the most alarming prospect of the present time is that so many of the "principles" to which we have long given at least lip-service have lost their authority, and we are left with the raw material of our conflicting demands without any clue to mutual accommodation[. . .]

Affectionately, [L.H.]

tp Wyzanski Papers, HLL, Box 2, Folder 10

218. *See* William Wordsworth, "Tintern Abbey," lines 37–41.

EPILOGUE

I have fallen into near idleness; I have taken part in not more than 25 or 26 cases this year

—Learned Hand to Felix Frankfurter, July 13, 1961

"PURITAN AND PAGAN": 1959–1961

At the end of his life, the principal features of Hand's character reveal him to be the double that Frankfurter repeatedly identifies throughout their correspondence: the puritan—who with a humorous skepticism continues to check on the truth of what he is told, even if that describes his own qualities as a person—and the pagan, who with a dedicated passion for duty continues to embrace the obligations he has always cherished, whatever the conditions in which he must perform them.

1959-1

On April 10, 1959, the United States Court of Appeals for the Second Circuit held an "extraordinary session" to commemorate LH's fifty years of service on the federal bench. The event, which included tributes by Justices Warren, Frankfurter, and Harlan, was reported by Anthony Lewis in the New York Times on April 11: "At the end of the day, Judge Hand responded to their tributes. He said they reminded him of the widow who listened to all the eulogies at her husband's wake and finally went up and looked in the coffin. Asked why, she said: 'After all they said, I didn't know it could be Mike who was there.'"

To Learned Hand from Walter Lippmann

April 11, 1959 3525 Woodley road, N.W., Washington, D.C.

I want to be included in the crowd which is telling you to your face how much they love and admire you. For me, having known you has been one of the best things in life.

Always yours, W.L.

ms with signature 106.19

To Walter Lippmann

April 14, 1959 Judge Learned Hand's Chambers

Dear Walter,

Your letter fills me with a gratitude and satisfaction that it is hard to put in words. I have never ceased to regret that you went to Washington—wise as that step was—for it interrupted an intimacy which was my support and my enlightenment. It has been particularly hard because now, in what I cannot disguise as not being very old age, my movement has become much limited. I wish you would let me know if at any time you are in New York so that we could arrange to meet.

This "celebration" was made by [Charles Edward] Clark, the Chief Judge, concededly for the "circuit," not for me.[1] It was trying but of course gratifying also. Remember me to Helen.

As ever, L.H.

ms with signature, Lippmann Papers, Sterling, Box 76 File 978

---

1. *See* Anthony Lewis, *Judge Hand, on Bench 50 Years*, N.Y. Times, Apr. 11, 1959, at 1, 12. The "celebration" was evidently for LH and not, as he claims, for the "circuit." See President Dwight D. Eisenhower's letter to LH, dated April 8, 1959, *in* Proceedings of a Special Session to Commemorate Fifty Years of Federal Judicial Service by the Honorable Learned Hand 16–17 (1959).

1960

First published in May 1952, The Spirit of Liberty *had sold 7,500 copies by August of that year. On September 8, 1952, Knopf offered to pay LH royalties, which LH refused to accept. On September 29, 1952, Irving Dilliard wrote to say that the volume had sold 9,000 copies, and on September 31, he sent LH a check, this time one representing a fraction of the royalties that Knopf had sent to him. LH returned the check to Dilliard on November 4, saying, "All the stuff was written con amore." On October 19, 1954, LH wrote to Dilliard that Knopf had informed him that the volume had sold 20,000 more copies; it had been translated into Turkish and Greek. On January 2, 1957, Jean Paul de Dadelson, of the International Press Institute, wrote LH about a forthcoming French translation and the foreword intended for French readers. A second edition of* The Spirit of Liberty *appeared in 1953; a third, much augmented, appeared in 1960.*

To Learned Hand from Alfred A. Knopf[2]

January 20, 1960 — Alfred A. Knopf, New York City

Dear Judge:

First of all, I would like to extend my personal congratulations and good wishes, together with those of all my associates here, to you on the occasion of your eighty-eighth birthday. It has been a great satisfaction to us to be associated with THE SPIRIT OF LIBERTY and a particular satisfaction to have found for that book something like the sale it deserves.[3] You have been reluctant in the past to accept any remuneration whatever from us, but just the same I am marking this birthday by enclosing our check to your order for one thousand dollars. If you do not wish this for yourself, then perhaps you will divide it among your grandchildren. In any case, I hope you will accept it in the spirit in which I send it. Believe me, with kind regards and every good wish,

Yours sincerely, Alfred A. Knopf

tp with ms signature 91.24

---

2. Alfred A. Knopf (1892–1984): founder of the publishing house Alfred A. Knopf.

3. Correspondence on the publication and sales of The Spirit of Liberty with Alfred A. Knopf is filed in 91.21-24, and with Irving Dilliard in 87.12-16. De Dadelson was concerned that the forward to the French edition clarify the differences between the civil law of France and the common law of the United States, a legacy of the common law of England: "As you know, [the] French people, having known absolutist monarchies and a few even more Caesaristic forms of arbitrary power, have but little respect for their judges. They have to be briefly explained what the 'common law' has made of the English judge, and how much further still the responsibilities of the American judge are stretched by his endless task of interpreting the XIV Amendment or other passage of his constitution." LH replied to de Dadelson on January 17, 1957, praising his skill "in translating not indeed only the words but the background or 'aura' of English law into the tradition of civil law." (tp with ms signature 87.26)

To Alfred A. Knopf

January 27, 1960

Dear Mr. Knopf:

The staggering enclosure in your letter of the 20th leaves me almost speechless, which is a rare experience for me. Frankly, I cannot understand why I should be entitled to so much bounty from you. It is rather I who should give to you, for it was you who took the chance, by no means negligible, that the book might be a "flop" and useful only as a "deduction." Now that it proved to get a certain degree of welcome, I can only credit it to your backing, and it gives me a gratification that I shall not forget, so ample that I should feel more in your debt as I always shall anyway.

Will you understand, I believe that you will, what I mean when I send it back with renewed thanks for the chance you gave me of spreading about my desultory talks among so many people? No, I could not be happy, even though I spread it among my grandchildren as you suggest. Don't ask me to make your credit balance any larger than it must be, as is. If you really feel like lightening your load of cash, maybe Irving Dilliard might be a good receptacle.[4]

Please tell your wife that I have received B.B.'s book[5] with the dedication. My God, I can't understand what all of you can be thinking about. I feel as though I were in some happy dream and wonder whether I shan't have to wake up. Or perhaps you will all see the facts as they are. That *would* be tough.

Gratefully yours, [Learned Hand]

tp 91.24

1961-2

To Felix Frankfurter

June 13, 1961 Judge Learned Hand's Chambers

F.F.:

What a pity we so seldom see each other, but I think of you very often and talk of you all the time; you are the best of them all, and I was glad that Yale has had the sense to know it. I suppose you must be over-driven; the production of such a work as §7 about

---

4. On March 22, Knopf wrote to say he was sending LH a case of wine. (tp with ms signature, 91.24) On March 25, LH thanked him for the gift. (tp. 91.24)

5. Berenson dedicated his book, ONE YEAR'S READING FOR FUN (1960), "To Judge Learned Hand, With Deep Affection."

Communists[6] fills me with weariness even in mere contemplation. How the Hell you manage I can't conceive.

I have fallen into near idleness; I have taken part in not more than 25 or 26 cases this year and I would take up some other job if I could find one[...] My back gets progressively worse and holds me fast. I go around in a wheeled chair. Apparently the docs have nothing to cure it; I suppose that I should lie back and thank God that I have had almost 90 years without becoming worse crippled than I am.

If by some happy chance you should be near Windsor do drop in; you have no idea what it would mean to me! My love to the Marquise. I have not heard anything about her for months and months[...]

Thine, L.H.

ms with signature 105D.26

To Learned Hand from Felix Frankfurter

June 15, 1961 3018 Dumbarton Ave., Washington, D.C.

Dear B:

[...]I can't bear to have you in such pain and I wish I could exorcise your concern that you don't toss off 60 or 70 opinions. For me the wonder is the dog performs not merely at all, but so well. I have just read your two latest admiralty opinions. What are you griping about? The old master appears in them. If it were not so, I wouldn't lie to you. What a Puritan conscience is driving you, with all your pagan admixture. Why in hell should you be working near 90 with the [same] head of steam that you did at 50 or 60 or 70 or even 80? Why should you, and why should you fret that you don't?!

This has been the heaviest docket since I've been here and the least edifying. How often I think with relief, for your sake, that the Fates kept you from this crowd, or the old Battalion of Death. It isn't merely of the intrinsic difficulty of making judicial determination of what so largely are, certainly under the Fourteenth Amendment, policy questions. The old Court—McReynolds and Co.—at least voted their convictions, confusing their narrow views with the Constitution. This crowd, too many of them, often enough don't do that; Chicane and log-rolling play a considerable part. John [Marshall] Harlan and

6. Section 7 of the Subversive Activities Control Act of 1950 mandated registration of Communist organizations and required, among other information, disclosure of the names and addresses of officers and members and a complete accounting of funds received and spent. The District of Columbia Court of Appeals upheld the registration requirement, which was later affirmed by the Supreme Court in an opinion by Frankfurter. *See* Communist Party of the United States v. Subversive Activities Control Bd. No. 12, 367 U.S. 1 (1961), *aff'g* 277 F.2d 78 (D.C. Cir. 1960).

[Potter] Stewart[7] and [Charles] Whittaker are outside these strictures. If the true story were told, it could hardly gain credence. Owen Roberts left because of his unwillingness to work with unscrupulous colleagues, in the full flush of his power, and Bob Jackson would have done so if John Lord O'Brian[8] and I had not nailed him down. "Oh Liberty what crimes are committed in thy name." You are sweet to say what you did about [the] Yale degree.

Ever thine, F.F.

ms with signature 105D.26

7. Potter Stewart (1915–1985): Associate Justice of the United States Supreme Court, 1958–1981.

8. John Lord O'Brian (1874–1974): attorney; General Counsel to the War Production Board, 1941–1944.

CASES CITED

BIOGRAPHIES

Dean Gooderham Acheson (1893–1971): Undersecretary of the Treasury, 1933; Assistant Secretary of State, 1941–1945; Undersecretary of State, 1945–1947; Secretary of State, 1949–1953.

Baron John Dalberg-Acton (1834–1902): Liberal Member of Parliament, 1859; Regius Professor of Modern History, Cambridge University.

James Barr Ames (1846–1910): Professor, Harvard Law School, 1872–1910.

Charles Fremont Amidon (1856–1937): Judge, United States District Court for the District of North Dakota, 1896–1928.

Hamilton Fish Armstrong (1893–1973): editor of FOREIGN AFFAIRS, 1928–1972.

John Austin (1790–1859): Professor of Jurisprudence, University of London.

Warren Austin (1877–1962): Senator from Vermont, 1931–1946; United States Ambassador to the United Nations, 1946–1953.

Newton D. Baker (1871–1937): attorney, Baker & Hostetler, Cleveland; Secretary of War, 1916–1921; member, the Permanent Court of Arbitration at The Hague, 1928–1937.

Simeon E. Baldwin (1840–1927): Professor, Yale Law School, 1869–1919; Governor of Connecticut, 1911–1915.

Arthur James Balfour (1848–1930): Prime Minister, 1902–1905; Foreign Secretary, 1916–1919.

Otto R. Barnett (1868–1945): attorney, Barnett & Truman, Chicago.

Joseph Beale (1861–1943): Professor, Harvard Law School.

James M. Beck (1861–1936): Assistant United States Attorney General, 1900–1903; Solicitor General, 1921–1925; and Representative from Pennsylvania, 1927–1934.

Bernard Berenson (1865–1959): art critic and connoisseur of Italian art; advisor to collectors and dealers on the provenance of works of art.

Isaiah Berlin (1909–1997): Professor of Social and Political Theory, Oxford University.

Alexander Bickel (1924–1974): Professor, Yale Law School, 1956–1974.

Francis Beverley Biddle (1886–1968): Chairman of the National Labor Relations Board, 1935; Judge, United States Court of Appeals for the Third Circuit, 1939; Solicitor General of the United States, 1940; Attorney General of the United States, 1941–1945.

Hugo Lafayette Black (1886–1971): Senator from Alabama, 1927–1937; Associate Justice of the United States Supreme Court, 1937–1971.

William Blackstone (1723–1789): Professor of Law, Oxford University; Justice of the Court of the King's Bench, 1770–1780.

William Borah (1865–1940): Senator from Idaho, 1907–1940; Chairman, Foreign Relations Committee, 1925–1933.

Henry de Bracton (1210–1268): Justice of the assize, 1245–1266; Chancellor of Exeter Cathedral, 1264–1268.

Louis Dembitz Brandeis (1856–1941): Associate Justice of the United States Supreme Court, 1916–1939.

John W. Bricker (1893–1986): Governor of Ohio, 1939–1945; Senator from Ohio, 1947–1975.

Henry Styles Bridges (1898–1961): Senator from New Hampshire, 1937–1961.

Herbert Brownell (1904–1996): Attorney General of the United States, 1953–1957.

William Jennings Bryan (1860–1925): Democratic nominee for President in 1896, 1900, and 1908; Secretary of State, 1913–1915.

Edward Burling (1871–1966): attorney, Covington & Burling, Washington, D.C.

Charles Culp Burlingham (1858–1959): attorney, Burlingham, Veeder, Masten & Feary, New York.

Pierce Butler (1866–1939): Associate Justice of the Supreme Court, 1922–1939.

James Byrne (1857–1942): attorney and founding member of the American Law Institute, 1922.

James Francis Byrnes (1879–1972): Representative from South Carolina, 1911–1925; Senator from South Carolina, 1931–1941; Associate Justice of the United States Supreme Court, 1941–1942; Secretary of State, 1945–1947; Governor of South Carolina, 1951–1955.

Francis G. Caffey (1868–1951): Judge, United States District Court for the Southern District of New York, 1929–1951.

Edmond N. Cahn (1906–1964): Professor, New York University Law School.

Benjamin Cardozo (1879–1938): Judge, New York Court of Appeals, 1914–1932; Associate Justice of the United States Supreme Court, 1932–1938.

Edward C. Carter (1878–1954): Officer of the YMCA, 1902–1922; member of the Institute of Pacific Relations, 1926–1948; chairman of the Russian War Relief Fund, 1941–1945.

Zechariah Chafee, Jr. (1885–1957): Professor, Harvard Law School, 1916–1956.

Harrie Brigham Chase (1889–1969): Judge, United States Court of Appeals for the Second Circuit, 1929–1954.

Charles Edward Clark (1889–1963): Professor, Yale Law School, 1919–1929; Dean, Yale Law School, 1929–1939; Judge, United States Court of Appeals for the Second Circuit, 1939–1963.

John H. Clarke (1857–1945): Associate Justice of the Supreme Court, 1916–1922.

Henry DeLamar Clayton, Jr. (1857–1929): Congressman from Alabama, 1897–1914; Judge, United States District Court for the Middle and Northern Districts of Alabama, 1914–1929.

Julius Cohen (1911–2005): Professor, University of Nebraska Law School, 1946–1957; Rutgers Law School, 1957–1981.

Morris R. Cohen (1880–1947): Professor of Philosophy, City College of New York, 1912–1938.

Arthur Holly Compton (1892–1962): Professor, Department of Physics, Washington University, 1920–1923, 1953–1962; Head, Office of Scientific Research and Development, 1941–1945; Chancellor, Washington University, 1945–1953.

James B. Conant (1893–1978): President, Harvard University, 1933–1953; Ambassador to Germany, 1953–1957.

Calvin Coolidge (1872–1933): President of the United States, 1923–1929.

Joseph P. Cotton (1875–1931): attorney; member of the New York State Commission on Workmen's Compensation, 1910; Undersecretary of State, 1929–1931.

Norman Cousins (1915–1990): journalist; on staff of the N.Y EVENING POST, 1934; the SATURDAY REVIEW, 1940; editor of the SATURDAY REVIEW, 1942–1972.

James M. Cox (1870–1957): Governor of Ohio, 1913–1915, 1917–1921.

Paul D. Cravath (1861–1940): attorney, Cravath, de-Gersdorff, Swaine & Wood, New York City; Director of the United States Council on Foreign Relations, 1921–1940.

Richard Croker (1841–1922): head of Tammany Hall, 1886–1902.

Herbert Croly (1869–1930): editor of THE NEW REPUBLIC, 1914–1930.

Charles P. Curtis (1891–1959): attorney, Curtis & Curtis, Boston.

Clarence Day (1874–1935): essayist and contributor, the NEW YORKER.

Winfred T. Denison (1873–1919): Assistant United States Attorney, Southern District, New York, 1906–1909; Assistant United States Attorney General, 1910–1914.

John Dewey (1859–1952): Professor of Philosophy, Columbia University, 1904–1952.

Thomas E. Dewey (1902–1971): Governor of New York, 1943–1955; Republican candidate for President of the United States, 1944, 1948.

Samuel Dickstein (1885–1954): Representative from New York, 1925–1945; Chairman of the Committee on Immigration and Naturalization, 1931–1947.

Everett Dirksen (1896–1969): Representative from Illinois, 1933–1947; Senator from Illinois, 1951–1969.

William O. Douglas (1898–1980): Chairman Securities and Exchange Commission, 1937–1939; Associate Justice of the United States Supreme Court, 1939–1975.

Ronald Dworkin (1931-): Professor of Philosophy and Frank Henry Sommer Professor of Law, New York University.

John Foster Dulles (1888–1959): Secretary of State, 1953–1959.

Max Eastman (1883–1969): publisher of THE MASSES, 1913–1917, a paper supporting radical reform.

Dwight David Eisenhower (1890–1969): Supreme Commander of Allied forces in Europe, 1943–1944; Chief of Staff, 1945–1948; President of Columbia University, 1948–1950; Supreme Commander of Allied Powers in Europe, 1951–1952; President of the United States, 1953–1958.

Charles W. Eliot (1834–1926): President, Harvard College, 1869–1909.

Lord Francis Raymond Evershed (1899–1966): Master of the Rolls, 1949–1962.

Herman Finkelstein (1903–1990): General Counsel of the American Society of Composers, Authors and Publishers.

Thomas K. Finletter (1893–1980): special assistant to Secretary of State Cordell Hull, 1941–1943; deputy director of the Office of Foreign Economic Coordinator, 1943–1944; consultant at the United Nations Conference on International Organization at San Francisco, 1945; Chairman, the Air Policy Commission, 1948; Secretary of the Air Force 1950–1953; Ambassador to the North Atlantic Treaty Organization, 1961–1965.

Simon Flexner (1863–1946): Director of the laboratories of the Rockefeller Institute for Medical Research in New York, 1901–1935; charter member of the Rockefeller Foundation.

Jerome New Frank (1889–1957): attorney; general counsel, the Agricultural Adjustment Administration, 1933–1935; special counsel, the Reconstruction Finance Association, 1935–1937; commissioner, the Securities and Exchange Commission, 1937–1941; Judge, United States Court of Appeals for the Second Circuit, 1941–1957.

Felix Frankfurter (1882–1965): Professor, Harvard Law School, 1914–1939; Associate Justice of the United States Supreme Court, 1939–1962.

Ernst Freund (1864–1932): Professor of Political Science, University of Chicago, 1894–1902; Professor, University of Chicago Law School, 1903–1932.

Henry J. Friendly (1903–1986): Judge, United States Court of Appeals for the Second Circuit, 1959–1986.

Alvan T. Fuller (1878–1958): Governor of Massachusetts, 1925–1929.

Lindley Garrison (1864–1932): Vice Chancellor of New Jersey, 1904–1913; Secretary of War, 1913–1916.

William Lloyd Garrison (1805–1879): editor of THE LIBERATOR; a founding member of The American Anti-Slavery Society.

John Chipman Gray (1839–1915): Professor, Harvard Law School, 1869–1913.

Sir Wilfred Greene (1883–1952): Lord Justice of Appeal, 1935–1937; Master of the Rolls, 1937–1949.

Thomas W. Gregory (1861–1933): Special Assistant to the United States Attorney General, 1913; Attorney General of the United States, 1914–1919.

Erwin Nathaniel Griswold (1904–1994): Solicitor General of the United States, 1967–1973; Dean, Harvard Law School, 1946–1967.

William D. Guthrie (1859–1935): Professor of Law, Columbia University.

Sir William John Haley (1901–1987): Director-General of the British Broadcasting Corporation, 1944–1952; editor THE TIMES, 1952–1966.

Augustus Noble Hand (1869–1954): the son of Richard Lockhart Hand, the brother of Learned Hand's father Samuel, and first cousin of Learned Hand; Judge, United States District Court for the Southern District, 1914–1928; Judge, United States Court of Appeals for the Second Circuit, 1928–1953.

Norman Hapgood (1868–1937): editor of COLLIER'S WEEKLY, 1903–1912; HARPER'S WEEKLY, 1913–1916; HEARST'S INTERNATIONAL MAGAZINE, 1923–1925.

Warren Gamaliel Harding (1865–1923): President of the United States, 1921–1923.

John Marshall Harlan (1833–1911): Associate Justice of the United States Supreme Court, 1877–1911.

John Marshall Harlan, II (1899–1971): Associate Justice of the United States Supreme Court, 1955–1971.

Jane Ellen Harrison (1860–1928): Lecturer, Newnham College, Cambridge University, 1898–1922.

Louis Henkin (1917–2010): United States Department of State, 1948–1956; Professor, University of Pennsylvania Law School, 1958–1962; Professor and University Professor, Columbia Law School, 1962–2010.

Frank H. Hiscock (1856–1946): Judge, New York State Court of Appeals, 1910–1916; Chief Judge, 1916–1926.

Alger Hiss (1904–1996): attorney, Choate, Hall & Stewart, Boston; assistant to Francis B. Sayre, Assistant Secretary of State, 1936; Director, Office of Special Policy Affairs, 1945; President, Carnegie Endowment for International Peace, 1945–1949; accused of being a Soviet spy in 1948 by the House Committee on Un-American Activities; convicted of perjury in connection with this charge in 1950; released from prison in 1954; readmitted to the Massachusetts Bar, 1975.

William Hitz (1872–1935): Judge, United States District Court for the District of Columbia, 1916–1931; Judge, United States Court of Appeals for the District of Columbia Circuit, 1931–1935.

Frank E. Holman (1886–1961): President, the American Bar Association, 1948–1949.

Oliver Wendell Holmes, Jr. (1831–1935): Associate Justice of the Massachusetts Supreme Judicial Court, 1882–1899; Chief Justice of the Massachusetts Supreme Judicial Court, 1899–1902; Associate Justice of the United States Supreme Court, 1902–1932.

George Chandler Holt (1843–1931): Judge, United States District Court for the Southern District of New York, 1903–1914.

Herbert Clark Hoover (1874–1964): Secretary of Commerce under Presidents Warren Harding and Calvin Coolidge; President of the United States, 1929–1933.

Charles Merrill Hough (1858–1927): Judge, United States District Court for the Southern District, 1906–1916; Judge, United States Court of Appeals for the Second Circuit, 1916–1927.

Edward M. House (1858–1938): advisor to President Wilson.

Charles Evans Hughes (1862–1948): Governor of New York, 1907–1910; Associate Justice of the United States Supreme Court, 1910–1916; Secretary of State, 1921–1925; Judge, the Permanent Court of International Justice, 1928–1930; Chief Justice of the United States, 1930–1941.

Joseph C. Hutcheson, Jr. (1853–1973): Judge, United States District Court for the Southern District of Texas, 1918–1930; Judge, United States Court of Appeals for the Fifth Circuit, 1931–1973.

Robert H. Jackson (1892–1954): United States Attorney General, 1940–1941; Associate Justice of the United States Supreme Court, 1941–1954; chief United States prosecutor at the Nuremberg Trials, 1945–1946.

William James (1842–1910): Professor of Psychology and Philosophy, Harvard University, 1873–1907.

Nelson Dean Jay (1883–1972): partner and later chairman, Morgan & Cie., Paris, 1920–1955.

William E. Jenner (1908–1985): Senator from Indiana, 1944–1945, 1947–1959.

Sir George Jessel (1824–1883): Master of the Rolls, Court of Chancery.

Alvin Johnson (1864–1971): economist; editor, The New Republic, 1915–1917; founder of The New School for Social Research, 1918.

Hiram Johnson (1866–1945): Governor of California, 1910–1916; Senator from California, 1917–1945.

George Frost Kennan (1904–2005): United States Foreign Service, 1927–1952; Ambassador to the Soviet Union, 1952–1953; Professor of Historical Studies, Institute for Advanced Study, 1953.

James Kent (1763–1847): Chancellor of New York State, 1814–1823.

Philip Kerr (1882–1940): Secretary to Lloyd George, 1916–1921; later Lord Lothian, British Ambassador to the United States, 1939–1940.

John Maynard Keynes (1883–1946): economist; Lecturer, Cambridge University; Director of the Bank of England, 1940–1945.

Harley M. Kilgore (1895–1956): Senator from West Virginia, 1941–1956; Chair, Antitrust and Monopoly Subcommittee of the Senate Committee on the Judiciary.

Freda Kirschwey (1893–1976): editor of THE NATION, 1918–1955.

Alfred A. Knopf (1892–1984): founder and publisher, the Alfred A. Knopf & Co.

Robert Martin La Follette (1855–1925): Governor of Wisconsin, 1901–1906; Senator from Wisconsin, 1906–1925.

James M. Landis (1899–1960): Professor, Harvard Law School; member, Securities and Exchange Commission, 1934–1937; Dean, Harvard Law School, 1938–1946.

Christopher Columbus Langdell (1826–1909): Dean, Harvard Law School.

Robert Lansing (1864–1928): Secretary of State, 1915–1920.

Harold Joseph Laski (1893–1950): economist; Professor of Political Science, London School of Economics, 1926–1950.

Owen Lattimore (1900–1989): Lecturer in History, Johns Hopkins University.

Charles Lindbergh (1902–1974): American aviator, author, inventor, and explorer. On May 20–21, 1927, Lindbergh piloted the first solo nonstop transatlantic flight from New York (Roosevelt Field) to Paris (Le Bourget Field) in the single-seat, single-engine monoplane. He was a member of the America First Committee, the foremost pressure group against American entry into the Second World War.

Walter Lippmann (1889–1974): journalist, author.

Philip Littell (1868–1843): editorial staff, the N.Y. GLOBE, 1910–1913; editor, THE NEW REPUBLIC, 1914–1923.

Henry Cabot Lodge, Jr. (1902–1985): Senator from Massachusetts, 1937–1944, 1947–1953; Representative to the United Nations, 1953–1960; Ambassador to Vietnam, 1965–1967; Ambassador to West Germany, 1968–1969.

A. Lawrence Lowell (1856–1943): Professor, Harvard Law School, 1898–1909; President, Harvard University, 1909–1933.

Henry T. Lummus (1876–1968): Associate Justice of the Supreme Judicial Court of Massachusetts, 1932–1955.

William Gibbs McAdoo (1863–1941): Secretary of the Treasury and Chairman of the Federal Reserve Board, 1914–1917; Senator from California, 1933–1938.

Joseph McCarthy (1908–1957): Senator from Wisconsin, 1947–1957; chairman, Senate Permanent Subcommittee on Investigations examining evidence of Communist influence in the United States.

John J. McCloy (1895–1989): President of the World Bank, 1947–1949; High Commissioner for Germany, 1949–1952.

Robert R. McCormick (1880–1955): journalist; publisher of the CHICAGO TRIBUNE.

Ramsay MacDonald (1866–1937): Prime Minister, 1924, 1929, 1931–1935.

Julian Mack (1866–1943): Judge, United States Court of Appeals for the Seventh Circuit, 1911–1929; Judge, United States Court of Appeals for the Sixth Circuit, 1930–1940.

Joseph McKenna (1843–1926): Associate Justice of the United States Supreme Court, 1898–1925.

William McKinley (1843–1901): President of the United States, 1897–1901.

Frank Douglas MacKinnon (1871–1946): Lord Justice of Appeal, 1907–1946.

James Clark McReynolds (1862–1946): United States Attorney General, 1913–1914; Associate Justice of the United States Supreme Court, 1914–1941.

Martin T. Manton (1880–1946): Judge, District Court for the Southern District of New York, 1916–1918; Judge, United States Court of Appeals for the Second Circuit, 1918–1939; convicted of bribery, 1939.

George Catlett Marshall (1880–1959): Army Chief of Staff, 1939–1945; Secretary of State, 1947–1949; Secretary of Defense, 1950–1951.

John Marshall (1755–1835): Chief Justice of the United States, 1801–1835.

Julius M. Mayer (1865–1925): Judge, United States District Court for the Southern District of New York, 1912–1921; Judge, United States Court of Appeals for the Second Circuit, 1921–1924.

Alexander Meiklejohn (1872–1964): President, Amherst College.

David Hunter Miller (1875–1961): Special Assistant to Paris Peace Conference, 1917–1919; drafted the covenant to the League of Nations, 1928; Judge, Permanent Court of International Justice, 1930; adviser to the State Department, 1931–1938.

Robert Millikan (1868–1953): Professor of Physics, University of Chicago; President of the California Institute of Technology, 1921–1945.

William DeWitt Mitchell (1874–1955): Solicitor General, 1925; Attorney General of the United States, 1929–1933.

Edward M. Morgan (1878–1966): Professor, Yale Law School, 1917–1925; Professor, Harvard Law School, 1925–1950; Professor, Vanderbilt Law School, 1950–1962.

Henry Morganthau (1856–1946): attorney; United States Ambassador to the Ottoman Empire, 1913–1916.

John Bassett Moore (1860–1947): Assistant Secretary of State, 1886–1891; Professor, Columbia Law School, 1891–1924; member, Permanent Court of Arbitration at the Hague, 1912–1921; Judge, Permanent Court of International Justice, 1921–1928.

Dwight Whitney Morrow (1873–1931): attorney and banker; chief civilian aide to General John J. Pershing during World War I; Ambassador to Mexico, 1927–1930; Senator from New Jersey, 1930–1931.

Frank Murphy (1890–1949): Governor General of the Philippines, 1930–1933; United States High Commissioner of the Philippines, 1935–1936; Governor of Michigan, 1937–1939; United States Attorney General, 1939–1940; Associate Justice of the United States Supreme Court, 1940–1949.

Gilbert Murray (1866–1957): Regius Professor of Greek, Oxford University.

Donald M. Nelson (1888–1959): Director, War Production Board, 1942–1945.

Richard Milhous Nixon (1913–1994): Representative from California, 1946–1950; Senator from California 1950–1952; Vice President of the United States, 1953–1961; President of the United States, 1969–1974.

George W. Norris (1861–1944): Senator from Nebraska, 1913–1943.

Charles Eliot Norton (1827–1908): editor of the NORTH AMERICAN REVIEW, 1864–1868; Professor of the History of Art, Harvard University, 1875–1898.

Gerald P. Nyes (1892–1971): Senator from North Dakota, 1925–1945.

John Lord O'Brian (1874–1974): United States Attorney for the Western District of New York, 1909–1921; Assistant Attorney General of the Antitrust Division, 1929–1941; General Counsel of the War Production Board, 1941–1945.

J. Robert Oppenheimer (1904–1969): Director of the atomic energy research project at Los Alamos, New Mexico, 1942–1945; Chairman, the advisory committee of the United States Atomic Energy Commission, 1946–1952; Director, the Institute for Advanced Study, Princeton, New Jersey, 1947–1967.

Robert Patterson (1891–1952): Judge, United States District Court for the Southern District of New York, 1930–1939; Judge, United States Court of Appeals for the Second Circuit, 1939–1940; Undersecretary of War, 1940–1945; Secretary of War, 1945–1947.

Rufus Peckham (1838–1909): Associate Justice of the United States Supreme Court, 1895–1909.

George Wharton Pepper (1867–1961): attorney, Pepper, Bodine, Stokes & Schoch, Philadelphia; Professor of Law, University of Pennsylvania, 1893–1910; Senator from Pennsylvania, 1922–1927; President, American Law Institute, 1936–1947.

George Walbridge Perkins (1862–1920): partner, J.P. Morgan & Co.; Executive Secretary of the Progressive Party, 1912.

Thomas Nelson Perkins (1870–1937): partner, Ropes, Gray, Boyden & Perkins, Boston; counsel to the War Industries Board, World War I; American Representative on the Reparations Committee.

Amos Pinchot (1872–1944): supported Theodore Roosevelt's Bull Moose campaign in 1912; founding member of the National Committee to Uphold Constitutional Government, 1937.

Mahlon Pitney (1858–1924): Associate Justice of the United States Supreme Court, 1912–1922.

Sir Frederick Pollock (1845–1937): Professor of Jurisprudence, Oxford University.

Roscoe Pound (1870–1964): Professor, Harvard Law School, 1910–1917; Dean, Harvard Law School, 1916–1936.

Thomas Reed Powell (1880–1955): Professor, Harvard Law School.

Nathan M. Pusey (1907–2001): President, Harvard University, 1953–1971.

Stanley Forman Reed (1884–1980): Solicitor General of the United States, 1935–1938; Associate Justice of the United States Supreme Court, 1938–1957.

James B. Reston (1909–1995): journalist, N.Y. Times, 1939–1940; correspondent for the United States Office of War Information, London, 1942–1945; diplomatic correspondent, N.Y. Times, 1953–1964; associate editor, N.Y. Times, 1964–1968; executive editor, N.Y. Times, 1968–1969; vice president, N.Y. Times, 1969–1974.

Elliot Richardson (1920–1999): Undersecretary of State, 1969–1970; Secretary of Health, Education, and Welfare, 1970–1973; Secretary of Defense, 1973; Attorney General, 1973; Secretary of Commerce, 1976–1977.

Owen Josephus Roberts (1875–1955): Associate Justice of the United States Supreme Court, 1930–1948.

Gilbert Ernstein Roe (1865–1929): attorney, Roe & McCombs, New York; counsel to Senator Robert La Follette, 1918.

Elihu Root (1845–1937): Secretary of War, 1899–1904; Secretary of State, 1905–1909; Senator from New York, 1909–1915; member, Permanent Court of Arbitration at The Hague, 1910.

Franklin Delano Roosevelt (1882–1945): Governor of New York, 1929–1933; President of the United States, 1933–1945.

Theodore Roosevelt (1858–1919): Assistant Secretary of the Navy, 1897–1898; commander of the 1st United States Volunteer Cavalry Regiment in the Spanish American War, 1898; Governor of New York, 1899–1900; Vice President of the United States, 1901; President of the United States, 1901–1908; presidential nominee of the Progressive Party, 1912.

Josiah Royce (1855–1916): Professor of Philosophy, Harvard University, 1882–1916.

George Rublee (1858–1957): attorney; served on The Federal Trade Commission, 1915–1916; Special Counsel to the Treasury Department, 1917; American Delegate to the Allied Maritime Transport Council, London, 1918–1919.

Bertrand Russell (1872–1970): mathematician and philosopher.

Wiley Blount Rutledge (1894–1949): Associate Justice of the United States Supreme Court, 1943–1949.

Arthur Salter (1881–1975): politician and economist.

Leverett Saltonstall (1892–1979): Governor of Massachusetts, 1939–1945; Senator from Massachusetts, 1945–1967.

George Santayana (1863–1952): philosopher, poet, and literary critic.

Alfred E. Smith (1873–1944): Governor of New York, 1919–1920, 1923–1928.

Young B. Smith (1891–1957): Dean, Columbia Law School, 1927–1952.

Herbert Spencer (1820–1903): biologist, philosopher.

Arthur E. Sutherland (1902–1978): Professor, Harvard Law School.

George Sutherland (1862–1942): Associate Justice of the United States Supreme Court, 1922–1938.

Thomas Walter Swan (1877–1975): Dean, Yale Law School, 1916–1926; Judge, United States Court of Appeals for the Second Circuit, 1926–1975.

Raymond B. Stevens (1874–1942): special counsel of the Federal Trade Commission, 1915–1917; United States representative to the Allied Maritime Transport Council, 1917–1918; vice chairman of the United States Shipping Board, 1917–1920; member and then Chairman, the Federal Tariff Commission, 1935–1942.

Potter Stewart (1915–1985): Associate Justice of the United States Supreme Court, 1958–1981.

Henry L. Stimson (1867–1950): United States Attorney for the Southern District of New York, 1906–1909; Secretary of War, 1911–1913; Governor General of the Philippines, 1927; Secretary of State, 1929–1933; Secretary of War, 1940–1945.

Harlan Fiske Stone (1872–1946): Attorney General of the United States, 1924–1925; Associate Justice of the United States Supreme Court, 1925–1941; Chief Justice of the United States, 1941–1946.

Harry E. Stone (1883–1959): Dean, West Virginia University, 1922–1959.

Oscar Solomon Straus (1850–1926): Secretary of Commerce and Labor, 1906–1909.

Robert A. Taft (1889–1953): Senator from Ohio, 1939–1953.

William Howard Taft (1857–1930): President of the United States, 1909–1913; Chief Justice of the United States, 1921–1930.

Roger Brooke Taney (1777–1864): Chief Justice of the United States, 1836–1864.

James Bradley Thayer (1831–1902): Professor, Harvard Law School, 1873–1902.

Webster Thayer (1857–1933): Judge of the Superior Court of Massachusetts, 1917–1933.

Arnold Toynbee (1889–1975): historian; Director of Studies, Royal Institute of International Affairs, 1929–1956.

Harry S. Truman (1884–1972): Vice President of the United States, 1944–1947; President of the United States, 1947–1952.

Harrison Tweed (1885–1969): attorney; President, the American Law Institute, 1945–1961.

Van Vechten Veeder (1867–1942): Judge, United States District Court for the Eastern District of New York.

Frederick Moore Vinson (1890–1953): Judge, United States Court of Appeals for the District of Columbia Circuit, 1938–1943; Director, Office of Economic Stabilization, 1943–1945; Secretary of the Treasury, 1945–1946; Chief Justice of the United States, 1946–1953.

James John Walker (1881–1946): Mayor of New York City, 1928.

John Walker, II (1906–1995): Curator, National Gallery, 1939–1956; Director, National Gallery, 1956–1996.

Henry Wallace (1888–1965): Secretary of Agriculture, 1933–1940; Vice President of the United States, 1941–1945, Secretary of Commerce, 1945–1946.

Graham Wallas (1858–1932): Professor of Political Science, University of London.

Thomas J. Walsh (1859–1935): Senator from Montana, 1913–1933.

Eugene Wambaugh (1856–1949): Professor, Harvard Law School, 1892–1925.

Henry G. Ward (1851–1933): Judge, United States Court of Appeals for the Second Circuit, 1907–1924.

Earl Warren (1891–1974): Governor of California, 1943–1953; Chief Justice of the United States, 1953–1969.

William E. Werner (1855–1916): Justice, New York Supreme Court, 1895–1904.

Edward Douglass White (1845–1921): Associate Justice of the United States Supreme Court, 1895–1910; Chief Justice of the United States, 1910–1921.

Alfred North Whitehead (1861–1947): English philosopher and mathematician, Professor of Philosophy, Harvard University, 1924–1937.

Charles Evans Whittaker (1901–1973): Associate Justice of the United States Supreme Court, 1957–1962.

George W. Wickersham (1858–1936): Attorney General of the United States, 1909–1913; President, American Law Institute, 1923–1936; President, the Council on Foreign Relations, 1933–1936.

John Henry Wigmore (1863–1943): Professor, Northwestern University Law School, 1893–1901; Dean, Northwestern University Law School, 1901–1921.

Samuel Williston (1861–1963): Professor, Harvard Law School, 1895–1938.

Woodrow Wilson (1856–1924): Governor of New Jersey, 1910–1912; President of the United States, 1913–1921.

Leonard Wood (1860–1927): Army Chief of Staff, 1910–1914; Governor General of the Philippines, 1921–1927.

Charles Wyzanski (1906–1986): solicitor, Department of Labor, 1933–1935; staff of the Solicitor General of the United States, 1935–1937; attorney, Ropes & Gray, Boston; Judge, United States District Court for Massachusetts, 1941–1971; Judge, the International Administrative Court in Geneva, 1950–1955.

BIBLIOGRAPHY

Acheson, Dean. *A Democrat Looks at His Party*. New York: Harpers, 1955.

———. *Present at the Creation: My Years at the State Department*. New York: W.W. Norton, 1969.

Alschuler, Albert W. *Law Without Values: the Life, Work, and Legacy of Justice Holmes*. Chicago: Chicago University Press, 2000.

Aristotle. *Selected Works*. Translated by Hippocrates G. Apostle and Lloyd P. Gerson. Grinnell, Iowa: Peripatetic Press, 1986.

Austin, John. *The Province of Jurisprudence Determined*. 1832.

———. *Lectures on Jurisprudence*. London: John Murray, 1869.

Balkin, Jack M. and Sanford Levinson, "Law and the Humanities: An Uneasy Relationship." *Yale Journal of Law & the Humanities* 18 (2006): 155–86.

Beale, Joseph. *A Selection of Cases on the Conflict of Laws*. Cambridge, MA: Harvard University Press, 1928.

Beard, Charles. *An Economic Interpretation of the Constitution of the United States*. New York: Macmillan, 1913.

Berenson, Bernard. *Venetian Painters of the Renaissance*. New York: G.P. Putnam, 1894.

———. *The Study and Criticism of Italian Art*. London: Bell, 1916.

———. *Aesthetics and History in the Visual Arts*. New York: Pantheon, 1949.

——— *The Italian Painters of the Renaissance*. Oxford: Clarendon Press, 1952.

———. *Seeing and Knowing*. New York: Macmillan, 1953.

———. *One Year's Reading for Fun*. New York: Alfred A. Knopf, 1960.

———. *The Selected Letters of Bernard Berenson*. Edited by A.K. McComb. Boston: Houghton Mifflin, 1964.

Berlin, Isaiah. *The Hedgehog and the Fox: An Essay on Tolstoy's View of History*. New York: Simon & Schuster, 1953.

———. *Historical Inevitability*. London: Oxford University Press, 1954.

———. *Four Essays on Liberty*. London: Oxford University Press, 1969.

———. *The Crooked Timber of Humanity: Chapters in the History of Ideas*. London: John Murray, 1990.

Berolzheimer, Fritz. *The World's Legal Philosophies*. Boston: Boston Book Co., 1912.

Bickel, Alexander. "The Original Understanding of the Segregation Decision." *Harvard Law Review* 69 (1955): 1–65.

———. *The Least Dangerous Branch: the Supreme Court at the Bar of Politics*. Indianapolis: Bobbs-Merrill, 1962.

Blackstone, Sir William. *Commentaries on the Laws of England*. Edited by William Carey Jones. 2 vols. San Francisco: Bancroft-Whitney Co., 1916.

Blaustein, Paul H. *Learned Hand on Patent Law*. White Plains, N.Y.: Pineridge Publishing House, 1983.

Boudin, Michael. "The Master Craftsman." *Stanford Law Review* 47 (1995): 363–86.

Bracton, Henry de. *De legibus et consuetudinibus Angliae. English and Latin. On the laws and customs of England*. Translated by Samuel E. Thorne. 6 vols. Cambridge, MA: Belknap Press of Harvard University Press, 1968–1977.

Brogan, D. W. *The Price of Revolution*. London: H. Hamilton, 1951.

Cahn, Edmond. *The Moral Decision: Right and Wrong in the Light of American Law*. Bloomington: Indiana University Press, 1955.

Chafee, Zechariah. "Freedom of Speech in War Time." *Harvard Law Review* 32 (1919): 932–73.

———. "A Contemporary State Trial: The United States versus Jacob Abrams et al." *Harvard Law Review* 33 (1920): 747–74.

———. *Freedom of Speech*. New York: Harcourt Brace and Howe, 1920.

Cohen, Morris R. "Rule versus Discretion." *Journal of Philosophy, Psychology, and Scientific Methods* 11, no. 8 (1914): 208–15.

———. *Reason and Nature: An Essay on the Meaning of the Scientific Method*. New York: Harcourt, Brace & Company, 1931.

———. *Law and the Social Order: Essays in Legal Philosophy*. New York: Harcourt, Brace & Company, 1933.

The Collected Works of Justice Holmes: Complete Public Writings and Selected Judicial Opinions. 3 vols. Edited by Sheldon M. Novick. London and Chicago: Chicago University Press, 1995.

Corwin, Edward S. "The Doctrine of Due Process of Law Before the Civil War." *Harvard Law Review* 24 (1911): 366–85 and *Harvard Law Review* 24 (1911): 460–79.

Cousins, Norman. "The Senators and Congressmen from New York." *The Saturday Review*, February 1, 1947.

Cox, Archibald. "Learned Hand and the Interpretation of Statutes." *Harvard Law Review* 60 (1947): 370–93.

———. *The Court and the Constitution*. Boston: Houghton Mifflin Co., 1987.

Cravath, Paul D. "Impressions of the Financial and Industrial Conditions in German." *Annals of the American Academy of Political and Social Science* 92 (1920): 5–12.

Croly, Herbert David. *The Promise of American Life*. New York: Macmillan Company, 1910.

Curtis, Charles P. "The Holmes–Laski Letters, 1916–1935, ed. Mark De Wolfe Howe." *Yale Law Journal* 63 (1953): 266–76.

Day, Clarence. *Life with Father*. New York: A.A. Knopf, 1935.

———. *Life with Mother*. New York: A.A. Knopf, 1937.

John Dewey, "What Outlawry of War Is Not." *The New Republic* (October, 3, 1923): 149–52.

Dworkin, Ronald. *Taking Rights Seriously*. Cambridge, MA: Harvard University Press, 1977.

———. *Law's Empire*. Cambridge, MA: Belknap Press of Harvard University Press, 1986.

———. "Mr. Liberty." *New York Review of Books* 41 no. 14 (1994).

———. *Freedom's Law: The Moral Reading of the American Constitution*. Cambridge MA: Harvard University Press, 1996.

———. *Justice in Robes*. Cambridge, MA: Belknap Press of Harvard University Press, 2006.

———. *Justice for Hedgehogs*. Cambridge, MA: Belknap Press of Harvard University Press, 2011.

Ely, John Hart. *Democracy and Distrust: A Theory of Judicial Review*. Cambridge, MA: Harvard University Press, 1980.

Evershed, Lord Francis Raymond. *The Impact of Statute on the Law of England*. London: Oxford University Press, 1957.

Farber, Daniel A. and Suzanna Sherry. *Desperately Seeking Certainty: The Misguided Quest for Constitutional Foundations*. Chicago: Chicago University Press, 2002.

Fairman, Charles. "The Supreme Court." *University of Chicago Law Review* 21 (1953): 40–78.

Ferrero, Guglielmo. *The Principles of Power: The Great Political Crises of History*. Translated by Theodore R. Jaeckel. New York: G. P. Putnam's Sons, 1942.

Finletter, Thomas K. *Can Representative Government Do the Job?* New York: Reynal & Hitchcock, 1945.

Frank, Jerome. *Law and the Modern Mind*. New York: Brentano's, 1930.

———. *Courts on Trial: Myth and Reality in American Justice*. Princeton: Princeton University Press, 1949.

———. "Some Reflections on Judge Learned Hand." *University of Chicago Law Review* 24 (1957): 666–705.

Frankfurter, Felix. "20 Years of Mr. Justice Holmes's Constitutional Opinions." 36 *Harvard Law Review* 36 (1923): 909–39.

———. "A National Policy for Enforcement of Prohibition." *Annals of the American Academy of Political and Social Science* 109 (1923): 193–95.

———. *The Case of Sacco and Vanzetti: A Critical Analysis for Lawyers and Laymen*. Boston: Little, Brown, 1927.

———. *Cases and Other Authorities on Federal Jurisdiction and Procedure*. Chicago: Callaghan, 1931.

———. "A Great Judge Retires: American Law Institute Honors Learned Hand." *American Bar Association Journal* 37 (1951): 502–04, 560–61.

———. "The Supreme Court in the Mirror of Justices." *University of Pennsylvania Law Review* 105 (1957): 781–96.

Frankfurter, Felix and Thomas G. Corcoran. "Petty Federal Offenses and the Constitutional Guaranty of Trial by Jury." *Harvard Law Review* 39 (1926): 917–1019.

Frankfurter, Felix and James M. Landis. *The Business of the Supreme Court: A Study in the Federal Judicial System*. New York: Macmillan, 1927.

———. *Of Law and Life and Other Things that Matter: Papers and Addresses of Felix Frankfurter, 1956–1963*. Edited by Philip B. Kurland. Cambridge, MA: Belknap Press of Harvard University, 1965.

———. *From the Diaries of Felix Frankfurter: With a Biographical Essay and Notes*. Edited by Joseph P. Lash. New York: W.W. Norton, 1975.

Freund, Ernst. "The Debs Case and Freedom of Speech" *The New Republic* (May 3, 1919): 13–15.

Freund, Paul. *On Understanding the Supreme Court*. Boston: Little, Brown, 1949.

Fried, Charles. *Saying What Law Is: The Constitution in the Supreme Court*. Cambridge, MA: Harvard University Press, 2004.

——— *Modern Liberty and the Limits of Government*. New York: W.W. Norton & Co., 2007.

Friedman, Barry. *The Will of the People: How Public Opinion Has Influenced the Supreme Court and Shaped the Meaning of the Constitution*. New York: Farrar, Straus and Giroux, 2009.

Gadamer, Hans-Georg. *Truth and Method*. Translation edited by Garrett Barden and John Cumming. New York: Seabury Press, 1975; translation revised by Joel Weinsheimer and Donald G. Marshall. New York, London: Continuum, 2009.

Ginsburg, Ruth Bader. Foreword to *Learned Hand: The Man and the Judge*, by Gerald Gunther, ix–xiii. 2nd ed. New York: Oxford University Press, 2011.

Goodnow, Frank J. *Social Reform and the Constitution*. New York: Macmillan, 1911.

Gormley, Ken. *Archibald Cox: Conscience of a Nation*. Reading, MA: Addison-Wesley, 1997.

Gray, John Chipman. *The Nature and the Sources of the Law*. New York: Columbia University Press, 1909.

Griffith, Kathryn. *Judge Learned Hand and the Role of the Federal Judiciary*. Norman, OK: University of Oklahoma Press, 1973.

Griswold, Erwin. *The 5th Amendment Today: Three Speeches*. Cambridge, MA: Harvard University Press, 1955.

Gunther, Gerald. "Learned Hand and the Origins of Modern First Amendment Doctrine: Some Fragments of History." *Stanford Law Review* 27 (1975): 719–73.

———. *Learned Hand: The Man and the Judge*. New York: Alfred A. Knopf, 1994; 2nd ed. New York: Oxford University Press, 2011.

Hadrian. *The Fragmentary Latin Poets*. Edited by Edward Courtney. New York: Oxford University Press, 2003.

Hamburger, Philip. "The Great Judge." In *Matters of State: A Political Excursion*, 1–12. Washington, D.C.: Counterpoint, 2000.

Hand, Learned. "Due Process of Law and the Eight-Hour Day." *Harvard Law Review* 21 (1907–1908): 495–509.

———. "An Unseen Reversal." *The New Republic* (January 9, 1915): 7–8.

———. "The Hope of the Minimum Wage." *The New Republic* (November 20, 1915): 66–68.

———. "The Normal Inequalities of Fortune." *The New Republic* (February 6, 1915): 5–7.

———. "Oliver Wendell Holmes, Jr., *Collected Legal Papers*." *Political Science Quarterly* 33 (1921): 528–30.

———. "The Legal Right to Starve." *The New Republic* (May 2, 1923): 254–55.

———. *The Spirit of Liberty*. Edited by Irving Dilliard. New York: Alfred A. Knopf, 1952; 1953; 1960.

———. *The Bill of Rights: The Oliver Wendell Holmes Lectures, 1958*. Cambridge, MA: Harvard University Press, 1958.

———. *The Bill of Rights: The Oliver Wendell Holmes Lectures, 1958*. With introduction by Charles Wyzanski. New York: Athenaeum, 1963.

Hand, Susan Train. *Letters of the Hand Family, 1796–1912*. New York: Edwin S. Gorham, 1923.

"The Hands: Distinguished Family of American Jurists." *Middlebury College News Letter* 47 no. 1 (Autumn 1972): 81–89.

Hapgood, Norman. *Industry and Progress*. New Haven: Yale University Press, 1911.

———. *The Advancing Hour*. New York: Boni & Liveright, 1920.

Harrison, Jane Ellen. *Prolegomena to the Study of Greek Religion*. Cambridge: The University Press, 1903.

——— *Themis: A Study of the Social Origins of Greek Religion*. Cambridge: University Press, 1912.

Henkin, Louis. *How Nations Behave: Law and Foreign Policy*. New York: Praeger, 1968.

———. *The Age of Rights*. New York: Columbia University Press, 1990.

——— *Constitutionalism, Democracy, and Foreign Affairs*. New York: Columbia University Press, 1990.

———. *Foreign Affairs and the United States Constitution*. (Oxford, UK: Oxford University Press, 1996.

Hirsch, H.N. *The Enigma of Felix Frankfurter*. New York: Basic Books, 1981.

Hobson, J. A. *Work and Wealth: A Human Valuation*. New York: Macmillan Co., 1914.

Holmes, Oliver Wendell, Jr. *The Common Law*. Boston: Little, Brown and Company, 1881.

———. *Speeches*. Boston: Little, Brown and Company, 1891.

———. *Collected Legal Papers*. New York: Harcourt Brace and Howe, 1920.

The Holmes–Laski Letters: The Correspondence of Mr. Justice Holmes and Harold J. Laski 1916–1935. Edited by Mark DeWolfe Howe. 2 vols. Cambridge, MA: Harvard University Press, 1953.

The Holmes-Pollock Letters: The Correspondence of Mr. Justice Holmes and Sir Frederick Pollock, 1874–1932. Edited by Mark DeWolfe Howe. 2 vols. Cambridge, MA: Harvard University Press, 1941.

Holmes and Frankfurter: Their Correspondence, 1912–1934. Edited by Robert M. Mennel and Christine L. Compston. Hanover and London: University Press of New England, 1996.

Howe, Mark DeWolfe. *Justice Oliver Wendell Holmes*. 2 vols. Cambridge, MA: Belknap Press of Harvard University Press, 1957–1963.

Hutcheson, Joseph C. "The Judgment Intuitive: The Function of the 'Hunch' in Judicial Decision." *Cornell Law Quarterly* 14 (1929): 274–88.

Huxley, Aldous. *The Perennial Philosophy* (New York, London: Harper & Brothers, 1945).

Huxley, Julian. *Evolutionary Humanism*. Melbourne: Australian Institute of International Affairs, 1954.

Ickes, M. Harold. "Who Killed the Progressive Party?" *The American Historical Review* 46 no. 2 (1941): 306–37.

James, William. *The Will to Believe, and Other Essays in Popular Philosophy*. Boston: 1896.

———. *Varieties of Religious Experience*. London: Longmans, Green, 1902.

———. *Pragmatism: A New Name for Some Old Ways of Thinking: Popular Lectures in Philosophy*. London: Longmans, Green and Co., 1907.

Jeans, Sir James Hopwood. *The Mysterious Universe*. New York: Macmillan, 1930.

Kalman, Laura. *The Strange Career of Legal Liberalism.* New Haven: Yale University Press, 1996.
Kellogg, Frederick R. "Learned Hand and the Great Train Ride." *The American Scholar* (Autumn 1987): 471–86.
Kennan, George F. *American Diplomacy, 1900–1950.* New York: New American Library, 1951.
———. *Realities of American Foreign Policy.* Princeton: Princeton University Press, 1954.
———. *Soviet-American Relations, 1917–1920.* Princeton: Princeton University Press, 1956–1958.
Kent, James. *Commentaries on American Law, 1826, 1830.* New York, Da Capo Press, 1971.
Keynes, John Maynard. *The Economic Consequences of the Peace.* London: Macmillan, 1919.
———. *A Treatise on Probability.* London: Macmillan, 1921.
———. *The General Theory of Employment, Interest and Money.* London: Macmillan, 1936.
———. *Two Memoirs.* New York: A. M. Kelley, 1949.
Langdell, Christopher Columbus. *A Selection of Cases on the Law of Contracts.* 1871. Littleton, CO: F.B. Rothman, 1980.
Laski, Harold Joseph. *Authority and the Modern State.* New Haven: Yale University Press, 1919.
———. *Political Thought in England, Locke to Bentham.* New York: Holt and Company, 1920.
———. *A Grammar of Politics.* New Haven: Yale University Press, 1925.
———. *Democracy in Crisis.* Chapel Hill: University of North Carolina Press, 1933.
———. *The Rise of European Liberalism.* London: George Allen & Unwin, 1936.
Lattimore, Owen. *Ordeal by Slander.* Boston: Little, Brown, 1950.
Lippmann, Walter. "The Outlawry of War." *Atlantic Monthly* (August 1923).
———. *The Phantom Public.* New York: Harcourt Brace and Company, 1925.
———. *Men of Destiny.* New York: Macmillan, 1927.
———. *A Preface to Morals.* New York: Macmillan, 1929.
———. *Inquiry into the Principles of the Good Society.* Boston: Little, Brown and Company, 1937.
——— *Essays in the Public Philosophy.* Boston: Little, Brown and Company, 1955.
Littell, Philip. *Books and Things.* New York: Harcourt, Brace and Howe, 1919.
———. *This Way Out.* New York: Coward-McCann, 1929.
Manz, William H. "*Brown v. Board of Education*: A Selected Bibliography." *Law Library Journal* 96 (2004): 245–66.
Mason, Alpheus Thomas. *Harlan Fiske Stone: Pillar of the Law.* New York: Viking Press, 1956.
McIlwain, Charles Howard. *Growth of Political Thought in the West from the Greeks to the Middle Ages.* New York: Macmillan, 1932.
Monroe, Alan H. "The Supreme Court and the Constitution." *American Political Science Review* 18 (1924): 737–59.
Moore, George Edward. *Principia Ethica.* Cambridge: At the University Press, 1903.
Morgan, Edmund. *Model Code of Evidence as Adopted and Promulgated by the American Law Institute of Philadelphia, Pennsylvania, May 15, 1942.* Philadelphia: American Law Institute, 1942.
Morgan, Edmund M. and John MacArthur Maguire. *Cases and Materials on Evidence.* Chicago: Foundation Press, 1942.
Murray, Gilbert. *The Rise of the Greek Epic.* Oxford: Clarendon Press, 1911.
O'Brian, John Lord. *National Security and Individual Freedom.* Cambridge: Harvard University Press, 1955.
Parrish, Michael E. *Felix Frankfurter: The Reform Years.* New York: The Free Press, 1982.
Pepper, George Wharton. "America and the League of Nations." *Journal of Comparative Legislation and International Law* 3 (1921): 21–30.
Philbin, Stephen H. "Judge Learned Hand and the Law of Patents and Copyrights." *Harvard Law Review* 60 (1947): 394–404.
Polenberg, Richard. *Fighting Faiths: The Abrams Case, the Supreme Court, and Free Speech.* New York: Viking, 1987.
Pollock, Sir Frederick. *The Principles of Contract.* 1876. London: Stevens, 1950.

———. *The Law of Torts: A Treatise on the Principle of Obligations Arising from Civil Wrongs in the Common Law*. 1887. London: Stevens and Sons, 1951.

Powell, Lewis F. Foreword to *Learned Hand: the Man and the Judge*, by Gerald Gunther, ix–xiv. New York: Alfred A. Knopf, 1994.

Posner, Richard A. "The Learned Hand Biography and the Question of Judicial Greatness." *Yale Law Journal* 104 (1994): 511–40.

———. *Law and Literature*. Cambridge, MA: Harvard University Press, 1998.

———. *How Judges Think*. Cambridge, MA: Harvard University Press, 2008.

Powe, Lucas A. Jr. *The Warren Court and American Politics*. Cambridge, MA: Belknap Press of Harvard University Press, 2000.

Proceedings of a Special Session to Commemorate Fifty Years of Federal Judicial Service by the Honorable Learned Hand. New York: United States Court of Appeals for the Second Circuit, 1959.

Radcliffe, Lord Cyril John. *The Problem of Power*. London: Secker & Warburg, 1952.

Reid, Robert T. and Earl Loreburn. *How the War Came*. London: Methuen & Co., Ltd., 1919.

The Remarkable Hands: An Affectionate Portrait. Edited by Marcia Nelson. New York: Foundation of the Federal Bar Council, 1983.

Rodell, Fred. *Woe Unto You, Lawyers!* New York: Reynal & Hitchcock, 1939.

Roosevelt, Franklin D. *The Public Papers and Addresses of Franklin D. Roosevelt, With a Special Introduction and Explanatory Notes by President Roosevelt*. Compiled by Samuel I. Rosenman. New York: Random House, 1938–1950.

———. *Roosevelt and Frankfurter: Their Correspondence—1928–1945*. Edited by Max Freemann. Boston: Little, Brown, 1967.

Roosevelt, Theodore. "Workmen's Compensation." *The Outlook* 98 (May 13, 1911): 49.

———. "The Trusts, the People and the Square Deal." *The Outlook* 99 (Nov. 18, 1911): 12.

———. "The Tobacco Trust and the Court." *The Outlook* 99 (Nov. 25, 1911): 13.

———. *The Conservation of Womanhood and Childhood*. New York: Funk & Wagnalls, 1912.

Royce, Josiah. *The Philosophy of Loyalty*. New York: Macmillan, 1908.

———. *William James and Other Essays on the Philosophy of Life*. New York: The Macmillan Company, 1911.

———. *The Problem of Christianity*. New York: Macmillan, 1913.

Russell, Bertrand. *A History of Western Philosophy and Its Connection with Political and Social Circumstances from the Earliest Times to the Present Day*. New York: Simon and Schuster, 1945.

———. *The Wisdom of the West: A Historical Survey of Western Philosophy in Its Social and Political Setting*. Garden City, NY: Doubleday, 1959.

———. *An Inquiry into Meaning and Truth*. London: G. Allen & Unwin, 1966.

Salter, Arthur. *Recovery, the Second Effort*. New York: The Century Co., 1932.

———. *The United States of Europe: And Other Papers*. Edited by W. Arnold-Forster. London: G. Allen & Unwin, 1933.

Santayana, George. *The Sense of Beauty: Being the Outlines of Aesthetic Theory*. New York: C. Scribner's Sons, 1896.

———. *The Life of Reason: Or, The Phases of Human Progress*. New York: C. Scribner's Sons, 1906.

———. *The Last Puritan: A Memoir in the Form of a Novel*. London: Constable & Co., 1935.

——— *The Realm of the Spirit. Book Fourth of Realms of Being*. New York: C. Scribner's Sons, 1940.

———. *Dominations and Powers; Reflections on Liberty, Society, and Government*. New York: Scribner, 1951.

Sayer, John. "Art and Politics, Dissent and Repression: The *Masses* Magazine versus the Government, 1917–1918." *American Journal of Legal History* 32 (1988): 42–78.

Schick, Marvin. *Learned Hand's Court*. Baltimore: Johns Hopkins Press, 1970.

Schrödinger, Erwin. *What is Life: The Physical Aspects of the Living Cell*. New York: Macmillan, 1945.

Shanks, Hershel. *The Art and Craft of Judging: The Decisions of Learned Hand.* New York: Macmillan, 1968.
Simon, James F. *The Antagonists: Hugo Black, Felix Frankfurter, and Civil Liberties in Modern America.* New York: Simon & Schuster, 1989.
Spencer, Herbert. *Social Statics, The Conditions Essential to Human Happiness Specified and the First of Them Developed.* 1851.
The Spirit of Liberty: The Learned Hand Centennial Exhibit, 1972. Cambridge, MA: Manuscript Division, Harvard Law School Library, 1972.
Steel, Ronald. *Walter Lippmann and the American Century.* Boston: Little, Brown, 1980.
———. "Letter on Lippmann and the *Schwimmer* Case." *New York Review of Books* 28 (April 2, 1981).
Stone, Geoffrey. *Perilous Times: Free Speech in Wartime from the Sedition Act of 1798 to the War on Terrorism.* New York: W.W. Norton, 2004.
Sutherland, Arthur E. *The Law at Harvard: A History of Ideas and Men, 1817–1967.* Cambridge, MA: The Belknap Press of Harvard University, 1967.
Thayer, James Bradley. "The Origin and Scope of the American Doctrine of Constitutional Law." *Harvard Law Review* 7 (1893) 129–56.
———. "The Presumption of Innocence in Criminal Cases." *Yale Law Journal* 6 (1897): 185–212.
———. *A Preliminary Treatise on Evidence at the Common Law*, 1898.
———. *A Selection of Cases on Evidence at the Common Law.* Cambridge, MA: C.W. Sever & Co., 1900.
———. *Legal Essays.* Boston: The Boston Book Company, 1908.
Toynbee, Arnold. *A Study of History.* 10 vols. London: Oxford University Press, 1934–1957.
Walker, John M. "Judicial Tendencies in Statutory Construction: Differing Views on the Role of the Judge." *New York University Annual Survey of America Law* 58 (2001): 203–39.
Wallas, Graham. *Human Nature in Politics.* London: A. Constable and Co., 1908.
———. *The Great Society; A Psychological Analysis.* New York: The Macmillan Co., 1914.
Webb, Sidney and Beatrice. *Industrial Democracy.* London: Longmans, Green, 1897.
White, G. Edward. *Earl Warren: A Public Life.* Oxford: Oxford University Press, 1982.
———. *Justice Oliver Wendell Holmes: Law and the Inner Self.* New York, Oxford: Oxford University Press, 1993.
Alfred North Whitehead, with Bertrand Russell. *Principia Mathematica.* Cambridge: University Press, 1910.
———. *The Organization of Thought, Educational and Scientific.* Philadelphia: J. B. Lippincott, 1916.
———. *An Enquiry Concerning the Principles of Natural Knowledge.* Cambridge: University Press, 1919.
———. *The Concept of Nature.* Cambridge: University Press, 1920.
———. *The Principle of Relativity with Application to Physical Science.* Cambridge: University Press, 1922.
———. *Science and the Modern World.* New York: Macmillan, 1926.
———. *Symbolism: Its Meaning and Effect.* New York: Macmillan, 1927.
———. *Process and Reality: An Essay in Cosmology.* Cambridge: University Press, 1929.
Williston, Samuel. *Commercial and Banking Law.* New York: American Institute of Banking, 1918.
———. *The Law of Contracts.* New York: Baker, Voorhis & Co., 1921.
———. *Restatement of the Law of Contracts, as adopted and promulgated by the American Law Institute.* St. Paul, American Law Institute, 1932.
———. *Life and Law: An Autobiography.* Boston: Little, Brown and Company, 1940.
Wigmore, John H. "Nemo Tenetur Seipsum Prodere" ("No One is Bound to Betray Himself"). *Harvard Law Review* 5 (1891): 71–88.

———. "The Privilege Against Self-Incrimination: Its History." *Harvard Law Review* 15 (1902): 610–37.

———. *A Treatise on the System of Evidence in Trials at Common Law, Including the Statutes and Judicial Decisions of All Jurisdictions of the United States*. Boston: Little, Brown, 1904–1905.

———. "*Abrams v. U.S.*: Freedom of Speech and Freedom of Thuggery in War-Time and Peace-Time." *Illinois Law Review* 14 (1920): 539–61.

Wyzanski, Charles, Jr. "Judge Learned Hand's Contributions to Public Law." *Harvard Law Review* 60 (1947): 348–69.

———. "History and Law." *University of Chicago Law Review* 26 (1959): 237–44.

———. *Whereas–A Judge's Premises: Essays in Judgment, Ethics and the Law*. Boston: Little, Brown and Company, 1964.

INDEX